An American Family

History and Descendants of Michael Arbogast
Born September 27 1732 in Freiburg, Baden-Württemberg, Germany

VOLUME TWO

Descendants of children
David Arbogast(b 1761 – d 1833),
Mary Elizabeth (b 1765 – d 1795)
Dorothy (b. 1767 – d.1839)
Michael (b. 1768 – d.1813)

Curtis Sharp, Eight Generation

Both justice and decency require that we should bestow on our forefathers an honorable remembrance.
Thucydides

"Hath this been in your days, or even in the days of your fathers? Tell your children of it, and let your children tell their children, and their children another generation.
Joel 1:1-3

Published 2017
CeateSpace

Contents

Contents 3
Introduction 5
Acknowledgements, Data Sources, Contributors 7
Immediate Family of Michael Arbogast and Mary Elizabeth Samuels. 10
    How best to use these listing 10
Descendants of David Arbogast Second Child of Michael and Mary Elizabeth Samuels 12
    Generation One 12
    Generation Two 13
    Generation Three 15
    Generation Four 19
    Generation Five 24
    Generation Six 28
Descendants of Mary Elizabeth Arbogast Third Child of Michael and Mary Elizabeth Samuels ...29
    Generation One 29
    Generation Two 29
    Generation Three 32
    Generation Four 38
    Generation Five 47
    Generation Six 63
    Generation Seven 81
    Generation Eight 101
    Generation Nine 119
    Generation Ten 131
Descendants of Michael Arbogast Forth Child of Michael and Mary Elizabeth Samuels 133
    Generation One 133
    Generation Two 134
    Generation Three 137
    Generation Four 142
    Generation Five 144
    Generation Six 147
    Generation Seven 151
    Generation Eight 158
    Generation Nine 164
Descendants of Dorothy Arbogast Fifth Child of Michael and Mary Elizabeth Samuels 166
    Generation One 166
    Generation Two 166

- Generation Three 169
- Generation Four 178
- Generation Five 189
- Generation Six 201
- Generation Seven 211
- Generation Eight 218
- Generation Nine 219

About The Author 221

Index 222

Introduction

Accumulating data on the ancestors of of my grandmother Nancy Elizabeth Arbogast, who Married William Alexander Gilmer Sharp September 24, 1868 started in 1995 and initiated an effort to honor all my grand parents by researching their history and identifying their descendants. The Sir names of my grandparents are Sharp, Morrison, Hill and Arbogast. How fascinating that I should be the off spring of four pioneering families who settled in the heart of the Alleghany Mountains.

The collection phase continued through the first dozen years of the 21 century. The not-to-be-ignored shadows of the tombs of my ancestors compelled me to lay aside the searching and pursue making the results available through the print media. This has been accomplished for my parents families, the Sharp and Morrison. Now the Arbogast, where the greatest amount of work by others resided. Fortunately the fruits of earlier and more diligent researchers were available. All are recognized and expanded in Acknowledgements. Starting on page 6.

Michael Arbogast came, and settled in the central Allegany's, and as the pages of countless documents, testify, the struggle for that elusive 'better life 'continued. But is it really important that we know our ancestors, why is it necessary or even desirable to count or identify them? On the other hand, why would one not do this? Didn't some not-to-be-forgotten Arbogast sail the stormy Atlantic and survive in the wilderness so that I might exist. If any thread of my emigrate ancestors had wiggled ever so much from the path they followed, I, Curtis Sharp, would have experienced an eternity of nonexistence.

It is not surprising, there are others with strong opinions of why count or identify our ancestors.

Leonard Morrison[1] offers a full and logical explanation in his 1880 publication The History of the Morison or Morrison Family.

> *"Our ancestors labored and suffered much for the attainment of the rich blessings which we enjoy. They rest from their labors; they have found "Sleep after toyle, port after stormie seas." It is not right in their descendants to allow their names and deeds to perish from the earth. To permit it would be unjust to the living and the dead; to those who have gone before us, and those who shall come after us. To prevent such a result is this volume published. It is a family record; to preserve its traditions, gathering up the fading memorials of its past, and transmit them to those who shall succeed us."*

Thucydides[2] put it another way.

> *"Both justice and decency require that we should bestow on our forefathers an honorable remembrance".*

This closely parallels that offered by Dr. William T. Price[3] author of Historical Sketches of Pocahontas County, West Virginia.

> *"Persons knowing but little of those gone before is very likely to care but little of those coming after them."*

Arthur C. Morrison[4], whose work made significant contributions to this book, observed in his introductory comments

> *"This book seeks to reunite descendants under a single roof."*

Another Morrison suggests[5]

> *"May we ever keep green the graves, and fresh in our memories the lives of our dear ones who have proceeded us to the beyond"*

And so Michael Arbogast came, leaving the hinder land of Baden-Württemberg, Germany. He put down roots in the heart of the Allegany Mountains near the head waters of eastern flowing rivers and western flowing rivers, straddling the Eastern North America continental divide in what is now Highland County. Here his family came into existence and expanded well over 15,000 ancestors.

Volumes II and III on the *History and Descendants of Michael Arbogast* eliminates some detail on the history of the Arbogast name, and the life of the pioneer Michael and needs to be reviewed to get a fuller

---

[1] The History of the Morison or Morrison Family by Leonard A. Morrison, Frederick William Leopold Thomas A. Williams & Company, 1880 - 468 p.

[2] Thucydides, The history of the Peloponnesian war, Vol. I, John Watts, 1753

[3] William T. Price, Historical Sketches of Pocahontas County, West Virginia, 1901, Heritage Books, 2003 .

[4] Arthur C. Morrison, Descendants of Nathanial Morrison of Virginia, 6th Edition, Glendora, CA, 198

[5] Morrison Genealogy, A History of a Branch of the Morrison Family by Granville Price Morrison, 1928.

history and appreciation of the family. This Volume (II) concentrates on the descendants of four of his children; David, Mary Elizabeth, Dorothy and Michael and does not contain a full review of the pioneer Michael. Volume III contains the descendants of his children Henry, Peter, John and George.

All descendants of Michael Arbogast are a part of this history and and history about him. This seems to diminish the rational of excluding any known descendants. Consequently, this volume includes some living persons. Other supporting points for doing this are:

(1) The *History of Pocahontas County West Virginia 1980*, references many living persons in this volume and is about ancestors and living family members;
(2) Some genealogy internet sites are now including birth dates of living persons[6]
(3) Current proliferation and instant availability of information through the social media, and the on-line search capabilities expand, rather than diminish, the availability of personal data.

It is inevitable that omissions, errors and deficiency are present in any book of this type and certainly in this one. We know many descendants are missing, and the data are not complete and may contain errors. As a matter of fact, considering all the potential data points that might be recorded for the nearly 30,000 descendants and spouses in all three volumes. , it is likely that more are missing than are present. It is appropriate to repeat the final words from the often-cited *Historical Sketches of Pocahontas County*.[i] "In submitting this book to the public, we are aware that there are imperfections and omissions that will be apparent to many readers."

The identified descendants of first son Odessus Adam (Volume One) nearly equals all the descendants from the other eight children.. The table below lists the descendants and spouses associated with each of the nine children of Michael Arbogast that is included in these three volumes. The are listed in birth order.

Child	descendent of each child	spouses of descendants	volume
Adam	8706	4619	I
David	261	101	II
Mary	1653	858	II
Michael	529	253	II
Dorothy	1011	436	II
Henry	1242	660	III
Peter	1420	741	III
John	2701	1338	III
George	1951	1054	III

Front and back cover pictures:
Front upper left: Mahalia Teter Hedrick and husband Solomon J. Hedrick. Mahalia is a granddaughter of Elizabeth L. Arbogast a grandchild of pioneer Michael Arbogast through son George
Front upper center: Sketch of the pioneer Michael Arbogast
Front upper right: Brown Arbogast and wife Francis Ervine Arbogast
Back upper left: A mid 19 century Midwest Arbogast reunion.
Back upper enter Albert Adair Arbogast and wife Veranda McBride
Back upper right: Robert Alexander Wymer and wife Eva Catherine Arbogast, daughter of Abraham Arbogast
Back lower left: John Morgan Tacy and Rosetta White Tacy family. The parents are centered.
Back lower center: James Summers and wife Elmira Frances Knapp

---

[6] Family Tree Maker, http://familytreemaker.genealogy.com/users/d/r/a/Angela-Draper/GENE8-0009.html#CHILD37, accessed Nov 16, 2014.

Acknowledgements, Data Sources, Contributors

Typically this subject area would appear near the end of the book. However, since much of the data collection for these Arbogast volumes was done by others, and early recognition of those responsible is totally justified.. First, volumes by Charles Joseph Eades are a most extensive accumulation of Arbogast data. And his able research assistant Amanda Arbogast Forbes warrants equal recognition. These contributions exceed all other

Their Work also contains excellent source documentation. Frequently there was multiple source documentation for each descendant, resulting in the source data greatly exceeding the data. Unfortunately, publisher imposed space limitation mandated the removal of the source data for each piece of data. However, to be sure each individual contribution is recognized all the source citations have been accumulated and are presented here in Acknowledgements, Data Sources, and Contributor. Also included in Acknowledgements, Data Sources, and Contributors, are numerous other citations not included in the work by Eades, such as the footnotes.

Dates from sources such as b. Wft Est. 1813-1850 or d. Wft Est. 1819-1887 have been deleted. Such dates provide no useful information. Many of these with Wft Est. born an death dates span in excess of 100 years.

- Arbogast Chorba of New Vernon, New Jersey Ref: Stalnaker 249 S/o Boston and Margaret (Hamilton) Stalnaker.
- A dozen Arbogast reunions who individually contributed data.
- **Amanda Arbogast Forbes** (AAF) research includes papers of Wilma Harper, 1850 and 1880 Census of Pendleton County, Court Records and County histories.
- (Amanda Arbogast Forbes AAF) research and papers, copy, Pendleton Co. Marriage Record. A.k.a. Eliza Ann & Ann Elizabeth. Ref: WBH; children and spouses from grandson Dr. William Kerr of Burnsville, WV. Lived in Burnsville, Upshur Co.
- Amanda Arbogast Forbs, (AAF) Principal Researcher for: Eades, Charles Joseph author of "Descendants of Michael Arbogast".+
- Ames Edward and Rita Wooddell for compiling the Pocahontas County Marriage Bonds 1822-52, and Minister Returns.
- Ancestry Family Trees Note: http://www.Ancestry.com/AMTCitationRedir.aspx?tid=16931876&pid=107>.
- Ancestry Family Trees Publication: Online publication - Provo, UT, USA: Ancestry.com. Original data: Family Tree files submitted by Ancestry members. Note: This information comes from 1 or more individual Ancestry Family Tree files. This source citation points you to a current version of those files. Note: The owners of these tree files may have removed or changed information since this source citation was created. Page: Ancestry Family Trees Note: Data: Repository: R2170648939 Name: Ancestry.com Address: <http://www.Ancestry.com> Note: Text: <http://trees.ancestry.com/pt/AMTCitationRedir.aspx?tid=16931876&pid=107>.
- Arthur C. Morrison, Descendants of Nathanial Morrison of Virginia, 6th Edition, Glendora, CA, 1988.
- Augusta Co. Marriage records
- Augusta county entry book 31 PG 64, 1765.
- Augusta County Courthouse Records, Staunton, VA.
- Barbara Black Lawyer, Industry, IL.
- Bockstruck, Lloyd D., "Naturalizations and Denizations in Colonial Virginia." In National Genealogical Society Quarterly, vol. 73:2 (June 1985), pp. 109-116.
- Capt. Peter Hull's Company of Cavalry. AAF's DAR Nat'l. #-484839. 1781
- Chalkley's Abstracts, Vol. I, p. 161.
  In National Genealogical Society Quarterly, vol. 73:2 (June 1985), pp. 109-116.
- Colonel Dean C. Davisson, Dayton, OH for his major contributions to sons David Michael and Peter
- Court Records Augusta County Virginia; August 22, 1770, page 117, Michael Arbocoast naturalized.
- DAR ancestor # A002973, Michael Arbogast Service, Birth and Death Records.
- Daughter of Richard David and Matilda Amanda (Meade) Robinson
- Daughter of Wilburn A. and Ellen Ivory (Hammond) Russell.
- Daughter. of Samuel Elliott and Josie Lee (Taylor) Elliott, Green Bank
- Deed Book 19, page 267, 130 acres on head of South Branch of Potowmack, Highland County, VA, patented to Michael Arbogast, undated, but adjacent entries indicate the year was 1773; Augusta Co., VA.
- Deed Book 23, page 90, 17 Aug 1779, is conveying property to Michael Armingcost.

- Descendants, by Mary Elizabeth (Nottingham) Skelton of Jamestown, = Durbin, WV.
- Doris (Snyder) Beverage.
- Dozens, hundreds even, of individuals that contributed single or multiple pieces of data and did not receive credit. You know who you are.
- Dr. Francis Yeager Dunham for preserving the records of Wilma Beard Harper.
- **Eades, Charles Joseph**, and Dunham, PhD, Frances (Yeager) et.al. "Descendants of Michael Arbogast (ca. 1734-1812), Vol. I-V, 1995-1996; Westbrook Publishing Co., 121 Yorktown Rd., Franklin, TN, 37064-3277AAT =
- Family and descendants from Tommie Arbogast Huggins and The Galford Ancestry, by Lloyd Pritt Galford, 1981, Gateway Press, Baltimore, MD.
- Find A Grave, all sites available of Michael Arbogast descendants
- From family records of Merle Arbogast Chorba of New Vernon, New Jersey, daughter of Dr. Hoyt Bailey Arbogast. Ref: Morton's Highland 344 S/o John and Matilda (Slaven) Wade.
- From Geo. O. Wilson, Jr., brother, Bridgewater, VA, 1995. Mary = children of Geo. Osborne Wilson and Bonnie Grace Gum.
- From obituary. She Married MAR 1916 in Elkins, Randolph Co., WV, Donald Harper, b. Jun 1 1892 in Tucker Co., WV, d. Feb 4 1974, buried in Maplewood Cem., Elkins, Randolph Co., WV
- From research and papers of Helen Rex Arbogast Huggins,
- From Wm. C. Varner
- From, The Lunsford Family, by Mrs. Ralph Lunsford, Cortland, OH, = undated, but believed to be written in 1982. Copy from =,
- From, William Nottingham, Jr. & Mary Arbogast of Pocahontas Co., = Descendants, by Mary Elizabeth (Nottingham) Skelton of Jamestown
- Glenn Huffman, Bridgewater, VA for his major contributions Highland and Pendleton Counties
- Highland County Courthouse Records, Monterey, VA.
- Highland History, Page 290.
- *Historical Sketches of Pocahontas County, West Virginia* William T. Price, Price Brothers Publishers, Marlinton, West Virginia, 1901
- *History of Pendleton (Highland) Co.*, by Morton, pages 257 332.
- Information from Avis Irene (Wimer) Arbogast family of Newport, PA
- Information from family records of Dolores J. Tacy Russell.
- Information from family records of James Collins, Essex, MD, a descendant.
- Information from family records of Lillian McCauley Griffith of = file. Daughter of John Horace and Gussie Belle (Evans) Gray.
- Information from Mrs. Sylvia (Taylor) Gum of Green Bank, WV
- Information from Pocahontas Co., WV, History, 1981, by Brambel Tracy.
- Information from records of Dolores Tacy Russell of Lebanon, PA
- Information from Tommie Arbogast Huggins and The Galford Ancestry, by Lloyd Pritt Galford, 1981, The Gateway Press, Baltimore, MD.
- Jane Weber Mason, Morgantown, WV
- Marriage and death date from A. Arbogast Forbes Papers .
- Mary E. (Nottingham) Skelton of Jamestown, PA
- Naturalized in Augusta Co., VA, 22 Aug 1770, #117, Chalkley's Abstracts, Vol. I, p. 161.zz
- Odessus Adam Arbogast Date and place of marriage from Pension Record, War of 1812. See deed of heirs, Deed Book 6, pp. 303 & 304 Pocahontas County Court Records. Storekeeper in Green Bank. AAF # A-7.(Amanda Arbogast Forbs file id.)
- Odessus Adam Arbogast, Birth 1759/60 from Rev. War Pension Applications.
- Peter Hull's Capt. 1781. Company of Cavalry. AAF's DAR Nat'l.#-484839.
- Pendleton County Courthouse Records, Franklin, VA
- *Pennsylvania German Pioneers*, 1993 edition, Strassberger, Ralph Beaver and Hincke, William John, editor of 1934 edition, pp. 410,411, Port of Philadelphia.
- Philip D. Arbogast letter. Daughter of Koichi and Yo (Kimura) Ido, Japan.
- Philip D. Arbogast. Lives in Tucson, AZ.
- Phyllis and John, Clendenin, WV, 1996.
- Real Estate Sources: See Deed Book 19, page 267, 130 acres on head of South Branch of Potowmack, Highland County, VA, patented to Michael Arbogast, undated, but adjacent entries indicate the year was 1773; Augusta Co., VA. Also Deed Book 23, page 90, 17 Aug 1779, conveying property to Michael Armingcost. This area is now Blue Grass, Highland Co., VA.
- Record from Evangelical Lutheran Church Records, Kehl, Baden, Germany

- Records of Augusta Co., VA, Page 195, citing Will Book VI, records appraisement of the estate of Barnet Lance by Peter Hull, Jno. Gum, Sr. and Michael Armengash, 20 Sep 1791.
- Records of Augusta Co., VA, Vol. III, by Chalkley, p.531, 560.
- Records of Jim and Rita Wooddell, January 1994. (These were extensive)
- Records of Sylvia (Taylor) Gum of Green Bank, WV
- Ref: Stalnaker 254.
- Robert B. Jordan, Brooklyn, NY, descendant. Married Wanda Watt. Children are Frank Cleland, Ruth Ann, and Mark Donavan Jordan.
- See Virginia Militia in the Revolutionary War, by McAllister, page 235. Adam received pension for service as Virginia Militiaman, living 1835. Also page 19, Indian Spy, 1776 or 1777; page 22, Pvt., Capt. Peter Hull's Co. during Yorktown Campaign, 1781; and, page 148, Muster Roll of that Company in 1779. See Pocahontas Co. History, by Price.
- Sharp, William Curtis, 2013 Author of these Arbogast volumes also wrote *John Sharp and Margaret Blain Sharp Family History*, .WC Sharp and MC Sharp and is the grandson of Nancy Elizabeth Arbogast.
- Sharron Wilkinson McNeeley, Dearborn Heights, MI
- Shirley Colaw Howell, Sumter, SC
- Source is AAF record A-371146, i.e. Amanda Arbogast Forbs. Source is a family tree chart done by Henry Miles Arbogast, his daughter, Marjorie Shrack or Marjorie's daughter, Louise Marsh and/or other descendants.
- Stalnaker Son of George Washington Salisbury and Mary Blaine (Mace) Salisbury.
- Sylvia (Arbogast) Arndorff, daughter of Fountain, Marlinton, WV, to Amanda (Arbogast) Forbes, 1991.
- The Church of Jesus Christ of Latter-day Saints, Ancestral File (R) (Copyright (c) 1987, June 1998, data as of 5 January 1998).
- The Family of John P. and Dinah (Nottingham) Varner, = Varner, R#1, Dayton, VA, in about 1962.
- The Galford Ancestry, by Lloyd Pritt Galford, 1981.
- *The History of the Morison or Morrison Family* by Leonard A. Morrison, Frederick William Leopold Thomas A. Williams & Company, 1880 - 468 p. Thucydides, *The history of the Peloponnesian war*, Vol. I, John Watts, 1753.
- The *Samuels Family Story*, Virginia, Kentucky, Indiana and Illinois, 1971 by Murial (Martens) Hoffman.
- The WBH is so often cited in this volume is Wilma Beard Harper.
- This information from, Records of Augusta Co., VA, Vol. III, by Chalkley, p.531, 560. Page 195, citing Will Book VI, records appraisement of the estate of Barnet Lance by Peter Hull, Jno. Gum, Sr. and Michael Armengash, 20 Sep 1791.
- Title: Ancestry Family Trees Publication: Online publication - Provo, UT, USA: Ancestry.com. Source: S2170648941 Repository: #R2170648939. Original data: Family Tree files submitted by Ancestry members. Note: This information comes from 1 or more individual Ancestry Family Tree files.
- Wesley Mullenneix of Naches, WA and Salton City, CA representing the Molynrux Family Association.
- Will recorded in Pocahontas Co. Will Book 3, page 4, copy Jacob Hull Arbogast is named as son in all histories but was not in will. Will probated in June 1852 term of Court, actual date of death unknown. Tombstone indicates 1760 birth.
- William Nottingham, Jr. & Mary Arbogast of Pocahontas

Immediate Family of Michael Arbogast and Mary Elizabeth Samuels.

The details and descendants of each child is presented in this Volume or in Volumes I and III.

<u>Children</u>

+	2	i.	Odessus Adam² Arbogast b. Oct 25 1759.
+	3	ii.	David Arbogast b. C 1761.
+	4	iii.	Mary Elizabeth Arbogast b. C 1765.
+	5	iv.	Michael Arbogast b. C 1768.
+	6	v.	Dorothy "Dolly" Arbogast b. 1765/1769.
+	7	vi.	Henry Arbogast b. Aug 22 1770.
+	8	vii.	Peter Arbogast b. Aug 22 1770.
+	9	viii.	John C. Arbogast b. C 1771.
+	10	ix.	George Arbogast b. Jun 09 1772.

How best to use these listing

Each descendant of of Adam **Odessus** Arbogast in all generations has been assigned a unique, person number. Following the unique number the descendant's name will appear in the listings, followed by, in parenthesis, the genealogical track of the person back to Adam **Odessus** Arbogast, who is person number 1. Following that in the paragraph is the personal information (birth, death, burial, notes, etc.) about the individual, their spouse(s), with the same information about them, and their children. Here is an example using the family of one of Adam's children Mary.

3. **Mary² Arbogast** (1.Odessus Adam¹), b. Jun 15 1782 in Augusta Co., VA, d. Oct 23 1858 in Siltington Creek, Pocahontas Co., WV, buried in Family Cem., Glade Hill, Pocahontas Co., WV.
   <u>She Married</u> **William Nottingham, Jr.**, b. Nov 5 1778 in Augusta Co., VA (son of William Nottingham, Sr. and Susannah O'Brien), d. Apr 14 1857 in Pocahontas Co., WV, buried in Family Cem., Glade Hill, Pocahontas Co., WV

+	16	i.	Henry³ Nottingham b. Jul 13 1804.
+	17	ii.	Margaret Nottingham b. Sep 25 1806.
+	18	iii.	Nancy Jane Nottingham b. Feb 14 1808.
+	19	iv.	Adam Nottingham b. Sep 12 1809.
+	20	v.	Mahalia Patsy Nottingham b. Jul 12 1811.
+	21	vi.	William Nottingham III b. Dec 25 1812.
	22	vii.	Mary Nottingham b. May 20 1814 in Bath Co., VA, buried in Family Cem., Glade Hill, Pocahontas Co., WV, d. 1840 in Pocahontas Co., WV.
+	23	viii.	Addison Nottingham b. Apr 2 1817.

Here, Mary Arbogast, who's unique number is "3", in front of her name is followed by her personal information and spouse, which will always be in bold, followed by her children. Note the superscript 2 following her name, meaning she is the second generation from Adam, being number one. Note that seven of her listed children have a plus (+) symbol in front of their unique number and one does not. Those with a (+) symbol in front of their unique number means they were <u>Married</u> with children and will appear later in the document identified by their unique number with their, spouse and children. The name of those descendants which did not have children (i.e. no + symbol in front of their name)appears once as a child below their parents names. If those descendants had a spouse it will appear with them in bold as well as the paragraph of personal information (birth, death, burial, notes, etc.). Their unique number or name will not appear again except in the index.

Those descendants who are parents of children (have a + symbol, to the left of their name) will initially only have their unique number, name and birth date (if available). However, the child's number and name will appear as a paragraph heading in the next generation, along with, in parenthesis, the genealogical track back to Adam Arbogast, personal information (birth, death, burial, notes, etc.), their spouse(s) and parents of the spouse(s) if available, notes about them, and their children, if any. Within the child's name will have a superscript number indicating which generation they are in.

Within those families with children, the children will be numbered i, ii, etc. The first child of a family will have a superscript showing their generation, and that of their siblings. This process repeats itself through all generations.

See in the example above. Mary is a second generation family and their third generation children. First is a person number. Then the person's name with a superscript number showing their generation from Adam. Following her name and within a set of parenthesis are the ancestors of the person back to $Adam^1$, then the descendants birth, death, etc. details, followed by any notes about the person. If the person has a spouse(s) it will be next in bold, followed by the parents of the spouse(s), and then their children, (numbered i, ii, etc.). In our example the family has eight children, each with its own unique number. Seven of the eight have a + symbol in front of their name, meaning it will appear in the next generation with their spouse and offspring. The children without a + symbol as well as their spouse, which will be in bold, if there is one, will not appear again in a listing. This process will repeat itself until all persons and all generations are listed.

Notice the first child in the listing has a superscript number. This indicates the number of generations this child is away from Adam Arbogast. For example $Henry^3$ Nottingham is three generation away, as is shown by the superscript ^{3}.

Descendants of David Arbogast Second Child of Michael and Mary Elizabeth Samuels

Generation One

David^1 Arbogast, b. About 1761 in Frederick, or, Pendleton Co., VA (son of Michael Arbogast and Mary Elizabeth Samuels Amanapas), d. About 1833 in Madison Co., IN. Migrated to Champaign Co., later Clark Co., OH with brothers, Michael, Jr., and Peter, about 1811. Peter remained in Ohio. David later relocated to Madison Co., IN, about 1830-1831, where he died.

Military: Pvt., Capt. Peter Hull's Co., 2nd Bn., Augusta Militia, during Yorktown Campaign, 1781, page 148, Virginia Militia in the Revolutionary War,

By McAllister. From "Mulanax - Bales" by Katherine and Alvin Mulanax, April 1980, pp. 83 &84, David is thought to have migrated to Madison Co., Indiana shortly after 1830 with his family and other relatives, including his niece, Catherine Arbogast Mulanax (daughter of Michael Arbogast, Jr.), and her husband, Joseph Mulanax. The Mulanax' report that three Arbogast bought land in Madison County in the 1830's, Jesse, Isaac and Jacob Arbogast. It is thought that they are sons of David Arbogast who came to Madison County about 1831.

According to Vera Arbogast Turner of Bloomington, IL, David purchased land in Madison Co., IN in 1833. Vera is descended through the son, Henry.

Deed, Sept.1799:David and Elizabeth Arbogast to Michael Arbogast 81 acres in Crab Apple Bottom, adjoining John Arbogast and his own land. Part of 315 acres patented 11-15-1791. Deed, Sept.3 1799:David and Elizabeth Arbogast to John Arbogast 50 acres in Crab Apple Bottom adjoining his own land and Michael Arbogast. Part of 315 acres patented 11-15-1791.

Married Jul 04 1785 in Augusta Co., VA, **Elizabeth Fleisher** (daughter of Peter Fleisher).Information from research of (AAF). Children are probably not in order of birth. (Galen Arbogast of Tabor, ND). Elizabeth is daughter of Peter Fleisher.

Children:

+ 2   i.   Anna Abigail^2 Arbogast b. Jun 17 1786.
+ 3   ii.   Henry Miles Arbogast b. Aug 29 1790.
+ 4   iii.   Barbary Arbogast b. Feb 09 1799.
+ 5   iv.   Enos Arbogast b. Feb 05 1802.
   6   v.   Jacob Arbogast, b. May 09 1810, d. Dec 14 1882.
                   Married Clark Co. OH marriage records Book 3. Marriage record says he was a widower when he Married **Elizabeth Hargadine**. Grave marker in Madison Co., IN, found by Katherine and Alvin Mulanax is engraved, Jacob Arbogast, died 14 Dec 1882, aged 72 years, 7 months and 5 days..
+ 7   vi.   Sarah (Sally) Arbogast b. About 1796.
   8   vii.   William Arbogast.
                   Married: Clark Co. OH marriage records Book 1-B, pg 251.Married Apr-11-1830 in Clark Co., OH, **Anna Jaynes**.
   9   viii.   Isaac Arbogast, b. About 1804 in Springfield, Clark Co., OH, d. About 1845 in Anderson, Madison Co., IN.
                   Married: **Elizabeth Farnsworth**, Clark Co. OH marriage records Book 1-B, pg 248.
   10   ix.   Elizabeth Arbogast.
                   She Married **Miles Elliott**.
   11   x.   Moses Arbogast, b. 1808 in Randolph Co., WV.

Generation Two

2. **Anna Abigail² Arbogast** (1.David¹), b. Jun 17 1786 in Virginia, d. Feb 10 1864 in Anderson, Madison Co., IN.
Information from a line of descent prepared by Ruth Moss Smith (Mrs. Leslie Smith) indicates date and place of death of Anna Abigail.
<u>Married</u> 1805 in Pendleton Co., WV, **John M. Moss**, b. 1 Jun 1788 in Pendleton Co., WV, d. Jun 1 1888 in Augusta Co., VA.

Children:

+	12	i.	William Jefferson³ Moss b. Sep-10-1810.
+	13	ii.	Montezuma Moss b. About 1811.
	14	iii.	Maud Betsy Moss b. in Virginia.
+	15	iv.	Eliza Moss b. Feb 15 1816.
	16	v.	James Moss b. Mar 30 1818 in Virginia, d. Jan 5 1865 in Madison Co., IL.
	17	vi.	Polly Ann Lewarky Moss b. About 1819 in Virginia.
+	18	vii.	Catherine Moss b. About 1821.
+	19	viii.	Isaac Moss b. About 1823.

3. **Henry Miles² Arbogast** (1.David¹), b. Aug 29 1790 in Pendleton Co., WV, d. Dec 6 1871 in Rutledge, DeWitt Co., IL, buried in McCord Cem., Fullerton, DeWitt Co., IL.
<u>Married</u> Feb 18 1809 in Augusta, Co., VA, **Mary Huffman**, b. Mar 24 1787 in Pendleton Co., WV (daughter of Christian Huffman and Catherine Colaw), d. Apr 12 1853 in DeWitt, DeWitt Co., IL, buried in McCord Cem., Fullerton, DeWitt Co., IL.

Children

+ 20   i.   William³ Arbogast b. Apr 10 1820.

   21   ii.   Henry J Arbogast b. May 29 1822 in Clark Co., OH, d. May 9 1903 in DeWitt, DeWitt Co., IL, buried in Campground Cem., Farmer City, DeWitt Co., IL.
He <u>Married</u> **Frances Harrold**, b. Dec 01 1825 in Grayson Co., VA.

+ 22   iii.   Mary Arbogast b. Jun 2 1824.

   23   iv.   Enos Arbogast b. Oct 13 1825 in Clark Co., OH, d. Nov 1 1913 in McLean Co., IL, buried in Greenwood Cem., Arrowsmith, McLean, IL.
<u>Married</u> Sep 06 1849 in McLean Co., IL, Mary Morgan, b. Sep 30 1827 in Greene Co., TN, d. Sep 30 1865 in Saybrook, McLean Co., IL.

   24   v.   Daniel Huffman Arbogast b. May 2 1827 in Clark Co., OH, Daniel was born in Clark county, Ohio, May 27th, 1827. David Arbogast and wife, the grandparents of the subject of this sketch, were natives of Germany. They emigrated to America and settled in Virginia. The family moved to Ohio at an early day and subsequently moved to Madison county, Indiana, where the grandparents died. Henry, his son (and father of D. H.), was born in Pendleton County, Virginia, in August 1791. He came from Clark county, Illinois, in October 1838, and the following winter settled near Lexington in McLean county. In March following he moved to DeWitt county and settled on section ten in DeWitt township, where he resided until a short time before his death. He died December 6th, 1871, in his eighty-seventh year. He <u>Married</u> Mary Huffman, daughter of Christian Huffman. She was born in Pendleton county, Virginia, in 1787. She died April 12th, 1853, in her sixty-seventy year. By the union of Henry and Mary Arbogast there were fifteen children, twelve of whom grew to maturity, and eight are still living. Daniel H. was in his twelfth year when the family came to DeWitt county. He here grew to manhood and remained at home at work on his father's farm, until he was twenty years of age, then he commenced working for himself. He worked for the farmers around in the neighborhood, rented land and raised a crop, and did such general work as fell to his hand. He soon after got into handling stock, and was principally engaged in that business from 1855 to 1870. In the latter year he commenced the manufacture of brick, and has given nearly all of his attention to that business since that time. He manufactured all the brick with a few

exceptions that are in the brick buildings now standing in Farmer City. Taking all-in-all Mr. Arbogast has been unusually successful. He has met, like most of men, with some reverses, yet has no particular reason to complain of his lot. On the 25th of February 1849 he was united in marriage to Miss Minerva Payn. She was born in Tennessee, May 29th, 1829. She is the daughter of John A. G. and Catherine Payn, who came to Indiana in 1830, and in 1841 settled in Will county, Illinois. Mrs. Arbogast was stopping with her grandfather Payn in this county when she was married. Nine children have been born to Mr. and Mrs. Arbogast; seven sons and two daughters. Their names in the order of their birth are, Elizabeth J., who is the wife of Arthur Webb; Lydia Ann, wife of John Sweeney; John, who Married Susan Muir; Amos, married Mary Griffith; Edward, Sherman, Walter; Grenade who died in his tenth year; and George who died in his infancy. Both he and his wife are members of the M. E. Church. Politically he has been a Republican since 1856, when he voted for John C. Fremont. His maternal grandfather Huffman was a soldier in the Revolution, and his father Henry was a soldier in the Indian War of 1817. Mr. Arbogast is a plain straightforward man, and much respected in the community.
From: http://www.rootsweb.ancestry.com/~ildewitt/biographies.htm
Married Feb 25 1849 in Santa Anna Twp., Dewitt Co., Il, **Minerva Payne**, b. May 29 1829 in Tennessee, d. Apr-01-1914.

- + 25 vi. George L Arbogast b. Jul 28 1829.
- 26 vii. Peter Arbogast b. 1812 in Pendleton Co., VA, d. 1874 in DeWitt, DeWitt Co., IL.
- 27 viii. Lydia Ann Arbogast b. 1831 in Clark Co., OH, d. AFT 1850 in DeWitt, DeWitt Co., IL.
- 28 ix. Jane Arbogast b. 1838 in DeWitt, DeWitt Co., IL, d. AFT 1850 in DeWitt, DeWitt Co., IL.
- + 29 x. Hugh Arbogast b. C1816.

4. **Barbary**^{2} **Arbogast** (1.David^1), b. Feb 09 1799 in Pendleton Co., WV, d. Mar 19 1885 in Paris, Edgar Co., IL, buried in Franklin Cem., Edgar Co., IL.
She Married **Henry Moss**, b. Jun-25-1790 in Augusta Co., VA, buried in Franklin Cem., Edgar Co., IL, d. Jan-09-1868 in Edgar Co. IL. Other children include Harrison Moss (1838).

Children:

- + 30 i. Elizabeth^3 Moss b. Feb-10-1822.
- 31 ii. Belimira Moss.
- 32 iii. Amanda Moss.
  Married ? Crabtree, Marshalltown, IA
- 33 iv. Henry S. Moss b. c 1834, d. Aug-09-1874 in Paris, Edgar Co., IL.
  Single-Religious fanatic-fasted & died-known as the meanest man on earth--Information from Stella R Jurey
- 34 v. Harriet Moss b. c 1836 in Clark Co., OH, d. 1914.
  Married **Joseph Glascow Arthur** 24 Aug 1871, Paris, IL. 1860 census 24, domestic, b. OH, b. Oct-23-1812, d. Sep-12-1987.
- 35 vi. Harrison Moss b. Sep 1 1838 in Clark Co., OH, d. Mar 1919. Farmer Edgar Twp., Edgar Co., IL. Married **Caroline R. McClain** 4 Oct 1870, , b. Aug-04-1849, d. Mar-14-1919. Children are Amanda (died in infancy), Bertha (Married **John Harris**), Blanche, and Faye (Married **Claude Reed**).
- + 36 vii. Alexandria Moss b. Apr-26-1841.

5. **Enos**^{2} **Arbogast** (1.David^1), b. Feb 05 1802 in Pendleton Co., WV, d. Apr 12 1853 in DeWitt, DeWitt Co., IL.
Information from Kay Ellen Martinson Fleming of Tucson,
Married Jun-01-1823 in Clark Co., OH, marriage records Book 1-B, pg 50**Catherine Fleming**, b. Mar-01-1806 in Clark Co., OH, d. Oct-16-1881 in Madison Co., IN.

Children:

+ 37	i.	Sanford Albert³ Arbogast b. Jan-26-1824.
38	ii.	Laura Louisa Arbogast b. C 1825, d. 1889.
+ 39	iii.	David Daniel Arbogast b. Nov-25-1826.
40	iv.	Jacob Arbogast b. Dec-15-1828.
		Married Apr-12-1853, **Sally Vinson**.
+ 41	v.	Henry J. Arbogast b. Oct-26-1830.
42	vi.	Benjamin Arbogast b. Apr-15-1832, d. Dec-01-1834.
+ 43	vii.	Albert Adair Arbogast b. Apr-17-1834.
44	viii.	Nancy Jane Arbogast b. 1841, d. 1862.
45	ix.	Enos Miles Arbogast b. c 1843, d. 1863.

7. **Sarah (Sally)² Arbogast** (1.David¹), b. About 1796.
   Source Henry Miles Arbogast, and descendants. Galen Arbogast of Tabor, SD,.
   Married Feb-19-1809 in Pendleton Co., VA, **Jacob Moss**, b. 1786.

   ### *Children:*

46	i.	Matilda³ Moss b. Nov-18-1854.
47	ii.	Lucinda Moss b. 1832 in Ohio.
48	iii.	Jacob Moss b. 1836 in Ohio.
49	iv.	Henry Moss b. 1839 in Ohio.

Generation Three

12. **William Jefferson³ Moss** (2.Anna Abigail² Arbogast, 1.David¹), b. Sep-10-1810 in Virginia, d. Apr 16 1865 in Anderson, Madison Co., IN.
    He Married **Elizabeth Gordon**, b. Sep 20 1813 (daughter of Philip Gordon and Nancy Smiley), d. Mar 27 1891 in Anderson, Madison Co., IN.

    ### *Children:*

50	i.	John L.⁴ Moss b. Feb 12 1837 in Madison Co., IN, d. Aug 29 1851 in Anderson, Madison Co., IN.
51	ii.	Nancy Jane Moss b. Dec 31 1839 in Madison Co., IN, d. Jan 2 1867 in Anderson, Madison Co., IN.
		She Married **Lemuell R. Webb**.
52	iii.	Margaret Ann Moss b. May 28 1841 in Madison Co., IN, d. Mar 6 1894 in Anderson, Madison Co., IN.
		She Married **Robert Wyson**, b. Feb 11 1838, d. Sep 13 1867 in Anderson, Madison Co., IN.
53	iv.	Leroy Franklin Moss b. Sep 10 1841 in Anderson, Madison Co., IN, d. Jan 28 1893 in Anderson, Madison Co., IN.
+ 54	v.	Samuel Robeson Moss b. 1846.
+ 55	vi.	Sanford Ross Moss b. Mar 12 1846.
+ 56	vii.	Isabel Nora Moss b. Nov 19 1853.

13. **Montezuma³ Moss** (2.Anna Abigail² Arbogast, 1.David¹), b. About 1811 in Virginia, buried Maplewood Cem. Anderson, Madison Co., IN
    He Married **Eliza Ann Davis,** b. 1836, d. 1885.

    ### *Children:*

57	i.	G. W.⁴ Moss b. 1858.
58	ii.	Sarah Alice Moss b. 1861.
		Married **Jerome Beachler**
59	iii.	N. A. Moss b. 1861.
60	iv.	Charles Lee Moss b. 1864.
		Married **Elnora Elizabeth Beck**
61	v.	E. M. Moss b. 1867.

15. **Eliza**[3] **Moss** (2.Anna Abigail[2] Arbogast, 1.David[1]), b. Feb 15 1816 in Ohio, d. Jul 30 1905 in Madison Co., IL.
    She Married **John Johnston**.
    ### *Children:*
    - 62   i.   James[4] Johnston.
    - 63   ii.   Emma Johnston b. 1853.
    - 64   iii.   Francis Johnston b. 1856.

18. **Catherine**[3] **Moss** (2.Anna Abigail[2] Arbogast, 1.David[1]), b. About 1821 in Virginia.
    She Married **Nancy Johnston**.
    ### *Children:*
    - 65   i.   Margaret[4] Moss b. 1855 in Indiana.
    - 66   ii.   Roma Moss b. 1855 in Indiana.
    - 67   iii.   Mike Moss b. 1859 in Indiana.

19. **Isaac**[3] **Moss** (2.Anna Abigail[2] Arbogast, 1.David[1]), b. About 1823, d. in Indiana.
    He Married **Martha (Unknown)**.
    ### *Children:*
    - 68   i.   Anna (Angelia)[4] Moss b. 1854 in Indiana.
    - 69   ii.   J. Thomas Moss b. 1856.
    - 70   iii.   James Moss b. 1859 in Indiana.
    - 71   iv.   William B. Moss b. 1867 in Indiana.

20. **William**[3] **Arbogast** (3.Henry Miles[2], 1.David[1]), b. Apr 10 1820 in Clark Co., OH, d. Dec 31 1861 in Arrowsmith, McLean Co., IL.
    Extract of a newspaper article, probably a Saybrook, IL, paper, telling of the reunion of all of William's 7 sons in 1906 or 1907. They had not been together since 1861. It was held on New Years Day at the farm of Enos, one mile west of Saybrook. A second gathering was held at the home of John L. on Jan 4th.
    John L., living on part of the old homestead.
    H. Harmon of Grant Co., Oregon.
    Enos A. of Cheney's Grove, IL.
    Ethan O. of Rooks Co., KS.
    Martin P. of Jefferson Co., IA.
    Ira of Kaboka, MO.
    James B. of Clifton, IL.

    Extract of cemetery record indicates William died 31 Dec 1862 at 40 yrs., 8 mos.
    and 20 days.
    Married Oct 5 1841 in McLean Co., IL, **Elizabeth Newcomb**, b. Jan 20 1917 in Clark Co., OH, d. Aug 1857.
    ### *Children:*
    - 72   i.   Millie Jane[4] Arbogast b. Mar-27-1843, d. Sep-27-1843.
    - + 73   ii.   John Lewis Arbogast b. Sep-09-1844.

22. **Mary**[3] **Arbogast** (3.Henry Miles[2], 1.David[1]), b. Jun 2 1824 in Clark Co., OH, d. Aug 29 1910 in Parnell, DeWitt Co., IL, buried in McCord Cem., Fullerton, DeWitt Co., IL.
    Married Mar 03 1844 in DeWitt, DeWitt Co., IL, **Robert McKinley**, b. Aug 02 1818 in Chillicothe, Ross Co., OH (son of William McKinley and Margaret Ralston), buried in McCord Cem., Fullerton, DeWitt Co., IL, d. Mar 07 1883 in Fullerton, DeWitt Co., IL.
    ### *Children:*
    - + 74   i.   John Warner[4] McKinley b. Feb 12 1845.
    - 75   ii.   Cornelius McKinley b. Aug 14 1849, d. Oct 11 1851.
    - + 76   iii.   Charles Lewis McKinley b. Sep 19 1852.

       77   iv.   George Haines McKinley b. Sep 07 1956.
                    (1) Married Nov 28 1883 in DeWitt, DeWitt Co., IL, **Emma L Barnes**, d. May 13 1895.
                    (2) Married Dec 30 1896 in DeWitt, DeWitt Co., IL, **Lottie Hollenback**, b. Feb 18 1873, d. Jun 26 1916.
       78   v.   Laura Susan McKinley b. Aug 06 1859, d. Oct 03 1894.

25. **George L³ Arbogast** (3.Henry Miles², 1.David¹), b. Jul 28 1829 in Clark Co., OH, d. Feb 26 1885 in DeWitt, DeWitt Co., IL, buried in McCord Cem., Fullerton, DeWitt Co., IL.
Married Oct 26 1858 in DeWitt, DeWitt Co., IL, **Martha Elizabeth Sappington**, b. Apr 25 1842 in Morgan Co., IL, buried in McCord Cem., Fullerton, DeWitt Co., IL, d. Mayb1931 in Farmer City, DeWitt, Co., IL.

                Children:
+ 79   i.   Stella Amanda⁴ Arbogast b. Oct 10 1859.
  80   ii.   Clarissa C Arbogast b. Aug 12 1861 in DeWitt, DeWitt Co., IL, d. May 29 1941 in DeWitt, DeWitt Co., IL.
  81   iii. Dora L Arbogast b. Sep 20 1863, d. Jan 19 1948 in Farmer City, DeWitt, Co., IL.
  82   iv.   Charles Preston Arbogast b. 1866, d. 1942.
  83   v.   Ida E Arbogast b. May 04 1872, d. May 1938.
                Married Oct 08 1891 in DeWitt, DeWitt Co., IL, **J Wes McConkey**, b. Feb 12 1870, d. Mar 28 1949.

29. **Hugh³ Arbogast** (3.Henry Miles², 1.David¹), b. C1816.
Married Nov-12-1837 in Clark Co., OH, **Nancy Curl**, b. Jan-14-1920 in OH (daughter of Jeremiah Curt and Margaret Swisher).

                Children:
  84   i.   George⁴ Arbogast.
  85   ii.   Bruce Arbogast.
  86   iii. John Wesley Arbogast. On 1880 census at Cheney's Grove Twp., McLean Co., IL Lists John W. Arbogast age 39 b. IL, wife Maggie age 39 b. IL, son Charles age 10 b. IL, and son Lewis age 8 b. IL. Address West Street Saybrook City, IL.
  87   iv.   Zeria W. Arbogast.
  88   v.   William Goodwin Arbogast.
  89   vi.   Rhoda Arbogast b. c1858. Married name Patton.
  90   vii. M.D. Arbogast.

30. **Eliza³ Moss** (4.Barbary² Arbogast, 1.David¹), b. Feb-10-1822 in Clark Co., OH, d. Jul-10-1903 in Edgar Co. IL.
She Married **John Arthur**, b. Oct-12-1819 in Pennsylvania, d. Oct-09-1898 in Edgar Co. IL.

                Children:
+ 91   i.   Athelinda⁴ Arthur b. c1848.
+ 92   ii.   Daniel Arthur.
  93   iii. Henry H. Arthur b. Oct-15-1854.
  94   iv.   John D. Arthur b. Apr-05-1919.
                Married **Lucy Keys**, 3 children. Lloyd Married **Margaret Hodge**, and Faith Married **Mr. Stout**
  95   v.   Addie Arthur b. Nov-19-1959, d. Jun-06-1947.
                Married **Simon Risser**, two children. John Married **Lorraine Scott** and Stella Married **Lester Christy**, and 2nd **Charles E. Jurey**.
  96   vi.   Mary J. Arthur b. 1852.
                Married **John Henry Harris**, Mary and John had 8 child:
                    Leonard Harris Married **Gertrude Taylor**,
                    Charles Harris Married **Lois Trogdon**,
                    John Harris Married **Bertha Moss**,
                    Myrtle Harris Married **Claude Thomas**,

Irma Harris Married **Charles B. Van Houton**, the 6th child died in infancy,
Hazel Harris Married **Dr. Frank Miller**, and
Amelia Harris Married **Floyd A. Johnson**.

36. **Alexandria**[3] **Moss** (4.Barbary[2] Arbogast, 1.David[1]), b. Apr-26-1841 in Clark Co., OH.
    He Married **Sarah A. Hazelton**, b. Jun-02-1843 in New Hampshire.

    ### *Children:*
    - 97   i.   Frank H.[4] Moss b. 1871, d. Aug-21-1963.
    - 98   ii.   Chester A. Moss.
    - 99   iii.   Josephine M. Moss.
    - 100   iv.   Mable A. Moss.
    - 101   v.   Maude A. Moss b. 1873, d. Sep 1874.

    They had a total of seven children, two died young.

37. **Sanford Albert**[3] **Arbogast** (5.Enos[2], 1.David[1]), b. Jan-26-1824, d. Apr-14-1892.
    Letter from Governor, National Soldiers Home, Topeka, KS, to Sanford Albert Arbogast, Parker, IN, 22 Oct 1912, confirming David's death and burial with full military honors. Effects sent to his daughter Ida L. Hall, Grand, OK, R# 2., 18 Apr 1912. Letter in Frances Arbogast files.
    Farmed near Muncie, IN, later to south of Parker, IN, they purchased the homestead which they transformed from a forest wilderness to a farm of unsurpassed fertility
    He Married **Isabella Hays**, b. Jul-15-1826 in Troy, Miami Co., Oh (daughter of James Hays and Sarah Wallace), buried in Windsor Cem., Randolph Co., IN, d. May 15 1900.

    ### *Children:*
    - 102   i.   Benjamin Hays[4] Arbogast b. Dec-08-1852, buried in Windsor Cem. Randolph Co., IN, d. Jul-29-1872.
    - 103   ii.   Louisa Acenith Arbogast b. Mar-11-1855, buried in Windsor Cem. Randolph Co., IN, d. Mar-26-0936.
      Married **George Duncan** b. 1845, d. 1902. Children: Herbert, Benjamin, Ivy, William, Catherine, Rollie and Oscar,
    - + 104   iii.   Robert Sprole Arbogast b. Feb-04-1858.
    - + 105   iv.   Frances Isabella Arbogast b. Jun-26-1860.
    - 106   v.   Henry Miles Arbogast b. Jan-29-1863, buried in Woodland Cem., Maxville, Randolph Co., IN, d. Oct-16-1929.
    - 107   vi.   Ethan Allan Arbogast b. Jul 1868, buried in Windsor Cem. Randolph Co., IN, d. Feb-12-1892.
    - 108   vii.   Sanford Albert Arbogast b. Sep-13-1865, d. Apr-03-1924.
      Married Jan-19-1889 in Parker, Randolph Co., IN, **Mary Des Moines**, b. Nov-20-1868 in Parker, Randolph Co., IN, buried in East Maplewood, Cem., Anderson, Madison Co., in, d. Dec-22-1948 in Anderson, Madison Co., IN.
    - 109   viii.   Ethan Allen Arbogast b. 1868, d. 1892.
    - + 110   ix.   Sarah Catherine Arbogast b. Jan 3 1848.
    - + 111   x.   Enos James Arbogast b. Jun-03-1850.

39. **David Daniel**[3] **Arbogast** (5.Enos[2], 1.David[1]), b. Nov-25-1826, d. Mar-24-1912 in Nat'l. Soldiers, Home, Topeka, Ks.
    Civil War Pension Files, notes from AAF, enlisted Jan 1863 yet another record indicates 14 Mar 1862 at St. Joseph, MO, applied for pension in 1893 after his wife died. Record indicates he was born 26 Nov 1825 in OH, died 24 Mar 1912, He lived at Troy, KS 1864-1874, Eureka, NV until 1879, then Butte, MT until 1886. In 1893 when applying for pension he lived at Salmon City, Lemhi Co., ID. In 1907 to National Home at Leavenworth, KS.
    He Married **Mercy Brevard**, b. Jun-10-1829 in Clark Co., OH, d. Aug-19-1887 in KS, married 20 Mar 1849 in Champaign Co., OH,

    ### *Children:*
    - 112   i.   Sarah Catherine[4] Arbogast b. Feb-28-1850.
    - 113   ii.   Stephen Faust Arbogast b. Jul-09-1851.

	114	iii.	Zebulon Brevard (Zeb) Arbogast, b. Aug-02-1852, d. Dec 1941 in Salmon, ID.
	115	iv.	Isaac Newton Arbogast b. Oct-21-1854.
+	116	v.	Rudolphus George Arbogast b. Jun-16-1860.
+	117	vi.	Ida Alice Arbogast b. Feb-02-1862.

41. **Henry J.**[3] **Arbogast** (5.Enos[2], 1.David[1]), b. Oct-26-1830.
<u>Married</u> JAN 1861 in Edgar Co. IL, **Mary Ann Roth**.

   Children:
   - 118   i.   Etta[4] Arbogast.
   - 119   ii. Thomas Jonathan Arbogast b. Jan-03-1862 in Edgar Co. IL, d. Aug-18-1862 in Springfield, Sangamon Co., IL.

43. **Albert Adair**[3] **Arbogast** (5.Enos[2], 1.David[1]), b. Apr-17-1834, d. Nov-30-1910.
<u>Married</u> Dec-31-1857, **Varenda Mc Bride**, b. Feb-18-1840, d. May-30-1915.

   Children:
   - 120   i.   Alfred[4] Arbogast.
   - 121   ii.   Sanford Barton Arbogast b. c 1860.
   - 122   iii. Enos Arbogast b. Jul-17-1867, d. Dec-29-1942.
   - 123   iv.   Louisa Catherine Arbogast b. Oct-02-1862, d. Jun-28-1938 in Dolson, Clark, IL.

Generation Four

54. **Samuel Robeson**[4] **Moss** (12.William Jefferson[3], 2.Anna Abigail[2] Arbogast, 1.David[1]), b. 1846 in Virginia.
He <u>Married</u> **Mary Ruth Rulon**, b. 1848 in Virginia, d. 1905 in Virginia.

   Children:
   - 124   i.   Minnie Bell[5] Moss b. Nov 21 1870 in Anderson, Madison Co., IN, d. Dec 9 1961 in Fairbury, Jefferson Co., NE.
   - + 125   ii.   William Jefferson Moss b. May 21 1872.
   - + 126   iii. Alfred Rulon Moss b. Nov 2 1873.
   - + 127   iv.   Simeon Martindale Moss b. Nov 27 1875.
   - + 128   v.   Vernon Laurence Moss b. 1888.

55. **Sanford Ross**[4] **Moss** (12.William Jefferson[3], 2.Anna Abigail[2] Arbogast, 1.David[1]), b. Mar 12 1846 in Alexander Co., IL.
One of the substantial men of Madison County, Indiana, who resides two miles West of the city of Anderson, was born near the place of of his present residence on the 12th of March, 1846. He is the son of Jefferson Moss, a pioneer of the county, who has been called to his reward, but whose memory is fondly cherished, not only by his descendants, but by all who knew him a quarter of a century ago. Sanford R was married to Martha Thornburgh, daughter of Thomas Thornburgh, an old and highly esteemed citizens of the county, August 14, 1876. No children have been born to bless their wedded life. Mr. Moss is extensively engaged in stock raising and trading, and has as high as two hundred fine head of cattle at a time on his extensive farm, which is also stocked at all times with, horses, hogs, sheep; in fact, all kinds of stock. He has a large fine brick residence on his farm, with conveniences calculated to make home desirable. Mr. Moss is an uncompromising Democrat of prominence and influence in the county, and always takes an active part in elections. When he announces himself in favor of a man for office, it will be upon investigation that he is competent and honest. He is not a member of any order or church, and is liberal in his notions generally. Quiet and unobtrusive in his bearing toward men, he glides along through life enjoying the comforts thereof in a modest and becoming manner, and the entire confidence of he community in which he lives.
Reference: "Those I Have Met, or Boys in Blue" by Samuel Harden son of William J & Elizabeth(Gordon) Moss.

(1) He Married **Martha Thornburg,** b. 1846, IN She was the daughter of Thomas Thornberg who came to Madison county from Ohio and for years was the owner and operator of a farm in Richland township. At the time of the death of her brother, Richard Thornberg, Mr. Moss and Martha adopted one of the latter's children, Thomas, which they reared and who is now a resident of Texas. Source Information History of Madison County, Indiana

Children:
- 129 i.   Mabelle K.^{5} Moss b. 1882.
- 130 ii. Josephine Winifred Moss b. 1884.
- 131 iii. Leroy Hartley Moss b. 1886.

(2) Married May 21 1873, **Mary Matilda Hartley**.

56. **Isabel Nora^4 Moss** (12.William Jefferson^3, 2.Anna Abigail^2 Arbogast, 1.David^1), b. Nov 19 1853 in Anderson, Madison Co., IN, d. Dec 15 1895 in Anderson, Madison Co., IN.
Married May 20 1873 in Anderson, Madison Co., IN, **Francis Marion Wertz**, b. Jul 20 1850, d. Apr 17 1930.

Children:
- 132 i.   Jesse^5 Wertz b. 1875, d. 1878.
- 133 ii. Chester Wertz b. 1879, d. 1881.
- 134 iii. Leroy Franklin Wertz b. 1884, d. 1967.
- 135 iv. Florence Marie Wertz b. 1892.

73. **John Lewis^4 Arbogast** (20.William^3, 3.Henry Miles^2, 1.David^1), b. Sep-09-1844 in Arrowsmith, McLean Co., IL, d. 0031918 in Tampa, Hillsborough Co., FL.
Information from letter from Mrs. Lynn Turner of Bloomington, IL,
He Married **Catherine Okey Henderson**, b. Dec-11-1947 in Maysville, Mason Co., KY, d. Aug-03-1924 in Moscow, Latah Co., Id.

Children:
- + 136 i.   Mary Elizabeth^5 Arbogast b. Jun-27-1868.
- + 137 ii. William Henderson Arbogast b. Feb-20-1870.
-   138 iii. Anna Belle Arbogast b. Dec-18-1873.
-   139 iv. Birdie Arbogast b. Apr-23-1875, d. May-15-1875.
-   140 v.   Sarah E. Arbogast b. Apr-22-1877.

74. **John Warner^4 McKinley** (22.Mary^3 Arbogast, 3.Henry Miles^2, 1.David^1), b. Feb 12 1845 in DeWitt, DeWitt Co., IL, d. Jan 17 1912 in Farmer City, DeWitt, Co., IL.
Married Mar 20 1866 in Fullerton, DeWitt Co., IL, **Zorado Jane Brown**, b. Jan 18 1850 in Fullerton, DeWitt Co., IL (daughter of James Madison Brown and Rhoda Kizer), buried in Maple Grove Cem., Farmer City, DeWitt Co., IL, d. Nov 17 1835 in Farmer City, DeWitt, Co., IL.

Children:
- + 141 i.   Joseph Franklin^5 McKinley b. Jun 24 1867.
- + 142 ii. Harriet Esther McKinley b. Dec 18 1868.
- + 143 iii. Mattie Susan McKinley b. Aug 06 1873.
- + 144 iv. Samuel A McKinley b. Jul 21 1884.
- + 145 v.   Anna B McKinley b. May 21 1887.
-   146 vi. John Schuyler McKinley b. 1890 in DeWitt, DeWitt Co., IL, d. 1891 in DeWitt, DeWitt Co., IL.
-   147 vii. Robert A McKinley b. Oct 10 1893 in DeWitt, DeWitt Co., IL, d. Jun 20 1966 in Farmer City, DeWitt, Co., IL.
         He Married **Ruby Windsor**.

76. **Charles Lewis^4 McKinley** (22.Mary^3 Arbogast, 3.Henry Miles^2, 1.David^1), b. Sep 19 1852, d. Sep 11 1902.
Married Feb 20 1878 in DeWitt, DeWitt Co., IL, **Estaline Roy**.

Children:

148	i.	Maxie Edith^5 McKinley b. Jun 02 1879, d. Mar 29 1936.
		Married Aug 01 1900, **Edward H Denison**, b. Feb 03 1876, d. Oct 25 1953.
149	ii.	Robert Frederick McKinley b. May 19 1883, d. Sep 05 1924.
		Married Feb 24 1904, **Ava Berry**.
150	iii.	Jessie Alice McKinley b. Aug 22 1890, d. Jul 07 1939.
		Married Sep 25 1907, **George Marvin Farabough**.

79. **Stella Amanda^4 Arbogast** (25.George L^3, 3.Henry Miles^2, 1.David^1), b. Oct 10 1859 in DeWitt, DeWitt Co., IL, d. May 29 1941 in Farmer City, DeWitt, Co., IL.
(1) Married Oct 30 1877, **Josephus Fuller**, b. 1854 in Greene Co., PA (son of David Smith Fuller and Mary Bowers), d. Aug 25 1937 in Bedford, Taylor Co., IA.

Children:

+ 151	i.	Iris Icelona^5 Fuller b. Jun 04 1878.
152	ii.	Fred Elmer Fuller b. Jul 25 1880.
		Married Nov 21 1902 in Texas, **Amrynth Brasher**, b. Jan 20 1882 in Lamar Co., TX, d. 1971.
153	iii.	Carl Lindsey Fuller b. Feb 28 1884 in Farmer City, DeWitt, Co., IL, d. May 24 1953 in Bedford, Taylor Co., IA.
		Married Dec 05 1905, **Pearl May Hamilton**, b. Apr 18 1884, d. Aug 27 1947 in Bedford, Taylor Co., IA.
154	iv.	Grace Fuller b. Jan 17 1886 in Farmer City, DeWitt, Co., IL, d. Feb 05 1932 in Farmer City, DeWitt, Co., IL.
		Married Apr 05 1911 in Farmer City, DeWitt, Co., IL, **Fred Afflack**, b. Sep 06 1882 in Atlanta, Logan Co., IL, d. Jan 19 1945 in Pekin, Tazewell Co., IL.
155	v.	George H Fuller b. Feb 22 1889 in Farmer City, DeWitt, Co., IL, d. May 28 1951 in Farmer City, DeWitt, Co., IL.
		Married Feb 23 1910 in Clinton, DeWitt Co., IL, **Jane Kendall**, b. Apr 03 1889 in Farmer City, DeWitt, Co., IL, d. Jul 20 1978 in Decatur, Macon Co., IL.

(2) Married 1891 in Monticello, Piatt Co., IL, **Hosea Call**, b. in Indiana, d. in St. Louis, St. Louis Co., MO.
(3) Married 1896 in Monticello, Piatt Co., IL, **Henry Ardillon Farmer**, b. 1862 in Farmer City, DeWitt, Co., IL, d. 1948 in Farmer City, DeWitt, Co., IL.

91. **Athelinda^4 Arthur** (30.Eliza^3 Moss, 4.Barbary^2 Arbogast, 1.David^1), b. c1848, d. 1923 in Paris, Edgar Co., IL.
She Married **George Washington Brown**, b. Jun-05-1839 in Hillsboro, Highland Co. VA, d. 1920 in Paris, Edgar Co., IL.

Children:

+ 156	i.	Ada Viola^5 Brown b. Aug-02-1869.
157	ii.	Ida Mae Brown b. Feb-04-1871 in Edgar Co. IL, d. Oct-19-1959 in Paris, Edgar Co., IL.
		Married **William Harvey Morris**, 8 children. Archie Edgar, Athalinda, Harvey William, Mary Jane, Charles Foster, Stella, Walter Frederick, and Virginia
158	iii.	John Arthur Brown b. Nov-06-1872 in Edgar Co. IL, d. Jun-27-1953.
		Married **Hattie Luvernia Ross**, 6 children. Geneva, George, Goldie Jane, Nora Guthrie, John Arthur, and Harmon Clemens.
159	iv.	Joseph Edgar Brown b. Sep-23-1874 in Edgar Co. IL, d. Mar-02-1957.
		Married **Samantha Azlee Alton**, 15 children. Mary Azlee, Courtley Edward, Ora Lee, Bertha Ellen, Daisy L., Ollie Burton, Bee Bell, Eva Linda, Ernestine, Maggie Mae, Irma Eddie, E. Vivian, Elser Rennole, John Henry, and Joseph Edgar, Jr.
160	v.	Ola Elizabeth Brown b. Oct-01-1876, d. Feb-02-1961.
		Married **Zachery T. North** 21 Aug 1902
161	vi.	Gertrude Harriet Brown b. Aug-02-1878 in Edgar Co. IL, d. Jul-20-1959.

Married **Alfred F. Claybaugh**, 3 children. Eila B. married Samuel J. Hinds, James Daniel (twin) married Aileen Trimble, Janet (twin) Lloyd Reynolds. Janet's child Barbara Jane Reynolds who married James T. Carroll and had a son, Thomas Carroll

- 162   vii.   James Cooper Brown b. Feb-03-1881 in Edgar Co. IL, d. 1947.
  Married **Anna Ethel Johnson**, 3 children. Dorthea Jane (Brown) Bitzer, Viola married Cecil Terrell, and Mary Genevieve married Foster Givens and had three sons, Billy Bob, James Edward, and Cecil Allen Givens.
- 163   viii.   George Washington Jr. Brown b. Mar-28-1883 in Eureka Springs, AR, d. Jul-09-1941.
  Married **Anna Henry**, 2nd **Bessie Duckworth**.
- 164   ix.   Charles Robert Brown, 21 Nov 1884, Paris, Edgar Co., Il, **d.** 15 Dec 1976, Edgar Co., Il.
- 165   x.   Harry Franklin Brown b. Sep-07-1886, d. Mar-25-1961 in Bell, CA.
  Married **Elizabeth Reagan** 9 Aug 1912, one child Walter Louis Brown.

92. **Daniel^4 Arthur** (30.Eliza^3 Moss, 4.Barbary^2 Arbogast, 1.David^1).
    (1) Married 1872, **Mary Harris**.
    ### *Children:*
    - 166   i.   Oliver Wendell^5 Arthur. He Married **Rachel Gillespie**.
    - 167   ii.   Nettie Arthur. She Married **George Taylor**.
    - 168   iii.   Bruce Arthur. He Married **Julia Patton**.

    (2) He Married **Charity Morris**. Charity: Children Ada, Lula, a third child died as infant, Lena, John Morris, Clarence E., and a seventh child died as infant

104. **Robert Sprole^4 Arbogast** (37.Sanford Albert^3, 5.Enos^2, 1.David^1), b. Feb-04-1858 in Randolph Co., IN, d. Oct-19-1921 in Delaware Co., IN.
     He Married **Leah Philena Neal**, b. Apr-16-1861 in Delaware Co., IN, d. May-02-1930 in Randolph Co., IN.
     ### *Children:*
     - + 169   i.   Grover C.^{5} Arbogast b. Apr-16-1961.
     - 170   ii.   Grace Arbogast b. 1882, d. Aug 1941.
     - 171   iii.   Lona Arbogast b. 1886, d. Feb-11-1922 in Elkhart.IN.

105. **Frances Isabella^4 Arbogast** (37.Sanford Albert^3, 5.Enos^2, 1.David^1), b. Jun-26-1860 in Randolph Co., IN, buried in Mount Tabor Cem, Muncie, Delaware Co, IN, d. Aug-16-1931 in Delaware Co., IN.
     She Married **John A Neel**, b. Jul-24-1851 in Delaware Co., IN, buried in Mount Tabor Cem, Muncie, Delaware Co, IN, d. Mar-05-1928 in Delaware Co., IN.
     ### *Children:*
     - 172   i.   Della Mae^5 Neel b. 1880, d. 1958.
     - + 173   ii.   Goldie Demoine Neel, b. 1887.
     - + 174   iii.   Ruth Ellen Neel b. 1891.

110. **Sarah Catherine^4 Arbogast** (37.Sanford Albert^3, 5.Enos^2, 1.David^1), b. Jan 3 1848, d. 23 Mar 1903.
     She Married **Daniel Brooks**, b. 1844, d. 1930.
     ### *Children:*
     - 175   i.   James W.^{5} Brooks.
       He Married **Helen Crantz**.
     - 176   ii.   Marietta Acenith Brooks b. Nov-16-1871, d. Aug-23-1950.
     - 177   iii.   Laura Dell Brooks b. 1874, d. 1938.
     - 178   iv.   Emery W. Brooks b. 1876 in 1942.
     - 179   v.   Ira S. Brooks b. 1882, d. 1947.
     - 180   vi.   Ethel Brooks b. 1891.
     - 181   vii.   Enos Brooks. Married(1) **Osis Clopp** ;(2) **Ella Brooks**

111. **Enos James⁴ Arbogast** (37.Sanford Albert³, 5.Enos², 1.David¹), b. Jun-03-1850, buried in Union Cem., Windsor, Randolph Co., IN, d. Jun-28-1922.
He Married **Cordelia Grace Benbow**, b. Jul-21-1848, d. Apr-17-1942.

Children:
- 182   i.   Claude⁵ Arbogast b. 1873, buried in Union Cem., Windsor, Randolph Co., IN, d. 1874.
- 183   ii.   Maude Isabella Arbogast b. 1875, buried in Union Cem., Windsor, Randolph Co., IN, d. 1878.
- + 184   iii.   Straud Deluca Arbogast b. Feb-24-1875.
- + 185   iv.   Meade Estella Arbogast b. Nov-20-1877.
- 186   v.   Sellah Ray Arbogast b. Apr-30-1880 in South Bend.IN, d. Apr-27-1948 in South Bend.IN.
  He Married **Agnes Jackson**.
- + 187   vi.   Ada Leah Arbogast b. Oct-15-1884.
- 188   vii.   Essie Opal Arbogast b. Apr 1887, d. Sep-30-1962 in Parker City, Randolph, IN.
- 189   viii.   May Lavonne Arbogast b. 1889, d. 1891.

116. **Rudolphus George⁴ Arbogast** (39.David Daniel³, 5.Enos², 1.David¹), b. Jun-16-1860, d. Feb-19-1947 in Big Horn County, Community Hosp., Hardin, Mt.
Married 18883 in KS or MO, **Itonia May Livingston**, b. Jan-01-1865 in De Kalb Co., MO (daughter of James W. Livingston and Emily Darthula Tarter), d. May-27-1930 in Wyota, MT.

Children:
- 190   i.   William David⁵ Arbogast b. Jul-28-1884 in Dalton, KS, d. Dec-12-1942 in Sheridan, WV.
  Married **Golda Wreathel Sausaman**, b. 28 Dec 1894, Canton, Oh, d. 21 Jun 1979, Sheridan, WY b. 28 Dec 1894, Canton, Oh d. 21 Jun 1979, Sheridan, WY
- 191   ii.   Lester James Arbogast b. Oct-14-1896 in Camp Cook, SD, d. Apr-02-1934 in Camp Sheridan, WY.
- 192   iii.   Henry Lawrence Arbogast b. Mar-29-1898 in Glendive, MT, d. Mar-16-1963 in Glendive, MT.
- 193   iv.   Clifford Rudolph Arbogast b. Jun-29-1903 in Glendive, Montana Territory, d. Jan-25-1991 in Big Horn, Sheridan Co., WY.
  Married **Louise Petros**, d. 3 Jul 1994, Hardin, Mt, d. 3 Jul 1994, Hardin, Mt
- 194   v.   Lora Alice Arbogast b. Apr-02-1907 in Glendive, MT, d. Dec-15-1989 in Huntsville, Madison Co., AL.
  Married **Fred Garfield Swanson**, b. 19 Sep 1884, Shabbona, Il, d. 14 Feb 1961, Vincent, Al, b. 19 Sep 1884, Shabbona, Il, d. 14 Feb 1961, Vincent, Al

117. **Ida Alice⁴ Arbogast** (39.David Daniel³, 5.Enos², 1.David¹), b. Feb-02-1862, d. Jan-31-1952 in Shattuck, Ellis Co., OK.
She Married **Christopher Luther Hall**, b. Sep-25-1952 in LA, d. Feb-27-1917 in Shattuck, Ellis Co., OK.

Children:
- 195   i.   Chester Roy⁵ Hall b. Sep-05-1883 in Robinson, KS.
- 196   ii.   Glen Wood Hall b. Jan-02-1885 in Robinson, KS.
- 197   iii.   Florence Gertrude Hall b. Oct-04-1887 in Robinson, KS, d. Aug-20-1890.
- 198   iv.   Ethel Mercy Hall, b. Oct-09-1890.
  Married Charles Lewis Nash, 1 May 1931. Taught school for 12 years prior to marriage. Had two girls and a boy. Colorado Springs, CO, 1964.
- 199   v.   Herschel Emit Hall b. Oct-09-1890. Married, had 2 boys and a girl. Barber, Bakersfield, CA, 1964.
- 200   vi.   Joseph Wesley Hal b. Mar-08-1893.
- 201   vii.   Herbert Hillary Hall b. Jun-10-1895. WWII Vet.

Generation Five

125. **William Jefferson⁵ Moss** (54.Samuel Robeson⁴, 12.William Jefferson³, 2.Anna Abigail² Arbogast, 1.David¹), b. May 21 1872 in Fairbury, Jefferson Co., NE, d. Jan 8 1953 in Fairbury, Jefferson Co., NE.
    Married Jun 28 1905 in Fairbury, Jefferson Co., NE, **Rena Ann Bower**, b. Oct 18 1878 in Bower, Jefferson Co., NE (daughter of Henry Theodore Bower and Mary Ann Norman), d. Feb 19 1964 in Fairbury, Jefferson Co., NE.
    ### *Children:*
    - 202 i. Melvin Henery⁶ Moss b. Oct 19 1906 in Fairbury, Jefferson Co., NE, d. Mar 18 1964 in Fairbury, Jefferson Co., NE.

        (1) Married May 10 1962 in New York City, NY, **Gladys Evelyn Pinnock**, b. Oct 23 1911 in London, England, d. Oct 31 1962 in Bristol, England.
        (2) He Married **Jesse Kidwell**.
    - 203 ii. Lavinia Mary Moss b. Dec 26 1909 in Fairbury, Jefferson Co., NE, d. Oct 10 1991 in Newark, New Castle Co., DE.
        Married Mar 28 1934 in Lincoln, Lancaster Co., NE, **Holger Heinrich Schaumann**, b. Mar 5 1906 in Chadron, Dawes Co., NE, d. Jun 8 1995 in Newark, New Castle Co., DE.
    - 204 iii. Paul Simeon Moss b. Aug 21 1911 in Fairbury, Jefferson Co., NE, d. Jun 8 1995 in Newark, New Castle Co., DE.
        Married Nov 25 1933 in Omaha, Douglas Co., NE, **Roberta Ruth Cole**, b. Sep 18 1911 in Alvin, Brazoria Co., TX, d. Feb 23 1979 in Denver, Arapaho Co., CO.

126. **Alfred Rulon⁵ Moss** (54.Samuel Robeson⁴, 12.William Jefferson³, 2.Anna Abigail² Arbogast, 1.David¹), b. Nov 2 1873 near Anderson, Madison Co., IN, d. Jan 26 1975 in Belleville, Republic Co., KS.
    Married Nov 24 1898 in Gilead, Thayer Co., NE, **Margaret Glenn**, b. Jun 22 1876 in El Paso, Woodford Co., IL, d. Nov 13 1952 in Los Angeles, Los Angeles Co., CA.
    ### *Children:*
    - 205 i. Ruth Margaret⁶ Moss b. Jun 28 1905 in Reynolds, Jefferson Co., NE, d. 1990.
        Married Jun 24 1931, **Leslie R. Smith**.
    - 206 ii. Naomi Mary Moss b. 1907, d. 1972.

127. **Simeon Martindale⁵ Moss** (54.Samuel Robeson⁴, 12.William Jefferson³, 2.Anna Abigail² Arbogast, 1.David¹), b. Nov 27 1875 in Anderson, Madison Co., IN, d. Oct 13 1948 in Fairbury, Jefferson Co., NE.
    Married Aug 19 1909, **Etta Crabtree**, b. Sep 16 1881 in Cass Co., NE.
    ### *Children:*
    - 207 i. John Crabtree⁶ Moss b. 1911.
    - 208 ii. Ruth Crabtree Moss.

128. **Vernon Laurence⁵ Moss** (54.Samuel Robeson⁴, 12.William Jefferson³, 2.Anna Abigail² Arbogast, 1.David¹), b. 1888 in Fairbury, Jefferson Co., NE, d. 1951 in Fairbury, Jefferson Co., NE.
    Married Sep 12 1909 in Western, Saline Co., NE, **Grace Marie Nottingham**, b. Oct 26 1889 in Tobias, Saline Co., NE, d. Dec 14 1928 in Omaha, Douglas Co., NE.
    ### *Children:*
    - 209 i. Rachel Aradene⁶ Moss b. 1910, d. 1988.
    - 210 ii. Lee Eugene Moss b. 1912, d. 1977.

136. **Mary Elizabeth**[5] **Arbogast** (73.John Lewis[4], 20.William[3], 3.Henry Miles[2], 1.David[1]), b. Jun-27-1868 in Arrowsmith, McLean Co., IL, d. Feb-16-1927 in Moscow, Latah Co., Id.
She Married **Dr. John H. Reid**, b. Sep-09-1844 in Arrowsmith, McLean Co., IL, d. Feb-03-1918 in Tampa, Hillsborough Co., FL.
Children:
    211 i. L. Wayne[6] Reid b. Sep-03-1889.
    212 ii. Harlan E. Reid.

137. **William Henderson**[5] **Arbogast** (73.John Lewis[4], 20.William[3], 3.Henry Miles[2], 1.David[1]), b. Feb-20-1870 in Arrowsmith, McLean Co., IL, d. Oct-25-1938 in Monmouth, McDonough Co., IL.
Newspaper story of her 95th birthday celebration in file. Pantographs, Bloomington - Normal, IL, Sun Dec 8, 1974, page C-16. The Church, Evangelical United Methodist, 400 W. Union, where her husband began his work in 1911, will celebrate the 62nd anniversary of the dedication of its sanctuary along with her birthday at the home of her daughter, Mrs. Lynn Turner, 211 W. Seminary. Rev. Arbogast retired in 1937, and they moved back to Bloomington. Rev. Arbogast had served many Churches in Illinois, including Conference Superintendent for southern Illinois beginning in 1920, which required almost constant travel.
Married Dec-27-1866 in Saybrook, McLean Co., IL, **Alta Menry Biehl**, b. Dec-25-1879 in West Salem, Edwards Co., IL (daughter of Henry Biehl, and Catherine Reiber), d. Jan-02-1976 in Normal' McLean Co. IL.

Children:
+ 213 i. John Lynn[6] Arbogast b. Mar-27-1903.
  214 ii. Paul B. Arbogast b. Mar-15-1906.
+ 215 iii. Vera Kathryn Arbogast b. Aug-13-1907.

141. **Joseph Franklin**[5] **McKinley** (74.John Warner[4], 22.Mary[3] Arbogast, 3.Henry Miles[2], 1.David[1]), b. Jun 24 1867, Dewitt Co. IL d. July 6, 1940 Bloomington, McLean, Co. IL
Married Feb 22 1888, **Mary Hester Gardner**. February 22, 1888, at Shelbyville, Illinois
Children:
  216 i. Cornelia[6] McKinley.
  217 ii. William McKinley.
  218 iii. Earl McKinley.
  219 iv. Joseph McKinley.
  220 v. James F McKinley b. Jul 27 1902.

142. **Harriet Esther**[5] **McKinley** (74.John Warner[4], 22.Mary[3] Arbogast, 3.Henry Miles[2], 1.David[1]), b. Dec 18 1868 in DeWitt, DeWitt Co., IL, d. Nov 14 1922 in Farmer City, DeWitt, Co., IL.
Married Aug 08 1887 in DeWitt, DeWitt Co., IL, **William Fuller**, b. Oct 11 1866 in Harp Twp., DeWitt Co., IL (son of David Smith Fuller and Mary Bowers), buried in McCord Cem., Fullerton, DeWitt Co., IL, d. Nov 08 1936.
Children:
  221 i. Walter W[6] Fuller b. 1891 in DeWitt, DeWitt Co., IL, d. 1941 in Farmer City, DeWitt, Co., IL.
  222 ii. Wayne McKinley Fuller b. Sep 25 1896 in DeWitt, DeWitt Co., IL, d. Aug 23 1959 in Burlington, Kit Carson Co., CO.
  223 iii. Willard Smith Fuller b. Sep 10 1898 in Farmer City, DeWitt Co., IL, d. Nov 17 1885 in Venice, Saratoga Co., FL.
  224 iv. Hazel Fuller.

143. **Mattie Susan**[5] **McKinley** (74.John Warner[4], 22.Mary[3] Arbogast, 3.Henry Miles[2], 1.David[1]), b. Aug 06 1873 in DeWitt, DeWitt Co., IL, d. Nov 14 1922 in Farmer City, DeWitt, Co., IL.
Married Nov 15 1893 in DeWitt, DeWitt Co., IL, **Arthur Thomas Powell**, b. Feb 27 1872, d. Jul 07 1947.
Children:

225 i. Rosella Zorada⁶ Powell b. Aug 24 1894.
226 ii. Delma Esther Powell.
227 iii. Dewett McKinley Powell b. Dec 16 1897, d. Jul 23 1935.

144. **Samuel A⁵ McKinley** (74.John Warner⁴, 22.Mary³ Arbogast, 3.Henry Miles², 1.David¹), b. Jul 21 1884, d. 1963.
(1) He Married **Nona Loudenslager**, b. Jan 23 1894.
   ### *Children:*
228 i. Joan⁶ McKinley.
229 ii. George Patrick McKinley b. Oct 16 1922, d. Dec 11 1944.
(2) Married Jan 17 1905, **Myrtle Danison**.

145. **Anna B⁵ McKinley** (74.John Warner⁴, 22.Mary³ Arbogast, 3.Henry Miles², 1.David¹), b. May 21 1887.
Married Sep 27 1911, **Ora H Reeser**, b. May 23 1885 (son of William Henry Reeser and Louisa A Miller), d. 1968.
   ### *Children:*
230 i. Harriet⁶ Reeser b. 1912, d. 1970 in Chicago, Cook Co., IL.
   She Married **E Baker**.
231 ii. Margaret Reeser.
   She Married **R Jackson**.

151. **Iris Icelona⁵ Fuller** (79.Stella Amanda⁴ Arbogast, 25.George L³, 3.Henry Miles², 1.David¹), b. Jun 04 1878 in Fullerton, DeWitt Co., IL, d. Jun 25 1972 in Farmer City, DeWitt, Co., IL.
Married Jun 17 1896 in DeWitt, DeWitt Co., IL, **John William Hammer**, b. Mar 18 1872 in Farmer City, DeWitt, Co., IL, d. Mar 30 1855.
   ### *Children:*
232 i. Lyle Frederick⁶ Hammer b. Apr 30 1899 in Farmer City, DeWitt, Co., IL, d. Jul 28 1993 in Farmer City, DeWitt, Co., IL.
233 ii. Vera Hammer b. Jan 31 1901 in Farmer City, DeWitt, Co., IL, d. Oct 06 1997 in Farmer City, DeWitt, Co., IL.
   Married Jul 14 1926 in Farmer City, DeWitt, Co., IL, **Lindsey H Denison**, b. Aug 04 1901 in Farmer City, DeWitt, Co., IL, d. Feb 06 1974 in Farmer City, DeWitt, Co., IL.

156. **Ada Viola⁵ Brown** (91.Athelinda⁴ Arthur, 30.Eliza³ Moss, 4.Barbary² Arbogast, 1.David¹), b. Aug-02-1869 in Clark Co., OH, d. Dec-28-1928 in Clark Co., OH.
She Married **William K. Easter**.
   ### *Children:*
234 i. Karl⁶ Easter.
235 ii. William Easter.
   their first died as infant.

169. **Grover C.⁵ Arbogast** (104.Robert Sprole⁴, 37.Sanford Albert³, 5.Enos², 1.David¹), b. Apr-16-1961 in Delaware Co., IN, buried in Mount Tabor Cem, Muncie, Delaware Co, IN, d. May-02-1930 in Randolph Co., IN.
He Married **Flora Mabel Orr**, b. Oct-26-1881 in Selma, Delaware, Co., IN (daughter of James Henry Orr and Edith Nims), d. Nov-11-1944 in Selma, Delaware, Co., IN.
   ### *Children:*
236 i. Sylva May⁶ Arbogast b. Sep-26-1906, d. Jun-06-1987.
   She received her master's degree at Columbia Teachers College in 1940 and attended Western Reserve Library School in Cleveland.
   Miss Arbogast taught at Selma High School from 1929 to 1936, Portland High School from 1936 to 1941, and Berea College, Berea, Ky., 1942 to 1946.

She then entered library work and was employed at Portland Public Library, the Fort Wayne Public Library and came to the Muncie Public Library in 1959 where she worked until her retirement in 1972. Miss Arbogast moved to Richmond in 1977.

    237 ii. Robert Guy Arbogast b. Dec-22-1910, buried in Mount Tabor Cem, Muncie, Delaware Co, IN, d. Jul-24-1924.

173. **Goldie Demoine⁵ Neel** (105.Frances Isabella⁴ Arbogast, 37.Sanford Albert³, 5.Enos², 1.David¹), b. 1887 in Delaware Co., IN, d. 1906 in Grand Rapids, Kent Co., MI.
She <u>Married</u> **Simon Harness Stephens,,** b. 1884 in Jamestown, Gree Co., OH, d. 1962 in Grand Rapids, Kent Co., MI.

          Children:
    238 i. Roger⁶ Stephens.
    239 ii. Howard E. Stephens, b. 1907 in Delaware Co., IN, d. in Sandusky, , OH.

174. **Ruth Ellen⁵ Neel** (105.Frances Isabella⁴ Arbogast, 37.Sanford Albert³, 5.Enos², 1.David¹), b. 1891.
She <u>Married</u> **Leslie Jones**.

          Children:
    240 i. Leslie⁶ Jones, Jr..
    241 ii. Robert Neal Jones.

184. **Straud Deluca⁵ Arbogast** (111.Enos James⁴, 37.Sanford Albert³, 5.Enos², 1.David¹), b. Feb-24-1875 in IN, d. Apr-19-1940.
He <u>Married</u> **Pearl Elmore**.

          Children:
    242 i. Mildred⁶ Arbogast b. 1905, d. 1959.
+ 243 ii. Elmore James Arbogast b. Jul-21-1915.

185. **Meade Estella⁵ Arbogast** (111.Enos James⁴, 37.Sanford Albert³, 5.Enos², 1.David¹), b. Nov-20-1877 in IN, buried in Woodlawn Cem., Farmland, In, d. Oct-04-1970 in Warren, Huntington Co., IN.
She <u>Married</u> **William Everett Hamilton**, b. May-26-1871 in IN, d. Jul-28-1942 in Muncie, Delaware Co., IN.

          Children:
+ 244 i. Ruby Rea⁶ Hamilton b. Apr-30-1901.
+ 245 ii. James Andrew Hamilton b. Sep-24-1902.
    246 iii. Esther Cordelia Hamilton b. Aug-19-1904 in Kempton, Tipton County, IN, d. Feb-08-1927 in Indianapolis, Marion County, IN.
    247 iv. Paul Harrick Hamilton b. May-24-1906 in New Waverly, IN, d. Mar-10-1998 in Yorktown, Delaware Co. IN.
    248 v. Charles Merrill Hamilton b. Mar-08-1911 in Santa Fe, IN, d. Feb-15-1988 in Salsbury, Rowan Co. NC.
He <u>Married</u> **Thelma Voyles**.
    249 vi. Mary Isabella Hamilton b. Sep-11-1912 in Santa Fe, IN, d. Jun-05-1952.
    250 vii. Lois Roberta Hamilton b. Jul-06-1917 in Ossian, IN, d. 100712004 in Warren, Huntington Co., IN.

187. **Ada Leah⁵ Arbogast** (111.Enos James⁴, 37.Sanford Albert³, 5.Enos², 1.David¹), b. Oct-15-1884, d. Jun-18-1908.
<u>Married</u> Sep-01-1904, **Arthur Kennedy**.

          Children:
    251 i. Rev. Harold⁶ Kennedy d. Dec-10-1965 in Muncie, Delaware Co., IN.

Generation Six

213. **John Lynn[6] Arbogast** (137.William Henderson[5], 73.John Lewis[4], 20.William[3], 3.Henry Miles[2], 1.David[1]), b. Mar-27-1903 in Forreston, IL, d. Aug-30-1979 in IN Univ. Hosp.
    He Married **Vivien Conrad**, b. Aug-13-1906.
    ### Children:
    - 252   i.   William[7] Arbogast.
    - 253   ii.   Anne Arbogast.

215. **Vera Kathryn[6] Arbogast** (137.William Henderson[5], 73.John Lewis[4], 20.William[3], 3.Henry Miles[2], 1.David[1]), b. Aug-13-1907 in Sherrard, Mercer Co., IL, d. Aug-23-1992 in Sherrard, Mercer Co., IL.
    Married Jun-17-1903, **Lynn Turner**, b. Jul-07-1906, d. Jan-04-1982.
    ### Children:
    - 254   i.   Vera Lynn[7] Turner.
    - 255   ii.   Bruce Ian Turner.
    - 256   iii.   Sylvia Warren Turner b. 1942, d. Aug-23-1992 in Lebanon, Warren Co., OH.

243. **Elmore James[6] Arbogast** (184.Straud Deluca[5], 111.Enos James[4], 37.Sanford Albert[3], 5.Enos[2], 1.David[1]), b. Jul-21-1915, d. Feb-07-1971.
    He Married **Maxine Davis**. **Maxine**: Source is Frances Arbogast files. Arbogast Floral Co., 6011 East 10th St.,
    Indianapolis, IN, 46219. Featured in June 1968 issue of Florists' Review.
    25th year as a retail florist. Son, Elliott, works with his parents in the
    business.
    ### Children:
    - 257   i.   Ann[7] Arbogast.
    - 258   ii.   Elliott Arbogast.
    - 259   iii.   Claire Arbogast.

244. **Ruby Rea[6] Hamilton** (185.Meade Estella[5] Arbogast, 111.Enos James[4], 37.Sanford Albert[3], 5.Enos[2], 1.David[1]), b. Apr-30-1901 in Ingalls, IN, d. Dec-23-1987 in ,Charlotte, Mecklenburg Co,, NC.
    Married Gilbert L. Jackson, son Douglas Jackson b. 1936. At West Palm Beach,
    FL, 1970, obit of mother.
    She Married **Gilbert Lee Jackson**, b. 1899.
    ### Children:
    - 260   i.   Douglas Lee[7] Jackson.

245. **James Andrew[6] Hamilton** (185.Meade Estella[5] Arbogast, 111.Enos James[4], 37.Sanford Albert[3], 5.Enos[2], 1.David[1]), b. Sep-24-1902 in Kempton, Tipton County, IN, buried in Elm Ridge Cem., near.
    Muncie, IN, d. Dec-07-1960 in Muncie, Delaware Co., IN.
    This family had additional children.
    He Married **Dorothea Marie Young**, b. 1906, d. 1970.
    ### Children:
    - 261   i.   Betty Jean[7] Hamilton b. Aug-28-1929 in Muncie, Delaware Co., IN, d. Jun-02-2002 in Sun Lakes, AZ.

Descendants of Mary Elizabeth Arbogast Third Child of Michael and Mary Elizabeth Samuels

Generation One

1. **Mary Elizabeth**[1] **Arbogast**, b. About 1765 in Augusta Co., VA (daughter of Michael Arbogast and Mary Elizabeth Samuels Amanapas), d. About 1795 in Pendleton Co., WV.
    Source is research and family records of Helen J. Gasch of Clarkston, WA.
    Married Apr 10 1785 in Augusta Co., VA, **James Mullenax**, b. About 1765 in Augusta Co., VA (son of John Mullenax and Rachel Jane Powell), d. Sep 06 1814 in Pendleton Co., WV, buried in Pendleton Co., WV. **James**: From *Mulanax - Bales Family History* by Alvin and Katherine Mulanax, April 1980, p. 93, James served as a Private in the Second Battalion of Augusta Militia in 1779. Also marriage to Mary Arbogast performed by John Rodgers. This book also records the year of death and place of burial. Sources indicated are *History of Highland County, Virginia* by Oren F. Morton and marriage records of Pendleton Co., VA/ WV.

    There is confusion about the name 'Mary Elizabeth', stemming from the confusion relating to her mother. The question comes down to whether the mother was Mary Elizabeth' or just Mary.

    The Jane Barnes Papers indicate year of death as 1814 since there was a public auction of his property on 6 Sep 1814. Jane also lists two land warrants for military service as Warrant # 12442, 2 Apr 1792, 10 ac on Crabbottom and # 1814,3 Jul 1794, 85 ac on Crabbottom. Jane also confirms data from others but indicates James was born in 1761 or 1762.

    ### *Children:*
    + 2   i.   Abraham[2] Mullenax b. About 1786.
    + 3   ii. Jacob Mullenax b. About 1790.
      4   iii. Rachel Mullenax, b. 1792 - 1793 in Pendleton Co., WV.
                Source is research and family records of Helen J. Gasch of Clarkston, WA. Marriage date is bond date.
                Married Sep 16 1813 in Pendleton Co., WV, **Joseph Thompson** (son of George Thompson, Sr. and Mary Wimer).
    + 5   iv. William Mullenax.
    + 6   v.   Joseph Mulanax b. a 1795.

Generation Two

2. **Abraham**[2] **Mullenax** (1.Mary Elizabeth[1] Arbogast), b. About 1786 in Augusta Co., VA, d. Before 1860 in Dry Run, Pendleton Co., WV. Information from *Mulanax - Bales Family Histories* by Alvin and Katherine Mulanax, April, 1980, p. 93. On 1860 census, wife, age 74
    Married 1804-1805 in Pendleton Co., WV, **Mary Hannah Kile**, b. in Augusta Co., VA (daughter of George Kile and Hannah Bogard), d. Jan 22 1872 in Mendota, Putnam Co., MO. **Mary**: Daughter of George KILE and Hanna BOG.

    ### *Children:*
    + 7   i.   James W.[3] Mullenax b. 1806.
      8   ii. Conrad Mullenax b. Aug 15 1807 in Pendleton Co., WV, d. Dec 18 1877 in Schuyler Co., MO. Buried Browns Cem., Coatesville, MO.
                (1) Married Oct 25 1825, **Mary Dove**, d. Aug 08 1852 in Ritchie Co., WV, Buried Browns Cem., Coatsville, MO.

			(2) Married Jul 31 1853 in Putnam Co., MO, **Flora Eva Motes**, b. Apr 20 1828, d. Feb 12 1912 in Coatesville, Schuyler Co., MO, buried in Browns Cem., Coatesville, Schuyler Co., MO.
+	9	iii.	Salathial Mullenax b. About 1808.
	10	iv.	Solomon Mullenax b. 1809, d. 1880.
+	11	v.	Mary Mullenax b. About 1815.
+	12	vi.	Elizabeth Ann Mullenax b. ABT 1817.
+	13	vii.	Margaret Mullenax b. Dec 26 1822.
	14	viii.	Abraham Mullenax, Jr. b. c 1825. Married Nov 21 1839, **Elizabeth Mullenax**.
	15	ix.	Jacob C. Mullenax b. About 1827, d. About 1850/1852. Married Aug 19 1849, **Margaret Nelson**, b. Jun 03 1831, d. 185/1852, buried in Franklin, Pendleton Co., VA.

3. **Jacob² Mullenax** (1.Mary Elizabeth¹ Arbogast), b. About 1790 in Pendleton Co., WV, d. Aug 1846 in Highland Co., VA.
Source is research and family records of Helen J. Gasch of Clarkston, WA.
Married Jan 24 1814 in Pendleton Co., WV, **Hannah Arbogast**, b. May 00 1790 in Crabbottom, Highland Co., VA (daughter of George Arbogast and Catherine Yeager), d. Jan 28 1856 in Crabbottom, Highland Co., VA. **Hannah**: Source AAF. Children, George, John and Catharine from "*Mullenax - Bales*, by Katherine and Alvin Mullenax, April 1980, Manhattan, Kansas. Hannah's death reported by son, John, 65 years, 8 mos. from supplemental information by Helen J. Gasch research and family group record in file.

Children:
+	16	i.	John H.³ Mullenax b. 1814.
+	17	ii.	George Mullenax b. About 1818.
+	18	iii.	Catharine Mullenax b. 1820.

5. **William² Mullenax** (1.Mary Elizabeth¹ Arbogast).
(1) Married 1814, **Christina Vance**,

Children:
+	19	i.	Joseph³ Mullenax.
+	20	ii.	Ruhana Mullenax b. 1816/17.
	21	iii.	Elizabeth Mullenax b. About 1821. Married in Randolph Co., WV, **Abel Long**, (son of George A. Long and Winnifred Wilfong.
	22	iv.	Mary Mullenax b. Apr 21 1819. (1) Married Aug 12 1845 in Ritchie Co., WV, **Lewis Rexrode**, b. 1823, d. 1863 in Battle of Beverly, Randolph Co., WV. (2) She Married **Solomon Vance**,
	23	v.	Samuel B. Mullenax b. 1823, d. c 1895.
+	24	vi.	Christina Mullenax b. May 6 1830.

(2) Married 1825, **Nancy Ann Murphy**,

Children:
	25	vii.	Lucinda Mullenax b. Apr 30 1834, d. 1900, b. 1832/33. (1) She Married **David Kincaid**, b. 1832/33, d. 1900. (2) She Married **Adam Gum**,
+	26	viii.	William Mullenax b. 1837.
+	27	ix.	Henry Clay Mullenax b. Feb 15 1838.
+	28	x.	Edward Mullenax b.
+	29	xi.	James K. Mullenax b.
	30	xii.	Abraham Mullenax b.
	31	xiii.	Susan Mullenax b.

Married **Henry Wiant**,
32   xiv. Martha Mullenax

6. **Joseph² Mulanax** (1.Mary Elizabeth¹ Arbogast), b. a 1795, d. Apr 12 1864 in Green City, Hickory Co., MO.
Title: Roots, *Ancestors & Wings Family Records & Stories*. Author: Kathy Taylor Spivey
These are records and stories handed down from family members and published records.
Page: Joseph Mulanax and his family were part of the great migration Westward. Date: 1816.
Note: Joseph Mulanax and his family were part of the great migration Westward to settle and make homes in the wilderness. From Virginia he pioneered in Clark County, Ohio in about 1816; then in Madison County, Indiana, and finally in Green County, Missouri, in about 1848, where he lived until he died in 1864 at the age of 69.

    Text: Joseph Mulanax and his family were part of the great migration Westward to settle and make homes in the wilderness. From Virginia he pioneered in Clark County, Ohio in about 1816; then in Madison County , Indiana, and finally in Green County, Missouri, in about 1848, where he lived until he died in1864 at the age of 69.Joseph Mullenax was born about 1795 in Virginia and died on April 12, 1864 in Gree ne County, Missouri. His first wife was Catherine "Kate" Arbogast, daughter of Michael Arbogast, Jr., and Barbara Buzzard. He Married Kate in about 1818. Kate died in Madison County, Indiana. Joseph married Mary Ann Davis in the same county in 1836. Mary Ann died on June 12, 1907. She was living with her daughter, Martha (Mrs. Cires Cowan) at the time of her death in Sparks, Oklahoma. Joseph Mulana x served as a private in the 5th Regiment, Virginia Militia during the war of 1812. He was a farmer, a carpenter, and a miller. Joseph Mullenax first appeared as head of a family in the 1820 Federal Census of Clark County, Ohio. They lived in Pleasant Township. Kate and Joseph were between the ages of 16-25 and they had one son under ten. Miles Elliot Mulanax, was born on September 20, 1820, so perhaps he was the son indicated in this census. Kate's mother Barbara Arbogast, lived on a farm in the same township and was listed in the same 1820 census as a widow between the ages of 26-44 with six boy s and two girls, all under the ages of 25.Joseph was a farmer most of his life. The 1830 Federal Census listed him and his family in Clark County, Ohio. He and Kate had 2 sons and 4 daughters at that time. Sometime after 1830, Joseph Mullenax and his family along with other friends and relatives, migrated to Madison County, Indiana. The land records of Malison County, Indiana show that Joseph Mulanax b ought 57.5 acres of land on June 13, 1833 and paid $71.88 for his land. This record was found in Book 4, Page 332 in the County Court House in Anderson, Indiana. This land was in Anderson Township, clos e to the town of Anderson, Indiana. The exact location was: Township 19 North, Range 7 East, the East half of the Northwest quarter in Section 10. The land was close to the Moss Islands in the White River just west of the city of Anderson, Indiana. Joseph's land is a beautiful flat farming land. He built the Moss Island Mills on this tract of land. In the "History of Madison County" by Samuel Harden (1874), there is a picture of the Moss Island Mills with this notation: "Moss Island Mills, these mills were built about the year 1836 by Joseph Mullenax. This mill was consumed by fire in 1873. This mil l is located 2 miles west of Anderson and is supplied with water from White River. The mill derived its name from a small island in the river. Frank Damis owned the mills after Joseph Mullenax. the 56. 5 acres were later owned by I. Moss in 1880."Joseph and Kate Mullenax had seven children who grew to adulthood. They were: Miles, Sarah, William, Catharine, Green berry, Elizabeth, and Mary. Kate died ab out 1835 in Madison County, Indiana. She had a daughter, Catharine, who was born in1835, so she may have died following childbirth. On June 7, 1836,

    Joseph Married **Mary Ann Davis** in Anderson, Indiana . She was also called "Polly." Mary Ann and Joseph had two children while they lived in Madison County, Indiana. They were Clotilla and Josephine. They had ten other children who were born in Missouri . They were: Joseph, Mahalia, Eliza, Alfred, Martha, Francis, Jacob, James, George, and John. Joseph and his second wife, Mary Ann, may have lived in the northwest corner of Missouri in Andrew, Buchanan o r Platte Counties for a short time in the 1840's and later moved down south to Green County, Missouri Federal Census of Missouri, in green County in Boone Township. In this census Joseph was 56, Mary Ann, his wife, was 30 years of age and they had eleven children still at home. Joseph bought land from Joseph Moss on May 6, 1848. It was 80 Acres plus. Its' location was in the east half of the southwest one quarter of Section 23, Township 31 (Boone Township), Range 24. He also bought part of the northwest and part of the southwest quarters of the same section. This transaction was found in Book F, Page 176 in the Greene

County, Missouri Court Records. On April 1, 1852, Joseph bought 320 acres of land from Samuel Julian. It was the southwest quarter of the northwest quarter in Section 34. This trans action was found in Book D, Page 131. Joseph received80 acres of bounty land fro having served during the War of 1812. This is on May 29, 1856, Land Warrant No. 31078. It was located in Township 27, Section 11, Range 33 and was the West half of the Northeast quarter of Section 11.
http://trees.ancestry.com/pt/AMTCitationRedir.aspx?tid=3521207&pid=-1433951232

(1) Married 1818 in Clark Co., OH, **Catherine Kate Arbogast**, b. 1805 in Pendleton Co., VA (daughter of Michael Arbogast and Barbara Buzzard), d. 1935 in Madison Co., IN. **Catherine**: Title: Public Member Trees
Author: Ancestry.com
Publication: Online publication - Provo, UT, USA: The Generations Network, Inc., 2006.Original data - Family trees submitted by Ancestry members. Original data: Family trees submitted by Ancestry members.

Children:

+ 33   i.   Miles Elliott^3 Mulanax b. Sep 06 1820.
+ 34   ii.   Elizabeth J. Mulanax b. 1827.
+ 35   iii.   William R. Mulanax b. Oct 10 1832.
   36   iv.   Greenberry Mulanax b. 1821 in Madison Co., IN.
   37   v.   Mary Mulanax b. 1929 in Ohio.
              Married Feb 04 1849 in Andrew Co., MO, **William Cass**.
   38   vi.   Sarah Mulanax b. 1830 in Clark Co., OH.
              Married Mar 13 1852 in Andrew Co., MO, **Joseph Dandrivan**, b. 1826 in Ohio.
   39   vii.   Catherine Mulanax b. 1935 in Madison Co., IN.

(2) Married Jun 7 1836 in Madison Co., IN, **Mary Ann Davis**, b. 1820 in Pasquotank Co., NC, d. Jun 12 1907.

Children:

+ 40   viii.   Joseph Riley Mullenax b. Jun 08 1841.
   41   ix.   Mahalia J Mullenax b. 1842.
              Married Jan 29 1861 in Green Co., MO, **William A. Perryman**.
   42   x.   Eliza C. Mullenax b. About 1845.
   43   xi.   Alfred C. Mullenax b. Feb 24 1846, d. Jul 06 1925, buried in Protem Cem., Taney Co., MO.
              Married Jan 25 1866 in Green Co., MO, **Martha Ann Matts**.
   44   xii.   Martha A. Mullenax.
              Married Mar 18 1866 in Green Co., MO, **Cires Cowan**.
   45   xiii.   Francis Benjamin Mullenax b. About 1850.
              Married Jun 22 1873, **Elizabeth Metts**.
   46   xiv.   Jacob L. Mullenax b. About 1850.
   47   xv.   James Wilson Mullenax b. Mar 24 1856, d. Jul 29 1931.
              He Married **Ida Cobb**.
   48   xvi.   George W. Mullenax b. About 1857.
   49   xvii.   John B. Mullenax b. About 1858.

Generation Three

7. **James W.**^{3} **Mullenax** (2.Abraham^2, 1.Mary Elizabeth^1 Arbogast), b. 1806 in Dry Run, Pendleton Co., WV, d. 1856 in Pendleton Co., WV.
Married Feb 28 1826 in Pendleton Co., WV, **Permelia Murphy**, b. 1803 in Dry Run, Pendleton Co., WV (daughter of Walter Murphy and Susannah Posten), d. After 1860 in Pendleton Co., WV.
Permelia: Daughter of Walter Murphy and Susannah Posten.

Children:

+ 50   i.   William Isaac^4 Mullenax b. Jul 5 1825.

	+ 51	ii.	John Wesley Mullenax b. Oct 15 1829.
	52	iii.	James P. Mullenax b. Feb 1832 in Dry Run, Pendleton Co., WV, d. Dec 12 1900 in Coyville, Wilson Co., KS. Married 1854, **Elizabeth Phares**, b. Jul 10 1841 in Churchville, Pendleton Co., WV (daughter of Adam Harness Phares and Pheobe Harper).
	53	iv.	Mary Mullenax b. 1836 in Pendleton Co., WV. Married 19 Aug 1849, **Solomon K. Nelson** in Pendleton Co. May have migrated to Hardy and/or Grant County
	54	v.	Sarah A. Mullenax b. 1838 in Dry Run, Pendleton Co., WV. Married 20 May 1858, **Jacob Nelson** in Pendleton Co.. Migrated to Kansas. Resident of Coyville in 1875, but not on 1880 census. Jacob, son of Elijah and Mary M. (Kinkead) Nelson
	55	vi.	Benjamin A. Mullenax b. 1840 in Dry Run, Pendleton Co., WV, d. Oct 22 1884 in Coyville, Wilson Co., KS. Married 22 Feb 1874, **Sidney Judy** in Pendleton Co.. Migrated to Kansas after Civil War, on 1880 census. Morton's Pendleton Co. History indicates marriage to Sarah Schrader, but unable to find any record of this. Death is from Wilson Co. Obituary in the Wilson Co. Citizen, via Mullenax Newsletter, Vol. VII, No.3, Sep. 1993, edited by Wesley L. Mullenneix

9. **Salathial^3 Mullenax** (2.Abraham^2, 1.Mary Elizabeth^1 Arbogast), b. About 1808.
(1) Married Jul 19 1829 in Pendleton Co., WV, **Catherine Grimes**, b. About 1808 in Pendleton Co., WV.
(2) Married Jan 13 1831, **Margaret Mullenax**, b. 1805 in Pendleton Co., WV.

   ### *Children:*
	56	i.	Abraham^4 Mullenax. He Married **Mary Mullenax**.
+	57	ii.	Charity Margaret Mullenax b. 1835.
+	58	iii.	Catherine Mullenax.
+	59	iv.	Isaac S. Mullenax b. 1838.
	60	v.	Jacob Mullenax b. 1853 in Pendleton Co., WV, d. 1880 in Putnam Co., MO. He Married **Winefred Lambert.**

11. **Mary^3 Mullenax** (2.Abraham^2, 1.Mary Elizabeth^1 Arbogast), b. About 1815.
There are several references to Margaret marrying Abraham Simmons and Robert Nelson. Additionally, Simmons Married Mary, sister of Margaret. The dates listed in various places does not accommodate this. At present both Margaret and Mary Mullenax have Abraham Simmons as a husband. Mary has a child with him, and Margaret has several.

Married Nov 17 1831 in Pendleton Co., WV, **Abraham Simmons**, b. 1811, buried in Indian Creek, Ritchie Co., WV. **Abraham**: info from Johns Marriage License from Doddridge Co, WV-Book 1-A Page118 68 Yr. in Grant, Ritchie, WV 1880 Census; Living with son John W. Simmons. A History of Pendleton County West Virginia by Oren Morton: p. 290 – Lists Leonard Simmons Married to Mary A., coming to South Fork by 1768 and died 1808.Children include Henry, Married to Susan. Henry was born Oct. 12, 1760 and died Sept. 7, 1825, and lived on the homestead. He has a child Abraham, but listed
as Married to Nancy.

   ### *Children:*
	61	i.	Mahulda^4 Simmons.
	61.2	ii	John Simmons, b. Mar 18, 1838 in Pendleton Co., VA, D. JAN 9, 1899 Richie Co., WV Married **Elizabeth Hourhood**. B. Dec 10 1836, Doddridge Co., VA. d. Aug 19 1913 Richie Co., WV

12. **Elizabeth Ann^3 Mullenax** (2.Abraham^2, 1.Mary Elizabeth^1 Arbogast), b. ABT 1817 in Pendleton Co., WV, d. BET. 1864 - 1865.

Married Jan 1 1833 in Pendleton Co., WV, **Eli Calhoun**, b. Dec 11 1815 in Pendleton Co., WV, d. Sep 30 1899 in Churchville, Pendleton Co., WV

Children:

	62	i. Ephraim[4] Calhoun b. ABT 1834 in Pendleton Co., WV, d. BEF 1882. He Married **Ann R. Simmons**, b. 1854, d. Before 1882.
+	63	ii. Annie Catherine Calhoun b. Jan 4 1841.
	64	iii. Allen Calhoun b. 1845 in Pendleton Co., WV.
+	65	iv. Susan Calhoun b. 1848.
	66	v. Jackson Calhoun b. ABT 1850 in Pendleton Co., WV.
	67	vi. Martha Calhoun b. ABT 1852 in Pendleton Co., WV.
+	68	vii. Phoebe (Susan) Calhoun.
	69	viii. James Calhoun b. 1857 in Pendleton Co., WV. He Married **America Bennett**, b. 1857.

13. **Margaret[3] Mullenax** (2.Abraham[2], 1.Mary Elizabeth[1] Arbogast), b. Dec 26 1822 in Pendleton Co., WV, buried in Indian Creek, Ritchie Co., WV. See above comments under 11. Mary Mullenax. From History of Pendleton County by Oren Morton: Abraham had a child named Margaret, but she Married **Robert J. Nelson.**
(1) Married Mar 19 1840 in Pendleton Co., WV, **Abraham Simmons**, b. 1811, buried in Indian Creek, Ritchie Co., WV.info from Johns Marriage License from Doddridge Co, WV-Book 1-A Page1 68 Yr. in Grant, Ritchie, WV 1880 Census; Living with son John W. Simmons. West *A History of Pendleton County Virginia* by Oren Morton: p. 290 – Lists Leonard Simmons Married to Mary A., coming to South Fork by 1768 and died 1808 Children include Henry, Married to Susan. Henry was born Oct. 12, 1760 and died Sept. 7, 1825, and lived on the homestead. He has a child Abraham, but listed as Married to Nancy ? Check on this marriage of Abraham Simmons and Margaret Mullenax.

Children:

+	70	i. John Wesley[4] Simmons b. 1836.
	71	ii. James Alfred Simmons. He Married **Mary Sinnett**.

(2) Married Mar 19 1840, **Robert J. Nelson**.

16. **John H.[3] Mullenax** (3.Jacob[2], 1.Mary Elizabeth[1] Arbogast), b. 1814 in Crabbottom, Highland Co., VA, d. Aug 19 1862 in Crabbottom, Highland Co., VA.
Married Mar 02 1837 in Crabbottom, Highland Co., VA, **Rachel Rexrode** (daughter of Christian Rexrode and Leah Seybert).

Children:

+	72	i. Emily Jane[4] Mullenax.
	73	ii. Ida Florence Mullenax.

17. **George[3] Mullenax** (3.Jacob[2], 1.Mary Elizabeth[1] Arbogast), b. About 1818 in Crabbottom, Highland Co., VA, d. in Crabbottom, Highland Co., VA.
He Married **Elizabeth Lambert** (daughter of John Lambert and Nancy (Unknown)).

Children:

+	74	i. Martha[4] Mullenax.

18. **Catharine[3] Mullenax** (3.Jacob[2], 1.Mary Elizabeth[1] Arbogast), b. 1820 in Crabbottom, Highland Co., VA, d. in Highland Co., VA.
Married Mar 14 1840 in Pendleton Co., WV, **George Vandevender**, b. About 1818 in Pendleton Co., WV, d. 1895 in Highland Co., VA.

Children:

	75	i. Almira J.[4] Mullenax b. 1840 Pend. Co., VA Married **John W. Simmons**, 1 Apr 1858, highland Co., VA
	76	ii. Jacob E. Mullenax.

Married **Margaret Colaw**, 1869, Highland Co., VA

19. **Joseph**[3] **Mullenax** (5.William[2], 1.Mary Elizabeth[1] Arbogast).
    Married 1840 in Pendleton Co., WV, **Abigail Phares**, b. 1833,.
    ### *Children:*
    + 77   i.   George[4] Mullenax b. 1845
      78   ii. Conrad Mullenax b..1843
      79   iii. Sarah C. Mullenax b., 1847

20. **Ruhana**[3] **Mullenax** (5.William[2], 1.Mary Elizabeth[1] Arbogast), b. 1816/17.
    Married in Highland Co., VA, **Nathan Wimer**, (son of George Wimer, Jr. and Susannah Zickefoose),
    ### *Children:*
      80   i.   James[4] Wimer.
      81   ii. Houston Wimer
      82   iii. Gennie Belle Wimer

24. **Christina**[3] **Mullenax** (5.William[2], 1.Mary Elizabeth[1] Arbogast), b. May 6 1830 in Pendleton Co., WV, d. Dec 16 1905 in Pendleton Co., WV, buried in Butchers Cem., Onego, Pendleton Co., WV.
    Married Aug 17 1848 in Pendleton Co., WV, **Daniel Waybright, Jr.**, b. 1823 in Pendleton Co., WV (son of Daniel Waybright and Rachel Arbogast), d. 1879 in Pendleton Co., WV.
    ### *Children:*
    + 83   i.   Abraham[4] Waybright b. May 5 1850.
    + 84   ii.   Mary Margaret Waybright b. Jan 14 1856.
    + 85   iii. William Washington Waybright b. Apr 1857.
      86   iv.   Henry Clay Waybright b. Feb 2 1864 in Pendleton Co., WV, d. Nov 5 1922.
    + 87   v.   Isaac Perry Waybright b. Mar 20 1866.
    + 88   vi.   Cordelia Waybright b. Jul 6 1869.
      89   vii. Lettie S. Waybright b. Aug 22 1873 in Crabbottom, Highland Co., VA, d. 20 Jan.
            Married Aug 24 1899, **James P. Davis**.
    + 90   viii. John Edward Waybright b. Mar 16 1875.

26. **William**[3] **Mullenax** (5.William[2], 1.Mary Elizabeth[1] Arbogast), b. 1837,
    (1) Married 1859 in Pendleton Co., WV, **Sarah Calhoun**,
    ### *Children:*
      91   i.   Tilden[4] Mullenax b. Feb 10 1876, d. 31 Jul.
            He Married **Emily Gertrude Hevener** (daughter of Jacob Pinkley Hevener and Phoebe J. Lunsford). Emily: Same person as #24385 in Adam Arbogast line.
      92   ii. Phoebe Mullenax b.
            Married, **Edward Hevener**
      93   iii. Martha Mullenax b.
      94   iv. Maude Mullenax b..
            Married, **William Hull,**
      95   v.   Garnett Mullenax.
            Married **George Kincaid,**
      96   vi. (infant) Son Mullenax b.
      97   vii. May Mullenax b.
            Married **William Hevener,**

    (2) Married, **Annie Waybright,**

27. **Henry Clay**[3] **Mullenax** (5.William[2], 1.Mary Elizabeth[1] Arbogast),
    (1) Married, **Lucinda Simmons**, b.
    ### *Children:*
    + 98   i.   Kenton L.[4] Mullenax b. Dec 10 1865.
      99   ii. Mavis A. Mullenax.

(2) Married, **Elizabeth Susan Calhoun**, b. Dec 27 1839,

    Children:

	100	iii.	Virginia Mullenax
			Married 1889, **Harrison Calhoun**,
	101	iv.	Lucy Bell Mullenax b. Mar 28 1868, d.
			Married, **Lemuel Waybright**,
	102	v.	Emily Mullenax b. Mar 20 1870, d. May 22 1870.
	103	vi.	Martha (Mattie) Mullenax b. Jun 10 1873, d. Feb 23 1945.
			Married Oct 26 1893, **Minor K. Simmons**, b. Sep 11 1871, d. Dec 30 1953.
	104	vii.	Salisbury Mullenax b. Apr 4 1875,
			Married **Margaret Newman**,
+	105	viii.	Henry Walter Mullenax b. Nov 28 1877.
	106	ix.	Adam D. Mullenax b. Mar 6 1881, d. Feb 27 1961.
			Married Sep 22 1915, **Myrtle M. Arbogast**, b. Aug 19 1887.
	107	x.	Cassie E. Mullenax b..
			Married, **Samuel Ralston**,
+	108	xi.	Aaron C. Mullenax

28. **Edward**[3] **Mullenax** (5.William[2], 1.Mary Elizabeth[1] Arbogast),
(1) Married **Winifred Calhoun**

    Children:

+	109	i.	Elizabeth S[4] Mullenax b. May 1858.
	110	ii.	Anna C. Mullenax b.
			Married, **Amby Harper**,
	111	iii.	Mary J. Mullenax, Matthew Potter,
	112	iv.	James Mullenax,
			Married in Pendleton Co., WV, **Sarah Moyers**, b.
	113	v.	Martha Mullenax,
			Married, **Sylvestor Nelson**,
	114	vi.	Emma Mullenax
			Married, **Norval High**,
	115	vii.	(infant) Daughter Mullenax b.

(2) Married 1859 in Pendleton Co., WV, **Mary Mowery**,

    Children:

116	viii.	Claude Mullenax b.
117	ix.	John Mullenax b.
		Married **Nora Rexrode**,
118	x.	Ernest Mullenax
		Married **Nettie Simmons**,

29. **James K.**[3] **Mullenax** (5.William[2], 1.Mary Elizabeth[1] Arbogast),
Married **Susan Lawrence**,

    Children:

119	i.	Minor[4] Mullenax b. Feb 1870, d. Oct 4 1932 in Boyer, Pocahontas Co., WV.
		(1) Married, **Charla Waybright**,
		(2) Married, **Eliza Vandevander**, b. 1871, d. 1898.
120	ii.	Ida Mullenax.
121	iii.	Christina Mullenax b.
122	iv.	Charlie Mullenax

33. **Miles Elliott**[3] **Mulanax** (6.Joseph[2], 1.Mary Elizabeth[1] Arbogast), b. Sep 06 1820 in Clark Co., OH, d. Mar 22 1896 in Jackson Co., KS.

Married Dec 10 1848 in Missouri, **Rachel Ellen Miller**, b. Oct 27 1833 in Ohio, d. 0616102 in Jackson Co., KS.

> ### *Children:*
> + 123   i.   Clotilda Adeline[4] Mulanax b. May 05 1853.
> + 124   ii. William Dallas Mulanax b. Dec 02 1854.
> + 125   iii. John Greenbury Mulanax b. Aug 27 1856.

34. **Elizabeth J.**[3] **Mulanax** (6.Joseph[2], 1.Mary Elizabeth[1] Arbogast), b. 1827 in Ohio, d. 1886. She Married **Jacob Matheny**.

> ### *Children:*
> 126   i.   Martha Jane[4] Matheny.

35. **William R.**[3] **Mulanax** (6.Joseph[2], 1.Mary Elizabeth[1] Arbogast), b. Oct 10 1832 in Madison Co., IN, d. May 10 1901 in Holton, Jackson Co., KS.
Married Dec 13 1855 in Andrew Co., MO, **Mary Ann Kincade**, b. Jan 07 1833 in Illinois, d. Dec 23 1906 in Holton, Jackson Co., KS.

> ### *Children:*
> + 127   i.   Matthew Elliott[4] Mulanax b. Jun 07 1858.
>   128   ii.   Elizabeth Jane Mulanax b. Jan 02 1860 in Holton, Jackson Co., KS.
>   Married 28 Nov 1880 in Jackson Co., KS, **William Coleman**.
>   129   iii. Rachel Elizabeth Mulanax b. Apr 15 1862 in Kansas.
>   (1) She Married **Jake Helm**.
>   (2) She Married **Floyd Beauchamp**.
> + 130   iv.   Jacob Allen Mulanax b. Oct 10 1864.
>   131   v.   Katherine Mulanax b. Jan 19 1866 in Kansas.
>   Married 20 May 1983, **Milton Curtis**.
>   132   vi.   Mary L. Mulanax b. May 30 1868 in Kansas.
>   (1) She Married **Joe Lightbody**.
>   (2) Married 17 Feb 1886, **Jake Helm**.
> + 133   vii. John William Mulanax b. Jan 07 1871.
>   134   viii. Nellie Mulanax b. About 1876 in Jackson Co., KS, d. Sept. 1907.
>   Married 6 Jun 1893 in Jackson Co., KS, **Bruce Fouch**.
>   135   ix.   Sarah E. Mulanax b. 2-11-1876.
> + 136   x.   Lucy Adeline Mulanax b. Aug 27 1878.
>   137   xi.   Jesse E. Mulanax b. Apr 28 1882, d. 9 Jan 1900.
>   He Married **(unknown) Perry**.

40. **Joseph Riley**[3] **Mullenax** (6.Joseph[2] Mulanax, 1.Mary Elizabeth[1] Arbogast), b. Jun 08 1841 in Missouri, d. Jul 8 1903. He married Mary Louise Perryman 29 Jan 1861 in Greene County, Missouri. She was visiting family in Northern California in 1912, passed away while there, and is buried in the Woodland Cemetery, Woodland, Yolo, California. They were the parents of 14 children. They moved back and forth between Greene County, Missouri and Coleman County, Texas. Some children stayed in Texas, while others migrated to Northern California and Washington state. They have many, many descendants.
Married Jan 29 1861 in Green Co., MO, **Mary Louise Perryman** (daughter of Thomas Perryman and Louise Wallace).

> ### *Children:*
> 138   i.   Steven N.[4] Mulanax b. Sep 24 1861 in Missouri, d. Nov 16 1934 .
> 139   ii. Mary L. Mulanax b. About 1864 in Missouri,. d in Oklahoma
>   Married **Nelson Hicks**
> 140   iii. George Cazwell Mulanax b. Feb 14 1866 in Missouri, d. Aug 23 1955. Burial: Suisun-Fairfield Cemetery Fairfield Solano County CA.
>   Married **Martha Ann Whitehead**, b. 1868 MO, D. Oct 15, 1942 Solano Co. CA

They had 10 children: Harley Sheridan, Joseph Hugh, Lillian Marcella, Sherman George, Lee Leslie, Charles Harrison, Addie Louella, Luther Edward, Myrtle Miami, and Cecil Clarence.

   141   iv.   Ella Mulanax b. About 1870 in Greene Co., MO.

   142   v.   Oliver Elliott Mulanax b. About 1871 in Greene Co., MO.
              Married **Lena Perryman**

   143   vi.   Lillian Mulanax b. Jan 1879 in Greene Co., MO, d. Seattle, WA.
              Married **Milton Kelly**

   144   vii.   Bertie Mulanax b. About 1873 in Greene Co., MO.

   145   viii.   Thomas Luther Mulanax b. About 1874 in Greene Co., MO.
              Married **Nettie Neff**

+ 146   ix.   Anna Louisa Mulanax b. May 10 1879.

   147   x.   James Harvey Mulanax b. June 1882 in Greene Co., MO, d. Apr 3 1964.
              Married **Hassie Fortnet Bragg** b 1885. D. Dec 1 1973 Turlock, CA. They had five children.

Generation Four

50. **William Isaac^4 Mullenax** (7.James W.^{3}, 2.Abraham^2, 1.Mary Elizabeth^1 Arbogast), b. Jul 5 1825 in Dry Run, Pendleton Co., WV, d. Sep 8 1901 in Elk Mountain, Pocahontas Co., WV, buried in Pocahontas Co., WV.

(1) He Married **Margaret Ann Waybright**, b. Feb 7 1858 in Pendleton Co., WV (daughter of Elijah Waybright and Catherine Helmick), d. 1916, buried in Maple Springs Cem., Eglon, Preston Co., WV.

              Children:

   148   i.   William Benny^5 Mullenax b. Jul 4 1883, d. Feb 22 1979 in Memorial General Hospital, Elkins, Randolph Co., WV.
              He Married **Susan Millie Martin**

   149   ii.   Arthur Mullenax b. 1891.

   150   iii.   Jesse Mullenax b. Jun 7 1895, d. Jan 1977 in Iowa.

   151   iv.   Dora Mullenax b. 1899.

   152   v.   Willie Mullenax b. 1894.
              Roots in tucker co. 1979, p. 30, tells of a William Benny Mullenax b. 7/4/1884, son of William Isaac Mullenax and Margaret Ann Waybright, Married **Susan Millie Martin** b. 1890. Other comments makes Willie fit the family.

(2) Married Oct 9 1847 in Franklin Co., WV, **Elizabeth Nelson**, b. Feb 9 1825 in Churchville, Pendleton Co., WV, d. Aug 28 1896 in Dry Run, Pendleton Co., WV.

              Children:

+ 153   vi.   Mary Permelia Catherine Mullenax b. Aug 7 1848.

   154   vii.   Margaret Ann Mullenax b. Jan 1 1850 in Dry Run, Pendleton Co., WV, d. Apr 12 1921.
              Married Jan 8 1873, **Anderson Nelson**.

+ 155   viii.   Elijah Mullenax b. Aug 30 1853.

+ 156   ix.   Annie Jane Mullenax b. Aug 14 1854.

+ 157   x.   James B. Mullenax b. Sep 25 1856.

+ 158   xi.   William Alexander Mullenax b. Jul 14 1858.

   159   xii.   Louisa Mullenax b. 1859 in Dry Run, Pendleton Co., WV.

   160   xiii.   Mary Virginia Mullenax b. Jul 13 1860 in Dry Run, Pendleton Co., WV, d. Apr 17 1919 in New Albany, Wilson Co., KS, buried Apr 20 1919 in Le Roy, McLean Co., IL.
              Married Jun 20 1881, **Howard Dice Harper**.

      161   xiv. Phoebe Ellen Mullenax b. May 20 1863 in Dry Run, Pendleton Co., WV, d. May 13 1946.
                  Married Oct 27 1880, **Nimrod Bennett**.
+ 162   xv. Solomon Key Mullenax b. May 07 1868.

51. **John Wesley⁴ Mullenax** (7.James W.³, 2.Abraham², 1.Mary Elizabeth¹ Arbogast), b. Oct 15 1829 in Crabbottom, Highland Co., VA, d. Feb 6 1907 in Whitmer, Randolph Co., WV.
Married Jun 7 1855 in Pendleton Co., WV, **Mary Catherine Judy**, b. Aug 20 1834 in Dry Run, Pendleton Co., WV, (daughter of Adam Judy and Mary Harper Hinkle), d. Jun 15 1898 in Big Run, Pendleton Co., WV. **Mary**: This information is provided for all BOYDs to research their family connection by the group Clan Boyd.
Note by unknown Arthur:: Regard all of this data as unsupported until you verify the accuracy at the original source. Some of the basis range from copies of original documents to guesses because it looks possible.
http://homepages.rootsweb.com/~clanboyd/index.htm

Children:

+ 163   i. Mary Jane⁵ Mullenax b. Oct 24 1852.
+ 164   ii. Isaac J. Mullenax.
   165   iii. John A. Mullenax d. Oct 11 1902 in Pendleton Co., WV.
             This information is provided for all BOYDs to research their family connection by the group Clan Boyd.
             NOTE: Regard all of this data as unsupported until you verify the accuracy at the original source. Some of the basis range from copies of original documents to guesses because it looks possible.
             http://homepages.rootsweb.com/~clanboyd/index.htm
+ 166   iv. Thomas Jefferson Mullenax b. Apr 05 1857.
+ 167   v. Virginia Susan Mullenax.
+ 168   vi. Phoebe Mullenax b. Oct 27 1864.
+ 169   vii. Martin Mullenax b. Nov 13 1865.
   170   viii. Elizabeth P. Mullenax d. in The Low Place near Dry Fork, Randolph Co., WV, b. Feb 02 1867 in The Low Place near Dry Fork, Randolph Co., WV.
             This information is provided for all BOYDs to research their family connection by the group Clan Boyd.
             She Married **Levi Lambert**, b. 1864.
   171   ix. Edward J. Mullenax d. Apr 01 1869 in The Low Place near Dry Fork, Randolph Co., WV, d. 1932 in Clarksburg, Harrison Co., WV, buried in Elkins, Randolph Co., WV.
   172   x. Alphra Mullenax d. Dec 01 1872 in The Low Place near Dry Fork, Randolph Co., WV, d. Mar 18 1894 in The Low Place near Dry Fork, Randolph Co., WV.

57. **Charity Margaret⁴ Mullenax** (9.Salathial³, 2.Abraham², 1.Mary Elizabeth¹ Arbogast), b. 1835.
She Married **Noah Teter**, b. 1830.

Children:
   173   i. James Albert⁵ Terer b. 1857.
             (1) He Married **Clorinda Jordan**, b. 1862.
             (2) He Married **Nettie Lamb**.
   174   ii. Frances Ina Teeter b. 1866.
             She Married **Job Lambert**, b. 1866.

58. **Catherine⁴ Mullenax** (9.Salathial³, 2.Abraham², 1.Mary Elizabeth¹ Arbogast).
She Married **Abraham Helmick**, b. 1841.

Children:
   175   i. Abraham⁵ Helmick, Jr. b. 1865.

59. **Isaac S.⁴ Mullenax** (9.Salathial³, 2.Abraham², 1.Mary Elizabeth¹ Arbogast), b. 1836, d. 1919.

He Married **Lucinda Teter**, b. Nov 30 1839. d. Apr 29 1926. Daughter of Phillip Teter and Sidnet Bland.

Children:

176	i.	Regania^5 Mullenax b. 1861.
177	ii.	Margaret A Mullenax b. 1865.
178	iii.	Luetta Mullenax b. 1870.
179	iv.	Noah Mullenax b. 1872.
180	v.	Sidney E. Mullenax b. 1875.
181	vi.	Pheobe Mullenax b. 1877.
182	vii.	Salathiel Mullenax b. May 18 1879, d. Feb 6 1960 Tucker Co., WV
		Married **Lillie Helmick** b. Apr 18 1889 Tucker Co., WV d. Nov 22 1961 Hambleton, Tucker Co. WV, daughter of Phillip Helmick and Martha helm rick.
	viii.	William Carter Mullenax b. Oct 36 1884, d. Nov 4 1944
		Married **Ethel Cora Knotts** b Feb 4 1895. D. Aug 4 1988

63. **Annie Catherine**^{4} **Calhoun** (12.Elizabeth Ann^3 Mullenax, 2.Abraham^2, 1.Mary Elizabeth^1 Arbogast), b. Jan 4 1841 in Pendleton Co., WV, b. ABT 1836 in Pendleton Co., WV, d. Apr 28 1875.
Married May 25 1858 in Pendleton Co., WV, **George Washington Lambert**, b. Mar 7 1838 in Dry Run, Pendleton Co., WV, d. Nov 16 1908.

Children:

183	i.	Margaret Ann^5 Lambert b. Jul 16 1860.
		(1) She Married Isaac **Grant Warner**, b. ABT 1858.
		(2) Married Sep 13 1881, **Francis Arnold Lambert**, b. ABT 1858.
184	ii.	Eli H. Lambert b. Jan 1 1863, d. Jun 22 1894.
		He Married **Elizabeth Mullenax**, b. ABT 1865.
+ 185	iii.	Jay Lambert b. Feb 24 1865.
+ 186	iv.	Solomon K. Lambert b. Mar 1 1867.
187	v.	Hester Jane Lambert.
188	vi.	Callie Coetta Lambert.

65. **Susan**^{4} **Calhoun** (12.Elizabeth Ann^3 Mullenax, 2.Abraham^2, 1.Mary Elizabeth^1 Arbogast), b. 1848 in Pendleton Co., WV.
She Married **Albinus Lambert**, b. 1842.

Children:

+ 189	i.	Elizabeth A.^{5} Lambert b. 1871.
190	ii.	Mahalia P. Lambert b. 1873.
		She Married **Jacob C. Arbogast**, b. in Virginia.
191	iii.	Philbert Lambert.
192	iv.	Cadden Lambert b. 1874.
		He Married **Cluetta Lambert**.
193	v.	Statten Lambert b. 1876.
194	vi.	Albinus Lambert, Jr..
195	vii.	Mary H. Lambert b. 1878.
		She Married **Edward White**.
196	viii.	Lucretia Lambert.
		She Married **Robert Smith**.
197	ix.	Ira Lambert.
		She Married **Zella Painter**.

68. **Phoebe (Susan)**^{4} **Calhoun** (12.Elizabeth Ann^3 Mullenax, 2.Abraham^2, 1.Mary Elizabeth^1 Arbogast), b. in Pendleton Co., WV.
She Married **Solomon Hinkle**.

Children:

+ 198	i.	William^5 Hinkle b. May 1826.

70. **John Wesley⁴ Simmons** (13.Margaret³ Mullenax, 2.Abraham², 1.Mary Elizabeth¹ Arbogast), b. 1836 in Pendleton Co., WV, d. Jan 9 1899 in Ritchie Co., WV, buried in Pleasant Hill, Grant, Ritchie Co., WV.
    REFN: 22
    Marriage book # 1-A Page 118 Doddridge Co. Place of Marriage A. Orrahood, Minster Ezekiel Bee
    Certificate of Death: Ritchie Co. WV Book 1 Pg.60.
    Married Oct 31 1856 in Doddridge Co., WV, **Elizabeth Ann Orrahood**, b. Dec 10 1836 in Hardy Co., WV, d. Aug 13 1913 in Cantwell, Ritchie Co., WV, buried Aug 20 1913 in Grant, Ritchie Co., WV Buried at Pleasant Grove Cem
    Info from Harrisville Newspaper.

    ### Children:
    - 199   i.   Mary⁵ Simmons b. 1858 in Ritchie Co., WV.
      She Married **Cameron Swadley** (son of Nicholas Swadley and Eliza Jane Sharp). Cameron: Lived in Indian Creek, Ritchie, WV.
    - 200   ii.   William Simmons b. 1860 in Ritchie Co., WV. Lived in Cokely, Ritchie, WV.
    - + 201   iii.   Sarah Lavina Simmons b. Sep 22 1861.
    - 202   iv.   Huldah C. Or Ulda Simmons b. 1865 in Ritchie Co., WV.
      She Married **George Layfield**. Lived in Addis Run, Ritchie, WV.
    - + 203   v.   Aaron Sharon Simmons b. Feb 21 1867.
    - 204   vi.   Norah A. Simmons b. 1875 in Ritchie Co., WV.
      She Married **William Layfield**. William: Lived at Elm Run, Ritchie, WV.
    - 205   vii.   Emery Simmons b. 1877. Lived in Harrisville, WV.

72. **Emily Jane⁴ Mullenax** (16.John H.³, 3.Jacob², 1.Mary Elizabeth¹ Arbogast).
    She Married **James J. Grogg**.

    ### Children:
    - + 206   i.   Louella Maer⁵ Grogg b. Apr 17 1874.

74. **Martha⁴ Mullenax** (17.George³, 3.Jacob², 1.Mary Elizabeth¹ Arbogast).
    Married Nov 24 1842, **Daniel Waybright, Jr.**, b. 1823 in Pendleton Co., WV (son of Daniel Waybright and Rachel Arbogast), d. 1879 in Pendleton Co., WV.

    ### Children:
    - + 207   i.   Columbus P.⁵ Waybright b. Jul 1845.
    - + 208   ii.   Mary Jane Waybright b. 1847.
    - + 209   iii.   Albert Waybright b. May 1848.

77. **George⁴ Mullenax** (19.Joseph³, 5.William², 1.Mary Elizabeth¹ Arbogast), b. 1818 in Crabbottom, Highland Co., VA.
    Married Aug 17 1838 in Pendleton Co., WV, **Sarah Simmons**, b.1820, VA,

    ### Children:
    - 210   i.   Louisa K.⁵ Mullenax.
    - 211   ii.   Henry A. Mullenax.
    - 212   iii.   Ann R. Mullenax.
    - 213   iv.   Martha E. Mullenax.
    - 214   v.   Ephraim A. Mullenax.
    - + 215   vi.   David Pillow Mullenax.
      Married **Elizabeth Snider** had a child Stephen Grover Mullenax
    - 216   vii.   Sarah F. Mullenax.
    - 217   viii.   John B. Mullenax.

83. **Abraham⁴ Waybright** (24.Christina³ Mullenax, 5.William², 1.Mary Elizabeth¹ Arbogast), b. May 5 1850 in Pendleton Co., WV, d. Apr 10 1885.
    He Married **Sarah Christina Wratchford**, b. Nov 8 1847, d. May 25 1930, buried in Waybright Cem., Pendleton Co., WV.

    ### Children:

	218	i.	Mary J^5 Waybright b. 1872.
	219	ii.	Abraham Waybright b. 1874.
+	220	iii.	Mary Christina Waybright b. Apr 23 1874.
	221	iv.	Rosetta Waybright b. May 18 1876, d. Jun 9 1892 in Randolph Co., WV, buried in Waybright Cem., Pendleton Co., WV. She <u>Married</u> Henry **Harrison Clayton**, b. Oct 17 1867 in Pendleton Co., WV, d. Jan 29 1937 in Randolph Co., WV.
	222	v.	Luther Waybright b. Jun 19 1878, d. Oct 15 1894, buried in Waybright Cem., Pendleton Co., WV.
	223	vi.	Verna Waybright b. Oct 18 1885, d. Jan 1982 in Parsons, Tucker Co., WV. <u>Married</u> 1903, **Walter W. Lambert**.

84. **Mary Margaret^4 Waybright** (24.Christina^3 Mullenax, 5.William^2, 1.Mary Elizabeth^1 Arbogast), b. Jan 14 1856 in Onego, Pendleton Co., WV, d. Nov 18 1932 in Whipped, ID.
Mary lived with 4 different men.
(1) She <u>Married</u> **David Huffman**, b. 1850 in Pendleton Co., WV, buried in Reed Cem., Pendleton Co., WV.

   Children:

	224	i.	Marian A.^{5} Huffman b. About 1875.
+	225	ii.	Mary Marcella Huffman b. Aug 27 1879.
+	226	iii.	Eve Frances Waybright b. Sep 24 1880.
+	227	iv.	Thaddeus Waybright b. Apr 12 1892.
	228	v.	Ica Chloe Waybright b. May 12 1894 in Onego, Pendleton Co., WV, d. Jun 28 1948 in Lewiston, Nez Perez Co., ID. <u>Married</u> Dec 1913, **Hetzel (John) Jordan**, b. May 20 1886 in Job, Randolph Co., WV, d. Feb 9 1964 in Lewiston, Nez Perez Co., ID.

(2) She <u>Married</u> **Simeon Harper**.
(3) She <u>Married</u> **Henry Cunningham**.
(4) She <u>Married</u> **John Sites**.

85. **William Washington^4 Waybright** (24.Christina^3 Mullenax, 5.William^2, 1.Mary Elizabeth^1 Arbogast), b. Apr 1857 in Pendleton Co., WV, d. Aft 1930 in Logan, Fayette Co., WV, buried in Chauncey, Logan Co., WV.
<u>Married</u> Jan 4 1885 in Pendleton Co., WV, **Mary A. Lewis**, b. Apr 1867 in Pendleton Co., WV.

   Children:

+	229	i.	Oscar Blaine^5 Waybright b. Oct 7 1887.
	230	ii.	Walter C. Waybright b. May 22 1890 in Pendleton Co., WV, d. Dec 1963. He <u>Married</u> **Fransina (Unknown)**.
+	231	iii.	Rettia C. Waybright b. Jul 1892.

87. **Isaac Perry^4 Waybright** (24.Christina^3 Mullenax, 5.William^2, 1.Mary Elizabeth^1 Arbogast), b. Mar 20 1866 in Pendleton Co., WV, d. Oct 5 1908 in Tucker Co., WV.
Isaac was a carpenter.
<u>Married</u> Jul 28 1893 in Randolph Co., WV, **Arthena Cunningham**, b. Apr 19 1873 in Pendleton Co., WV, d. Nov 9 1948.

   Children:

+	232	i.	Solomon Robert^5 Waybright b. Apr 11 1894.
	233	ii.	Silva Gladys Waybright b. Feb 14 1897 in Randolph Co., WV.
	234	iii.	Oliver Waybright b. Jan 19 1899 in Randolph Co., WV, d. May 22 1899 in Randolph Co., WV.
	235	iv.	Cecil Waybright b. Dec 8 1899 in Randolph Co., WV, d. 26 Jan in Randolph Co., WV.
	236	v.	Mary Jane Waybright b. Mar 22 1904 in Hendricks, Tucker Co., WV, d. Jul 28 1964. She <u>Married</u> **Joseph Bragg**.

88. **Cordelia**[4] **Waybright** (24.Christina[3] Mullenax, 5.William[2], 1.Mary Elizabeth[1] Arbogast), b. Jul 6 1869 in Crabbottom, Highland Co., VA, d. Jan 20 1955 in Parsons, Tucker Co., WV, buried in Parsons, Tucker Co., WV.
Married Dec 6 1899, **Samuel Henry Arbogast**, b. Aug 2 1881 in Pendleton Co., WV (son of John B. (Jack) Arbogast and Othelia Ann Ramsey), d. Feb 22 1920 in Pendleton Co., WV, buried in Arbogast Cem., Roaring Creek Pendleton Co., WV.

   Children:
   + 237   i.   Perlie[5] Arbogast b. Jun 16 1900.
   + 238   ii.   Wilbur Arbogast b. Jun 2 1901.
     239   iii. Jasper Arbogast b. Jan 24 1903 in Pendleton Co., WV, d. Apr 1984 in Dilliner, Greene Co., PA.
                 He Married **Gladys Roy**.
     240   iv.   Henry Clay Arbogast b. Jun 9 1905 in Pendleton Co., WV, d. Sep 28 1985 in Elkins, Randolph Co., WV, buried in Mountain State Memorial Gardens Elkins Randolph Co., WV.
                 Married 1923, **Gertrude Ellen Teter**, d. Jul 19 1970 in Elkins, Randolph Co., WV, buried in Parsons, Tucker Co., WV.
     241   v.   Chloe Arbogast b. Jul 7 1907 in Pendleton Co., WV.
                 She Married **Allen Isner**.
     242   vi.   Mary Susan Arbogast b. Aug 6 1909 in Pendleton Co., WV, d. Feb 10 1990 in Akron, Summit Co., OH, buried in Crown Hill Cem., Twinsburg, OH.
                 Married Jun 21 1929, **Wilbur Gay Loughry**.
     243   vii. Hazel Mae Arbogast b. Feb 16 1911 in Pendleton Co., WV, d. Jul 10 1978 in Randolph Co., WV, buried in Tucker Co., WV.
                 She Married **Arthur B Parsons**, b. Oct 15 1904 in Slip Hill, Kanawha Co., WV, d. Aug 25 1965 in Toms River, Ocean Co., NJ.

90. **John Edward**[4] **Waybright** (24.Christina[3] Mullenax, 5.William[2], 1.Mary Elizabeth[1] Arbogast), b. Mar 16 1875 in Dry Fork, Randolph Co., WV, d. Jan 29 1958 in Laurel Run, South Parsons, Tucker Co., WV, buried Feb 1958 in Parsons, Tucker Co., WV.
Married Mar 7 1898 in Pendleton Co., WV, **Sophia Catherine Clayton**, b. Oct 15 1881 in Job, Randolph Co., WV, d. Oct 1973 in Parsons, Tucker Co., WV, buried in Parsons, Tucker Co., WV.

   Children:
   + 244   i.   Clifton Mason[5] Waybright b. Jul 28 1899.
   + 245   ii.   Guy Daniel Waybright b. Dec 5 1901.
   + 246   iii. Burley McCoy Waybright b. Oct 30 1904.
   + 247   iv.   Edna Margaret Waybright b. Apr 23 1907.
     248   v.   Martha Elizabeth Waybright b. Feb 16 1910 in Onego, Pendleton Co., WV, d. Mar 23 1991.
                 She Married **Walter Hedrick**, b. Mar 5 1904 in West Virginia, d. Jul 1980 in Buckhannon, Upshur Co., WV, buried Jul 1980 in Buckhannon, Upshur Co., WV.
     249   vi.   James Albert Waybright b. Sep 19 1912 in Onego, Pendleton Co., WV, d. Apr 18 1989.
                 He Married **Philope Humphrey**.
     250   vii. Jessie Susan Waybright b. Oct 2 1915 in Dry Fork, Randolph Co., WV, d. Nov 1987 in Parsons, Tucker Co., WV.
                 She Married **Roy Hottle**.
     251   viii. Ethel Virginia Waybright b. Jul 7 1919 in Davis, Tucker Co., WV.
                 Married Oct 5 1940 in West Virginia, Vincent Carr. Vincent:
     252   ix.   Virgil Lee Waybright b. Aug 16 1922 in Montrose, Randolph Co., WV.
                 Married Aug 17 1940, **Mary Belle McClintic**, b. Aug 4 1923.
     253   x.   Edger Roy Waybright b. Apr 23 1925 in Montrose, Randolph Co., WV.

98. **Kenton L.**[4] **Mullenax** (27.Henry Clay[3], 5.William[2], 1.Mary Elizabeth[1] Arbogast), b. Dec 10 1865, d. 1946 in Camille, Prince George's Co., MD.
Married May-04-1898 in Highland Co., VA, **Ollie A. Arbogast**, b. Nov 23 1879 in Crabbottom, Highland Co., VA (daughter of William Henry Arbogast and Barbara Ellen Fleiisher), d. Feb 01 1963 in Highland Co., VA.

   Children:
   - \+ 254   i.   Mavis A.[5] Mullenax b. Apr-28-2005.
   - 255   ii.   Ronald Jones Arbogast b. Apr-19-1908, d. Sep-24-1970.
   He Married **Rebecca M. Cox**, d. 17 Dec 1957.
   - \+ 256   iii.   Claris Ella Mullenax b. Oct-15-1910.
   - 257   iv.   Ruby Mae Mullenax b. Feb-15-1915.
   Married May-07-1960, **Leonard Christebson**.
   - \+ 258   v.   Kenton Dexter Mullenax b. Jul-11-1917.

105. **Henry Walter**[4] **Mullenax** (27.Henry Clay[3], 5.William[2], 1.Mary Elizabeth[1] Arbogast), b. Nov 28 1877, d. Jan 17 1961. Operated the poor house at Blue Grass from 1912 to 1952
Married, **Mamie Katherine Collins**, about 1897, b. Apr 20 1882, d. Feb 12 1967.

   Children:
   - 259   i.   Esta Belle[5] Mullenax b. Nov 8 1899 in Blue Grass, Highland Co., WV, d. Jul 10 1964 in Canton, Stark Co., OH.
   Married Jul 20 1921, **William Ashley Hoover**, b. Oct 12 1889,
   - \+ 260   ii.   Monna Lee Mullenax b. Aug 31 1901.
   - 261   iii.   Hazel Gray Mullenax b. Jul 9 1903, d. Sep 26 1903.
   - 262   iv.   Thelma Gertrude Mullenax.
   She Married **Ray Mullenax**,
   - 263   v.   Joseph Mullenax .
   - 264   vi.   Fred Mullenax .
   He Married **Ella Vaiden Dahmer**,
   - 265   vii.   Gladys Mae Mullenax .
   She Married **John Swecker**, b. Mar 29 1899, d. 1976.
   - 266   viii.   Edith Virginia Mullenax .
   - 267   ix.   Benjamin W. Mullenax .
   - 268   x.   John William Mullenax .
   He Married **Edith Parsons**, b. Jul 12 1920, d. May 13 1979.
   - 269   xi.   Geneva Katherine Mullenax b. Jul 22 1913, d. 1986.
   Married, **Roscoe W. Fox**, b. Aug 4 1909, d. Dec 12 1990.

108. **Aaron C.**[4] **Mullenax** (27.Henry Clay[3], 5.William[2], 1.Mary Elizabeth[1] Arbogast), b.He Married **Arbelia Wimer**, b. 1886 (daughter of Jeremiah Emanuel Wimer and Ellen Catherine Rexrode).

   Children:
   - \+ 270   i.   Ollie Elizabeth[5] Mullenax b. Mar 2 1905.
   - 271   ii.   Elva Mullenax.
   - 272   iii.   Lester Mullenax.
   - 273   iv.   Calhoun Mullenax b. 1910, d. 1989.
   He Married **Haxel** Mullenax.
   - 274   v.   Merle Mullenax b. 1915.
   - \+ 275   vi.   Nellie Susan Mullenax b. Jun 6 1912.

109. **Elizabeth S**[4] **Mullenax** (28.Edward[3], 5.William[2], 1.Mary Elizabeth[1] Arbogast), b. May 1858.
Married 1879, **Jefferson D Rexroad**, b. About 1862 in Dry Fork, Randolph Co., WV (son of Nicholas Rexroad and Elizabeth Waybright).

   Children:
   - \+ 276   i.   Kemper D[5] Rexroad b. June 1881.
   - 277   ii.   Arthur Rexroad b. Apr 1883.
   - 278   iii.   Clinton D Rexroad b. 1884.

279   iv.   Forrest Rexroad b. Mar 1888.
280   v.   Lena Rexroad b. Apr 1889.
          She Married **Ira H Rexroad**, b. 1892 in Highland Co., VA (son of Benjamin Rexroad and Delia Weese).
281   vi.   Grace Rexroad b. 1894, d. 1918, buried in Blue Grass Cem., Highland Co., VA.
          She Married **William Hover**, b. About 1893 in Pocahontas Co., WV.
282   vii.   Robert Rexroad b. June 1896.
283   viii.   Mary E Rexroad b. July 1899.

123. **Clotilda Adeline[4] Mulanax** (33.Miles Elliott[3], 6.Joseph[2], 1.Mary Elizabeth[1] Arbogast), b. May 05 1853 in Montana, d. Jun 01 1920 in Jackson Co., KS.
Married Jan 02 1873 in Kansas, **John H. Renfro**, b. About 1849 in Missouri. **John**: Repository: Name: Anita Lorraine (Groce) Stiner
Post Falls, Idaho 83854
Title: *Notes of Dorothy Mulanax* Author: Dorothy Mulanax, Publication: sent to Anita Stiner by Thelma Louise (Kelley) Groce

Children:
284   i.   Mary Agnus.[5] Renfro b. 1873.
          She Married **Henry Ray**.
285   ii.   Rachel Ann Renfro b. 1875.
          Married 1898, **Lewis England**.
286   iii.   Jesse Renfro b. 1879.
287   iv.   Lucy Renfro b. 1882.
288   v.   Flora Renfro b. 1883.
          Married 1911, **John Krumrey**.

124. **William Dallas[4] Mulanax** (33.Miles Elliott[3], 6.Joseph[2], 1.Mary Elizabeth[1] Arbogast), b. Dec 02 1854 in Missouri, d. Jun 01 1920 in Jackson Co., MO.
Married Sep 17 1876, **Mary Renfro**, b. in Missouri (daughter of James Renfro and Ann Overly), buried in South Cedar Cem., Denison, Jackson Co., KS, d. May 04 1884 in Denison, Jackson Co., KS.

Children:
+ 289   i.   James Lewis[5] Mulanax b. Jul 27 1877.
290   ii.   Arthur Dallas Mulanax b. Oct 17 1880 in Kansas, d. Sep 28 1945 in Topeka, Shawnee Co., KS.
          He Married **Mary E. Campbell**.
291   iii.   Harry Edgar Mulanax b. Dec 13 1881 in Kansas, buried in Holton, Jackson Co., KS, d. Aug 06 1955 in Holton, Jackson Co., KS.
          Married Dec 25 1901 in Holton, Jackson Co., KS, **Cora Spiker**.
292   iv.   George Ellet Mulanax b. Apr 29 1884, buried in Cassoday, Butler Co., KS, d. Oct 31 1951 in Cassoday, Butler Co., KS.
          Married Mar 22 1905 in Topeka, Shawnee Co., KS, **Myrtle Martin**.

125. **John Greenbury[4] Mulanax** (33.Miles Elliott[3], 6.Joseph[2], 1.Mary Elizabeth[1] Arbogast), b. Aug 27 1856 in Missouri, d. Aug 20 1930 in Denison, Jackson Co., KS, buried in South Cedar Cem., Denison, Jackson Co., KS.
Title: 1880 United States Federal Census, Ancestry.com and The Church of Jesus Christ of Latter-day Saints
(1) Married Sep 05 1977 in Denison, Jackson Co., KS, **Flora Ellen Kirkpatrick**, b. Dec 27 1858 in Muskingum Co., OH (daughter of James W. Kirkpatrick and Eleanor Ann Lyons), buried in South Cedar Cem., Denison, Jackson Co., KS, d. Jun 20 1889 in Denison, Jackson Co., KS.

Children:
+ 293   i.   Flora Adeline[5] Mulanax b. 0828879 . Denison, Jackson Co., KS. D Jan 12 1952 Springtown, AR
          Married **Frank Francis Blaikie b.** 5 Oct 1862, Coldingham, Scotland d. 15 Nov 1941, Springtown, Benton Co., AR

	294	ii.	Rachel Ellen Mulanax b. Aug 28 1878 in Denison, Jackson Co., KS, d. Apr 04 1957.
	295	iii.	Ida May Mulanax b. Apr 27 1883 in Kansas, d. Aug 05 1919 in Kansas.
	296	iv.	(infant) Mulanax b. May 17 1884 in Jackson Co., KS, d. May 17 1884 in Jackson Co., KS.
	297	v.	John W. Mulanax b. Aug 26 1886 in Kansas, d. Mar 29 1905 in Kansas.
	298	vi.	Anna M. Mulanax b. Jun 01 1889 in Kansas, d. Aug 16 1889 in Kansas.

(2) He Married **Rachel McRaynolds**, d. 1930 in Kansas.

127. **Matthew Elliott⁴ Mulanax** (35.William R.³, 6.Joseph², 1.Mary Elizabeth¹ Arbogast), b. Jun 07 1858 in Grant Twp., Jackson Co., KS, d. Aug 11 1928 in Mayetta, Jackson Co., KS, buried Aug 13 1928 in Mayetta, Jackson Co., KS.
Married Feb 13 1881 in Doniphan Co., KS, **Olive Lavina Payne**.

Children:
- 299 i. Joseph M.⁵ Mulanax b. Jun 26 1886 in Jackson Co., KS, buried in Olive Hill Cem., Horton, Brown Co., KS, d. Jun 08 1894 in Jackson Co., KS.
- 300 ii. Walter Mulanax b. Nov 09 1888 in Jackson Co., KS, d. Oct 08 1964.
  He Married **Bessie Sharrai**.
- + 301 iii. Mary Aceneth Mulanax b. Oct 10 1890.
- 302 iv. Kate Mulanax b. Sep 17 1892 in Jackson Co., KS, d. Sep 1962 in Topeka, Shawnee Co., KS.
  She Married **Jess Martin**.
- 303 v. Grace Mulanax b. Aug 23 1895, buried in Olive Hill Cem., Horton, Brown Co., KS, d. Dec 05 1895 in Jackson Co., KS.
- 304 vi. Leroy Mulanax b. May 10 1896 in Jackson Co., KS, d. Aug 15 1961 in Jackson Co., KS.
  He Married **Elizabeth Lavier**.
- + 305 vii. Louis Mulanax b. Oct 19 1898.
- + 306 viii. Alfred Mulanax b. Feb 11 1901.

130. **Jacob Allen⁴ Mulanax** (35.William R.³, 6.Joseph², 1.Mary Elizabeth¹ Arbogast), b. Oct 10 1864 in Jackson Co., KS, d. 19 Apr 1944 in Torrington, Goshen Co., WY.
Married 15 Feb 1992 in Pottawattamie Co., KS, **Maymie Alice Brooks Bennett**, b. 1854, d. 1929 in Laramie, Laramie Co., WY.

Children:
- 307 i. Violet⁵ Mulanax b. 27 Jan 1896, d. 26 Apr 1930.
  She Married **William Alvin Shaw**.
- 308 ii. Bessie Mulanax.
- 309 iii. Hazel Mulanax d. 1964.
  She Married **Fred Cooley**.
- 310 iv. Raymond Mulanax.
- 311 v. Ed Barnett Mulanax.

133. **John William⁴ Mulanax** (35.William R.³, 6.Joseph², 1.Mary Elizabeth¹ Arbogast), b. Jan 07 1871 in Kansas, d. 28 Dec 1938 in Lafayette, Yamhill Co., OR, buried in Evergreen Cem., McMinnville, Yamhill Co., OR.
Married 23 Dec 1896 in Jackson Co., KS, **Sarah Ellen Osburn**, b. 25 Aug 1876 in Havensville, Pottawatomie Co., KS, d. 18 Sep 1940 in Lafayette, Yamhill Co., OR, buried in Evergreen Cem., McMinnville, Yamhill Co., OR.

Children:
- 312 i. Gertrude May⁵ Mulanax b. 10 Mar 1898 in Havensville, Pottawatomie Co., KS, d. 5 Oct 1961.
- + 313 ii. Calvin Silas Mulanax b. 16 Aug 1903.
- 314 iii. Alice Ruby Mulanax b. 21 May 1907.
- + 315 iv. Edith Pearl Mulanax b. 25 May 1909.

+ 316 v. Ruby Ann Mulanax b. 25 Aug 1916.

136. **Lucy Adeline**[4] **Mulanax** (35.William R.[3], 6.Joseph[2], 1.Mary Elizabeth[1] Arbogast), b. Aug 27 1878 in Denison, Jackson Co., KS, d. 24 Nov 1945 in Douglas, Converse Co., WY, buried in Holton, Jackson Co., KS.
Married 10 Mar 1897 in Jackson Co., KS, **James William Hager**, b. 17 Apr 1872 at Avoca, Jackson Co., KS (son of David Hammond Hagar and Laura Gish), d. 17 Nov 1937 in Topeka, Shawnee Co., KS, buried in Holton, Jackson Co., KS.

Children:
- 317 i. Estella May[5] Hager b. 1 Oct 1898 in Avoca, Jackson Co., KS, d. 17 Feb 1952 in Kansas, buried in Holton, Jackson Co., KS.
Married About 1922, **Frank Zibell**.
- 318 ii. Edith Asele Hager b. 18 Dec 1900 in Avoca, Jackson Co., KS, buried in Holton, Jackson Co., KS, d. 17 Jan 1978 in Arkansas.
Married 27 Mar 1920, **Ray A. McKinsey**.
- + 319 iii. William Roy Hager b. 7 Jan 1903.
- 320 iv. Laura Maude Hagar b. 28 Dec 1904 in Avoca, Jackson Co., KS, d. About 1987 in Douglas, Converse Co., WY.
Married 3 Mar 1923, **John S. Townend**.

146. **Anna Louisa**[4] **Mulanax** (40.Joseph Riley[3] Mullenax, 6.Joseph[2] Mulanax, 1.Mary Elizabeth[1] Arbogast), b. May 10 1879 in Greene Co., MO, d. Dec 17 1934 in Seattle, King Co., WA.
Married Aug 26 1897 in Missouri, **Milton Ephraim Kelley**, b. Oct 6 1877 in Waco, McLennan Co., TX (son of Thomas Benton Kelley and Nancy Emiline Goss), d. 1979 in Seattle, King Co., WA.

Children:
- 321 i. Hobart William[5] Kelley b. 1899 in Glen Cove, Coleman Co., TX, d. 1921.
Married About 1920 in Washington, **Marie Clark**, b. About 1903 in Glen Cove, Coleman Co., TX, d. in Seattle, King Co., WA.
- + 322 ii. Mary Evelyn Kelley b. Sep 8 1901.
- + 323 iii. Thelma Louise Kelley b. Jul 13 1903.
- 324 iv. Joseph Henry Kelley b. Jan 22 1905 in Glen Cove, Coleman Co., TX, d. Nov 8 1980 in Seattle, King Co., WA.
- 325 v. Irene Marie Kelley b. Aug 15 1906 in Glen Cove, Coleman Co., TX, d. in Glen Cove, Coleman Co., TX.
- 326 vi. G. Vernon Kelley b. Aug 19 1907 in Glen Cove, Coleman Co., TX.
Married Jul 15 1937 in Seattle, King Co., WA, **Jessie Langenbacker**, b. Jan 15 1913, d. Nov 30 1982 in Seattle, King Co., WA.
- 327 vii. James Fay Kelley b. 1911 in Glen Cove, Coleman Co., TX.
Married About 1936 in Seattle, King Co., WA, **Madeline V. McGraff**, b. Jan 15 1913 in Seattle, King Co., WA, d. 1980 in Salinas, Monterey Co., CA.
- 328 viii. Luther Elliot Kelley b. Aug 23 1918 in Richmond, Contra Costa Co., CA.
Married About 1937 in Seattle, King Co., WA, **Mary Clark**, b. About 1918, d. in Port Orchard, Kitsap Co., WA.
- + 329 ix. Anna Jane Kelley b. Oct 29 1919.
- 330 x. Robert Harold Kelley b. Jan 25 1924 in Seattle, King Co., WA, d. Aug 27 1995 in Seattle, King Co., WA.

Generation Five

153. **Mary Permelia Catherine**[5] **Mullenax** (50.William Isaac[4], 7.James W.[3], 2.Abraham[2], 1.Mary Elizabeth[1] Arbogast), b. Aug 7 1848 in Dry Run, Pendleton Co., WV, d. Apr 16 1932 in Pocahontas Co., WV, buried Apr 18 1932 in Thornwood, Pocahontas Co., WV.

Married Jun 15 1868 in Churchville, Pendleton Co., WV, **Churchill Waybright**, b. Aug 3 1844 in Blue Grass, Highland Co., WV (son of John R. Allen and Alice Waybright), d. Jul 11 1911 in Thornwood, Pocahontas Co., WV, buried in Bartow, Pocahontas Co., WV. **Churchill**: Allen took his mothers maiden name.

Children:
- 331   i.   Sarah P^6 Waybright b. About 1867.
- + 332   ii.   Wilber Allen Waybright b. Jul 8 1869.
- 333   iii.   Clara Ann Waybright b. May 15 1871 in Dry Run, Pendleton Co., WV.
  Married 1912, **Minor Mullenax**.
- + 334   iv.   Amby Stanton Waybright b. Sep 30 1873.
- 335   v.   James Buckhannan Waybright b. Apr 10 1875 in Dry Run, Pendleton Co., WV, d. Apr 9 1950.
  Married Mar 4 1897 in Back Mt. Cem., Pocahontas Co., WV, **Louise Murphy**.
- + 336   vi.   Fransina Lee Waybright b. Mar 28 1877.

155. **Elijah^5 Mullenax** (50.William Isaac^4, 7.James W.^{3}, 2.Abraham^2, 1.Mary Elizabeth^1 Arbogast), b. Aug 30 1853 in Dry Run, Pendleton Co., WV, d. Jan 20 1928, buried in Elk Mt. Cem., Pendleton. Co., WV.
He Married **Elizabeth C Hinkle**, b. Mar 1855 in Dry Run, Pendleton Co., WV (daughter of William Hinkle and Martha Ann Waybright), d. Jan 20 1928.

Children:
- + 337   i.   Dolly^6 Mullenax b. Mar 04 1879.
- + 338   ii.   Lura Mullenax b. Jun 28 1881.
- + 339   iii.   Mcclelland Mullenax b. Oct 25 1883.
- + 340   iv.   Martha Ellen Mullenax b. Feb 1891.
- + 341   v.   Betty Alice Mullenax b. Feb 28 1891.

156. **Annie Jane^5 Mullenax** (50.William Isaac^4, 7.James W.^{3}, 2.Abraham^2, 1.Mary Elizabeth^1 Arbogast), b. Aug 14 1854 in Dry Run, Pendleton Co., WV, d. Jun 23 1925.
Married Aug 4 1874 in Dry Run, Pendleton Co., WV, **Silas Clark Halterman**.

Children:
- + 342   i.   Joseph Clark^6 Halterman b. Feb 22 1887.

157. **James B.^{5} Mullenax** (50.William Isaac^4, 7.James W.^{3}, 2.Abraham^2, 1.Mary Elizabeth^1 Arbogast), b. Sep 25 1856 in Dry Run, Pendleton Co., WV, d. Aug 14 1896.
(1) Married 1880, **Amanda M. Bennett**.

Children:
- + 343   i.   Emory R^6 Mullenax b. Oct 20 1884.

(2) Married 1878, **Sallie Dean Bennett**.

Children:
- + 344   ii.   Sallie Denie Mullenax b. Aug 1879.

158. **William Alexander^5 Mullenax** (50.William Isaac^4, 7.James W.^{3}, 2.Abraham^2, 1.Mary Elizabeth^1 Arbogast), b. Jul 14 1858 in Dry Run, Pendleton Co., WV, d. Sep 1 1945.
Married 1894, **Elizabeth J. Warner**.

Children:
- 345   i.   Ellen^6 Mullenax b. 1890.
- 346   ii.   Virgie Mullenax b. 1898.

162. **Solomon Key^5 Mullenax** (50.William Isaac^4, 7.James W.^{3}, 2.Abraham^2, 1.Mary Elizabeth^1 Arbogast), b. May 07 1868 in Dry Run, Pendleton Co., WV, d. May 13 1946 in Pocahontas Co., WV, buried in Arbovale Cem., Arbovale, Pocahontas Co., WV.
(1) Married Dec 31 1890, **Charlotte Ellen Bennett**, b. Apr 17 1875, d. Dec 11 1901 in Pocahontas Co., WV, buried in Arbovale Cem., Arbovale, Pocahontas Co., WV.

Children:

+	347	i.	Nellie Mae⁶ Mullenax b. Apr 21 1892.
+	348	ii.	Tiffin Rinehart Mullenax b. Sep 04 1894.
	349	iii.	Vivian Lucille Mullenax b. May 17 1897, d. Mar 24 1937.
			Married Jul 5 1915, J. **Stanley Robertson**.
	350	iv.	Elva Mullenax b. Apr 15 1900, d. Aug 24 1900.

(2) He Married **Daisy Margaret Mick**, b. Jul 14 1889 in Pendleton Co., WV, d. Aug 01 1979.

Children:

+	351	v.	Virgil Craig Mullenax b. Sep 11 1907.
+	352	vi.	Wilma Grethel Mullenax b. May 06 1910.
	353	vii.	Basil Kay Mullenax b. Jun 05 1913.
			He Married **Nina Bridat**.
+	354	viii.	Raymond Rafe Mullenax b. Aug 02 1916.
+	355	ix.	Inez Catherine Mullenax b. Apr 4 1919.
	356	x.	Crystabelle Mullenax b. Sep 20 1921.
			She Married **Roscoe Warner**.
	357	xi.	Stanley Domaine Mullenax b. Nov 26 1923, d. 13 Sep1952 in Los Angeles, Los Angeles Co., CA.
			He Married **Ann Cinders**.
	358	xii.	William Vivian Mullenax b. Apr 04 1926, d. Apr 23 1926.
	359	xiii.	Gerald Allen Mullenax b. Oct 16 1927, d. Mar 20 1975.
			He Married Ruby **Vandevender**.
+	360	xiv.	Edward Lee Mullenax b. Apr 20 1930.

163. **Mary Jane⁵ Mullenax** (51.John Wesley⁴, 7.James W.³, 2.Abraham², 1.Mary Elizabeth¹ Arbogast), b. Oct 24 1852 in Pendleton Co., WV, d. UNKNOWN.
This information is provided for all BOYDs to research their family connection by the group Clan Boyd.
NOTE: Regard all of this data as unsupported until you verify the accuracy at the original source.
Married 1868 in Pendleton Co., WV, **Elemuel Jefferson Bennett**, b. Dec 13 1848 in Pendleton Co., WV

Children:

	361	i.	John Adam⁶ Bennett b. 1870 in Pendleton Co., WV.
+	362	ii.	Oscela Martin Bennett b. 1871.
	363	iii.	Cora Ellen Bennett
	364	iv.	Ida Florence Bennett b. 1873 in Pendleton Co., WV.
+	365	v.	Florrie Dean Bennett b. 1874.
	366	vi.	Martha (Mattie) Bennett b. 1877 in Pendleton Co., WV.
	367	vii.	Azora M. Bennett b. Dec 14 1878 in Pendleton Co., WV.
	368	viii.	Zenia Bennett b. Oct 12 1889 in Pendleton Co., WV.
	369	ix.	Katie Bennett
	370	x.	Willie Bennett b. 1891 in Pendleton Co., WV.
	371	xi.	Edward J. Bennett b. 1893 in Pendleton Co., WV.
	372	xii.	Thomas J. Bennett b. 1895 in Pendleton Co., WV.

164. **Isaac J.⁵ Mullenax** (51.John Wesley⁴, 7.James W.³, 2.Abraham², 1.Mary Elizabeth¹ Arbogast).
This information is provided for all BOYDs to research their family connection by the group Clan Boyd.
NOTE: Regard all of this data as unsupported until you verify the accuracy at the original source. Some of the basis range from copies of original documents to guesses because it looks possible.
Married Oct 13 1875 in Dry Run, Pendleton Co., WV, **Rosetta Myers**, b. May 08 1861 in Crabbottom, Highland Co., VA (daughter of John William Myers and Martha Ann Mullenax), d. Jan 08 1934 in Staunton, Augusta Co., VA, buried in Green Hill Cem., Circleville, Pendleton Co., WV.
Rosetta: Rosetta was the child of John William Myers and and Martha Ann Mattie. Rosetta never

married. They intended to, but John entered the Civil war, was captured, released in 1865, and went home to claim his daughter..

Children:
- 373   i.   Viola[6] Mullenax b. Jan 16 1877 in Cherry Grove, Pendleton Co., WV, d. Jul 14 1963 in Thornrose Cem., Staunton, Augusta Co., VA.
- 374   ii.   Strickler J. Mullenax b. Dec 02 1878 in Cherry Grove, Pendleton Co., WV, d. Jan 16 1879 in Pendleton Co., WV.
- 375   iii.   Ida Jane Mullenax b. Dec 01 1879 in Cherry Grove, Pendleton Co., WV, d. May 26 1961 in Thornrose Cem., Staunton, Augusta Co., VA.
- 376   iv.   Pheobe Ann Mullenax b. May 23 1882 in Whitmer, Randolph Co., WV, d. Feb 11 1885 in Randolph Co., WV.
- 377   v.   Levie Mullenax b. Sep 11 1886 in Whitmer, Randolph Co., WV, d. Feb 09 1955 in Loudoun Co., VA, buried Lovettsville, VA.
- 378   vi.   Etta Mullenax b. Jun 30 1889 in Whitmer, Randolph Co., WV, d. 1889 in Randolph Co., WV.
- 379   vii.   Mattie Mullenax b. Oct 20 1890 in Whitmer, Randolph Co., WV, d. Oct 18 1971 in Randolph Co., WV.
- 380   viii.   John William Mullenax b. Jul 19 1893 in Cherry Grove, Pendleton Co., WV, d. Jun 18 1946 in Charlottesville, Albemarle Co., VA, buried in Green Hill Cem., Churchville, Lewis Co., WV.
- 381   ix.   Bishop Marvin Mullenax b. Apr 18 1896 in Cherry Grove, Pendleton Co., WV, d. May 12 1931, buried in Green Hill Cem., Churchville, Lewis Co., WV.
- + 382   x.   Charles Edward Vivian Mullenax b. Jul 28 1900.
- 383   xi.   Elva Lenor Mullenax b. Oct 11 1902, d. Jan 12 1990 in Thornrose Cem., Staunton, Augusta Co., VA.

166. **Thomas Jefferson[5] Mullenax** (51.John Wesley[4], 7.James W.[3], 2.Abraham[2], 1.Mary Elizabeth[1] Arbogast), b. Apr 05 1857 in Dry Run, Pendleton Co., WV.
Married 1880, **Virginia Dove**, b. 10 Dec 1859, d. 28 Oct 1938, Elkins, Randolph. Co., WV.

Children:
- 384   i.   Sedgwick L.[6] Mullenax b. Feb 1880.
- 385   ii.   John W. Mullenax.
- 386   iii.   Harnass Mullenax.
- 387   iv.   Katie E. Mullenax.
- 388   v.   Jeddy D. Mullenax.
- 389   vi.   Wandy F. Mullenax.
- 390   vii.   Silvie P. Mullenax.

167. **Virginia Susan[5] Mullenax** (51.John Wesley[4], 7.James W.[3], 2.Abraham[2], 1.Mary Elizabeth[1] Arbogast), d. Apr 07 1860.
Married 1877 in Pendleton Co., WV, **Alonzo John Gibson**, b. 1854 in Randolph Co., WV, d. 1935 in Beverly, Randolph Co., WV.

Children:
- 391   i.   William[6] Gibson.
- 392   ii.   Effie Viola Gibson.
- 393   iii.   John Gibson.
- 394   iv.   Ethel Victoria Gibson.
- 395   v.   Eddie Oliver Gibson.
- 396   vi.   Flossie Margaret Gibson.
- 397   vii.   Mary Catherine Gibson.
  Married **Forrest Stalnaker** b. 1895, d 1975

168. **Phoebe⁵ Mullenax** (51.John Wesley⁴, 7.James W.³, 2.Abraham², 1.Mary Elizabeth¹ Arbogast), d. Jan 10 1929 in Beverly, Randolph Co., WV, b. Oct 27 1864.
Married 1883, **Christopher Armentrout**, b. 1843.

Children:
- 398   i.   Ola E.⁶ Armentrout.
- 399   ii.   Vista G. Armentrout.
- 400   iii. Carney L. Armentrout.
- 401   iv.   Elva T. Armentrout.
- 402   v.   Vivav. Armentrout.
- 403   vi.   Vergie F. Armentrout.

169. **Martin⁵ Mullenax** (51.John Wesley⁴, 7.James W.³, 2.Abraham², 1.Mary Elizabeth¹ Arbogast), b. Nov 13 1865 in Churchville, Pendleton Co., WV, d. Feb 9 1933 in Whitmer, Randolph Co., WV. He Married **Rachel Elizabeth Teter**, b. Nov 08 1867 in Bland Hills, Pendleton Co., WV, d. Feb 05 1959 in Elkins, Randolph Co., WV, buried in Whitmer, Randolph Co., WV.

Children:
- 404   i.   Richard Dickson⁶ Mullenax b. Dec 07 1887 in Cherry Grove, Pendleton Co., WV, d. May 03 1964, buried in Mullenax Cem., Dry Fork, Randolph Co., WV.
  Married **Grace Adamson**, 1907, Randolph Co., WV.
- + 405   ii.   Lena Ester Mullenax b. Feb 02 1890.
  Married **Jonah Elmer Buckbee**, b. 7 Aug 1887, Tucker Co., WV , d. 11 Feb 1975,Tampa, FL
- 406   iii. Stella Mullenax b. Dec 02 1892 in Dry Run, Pendleton Co., WV, d. About 1946 in Baltimore, MD, buried in Maplewood Cem., Elkins, WV.
  Married **Hugh Lambert**, 1910.
- 407   iv.   Charles B. Mullenax b. Jan 03 1894, d. Aug 31 1956 in Elkins, Randolph Co., WV, buried in Armentrout Cem., Whitmer, Randolph Co., WV.
  Married **Opal Amy Mallow**, 20 Aug 1922
- 408   v.   Lillie Mullenax b. Sep 05 1896 in The Low Place near Dry Fork, Randolph Co., WV, d. Jul 18 1974 in Endicott, Broome Co., NY.
  Married **Winebert Bible**, Nov 1913.
- 409   vi.   Valley Mullenax b. Jan 08 1898 in The Low Place near Dry Fork, Randolph Co., WV, d. Feb 12 1944 in Preston Co., WV, buried in Armentrout Cem., Elkins, WV.
  Married **Ray Bennett**, Denver, CO.
- 410   vii. Kenneth Oscar Mullenax b. Feb 26 1900 in The Low Place near Dry Fork, Randolph Co., WV, d. in Brownsville, Fayette Co., PA, buried in Memorial Park, Waynesburg, Greene Co., PA.
  Married **Elva Rebecca Cunningham**, Mar 1918, Cumberland. MD
- 411   viii. Rachel Mullenax b. Feb 16 1902 in The Low Place near Dry Fork, Randolph Co., WV, d. Apr 06 1986 in New Smyrna Beach, FL, Israel Cem., Montrose, VA.
  Married **Ona T. Hedrick**, 26 Dec 1921, Elkins, Randolph Co., WV. Cremated, ashes buried
- 412   ix.   Martin Mullenax, Jr. b. Feb 16 1902 in The Low Place near Dry Fork, Randolph Co., WV, d. Dec 23 1984 in Mt. St. Memorial Garden, Gilman, WV.
  Married **Gladys Mallow**, 2 Sep 1922, Whitmer, WV

185. **Jay⁵ Lambert** (63.Annie Catherine⁴ Calhoun, 12.Elizabeth Ann³ Mullenax, 2.Abraham², 1.Mary Elizabeth¹ Arbogast), b. Feb 24 1865 in Dry Run, Pendleton Co., WV, d. Feb 14 1938.
(1) Married Nov 8 1884 in Pendleton Co., WV, **Frances Ina Teter**, b. ABT 1867.

Children:
- + 413   i.   Curtis C.⁶ Lambert.

(2) Married Mar 6 1907 in Pendleton Co., WV, **Arnetta C. Lambert**, b. ABT 1867.

186. **Solomon K.⁵ Lambert** (63.Annie Catherine⁴ Calhoun, 12.Elizabeth Ann³ Mullenax, 2.Abraham², 1.Mary Elizabeth¹ Arbogast), b. Mar 1 1867 in Dry Run, Pendleton Co., WV, d. Oct 29 1946 in Durbin, Pocahontas Co., WV.
(1) Married ABT 1887, **Ida Lambert**, b. ABT 1869.
(2) Married Mar 8 1889 in North Fork, Pendleton Co., VA, **Ellen Jane Cunningham**, b. Oct 28 1869 in West Virginia, d. Jun 30 1929 in Boyer, Pocahontas Co., WV. **Ellen**:

Children:
- 414   i.   Turlie⁶ Lambert b. Mar 21 1890 in West Virginia, d. Jul 10 1976.
  Married Aug 10 1913, **Leila Modelia Wimer**, b. Apr 18 1890 in West Virginia, d. Sep 10 1966.
- 415   ii.   George Edward Lambert b. Aug 3 1892 in West Virginia, d. Aug 4 1985 in Greenville, Mercer Co., PA.
  (1) Married Dec 25 1915, **Zadie White**, b. Dec 14 1899, d. Mar 24 1919.
  (2) Married Dec 19 1920, **Wilma J. Hallon**, b. Oct 15 1900, d. Nov 30 1987 in Greenville, Mercer Co., PA.
- + 416   iii.   Flotie V. Lambert b. Apr 21 1895.
- + 417   iv.   Uxter Lambert b. Apr 15 1898.
- + 418   v.   Lillie Lambert b. Oct 6 1899.
- 419   vi.   Moody Lambert b. Aug 18 1901 in West Virginia, d. Jan 29 1902 in West Virginia.
- 420   vii.   Elsie Bird Lambert b. Apr 21 1903 in Boyer, Pocahontas Co., WV, d. Jul 23 1987 in Mercer, Mercer Co., PA.
  She Married **(unknown) Hite**.
- 421   viii.   Robert Lambert b. Mar 23 1906 in Pendleton Co., WV, d. May 31 1980.
- 422   ix.   Jay Lambert b. Sep 11 1908 in West Virginia, d. Jul 9 1916 in West Virginia.
- 423   x.   Bessie Ann Lambert b. Apr 21 1910 in West Virginia, d. Apr 5 1991.
  Married JUL 1927, **Thornton George Puffenbarger**, b. Apr 25 1901, d. Sep 17 1974.

189. **Elizabeth A.⁵ Lambert** (65.Susan⁴ Calhoun, 12.Elizabeth Ann³ Mullenax, 2.Abraham², 1.Mary Elizabeth¹ Arbogast), b. 1871.
She Married **Stewart Raines**, b. 1847.

Children:
- + 424   i.   Lillie⁶ Raines b. Sep 26 1890.
  Married **Adam Collins**. Their children; Dale, Dert, Nora, Goldie, Franklin, Mabel
- 425   ii.   Sylvia Raines.
- 426   iii.   Kenney Raines.
- 427   iv.   Fred Raines.
- 428   v.   Walter Raines.
- 429   vi.   Kate Raines.
- 430   vii.   Martha Raines.
- + 431   viii.   Marshall Raines.

198. **William⁵ Hinkle** (68.Phoebe (Susan)⁴ Calhoun, 12.Elizabeth Ann³ Mullenax, 2.Abraham², 1.Mary Elizabeth¹ Arbogast), b. May 1826 in Pendleton Co., WV, d. 1907, buried in Dry Run Cem., Cherry Grove, Pendleton Co., WV.
Married Sep 14 1847 in Highland Co., VA, **Martha Ann Waybright**, b. May 30 1830 in Pendleton Co., WV (daughter of Daniel Waybright and Rachel Arbogast), d. Nov 7 1883, buried in Dry Run Cem., Cherry Grove, Pendleton Co., WV.

Children:
- + 432   i.   Elbridge L.⁶ Hinkle b. Jul 1848.
- + 433   ii.   Susan Hinkle b. Mar 25 1853.
- + 434   iii.   Elizabeth C Hinkle b. Mar 1855.
- + 435   iv.   Eliza Ann Hinkle b. Oct 31 1856.
- + 436   v.   Catherine Beam Hinkle b. 1859.

+ 437 vi. Isaac Harness Hinkle b. 1862.
438 vii. Jasper Triplett Hinkle b. Mar 18 1865 in Dry Run, Pendleton Co., WV.
He Married **Florence Warner**, b. Jun 15 1883 in Riverton, Pendleton Co., WV.
439 viii. Leonard Harper Hinkle b. 1867 in Dry Run, Pendleton Co., WV.
He Married **Sarah Catherine Hammer**, b. Mar 16 1875, d. Jul 04 1950. Sarah: Child of Leonard Hammer and Sarah Trimble.
440 ix. (unknown) Hinkle b. May 1870 in Dry Run, Pendleton Co., WV.
441 x. Pauline Hinkle b. 1873 in Dry Run, Pendleton Co., WV.
She Married **Philip M. Hinkle**, b. 1874.

201. **Sarah Lavina[5] Simmons** (70.John Wesley[4], 13.Margaret[3] Mullenax, 2.Abraham[2], 1.Mary Elizabeth[1] Arbogast), b. Sep 22 1861 in Pendleton Co., WV, d. Dec 28 1897 in Ritchie Co., WV, buried in West Virginia.
Married Sep 11 1879, **Robert Louis Smith**, b. Jan 25 1855 in Cokeley, Ritchie Co., WV (son of Jacob Smith and Mary Wade Zickafoose), d. Sep 21 1931 in Parkersburg, Wood Co., WV, buried in Cedar Grove Cem., Parkersburg, Wood Co., WV. Robert Lewis Smith farmed 200 acres. He married Levina Simmons, and they had little money but had all the things they needed. They lived in Smithville, near Harrisville. Their children were Ezra, Ralph, Myrtle, Elizabeth, Blanche, and Charlie. Ralph lived in Talmadge, Ohio (and Akron?) and had a son and a daughter. Charlie lived in McConnelsville, OH. And was Married to Ollie and had a big family. Elizabeth, or Aunt Lib, lived on Rt. 7 near Marietta. Levina died when Charlie was born. Robert's sister, Mel, took care of the children then. Robert gave up farming and tried running a country store. He went broke on the store and returned to farming. Robert remarried to a woman
whose first name was Isoprene, and they had 3 children Pauline (Married to **Edwin Scott**), Edith (Married to **Nick Nichols**. Isoprene was a little grouchy, and Walter and Blanche's children remember having to be especially nice when Grandma Isoprene visited. When Walter and Blanche lived in Gnadenhutten, Ohio, Robert and Isoprene lived with them for a while. Florence Ruth Clark Garris reports that she spoiled one visit by singing, "Grandma Isoprene fell down and broke her bean" (Florence Ruth thinks he may be buried in St. Mary's WV, where he and Isoprene lived.)
   Children:
+ 442 i. Ezra J.[6] Smith b. Jan 12 1881.
+ 443 ii. Blanche Alma Smith b. Sep 16 1886.
+ 444 iii. Mirta B. Or Myrtle Smith b. Jan 8 1890.
+ 445 iv. Mary Elizabeth Smith b. Jan 8 1892.
+ 446 v. Richard Ralph Smith b. May 1894.
+ 447 vi. Charles W. Smith b. Oct 11 1922.

203. **Aaron Sharon[5] Simmons** (70.John Wesley[4], 13.Margaret[3] Mullenax, 2.Abraham[2], 1.Mary Elizabeth[1] Arbogast), b. Feb 21 1867 in Ritchie Co., WV, d. Mar 3 1952 in Ritchie Co., WV. Lived in Cantwell, Ritchie, WV.
(1) Married Nov 17 1915, **Mary Jane (Chambers) Lemon**, b. 1878 in Ritchie Co., WV, d. 1953 in Ritchie Co., WV. **Mary**: Daughter of Charles Newton Lemon and Arvilla Jame Tingler.
(2) Married Feb 18 1887, **Margaret A. Moore**.
   Children:
448 i. Emmett[6] Simmons b. Oct 29 1888, d. 1976.
449 ii. Winnie B Simmons.
450 iii. Vesta Simmons.
451 iv. Everret Simmons.

206. **Louella Maer[5] Grogg** (72.Emily Jane[4] Mullenax, 16.John H.[3], 3.Jacob[2], 1.Mary Elizabeth[1] Arbogast), b. Apr 17 1874 in Crabbottom, Highland Co., VA, d. Apr 12 1949 in Boyer, Pocahontas Co., WV.
Married Aug 19 1890 in Pocahontas Co., WV, **Andrew Morgan Collins**, b. in Pocahontas Co., WV, d. Nov 28 1942 in Boyer, Pocahontas Co., WV.
   Children:

+ 452 i. Floyd William⁶ Collins b. Nov 25 1893.
+ 453 ii. Cecil Morgan Collins b. Aug 14 1896.

207. **Columbus P.⁵ Waybright** (74.Martha⁴ Mullenax, 17.George³, 3.Jacob², 1.Mary Elizabeth¹ Arbogast), b. Jul 1845 in Pendleton Co., WV, d. in Huntington, Cabell Co., WV.
Married Dec 7 1865, **Phoebe Jane Huffman**, b. 1848 in Pendleton Co., WV.
Children:
454 i. Mona⁶ Waybright.
455 ii. (infant) Waybright b. Jul 27 1860 in Pendleton Co., WV.
456 iii. Mary Bella Waybright b. 1867 in Pendleton Co., WV.
457 iv. Martha J. Waybright b. Aug 1870 in Pendleton Co., WV.

208. **Mary Jane⁵ Waybright** (74.Martha⁴ Mullenax, 17.George³, 3.Jacob², 1.Mary Elizabeth¹ Arbogast), b. 1847. Daughter of Daniel Waybright and Martha Mullenax

She Married **Perry Vance**, b. 1843.
Children:
458 i. Phoebe C.⁶ Vance b. About 1866.
459 ii. Martha E Vance b. About 1868.
460 iii. Sarah Vance b. About 1869.
461 iv. Mary J Vance b. About 1869.

209. **Albert⁵ Waybright** (74.Martha⁴ Mullenax, 17.George³, 3.Jacob², 1.Mary Elizabeth¹ Arbogast), b. May 1848 in Whitmer, Randolph Co., WV, d. Feb 27 1909, buried in Seneca Creek, Pendleton Co., VA/WV.
Married Oct 20 1876 in Pendleton Co., WV, **Dorothy Dolly**, b. Apr 16 1858 in Pendleton Co., WV, d. Oct 29 1904, buried in Waybright Cem., Pendleton Co., WV.
Children:
462 i. Lloyd⁶ Waybright b. Jan 1878 in Pendleton Co., WV.
463 ii. Rosie Waybright b. May 1882 in Pendleton Co., WV.
464 iii. Jasper Waybright b. Oct 3 1884 in Pendleton Co., WV, d. Feb 18 1904 in Onego, Pendleton Co., WV, buried in Seneca Creek, Pendleton Co., VA/WV.
He Married **Rachel Turner**.
465 iv. Henry V. Waybright b. Sep 1887 in Pendleton Co., WV.
+ 466 v. Bert Waybright b. Oct 1890.
467 vi. Myrtle Waybright b. Aug 1893.
468 vii. Martha Jane Waybright b. Aug 1895 in Pendleton Co., WV.
She Married **Frank Huffman**.
469 viii. Arthur Waybright b. Apr 1897 in Pendleton Co., WV.

215. **David Pillow⁵ Mullenax** (77.George⁴, 19.Joseph³, 5.William², 1.Mary Elizabeth¹ Arbogast).
He Married **Elizabeth Snider**.
Children:
+ 470 i. Steven Grove⁶ Mullenax.

220. **Mary Christina⁵ Waybright** (83.Abraham⁴, 24.Christina³ Mullenax, 5.William², 1.Mary Elizabeth¹ Arbogast), b. Apr 23 1874 in Pendleton Co., WV, d. Jun 3 1960, buried in Waybright Cem., Pendleton Co., WV.
Married Jan 3 1893 in Harman, Randolph Co., WV, **John Robert Adamson**, b. Aug 26 1867 in Pendleton Co., WV, d. Feb 21 1943, buried in Joseph Adamson Cem., Pendleton Co., WV.
Children:
471 i. Nellie C.⁶ Adamson b. May 1894 in Pendleton Co., WV.
472 ii. Rosa N. Adamson b. Oct 3 1894 in Pendleton Co., WV, d. Feb 16 1973.
She Married **(unknown) Malberg**.
473 iii. Fred A. Adamson b. Oct 31 1896 in Pendleton Co., WV, d. Apr 1972.

	474	iv.	Glenn Adamson b. Apr 3 1899 in Pendleton Co., WV, d. Sep 28 1968.
	475	v.	Verner C. Adamson b. 1902 in Pendleton Co., WV.
	476	vi.	Albert C Adamson b. Apr 10 1903 in Pendleton Co., WV, d. Aug 1986.
	477	vii.	Rula K. Adamson b. 1907 in Pendleton Co., WV.

225. **Mary Marcella**[5] **Huffman** (84.Mary Margaret[4] Waybright, 24.Christina[3] Mullenax, 5.William[2], 1.Mary Elizabeth[1] Arbogast), b. Aug 27 1879 in Onego, Pendleton Co., WV, d. Mar 11 1950 in Lewiston, Nez Perez Co., ID.
Married Aug 27 1906, **Fleet Jordan**, b. Jan 14 1875 in Churchville, Pendleton Co., WV, d. Dec 22 1965 in Lewiston, Nez Perez Co., ID.

Children:
| | 478 | i. | Glen Weed[6] Jordan b. May 16 1902 in Whitmer, Randolph Co., WV, d. Apr 5 1978 in Lewiston, Nez Perez Co., ID. |

Married Mar 29 1928, **Florna Jane Carr**.

226. **Eve Frances**[5] **Waybright** (84.Mary Margaret[4], 24.Christina[3] Mullenax, 5.William[2], 1.Mary Elizabeth[1] Arbogast), b. Sep 24 1880 in Onego, Pendleton Co., WV, d. Aug 1 1961 in Wayne, Ashtabula Co., OH, buried in Wayne, Ashtabula Co., OH.
Married Jun 14 1897 in Onego, Pendleton Co., WV, **Hayes Wheeler Kisamore**, b. May 19 1876 in Onego, Pendleton Co., WV, d. Mar 24 1983 in Morgan, Ashtabula Co., OH, buried in Wayne, Ashtabula Co., OH.

Children:
	479	i.	Ethel May[6] Kisamore b. Aug 27 1898 in Onego, Pendleton Co., WV, d. Nov 12 1984. Married 24 Aug, **Thomas Roach**.
	480	ii.	Marjorie Ettie Kisamore b. Oct 21 1900 in Onego, Pendleton Co., WV, d. Jul 13 1901.
	481	iii.	Zernie Kisamore b. Jul 7 1902 in Onego, Pendleton Co., WV. She Married **Allie Winch**.
	482	iv.	Byron Stanley Kisamore b. Jun 22 1904 in Onego, Pendleton Co., WV, d. May 2 1982. Married Sep 27 1928, **Patsey Ethel Farence**.
	483	v.	Elaine Kisamore b. Aug 13 1906 in Onego, Pendleton Co., WV, d. Mar 28 1913.
	484	vi.	Gola Kisamore b. Dec 11 1908 in Onego, Pendleton Co., WV, d. Feb 18 1966. She Married **Fredwin Holcomb**.
	485	vii.	Mary Frances Kisamore b. Jul 24 1912 in Onego, Pendleton Co., WV, d. Feb 9 1981. Married May 25 1946, **Vern Niles Birdette**.
	486	viii.	Nina Elizabeth Kisamore b. Feb 14 1916 in Unus, Greenbrier Co., WV, d. Dec 12 1994. She Married **Harold V Heath**.
	487	ix.	Ruth Virginia Kisamore b. Apr 1 1918 in Falling Springs, Greenbrier Co., WV. She Married **William Heath**.
	488	x.	Oliver Wayne Kisamore b. Mar 30 1922 in Wayne, Ashtabula Co., OH, d. Aug 13 1944.

227. **Thaddeus**[5] **Waybright** (84.Mary Margaret[4], 24.Christina[3] Mullenax, 5.William[2], 1.Mary Elizabeth[1] Arbogast), b. Apr 12 1892 in Onego, Pendleton Co., WV, d. Jan 22 1977 in West Virginia.
Married Oct 27 1917 in Onego, Pendleton Co., WV, **Alpha Hollie Elza**, b. Sep 25 1899 in Whitmer, Randolph Co., WV, d. Mar 1987.

Children:
	489	i.	Mary Margaret[6] Waybright b. Sep 12 1919 in Whitmer, Randolph Co., WV. Married Dec 5 1942, **Earl Frederick Kerr**.
+	490	ii.	Mary Waybright b. 1920.
	491	iii.	Paul Waybright b. Dec 13 1923 in Whitmer, Randolph Co., WV, d. Jan 11 1925.

492 iv. Leonard Thaddeus Waybright b. Apr 22 1926 in Whitmer, Randolph Co., WV, d. May 23 1999 in Clarksburg, Harrison Co., WV, buried May 27 1999 in WV National Cem., Grafton, Taylor Co., WV.
U.S. Navy S2C.
<u>Married</u> Dec 20 1945, **Betty Loraine Tolliver.**

493 v. James Herman Waybright b. Aug 17 1929 in Whitmer, Randolph Co., WV.
James H. PFC Infantry 14 th Inf. Regt 25th div. wounded 12 Mar 1952 North Korea by missile, returned to duty

229. **Oscar Blaine**[5] **Waybright** (85.William Washington[4], 24.Christina[3] Mullenax, 5.William[2], 1.Mary Elizabeth[1] Arbogast), b. Oct 7 1887 in Pendleton Co., WV, d. Mar 15 1926 in Barnabas, Logan Co., WV, buried in Cham Cem., Barnabas Logan Co., WV.
<u>Married</u> Jul 9 1908, **Rosa Lee Loughrey**, b. 1891, d. Feb 10 1919 in Tucker Co., WV, buried in Tucker Co., WV.

    Children:
494 i. Verlin[6] Waybright d. 1921.
495 ii. Dove Waybright b. 1910 in Parsons, Tucker Co., WV.
She <u>Married</u> **Filmore Neace**, b. Aug 6 1906, d. Jun 1957.
+ 496 iii. Darl Blaine Waybright b. Jun 16 1913.

231. **Rettia C.**[5] **Waybright** (85.William Washington[4], 24.Christina[3] Mullenax, 5.William[2], 1.Mary Elizabeth[1] Arbogast), b. Jul 1892 in Pendleton Co., WV, d. 1950.
<u>Married</u> in Tucker Co., WV, **Nathan Andrew Warren Loughrey**, b. 1887, d. in Hendricks, Tucker Co., WV.

    Children:
497 i. Viola[6] Loughrey b. Aug 28 1908 in Hendricks, Tucker Co., WV, d. Feb 6 1996 in Maryland.
She <u>Married</u> **Andrew Brewster**.
498 ii. Georgia Virginia Loughrey b. 1912.
<u>Married</u> Jul 12 1933 in Tucker Co., WV, **William Shirley McDonald**.
499 iii. Rosalie Loughrey b. Aug 18 1913 in Hendricks, Tucker Co., WV, d. Feb 17 1989 in Fairview Memorial Hospital, Elmhurst, Moscow, PA.
She <u>Married</u> **Willard James Scheitlin**.
500 iv. James Patrick Loughrey b. Feb 24 1919 in Hendricks, Tucker Co., WV, d. Apr 1980 in Fairview Memorial Hospital, Elmhurst, Moscow, PA.
He <u>Married</u> **Mildred Barb**.

232. **Solomon Robert**[5] **Waybright** (87.Isaac Perry[4], 24.Christina[3] Mullenax, 5.William[2], 1.Mary Elizabeth[1] Arbogast), b. Apr 11 1894 in Randolph Co., WV, d. Mar 9 1967 in Detroit, Wayne Co., MI, buried in Woodlawn Cem., Detroit Wayne Co., MI.
<u>Married</u> Aug 11 1923 in Detroit, Wayne Co., MI, **Erma Blanche Gennette**, b. Dec 13 1900 in Hancock Houghton Co., MI, d. Feb 10 1982 in Monroe, Monroe Co., MI, buried Feb 13 1982 in St. Joseph Catholic, Monroe City, Monroe Co., MI.

    Children:
501 i. Donald Henry[6] Waybright b. May 13 1929 in Detroit, Wayne Co., MI.

237. **Perlie**[5] **Arbogast** (88.Cordelia[4] Waybright, 24.Christina[3] Mullenax, 5.William[2], 1.Mary Elizabeth[1] Arbogast), b. Jun 16 1900 in Pendleton Co., WV, d. Deceased in Baltimore, Baltimore Co., MD.
(1) She <u>Married</u> **Gary Kisamore**.

    Children:
502 i. Harry[6] Kisamore b. 1918, d. 1918.
+ 503 ii. Margie Kisamore b. Jul 27 1919.
504 iii. Grace Kisamore.

	+ 505	iv.	Troy Kisamore.
	+ 506	v.	Glen Kisamore b. Oct 13 1927.
	507	vi.	Goldie Kisamore b. Oct 13 1927.
	+ 508	vii.	Guy Kisamore b. Jan 18 1934.
	509	viii.	Ralph Hugh Kisamore b. Jan 18 1934, d. Dec 24 1978.
	510	ix.	Valley Kisamore.

(2) She Married **John Nestor**.

(3) She Married **Okey Kittle**, b. Feb 06 1900.

238. **Wilbur^5 Arbogast** (88.Cordelia^4 Waybright, 24.Christina^3 Mullenax, 5.William^2, 1.Mary Elizabeth^1 Arbogast), b. Jun 2 1901 in Pendleton Co., WV, d. Oct 16 1977 in Akron, Summit Co., OH, buried in Crown Hill Cem., Akron, Summit Co., OH.
Married May 23 1926 in Parsons, Tucker Co., WV, **Effie May Hardy**, b. Aug 02 1908 in Hendricks, Tucker Co., WV, buried in Tucker Co., WV. **Effie**: Daughter of Ed Hardy and Jean Hawkins.

Children:

	511	i.	Rose Joy^6 Arbogast b. Apr 05 1927, d. Apr 05 1927.
	+ 512	ii.	Samuel Henry Arbogast b. Jul 10 1928.
	+ 513	iii.	Lovie May Arbogast b. Aug 18 1929.
	+ 514	iv.	Wilbur Junior Arbogast b. Jun 21 1932.
	515	v.	Margaret Arbogast.
	516	vi.	Betty Virginia Arbogast b. Mar 12 1936 in Montrose, Randolph Co., WV, d. Apr 06 1994 in Garrard's Fort, Greene Co., PA. Married Dec 18 1954 in Waynesburg, Greene Co., PA, **Kramer Darr**, b. Jun 14 1921 in Waynesburg, Greene Co., PA, d. May 14 1976 in Waynesburg, Greene Co., PA.
	517	vii.	Ruby Jane Arbogast b. Nov 22 1937.
	518	viii.	Pauline Faye Arbogast b. Sep 10 1939.
	519	ix.	Roselee Arbogast b. Apr 16 1941.
	520	x.	Carl Lee Arbogast b. Nov 1943, d. Nov 1943.

244. **Clifton Mason^5 Waybright** (90.John Edward^4, 24.Christina^3 Mullenax, 5.William^2, 1.Mary Elizabeth^1 Arbogast), b. Jul 28 1899 in Onego, Pendleton Co., WV, d. Mar 23 1960 in Cassity Cem., Cassity, Randolph Co., WV, buried in Maplewood Cem., Elkins, Randolph Co., WV.
Married Sep 10 1918, **Mary Elizabeth Bennett**, b. Oct 18 1903 in Dry Run, Pendleton Co., WV, d. May 14 1973 in Elkins, Randolph Co., WV.

Children:

	521	i.	Gerald Mason^6 Waybright b. Sep 22 1919 in Parsons, Tucker Co., WV, d. Jan 10 1987 in Baltimore, Baltimore Co., MD. Married Sep 8 1940 in Red House, Garrett Co., MD, **Wila Jenieva Hart**, b. May 7 1918 in Karens, Tucker Co., WV, d. Nov 1997 in Baltimore, Baltimore Co., MD.
	522	ii.	Elmer Lewis Waybright b. Nov 10 1921, d. 1936.
	523	iii.	Harold Burton Waybright b. Apr 22 1924 in Kerens, Randolph Co., WV, d. Aug 4 1991 in Elkins, Randolph Co., WV.
	524	iv.	Katheryn Mary Waybright b. May 20 1926 in Randolph Co., WV. She Married **Edward Earl Flemming**, b. 1921, d. May 1 1997 in Illinois, buried in River Bend Cem., Will Co., IL. Edward:
	525	v.	Clarice June Waybright b. Jun 21 1929 in Randolph Co., WV. She Married **Bernard Thomas**.
	526	vi.	Betty Jean Waybright b. Aug 23 1932 in Clover, Roane Co., WV, d. Mar 2 1995. Married Mar 11 1953 in Cold Water, Branch Co., MI, Carl **Thomas Ash**, b. Mar 21 1930 in Cold Water, Branch Co., MI, d. Mar 2 1995 in Cold Water, Branch Co., MI, buried Mar 5 1995 in Oak Grove Cem., Coldwater Branch Co., MI.

245. **Guy Daniel⁵ Waybright** (90.John Edward⁴, 24.Christina³ Mullenax, 5.William², 1.Mary Elizabeth¹ Arbogast), b. Dec 5 1901 in Onego, Pendleton Co., WV, d. Nov 29 1965 in Cuyahoga Falls Summit Co., OH.
He Married **Toy Helen Bennett**, b. Apr 22 1908 in Dry Fork, Randolph Co., WV.
Children:
- 527 i. Stanley Guy⁶ Waybright b. Jan 2 1923 in Montrose, Randolph Co., WV.
  Married Dec 22 1946, **Kitty Lou Rhodes**.
- 528 ii. Robert Lewis Waybright b. Aug 22 1924 in Montrose, Randolph Co., WV.
  Married Dec 19 1944, **Wilma Gatewood**, b. 1926 (daughter of Willie Nathen Gatewood and Hassie Blanche Wimer).
- 529 iii. Glenn McCoy Waybright b. Aug 9 1926 in Montrose, Randolph Co., WV.
  Married Jul 31 1947 in Oakland, Garrett Co., MD, **Cora Eleanor Toothman**, b. Mar 20 1928 in Pennsboro, Ritchie Co., WV.

246. **Burley McCoy⁵ Waybright** (90.John Edward⁴, 24.Christina³ Mullenax, 5.William², 1.Mary Elizabeth¹ Arbogast), b. Oct 30 1904 in Dry Fork, Randolph Co., WV, d. May 16 1967.
Married Feb 22 1930 in Porterwood Tucker Co., WV, **Violet Elizabeth Miller**, b. May 18 1912 in Hambleton Tucker Co., WV, d. Feb 10 1964 in Mount Pifer Cem., Tucker Co., WV.
Children:
- 530 i. June Elizabeth⁶ Waybright b. Jan 7 1931 in Porterwood Tucker Co., WV, d. Oct 24 1985 in St. Frances Cabini Hospital, Alexandria, Rapides Co., LA, buried Oct 27 1985 in Alexandria Rapides Co., Louisiana.
  Married May 22 1948, **William Russell Clingerman**.
- 531 ii. Grace Marie Waybright b. Oct 17 1933 in Porterwood Tucker Co., WV, d. Jul 17 1979, buried in Mount Pifer Cem., Tucker Co., WV.
  She Married **Nobel Edward Auvil**. Nobel:
- 532 iii. Ella Catherine Waybright b. Aug 13 1934 in Kearns WV, d. Apr 21 1939.
- 533 iv. Vavil Virginia Waybright b. Apr 10 1936 in Kerens, Randolph Co., WV, d. Nov 8 1994.
- + 534 v. Ellis Paul Waybright b. Mar 12 1941.

247. **Edna Margaret⁵ Waybright** (90.John Edward⁴, 24.Christina³ Mullenax, 5.William², 1.Mary Elizabeth¹ Arbogast), b. Apr 23 1907 in Onego, Pendleton Co., WV, d. Dec 30 1990.
She Married **Odes Botkin**, b. Oct 17 1905 in West Virginia, d. Apr 1982 in Elkins, Randolph Co., WV.
Children:
- 535 i. John⁶ Botkin.
  He Married **Josephine Pennington**.
- 536 ii. Wanda Botkin.
- 537 iii. Margaret Botkin.
- 538 iv. Thomas Botkin.
- 539 v. Susan Botkin.
- 540 vi. Jack Botkin b. 23 May in West Virginia.
- 541 vii. Odes Botkin b. Aug 15 1926 in West Virginia, d. Dec 6 1992.
- 542 viii. James Botkin b. May 22 1932 in West Virginia, d. Jan 21 1965 in Korea.

254. **Mavis A.⁵ Mullenax** (98.Kenton L.⁴, 27.Henry Clay³, 5.William², 1.Mary Elizabeth¹ Arbogast), b. Apr-28-2005 in Crabbottom, Highland Co., VA, d. Mar-14-1952 in Highland Co., VA.
Married Sep-13-1920, **John H. Hevener**.
Children:
- 543 i. Kathleen Hope⁶ Hevener b. Jul-20-1921 in NY.
  Married May-11-1944, **Ernest A. Thompson**.
- + 544 ii. Madelyn Gayle Hevener b. Feb-03-1923.

256. **Claris Ella**[5] **Mullenax** (98.Kenton L.[4], 27.Henry Clay[3], 5.William[2], 1.Mary Elizabeth[1] Arbogast), b. Oct-15-1910.
Married Feb-11-1931, **James Arthur Jerman**.
Children:
    545   i.   James Arthur[6] Jerman, Jr. b. Oct-24-1931, d. Feb-14-1968.

258. **Kenton Dexter**[5] **Mullenax** (98.Kenton L.[4], 27.Henry Clay[3], 5.William[2], 1.Mary Elizabeth[1] Arbogast), b. Jul-11-1917.
Married Jun-17-1941, **Gertrude Maequess**, d. Oct-15-1956.
Children:
+ 546   i.   Wanda Dran[6] Mullenax b. Feb-27-1944.
   547 ii. Kenton Dexter Mullenax, Jr. b. Apr-16-1952.
       (1) Married Nov-16-1981, **Donna Cotherman**.
       (2) He Married **Helen Gregory**.

260. **Monna Lee**[5] **Mullenax** (105.Henry Walter[4], 27.Henry Clay[3], 5.William[2], 1.Mary Elizabeth[1] Arbogast), b. Aug 31 1901, d. Jan 24 1993.   Child of Henry Walter Mullenax and Mamie Collins.
Married Feb 28 1922 in Crabbottom, Highland Co., VA, **Glen Hammer**, b. Apr 23 1903 in Crabbottom, Highland Co., VA (son of Luther Hammer and Esther Waybright), d. Mar 5 1995 in Augusta Co., VA, buried Mar 8 1995 in Monterey Cem., Monterey, Highland Co., VA.
Children:
   548 i.   Robert G.[6] Hammer.
   549 ii. C. E. Hammer.

270. **Ollie Elizabeth**[5] **Mullenax** (108.Aaron C.[4], 27.Henry Clay[3], 5.William[2], 1.Mary Elizabeth[1] Arbogast), b. Mar 2 1905 in Blue Grass Cem., Highland Co., VA, d. Jun 11 1998 in Churchville, Pendleton Co., WV.
Married Apr 19 1924 in Crabbottom, Highland Co., VA, **Kenny Waybright**, b. Jul 26 1904 in Cherry Grove, Pendleton Co., WV (son of Jesse Waybright and Attie Bessie Rexrode), d. Oct 28 1990 in Staunton, Augusta Co., VA, buried in Arbovale Cem., Arbovale, Pocahontas Co., WV.
Children:
+ 550   i.   William Nevin[6] Waybright b. Jan 25 1925.
   551 ii. Lucille Mae Waybright b. Apr 27 1927 in Blue Grass Cem., Highland Co., VA.
       Married May 10 1947 in Churchville, Pendleton Co., WV, **Stanley Miller Back**, b. Aug 23 1925 in Churchville, Pendleton Co., WV. Stanley:
+ 552 iii. George Samuel Waybright, Sr..
+ 553 iv. Dollie Elizabeth Waybright.
   554 v. George Samuel Waybright.
       S/o Kennie and Ollie (Mullenax) Waybright. Both Kennie and Ollie were descendants of John Arbogast, Volume I. Kennie is #22073 and Ollie's mother Arbelia (Wimer) Mullenax is #23236. The marriage to Naomi Wenger was George's second marriage.
       Married Apr 1 1976 in Staunton, Augusta Co., VA, Naomi Gay Wenger, b. Feb 8 1932 (daughter of Leonard C. Wenger and Maudie Dolin). Naomi: Ref: Pocahontas 1981: 482.

275. **Nellie Susan**[5] **Mullenax** (108.Aaron C.[4], 27.Henry Clay[3], 5.William[2], 1.Mary Elizabeth[1] Arbogast), b. Jun 6 1912 in Highland Co., VA, buried in Puffenbarger Cem. Monterey Highland Co., VA, d. Dec 4 1959 in Highland Co., VA.
She Married **Ray Waybright**, b. Nov 28 1905 in Straight Creek, Pendleton/Highland Co., VA (son of Ira Waybright and Mary Ettie Rexrode), d. Dec 28 1959 in Highland Co., VA, buried in Puffenbarger Cem. Monterey Highland Co., VA.
Children:
   555 i.   Randolph Ray[6] Waybright b. Sep 14 1931 in Cave, Pendleton Co., WV, d. Nov 24 1993.

556   ii.   Ocie Aaron Waybright b. Dec 24 1944 in Cave, Pendleton Co., WV, d. Nov 23 1967, buried in Rohrbaugh Farm, Highland Co., VA.

276. **Kemper D^5 Rexroad** (109.Elizabeth S^4 Mullenax, 28.Edward^3, 5.William^2, 1.Mary Elizabeth^1 Arbogast), b. June 1881.
Married Jan 14 1907 in Highland Co., VA, **Linnie M Newman**, b. About 1882. **Linnie**: Child of Salisbury Newman and Phebe Rymer.

Children:
557   i.   Edwin C^6 Rexroad b. About 1910.

289. **James Lewis^5 Mulanax** (124.William Dallas^4, 33.Miles Elliott^3, 6.Joseph^2, 1.Mary Elizabeth^1 Arbogast), b. Jul 27 1877 in Kansas, buried in Denison, Jackson Co., KS, d. Nov 24 1952 in Abilene, Dickinson Co., KS.
Married Nov 04 1896 in Meriden, Jefferson Co., KS, **Mary Willella Bales**, b. Feb 14 1878 in Hancock Co., IN (daughter of John Bales and Sarah Jane Smith), d. Oct 01 1960 in Abilene, Dickinson Co., KS.

Children:
558   i.   Claude Arthur^6 Mulanax b. Nov 27 1900 in Kansas, d. Nov 09 1986 in Riverside, Riverside Co., CA.
               (1) Married Aug 07 1921, **Grace Moore**.
               (2) He Married **Dolly Millikan**.
559   ii.   Curtis Mulnanx b. Mar 16 1901 in Jackson Co., KS, d. Mar 16 1901 in Jackson Co., KS.
+ 560   iii.   Hazel Marie Mulnanx b. Jun 01 1904.
561   iv.   Louise Ernest Mulnanx b. Sep 09 1907 in Denison, Jackson Co., KS, d. Sep 15 1972 in Enterprise, Dickinson Co., KS.
           He Married **Velma A. Cline**.
562   v.   (infancy) Mulnanx b. Mar 29 1910 in Denison, Jackson Co., KS, d. Mar 29 1910 in Denison, Jackson Co., KS.
+ 563   vi.   Alvin Edgar Mulnanx b. Apr 01 1912.
564   vii.   Lyle Verne Mulanax b. May 22 1914 in Denison, Jackson Co., KS, d. Nov 19 1973 in Abilene, Dickinson Co., KS.
           Married Nov 12 1935 in Enterprise, Dickinson Co., KS, **Marian A. Knox**.
565   viii.   Faye Ammelia Mulanax b. Nov 26 1916 in Denison, Jackson Co., KS.
           Married Jun 21 1936 in Enterprise, Dickinson Co., KS, Harold Laughlin.

293. **Flora Adeline^5 Mulanax** (125.John Greenbury^4, 33.Miles Elliott^3, 6.Joseph^2, 1.Mary Elizabeth^1 Arbogast), b. 0828879 in Jackson Co., KS, d. Jan 12 1953 in Springtown, Benton Co., AR.
Married Oct 02 1895 in Holden, Jackson Co., KS, **Frank Francis Blaikie**, b. Oct 05 1862 in Coldingham, Scotland, buried in Gentry Cem., Gentry, Benton Co., AR, d. Nov 15 1941 in Springtown, Benton Co., AR.

Children:
566   i.   Maude^6 Blaikie b. Jul 26 1896 in Kansas, d. Sep 08 1976 in Oklahoma.
567   ii.   Flora Jane Blaikie b. Sep 23 1897 in Kansas, d. Jan 19 1985 in Oklahoma.
+ 568   iii.   Maggie May Blaikie b. Jun 19 1899.
569   iv.   Ellen E. Blaikie b. Oct 22 1900 in Jackson Co., KS, d. Oct 20 1987 in Oklahoma.
570   v.   John W. Blaikie b. Jul 20 1902 in Jackson Co., KS, d. May 21 1966 in Oklahoma.
571   vi.   Jessie A. Blaikie b. Dec 22 1905 in Jackson Co., KS.
572   vii.   Nora Bell Blaikie b. Jun 03 1911.
573   viii.   Robert F. Blaikie b. Jul 22 1912, d. in Gentry, Benton Co., AR.

301. **Mary Aceneth^5 Mulanax** (127.Matthew Elliott^4, 35.William R.^{3}, 6.Joseph^2, 1.Mary Elizabeth^1 Arbogast), b. Oct 10 1890 in Denison, Jackson Co., KS, d. Sep 03 1955.

Married May 03 1905 in Jackson Co., KS, **Riley Newton Osburn**, b. Apr 27 1881 in Havensville, Pottawatomie Co., KS (son of Stephen Osburn and Perthena Ann Smalley), d. Mar 22 1942 in McMinnville, Yamhill Co., OR.

Children:

- \+ 574   i.   Bessie Lee[6] Osburn b. Feb 24 1906.
- \+ 575   ii.   Charley Calvin Osburn b. Jul 24 1907.
- \+ 576   iii.   Cleo Faye Osburn b. Feb 03 1909.
- \+ 577   iv.   Samuel Stephen Osburn b. Oct 23 1910.
- \+ 578   v.   Parthena Ann Osburn b. Oct 25 1912.
- \+ 579   vi.   Mable Marie Osburn b. Apr 23 1915.
- \+ 580   vii.   Myrtle May Osburn b. Apr 23 1915.
- \+ 581   viii.   Minnie Belle Osburn b. Oct 30 1916.
- \+ 582   ix.   Francis Paul Osburn b. Oct 14 1928.
- \+ 583   x.   Theodore Harvey Osburn b. Oct 13 1920.
- \+ 584   xi.   Mary Helen Rose Osburn b. Feb 26 1922.
- 585   xii.   Jim Conrad Burton Osburn b. Jun 17 1924, buried in Marcola Cem., Lane Co., OR, d. Apr 16 1989 in Marcola, Lane Co., OR.
  He Married **Clarabelle Jones**, b. 13 Aug 1930 in Ontario, Vernon Co., WI (daughter of William Samuel Jones and Claudia Bell Todd).
- 586   xiii.   Riley Matthew Osburn b. Jul 05 1926 in Ontario, Malheur Co., OR.
  He Married **Beatrice Faye Guther**, b. 20 Jan 1923 in Lakeview, Lake Co., OR.
- \+ 587   xiv.   Zella Jane Osburn b. Oct 04 1928.
- 588   xv.   Vance Vernon Osburn b. Jan 18 1931 in Payette, Payette Co., ID.

305. **Louis[5] Mulanax** (127.Matthew Elliott[4], 35.William R.[3], 6.Joseph[2], 1.Mary Elizabeth[1] Arbogast), b. Oct 19 1898 in Jackson Co., KS, d. Mar 1963 in Mayetta, Jackson Co., KS.
Married 27 Jan 1921 in Jackson Co., KS, **Eunice Lavier** (daughter of Joe Lavier and Martha Battesse).

Children:

- 589   i.   James Matthew[6] Mulanax b. in Jackson Co., KS.
  Married 18 Jul 1953 in Jackson Co., KS, Dorothy Nozhachum.
- 590   ii.   Kenneth Mulanax.
  Married 29 Jul 1967 in Jackson Co., KS, **Elizabeth Stueve**.
- 591   iii.   Irvan Mulanax.
  (1) He Married **Jeanie Hannerhan**.
  (2) He Married **Janice Thompson**.
- 592   iv.   William Mulanax b. in Jackson Co., KS.
  He Married **Mary Fitzgerald**.
- 593   v.   Elta Vera Mulanax b. in Jackson Co., KS.
  She Married **Clayton H. Ray**.
- 594   vi.   Cora Vivena Mulanax b. in Jackson Co., KS.
  She Married **Abe Walkenstick**.

306. **Alfred[5] Mulanax** (127.Matthew Elliott[4], 35.William R.[3], 6.Joseph[2], 1.Mary Elizabeth[1] Arbogast), b. Feb 11 1901 in Jackson Co., KS, buried in Evergreen Cem., McMinnville, Yamhill Co., OR, d. Aug 1956.
He Married **Ruby Ann Mulanax**, b. 25 Aug 1916 (daughter of John William Mulanax and Sarah Ellen Osburn), d. 21 Dec 1966 in Evergreen Cem., McMinnville, Yamhill Co., OR.

Children:

- 595   i.   Matthew William[6] Mulanax b. 1940.

313. **Calvin Silas[5] Mulanax** (133.John William[4], 35.William R.[3], 6.Joseph[2], 1.Mary Elizabeth[1] Arbogast), b. 16 Aug 1903 in Havensville, Pottawatomie Co., KS, buried in Evergreen Cem., McMinnville, Yamhill Co., OR, d. 24 Apr 1966 in Portland, Multnomah Co., OR.

Married 20 Mar 1927 in Portland, Multnomah Co., OR, **Marguerite Barbara Deets**, b. 11 Sep 1906 in Kearny Co., KS, buried in Evergreen Cem., McMinnville, Yamhill Co., OR, d. 2 Apr 1994.

Children:
+ 596   i.   Dorothy Ellen^6 Mulanax b. 3 Apr 1929.

315. **Edith Pearl^5 Mulanax** (133.John William^4, 35.William R.^{3}, 6.Joseph^2, 1.Mary Elizabeth^1 Arbogast), b. 25 May 1909.
She Married **Ernest Alexander**.

Children:
597   i.   Bidwell William^6 Alexander.

316. **Ruby Ann^5 Mulanax** (133.John William^4, 35.William R.^{3}, 6.Joseph^2, 1.Mary Elizabeth^1 Arbogast) (See marriage to number 306.)

319. **William Roy^5 Hager** (136.Lucy Adeline^4 Mulanax, 35.William R.^{3}, 6.Joseph^2, 1.Mary Elizabeth^1 Arbogast), b. 7 Jan 1903 in Avoca, Jackson Co., KS, buried in Casper City Cem., Casper, WY, d. 26 Feb 1971 in Casper, Natrona Co., KY.
(1) Married 14 Apr 1923, **Pearl McQueen**.

(2) Married 21 Dec 1925 in Douglas, Converse Co., WY, **Martha Markyton**, b. 14 Jun 1908 in Clarkston, Colfax Co., NE (daughter of John Markyston and Julie Koukal), buried in Casper City Cem., Casper, WY, d. 22 Dec 1977 in Casper, Natrona Co., KY.

Children:
+ 598   i.   Ardath Lenore^6 Hagar b. 23 Feb 1937.

322. **Mary Evelyn^5 Kelley** (146.Anna Louisa^4 Mulanax, 40.Joseph Riley^3 Mullenax, 6.Joseph^2 Mulanax, 1.Mary Elizabeth^1 Arbogast), b. Sep 8 1901 in Glen Cove, Coleman Co., TX, d. Dec 30 1986.
Married About 1917 in Seattle, King Co., WA, **Charles Hobart Mahler**, b. About 1898 in California, d. in Oakland, Alameda Co., CA.

Children:
599   i.   Charles^6 Mahler.
600   ii.   Mary Mahler.
601   iii.   Barbara Joy Mahler.

323. **Thelma Louise^5 Kelley** (146.Anna Louisa^4 Mulanax, 40.Joseph Riley^3 Mullenax, 6.Joseph^2 Mulanax, 1.Mary Elizabeth^1 Arbogast), b. Jul 13 1903 in Glen Cove, Coleman Co., TX, d. Jan 2 1993 in Seattle, King Co., WA.
Married Sep 24 1922 in Monroe, Snohomish Co., WA, **Cecil Leroy Groce**, b. Apr 15 1894 in Marienville, Jenks Twp., Forest, Co., PA, d. Oct 15 1965 in Livermore, Alameda Co., CA.

Children:
+ 602   i.   Anita Lorraine^6 Groce.
603   ii.   Don Romaine Groce b. Oct 29 1928 in Seattle, King Co., WA, d. Aug 8 1992 in Seattle, King Co., WA.
604   iii.   Glen Ramon Groce b. Oct 26 1931 in Seattle, King Co., WA, d. May 6 1986 in Tacoma, Pierce Co., WA.
605   iv.   Terrance Renaldo Groce b. Oct 13 1932 in Seattle, King Co., WA, d. Aug 31 1975 in Seattle, King Co., WA.

329. **Anna Jane^5 Kelley** (146.Anna Louisa^4 Mulanax, 40.Joseph Riley^3 Mullenax, 6.Joseph^2 Mulanax, 1.Mary Elizabeth^1 Arbogast), b. Oct 29 1919 in Machias, Snohomish Co., WA, d. Apr 28 2003 in Phoenix, Jackson Co., AZ.
(1) Married About 1937 in Seattle, King Co., WA, **Raymond Patton**, b. 1916 in Seattle, King Co., WA, d. 1980 in Salinas, Monterey Co., CA.

Children:

606	i.	Michael R.⁶ Patton b. Sep 22 1937 in Seattle, King Co., WA, d. 1992 in Culver City, Los Angles Co., CA.
607	ii.	Patrick H. Patton b. Apr 5 1939 in Seattle, King Co., WA, d. Feb 10 1995 in Boise, Ada Co., ID.

(2) <u>Married</u> Nov 5 1948 in Seattle, King Co., WA, **Walter Mechem**, b. Aug 10 1910 in Raymond, Union Co., OH, d. March 2001 in Medford, Jackson Co., OR.

Generation Six

332. **Wilber Allen⁶ Waybright** (153.Mary Permelia Catherine⁵ Mullenax, 50.William Isaac⁴, 7.James W.³, 2.Abraham², 1.Mary Elizabeth¹ Arbogast), b. Jul 8 1869 in Dry Run, Pendleton Co., WV, d. Jun 2 1958 in Elkins, Randolph Co., WV, buried in Old Fellows Cem., Elkins, Randolph Co., WV.

<u>Married</u> 1893, **Sena White**, b. Mar 8 1875 in Dry Run, Pendleton Co., WV, d. Apr 12 1963 in Canton, Stark Co., OH, buried in Old Fellows Cem., Elkins, Randolph Co., WV.

Children:
+ 608	i.	Iona Patrica⁷ Waybright b. Apr 24 1894.
609	ii.	Morris Waybright b. Sep 30 1905 in Rich Mountain, Pendleton Co., WV. <u>Married</u> in Franklin Co., WV, Kitty Belle Sponaugle, b. Apr 24 1912 in Churchville, Pendleton Co., WV (daughter of Herman Henry Sponaugle and Etta Beulah Warner).

334. **Amby Stanton⁶ Waybright** (153.Mary Permelia Catherine⁵ Mullenax, 50.William Isaac⁴, 7.James W.³, 2.Abraham², 1.Mary Elizabeth¹ Arbogast), b. Sep 30 1873 in Dry Run, Pendleton Co., WV, d. Jul 12 1935 in Thornwood, Pocahontas Co., WV, buried in Thornwood, Pocahontas Co., WV.
<u>Married</u> Sep 30 1902 in Cumberland, Alleghany Co., MD, **Charlotte Nelson**, b. Apr 17 1883 in Pendleton Co., WV, d. Dec 27 1980, buried in Arbovale Cem., Arbovale, Pocahontas Co., WV.

Children:
+ 610	i.	Ollie Katherine⁷ Waybright b. Sep 30 1903.
+ 611	ii.	Grace Elizabeth Waybright b. Jun 16 1905.
+ 612	iii.	Gertrude Lee Waybright b. Dec 2 1907.
+ 613	iv.	Rella K Waybright b. Sep 29 1908.
614	v.	Emery Henry Waybright b. Jun 1 1910 in Pocahontas Co., WV, d. Apr 3 1989 in Bartow, Pocahontas Co., WV. He <u>Married</u> **Margie K Varner**, b. May 23 1911 in Pocahontas Co., WV, d. Feb 7 1985 in Randolph Co., WV, buried in Arbovale Cem., Arbovale, Pocahontas Co., WV.
+ 615	vi.	Edna Alice Waybright b. Mar 27 1912.

336. **Fransina Lee⁶ Waybright** (153.Mary Permelia Catherine⁵ Mullenax, 50.William Isaac⁴, 7.James W.³, 2.Abraham², 1.Mary Elizabeth¹ Arbogast), b. Mar 28 1877 in Dry Run, Pendleton Co., WV, d. Apr 25 1929 in Pocahontas Co., WV, buried in Warner Cem., Hunting Ground, Pendleton Co., VA/WV.
<u>Married</u> 1897 in Pendleton Co., WV, **John W. Warner**, b. May 15 1874 in Pendleton Co., WV, d. Sep 5 1960, buried in Warner Cem., Hunting Ground, Pendleton Co., VA/WV.

Children:
+ 616	i.	Bertie Catherine⁷ Warner b. Jul 9 1903.
617	ii.	Myrtle R. Warner b. Nov 25 1907 in Churchville, Pendleton Co., WV. (1) <u>Married</u> Dec 3 1924, **Robert C. Bennett**, b. Apr 1904. (2) She <u>Married</u> **Bead Sponaugle**, b. Apr 1908.
618	iii.	Emory J. Warner b. Jan 9 1913 in Churchville, Pendleton Co., WV, d. Apr 19 1994. He <u>Married</u> **Tina Judy** (daughter of Olie Judy and Tina Warner).

337. **Dolly**[6] **Mullenax** (155.Elijah[5], 50.William Isaac[4], 7.James W.[3], 2.Abraham[2], 1.Mary Elizabeth[1] Arbogast), b. Mar 04 1879 in Pendleton Co., WV, d. Jul 10 1957 Harrisonburg, VA, buried in Arbovale Cem., Arbovale, Pocahontas Co., WV.
(1) Married Nov 22 1894, **Solomon Harvey Johnston**, b. Jan 01 1871, d. Aug 26 1962, buried in Arbovale Cem., Arbovale, Pocahontas Co., WV.

Children:

- 619   i.   Mona[7] Johnston b. Feb 10 1896.
  She Married **Lacy Bowling**.
- 620   ii.   Otis Johnston b. Jul 7 1897, d. Jun 20 1920.
- + 621   iii.   Cletis Johnston b. Jul 31 1902.
- 622   iv.   William Johnston b. Oct 26 1904.
  He Married **Elizabeth Matheney**.
- + 623   v.   Jesse Johnston b. Jul 2 1907.
- 624   vi.   Judith Johnston b. Sep 25 1909 in Bartow, Pocahontas Co., WV, d. Jul 26 1990.
  Married Jun 26 1939, **Paul Lowell Bennett**, d. Nov 25 1981.
- + 625   vii.   Georgia Ellen Johnston b. Oct 01 1911.
- 626   viii.   Mildred Johnston b. Dec 30 1913, d. 1992.
  She Married **W. l. Willey**.
- 627   ix.   Virginia Johnston b. Oct 27 1916.
  She Married **Carl Mallow**.
- 628   x.   Merle Johnston b. Sep 9 1922.
  He Married **Mary Musser**.
- 629   xi.   Cletus Johnston.
  She Married **Ollice C Warner**, b. Mar-01-1915 (son of Charles Warner and Maryellen Wimer).

(2) She Married **Solomon Johnson**.

338. **Lura**[6] **Mullenax** (155.Elijah[5], 50.William Isaac[4], 7.James W.[3], 2.Abraham[2], 1.Mary Elizabeth[1] Arbogast), b. Jun 28 1881, d. Dec 11 1961.

She Married **Pet Warner**, b. Sep 29 1877, d. Sep 22 1952 in Warner Cem., Hunting Ground, Pendleton Co., VA/WV.

Children:

- 630   i.   Jenna[7] Warner b. Sep 18 1902.
  Married Mar 10 1951, **Otha Lambert**, d. 1968.
- + 631   ii.   Verlie Warner b. Dec 27 1903.
- 632   iii.   Evelyn Warner b. Jan 23 1907.
  She Married **Richard Phares**.
- + 633   iv.   Betty Warner b. Jul 26 1913.
- + 634   v.   Judith Warner b. Dec 18 1915.
- 635   vi.   Argle Warner b. Feb 26 1922.

339. **Mcclelland**[6] **Mullenax** (155.Elijah[5], 50.William Isaac[4], 7.James W.[3], 2.Abraham[2], 1.Mary Elizabeth[1] Arbogast), b. Oct 25 1883, d. 1961.
He Married **Anna B. Cummingham**, b. 1882, d. 1943.

Children:

- + 636   i.   Brooks Burdette[7] Mullenax b. Apr 23 1918.

340. **Martha Ellen**[6] **Mullenax** (155.Elijah[5], 50.William Isaac[4], 7.James W.[3], 2.Abraham[2], 1.Mary Elizabeth[1] Arbogast), b. Feb 1891.
She Married **Otha Lambert**, d. 1968.

Children:

- + 637   i.   Harlan[7] Mullenax b. May 11 1912.

+ 638 ii. Halcie Mullenax.

341. **Betty Alice**[6] **Mullenax** (155.Elijah[5], 50.William Isaac[4], 7.James W.[3], 2.Abraham[2], 1.Mary Elizabeth[1] Arbogast), b. Feb 28 1891 in Churchville, Pendleton Co., WV, d. Sep 09 1941 in Beverly, Randolph Co., WV.
Married Apr 25 1938, **David Frederick Hulver**.
Children:
- 639 i. Hinkle[7] Hulver.
- 640 ii. Mildred Hulver.
  She Married **George Fencemaker**.
- 641 iii. Irene Hulver. Died in teens, accident top Allegheny Mountain

342. **Joseph Clark**[6] **Halterman** (156.Annie Jane[5] Mullenax, 50.William Isaac[4], 7.James W.[3], 2.Abraham[2], 1.Mary Elizabeth[1] Arbogast), b. Feb 22 1887, d. Nov 16 1960.
Ref: Pocahontas 1981: 439 S/o Silas Clark and Annie Jane (Mullenax) Halterman; Joseph is a descendant of Mary Arbogast. See Volume III for his lineage under # 15714.
Married Jan 6 1915, **Cora Belle Wooddell**, b. Nov 6 1898 in Arbovale Cem., Arbovale, Pocahontas Co., WV (daughter of Charles Stewart Warwick Wooddell and Virginia Lee Spencer), d. Dec 27 1971 in Meadville, Crawford Co., PA. **Cora**: Ref: Pocahontas 1981: 419.

Children:
- + 642 i. Lena Virginia[7] Halterman b. Dec 24 1915.
- 643 ii. Jesse Halterman b. Sep 6 1917, d. Jun 25 1935, buried in Family Cem., Griffin Run, Pocahontas Co., WV.
- 644 iii. Mary Jane Halterman b. Mar 13 1920.
  She Married **Albert Deeter**.
- 645 iv. Violet Halterman b. May 6 1922, d. May 29 1974.
  (1) She Married **Thomas Grossman**.
  (2) Married Jan 24 1939, **Ronald John Phillips**.
- + 646 v. Fairy Dare Halterman b. Nov 4 1924.
- 647 vi. Joseph R. Halterman b. Jun 17 1928.
- + 648 vii. Charlsie Halterman b. Nov 5 1932.

343. **Emory R**[6] **Mullenax** (157.James B.[5], 50.William Isaac[4], 7.James W.[3], 2.Abraham[2], 1.Mary Elizabeth[1] Arbogast), b. Oct 20 1884, d. Apr 11 1932.
He Married **Mamie Hoover**.
Children:
- + 649 i. Paul[7] Mullenax b. Mar 3 1918.
- + 650 ii. Richard Emory Mullenax b. Oct 16 1928.

344. **Sallie Denie**[6] **Mullenax** (157.James B.[5], 50.William Isaac[4], 7.James W.[3], 2.Abraham[2], 1.Mary Elizabeth[1] Arbogast), b. Aug 1879 in Pendleton Co., WV, d. Oct 25 1958 in Pocahontas Co., WV.
She Married **Fallen Lambert**, b. May 30 1876 in Pendleton Co., WV, d. Nov 7 1938.
Children:
- + 651 i. Gus[7] Warner b. Jun 27 1900.
- + 652 ii. Georgia Lambert b. Apr 28 1903.
- + 653 iii. Roy D. Lambert b. Jun 08 1905.
- + 654 iv. Russell Lambert b. Oct 11 1907.
- + 655 v. Orie Basil Lambert b. Jan 22 1910.
- + 656 vi. Jessie Lambert b. Oct 13 1912.
- + 657 vii. Rhoda Martha Lambert b. Nov 16 1914.
- + 658 viii. Dewey Judy Lambert b. Mar 18 1917.

347. **Nellie Mae**[6] **Mullenax** (162.Solomon Key[5], 50.William Isaac[4], 7.James W.[3], 2.Abraham[2], 1.Mary Elizabeth[1] Arbogast), b. Apr 21 1892, d. Oct 06 1972.

Married Aug 09 1913 in Randolph Co., WV, **Virgil McQuain Calhoun**, b. Jun 19 1887, d. Aug 15 1929 in Pocahontas Co., WV, buried in Circleville, Pendleton Co., WV.

Children:
	659	i.	Virgil Mullenax[7] Calhoun b. Jul 28 1914.
+	660	ii.	Sherron Virginia Calhoun b. Aug 28 1915.
+	661	iii.	Shellace Tiffin Calhoun b. Oct 06 1917.
+	662	iv.	Harold Kay Calhoun b. Jan 01 1920.
	663	v.	Ronald Victor Calhoun b. Dec 23 1921 in Pocahontas Co., WV, d. Aug 15 1985 in Alleghany Co., PA, buried in Arbovale Cem., Arbovale, Pocahontas Co., WV.

348. **Tiffin Rienhart[6] Mullenax** (162.Solomon Key[5], 50.William Isaac[4], 7.James W.[3], 2.Abraham[2], 1.Mary Elizabeth[1] Arbogast), b. Sep 04 1894, d. Jan 05 1984.
Married Dec 26 1922, **Letha Armentrout**, b. c1890 in Randolph Co., WV, d. Feb 16 1983 in Larwill, Whitney Co., IN,.

Children:
664	i.	William Kay[7] Mullenax b. Jan 10 1924.
		Married Oct 06 1945, **Betty Blazer**.
665	ii.	Letha Carol Mullenax b. May 23 1925.
		Married Aug 06 1946, **Jesse Waybright**.
666	iii.	Thorald Tiffin Mullenax b. Feb 04 1928, d. Dec 30 1947 in Arbovale Cem., Arbovale, Pocahontas Co., WV.
667	iv.	George Fry Mullenax b. Feb 22 1934.
		Married Apr 03 1952, **Janer Dell**.
668	v.	Fannie Margaret Mullenax b. Nov 23 1936.
		Married Sep 25 1955, **Roger Davenport**.
669	vi.	Tiffin Rinehart Mullenax b. Apr 07 1940.
		He Married **Alice Oryall**.

351. **Virgil Craig[6] Mullenax** (162.Solomon Key[5], 50.William Isaac[4], 7.James W.[3], 2.Abraham[2], 1.Mary Elizabeth[1] Arbogast), b. Sep 11 1907, d. Nov 20 2000.
Married 1929, **Myrtle Nellie Eye**, b. Jun 01 1909.

Children:
+	670	i.	Helen[7] Mullenax.
+	671	ii.	Bonnie Mullenax.
+	672	iii.	Donald C. Mullenax.
	673	iv.	Galen Mullenax.
			He Married **Eva Jean Varner**.

352. **Wilma Grethel[6] Mullenax** (162.Solomon Key[5], 50.William Isaac[4], 7.James W.[3], 2.Abraham[2], 1.Mary Elizabeth[1] Arbogast), b. May 06 1910, d. Jul 08 1978.
(1) She Married **Otis White**.

(2) She Married **Lester Nelson**, b. Oct 02 1916 in Pocahontas Co., WV, d. Nov 07 1983 in Baltimore, Baltimore Co., MD.

Children:
674	i.	Helen[7] Nelson.
		She Married **A. Grogg**.
675	ii.	Donna Nelson.
		She Married **Unknown Hammacker**.
676	iii.	Jerry Nelson.
677	iv.	John Nelson.
678	v.	David Nelson.

354. **Raymond Rafe[6] Mullenax** (162.Solomon Key[5], 50.William Isaac[4], 7.James W.[3], 2.Abraham[2], 1.Mary Elizabeth[1] Arbogast), b. Aug 02 1916, d. Feb 23 1945 in KIA, buried in Luxembourg.

Killed in Action WWII, Luxemburg, buried there in US Cem.
He Married **Lula Mae Gillespie**, b. Jul 10 1920 (daughter of Harry Clifford Gillespie and Rosa Bell McQuain), d. Apr 18 1987.

> ***Children:***
> 679   i.   Raymond[7] Mullenax.
> 680   ii.   Douglas Mullenax.
> 681   iii.   Randall Mullenax.

355. **Inez Catherine**[6] **Mullenax** (162.Solomon Key[5], 50.William Isaac[4], 7.James W.[3], 2.Abraham[2], 1.Mary Elizabeth[1] Arbogast), b. Apr 4 1919.
Married Mar 05 1938, **Harlan Tallman**.

> ***Children:***
> 682   i.   Bonnie[7] Tallman.
> She Married **Calvin Kieth Plyler**, b. Feb 25 1927, d. Aug 13 1983, buried in Mountain View Cem., Marlinton, Pocahontas Co., WV.

360. **Edward Lee**[6] **Mullenax** (162.Solomon Key[5], 50.William Isaac[4], 7.James W.[3], 2.Abraham[2], 1.Mary Elizabeth[1] Arbogast), b. Apr 20 1930.
He Married **Betty Brown**.

> ***Children:***
> + 683   i.   Debra Elizabeth[7] Mullenax b. May 14 1955.

362. **Oscela Martin**[6] **Bennett** (163.Mary Jane[5] Mullenax, 51.John Wesley[4], 7.James W.[3], 2.Abraham[2], 1.Mary Elizabeth[1] Arbogast), b. 1871 in Pendleton Co., WV.
http://homepages.rootsweb.com/~clanboyd/index.htm.
Married Jul 11 1909 in Harman, Randolph Co., WV, **Texanna Smith**, b. Apr 10 1890 in Harman, Randolph Co., WV, d. Sep 14 1954 in Elkins, Randolph Co., WV, buried UNKNOWN in Harman, Randolph Co., WV. **Texanna**: This information is provided for all BOYDs to research their family connection by the group Clan Boyd.
NOTE: Regard all of this data as unsupported until you verify the accuracy at the original source. Some of the basis range from copies of original documents to guesses because it looks possible.

> ***Children:***
> + 684   i.   Grace Marie[7] Bennett b. Dec 1 1909.
>   685   ii.   Merle Bennett b. 1910 in Harman, Randolph Co., WV, d. Dec 9 1949 in Webster Springs, Webster Co., WV, buried Dec 13 1949 in Harman, Randolph Co., WV.
>   686   iii.   Paul Bennett b. 1915 in Harman, Randolph Co., WV, d. 1990 in Elkins, Randolph Co., WV, buried 1990 in Mill Creek, Randolph Co., WV.
> http://homepages.rootsweb.com/~clanboyd/index.htm.

365. **Florrie Dean**[6] **Bennett** (163.Mary Jane[5] Mullenax, 51.John Wesley[4], 7.James W.[3], 2.Abraham[2], 1.Mary Elizabeth[1] Arbogast), b. 1874 in Pendleton Co., WV.
Married About 1893, **Seymore Roy**.

> ***Children:***
> 687   i.   Lester Lee[7] Roy b. 1894.
> 688   ii.   Stilman Roy b. 1895.

382. **Charles Edward Vivan**[6] **Mullenax** (164.Isaac J.[5], 51.John Wesley[4], 7.James W.[3], 2.Abraham[2], 1.Mary Elizabeth[1] Arbogast), b. Jul 28 1900, d. Oct 17 1973.
(1) Married May 11 1925, **Helen Musetta**, b. in Phoenix, Jackson Co., AZ, d. Feb 12 1928.

> ***Children:***
> + 689   i.   Helen J.[7] Mullenax b. Jul 25 1926.

(2) Married Jul 25 1945, **Lauretta Sternes McKee**.

405. **Lena Ester⁶ Mullenax** (169.Martin⁵, 51.John Wesley⁴, 7.James W.³, 2.Abraham², 1.Mary Elizabeth¹ Arbogast), b. Feb 02 1890 in Randolph Co., WV, d. Apr 27 1965 in Jane Lew, Lewis Co., WV, buried in Forest Lawn Cem., Weston, Lewis Co., WV.
She Married **John Elmer Buckbee**, b. Aug 07 1887 in Tucker Co., WV, d. Feb 11 1975 in Tampa, Pasco Co., FL.

Children:
+ 690   i.   Grethel Mae⁷ Buckbee b. Feb 11 1907.
   691   ii.   Guy Carleston Buckbee b. Nov 22 1910 in Whitmer, Randolph Co., WV, d. Dec 16 1979 in Jane Lew, Lewis Co., WV.
   692   iii.   Maudie Irene Buckbee b. Jan 12 1912 in Benwood, Marshall Co., WV.

413. **Curtis C.⁶ Lambert** (185.Jay⁵, 63.Annie Catherine⁴ Calhoun, 12.Elizabeth Ann³ Mullenax, 2.Abraham², 1.Mary Elizabeth¹ Arbogast).
Married Aug 26 1911 in Pocahontas Co., WV, **Meno C. Gladwell**, b. APR 1892 in Pocahontas Co., WV (daughter of William Alexander Gladwell and Nancy Luverta Arbogast). **Meno**: Names of sons from sister Mary Gladwell's obituary.

Children:
   693   i.   William L.⁷ Lambert.
   694   ii.   Francis Lambert.

416. **Flotie V.⁶ Lambert** (186.Soloman K.⁵, 63.Annie Catherine⁴ Calhoun, 12.Elizabeth Ann³ Mullenax, 2.Abraham², 1.Mary Elizabeth¹ Arbogast), b. Apr 21 1895 in West Virginia.
She Married **Floyd Sr. Slayton**, b. Apr 8 1903 in West Virginia, d. DEC 1973 in Columbus, Franklin Co., OH.

Children:
   695   i.   Jada⁷ Teter b. Jun 10 1919, d. Dec 20 1921 in West Virginia.
   696   ii.   Floyd Jr. Slayton b. Jun 5 1921 in West Virginia, d. FEB 1973.

417. **Uxter⁶ Lambert** (186.Soloman K.⁵, 63.Annie Catherine⁴ Calhoun, 12.Elizabeth Ann³ Mullenax, 2.Abraham², 1.Mary Elizabeth¹ Arbogast), b. Apr 15 1898 in West Virginia, d. Mar 17 1972 in Fort Spring, Greenbrier Co., WV.
Married Dec 6 1919, **Mary Elizabeth White**, b. Aug 1 1901, d. Aug 19 1991.

Children:
+ 697   i.   Donald Woodrow⁷ Lambert.

418. **Lillie⁶ Lambert** (186.Soloman K.⁵, 63.Annie Catherine⁴ Calhoun, 12.Elizabeth Ann³ Mullenax, 2.Abraham², 1.Mary Elizabeth¹ Arbogast), b. Oct 6 1899 in West Virginia, d. Apr 30 1928.
(1) She Married **Brown Hull**, b. ABT 1897

Children:
   698   i.   Rachel⁷ Elizabeth b. Apr 11 1921 in Virginia, d. Jun 19 1985 in Durbin, Pocahontas Co., WV.

(2) She Married **Amos Simmons**, b. ABT 1897. .

424. **Lillie⁶ Raines** (189.Elizabeth A.⁵ Lambert, 65.Susan⁴ Calhoun, 12.Elizabeth Ann³ Mullenax, 2.Abraham², 1.Mary Elizabeth¹ Arbogast), b. Sep 26 1890 in Pendleton Co., WV, d. May 12 1984 in Randolph Co., WV, buried in Hosterman Cem., Back Mountain, Pocahontas Co., WV.
She Married **Adam Collins**.

Children:
   699   i.   Franklin D.⁷ Collins.
   700   ii.   Goldie Collins.
   701   iii.   Nors Collins.
   702   iv.   Delbert Collins.
   703   v.   Dale Collins.

+ 704 vi. Mabel Caroline Collins b. Jul 2 1912.

431. **Marshall**[6] **Raines** (189.Elizabeth A.[5] Lambert, 65.Susan[4] Calhoun, 12.Elizabeth Ann[3] Mullenax, 2.Abraham[2], 1.Mary Elizabeth[1] Arbogast).
He Married **Martha Jane Waybright**, b. Jan 5 1910 in Blue Grass Cem., Highland Co., VA (daughter of Jesse Waybright and Attie Bessie Rexrode), d. Jun 12 1983 in Waynesboro Community Hospital, Waynesboro, Augusta Co., VA, buried in Augusta Memorial Park Waynesboro, Franklin Co.,, VA.

Children:
705 i. Delbert[7] Raines.
706 ii. Russell Raines b. 1926.
707 iii. Una Raines b. Jul 6 1930, d. Nov 30 1993.
 She Married **Camon Wolfe**.

432. **Elbridge L.**[6] **Hinkle** (198.William[5], 68.Phoebe (Susan)[4] Calhoun, 12.Elizabeth Ann[3] Mullenax, 2.Abraham[2], 1.Mary Elizabeth[1] Arbogast), b. Jul 1848 in Dry Run, Pendleton Co., WV, d. Aug 1924 in Crabbottom, Highland Co., VA.
He Married **Sarah S Nelson**, b. 1845. **Sarah**: Child of Absolon Nelson and Susannah Calhoun.

Children:
708 i. Clara[7] Hinkle b. About 1873.
+ 709 ii. Fannie May Hinkle b. May 27 1877.

433. **Susan**[6] **Hinkle** (198.William[5], 68.Phoebe (Susan)[4] Calhoun, 12.Elizabeth Ann[3] Mullenax, 2.Abraham[2], 1.Mary Elizabeth[1] Arbogast), b. Mar 25 1853 in Dry Run, Pendleton Co., WV, d. Jan 25 1916 in Dry Run, Pendleton Co., WV.
Married Feb 4 1877, **Jacob Harper Rymer**, b. Aug 30 1858, d. Feb 15 1940 in Dry Run, Pendleton Co., WV. **Jacob**: Son of George W. Rymer and Margaret Harper.

Children:
710 i. Mattie[7] Rymer b. Jun 25 1879, d. May 02 1914.
 She Married **Will Simmons**.
+ 711 ii. Clyde Rymer b. Mar 30 1881.
+ 712 iii. Sudie R Rymer b. Feb 12 1886.

434. **Elizabeth C**[6] **Hinkle** (198.William[5], 68.Phoebe (Susan)[4] Calhoun, 12.Elizabeth Ann[3] Mullenax, 2.Abraham[2], 1.Mary Elizabeth[1] Arbogast) (See marriage to number 155.)

435. **Eliza Ann**[6] **Hinkle** (198.William[5], 68.Phoebe (Susan)[4] Calhoun, 12.Elizabeth Ann[3] Mullenax, 2.Abraham[2], 1.Mary Elizabeth[1] Arbogast), b. Oct 31 1856 in Dry Run, Pendleton Co., WV, d. Mar 5 1926 in Pendleton Co., WV.
Married Apr 1883 in Pendleton Co., WV, **Benjamin B. Phares**, b. May 1858 in Churchville, Pendleton Co., WV, d. Apr 1917 in Pendleton Co., WV. **Benjamin**: Son of Benjamin Phares and Catherine Bennett.

Children:
+ 713 i. Cleat[7] Phares b. Sep 19 1884.
714 ii. Martha Phares b. 1890.
715 iii. Bulah Phares b. Sep 1894.

436. **Catherine Beam**[6] **Hinkle** (198.William[5], 68.Phoebe (Susan)[4] Calhoun, 12.Elizabeth Ann[3] Mullenax, 2.Abraham[2], 1.Mary Elizabeth[1] Arbogast), b. 1859 in Dry Run, Pendleton Co., WV.
She Married **Abraham Lantz Cunningham**, b. Abt 1854 in Dry Run, Pendleton Co., WV.

Children:
716 i. Zena[7] Cunningham.
717 ii. Willie Cunningham.

718	iii.	Hinkle Cunningham.
719	iv.	Chloe Cunningham.
720	v.	Vella J Cunningham.

437. **Isaac Harness⁶ Hinkle** (198.William⁵, 68.Phoebe (Susan)⁴ Calhoun, 12.Elizabeth Ann³ Mullenax, 2.Abraham², 1.Mary Elizabeth¹ Arbogast), b. 1862 in Dry Run, Pendleton Co., WV, d. 1950, buried in Blue Grass Cem., Highland Co., VA.
Married Jun 17 1901 in Highland Co., VA, **Phoebe J Stone Nicholas**, b. 1864.

   ### Children:
	721	i.	Isaac Harness⁷ Hinkle, Jr. b. Mar 12 1893.
	722	ii.	Salma Hinkle.
+	723	iii.	Martha Ann Hinkle b. May 11 1902.

442. **Ezra J.⁶ Smith** (201.Sarah Lavina⁵ Simmons, 70.John Wesley⁴, 13.Margaret³ Mullenax, 2.Abraham², 1.Mary Elizabeth¹ Arbogast), b. Jan 12 1881 in Ritchie Co., WV, d. Feb 2 1958 in Harrisville, Ritchie Co., WV, buried Feb 5 1958 in Akron, Summit Co., OH., Buried Rosehill Cem. Akron, OH.

    He Married **Lu Cinda Cunningham**.

    ### Children:
724	i.	Virgina⁷ Smith.
725	ii.	Leland D. Smith b. Aug 1 1917, d. Sep 4 1959, buried in Akron, Summit Co., OH. Buried at Rose Hill Burial Park.

443. **Blanche Alma⁶ Smith** (201.Sarah Lavina⁵ Simmons, 70.John Wesley⁴, 13.Margaret³ Mullenax, 2.Abraham², 1.Mary Elizabeth¹ Arbogast), b. Sep 16 1886 in Ritchie Co., WV, d. Feb 8 1967 in Millersburg, Holmes Co., OH, buried in Smith Chapel, Center Twp., Morgan Co., OH.
See Rev. Walter Clark for more information on Blanche Smith.   Blancheand her siblings went to Ritchie Co. W.Va. schools. Blanche Married **Walter Clark**, and they eventually moved to Ohio. Their oldest son, Curtis, told of their yearly trips back to W.Va. to visit. They travelled in a horse and surrey, going from Center Bend to Marietta (about 25 miles) the first day. One   of Walter's uncles had a store in Marietta, and they'd stay with him. The next day, they'd travel on to William Clark's to visit for a week. But Blanche's home was too far away to visit until 1918, when the Clark's got an automobile. One one of the surrey trips, Blanche was pregnant and became sick. Walter was told that beer would help. In spite of his religious convictions against alcohol, he some warm beer for her. But she had to keep it hidden under the surrey seat.
Charlie Smith, Blanche's brother, lived with Walter and Blanche part of the time. He was raised by Aunt Mel as his mother died when he was born. Aunt Mel   came into some oil money. She used the money to educate missionaries, but willed Charlie what was left when she died. Charlie then left a Model-T Ford with Walter and blanche while he went travelling. This was their first car. Mel's sister Martha Married a Rexroad, and Mel loaned money to Claude Rexroad to start a business. The business broke up and Mel lost her money. Thus Blanche was always mad a Claude Rexroad and his family.
Walter and Blanche had 9 children: Curtis, Ethel, Edra, Dale, Bob, Arlene, Leman, Dorothy, and Florence Ruth. Blanche moved to Newcomerstown after Walter's death, which was where her son Leman lived and near Edra and Bob. She
died in 1966 or 1967. Blanche was a warm woman, and was especially fond of Ruth, her baby, and Ruth's children. She sponsored Easter egg hunts at her home, and in her later years would visit her children for a couple of weeks at
a time. She suffered from Alzheimer's or dementia of some sort in her last couple of years and lived in a rest home, where she occasionally attempted to lead a revolt of the ladies to return to their homes.

Married Jan 23 1905 in Ritchie Co., WV, **Walter Clark**, b. Sep 13 1876 in Crooked Tree, Noble, OH, d. Jun 19 1958 in Family Farm, Center Twp., Morgan, Co., OH, buried in Smith Chapel, Center Twp., Morgan Co., OH. **Walter**: REFN: 4

Walter worked on the oil rigs in West Virginia, as the farm was not too prosperous. As a young man, he drank a little. He Married Blanche Smith and built a house in Devil Hole, near Cairo, West Virginia, near his father. It is here that family members are buried on the homestead. Walter gave up working on the oil rigs when a co-worker was suddenly killed on the job. Walter and Blanche lived with his parents a while. Then Blanche came into some oil money. Walter made a trip to Ohio and selected a home on the hill above Center Bend, near Beverly Ohio. In February or March, 1912, Walter, Blanche, and their oldest son Curtis (who was born at Devil Hole) took the train from Cairo to Relief, Ohio. Relief Station is located across the Muskingum River from the Lawrence Dietz farm, near Ohio Power's Muskingum River Plant and near Center Bend, but on the other side of the river. The river was frozen, and a man with a sled drove them across the river to the house, which Blanche hadn't seen before. Walter and Blanche wanted the better schools and land in Ohio, but still needed money. Walter started filling in for preachers, as he sometimes had at the log church in W. Va. He could use the cash. But he also felt he had a "call." He only had a 6th grade education, but he studied English, history, and religious courses to get a preacher's license. He was a Methodist. In 1920 he started preaching at Fletcher. He quit in a dispute, built his own church benches, and started preaching at the old Hackney store in Center Twp., Morgan Co. He moved on to Smith's Chapel, near Hackney, a Methodist Church. Before he retired, he had preached in many places - the Reinersville Circuit, Lima, all around Stockport, and others. He was said to be a dramatic hellfire and brimstone preacher who left sinners shaking in their seats. Walter also continued farming whenever at his home in Center Bend, until he fell off a wagon after retiring and was unable to work longer. Walter and Blanche had a big garden, fruit trees, grapes, and berries, and lots of good things to eat.

It was always fun to visit them. They had no indoor plumbing. We used an outdoor toilet and chamber pots at night. It was the grandchildren's job to empty and clean the chamber pots. The grandchildren also locked each other in the outdoor toilet, which smelled awful, for fun. Water was pumped by hand. A pot-bellied coal-fired stove warmed the living room. No card playing or dancing was allowed and shorts were frowned upon, but dominoes was a favorite. They had a television with a rotor antenna, and Walter like to watch boxing matches. There were always many children and grandchildren of all ages visiting. On a porch swing, the relatives would tell ghost stories at night while the heat lightning flashed. Or they'd head out to the nearby plowed field to look for Indian overheads, or hike over the hill toward the river to play on the huge "Indian rocks." The younger grandchildren would play pirate in the cherry tree, or try to start leaf fires by rubbing sticks together, or play in the barn. Or they might be asked to pick fruit (which was half eaten), gather eggs, or help crank ice cream, a big favorite. In the summer, children took baths outside in round metal wash tubs. Walter loved to fish, and his children and grandchildren often went along. Blanche put coffee grounds around a certain bush to attract earthworms as bait. Grandchildren would help pick worms off the Catawba tree, or go with Walter at night to look for night crawlers with a flashlight, or go with relatives to wade in the shallow creeks looking for crawdads. Walter had a favorite fishing rock down at Center Bend, and used to have a trot line across the river. He also had a favorite rocking chair at home, and liked to rock and chew tobacco, spit in a coffee can. He was tall and thin. He had an old car with running boards. Walter died after an illness in 195-. I (Dianne Garris Com.

Children:

726   i.   Luther Curtis[7] Clark b. Oct 29 1905 in Devils Hole, near Grant, Ritchie Co., WV, d. Feb 25 1997 in Marietta, Washington Co., OH, buried in Smith Chapel, Center Twp., Morgan Co., OH.

Curtis Clark was a 1924 graduate of Beverly High school, where he played baseball, basketball, and track. He pitched on several barnyard baseball teams in the Hackney, Oh. area. He taught in a one-room school house in Center Township starting in 1928, and retired from the Fort Frye district in 1972. He was the teacher of Richard Combs,

who always remembers a saying Curt taught him. "Once a task is first begun, never leave it til it's done. Be the labor great or small, do it well or not at all." Curtis was a chairman of the Republic Party in Morgan County and once attended the Republican National Convention. He was a Center Township Clerk from 1948 to 1974.. She died on April 20, 1994. Their children are Herman, Norman, Cecil, Edward, Gerald, Ronald, and Edna Pennock Phillis.
He <u>Married</u> **Lucille Faye Welch** March 9, 1929.

+ 727   ii.   Ethel Clark b. Feb 24 1907.
   728   iii.   Edra Mae Clark b. Apr 18 1909 in Ritchie Co., WV, d. Aug 1 1988 in Ohio.
<u>Married</u> Jun 11 1930, **John R. Hursey**, b. 1904 in Ohio.
   729   iv.   Olive Arlene Clark b. Oct 18 1910 in Ritchie Co., WV, d. May 1 1998 in Danville, Knox Co., OH, buried May 5 1998 in Millersburg, Holmes Co., OH.
Nurse at Joel Pomerene Memorial Hospital, Millersburg, OH.
Buried at Oak Hill Cemetery, Millersburg, OH
Retired 1972
Services at Alexander Funeral Home, Millersburg, OH.
<u>Married</u> May 1 1935, **Vernon E. Close**, b. Dec 9 1911 in Ohio, d. Jun 20 1950 in Holmes Co., OH.
   730   v.   Robert William Clark b. Mar 22 1912 in Center TWP., Morgan Co., OH, d. Nov 13 1982 in Dennison, Tuscarawas Co., OH, buried in Gnadenhutten, Tuscarawas Co., OH.
<u>Married</u> May 1 1939 in Stockport, Morgan Co., OH, **Mildred Schriener**, b. Feb 12 1914 in Ohio.
   731   vi.   Walter Dale Clark b. Mar 10 1914 in Center TWP., Morgan Co., OH, d. Aug 29 1981 in Ohio, buried Aug 31 1981 in Huntington, Lorain Co., OH. Methodist Minister at Huntington OH.
<u>Married</u> Apr 18 1936, **Helen Jean Taylor** (daughter of Robert Daniel Taylor and Thelma Gertrude Carpenter).
   732   vii.   Dorothy Elvira Clark b. Oct 1 1915 in Center TWP., Morgan Co., OH.
<u>Married</u> Apr 8 1939 in Michigan, **L. Merton Wilson**, b. Sep 21 1906 in Vestaburg, Montcalm Co., MI, d. Oct 29 1989 in Vestaburg, Montcalm Co., MI, buried Nov 1 1989 in Vestaburg, Montcalm Co., MI. L.: Buried at Ferris Center Cemetery
School Teacher
Farmer.
   733   viii.   Leman Dwight Clark b. Apr 30 1922 in Center TWP., Morgan Co., OH, d. Feb 5 1988 in Newcomerstown, Tuscarawas Co., OH.
<u>Married</u> Dec 18 1948 in Ohio, **Freda Fay Guy**, b. Aug 27 1927.
   734   ix.   Florence Ruth Clark b. Aug 31 1926 in Family Farm, Center Twp., Morgan, Co., OH.
<u>Married</u> Jan 2 1948 in Portsmouth, Scioto Co., OH, **Noah Vernon Garris**, b. Feb 13 1929 in Logan, Fayette Co., WV. Noah: Has three children..

444. **Mirta B. Or Myrtle**[6] **Smith** (201.Sarah Lavina[5] Simmons, 70.John Wesley[4], 13.Margaret[3] Mullenax, 2.Abraham[2], 1.Mary Elizabeth[1] Arbogast), b. Jan 8 1890 in Ritchie Co., WV, d. Jul 10 1963 in Harrisville, Ritchie Co., WV, buried Jul 12 1963 in Harrisville, Ritchie Co., WV.
Also named Myrtle.
She <u>Married</u> **Irvine James Morris**, b. Jan 4 1875, d. Dec 26 1951, buried Dec 29 1951 in Harrisville, Ritchie Co., WV.

         Children:
   735   i.   Alma[7] Morris.
   736   ii.   Dana Morris.
   737   iii.   Farnsworth Morris.

445. **Mary Elizabeth**[6] **Smith** (201.Sarah Lavina[5] Simmons, 70.John Wesley[4], 13.Margaret[3] Mullenax, 2.Abraham[2], 1.Mary Elizabeth[1] Arbogast), b. Jan 8 1892 in Ritchie Co., WV, d. May 23 1979, buried in Elizabeth, Wirt Co., WV.
Buried in Knights of Pythias Cem. Elizabeth.

She Married **Henry Lee Bryan**, b. Jun 21 1886 in West Virginia, d. Mar 6 1954, buried Mar 8 1954 in Elizabeth, Wirt Co., WV. **Henry**: Elizabeth Methodist Church.

Children:
- 738   i.   Doris[7] Bryan.
- 739   ii.   Gertude Bryan b. Apr 19 1910, d. Jun 4 1991.
- 740   iii.   Gilbert Jennings Bryan b. May 23 1914 in Spencer, Rhone Co., WV, d. May 27 1995 in Elizabeth, Wirt Co., WV, buried May 31 1995 in Elizabeth, Wirt Co., WV.
  Br in Pythias Cem. Elizabeth died of Brain Cancer.
  Graduated Elizabeth High School in 1932
  Graduate of the McSweeny Auto, Tractor & Electrical School in Cleveland, OH
  Former owner of Standard Oil Service station Elizabeth, WV
  Retired from Ford Brothers Garage in Marietta, OH
  Baptized in the Elizabeth Methodist Church.
- 741   iv.   Lorraine Bryan.

446. **Richard Ralph[6] Smith** (201.Sarah Lavina[5] Simmons, 70.John Wesley[4], 13.Margaret[3] Mullenax, 2.Abraham[2], 1.Mary Elizabeth[1] Arbogast), b. May 1894 in Ritchie Co., WV.   WORLD WAR 1 VET.
(1) He Married **Zelda (Unknown)**.

Children:
- 742   i.   Richard[7] Smith.
- 743   ii.   Alice Smith.

447. **Charles W.[6] Smith** (201.Sarah Lavina[5] Simmons, 70.John Wesley[4], 13.Margaret[3] Mullenax, 2.Abraham[2], 1.Mary Elizabeth[1] Arbogast), b. Oct 11 1922 in Marietta, Washington Co., OH.
He Married **Ollie Washburn**, b. Jun 23 1904 in Washburn, Ritchie Co., WV.

Children:
- 744   i.   Herman Ray[7] Smith b. Dec 30 1923 in Ritchie Co., WV.
- 745   ii.   Dale Smith b. Sep 8 1924 in Ritchie Co., WV.
- 746   iii.   Evajene Faynell Smith b. Mar 19 1925 in Ritchie Co., WV.
- 747   iv.   Myrtle Marie Smith b. Feb 11 1927 in Ritchie Co., WV.
- 748   v.   Clifford Clem Smith b. Aug 28 1933 in Ritchie Co., WV, d. Aug 28 1934 in Ritchie Co., WV.
- 749   vi.   Dane Avery Smith b. Sep 29 1940 in Ritchie Co., WV, d. Dec 4 1986 in Ohio.
  Died of Brain Cancer.

452. **Floyd William[6] Collins** (206.Louella Maer[5] Grogg, 72.Emily Jane[4] Mullenax, 16.John H.[3], 3.Jacob[2], 1.Mary Elizabeth[1] Arbogast), b. Nov 25 1893, d. May 20 1968 in Frank, Pocahontas Co., WV.
Ref: Pocahontas 1981: 257 S/o Andrew Morgan and Louella Mae (Grogg) Collins. Louella is the same person as #7634, a descendant of George; see Volume III for her lineage.
Married Nov 26 1914 in Pocahontas Co., WV, **Bertie Ruth Ervine**, b. Jul 18 1894 (daughter of Edward Newton Ervine and Phoebe Rebecca Bright), d. May 20 1962.

Children:
- + 750   i.   Paul Hunter[7] Collins b. Dec 9 1915.
- 751   ii.   Donald Eugene Collins b. 1917, d. 1936 in Circleville, Pendleton Co., WV. Died in accident.

453. **Cecil Morgan[6] Collins** (206.Louella Maer[5] Grogg, 72.Emily Jane[4] Mullenax, 16.John H.[3], 3.Jacob[2], 1.Mary Elizabeth[1] Arbogast), b. Aug 14 1896 in Boyer, Pocahontas Co., WV, d. Apr 13 1952 in Hospital, Columbus, Franklin Co., OH, buried in Union Cem., Olentangy River, Columbus, Franklin Co., OH.
He Married **Iona Patrice Waybright**, b. Apr 24 1894 in Job, Randolph Co., WV (daughter of Wilber Allen Waybright and Sena White), d. Dec 08 1965 in Elkins, Randolph Co., WV.

Children:
- + 752   i.   Harold Cecil[7] Collins b. Aug 13 1916.

       753   ii.   Wilma Dell Collins b. Jan 10 1918 in Sitlington Creek, Pocahontas Co., WV, d. Jul 14 1918 in Sitlington Creek, Pocahontas Co., WV.
+ 754   iii.   Bernard Morris Collins b. Jan 30 1920.
   755   iv.   Ruby Mae Collins b. Feb 10 1925 in Laurel Lick, Boyer, Pocahontas Co., WV, d. Sep 1925 in Laurel Lick, Boyer, Pocahontas Co., WV.

466. **Bert**[6] **Waybright** (209.Albert[5], 74.Martha[4] Mullenax, 17.George[3], 3.Jacob[2], 1.Mary Elizabeth[1] Arbogast), b. Oct 1890 in Pendleton Co., WV.
(1) He Married **Minnie V. (Unknown)**, b. Oct 3 1891, d. Jan 1981 in Alleghany Co., MD.
         Children:
   756   i.   Ruth V.[7] Waybright.
   757   ii.   (unknown) Waybright.
   758   iii. (unknown) Waybright.
   759   iv. Edsel Waybright b. Jul 24 1919.
   760   v.   Gerald Waybright b. Jul 10 1922.

(2) He Married **Artie Dolly Hedrick**, b. May 10 1894, d. Jan 15 1968 in Elkins, Randolph Co., WV.
         Children:
+ 761   vi. Bricel Waybright b. Dec 13 1911.

470. **Steven Grove**[6] **Mullenax** (215.David Pillow[5], 77.George[4], 19.Joseph[3], 5.William[2], 1.Mary Elizabeth[1] Arbogast).
         Children:
   762   i.   Geraldine M.[7] Mullenax.
                  She Married Rev. **Donald E. Richards**.

490. **Mary**[6] **Waybright** (227.Thaddeus[5], 84.Mary Margaret[4], 24.Christina[3] Mullenax, 5.William[2], 1.Mary Elizabeth[1] Arbogast), b. 1920. D/o Thaddeus and Alpha Hollie (Elza) Waybright. .
Married Dec 3 1942, **Earl Frederick Kerr**, b. Sep 18 1918 in Randolph Co., WV (son of Orville Erry Kerr and Jessie Lucy Louk), d. Aug 6 1990.
         Children:
+ 763   i.   Margaret Ann[7] Kerr b. Jan 6 1949.

496. **Darl Blaine**[6] **Waybright** (229.Oscar Blaine[5], 85.William Washington[4], 24.Christina[3] Mullenax, 5.William[2], 1.Mary Elizabeth[1] Arbogast), b. Jun 16 1913 in Parsons, Tucker Co., WV, d. May 24 1999 in Logan General Hospital, Logan Co., WV, buried May 27 1999 in Highland Memorial Gardens Logan Co., WV. Darl was a retired miner from Island Creek Coal National mines with 35 years of service.
Married Dec 17 1934 in Logan, Fayette Co., WV, **Mamie Tennessee Taylor**, b. Jun 5 1912 in Johnson City, Washington Co., TN, d. Mar 28 1998 in Logan General Hospital, Logan Co., WV, buried in Highland Memorial Gardens Logan Co., WV.
         Children:
   764   i.   Edna Lois[7] Brewer b. Feb 1 1934 in Monaville Logan Co., WV, d. Apr 2 1988, buried in Highland Memorial Gardens Logan Co., WV.

503. **Margie**[6] **Kisamore** (237.Perlie[5] Arbogast, 88.Cordelia[4] Waybright, 24.Christina[3] Mullenax, 5.William[2], 1.Mary Elizabeth[1] Arbogast), b. Jul 27 1919 in Pendleton Co., WV, d. Mar 17 1990 in Tucker Co., WV.
Married Jun 26 1938 in Tucker Co., WV, **George Clarence Gatto**, b. Jul 27 1917 in Henry, Grant Co., WV.
         Children:
+ 765   i.   Kathryn Mae[7] Gatto b. Mar 16 1939.

505. **Troy**[6] **Kisamore** (237.Perlie[5] Arbogast, 88.Cordelia[4] Waybright, 24.Christina[3] Mullenax, 5.William[2], 1.Mary Elizabeth[1] Arbogast), b. in Tucker Co., WV.

(1) He Married **Lucille Taylor**.
Children:
- 766   i.   Troy Eugene⁷ Kisamore b. Aug 03 1947.
- 767   ii.   Gary Williams Kisamore b. Nov 18 1948.
- 768   iii.   Gloria Dale Kisamore.

(2) He Married **Lorena (Unknown)**.
Children:
- 769   iv.   Troy Kisamore, Jr..

506. **Glen⁶ Kisamore** (237.Perlie⁵ Arbogast, 88.Cordelia⁴ Waybright, 24.Christina³ Mullenax, 5.William², 1.Mary Elizabeth¹ Arbogast), b. Oct 13 1927 in Barbour Co., WV.
Married Dec 24 1949 in Elkins, Randolph Co., WV, **Maria Bertha Kirkpatrick**, b. Jun 06 1929 in St. George, Washington Co., UT.
Children:
- 770   i.   Glen⁷ Kisamore, Jr. b. Feb 14 1952 in Baltimore, Baltimore Co., MD.
- + 771   ii.   Diana Marie Kisamore b. Aug 27 1954.

508. **Guy⁶ Kisamore** (237.Perlie⁵ Arbogast, 88.Cordelia⁴ Waybright, 24.Christina³ Mullenax, 5.William², 1.Mary Elizabeth¹ Arbogast), b. Jan 18 1934 in Tucker Co., WV, d. Dec 24 1978 in Tucker Co., WV.
Married Apr 28 1953 in Oakland, Garrett Co., MD, **Mary Bell**, b. Dec 15 1934 in Tucker Co., WV.
Children:
- + 772   i.   Olive Pearl⁷ Kisamore b. Jul 26 1954.
- 773   ii.   Bernetti Ann Kisamore b. Oct 24 1955 in Tucker Co., WV, d. Oct 24 1955 in Tucker Co., WV.

512. **Samuel Henry⁶ Arbogast** (238.Wilbur⁵, 88.Cordelia⁴ Waybright, 24.Christina³ Mullenax, 5.William², 1.Mary Elizabeth¹ Arbogast), b. Jul 10 1928, d. Feb 13 1986 in Morgantown, Monongalia Co., WV.
Married Oct 15 1947, **Iva Marie Cree**, b. Jan 16 1931, d. Feb 13 1986 in Morgantown, Monongalia Co., WV, buried in Garards Fort, Greene Co., PA.
Children:
- + 774   i.   David Lee⁷ Arbogast b. Feb 14 1948.
- 775   ii.   Doyle Edward Arbogast b. 1950, d. May 16 1954.
- 776   iii.   Robert Allen Arbogast b. Jan 28 1951.
- + 777   iv.   Linda Arbogast b. Jul 06 1952.
- + 778   v.   Donald Arbogast b. May 05 1958.
- 779   vi.   Donna Darlene Arbogast b. Nov 1958, d. Nov 1958 in Garards Fort, Greene Co., PA.
- + 780   vii.   Connie Sue Arbogast b. Mar 16 1961.

513. **Lovie May⁶ Arbogast** (238.Wilbur⁵, 88.Cordelia⁴ Waybright, 24.Christina³ Mullenax, 5.William², 1.Mary Elizabeth¹ Arbogast), b. Aug 18 1929, d. Mar 10 1985 in Washington, PA, buried Garards Fort, Greene Co., PA.
Married Jul 31 1948, **Lloyd Francis Conrad**, b. Sep 1927. **Lloyd**: Son of Samuel and Martha Conrad.
Children:
- + 781   i.   Larry Francis⁷ Conrad b. May 13 1949.
- + 782   ii.   Randy Conrad b. Jul 25 1954.
- + 783   iii.   Patricia Ann Conrad b. Oct 31 1955.
- + 784   iv.   Debra Conrad b. Oct 08 1957.
- + 785   v.   Jerry Conrad b. Mar 08 1961.
- 786   vi.   Michael Conrad b. May 16 1962.
  He Married **Sue Davis**, b. Aug 08 1992.
- 787   vii.   Ricky Gene Conrad b. Nov 02 1971.

514. **Wilbur Junior**[6] **Arbogast** (238.Wilbur[5], 88.Cordelia[4] Waybright, 24.Christina[3] Mullenax, 5.William[2], 1.Mary Elizabeth[1] Arbogast), b. Jun 21 1932, d. May 19 1978 in Garards Fort, Greene Co., PA.
He Married **Mary Jane Fordyce**, b. Nov 25 1941.
   Children:
   788   i.   James Edward[7] Arbogast b. Apr 16 1958.
 + 789   ii. Roger Lee Arbogast b. Jan 04 1960.

534. **Ellis Paul**[6] **Waybright** (246.Burley McCoy[5], 90.John Edward[4], 24.Christina[3] Mullenax, 5.William[2], 1.Mary Elizabeth[1] Arbogast), b. Mar 12 1941 in Elkins, Randolph Co., WV, d. Feb 22 1982.
   Children:
   790   i.   Anthony Burl[7] Waybright.
   791   ii. Jeffrey Lynn Waybright b. Mar 23 1967, d. Mar 23 1967.
   792   iii. Ellis Paul Waybright b. Feb 5 1968, d. May 29 1995.

544. **Madelyn Gayle**[6] **Hevener** (254.Mavis A.[5] Mullenax, 98.Kenton L.[4], 27.Henry Clay[3], 5.William[2], 1.Mary Elizabeth[1] Arbogast), b. Feb-03-1923 in MD.
Married Jun-18-1942, **Russell C Turner, Jr.**.
   Children:
   793   i.   Sherren Lee[7] Turner b. Oct-04-1945.
   794   ii. Sondra Jat Terner b. May-02-1948.

546. **Wanda Dran**[6] **Mullenax** (258.Kenton Dexter[5], 98.Kenton L.[4], 27.Henry Clay[3], 5.William[2], 1.Mary Elizabeth[1] Arbogast), b. Feb-27-1944.
Married May-06-1961, **Richard Theodore Hebb**.
   Children:
   795   i.   Richard[7] Kenton b. 0211962.
             Married Aug-28-1981, **Belinda Hix**.

   796   ii. Sherry Lynn Hebb b. Sep-16-1964.

550. **William Nevin**[6] **Waybright** (270.Ollie Elizabeth[5] Mullenax, 108.Aaron C.[4], 27.Henry Clay[3], 5.William[2], 1.Mary Elizabeth[1] Arbogast), b. Jan 25 1925 in Blue Grass Cem., Highland Co., VA, d. Oct 8 1997 in Arbovale Cem., Arbovale, Pocahontas Co., WV, buried Oct 11 1997 in Boyer, Pocahontas Co., WV.
He Married **Millie Ryder**.
   Children:
 + 797   i.   William Nevin[7] Waybright.
   798   ii. Timothy Scott Waybright b. Sep 5 1955 in Marlinton, Pocahontas Co., WV, d. Jun 10 1995.
   799   iii. (unknown) Waybright b. May 13 1961 in Marlinton, Pocahontas Co., WV, d. May 13 1961 in Marlinton, Pocahontas Co., WV.

552. **George Samual**[6] **Waybright, Sr.** (270.Ollie Elizabeth[5] Mullenax, 108.Aaron C.[4], 27.Henry Clay[3], 5.William[2], 1.Mary Elizabeth[1] Arbogast).
Married Feb 21 1954, **Anna B. Wilfong**, b. May 30 1936.
   Children:
   800   i.   Diana Kay[7] Waybright b. Jan 27 1955.
             She Married **Gary Lane Cash**.
 + 801   ii. George Samuel Waybright, Jr. b. Feb 3 1957.

553. **Dollie Elizabeth**[6] **Waybright** (270.Ollie Elizabeth[5] Mullenax, 108.Aaron C.[4], 27.Henry Clay[3], 5.William[2], 1.Mary Elizabeth[1] Arbogast). Dau. of Kennie and Ollie Elizabeth (Mullenax) Waybright.
Married Aug 19 1961, **William Dale Varner**, b. Oct 4 1941 (son of William Oaklyn Varner and Anna Mae Sayre). **William**: Same person as #24435 in Dollie's line to Mary Arbogast.

Children:
+ 802   i.   Penelope Kaye⁷ Varner b. May 26 1962.
    803   ii.   Jenifer Lynn Varner b. May 16 1966.
                From Wm. C. Varner.

560. **Hazel Marie**⁶ **Mulnanx** (289.James Lewis⁵ Mulanax, 124.William Dallas⁴, 33.Miles Elliott³, 6.Joseph², 1.Mary Elizabeth¹ Arbogast), b. Jun 01 1904 in Denison, Jackson Co., KS.
Married May 15 1922, **Lester Earl Townsend**, b. Jun 26 1900 in Jackson Co., KS, buried in Denison, Jackson Co., KS, d. Sep 23 1969 in Topeka, Shawnee Co., KS.
Children:
    804   i.   (infant)⁷ Townsend b. 1922, d. 1923.
    805   ii.   Virginia Louise Townsend b. Jul 13 1924 in Denison, Jackson Co., KS, buried in Denison, Jackson Co., KS, d. May 02 1971 in Topeka, Shawnee Co., KS.
+ 806   iii.   Lester Lou Townsend b. Sep 09 1927.

563. **Alvin Edgar**⁶ **Mulnanx** (289.James Lewis⁵ Mulanax, 124.William Dallas⁴, 33.Miles Elliott³, 6.Joseph², 1.Mary Elizabeth¹ Arbogast), b. Apr 01 1912 in Denison, Jackson Co., KS, buried in Denison Cem., Jackson Co., KS, d. Apr 24 1987 in Manhattan, Riley Co., KS.
He Married **Alma Katherine Schiller, R.n.**, b. Sep 04 1914 in Kirwin, Phillips Co., KS (daughter of Frank William Schiller and Edith May Thomas).
Children:
+ 807   i.   Roger Lewis⁷ Mulanax b. Jul 15 1945.

568. **Maggie May**⁶ **Blaikie** (293.Flora Adeline⁵ Mulanax, 125.John Greenbury⁴, 33.Miles Elliott³, 6.Joseph², 1.Mary Elizabeth¹ Arbogast), b. Jun 19 1899 in Jackson Co., KS, d. Oct 13 1929 in Grant Co., OK.
Married May 15 1925 in Bentonville, Benton Co., OK, **Leslie Howard Nelson**, b. Oct 16 1900 in Columbia, Kingfish Co., OK (son of George Monroe Nelson and Nellie Beatty Moore), buried in Cherry Hill, Polk Co., AR, d. Feb 02 1990 in Mena, Polk Co., AR.
Children:
    808   i.   Vera Dean⁷ Nelson b. Apr 02 1926 in Pond Creek, Grant Co., OK, d. Apr 13 1926 in Pond Creek, Grant Co., OK.
    809   ii.   Jean Earl Nelson b. Dec 20 1927 in Pond Creek, Grant Co., OK, d. Dec 26 1927 in Pond Creek, Grant Co., OK.
+ 810   iii.   Jane Earline Nelson b. Dec 20 1927.
    811   iv.   Cleo May Nelson b. Oct 13 1929 in Perry, Noble Co., OK, d. Oct 13 1929 in Perry, Noble Co., OK.

574. **Bessie Lee**⁶ **Osburn** (301.Mary Aceneth⁵ Mulanax, 127.Matthew Elliott⁴, 35.William R.³, 6.Joseph², 1.Mary Elizabeth¹ Arbogast), b. Feb 24 1906, buried in Springfield, Lane Co., OR, d. Jul 16 1976 in Springfield, Lane Co., OR.
Married Sep 08 1924 in Idaho, **James William Newton Franklin**, b. Apr 06 1883 in Buffalo, Dallas Co., MO (son of James Benton Franklin and Liza Slack), d. May 29 1954 in Silverton, Marion Co., OR.
Children:
+ 812   i.   Francis Billey⁷ Franklin b. Jun 23 1925.
+ 813   ii.   Vernon Newton Franklin b. Feb 27 1927.
+ 814   iii.   Wayne Russell Franklin b. Oct 12 1928.
+ 815   iv.   Maty Ann Franklin b. Jul 10 1930.
+ 816   v.   Gladys Faye Franklin b. Mar 28 1932.
+ 817   vi.   Lois Ruth Franklin b. Mar 06 1934.
+ 818   vii.   Betty Jean Franklin b. Nov 10 1935.
+ 819   viii.   Bonnie Jean Franklin b. Sep 10 1937.
+ 820   ix.   James Lee Franklin b. Sep 10 1937.
+ 821   x.   John Allen Franklin b. Apr 09 1939.

+ 822   xi.   Alman Ray Franklin b. Sep 05 1941.

575. **Charley Calvin⁶ Osburn** (301.Mary Aceneth⁵ Mulanax, 127.Matthew Elliott⁴, 35.William R.³, 6.Joseph², 1.Mary Elizabeth¹ Arbogast), b. Jul 24 1907 in Paxton, Harvey Co., KS, buried in Riverside Cem., Payette Co., ID, d. Nov 02 1973 in Bellingham, Whatcom Co., WA.
Married Oct 06 1931 in Payette, Payette Co., WA, **Agnus Virenda Corbit**, b. Feb 02 1924 in Idaho Falls, Bonneville Co., ID (daughter of Ira Alfred Corbit and Susie A. Meeds), buried in Riverside Cem., Payette Co., ID, d. Feb 27 1974 near Bellingham, Whatcom Co., WA.

        Children:
+ 823   i.   Ethel Fern⁷ Osburn b. Aug 24 1932.
   824   ii.   Charleyn Joy Osburn b. Apr 19 1934 in Wendell, Gooding Co., ID.
                 Married Nov 26 1965 in Oregon Falls, OR, **Clarie Gerald Harris**.
+ 825   iii.   Billie Lorreen Osburn b. May -2 1936.
+ 826   iv.   Kathryn Machiel Osburn b. Mar 22 1939.

576. **Cleo Faye⁶ Osburn** (301.Mary Aceneth⁵ Mulanax, 127.Matthew Elliott⁴, 35.William R.³, 6.Joseph², 1.Mary Elizabeth¹ Arbogast), b. Feb 03 1909, d. May 29 1968.
She Married **Christopher Thomas Soron**, b. Jul 26 1898 in Denver, Arapaho Co., CO (son of Thomas Soran and Anne Meade).

        Children:
+ 827   i.   Mary Virginia⁷ Soron b. Aug 10 1929.
   828   ii.   Annastasia Soran b. Jan 17 1913, d. Jun 1931.
+ 829   iii.   Thomas Christopher Soran b. Jan 31 1933.
   830   iv.   Rita (Louise) Soran b. Jun 02 1934.
                 Married Sep 11 1954, **Leo Echel**.
   831   v.   Patricia Soran b. Jul 08 1935.
                 She Married **Lenard McMahan**.
   832   vi.   Christopher Soran b. Apr 17 1937 in Boise, Ada Co., ID, d. Jan 02 1939.
   833   vii.   Michael Thomas Soran b. Jan 26 1941.
                 Married 1958, **Donna McHugh**.
+ 834   viii. Cordelia Soran b. Jan 20 1941.
+ 835   ix.   Stephen Michael Soran b. Dec 10 1943.
   836   x.   Phillip Stephen Soran b. May 21 1945 in Denver, Denver Co., CO.
                 Married Nov 11 1967, **Mary Theresa Thurston**.
   837   xi.   Matthew Richard Soran b. Jul 29 1947 in Twin Falls Co., ID, d. 1967.
                 He Married **Barbara Ann Friskie**.

577. **Samuel Stephen⁶ Osburn** (301.Mary Aceneth⁵ Mulanax, 127.Matthew Elliott⁴, 35.William R.³, 6.Joseph², 1.Mary Elizabeth¹ Arbogast), b. Oct 23 1910 in Avoca, Jackson Co., KS, buried in Midvale, Washington Co., ID, d. Dec 1984 in Midvale, Washington Co., ID.
Married Apr 04 1934 in Payette, Payette Co., ID, **Thelma Head**, b. Jun 24 1914 (daughter of Marion Head and Alzona Head).

        Children:
+ 838   i.   Patricia Lee⁷ Osburn b. Jun 29 1935.
+ 839   ii.   Betty Jane Osburn b. Jun 19 1937.
+ 840   iii.   Linda Gail Osburn b. Jun 15 1940.
+ 841   iv.   John Franklin Osburn b. Aug 31 1943.
+ 842   v.   Connie Jean Osburn b. Mar 02 1950.

578. **Parthena Ann⁶ Osburn** (301.Mary Aceneth⁵ Mulanax, 127.Matthew Elliott⁴, 35.William R.³, 6.Joseph², 1.Mary Elizabeth¹ Arbogast), b. Oct 25 1912 in Emmett, Pottawatomie Co., KS.
Married 20 Jun 1934 in Boise, Ada Co., ID, **Floyd Edward Van Horn**, b. 3 Mar 1908 in Solomon, Dixon Co., KS.

        Children:
   843   i.   Billie Floyd⁷ Van Horn b. 2 Nov 1936 in Boise, Ada Co., ID.

Married 5 May 1956, **Marilyn Jean King**.
844   ii.   Jackie Dean Van Horn b. 2 Dec 1939 in Boise, Ada Co., ID.
Married 25 May 1961, **Dorris Lea De Mott**.
845   iii.   Judith Ann Van Horn b. 21 Sep 1941 in Boise, Ada Co., ID.
Married 5 Jun 1959, **Delloyd Bowen**.

579. **Mable Marie^6 Osburn** (301.Mary Aceneth^5 Mulanax, 127.Matthew Elliott^4, 35.William R.^{3}, 6.Joseph^2, 1.Mary Elizabeth^1 Arbogast), b. Apr 23 1915 in Elkton, Mower Co., MN, buried in Marcola, Lane Co., OR, d. May 17 1981 in Springfield, Lane Co., OR.
Married 16 Apr 1933 in Payette, Payette Co., ID, **Archaball Allen**, b. 7 Dec 1909 in Deerhead, Barber Co., KS, d. in Marcola, Lane Co., OR.
      Children:
+ 846   i.   Doris Acentha^7 Allen b. 22 Feb 1934.
+ 847   ii.   Opal Jane Allen b. 30 May 1935.

580. **Myrtle May^6 Osburn** (301.Mary Aceneth^5 Mulanax, 127.Matthew Elliott^4, 35.William R.^{3}, 6.Joseph^2, 1.Mary Elizabeth^1 Arbogast), b. Apr 23 1915 in Elkton, Mower Co., MN.
Married 20 Oct 1931 in Vale, Malheur Co., OR, **Carol Thomas Fulton**, b. 9 Jun 1910 in Iowa.
      Children:
+ 848   i.   Eunice Marie^7 Fulton b. 12 May 1932.
   849   ii.   Lamont Fulton b. 29 Dec 1942 in Payette, Payette Co., ID.
Married 1951, **Carol Thornton**.

581. **Minnie Belle^6 Osburn** (301.Mary Aceneth^5 Mulanax, 127.Matthew Elliott^4, 35.William R.^{3}, 6.Joseph^2, 1.Mary Elizabeth^1 Arbogast), b. Oct 30 1916 in Payette, Payette Co., ID, buried in Jupiter Haven Cem., Prineville, Crook Co., OR, d. Jun 03 1994 in Prineville, Crook Co., OR.
She Married **Lester Thomas Garside**, b. 19 Jul 1914 in Ontario, Malheur Co., OR.
      Children:
850   i.   Lawrence Addison^7 Garside b. 25 Jul 1934 in Payette, Payette Co., ID.
He Married **Ruby Smith**.
851   ii.   Mearl Lester Garside b. 25 Nov 1935 in Payette, Payette Co., ID.
852   iii.   Cinthea Loreda Garside b. 15 Jul 1945 in Lakeview, Lake Co., OR.
She Married **Duane Morgan**.

582. **Francis Paul^6 Osburn** (301.Mary Aceneth^5 Mulanax, 127.Matthew Elliott^4, 35.William R.^{3}, 6.Joseph^2, 1.Mary Elizabeth^1 Arbogast), b. Oct 14 1928 in Poapie, Mower Co., MN, d. Jul 29 1989 in Vancouver, Clark Co., WA.
(1) Married 17 Apr 1941 in Weiser, Washington Co., ID, **Dorothy Grace Windle**, b. 24 May 1925 in Payette, Payette Co., ID.

      Children:
853   i.   Ronald^7 Osburn b. 22 Oct 1942 in La Grange, Cook Co., OR.
    (1) Married 1966, **Lillian Hardy**.
    (2) Married Mar 1971, **Diane Slone**.
854   ii.   Mary Osburn b. 1 Apr 1944 in Payette, Payette Co., ID.
    (1) Married 2 May 1964, **Wilber Skinner**.
    (2) Married 23 Nov 1971, **Norman Johnson**.
    (3) She Married **(unknown) Fraizer**.
855   iii.   Joyce Osburn b. 13 Oct 1945 in Ontario, Malheur Co., OR.
She Married **(unknown) Gilbertson**.

(2) He Married **Dessa Evelon Wilson**, b. 29 Jun 1950 in Plymouth, Payette Co., ID.
      Children:
856   iv.   Andrea Osburn b. 14 Dec 1950.
Married Aug 1973, **Richard Guthery**.

857 v. Daniel Osburn b. 16 Feb 1952.
858 vi. Julie Osburn b. 27 Apr 1953.
    She Married **Ivan Lamarr**.
859 vii. Lynn Osburn b. 3 Jan 1955.
860 viii. Stanley Osburn.
861 ix. Jerry Osburn b. 6 Apr 1958.

583. **Theodore Harvey**[6] **Osburn** (301.Mary Aceneth[5] Mulanax, 127.Matthew Elliott[4], 35.William R.[3], 6.Joseph[2], 1.Mary Elizabeth[1] Arbogast), b. Oct 13 1920 in Plainview, Wabasha Co., MN, buried in Riverside Cem., Payette Co., ID, d. Aug 03 1985 in Payette, Payette Co., ID.
(1) He Married **Ellen Lila Windle**, b. 11 Jun 1921 in Payette, Payette Co., ID (daughter of Burrel Windle and Elizabeth Mickelson).
   Children:
+ 862 i. Sandra[7] Osburn b. 1 Oct 1941.
+ 863 ii. Laurie Joan Osburn b. 22 May 1943.
  864 iii. (infant) Osburn b. 1945, d. 1945.

(2) He Married **Edith Hoyle Tomasson**.
   Children:
  865 iv. Stephen Wayne Osburn b. 27 Jun 1956 in Ontario, Malheur Co., OR.
    He Married **Connie Haines**.
  866 v. Rita Faye Osburn b. 1957, d. 1970.
  867 vi. Teddy Lea Osburn b. 13 Sep 1958.

584. **Mary Helen Rose**[6] **Osburn** (301.Mary Aceneth[5] Mulanax, 127.Matthew Elliott[4], 35.William R.[3], 6.Joseph[2], 1.Mary Elizabeth[1] Arbogast), b. Feb 26 1922 in Plainview, Wabasha Co., MN.
Married 20 Sep 1942 in Payette, Payette Co., ID, **Jesse William Compton**, d. 1969.
   Children:
+ 868 i. Carlotta Aceneth[7] Compton b. 13 Sep 1942.
+ 869 ii. Jesse William Compton, Jr. b. 1 Oct 1946.
  870 iii. Timothy Jay Compton b. 16 Jun 1949, d. 18 Mar 1973.

587. **Zella Jane**[6] **Osburn** (301.Mary Aceneth[5] Mulanax, 127.Matthew Elliott[4], 35.William R.[3], 6.Joseph[2], 1.Mary Elizabeth[1] Arbogast), b. Oct 04 1928 near Wenatchee, Chelan Co., WA.
She Married **Lyle Ames Wheeler**, b. 19 Oct 1922 in Kennewick, Benton Co., WA.
   Children:
+ 871 i. Lyle Anthony[7] Wheeler b. 5 Aug 1957.
  872 ii. Scott Matthew Wheeler.
    He Married **Connie Hayes**, b. 29 Dec 1958 in Springfield, Lane Co., OR.

596. **Dorothy Ellen**[6] **Mulanax** (313.Calvin Silas[5], 133.John William[4], 35.William R.[3], 6.Joseph[2], 1.Mary Elizabeth[1] Arbogast), b. 3 Apr 1929 in Portland, Multnomah Co., OR.
She Married **Curtis Fay Myrick**, b. 31 Jan 1927 in Pendleton, Umatilla Co., OR.
   Children:
+ 873 i. Clinton Jay[7] Myrick b. 1 Jun 1953.
+ 874 ii. Calvin Curtis Myrick b. 4 Feb 1957.
+ 875 iii. Cynthia Marguerite Myrick b. 9 Apr 1963.

598. **Ardath Lenore**[6] **Hagar** (319.William Roy[5] Hager, 136.Lucy Adeline[4] Mulanax, 35.William R.[3], 6.Joseph[2], 1.Mary Elizabeth[1] Arbogast), b. 23 Feb 1937 in Douglas, Converse Co., WY.
Married 10 Dec 1954 in Lincoln, Lancaster Co., NE, **Paul Elton Brown**, b. 7 Oct 1932 in Cochran, Bleckley Co., GA.
   Children:
  876 i. Martha Laree[7] Brown b. 4 Jan 1958 in Atlanta, Fulton Co., GA.
  877 ii. Lenore Ann Brown b. 18 Jul 1959 in De Kalb Co., GA.

Married 8 Nov 1991 in Knoxville, Knox Co., TN, **Gary Eugene Poteat**.

602. **Anita Lorraine⁶ Groce** (323.Thelma Louise⁵ Kelley, 146.Anna Louisa⁴ Mulanax, 40.Joseph Riley³ Mullenax, 6.Joseph² Mulanax, 1.Mary Elizabeth¹ Arbogast).
(1) She Married **Stanley Carl Bohlin**, b. Jul 30 1922 in Seattle, King Co., WA, d. Jun 26 2003 in Anacortes, Skagit Co., WA.
   Children:
   878   i.   Anna Thelita⁷ Bohlin b. Oct 5 1942 in Seattle, King Co., WA, d. Aug 27 1996 in Anacortes, Skagit Co., WA.
   879   ii. Timothy Carl Bohlin b. Mar 22 1944 in Salinas, Monterey Co., CA, d. Oct 5 1976 in Tacoma, Pierce Co., WA.
(2) She Married **August Edward Van Der Wastein Or Stiner**, b. Mar 23 1899 in Illinois, d. in Centralia, Lewis Co., WA.

Generation Seven

608. **Iona Patrica⁷ Waybright** (332.Wilber Allen⁶, 153.Mary Permelia Catherine⁵ Mullenax, 50.William Isaac⁴, 7.James W.³, 2.Abraham², 1.Mary Elizabeth¹ Arbogast) (See marriage to number 453.)

610. **Ollie Katherine⁷ Waybright** (334.Amby Stanton⁶, 153.Mary Permelia Catherine⁵ Mullenax, 50.William Isaac⁴, 7.James W.³, 2.Abraham², 1.Mary Elizabeth¹ Arbogast), b. Sep 30 1903 in Winterburn Pocahontas Co., WV, d. Jan 2 1999 in Crystal Springs Nursing home Elkins Pendleton Co., WV, buried Jan 5 1999 in Arbovale Cem., Arbovale, Pocahontas Co., WV.
She Married **Carl Elza**, b. Apr 25 1902, d. Feb 1983.
   Children:
   880   i.   Clinton Charles⁸ Elza b. Mar 28 1923.

611. **Grace Elizabeth⁷ Waybright** (334.Amby Stanton⁶, 153.Mary Permelia Catherine⁵ Mullenax, 50.William Isaac⁴, 7.James W.³, 2.Abraham², 1.Mary Elizabeth¹ Arbogast), b. Jun 16 1905 in Pocahontas Co., WV, d. 1993.
(1) She Married **Charles Vandevander**.
   Children:
   881   i.   Dollie Irene⁸ Vandevander b. Sep 30 1921.
   882   ii.   Lottie Mae Vandevander b. Oct 24 1924, d. Jan 1 1970.
   883   iii. Vervie Vandevander b. Oct 26 1926.
   884   iv.   Merle Vandevander b. Jul 19 1929.

(2) She Married **George Starks**, b. Nov 5 1904, d. Dec 24 1980. **George**:

612. **Gertrude Lee⁷ Waybright** (334.Amby Stanton⁶, 153.Mary Permelia Catherine⁵ Mullenax, 50.William Isaac⁴, 7.James W.³, 2.Abraham², 1.Mary Elizabeth¹ Arbogast), b. Dec 2 1907 in Pocahontas Co., WV.
She Married **Sterling Bruce Gum**, b. Oct 18 1897 in Green Bank, Pocahontas Co., WV (son of William Crawford Gum and Rubina Ruth Sutton), d. May 13 1980 in Marlinton, Pocahontas Co., WV.
   Children:
   + 885   i.   Sterling Lee⁸ Gum b. May 2 1925.

613. **Rella K⁷ Waybright** (334.Amby Stanton⁶, 153.Mary Permelia Catherine⁵ Mullenax, 50.William Isaac⁴, 7.James W.³, 2.Abraham², 1.Mary Elizabeth¹ Arbogast), b. Sep 29 1908 in Pocahontas Co., WV, d. Jul 22 2001.

She Married **Henry Parker Arbogast**, b. May 1 1892 in Pocahontas Co., WV (son of Adam Crawford Arbogast and Rachel Nettie Galford), d. Sep 11 1979 in Pocahontas Co., WV, buried in Arbovale Cem., Arbovale, Pocahontas Co., WV. **Henry:** The line of Parker Henry from Tommie Arbogast Huggins and her copy of The Galford Ancestry, by Lloyd Pritt Galford, 1981, Gateway Press, Baltimore, MD; copy in file. For family with Rella Waybright see #15691.

Children:

+ 886   i.   Rev. James Bert^8 Arbogast b. Aug 11 1927.

615. **Edna Alice**^{7} **Waybright** (334.Amby Stanton^6, 153.Mary Permelia Catherine^5 Mullenax, 50.William Isaac^4, 7.James W.^{3}, 2.Abraham^2, 1.Mary Elizabeth^1 Arbogast), b. Mar 27 1912 in Pocahontas Co., WV, d. May 28 1993.
She Married **Grant Vandevander**.

Children:

887   i.   Helen Kathleen^8 Vandevander b. Jul 10 1928.
888   ii.   Eugene Charles Vandevander b. Feb 01 1930.
889   iii.   Grant Vandevander b. Jul 23 1934.
890   iv.   Francis Marie Vandevander b. Aug 28 1936.

616. **Bertie Catherine**^{7} **Warner** (336.Fransina Lee^6 Waybright, 153.Mary Permelia Catherine^5 Mullenax, 50.William Isaac^4, 7.James W.^{3}, 2.Abraham^2, 1.Mary Elizabeth^1 Arbogast), b. Jul 9 1903 in Churchville, Pendleton Co., WV, d. Feb 14 1937.
Married Oct 4 1923, **Fred Marshall Wimer**, b. Mar 1903, d. Nov 1961.

Children:

891   i.   Dessie Ina^8 Wimer b. Mar-12-1922 in Hunting Ground, Pendleton Co. WV.
        She Married **Lynn Lambert**, b. May-28-1916 in Riverton, Pendleton, West Virginia (son of J. Elmer Lambert and Maggie Hedrick).
892   ii.   Floyd Herman Wimer b. Mar-24-1924, d. Dec-18-1975.
        He Married **Mary Ruth Armstrong**, b. Nov-22-1920 in Harmon, WV (daughter of Eli Armstrong and Kate Warner), d. Aug-31-1980 in Baltimore, Baltimore Co., MD.
893   iii.   Omer John Wimer b. Mar-14-1926 in Hunting Ground, Pendleton Co. WV.
        He Married **Viva Georgia Lambert**, b. Oct-25-1930 (daughter of Cam lambert and Tressie Bennett).
894   iv.   Homer Sylvarius Wimer b. Mar-14-1926 in Hunting Ground, Pendleton Co. WV, d. Jul-11-1986 in Baltimore, Baltimore Co., MD.
        He Married **Oddie Mclamb**, b. Apr-18-1916 in Columbia Co. SC (daughter of Cager McLamb and Hattie Watts).
895   v.   Berlie Brooks Wimer b. Feb-10-1928 in Hunting Ground, Pendleton Co. WV.
        He Married **Maxine Carrie Hartman**, b. Jul-24-1935 (daughter of Charles Okey Hartman and Pauline Elza Eye).
896   vi.   Eston Jennings Wimer b. Nov-03-1935 in Hunting Ground, Pendleton Co. WV.
        He Married **Lois Ann Holtz**, b. Jun-21-1937 in Minot, ND (daughter of Arthur Holtz and Mabel Forthun).
+ 897   vii.   Bobby MCarthur Wimer b. May-10-1942.

621. **Cletis**^{7} **Johnston** (337.Dolly^6 Mullenax, 155.Elijah^5, 50.William Isaac^4, 7.James W.^{3}, 2.Abraham^2, 1.Mary Elizabeth^1 Arbogast), b. Jul 31 1902, d. Nov 03 1993.
Married Oct 27 1938, **Ollie K. Warner**, b. Mar 1 1915.

Children:

+ 898   i.   Mary Leta^8 Johnson.
+ 899   ii.   Buford C Johnston.
   900   iii.   Ann Lynn Johnston.

623. **Jesse**^{7} **Johnston** (337.Dolly^6 Mullenax, 155.Elijah^5, 50.William Isaac^4, 7.James W.^{3}, 2.Abraham^2, 1.Mary Elizabeth^1 Arbogast), b. Jul 2 1907, d. Dec 18 1971 in Bartow, Pocahontas Co., WV.
He Married **Monna Raines**.

Children:
 901 i. Odell Raines[8] Johnston.
    He Married **Mildred Lambert**.

625. **Georgia Ellen[7] Johnston** (337.Dolly[6] Mullenax, 155.Elijah[5], 50.William Isaac[4], 7.James W.[3], 2.Abraham[2], 1.Mary Elizabeth[1] Arbogast), b. Oct 01 1911, d. Mar 20 1975, buried in Pine Hill Cem., Brandywine, Pendleton Co., WV.
She Married **Harry Srtife Eye**, b. 1909.
Children:
 902 i. Richard Hull[8] Eye b. Jul 09 1937, d. Jul 24 1968.
 903 ii. James Lee Eye b. Jan 30 1939.
 904 iii. Terry Sue Eye b. Sep 03 1943.

631. **Verlie[7] Warner** (338.Lura[6] Mullenax, 155.Elijah[5], 50.William Isaac[4], 7.James W.[3], 2.Abraham[2], 1.Mary Elizabeth[1] Arbogast), b. Dec 27 1903, d. Nov 29 1969 in Circleville, Pendleton Co., WV, buried in Hunting Ground, Pendleton Co., (W)VA.
Married Apr-09-1928, **Ona Lucy Sponaugle**, b. Nov-21-1909 in Circleville Pendleton Co., WV (daughter of John Alonzo Sponaugle and Mary Dessie Vandevander), d. Dec-19-1992.
Children:
+ 905 i. Mildred Mary[8] Warner b. Sep 1928.
 906 ii. Hilda Warner b. c 1931 in Cherry Grove, Pendleton Co., WV, d. Feb-26-1987 in Port St. Lucie, FL.
    She Married **Eldon J Wimer** (son of Charles Amos Wimer and Zoe Etta Thompson).
 907 iii. Geneva Warner.
 908 iv. Francis Warner.
 909 v. Jerrol Warner.
 910 vi. Jimmy Warner.
 911 vii. Johnnie Warner.
 912 viii. Caroline Ruth Warner.
 913 ix. Dennis Warner.
 914 x. Gail Warner.
 915 xi. Kermit Warner.

633. **Betty[7] Warner** (338.Lura[6] Mullenax, 155.Elijah[5], 50.William Isaac[4], 7.James W.[3], 2.Abraham[2], 1.Mary Elizabeth[1] Arbogast), b. Jul 26 1913.
She Married **Conda Roy Sponaugle**, b. May-20-1912 in Circleville Pendleton Co., WV (son of John Alonzo Sponaugle and Mary Dessie Vandevander).
Children:
 916 i. Genevieve[8] Sponaugle.
 917 ii. Norms Jean Sponaugle.
    She Married **Kelley M. Mullenax**.
 918 iii. Billy Roy Sponaugle.
 919 iv. Brenda Sponaugle.

634. **Judith[7] Warner** (338.Lura[6] Mullenax, 155.Elijah[5], 50.William Isaac[4], 7.James W.[3], 2.Abraham[2], 1.Mary Elizabeth[1] Arbogast), b. Dec 18 1915.
She Married **Brison Jay Sponaugle**, b. Apr 03 1911 in Hunting Ground, Pendleton Co., (W)VA (son of Gilbert Kenton Sponaugle and Annie Pressie Mallow), d. Jun 13 1992.
Children:
 920 i. M. Elaine[8] Sponaugle.
    She Married **(unknown) Alt**.
 921 ii. Jenny K. Sponaugle.
    Married 0, **(unknown) Halterman**.
+ 922 iii. Harold Michael Sponaugle b. May-18-1936.

636. **Brooks Burdette⁷ Mullenax** (339.Mcclelland⁶, 155.Elijah⁵, 50.William Isaac⁴, 7.James W.³, 2.Abraham², 1.Mary Elizabeth¹ Arbogast), b. Apr 23 1918, d. Dec 15 1968 in Fayetteville, Cumberland Co., NC.
S/o McClelland and Anna B. (Calhoun) Mullenax; Brooks is same person as #22355 and is a descendant of both John (Volume I) and Mary (Volume III).
Married Jun 5 1944, **Nell Lorraine Beard**, b. Mar 19 1920 (daughter of Samuel Bryant Monroe Beard and Mary Inez Brown), d. Nov 15 2001 in Wake Medical Center, Raleigh Co., NC.
   Children:
+ 923   i.   Carolyn Jean⁸ Mullenax b. Nov 9 1952.

637. **Harlan⁷ Mullenax** (340.Martha Ellen⁶, 155.Elijah⁵, 50.William Isaac⁴, 7.James W.³, 2.Abraham², 1.Mary Elizabeth¹ Arbogast), b. May 11 1912.
(1) Married Dec 05 1934, **Ruby M. Johnson**.
   Children:
924   i.   Doris Lee⁸ Mullenax b. Oct 06 1934.

(2) He Married **Ruth Bennett**.
   Children:
+ 925   ii.   David Lee Mullenax b. May 24 1949.

638. **Halcie⁷ Mullenax** (340.Martha Ellen⁶, 155.Elijah⁵, 50.William Isaac⁴, 7.James W.³, 2.Abraham², 1.Mary Elizabeth¹ Arbogast).
She Married **Virgil Vandevander** (son of Wayne Sylvester Vandevender and Lena Tingler).
   Children:
926   i.   Wayne⁸ Vandevander.
927   ii.   Randall Vandevander.
928   iii.   Billy D. Vandevander.
929   iv.   Robert Vandevander.

642. **Lena Virginia⁷ Halterman** (342.Joseph Clark⁶, 156.Annie Jane⁵ Mullenax, 50.William Isaac⁴, 7.James W.³, 2.Abraham², 1.Mary Elizabeth¹ Arbogast), b. Dec 24 1915.
Married Nov 23 1938 in Unsure, **Clarence Wimer Hise**, b. Feb 15 1914, d. Aug 14 2003.
   Children:
930   i.   Shirley Marie⁸ Hise b. Jun 25 1939.
931   ii.   Nancy Louise Hise b. Mar 12 1941.
    (1) She Married **Herman Puffenbarger**.
    (2) Married Oct 9 1976, **Vernon Harold Newman**.
932   iii.   Clarence Wilmer Hise II b. Dec 46 1943.
    Married Jun 8 1972, **Darlene Turner**.
+ 933   iv.   Ralph Gerald Hise II b. Oct 1 1946.

646. **Fairy Dare⁷ Halterman** (342.Joseph Clark⁶, 156.Annie Jane⁵ Mullenax, 50.William Isaac⁴, 7.James W.³, 2.Abraham², 1.Mary Elizabeth¹ Arbogast), b. Nov 4 1924 in Bartow, Pocahontas Co., WV, d. May 2 1994 in Dunmore, Pocahontas Co., WV.
Married Dec 18 1941 in Cochranton, Crawford Co., PA, **William Winfred Sheets**, b. Feb 2 1915 (son of Grover Cleveland Sheets and Nina Elizabeth Taylor), d. Aug 12 1994. **William**: Ref: Pocahontas 1981: 439 20 Mil: WWII.
   Children:
+ 934   i.   Mary Frances⁸ Sheets b. Jan 4 1943.
+ 935   ii.   Robert Clark Sheets b. Mar 26 1947.
+ 936   iii.   Roy Wetzel Sheets b. Jan 13 1951.

648. **Charlsie⁷ Halterman** (342.Joseph Clark⁶, 156.Annie Jane⁵ Mullenax, 50.William Isaac⁴, 7.James W.³, 2.Abraham², 1.Mary Elizabeth¹ Arbogast), b. Nov 5 1932.
Ref: Pocahontas 1981: 419.

Married Aug 19 1950, **Clarence Walter Seeley**, b. Mar 28 1930 in Venango Co., PA.
Children:
- 937   i.   Ann Marie[8] Seeley b. Sep 19 1951.
  Married Jan 15 1973, Richard Allen Johnson, b. Nov 6 1946 in Forest Co., PA.
  Richard: S/o Francis Bernard and Elmeda Marie (Mealy) Johnson.
- 938   ii.   Carmen Cora Seeley b. May 25 1957.

649. **Paul[7] Mullenax** (343.Emory R[6], 157.James B.[5], 50.William Isaac[4], 7.James W.[3], 2.Abraham[2], 1.Mary Elizabeth[1] Arbogast), b. Mar 3 1918.
Married Dec 2 1940 in Oakland, Garrett Co., MD, **Gayle Marie Cassell**, b. Mar 17 1922 in Back Mountain, Pocahontas Co., WV (daughter of Willis Cassell and Eva Pearl Drumheller).
Children:
- 939   i.   Sandra Jean[8] Mullenax b. Aug 2 1942, d. Nov 29 1942.
- + 940   ii.   Karen Sue Mullenax b. Jun 12 1945.
- + 941   iii.   Janice Lee Mullenax b. Jul 4 1948.
- 942   iv.   Paula Marie Mullenax b. Jul 4 1948.
- + 943   v.   Louise Grey Mullenax b. Jun 25 1950.

650. **Richard Emory[7] Mullenax** (343.Emory R[6], 157.James B.[5], 50.William Isaac[4], 7.James W.[3], 2.Abraham[2], 1.Mary Elizabeth[1] Arbogast), b. Oct 16 1928.
Married May 29 1947 in Oakland, Garrett Co., MD, **Crystal Belle Wooddell**, b. Mar 9 1932 in Boyer, Pocahontas Co., WV (daughter of Baine Wesley Wooddell and Margie Marie Vandevender), d. Dec 22 2001 in Davis Memorial Hospital, Elkins, Randolph Co., WV.
Children:
- + 944   i.   Connie Jean[8] Mullenax b. Mar 13 1949.
- + 945   ii.   Sonya Mullenax.
- 946   iii.   Michael Mullenax.
- + 947   iv.   Kelly Blaine Mullenax.

651. **Gus[7] Warner** (344.Sallie Denie[6] Mullenax, 157.James B.[5], 50.William Isaac[4], 7.James W.[3], 2.Abraham[2], 1.Mary Elizabeth[1] Arbogast), b. Jun 27 1900, d. Mar 10 1971 in Akron, Summit Co., OH.
It is unclear the relationship of this child to the Lambert family. Maybe adopted. He has been added as a child of Fallen Lambert and Sallie Mullenax, but not his off springs.
He Married **Kathryn Hoffa**, b. 22 Dec 1887, d. 2 Jun 1966 in Ohio.
Children:
- + 948   i.   Shirley Ann[8] Warner b. 12 Nov 1928.
- 949   ii.   Robert G. Warner b. 26 Jun 1927, d. 7 May 1986.

652. **Georgia[7] Lambert** (344.Sallie Denie[6] Mullenax, 157.James B.[5], 50.William Isaac[4], 7.James W.[3], 2.Abraham[2], 1.Mary Elizabeth[1] Arbogast), b. Apr 28 1903, d. Jun 4 1985 in Boyer, Pocahontas Co., WV.
She Married **James Lester Simmons**, b. 1898 in Pocahontas Co., WV, d. Apr 30 1974 in Randolph Co., WV.
Children:
- 950   i.   Keith[8] Simmons b. Aug 21 1918, d. Jul 11 1944.
- + 951   ii.   Dewey Hunter Simmons b. Feb 19 1922.
- + 952   iii.   Edward Lee Simmons b. Jul 5 1925.
- + 953   iv.   Roy Lester Simmons b. Sep 5 1927.
- 954   v.   Irma Simmons b. Sep 3 1928.
  She Married **John Hendricks**.
- 955   vi.   Emma Simmons b. Apr 3 1932.
- + 956   vii.   Martha M. Simmons b. May 24 1935.
- + 957   viii.   Clara Simmons b. Oct 6 1940.
- + 958   ix.   Sadie Simmons b. Feb 24 1947.

653. **Roy D.**[7] **Lambert** (344.Sallie Denie[6] Mullenax, 157.James B.[5], 50.William Isaac[4], 7.James W.[3], 2.Abraham[2], 1.Mary Elizabeth[1] Arbogast), b. Jun 08 1905, d. Apr 30 1976 in Harrisonburg, Rockingham Co., VA, buried in Arbovale Cem., Arbovale, Pocahontas Co., WV.
(1) Married Feb 17 1939, **Sylvia Hedrick**, b. Apr 1 1914 in Cherry Grove, Pendleton Co., WV (daughter of Will Hedrick and Martha Hedrick), d. Aug 28 1986 in Elkins, Randolph Co., WV, buried in Arbovale Cem., Arbovale, Pocahontas Co., WV.

Children:
+ 959   i.   Janet Lee[8] Lambert b. Nov 17 1939.
+ 960   ii.   Francis Lambert b. Oct 14 1942.
+ 961   iii. Keith Fallen Lambert b. Nov 24 1942.
+ 962   iv.   Joan Dare Lambert b. May 5 1943.
  963   v.   Roy Allen Lambert b. Jun 1 1944.
+ 964   vi.   Charlotte Lambert b. Feb 12 1950.
+ 965   vii. Donald Curtis Lambert b. May 26 1954.

(2) He Married **Ruby Griffin**, b. Feb 29 1912 in Durbin, Pocahontas Co., WV, d. Sep 21 1982 in Warren, OH.

Children:
  966   viii. Ethel Marie Lambert b. Jun 20 1931.

654. **Russell**[7] **Lambert** (344.Sallie Denie[6] Mullenax, 157.James B.[5], 50.William Isaac[4], 7.James W.[3], 2.Abraham[2], 1.Mary Elizabeth[1] Arbogast), b. Oct 11 1907 in Pendleton Co., WV, d. Oct 31 1985 in Akron, Summit Co., OH.
He Married **Gladys Mae McBride**, b. Nov 2 1907 in Ohio, d. Feb 4 1984 in Akron, Summit Co., OH.

Children:
+ 967   i.   Earl Russell[8] Lambert b. Jul 25 1929.
+ 968   ii.   Kenneth Lambert b. Jan 25 1938.

655. **Orie Basil**[7] **Lambert** (344.Sallie Denie[6] Mullenax, 157.James B.[5], 50.William Isaac[4], 7.James W.[3], 2.Abraham[2], 1.Mary Elizabeth[1] Arbogast), b. Jan 22 1910 in Pendleton Co., WV, d. Jul 18 1988.
Married May 25 1932 in Monterey, Highland Co., VA, **Rheda Catherine Puffenbarger**, b. May 3 1910 in Monterey, Highland Co., VA, d. Jun 25 1995 in Bartow, Pocahontas Co., WV.

Children:
+ 969   i.   Hilda Josephine[8] Lambert b. Feb 24 1932.
  970   ii.   Margaret Deanie Lambert b. Mar 19 1934, d. Jul 19 1934 in Harrisonburg, Rockingham Co., VA.
+ 971   iii. Gladys Marie Lambert b. Nov 18 1936.
+ 972   iv.   Shirley Mae Lambert b. Mar 12 1938.
+ 973   v.   Doris Ann Lambert b. Mar 27 1941.

656. **Jessie**[7] **Lambert** (344.Sallie Denie[6] Mullenax, 157.James B.[5], 50.William Isaac[4], 7.James W.[3], 2.Abraham[2], 1.Mary Elizabeth[1] Arbogast), b. Oct 13 1912, d. Jan 12 1992.
D/o Fallen and Sallie Ardena (Mullenax) Lambert. Jessie is a = Mary Arbogast, of Michael. See Vol. III for her lineage.
She Married **Miller David Varner**, b. Dec 25 1910 (son of David Mauzy Varner and Loleta Ann Beverage).

Children:
+ 974   i.   David F.[8] Varner b. Mar 22 1930.
  975   ii.   Clinton Lee Varner b. Feb 5 1932. Married, children are Eleanor Lee and Clinton Lee Varner, Jr.

657. **Rhoda Martha[7] Lambert** (344.Sallie Denie[6] Mullenax, 157.James B.[5], 50.William Isaac[4], 7.James W.[3], 2.Abraham[2], 1.Mary Elizabeth[1] Arbogast), b. Nov 16 1914 in Pendleton Co., WV. Parents' names from marriage record. D/o Fallen and Ardena Marie (Mullenax) Lambert. Rhoda Martha is the same person as #13918, a descendant of both John (Volume I) and Mary (Volume III). See those volumes for her lineage.
Married Jun 15 1938 in Highland Co., VA, **Ernest McKinley Arbogast**, b. Apr 8 1920 in Pocahontas Co., WV (son of James Lawrence Arbogast and Bessie Catherine Simmons), d. Sep 5 2002 in Parma, Cuyahoga Co., OH.

Children:
+ 976   i.   Ernest McKinley[8] Arbogast b. Oct 18 1939.

658. **Dewey Judy[7] Lambert** (344.Sallie Denie[6] Mullenax, 157.James B.[5], 50.William Isaac[4], 7.James W.[3], 2.Abraham[2], 1.Mary Elizabeth[1] Arbogast), b. Mar 18 1917, d. May 2 1984 in Meadville, Crawford Co., PA.
He Married **Mildred Hinkle**, b. May 17 1925 (daughter of Edward Hinkle and Mary Phares).

Children:
+ 977   i.   Betty[8] Lambert b. Jan 20 1945.
+ 978   ii.   Edward Judy Lambert b. Nov 16 1947.
+ 979   iii.   Roger Lee Lambert b. Jul 28 1948.
+ 980   iv.   James Eugene Lambert b. Jul 3 1951.
  981   v.   Gary Allen Lambert b. Dec 23 1952, d. Aug 1 1955.
+ 982   vi.   Larry Dale Lambert b. May 19 1955.
+ 983   vii.   Debra Kay Lambert b. Jun 1 1957.
+ 984   viii.   Patty Jean Lambert b. Aug 31 1958.
+ 985   ix.   Brenda Lee Lambert b. Sep 26 1962.

660. **Sherron Virginia[7] Calhoun** (347.Nellie Mae[6] Mullenax, 162.Solomon Key[5], 50.William Isaac[4], 7.James W.[3], 2.Abraham[2], 1.Mary Elizabeth[1] Arbogast), b. Aug 28 1915.
(1) Married Sep 30 1933, **Delbert Waybright**, b. Jun 3 1920 in Highland Co., VA (son of Clarence Waybright and Mary Ellen Wimer).

Children:
+ 986   i.   Ralph David[8] Waybright b. Apr 19 1949.

(2) Married Sep 30 1933, **Charles Edward Bryant**, b. Nov 29 1913.

Children:
+ 987   ii.   Charles Edward Bryant b. Mar 17 1938.
+ 988   iii.   Harold McQuain Bryant b. Mar 17 1938.
+ 989   iv.   Richard Gale Bryant b. Aug 16 1941.

661. **Shellace Tiffin[7] Calhoun** (347.Nellie Mae[6] Mullenax, 162.Solomon Key[5], 50.William Isaac[4], 7.James W.[3], 2.Abraham[2], 1.Mary Elizabeth[1] Arbogast), b. Oct 06 1917, d. Aug 21 1969.
Married Jan 25 1946, **Lyda McDermott**.

Children:
  990   i.   Schallace Tiffin[8] Calhoun b. Oct 12 1948 in Munich, Germany.

662. **Harold Kay[7] Calhoun** (347.Nellie Mae[6] Mullenax, 162.Solomon Key[5], 50.William Isaac[4], 7.James W.[3], 2.Abraham[2], 1.Mary Elizabeth[1] Arbogast), b. Jan 01 1920, d. Nov 30 1992 in Thornwood, Pocahontas Co., WV.
Married 1961, **Marguerite Rowe Borrow**.

Children:
  991   i.   Carry Evans[8] Calhoun b. Dec 04 1961.

670. **Helen[7] Mullenax** (351.Virgil Craig[6], 162.Solomon Key[5], 50.William Isaac[4], 7.James W.[3], 2.Abraham[2], 1.Mary Elizabeth[1] Arbogast).
She Married **(unknown) Loftice**.

Children:
- 992 i. Brenda⁸ Loftice.
- 993 ii. Brent Loftice.
- 994 iii. Kimberly Loftice.

671. **Bonnie⁷ Mullenax** (351.Virgil Craig⁶, 162.Solomon Key⁵, 50.William Isaac⁴, 7.James W.³, 2.Abraham², 1.Mary Elizabeth¹ Arbogast).
She Married **John Teeple**.
Children:
- 995 i. Bonita⁸ Teeple.
- 996 ii. Harry Teeple.
- 997 iii. Craig Teeple.
- 998 iv. Jennifer Teeple.

672. **Donald C.⁷ Mullenax** (351.Virgil Craig⁶, 162.Solomon Key⁵, 50.William Isaac⁴, 7.James W.³, 2.Abraham², 1.Mary Elizabeth¹ Arbogast).
He Married **Jo Ann Hull Brock**, b. Dec 11 1943.
Children:
- 999 i. Connie⁸ Mullenax.

683. **Debra Elizabeth⁷ Mullenax** (360.Edward Lee⁶, 162.Solomon Key⁵, 50.William Isaac⁴, 7.James W.³, 2.Abraham², 1.Mary Elizabeth¹ Arbogast), b. May 14 1955.D/o Edward Lee and Betty (Brown) Mullenax.
of Mary; see Volume III for her lineage.
Married Oct 10 1976, **Robert Francis Ervine**, b. Sep 20 1953 in Marlinton, Pocahontas Co., WV (son of Dewey Hunter Ervine and Anna Pauline Plyler).
Children:
- 1000 i. Donald Robert⁸ Ervine b. Aug 31 1978.
- 1001 ii. Jason Edward Ervine b. Nov 19 1981.

684. **Grace Marie⁷ Bennett** (362.Oscela Martin⁶, 163.Mary Jane⁵ Mullenax, 51.John Wesley⁴, 7.James W.³, 2.Abraham², 1.Mary Elizabeth¹ Arbogast), b. Dec 1 1909 in Harman, Randolph Co., WV, d. Aug 31 1988 in Phoenix, Jackson Co., AZ, buried Sep 3 1988 in Phoenix, Jackson Co., AZ.
http://homepages.rootsweb.com/~clanboyd/index.htm.
(1) She Married **George Daniel Saum, Sr.**, b. Jul 7 1904 in Elkins, Randolph Co., WV, d. Jun 8 1971 in Cumberland, Alleghany Co., MD. **George**:
http://homepages.rootsweb.com/~clanboyd/index.htm.
Children:
- 1002 i. George Daniel⁸ Saum, Jr. b. Dec 1 1931 in Bemis, Randolph County WV, d. Mar 26 1984 in Cheverly, Prince George Co., MD, buried UNKNOWN in Arlington National Cem., Arlington, VA.

(2) Married Apr 17 1934 in Elkton, Cecil Co., MD, **Joseph Jerome Harris**, b. Jul 25 1906 in Whitmer, Randolph Co., WV, d. Apr 25 1973 in Phoenix, Jackson Co., AZ.

689. **Helen J.⁷ Mullenax** (382.Charles Edward Vivan⁶, 164.Isaac J.⁵, 51.John Wesley⁴, 7.James W.³, 2.Abraham², 1.Mary Elizabeth¹ Arbogast), b. Jul 25 1926.
Married Jun 13 1948 in Later Divorced, **Richard Donald Gasch**.
Children:
- 1003 i. David Noel⁸ Gasch b. Dec 11 1949 in McCook, Red Willow Co., NE.

690. **Grethel Mae⁷ Buckbee** (405.Lena Ester⁶ Mullenax, 169.Martin⁵, 51.John Wesley⁴, 7.James W.³, 2.Abraham², 1.Mary Elizabeth¹ Arbogast), b. Feb 11 1907, d. Aug 08 1990.
Married Jan 17 1925 in Red House, Garrett Co., MD, **John Herbert Kyer**, b. Feb 12 1899 in Webster Co., WV, d. Nov 08 1982 in Weston, Lewis Co., WV.

Children:
+ 1004 i. Helen Grethel⁸ Kyer b. Aug 29 1925.
   1005 ii. Geraldine Marie Kyer b. Aug 09 1927 in Weston, Lewis Co., WV.
+ 1006 iii. Lucille Zenna Kyer.
+ 1007 iv. John Herbert Kyer, Jr. b. Jun 03 1940.

697. **Donald Woodrow⁷ Lambert** (417.Uxter⁶, 186.Soloman K.⁵, 63.Annie Catherine⁴ Calhoun, 12.Elizabeth Ann³ Mullenax, 2.Abraham², 1.Mary Elizabeth¹ Arbogast).
He Married **Marilyn Lee Gum**, b. Dec 28 1935 in Bartow, Pocahontas Co., WV (daughter of Robert Dale Gum and Chessa Lee Ervine), d. Feb 6 1999 in Painesville, Lake Co., OH.

Children:
1008 i. Beth⁸ Lambert.
1009 ii. Lannas Lambert.

704. **Mabel Caroline⁷ Collins** (424.Lillie⁶ Raines, 189.Elizabeth A.⁵ Lambert, 65.Susan⁴ Calhoun, 12.Elizabeth Ann³ Mullenax, 2.Abraham², 1.Mary Elizabeth¹ Arbogast), b. Jul 2 1912 in Hosterman Cem., Back Mountain, Pocahontas Co., WV, d. Oct 5 1952 in Bartow, Pocahontas Co., WV.
D/o Adam and Lillie (Raines) Collins; Mabel is the same person as #15986, a descendant of Mary; see Volume III for her lineage.
She Married **Earl Cranson Wilfong**, b. Jan 26 1908 in Bartow, Pocahontas Co., WV (son of Norman J. Wilfong and Effie Bly Ervine), d. Sep 21 1984 in Washington, D.C., buried in Arbovale Cem., Arbovale, Pocahontas Co., WV. **Earl**: Dates and names of children from obituary.

Children:
1010 i. Gerald Gray⁸ Wilfong b. Aug 10 1929 in Bartow, Pocahontas Co., WV, d. Jun 4 1933 in Bartow, Pocahontas Co., WV.
1011 ii. Patricia Lou Wilfong b. Dec 20 1935 in Bartow, Pocahontas Co., WV, d. Feb 9 1938.
1012 iii. Erlene Wilfong b. Oct. 25 ?.
She Married **Lawrence Brown**.
+ 1013 iv. Linda Carol Wilfong b. Apr 28 1938.
1014 v. Greta Jewell Wilfong b. May 24 ?.
She Married **(unknown) Tuck**.
1015 vi. Deloris Kay Wilfong b. May 27 1943.
(1) She Married **(unknown) Jeans**.
(2) She Married **William Davis**.
1016 vii. Archie Wilfong b. Oct. 25 ? in Bartow, Pocahontas Co., WV.
1017 viii. Robert Cranston Wilfong.
He Married **Eve Hamel**.
1018 ix. Dharl Lane Wilfong b. May 13 ? in Bartow, Pocahontas Co., WV.
He Married **Mary Petra**.
1019 x. Daniel James Wilfong b. May 27 1943 in Bartow, Pocahontas Co., WV.
Married Jul 15 1967 in Durbin, Pocahontas Co., WV, **Barbara Jean Banton**.
+ 1020 xi. Phyllis Jean Wilfong b. Nov 20 1946.

709. **Fannie May⁷ Hinkle** (432.Elbridge L.⁶, 198.William⁵, 68.Phoebe (Susan)⁴ Calhoun, 12.Elizabeth Ann³ Mullenax, 2.Abraham², 1.Mary Elizabeth¹ Arbogast), b. May 27 1877, d. Jan 10 1933.
Married Jun 12 1899 in Highland Co., VA, **Albert Simmons**, b. Feb 09 1872, d. Jul 08 1934, buried in Blue Grass Cem., Highland Co., VA.

Children:
1021 i. Ethel S⁸ Simmons b. Apr 1900.
+ 1022 ii. Ralph Scott Simmons b. Jan 18 1903.
1023 iii. Elbridge H Simmons b. 1904.
1024 iv. Roxie Simmons b. 1906.
1025 v. Roy Simmons b. 1906.
1026 vi. Sylvia H Simmons b. 1912.

711. **Clyde⁷ Rymer** (433.Susan⁶ Hinkle, 198.William⁵, 68.Phoebe (Susan)⁴ Calhoun, 12.Elizabeth Ann³ Mullenax, 2.Abraham², 1.Mary Elizabeth¹ Arbogast), b. Mar 30 1881, d. Mar 22 1956.
He Married **Sallie Cook**, b. Oct 13 1885, d. Dec 11 1970.
   Children:
   1027 i. Mary⁸ Rymer b. 1908.
 + 1028 ii. Virgil Rymer b. Nov 03 1908.

712. **Sudie R⁷ Rymer** (433.Susan⁶ Hinkle, 198.William⁵, 68.Phoebe (Susan)⁴ Calhoun, 12.Elizabeth Ann³ Mullenax, 2.Abraham², 1.Mary Elizabeth¹ Arbogast), b. Feb 12 1886, d. Jun 29 1966.
Married c 1907, **Charlie N Bennett**, b. Sep 24 1885, d. Sep 25 1941.
   Children:
   1029 i. John⁸ Bennett.
   1030 ii. Ada Bennett.

713. **Cleat⁷ Phares** (435.Eliza Ann⁶ Hinkle, 198.William⁵, 68.Phoebe (Susan)⁴ Calhoun, 12.Elizabeth Ann³ Mullenax, 2.Abraham², 1.Mary Elizabeth¹ Arbogast), b. Sep 19 1884, d. May 22 1938.
He Married **Edith C Hammer**, b. May 22 1884, d. Oct 10 1937.

   Children:
 + 1031 i. Elmer P.⁸ Phares b. 1908.
   1032 ii. Myrtle K Phares b. Apr 16 1911, d. Dec 26 1980.
        She Married **Ramsey Teter**, b. Apr 09 1910. Ramsey: Son of Ambrose Teter and Ann Rebecca Warner.

723. **Martha Ann⁷ Hinkle** (437.Isaac Harness⁶, 198.William⁵, 68.Phoebe (Susan)⁴ Calhoun, 12.Elizabeth Ann³ Mullenax, 2.Abraham², 1.Mary Elizabeth¹ Arbogast), b. May 11 1902, d. Oct 12 1992.
She Married **Charles A Warner**.
   Children:
   1033 i. Genevieve⁸ Warner.
   1034 ii. Ann Warner.
   1035 iii. Harold Warner.
   1036 iv. Jack T Warner.
   1037 v. Charles J Warner.
   1038 vi. John Edward Warner.

727. **Ethel⁷ Clark** (443.Blanche Alma⁶ Smith, 201.Sarah Lavina⁵ Simmons, 70.John Wesley⁴, 13.Margaret³ Mullenax, 2.Abraham², 1.Mary Elizabeth¹ Arbogast), b. Feb 24 1907 in Ritchie Co., WV, d. Apr 17 1995 in Port Washington, Tuscarawas Co., OH, buried Apr 20 1995 in Smith Chapel, Center Twp., Morgan Co., OH.
Married Dec 25 1926, **John Russell Freeland I**, b. Oct 1 1903, d. Apr 7 1988 in Florida, buried in Smith Chapel, Center Twp., Morgan Co., OH.
   Children:
   1039 i. John Russell⁸ Freeland II b. Jan 24 1931, d. Aug 14 1998 in Newcomerstown, Tuscarawas Co., OH, buried Aug 18 1998 in Early Cem. Guernsey County OH. Died of a Heart Attack at home. Cremated.

750. **Paul Hunter⁷ Collins** (452.Floyd William⁶, 206.Louella Maer⁵ Grogg, 72.Emily Jane⁴ Mullenax, 16.John H.³, 3.Jacob², 1.Mary Elizabeth¹ Arbogast), b. Dec 9 1915.
He Married **Georgia Goodsell Frazier**.
   Children:
   1040 i. Karyl Lynn⁸ Collins.
   1041 ii. Kaye Adair Collins.

752. **Harold Cecil⁷ Collins** (453.Cecil Morgan⁶, 206.Louella Maer⁵ Grogg, 72.Emily Jane⁴ Mullenax, 16.John H.³, 3.Jacob², 1.Mary Elizabeth¹ Arbogast), b. Aug 13 1916 in Columbus, Franklin Co., OH, d. Jul 8 1986 in Cleveland, Cuyahoga Co., OH.

   He Married **Evalene S Hickman**, b. 1920 in Big Springs, Meigs Co., TN.
   ### *Children:*
   + 1042   i.   Lowell Jene⁸ Collins b. Aug 09 1939.
   + 1043   ii. Atlos Martin Collins b. Oct 25 1942.

754. **Bernard Morris⁷ Collins** (453.Cecil Morgan⁶, 206.Louella Maer⁵ Grogg, 72.Emily Jane⁴ Mullenax, 16.John H.³, 3.Jacob², 1.Mary Elizabeth¹ Arbogast), b. Jan 30 1920 in Bartow, Pocahontas Co., WV, d. Sep 28 2002 in Northfield, Franklin Co., MA.
   He Married **Mildred Lee Varner**, b. 1924, d. Sep 28 1983 in Arbovale Cem., Arbovale, Pocahontas Co., WV.
   ### *Children:*
   + 1044   i.   Carol Lee⁸ Collins.
   + 1045   ii. Rebecca Jeanne Collins.

761. **Bricel⁷ Waybright** (466.Bert⁶, 209.Albert⁵, 74.Martha⁴ Mullenax, 17.George³, 3.Jacob², 1.Mary Elizabeth¹ Arbogast), b. Dec 13 1911 in Whitmer, Randolph Co., WV, d. Nov 12 1966 in Elkins, Randolph Co., WV.
   He Married **Dollie Vorden Fansler**, b. 1916, d. 1971.
   ### *Children:*
   1046   i.   Thomas L.⁸ Waybright d. 1991.
                He Married **Marla (Unknown)**.
   1047   ii. Bricel Roy Waybright.
   1048   iii. Retha Waybright.
                (1) She Married **Neal Smith**.
                (2) She Married **Roy Ware** (son of Jacob G. Ware and Sarah M Hamrick).
   1049   iv. Richard L. Waybright b. Jun 6 1933, d. Aug 1987 in Dundalk Baltimore Co., MD.
   1050   v.   Billy Keith Waybright b. Jun 30 1935, d. Mar 1980.
   1051   vi. Kenneth Gene Waybright b. Mar 4 1937 in Elkins, Randolph Co., WV, d. Oct 11 1993 in Las Vegas, Clark Co., NV.

763. **Margaret Ann⁷ Kerr** (490.Mary⁶ Waybright, 227.Thaddeus⁵, 84.Mary Margaret⁴, 24.Christina³ Mullenax, 5.William², 1.Mary Elizabeth¹ Arbogast), b. Jan 6 1949.
   She Married **Robert Nicholas Beckwith**, b. Dec 12 1945 in Morristown, Morris Co., NJ (son of Walton Beckwith and Olga Markom). **Robert**: Ref: Randolph 1991: 33; information from Robert S/o Walton and Olga (Markom) Beckwith.
   ### *Children:*
   1052   i.   Beth Ann⁸ Beckwith b. Oct 3 1969.
   1053   ii. Tracy Lynn Beckwith b. Nov 23 1971.

765. **Kathryn Mae⁷ Gatto** (503.Margie⁶ Kisamore, 237.Perlie⁵ Arbogast, 88.Cordelia⁴ Waybright, 24.Christina³ Mullenax, 5.William², 1.Mary Elizabeth¹ Arbogast), b. Mar 16 1939 in Tucker Co., WV.
   Married Feb 14 1959 in Washington, D.C., **Dwight Gorden Hoppes**.
   ### *Children:*
   1054   i.   Dwayne Allen⁸ Hoppes b. Aug 31 1960 in Wichita, Sedgwick Co., KS.
                Married Oct 25 1987, **Janet Shepler**.

771. **Diana Marie⁷ Kisamore** (506.Glen⁶, 237.Perlie⁵ Arbogast, 88.Cordelia⁴ Waybright, 24.Christina³ Mullenax, 5.William², 1.Mary Elizabeth¹ Arbogast), b. Aug 27 1954 in Baltimore, Baltimore Co., MD.
   Married 1972, **David Personeus**.

Children:
1055 i. Mary Alicia[8] Personeus b. Sep 06 1972.
1056 ii. Melissa Personeus b. Jan 31 1981.

772. **Olive Pearl[7] Kisamore** (508.Guy[6], 237.Perlie[5] Arbogast, 88.Cordelia[4] Waybright, 24.Christina[3] Mullenax, 5.William[2], 1.Mary Elizabeth[1] Arbogast), b. Jul 26 1954 in Tucker Co., WV. Married in Baltimore, Baltimore Co., MD, **Henry Ross**.
   Children:
   1057 i. Henry[8] Ross, Jr. b. Mar 15 1973.
   1058 ii. Selena Ross b. Jul 26 1975 in Baltimore, Baltimore Co., MD.
   1059 iii. Christopher Guy Ross b. Dec 30 1977 in Baltimore, Baltimore Co., MD.

774. **David Lee[7] Arbogast** (512.Samual Henry[6], 238.Wilbur[5], 88.Cordelia[4] Waybright, 24.Christina[3] Mullenax, 5.William[2], 1.Mary Elizabeth[1] Arbogast), b. Feb 14 1948 in Waynesburg, Greene Co., PA. He Married **Linda Cummings**, b. Jul 11 1950.
   Children:
   + 1060 i. Quinten[8] Arbogast b. Aug 21 1970.
   1061 ii. Duane Arbogast b. Jul 1973.

777. **Linda[7] Arbogast** (512.Samual Henry[6], 238.Wilbur[5], 88.Cordelia[4] Waybright, 24.Christina[3] Mullenax, 5.William[2], 1.Mary Elizabeth[1] Arbogast), b. Jul 06 1952 in Waynesburg, Greene Co., PA. She Married **Donnie Ray Higgins**, b. Aug 08 1947.
   Children:
   1062 i. Brandy[8] Huggins b. Feb 14 1980.
   1063 ii. Heather Higgins b. Dec 24 1982.
   1064 iii. Samuel Raymond Higgins b. Feb 16 1990.

778. **Donald[7] Arbogast** (512.Samual Henry[6], 238.Wilbur[5], 88.Cordelia[4] Waybright, 24.Christina[3] Mullenax, 5.William[2], 1.Mary Elizabeth[1] Arbogast), b. May 05 1958. Married Apr 17 1982, **Kathy Dean**, b. Oct 18 1961.
   Children:
   1065 i. Nichol[8] Arbogast b. Sep 25 1982.
   1066 ii. Travis Arbogast b. Jan 23 1984.

780. **Connie Sue[7] Arbogast** (512.Samual Henry[6], 238.Wilbur[5], 88.Cordelia[4] Waybright, 24.Christina[3] Mullenax, 5.William[2], 1.Mary Elizabeth[1] Arbogast), b. Mar 16 1961 in Waynesburg, Greene Co., PA. She Married **Kenneth Frost**, b. Apr 07 1952.
   Children:
   1067 i. Joshua[8] Frost b. Feb 27 1982.
   1068 ii. Jeff Frost b. Apr 01 1983.
   1069 iii. Jonathan Frost b. May 20 1986.

781. **Larry Francis[7] Conrad** (513.Lovie May[6] Arbogast, 238.Wilbur[5], 88.Cordelia[4] Waybright, 24.Christina[3] Mullenax, 5.William[2], 1.Mary Elizabeth[1] Arbogast), b. May 13 1949 in Waynesburg, Greene Co., PA. Married Dec 30 1972, **Nadine Polize**.
   Children:
   1070 i. Nichole[8] Conrad b. 1972, d. Mar 11 1973.
   1071 ii. Heidi Conrad b. Jun 02 1975 in Morgantown, Monongalia Co., WV.
   1072 iii. Larry Francis Conrad b. Mar 03 1979 in Morgantown, Monongalia Co., WV.

782. **Randy[7] Conrad** (513.Lovie May[6] Arbogast, 238.Wilbur[5], 88.Cordelia[4] Waybright, 24.Christina[3] Mullenax, 5.William[2], 1.Mary Elizabeth[1] Arbogast), b. Jul 25 1954.

He <u>Married</u> **Debra White**.
Children:
- 1073 i.   Darla Renna[8] Conrad b. Aug 18 1975 in Waynesburg, Greene Co., PA.
- 1074 ii. Christie Lynn Conrad b. Sep 20 1976 in Waynesburg, Greene Co., PA.
- 1075 iii. Robert Lee Conrad b. in Waynesburg, Greene Co., PA.

783. **Patricia Ann[7] Conrad** (513.Lovie May[6] Arbogast, 238.Wilbur[5], 88.Cordelia[4] Waybright, 24.Christina[3] Mullenax, 5.William[2], 1.Mary Elizabeth[1] Arbogast), b. Oct 31 1955.
She <u>Married</u> **Gary Sappington**, b. Dec 31 1929 in Garards Fort, Greene Co., PA.
Children:
- 1076 i. Angela Mae[8] Conrad b. Nov 03 1982 in Morgantown, Monongalia Co., WV.
- 1077 ii. Justin Lloyd Conrad b. Feb 18 1986 in Morgantown, Monongalia Co., WV.

784. **Debra[7] Conrad** (513.Lovie May[6] Arbogast, 238.Wilbur[5], 88.Cordelia[4] Waybright, 24.Christina[3] Mullenax, 5.William[2], 1.Mary Elizabeth[1] Arbogast), b. Oct 08 1957. Debra had two other children Glen E. Miller b 11-21-1978, at Uniontown, PA and Nichole Catherine Miller, b 1-11-1979 in Uniontown, PA. She also <u>Married</u> **Lane Harbarger**.
She <u>Married</u> **Billy King**, b. in Morgantown, Monongalia Co., WV.
Children:
- 1078 i. William Authur[8] King b. Jan 03 1975 in Morgantown, Monongalia Co., WV.

785. **Jerry[7] Conrad** (513.Lovie May[6] Arbogast, 238.Wilbur[5], 88.Cordelia[4] Waybright, 24.Christina[3] Mullenax, 5.William[2], 1.Mary Elizabeth[1] Arbogast), b. Mar 08 1961 in Waynesburg, Greene Co., PA.
He <u>Married</u> **Debbie Stewart**.
Children:
- 1079 i. Jerry Lee[8] Conrad b. Dec 01 1982.
- 1080 ii. Jonathan Conrad b. Oct 08 1985.

789. **Roger Lee[7] Arbogast** (514.Wilbur Junior[6], 238.Wilbur[5], 88.Cordelia[4] Waybright, 24.Christina[3] Mullenax, 5.William[2], 1.Mary Elizabeth[1] Arbogast), b. Jan 04 1960 in Waynesburg, Greene Co., PA.
(1) He <u>Married</u> **Lisa Murray**.
Children:
- 1081 i. Misty Lea[8] Arbogast b. Mar 10 1982.

(2) He <u>Married</u> **Sherry Murray**.
Children:
- 1082 ii. Narhon Scott Murray b. Jun 30 1988 in Morgantown, Monongalia Co., WV.

797. **William Nevin[7] Waybright** (550.William Nevin[6], 270.Ollie Elizabeth[5] Mullenax, 108.Aaron C.[4], 27.Henry Clay[3], 5.William[2], 1.Mary Elizabeth[1] Arbogast).
He <u>Married</u> **Regina Cassell**.
Children:
- 1083 i. Nevette Lagina[8] Waybright b. Jun 26 1972.
- 1084 ii. Javan Seth Waybright b. Jun 2 1977.

801. **George Samuel[7] Waybright Jr.** (552.George Samual[6], 270.Ollie Elizabeth[5] Mullenax, 108.Aaron C.[4], 27.Henry Clay[3], 5.William[2], 1.Mary Elizabeth[1] Arbogast), b. Feb 3 1957 in Marlinton, Pocahontas Co., WV, d. Jan 1 1992.
He <u>Married</u> **Vickie Lynn McCarty**.
Children:
- 1085 i. Kagun Eugene[8] Waybright.

802. **Penelope Kaye**^{7} **Varner** (553.Dollie Elizabeth^6 Waybright, 270.Ollie Elizabeth^5 Mullenax, 108.Aaron C.^{4}, 27.Henry Clay^3, 5.William^2, 1.Mary Elizabeth^1 Arbogast), b. May 26 1962.

      Children:
    1086 i.   Autumn Grace^8 Hunter b. Nov 14 1979, d. Dec 4 1991.

806. **Lester Lou**^{7} **Townsend** (560.Hazel Marie^6 Mulnanx, 289.James Lewis^5 Mulanax, 124.William Dallas^4, 33.Miles Elliott^3, 6.Joseph^2, 1.Mary Elizabeth^1 Arbogast), b. Sep 09 1927.
Married Aug 07 1948, **Peggy Redro**, b. Sep 04 1928 in Junction City, Geary Co., KS.

      Children:
    1087 i.   Lester John^8 Townsend b. Nov 24 1949 in Manhattan, Riley Co., KS.
+ 1088 ii.   Louis Scott Townsend b. Sep 07 1953.
+ 1089 iii. Harry Steve Townsend b. Nov 11 1958.
+ 1090 iv. Kevin Lee Townsend b. Nov 03 1959.

807. **Roger Lewis**^{7} **Mulanax** (563.Alvin Edgar^6 Mulnanx, 289.James Lewis^5 Mulanax, 124.William Dallas^4, 33.Miles Elliott^3, 6.Joseph^2, 1.Mary Elizabeth^1 Arbogast), b. Jul 15 1945 in Hot Springs, Garland Co., AR.
Married Jun 01 1970 in Manhattan, Riley Co., KS, **Joann Lefeber**, b. Nov 02 1947 in Chicago, Cook Co., IL (daughter of John Lefeber and Hazel Ann Sterrett).

      Children:
    1091 i.   Douglas Lefeber^8 Mulanax b. Jun 03 1972 in Youngstown, Mahoning Co., OH.

810. **Jane Earline**^{7} **Nelson** (568.Maggie May^6 Blaikie, 293.Flora Adeline^5 Mulanax, 125.John Greenbury^4, 33.Miles Elliott^3, 6.Joseph^2, 1.Mary Elizabeth^1 Arbogast), b. Dec 20 1927 in Pond Creek, Grant Co., OK.
Married Jun 14 1947 in Mena, Polk Co., AR, **William Jackson Barnes**, b. Sep 02 1927 in Mena, Polk Co., AR (son of Harvey L. Barnes and Gertrude Kellar).

      Children:
+ 1092 i.   Beverly Sue^8 Barnes b. Jun 30 1948.
+ 1093 ii.   Joane Sue Barnes b. Dec 15 1950.
+ 1094 iii. Betty Lovella Barnes b. Oct 05 1952.
    1095 iv. William Jack Barnes b. Sep 05 1954.
              (1) Married Jun 01 1974 in Mena, Polk Co., AR, **Barbara Bell.**
              (2) He Married **Scheryl Campbell`**.

812. **Francis Billey**^{7} **Franklin** (574.Bessie Lee^6 Osburn, 301.Mary Aceneth^5 Mulanax, 127.Matthew Elliott^4, 35.William R.^{3}, 6.Joseph^2, 1.Mary Elizabeth^1 Arbogast), b. Jun 23 1925 in Twin Falls Co., ID.
Married Apr 23 1950 in Springfield, Greene Co., MO, **Eunice Marie Loony**, b. Apr 23 1932 in Halfway, Polk Co., MO.

      Children:
+ 1096 i.   Randy Gale^8 Franklin b. Jun 26 1951.
    1097 ii.   Ronald Dale Franklin b. Dec 18 1952 in Springfield, Greene Co., MO.
              He Married **Mary Jane Edwards**, b. Aug 12 1960.
+ 1098 iii. Cheryl Lynn Franklin b. Aug 07 1954.

813. **Vernon Newton**^{7} **Franklin** (574.Bessie Lee^6 Osburn, 301.Mary Aceneth^5 Mulanax, 127.Matthew Elliott^4, 35.William R.^{3}, 6.Joseph^2, 1.Mary Elizabeth^1 Arbogast), b. Feb 27 1927 in Denver, Denver Co., CO.
Married Apr 10 1948 in Buffalo, Dallas Co., MO, **Ailene Oleta Cansler**, b. Sep 09 1931 in Halfway, Polk Co., MO.

      Children:
+ 1099 i.   Ricky Michael^8 Franklin b. Aug 16 1950.
+ 1100 ii.   Brent Mitchell Franklin b. Dec 31 1952.

+ 1101 iii. Kevin Kyle Franklin b. Mar 19 1958.
  1102 iv. Darren Vern Franklin b. Mar 08 1965 in Pekin, Tazewell Co., IL.

814. **Wayne Russell**[7] **Franklin** (574.Bessie Lee[6] Osburn, 301.Mary Aceneth[5] Mulanax, 127.Matthew Elliott[4], 35.William R.[3], 6.Joseph[2], 1.Mary Elizabeth[1] Arbogast), b. Oct 12 1928.
He Married **Lois Ann Jones**, b. Jan 01 1935 in Ontario, Vernon Co., WI.
Children:
+ 1103 i. Galen Wayne[8] Franklin b. May 01 1952.
  1104 ii. Gary Lee Franklin b. Jul 28 1954 in Eugene, Lane Co., OR.
        Married Sep 21 1985 in Eugene, Lane Co., OR, **Debbie Faye Keefe**, b. May 05 1955 in Eugene, Lane Co., OR.
+ 1105 iii. Terry Lynn Franklin b. Oct 12 1955.

815. **Maty Ann**[7] **Franklin** (574.Bessie Lee[6] Osburn, 301.Mary Aceneth[5] Mulanax, 127.Matthew Elliott[4], 35.William R.[3], 6.Joseph[2], 1.Mary Elizabeth[1] Arbogast), b. Jul 10 1930 in Buffalo, Dallas Co., MO.
Married Aug 24 1950 in Reno, Washoe Co., NV, **Earl Claude Bruce**, b. Aug 06 1928.
Children:
+ 1106 i. Shirley Ann[8] Bruce b. Mar 04 1941.
+ 1107 ii. Janell Kay Bruce b. Nov 20 1953.
+ 1108 iii. Liessa Gay Bruce b. Aug 15 1961.

816. **Gladys Faye**[7] **Franklin** (574.Bessie Lee[6] Osburn, 301.Mary Aceneth[5] Mulanax, 127.Matthew Elliott[4], 35.William R.[3], 6.Joseph[2], 1.Mary Elizabeth[1] Arbogast), b. Mar 28 1932 in Long Lane, Dallas Co., MO.
Married May 23 1950 in Reno, Washoe Co., NV, **Harry Wayne Crabtree**, b. Dec 16 1926 in Missouri.
Children:
+ 1109 i. Harry James[8] Crabtree b. Mar 23 1951.
  1110 ii. Sheldon DeWayne Crabtree b. May 18 1952 in Eugene, Lane Co., OR, d. Mar 23 1952 in Eugene, Lane Co., OR.
  1111 iii. Sonya Faye Crabtree b. Aug 28 1953 in Silverton, Marion Co., OR, d. Apr 01 1956 in Eugene, Lane Co., OR.
  1112 iv. Larry Dean Crabtree b. Mar 12 1955 near Silverton, Marion Co., OR.
        Married Sep 14 1971 in Reno, Washoe Co., NV, **Carolyn Kay Bunch**, b. Dec 06 1958.

817. **Lois Ruth**[7] **Franklin** (574.Bessie Lee[6] Osburn, 301.Mary Aceneth[5] Mulanax, 127.Matthew Elliott[4], 35.William R.[3], 6.Joseph[2], 1.Mary Elizabeth[1] Arbogast), b. Mar 06 1934 in Long Lane, Dallas Co., MO.
Married Jun 06 1934 in Springfield, Lane Co., OR, **Gilman Joseph Fennimore**, b. Mar 24 1932 in Silverton, Marion Co.

Children:
+ 1113 i. Charmaine Marie[8] Fennimore b. Jul 15 1957.
+ 1114 ii. Gilman Joseph Fennimore, Jr. b. Jul 23 1958.
+ 1115 iii. Cassandra Lou Fennimore b. Aug 21 1960.

818. **Betty Jean**[7] **Franklin** (574.Bessie Lee[6] Osburn, 301.Mary Aceneth[5] Mulanax, 127.Matthew Elliott[4], 35.William R.[3], 6.Joseph[2], 1.Mary Elizabeth[1] Arbogast), b. Nov 10 1935.
Married Nov 11 1961 in Reno, Washoe Co., NV, **Vernon George Hoag**, b. Sep 25 1935 in Dixon, Logan Co., ND.
Children:
+ 1116 i. Teresa Jean[8] Hoag b. Jun 08 1957.
  1117 ii. Valerie Lea Hoag b. Jun 23 1962 in Eugene, Lane Co., OR.
  1118 iii. Todd Vernon Hoag b. Jul 19 1963 in Eugene, Lane Co., OR.

819. **Bonnie Jean⁷ Franklin** (574.Bessie Lee⁶ Osburn, 301.Mary Aceneth⁵ Mulanax, 127.Matthew Elliott⁴, 35.William R.³, 6.Joseph², 1.Mary Elizabeth¹ Arbogast), b. Sep 10 1937, d. Jul 06 1989 in Eugene, Lane Co., OR.
Married Jan 30 1955 in Woodburn, Marion Co., OR, **Oscar Larson, Jr.**, b. May 01 1955 in Oshkosh, Winnebago Co., WI.
Children:
+ 1119   i.   Gregory Allen⁸ Larson b. Jul 08 1956.
+ 1120   ii.   Michael Ray Larson b. Feb 02 1958.
   1121   iii.   Kimberly Lee Larson b. Oct 01 1960 in Springfield, Lane Co., OR.

820. **James Lee⁷ Franklin** (574.Bessie Lee⁶ Osburn, 301.Mary Aceneth⁵ Mulanax, 127.Matthew Elliott⁴, 35.William R.³, 6.Joseph², 1.Mary Elizabeth¹ Arbogast), b. Sep 10 1937.
He Married **Tomi Jean Hatfield**, b. Jul 10 1939 in Buckholts, Milam Co., TX.
Children:
   1122   i.   Colleen Ann⁸ Franklin b. Jan 04 1958 in Eugene, Lane Co., OR.
           Married Jul 02 1981 in Eugene, Lane Co., OR, **Bryan Clough**, b. May 19 1959 in Fresno, Fresno Co., CA.
   1123   ii.   John James Franklin b. May 09 1959.
+ 1124   iii.   William Douglas Franklin b. Feb 17 1963.
   1125   iv.   James Paul Franklin b. Oct 26 1968 in Eugene, Lane Co., OR.

821. **John Allen⁷ Franklin** (574.Bessie Lee⁶ Osburn, 301.Mary Aceneth⁵ Mulanax, 127.Matthew Elliott⁴, 35.William R.³, 6.Joseph², 1.Mary Elizabeth¹ Arbogast), b. Apr 09 1939.
Married Jan 16 1960 in Springfield, Lane Co., OR, **Malba May Sizemore**, b. Dec 31 1942.
Children:
+ 1126   i.   Brandel Allen⁸ Franklin b. Aug 16 1960.
   1127   ii.   Mark Lee Franklin b. Sep 26 1962 in Springfield, Lane Co., OR.
   1128   iii.   Angelia Joy Franklin b. May 19 1964 in Springfield, Lane Co., OR.
   1129   iv.   Melissa Robyn Franklin b. Apr 04 1966 in Springfield, Lane Co., OR.
   1130   v.   Robyn Melinda Franklin b. Aug 29 1968 in Springfield, Lane Co., OR.

822. **Alman Ray⁷ Franklin** (574.Bessie Lee⁶ Osburn, 301.Mary Aceneth⁵ Mulanax, 127.Matthew Elliott⁴, 35.William R.³, 6.Joseph², 1.Mary Elizabeth¹ Arbogast), b. Sep 05 1941.
Married Jul 03 1962 in Springfield, Lane Co., OR, **Shirley Dawn Nelson**, b. Nov 21 1942 in Chicago, Cook Co., I
Children:
+ 1131   i.   Tony Ray⁸ Franklin b. Sep 14 1963.
   1132   ii.   Wendy Lee Franklin b. May 05 1968.

823. **Ethel Fern⁷ Osburn** (575.Charley Calvin⁶, 301.Mary Aceneth⁵ Mulanax, 127.Matthew Elliott⁴, 35.William R.³, 6.Joseph², 1.Mary Elizabeth¹ Arbogast), b. Aug 24 1932 in Boise, Ada Co., ID.
Married Jun 19 1950 in Winnemucca, Humboldt Co., NV, **Charles Isadore Arnold, Jr.**, b. Jul 03 1928 in Azalea, Green Co., IA (son of Charles Isadore Arnold and Pearl Mable Berry).
Children:
+ 1133   i.   Donald Gene⁸ Arnold b. Jan 14 1951.
+ 1134   ii.   Shelly Lynn Arnold b. Jun 23 1956.

825. **Billie Lorreen⁷ Osburn** (575.Charley Calvin⁶, 301.Mary Aceneth⁵ Mulanax, 127.Matthew Elliott⁴, 35.William R.³, 6.Joseph², 1.Mary Elizabeth¹ Arbogast), b. May -2 1936 in Payette, Payette Co., ID.
Married Apr 04 1959 in Bellingham, Whatcom Co., WA, **Keith Duane Fagerberg**, b. May 05 1934 in Kirtland, King Co., WA (son of Theodore Fagerburd and Edna Lura Bluch).
Children:
+ 1135   i.   Juanita Raquelle⁸ Fagerburg b. Jan 10 1960.
+ 1136   ii.   Martin Kerry Fagerburg b. Jan 06 1961.

826. **Kathryn Machiel⁷ Osburn** (575.Charley Calvin⁶, 301.Mary Aceneth⁵ Mulanax, 127.Matthew Elliott⁴, 35.William R.³, 6.Joseph², 1.Mary Elizabeth¹ Arbogast), b. Mar 22 1939 in Payette, Payette Co., ID.
She Married **Harold Glen Vail**, b. Oct 12 1933 in Sumas, Whatcom Co., WA (son of Glen Burton Vail and Sadie L. House).

Children:
- 1137 i. Charles Anthony⁸ Vail b. Apr 24 1959 in Bellingham, Whatcom Co., WA.
  He Married **Paula Huffine**, b. May 12 1960 in Wichita, Sedgwick Co., KS.
- + 1138 ii. Kimberly Cherise Vail b. Oct 02 1960.

827. **Mary Virginia⁷ Soron** (576.Cleo Faye⁶ Osburn, 301.Mary Aceneth⁵ Mulanax, 127.Matthew Elliott⁴, 35.William R.³, 6.Joseph², 1.Mary Elizabeth¹ Arbogast), b. Aug 10 1929 in Emmett, Gem Co., ID, d. Nov 23 1990 in Spokane, Spokane Co., WA.
She Married **Robert Sullivan**, b. in Butte, Silver Bow Co., MT, buried in Holy Cross Cem., Spokane, WA.

Children:
- 1139 i. Delores Ann⁸ Sullivan.
  Married in Spokane, Spokane Co., WA, **Gene Bonderman**.
- 1140 ii. Faye Elizabeth Sullivan.
  She Married **Scott Ellern**.
- 1141 iii. Dayle Marie Sullivan b. in Spokane, Spokane Co., WA.
  She Married **Randy L. Lewis**.
- 1142 iv. Timothy Albert Sullivan b. in Spokane, Spokane Co., WA.
  Married in Spokane, Spokane Co., WA, **Laurie Bonderman**.
- 1143 v. John Albert Sullivan.
- 1144 vi. Patricia J. Sullivan.
- 1145 vii. Michelle T. Sullivan.
- 1146 viii. Rita J. Sullivan.
- 1147 ix. Robert Patrick Sullivan.
- 1148 x. Todd Tyse Sullivan.

829. **Thomas Christopher⁷ Soran** (576.Cleo Faye⁶ Osburn, 301.Mary Aceneth⁵ Mulanax, 127.Matthew Elliott⁴, 35.William R.³, 6.Joseph², 1.Mary Elizabeth¹ Arbogast), b. Jan 31 1933.
Married Aug 25 1956, **Cscelia Schweiger**.

Children:
- 1149 i. Thomas Christophor⁸ Soran b. in Hoquiam, Grays Harbor Co., WA.
- 1150 ii. Joseph Soran b. in Hoquiam, Grays Harbor Co., WA.
- 1151 iii. Mary Soran.
- 1152 iv. Louise Soran.
- 1153 v. Steve Soran.
- 1154 vi. Tony Soran.
  Married in Tacoma, Pierce Co., WA, **Mary Fitzpatrick**.
- 1155 vii. Christopher Soran.
- 1156 viii. Tim Soran.
- 1157 ix. Joan Soran b. 1968 in Everett, Snohomish Co., WA.

834. **Cordelia⁷ Soran** (576.Cleo Faye⁶ Osburn, 301.Mary Aceneth⁵ Mulanax, 127.Matthew Elliott⁴, 35.William R.³, 6.Joseph², 1.Mary Elizabeth¹ Arbogast), b. Jan 20 1941 in Boise, Ada Co., ID.
(1) Married 1958, **Byron James Hobbs**.
(2) Married Jun 09 1973 in Coeur d'Alene, Kootenai Co., ID, **Paul Charles Kemble**, b. May 30 1937 in Martinez, Contra Costa, CA.

Children:
- 1158 i. Samuel Crispin⁸ Kemble b. Jan 30 1976 in Spokane, Spokane Co., WA, d. Jan 31 1976.

1159 ii. Kyle Crispin Kemble b. Sep 15 1978 in Spokane, Spokane Co., WA.

835. **Stephen Michael**[7] **Soran** (576.Cleo Faye[6] Osburn, 301.Mary Aceneth[5] Mulanax, 127.Matthew Elliott[4], 35.William R.[3], 6.Joseph[2], 1.Mary Elizabeth[1] Arbogast), b. Dec 10 1943 in Denver, Denver Co., CO.
Married Jul 05 1969 in Spokane, Spokane Co., WA, **Roberta Ann Schell**, b. Sep 09 1946 in Spokane, Spokane Co., WA (daughter of Robert Schell and Elsie Baldasty).
Children:
1160 i. Eric[8] Soran b. Oct 01 1980 in Tacoma, Pierce Co., WA.
1161 ii. Elizabeth Jo Beth Soran b. May 06 1985 in Tacoma, Pierce Co., WA.

838. **Patricia Lee**[7] **Osburn** (577.Samual Stephen[6], 301.Mary Aceneth[5] Mulanax, 127.Matthew Elliott[4], 35.William R.[3], 6.Joseph[2], 1.Mary Elizabeth[1] Arbogast), b. Jun 29 1935 in Payette, Payette Co., ID.
She Married **Lawrence Wade Kitchek**, b. 1 Apr 1956 in Eugene, Lane Co., OR.
Children:
1162 i. Vance Wade[8] Kitchek b. 12 Oct 1956 in Eugene, Lane Co., OR.
1163 ii. Kim Bryan Kitchek b. 10 Jan 1958 in Eugene, Lane Co., OR.

839. **Betty Jane**[7] **Osburn** (577.Samual Stephen[6], 301.Mary Aceneth[5] Mulanax, 127.Matthew Elliott[4], 35.William R.[3], 6.Joseph[2], 1.Mary Elizabeth[1] Arbogast), b. Jun 19 1937 in Payette, Payette Co., ID.
Married 2 Jun 1957 in Eugene, Lane Co., OR, **Alvin Delano Schnell**, b. 20 Apr 1937 in Council, Adams Co., ID (son of Walter Schnell and Louise Heinrick).
Children:
+ 1164 i. Leland Gary[8] Schnell b. 7 Apr 1858.
1165 ii. Danise Dawn Schnell b. 1 Jul 1990 in Midvale, Washington Co., ID.
Married 1 Jul 1990 in Midvale, Washington Co., ID, **Ivan Ray Wolfe**, b. 10 Aug 1970 in Ontario, Malheur Co., OR (son of Janes Wolfe and Carol Matthews).
+ 1166 iii. Heather Susan Schnell b. 1 Dec 1966.

840. **Linda Gail**[7] **Osburn** (577.Samual Stephen[6], 301.Mary Aceneth[5] Mulanax, 127.Matthew Elliott[4], 35.William R.[3], 6.Joseph[2], 1.Mary Elizabeth[1] Arbogast), b. Jun 15 1940.
Married 5 May 1962 in Las Vegas, Clark Co., NV, **Robert Pyanowski**.
Children:
1167 i. Douglas Kent[8] Pyanowski b. 26 Nov 1962 in Loma Linda, San Bernardino Co., CA.

841. **John Franklin**[7] **Osburn** (577.Samual Stephen[6], 301.Mary Aceneth[5] Mulanax, 127.Matthew Elliott[4], 35.William R.[3], 6.Joseph[2], 1.Mary Elizabeth[1] Arbogast), b. Aug 31 1943.
Married 23 Nov 1963 in Newport, Washington Co., OH, **Marjorie Bailor**.
Children:
1168 i. Jeffery Todd[8] Osburn b. 21 Nov 1966 in Eugene, Lane Co., OR.

842. **Connie Jean**[7] **Osburn** (577.Samual Stephen[6], 301.Mary Aceneth[5] Mulanax, 127.Matthew Elliott[4], 35.William R.[3], 6.Joseph[2], 1.Mary Elizabeth[1] Arbogast), b. Mar 02 1950.
Married April 1970, **Runen Plates**.
Children:
1169 i. Angeline Alicia[8] Plates b. 26 Oct 1970 in Eugene, Lane Co., OR.
1170 ii. Enoc Ruben Plates b. 5 Jun 1973 in Maryland.

846. **Doris Acentha**[7] **Allen** (579.Mable Marie[6] Osburn, 301.Mary Aceneth[5] Mulanax, 127.Matthew Elliott[4], 35.William R.[3], 6.Joseph[2], 1.Mary Elizabeth[1] Arbogast), b. 22 Feb 1934 at Payette, Payette Co., ID
Married 28 Sep 1952 in Springfield, Lane Co., OR, **Wesley Ray Sisco**, b. 13 Apr 1933 in Soper, Choctaw Co., OK.
Children:

+ 1171 i. Rebecca Rae^8 Sisco b. 17 Oct 1953.
+ 1172 ii. Tanya Mae Sisco b. 17 Oct 1955.
+ 1173 iii. Wesley Ray Sisco, Jr. b. 25 Mar 1959.

847. **Opal Jane**^{7} **Allen** (579.Mable Marie^6 Osburn, 301.Mary Aceneth^5 Mulanax, 127.Matthew Elliott^4, 35.William R.^{3}, 6.Joseph^2, 1.Mary Elizabeth^1 Arbogast), b. 30 May 1935 in Payette, Payette Co., ID, d. 17 Nov 1992 in Eugene, Lane Co., OR.
(1) Married 25 Nov 1954, **Donald Lewis O'Brien**.
Children:
1174 i. Clayton Lewis^8 O'Brien b. Nov 1955 in Roseburg, Douglas Co., OR.
Married 30 Aug 1974, Nancy Jean Hill, b. 31 Mar 1956 in Eugene, Lane Co., OR.

(2) She Married **Francis Merle Wallace**.
Children:
1175 ii. Allen Merle Wallace b. 20 Apr 1965.
1176 iii. Christopher Loy Wallace.

848. **Eunice Marie**^{7} **Fulton** (580.Myrtle May^6 Osburn, 301.Mary Aceneth^5 Mulanax, 127.Matthew Elliott^4, 35.William R.^{3}, 6.Joseph^2, 1.Mary Elizabeth^1 Arbogast), b. 12 May 1932 in Payette, Payette Co., ID.
Married 30 Mar 1951, **David Norman Swafford**, b. 24 Nov 1931 in Wendling, Lane Co., OR.
Children:
1177 i. Debra L.^{8} Swafford b. 21 Jul 1951 in Roseburg, Douglas Co., OR.
1178 ii. Michelle M. Swafford b. 20 Jan 1955.
1179 iii. Jeff N. Swafford b. 4 Feb 1959.
1180 iv. Steve J. Swafford b. 1 Jan 1961.

862. **Sandra**^{7} **Osburn** (583.Theodore Harvey^6, 301.Mary Aceneth^5 Mulanax, 127.Matthew Elliott^4, 35.William R.^{3}, 6.Joseph^2, 1.Mary Elizabeth^1 Arbogast), b. 1 Oct 1941 in Coos Bay, Coos Co., OR.
(1) She Married **Wallace Zielienski**.

(2) She Married **Lawrence Martin**.
Children:
1181 i. John Lawrence^8 Martin b. 1 Aug 1962.
1182 ii. Terry Lila Martin b. 1 Jul 1963.
1183 iii. David Vernon Martin.

(3) She Married **Steve Black**.
Children:
1184 iv. Nathan Milo Black b. 26 Apr 1975.
1185 v. Amy Rachel Black b. 5 Jul 1976.

863. **Laurie Joan**^{7} **Osburn** (583.Theodore Harvey^6, 301.Mary Aceneth^5 Mulanax, 127.Matthew Elliott^4, 35.William R.^{3}, 6.Joseph^2, 1.Mary Elizabeth^1 Arbogast), b. 22 May 1943 in Payette, Payette Co., ID.

She Married **Jerry Loomis**, b. 1 Jul 1966 in Mountain Grove, Ozarks Co., MO.
Children:
1186 i. Brenden Phillips^8 Loomis b. 8 May 1968.
1187 ii. Deborah Kate Lommis b. 1 Mar 1970.

868. **Carlotta Aceneth**^{7} **Compton** (584.Mary Helen Rose^6 Osburn, 301.Mary Aceneth^5 Mulanax, 127.Matthew Elliott^4, 35.William R.^{3}, 6.Joseph^2, 1.Mary Elizabeth^1 Arbogast), b. 13 Sep 1942 in Boise, Ada Co., ID.
(1) She Married **Smith B. Prowell**.

Children:
1188 i. Randy Ray⁸ Prowell b. 5 May 1959 in Roseburg, Douglas Co., OR.
1189 ii. Ronnie Jay Prowell b. 23 Jun 1960 in Roseburg, Douglas Co., OR.
1190 iii. Diane Kay Prowell b. 60 Apr 1966 in Springfield, Lane Co., OR.
He Married **Linda Lydie**.

(2) She Married **Robert Bunnell**.

869. **Jesse William⁷ Compton, Jr.** (584.Mary Helen Rose⁶ Osburn, 301.Mary Aceneth⁵ Mulanax, 127.Matthew Elliott⁴, 35.William R.³, 6.Joseph², 1.Mary Elizabeth¹ Arbogast), b. 1 Oct 1946.
(1) Married 23 Sep 1970, **Myrna Ricken**.

(2) He Married **Carol McCarty**.
Children:
1191 i. Jesse Caleb⁸ Compton b. 31 Dec 1976 in Eugene, Lane Co., OR.
1192 ii. Lacey Celine Compton b. 5 Mar 1979 in Eugene, Lane Co., OR.

(3) He Married **Terry Lynn Langnes**, b. 5 Sep 1952 in San Angelo, Tom Green Co., TX.
Children:
1193 iii. Kelley Corrine Compton b. 6 Mar 1984 in Eugene, Lane Co., OR.

871. **Lyle Anthony⁷ Wheeler** (587.Zella Jane⁶ Osburn, 301.Mary Aceneth⁵ Mulanax, 127.Matthew Elliott⁴, 35.William R.³, 6.Joseph², 1.Mary Elizabeth¹ Arbogast), b. 5 Aug 1957 in Springfield, Lane Co., OR.
He Married **Patricia Conner**, b. 17 Apr 1958.
Children:
1194 i. Shannon Diane⁸ Wheeler b. 15 Feb 1988 in Portland, Multnomah Co., OR.

873. **Clinton Jay⁷ Myrick** (596.Dorothy Ellen⁶ Mulanax, 313.Calvin Silas⁵, 133.John William⁴, 35.William R.³, 6.Joseph², 1.Mary Elizabeth¹ Arbogast), b. 1 Jun 1953.
He Married **Kathleen Marie Forsman**, b. 13 Oct 1954 in Fort Ord, Monterey Co., CA.
Children:
1195 i. Daniel Jay⁸ Myrick b. 26 Feb 1980 in Dover, Kent Co., DE.
1196 ii. David Curtis Myrick b. 9 Jul 1982 in Dover, Kent Co., DE.

874. **Calvin Curtis⁷ Myrick** (596.Dorothy Ellen⁶ Mulanax, 313.Calvin Silas⁵, 133.John William⁴, 35.William R.³, 6.Joseph², 1.Mary Elizabeth¹ Arbogast), b. 4 Feb 1957 in Portland, Multnomah Co., OR.
(1) Married 9 Apr 1977, **Donna A. Hamilton**.

(2) He Married **Vicki Kay Eckert**, b. 9 Sep 1959 in Boulder, Boulder Co., CO.
Children:
1197 i. Marissa Mary⁸ Myrick b. 29 May 1988 in Honolulu, Honolulu Co., HI.

875. **Cynthia Marguerite⁷ Myrick** (596.Dorothy Ellen⁶ Mulanax, 313.Calvin Silas⁵, 133.John William⁴, 35.William R.³, 6.Joseph², 1.Mary Elizabeth¹ Arbogast), b. 9 Apr 1963 in Portland, Multnomah Co., OR.
She Married **Dunan Arthur Howell**, b. 4 Apr 1963 in Hawaii.
Children:
1198 i. Anna Elizabeth⁸ Howell b. 23 May 1985 in Upper Haayford, Oxfordshire, England.
1199 ii. Jamin Arthur Howell b. 10 May 1988 in Milwaukie, Clackamas Co., OR.
1200 iii. Rebecca Estella Howell b. in Milwaukie, Clackamas Co., OR.

Generation Eight

885. **Sterling Lee⁸ Gum** (612.Gertrude Lee⁷ Waybright, 334.Amby Stanton⁶, 153.Mary Permelia Catherine⁵ Mullenax, 50.William Isaac⁴, 7.James W.³, 2.Abraham², 1.Mary Elizabeth¹ Arbogast), b. May 2 1925 in Bartow, Pocahontas Co., WV, d. Jul 27 1972 in Bartow, Pocahontas Co., WV.
He Married **Thelma Delores Slaven**, b. Nov 12 1930 in Pocahontas Co., WV (daughter of Dallas Slaven and Alice Seiler), d. Dec 25 2002 in Martinsburg, Berkeley Co., WV.
   ### Children:
   - 1201 i. Donna Lee⁹ Gum b. Apr 10 1954 in Marlinton, Pocahontas Co., WV.
     She Married **(unknown) Means**.
   - 1202 ii. Sandra Gum.
     She Married **(unknown) Mullin**.
   - 1203 iii. Beverly Ann Gum b. o5241956 in Marlinton, Pocahontas Co., WV.
   - 1204 iv. Pamela Marie Gum b. Mar 29 1957 in Bartow, Pocahontas Co., WV.
     She Married **(unknown) Butts**.
   - 1205 v. David Sterling Gum b. Apr 15 1959 in Bartow, Pocahontas Co., WV.
   - 1206 vi. Jacqueline Jean Gum b. Mar 8 1961 in Marlinton, Pocahontas Co., WV.
     She Married
   - 1207 vii. Patricia Jo Gum b. Dec 17 1965 in Marlinton, Pocahontas Co., WV.
     She Married **(unknown) Offutt**.
   - 1208 viii. Tamara Gum.

886. **Rev. James Bert⁸ Arbogast** (613.Rella K⁷ Waybright, 334.Amby Stanton⁶, 153.Mary Permelia Catherine⁵ Mullenax, 50.William Isaac⁴, 7.James W.³, 2.Abraham², 1.Mary Elizabeth¹ Arbogast), b. Aug 11 1927.
Ref: Names of wife and children given by Jim and Rita Wooddell 1994.
He Married **Rheba Hoffman**, b. Dec 11 1929 (daughter of Brown Hoffman and Mary Ann Stalnaker). Rheba: Ref: Stalnaker 259.
   ### Children:
   - + 1209 i. Sue Ellen⁹ Arbogast.
   - + 1210 ii. Sherry Lynn Arbogast.

897. **Bobby MCarthur⁸ Wimer** (616.Bertie Catherine⁷ Warner, 336.Fransina Lee⁶ Waybright, 153.Mary Permelia Catherine⁵ Mullenax, 50.William Isaac⁴, 7.James W.³, 2.Abraham², 1.Mary Elizabeth¹ Arbogast), b. May-10-1942 in Hunting Ground, Pendleton Co. WV.
He Married **Patricia Vandevander** (daughter of Arlie Vandevander and Mary Harper).
   ### Children:
   - 1211 i. Timothy Allen⁹ Wimer b. Feb-19-1967, d. Jul-22-1985 in auto acc., Circleville, WV.

898. **Mary Leta⁸ Johnson** (621.Cletis⁷ Johnston, 337.Dolly⁶ Mullenax, 155.Elijah⁵, 50.William Isaac⁴, 7.James W.³, 2.Abraham², 1.Mary Elizabeth¹ Arbogast).
She Married **James Morgan Rexrode** (son of Cecil Clark Rexrode and Jessie Wilfong).
   ### Children:
   - 1212 i. Theresa Iola⁹ Rexrode.
     She Married **Richard Creed**, b. Jun 19 1992 in Bozeman, Gallatin Co., MT.
   - 1213 ii. Kim Rexrode.

899. **Buford C⁸ Johnston** (621.Cletis⁷, 337.Dolly⁶ Mullenax, 155.Elijah⁵, 50.William Isaac⁴, 7.James W.³, 2.Abraham², 1.Mary Elizabeth¹ Arbogast).
He Married **Patrice Sponaugle** (daughter of Herbert Charles Sponaugle and Sally Nola "Sallie" Sponaugle).
   ### Children:
   - 1214 i. Mary Ann⁹ Johnston.
     She Married **William Vandevender**.

1215 ii. Janet L Johnston.
She Married **Danny Vandevender**.
1216 iii. Ricky Johnston b. 1960.
1217 iv. Dotty Johnston b. 1964.

905. **Mildred Mary**[8] **Warner** (631.Verlie[7], 338.Lura[6] Mullenax, 155.Elijah[5], 50.William Isaac[4], 7.James W.[3], 2.Abraham[2], 1.Mary Elizabeth[1] Arbogast), b. Sep 1928 in Hunting Ground, Pendleton Co., (W)VA.
She Married **Warden Guy Hartman**, b. Jan-11-1922 (son of Elemuel Ake Hartman and Mona Wimer), buried in Cedar Hill Cem., Pendleton Co., WV, d. Sep-30-1968.
   Children:
   1218 i. Dorothy Louise[9] Hartman.
   She Married **Jimmy Stewart**.
+ 1219 ii. Steven Guy Hartman.

922. **Harold Michael**[8] **Sponaugle** (634.Judith[7] Warner, 338.Lura[6] Mullenax, 155.Elijah[5], 50.William Isaac[4], 7.James W.[3], 2.Abraham[2], 1.Mary Elizabeth[1] Arbogast), b. May-18-1936.
(1) He Married **Peter Hebert**.

(2) Married Dec-31-1956 in Oakland, Garrett Co., MD, **Patricia Louvon Judy**, b. Apr-15-1937 in Smith Creek, Pendleton Co., WV (daughter of Early Thomas Judy and Monna Roxie Sponaugle).
   Children:
   1220 i. Tamara Jo[9] Sponaugle b. Sep-11-1970 in Cleveland, Cuyahoga Co., OH.

923. **Carolyn Jean**[8] **Mullenax** (636.Brooks Burdette[7], 339.Mcclelland[6], 155.Elijah[5], 50.William Isaac[4], 7.James W.[3], 2.Abraham[2], 1.Mary Elizabeth[1] Arbogast), b. Nov 9 1952 in Fuerth, Germany.
(1) She Married **Andrew Smith**.
(2) She Married **John Hair II**.
   Children:
   1221 i. A. Forbes[9] Hair.

925. **David Lee**[8] **Mullenax** (637.Harlan[7], 340.Martha Ellen[6], 155.Elijah[5], 50.William Isaac[4], 7.James W.[3], 2.Abraham[2], 1.Mary Elizabeth[1] Arbogast), b. May 24 1949.
He Married **Juanita Mallow**.
   Children:
   1222 i. Brenda Lyn[9] Mullenax.
   1223 ii. Lonnie Lee Mullenax.

933. **Ralph Gerald**[8] **Hise II** (642.Lena Virginia[7] Halterman, 342.Joseph Clark[6], 156.Annie Jane[5] Mullenax, 50.William Isaac[4], 7.James W.[3], 2.Abraham[2], 1.Mary Elizabeth[1] Arbogast), b. Oct 1 1946.
(1) Married Nov 27 1974, **Mary Frances Smith**.

(2) He Married **Mary Francis Smith** (daughter of George Smith and Norma Judy).
   Children:
   1224 i. Laure[9] Hise.
   1225 ii. Luke Hise.
   1226 iii. Lee Hise.
   1227 iv. Benjamin Jeremiah Hise.

934. **Mary Frances**[8] **Sheets** (646.Fairy Dare[7] Halterman, 342.Joseph Clark[6], 156.Annie Jane[5] Mullenax, 50.William Isaac[4], 7.James W.[3], 2.Abraham[2], 1.Mary Elizabeth[1] Arbogast), b. Jan 4 1943.
(1) Married Feb 26 1961, **Larry Addison Staton**, b. Jul 13 1935, d. Jul 4 1982.
   Children:
   1228 i. Max Addison[9] Staton b. Jul 31 1963.

(2) Married Jun 1 1973, **George William Dillon**.
Children:
1229   ii.   Kristi Dare Dillon b. Jun 18 1977.

935. **Robert Clark[8] Sheets** (646.Fairy Dare[7] Halterman, 342.Joseph Clark[6], 156.Annie Jane[5] Mullenax, 50.William Isaac[4], 7.James W.[3], 2.Abraham[2], 1.Mary Elizabeth[1] Arbogast), b. Mar 26 1947.
Married Sep 19 1966, **Karen Kay Wright** (daughter of Grover Wright and Maude Burns).
Children:
1230   i.   Stephen Mark[9] Sheets b. Jul 1 1967.
1231   ii.   Bryan Robert Sheets b. Feb 16 1973.

936. **Roy Wetzel[8] Sheets** (646.Fairy Dare[7] Halterman, 342.Joseph Clark[6], 156.Annie Jane[5] Mullenax, 50.William Isaac[4], 7.James W.[3], 2.Abraham[2], 1.Mary Elizabeth[1] Arbogast), b. Jan 13 1951.
Married Mar 26 1969, **Carolyn Sue Lambert** (daughter of Kenneth Lambert and Carolyn (Unknown)).
Children:
1232   i.   Todd Loran[9] Sheets b. Apr 14 1969.
1233   ii.   William Wetzel Sheets b. Sep 27 1973.

940. **Karen Sue[8] Mullenax** (649.Paul[7], 343.Emory R[6], 157.James B.[5], 50.William Isaac[4], 7.James W.[3], 2.Abraham[2], 1.Mary Elizabeth[1] Arbogast), b. Jun 12 1945.
Married Jun 12 1967, **Gerald Wayne Senger II**.
Children:
1234   i.   Gerald Wayne[9] Senger III b. Jun 2 1971.
1235   ii.   Jonathan Paul Senger b. Apr 12 1975.
1236   iii.   Kara Anna- Marie Senger b. May 15 1977.

941. **Janice Lee[8] Mullenax** (649.Paul[7], 343.Emory R[6], 157.James B.[5], 50.William Isaac[4], 7.James W.[3], 2.Abraham[2], 1.Mary Elizabeth[1] Arbogast), b. Jul 4 1948.
Married Dec 5 1969 in Boyer, Pocahontas Co., WV, **Richard Stanley Carter**.
Children:
+ 1237   i.   Mary Ann[9] Carter b. Nov 21 1976.

943. **Louise Grey[8] Mullenax** (649.Paul[7], 343.Emory R[6], 157.James B.[5], 50.William Isaac[4], 7.James W.[3], 2.Abraham[2], 1.Mary Elizabeth[1] Arbogast), b. Jun 25 1950.
Married Jul 24 1971 in Boyer, Pocahontas Co., WV, **Howard Ellet Shinaberry**, b. Sep 14 1949 in Durbin, Pocahontas Co., WV (son of Henry Shinaberry and Melvina Sheets).
Children:
+ 1238   i.   Ronald[9] Gordon b. Aug 23 1975.
1239   ii.   Brandon Christin Shinaberry.
1240   iii.   Seth Adam Shinaberry b. May 18 1978.
1241   iv.   Joshua Daryl Shinaberry b. Jan 12 1981.

944. **Connie Jean[8] Mullenax** (650.Richard Emory[7], 343.Emory R[6], 157.James B.[5], 50.William Isaac[4], 7.James W.[3], 2.Abraham[2], 1.Mary Elizabeth[1] Arbogast), b. Mar 13 1949 in Ohio Co., WV.
D/o Richard Emery and Crystal Belle (Wooddell) Mullenax.
Married Oct 16 1965 in Highland Co., VA, **James Edward Cassell**, b. May 10 1948 in Marlinton, Pocahontas Co., WV (son of Edward Clarence Cassell and Irene May Arbogast).
Children:
+ 1242   i.   James Richard[9] Cassell b. Aug 19 1967.
+ 1243   ii.   Crissy Jo Cassell b. Nov 14 1969.

945. **Sonya[8] Mullenax** (650.Richard Emory[7], 343.Emory R[6], 157.James B.[5], 50.William Isaac[4], 7.James W.[3], 2.Abraham[2], 1.Mary Elizabeth[1] Arbogast).

She Married **Raymond Hess**.
Children:
+ 1244 i. Lauri Ann[9] Hess.

947. **Kelly Blaine[8] Mullenax** (650.Richard Emory[7], 343.Emory R[6], 157.James B.[5], 50.William Isaac[4], 7.James W.[3], 2.Abraham[2], 1.Mary Elizabeth[1] Arbogast).
(1) Married in Arbovale Cem., Arbovale, Pocahontas Co., WV, **John Allen Wright**, b. Apr 10 1964 in Baltimore, Baltimore Co., MD (son of John Wright), d. Apr 29 2003 in Hanahan, Berkeley Co., SC.
Children:
1245 i. Collin David[9] Wright.

(2) Married Sep 3 1988 in College Park Church of Christ, Winchester, VA, **Michael Allen Sager**.
Children:
1246 ii. Corysager.
1247 iii. Jordan Sager.

948. **Shirley Ann[8] Warner** (651.Gus[7], 344.Sallie Denie[6] Mullenax, 157.James B.[5], 50.William Isaac[4], 7.James W.[3], 2.Abraham[2], 1.Mary Elizabeth[1] Arbogast), b. 12 Nov 1928.
She Married **Edward Louis Crabtree**, b. 17 Jun 1922.
Children:
+ 1248 i. John E.[9] Crabtree b. 9 Jan 1951.
  1249 ii. Ted L. Crabtree b. 5 Jun 1958.
  1250 iii. Edward J. Crabtree b. 9 Sep 1959.

951. **Dewey Hunter[8] Simmons** (652.Georgia[7] Lambert, 344.Sallie Denie[6] Mullenax, 157.James B.[5], 50.William Isaac[4], 7.James W.[3], 2.Abraham[2], 1.Mary Elizabeth[1] Arbogast), b. Feb 19 1922.
He Married **Belva Kline**.
Children:
  1251 i. Edward Lee[9] Simmons.
+ 1252 ii. Lertie Simmons b. Oct 16 1948.
+ 1253 iii. Shirley Marie Simmons b. Apr 3 1950.
+ 1254 iv. Rose Mary Simmons b. Feb 1 1953.
  1255 v. Dewey Hunter Simmons, II b. May 26 1960.
  1256 vi. Gladys Simmons b. Mar 27 1963.
  1257 vii. Larry Simmons b. Oct 6 1965.
  He Married Christine Cody.

952. **Edward Lee[8] Simmons** (652.Georgia[7] Lambert, 344.Sallie Denie[6] Mullenax, 157.James B.[5], 50.William Isaac[4], 7.James W.[3], 2.Abraham[2], 1.Mary Elizabeth[1] Arbogast), b. Jul 5 1925 in Bemis, Randolph County WV, d. Feb 10 1990 in Tampa, Pasco Co., FL.
Married Jan 9 1960, **Kathleen Ruggles**, b. Mar 21 1930.
Children:
  1258 i. Paul[9] Simmons b. May 16 1951.
+ 1259 ii. Barbara Joan Simmons b. Aug 18 1953.
+ 1260 iii. Sondra Simmons b. Dec 6 1955.
+ 1261 iv. Kathleen Marie Simmons b. Dec 24 1958.
+ 1262 v. Judy Simmons b. Oct 26 1960.
+ 1263 vi. Georgie Elizabeth Simmons b. Sep 24 1962.
+ 1264 vii. Kevin Lee Simmons b. May 3 1964.
  1265 viii. James Orie Simmons b. Aug 30 1966.
+ 1266 ix. Charles Blaine Simmons b. Nov 4 1971.

953. **Roy Lester[8] Simmons** (652.Georgia[7] Lambert, 344.Sallie Denie[6] Mullenax, 157.James B.[5], 50.William Isaac[4], 7.James W.[3], 2.Abraham[2], 1.Mary Elizabeth[1] Arbogast), b. Sep 5 1927, d. Aug 12 1992.
He Married **Geraldine Butcher**.
Children:
+ 1267   i.   Bruce Allen[9] Simmons b. Feb 28 1957.
+ 1268   ii.   Roy Lester Simmons b. Jun 23 1958.
+ 1269   iii.   Roxanna Yvonne Simmons b. May 4 1963.

956. **Martha M.[8] Simmons** (652.Georgia[7] Lambert, 344.Sallie Denie[6] Mullenax, 157.James B.[5], 50.William Isaac[4], 7.James W.[3], 2.Abraham[2], 1.Mary Elizabeth[1] Arbogast), b. May 24 1935, d. Aug 7 2002 in Washington, PA.
(1) She Married **Buck Butcher**.
Children:
1270   i.   Shelda[9] Butcher.
       She Married **(unknown) Vandevander**.
1271   ii.   Charlene Butcher.
1272   iii.   Debra Butcher.
1273   iv.   Delores Butcher.
1274   v.   Alva Butcher.
1275   vi.   Randall Butcher.

(2) She Married **Kenneth Williams**.
Children:
1276   vii.   Patricia Russell Williams.
1277   viii.   Trenia Williams.
1278   ix.   Kenneth J. Williams.
1279   x.   Elizabeth Williams.

957. **Clara[8] Simmons** (652.Georgia[7] Lambert, 344.Sallie Denie[6] Mullenax, 157.James B.[5], 50.William Isaac[4], 7.James W.[3], 2.Abraham[2], 1.Mary Elizabeth[1] Arbogast), b. Oct 6 1940, d. Jun 17 1971 in Minnesota.
She Married **Harold Hayse**, b. Apr 15 1940.
Children:
+ 1280   i.   Cheryl Annetta[9] Hayse b. Jan 2 1959.
+ 1281   ii.   Darlene Francis Hayse b. May 25 1960.
1282   iii.   Gragery Allen Hayse b. Aug 15 1964.
       He Married **Boinnie Smith**, b. Jan 27 1964.

958. **Sadie[8] Simmons** (652.Georgia[7] Lambert, 344.Sallie Denie[6] Mullenax, 157.James B.[5], 50.William Isaac[4], 7.James W.[3], 2.Abraham[2], 1.Mary Elizabeth[1] Arbogast), b. Feb 24 1947.
She Married **Wilmouth Lambert**, b. Sep 16 1937.
Children:
+ 1283   i.   Theresa[9] Lambert b. Nov 14 1966.
+ 1284   ii.   Diana F. Lambert b. Oct 17 1967.
+ 1285   iii.   Richard W. Lambert b. May 19 1971.
1286   iv.   Peggy L. Lambert b. Mar 13 1975.
       Married Jul 31 1993, Frank K. Smith, b. Nov 11 1972.

959. **Janet Lee[8] Lambert** (653.Roy D.[7], 344.Sallie Denie[6] Mullenax, 157.James B.[5], 50.William Isaac[4], 7.James W.[3], 2.Abraham[2], 1.Mary Elizabeth[1] Arbogast), b. Nov 17 1939.
(1) She Married **Robert Lee Brown**, b. Oct 9 1930 (son of Warren Brown and Grace Johnson).
Children:
+ 1287   i.   Carolyn Sue[9] Brown b. Feb 16 1957.
+ 1288   ii.   Phyllis Ann Brown b. Jun 4 1958.

+ 1289 iii. Barbara Sue Brown b. May 30 1960.
+ 1290 iv. Roberta Jane Brown b. Apr 9 1961.
   1291 v. Joseph Lynn Brown b. Apr 11 1962, d. Apr 11 1962.
   1292 vi. Robert Lee Brown b. Nov 8 1963.

(2) She Married **Josea Gordilla**, b. Mar 21 1931.

960. **Francis**[8] **Lambert** (653.Roy D.[7], 344.Sallie Denie[6] Mullenax, 157.James B.[5], 50.William Isaac[4], 7.James W.[3], 2.Abraham[2], 1.Mary Elizabeth[1] Arbogast), b. Oct 14 1942.
(1) He Married **(unknown) Howeyshell**.
Children:
+ 1293 i. Brenda Kay[9] Howeyshell b. May 21 1961.

(2) He Married **Earl Turner**, b. Jul 6 1936.
Children:
+ 1294 ii. Lewis Earl Turner b. Mar 9 1965.

961. **Keith Fallen**[8] **Lambert** (653.Roy D.[7], 344.Sallie Denie[6] Mullenax, 157.James B.[5], 50.William Isaac[4], 7.James W.[3], 2.Abraham[2], 1.Mary Elizabeth[1] Arbogast), b. Nov 24 1942.
He Married **Peggy Marie O'Neal**, b. Apr 13 1950.
Children:
+ 1295 i. Jeffery Allen[9] Lambert b. Apr 18 1971.
   1296 ii. Michael David Lambert b. Nov 16 1972.

962. **Joan Dare**[8] **Lambert** (653.Roy D.[7], 344.Sallie Denie[6] Mullenax, 157.James B.[5], 50.William Isaac[4], 7.James W.[3], 2.Abraham[2], 1.Mary Elizabeth[1] Arbogast), b. May 5 1943.
Married May 16 1959 in Elkins, Randolph Co., WV, **Robert Allen Woods**, b. Feb 17 1939 (son of James Woods and Mae Howell).
Children:
+ 1297 i. Robert Allen[9] Woods, II b. May 14 1961.
+ 1298 ii. Robert Lynn Woods b. Aug 21 1963.

964. **Charlotte**[8] **Lambert** (653.Roy D.[7], 344.Sallie Denie[6] Mullenax, 157.James B.[5], 50.William Isaac[4], 7.James W.[3], 2.Abraham[2], 1.Mary Elizabeth[1] Arbogast), b. Feb 12 1950.
(1) He Married **William Edward Deeter**.
Children:
   1299 i. William Edward[9] Deeter, II b. Aug 20 1967.
+ 1300 ii. Sherrie Marie Deeter b. Aug 2 1970.

(2) He Married **Donald Ritchie**.

965. **Donald Curtis**[8] **Lambert** (653.Roy D.[7], 344.Sallie Denie[6] Mullenax, 157.James B.[5], 50.William Isaac[4], 7.James W.[3], 2.Abraham[2], 1.Mary Elizabeth[1] Arbogast), b. May 26 1954.
He Married **Sheryl (Unknown)**.
Children:
   1301 i. Elizabeth[9] Lambert.
   1302 ii. Crystal Lambert.

967. **Earl Russell**[8] **Lambert** (654.Russell[7], 344.Sallie Denie[6] Mullenax, 157.James B.[5], 50.William Isaac[4], 7.James W.[3], 2.Abraham[2], 1.Mary Elizabeth[1] Arbogast), b. Jul 25 1929 in Ohio, d. Feb 23 1998 in North Carolina.

He Married **Pat Ann Warwick**, b. Sep 14 1931 in Ohio.
Children:

1303 i. David Russell⁹ Lambert b. Dec 1 1956.

968. **Kenneth⁸ Lambert** (654.Russell⁷, 344.Sallie Denie⁶ Mullenax, 157.James B.⁵, 50.William Isaac⁴, 7.James W.³, 2.Abraham², 1.Mary Elizabeth¹ Arbogast), b. Jan 25 1938.
(1) He Married **Lee Ann Warwick**, b. May 2 1956.

(2) He Married **Carolyn (Unknown)**, b. Oct 24 1940.
Children:
1304 i. Tony⁹ Lambert b. May 1 1960.
1305 ii. Keith Lambert b. Feb 12 1962.
1306 iii. Kimberly Lambert b. Sep 22 1964.
+ 1307 iv. Carolyn Sue Lambert.
1308 v. Misty Lambert b. Sep 28 1977.

969. **Hilda Josephine⁸ Lambert** (655.Orie Basil⁷, 344.Sallie Denie⁶ Mullenax, 157.James B.⁵, 50.William Isaac⁴, 7.James W.³, 2.Abraham², 1.Mary Elizabeth¹ Arbogast), b. Feb 24 1932 in Monterey, Highland Co., VA.
(1) Married Sep 6 1949 in Oakland, Garrett Co., MD, **Clawson Emerson Sheets, II**, b. Oct 3 1926 in Greenbrier Co., WV (son of Clawson Sheets and Bessie Fogus).
Children:
+ 1309 i. Sandra Jean⁹ Sheets b. Mar 29 1950.
+ 1310 ii. Donna Faye Sheets b. Aug 12 1951.
+ 1311 iii. Larry Allen Sheets b. Dec 6 1952.
+ 1312 iv. Diana Kay Sheets b. Jun 3 1954.
+ 1313 v. Teresa Allen Sheets b. Dec 16 1959.
+ 1314 vi. Thomas Wayne Sheets b. Dec 22 1964.

(2) She Married **William Wilson Brock**, b. Dec 14 1931 in Hightown, Highland Co., VA (son of William Brock and Cornelia Bratton). **William**: S/o William Wilson and Cornelia Fulton (Bratton) Brock.

971. **Gladys Marie⁸ Lambert** (655.Orie Basil⁷, 344.Sallie Denie⁶ Mullenax, 157.James B.⁵, 50.William Isaac⁴, 7.James W.³, 2.Abraham², 1.Mary Elizabeth¹ Arbogast), b. Nov 18 1936 in Boyer, Pocahontas Co., WV, d. Sep 3 1967 in Portsmouth, VA.
Married in Boyer, Pocahontas Co., WV, **Daniel Funkhouser**, b. Feb 24 1934 in Mount Jackson, Shenandoah Co., VA.
Children:
+ 1315 i. Vickie Lynn⁹ Funkhouser b. May 10 1960.
1316 ii. Daniel Curtis Funkhouser.
1317 iii. Douglas Funkhouser b. Aug 3 1967.

972. **Shirley Mae⁸ Lambert** (655.Orie Basil⁷, 344.Sallie Denie⁶ Mullenax, 157.James B.⁵, 50.William Isaac⁴, 7.James W.³, 2.Abraham², 1.Mary Elizabeth¹ Arbogast), b. Mar 12 1938 in Pocahontas Co., WV.
Married 1963, **Dorral Dainwood Roach**, b. Jul 7 1929 in Greenbrier Co., WV (son of James Roach and Gladys Simmons).
Children:
+ 1318 i. Travis Lee⁹ Roach b. Jun 20 1962.
1319 ii. Darrell Dwayne Roach b. Jul 16 1964.
+ 1320 iii. Tina Marie Roach b. Mar 25 1968.
+ 1321 iv. Kathy Lunn Roach b. Feb 7 1970.

+ 1322 v. Beth Ann Roach b. Oct 2 1971.

973. **Doris Ann⁸ Lambert** (655.Orie Basil⁷, 344.Sallie Denie⁶ Mullenax, 157.James B.⁵, 50.William Isaac⁴, 7.James W.³, 2.Abraham², 1.Mary Elizabeth¹ Arbogast), b. Mar 27 1941.
She Married **Richard D. Greathouse**, b. Apr 7 1939 in Arbovale Cem., Arbovale, Pocahontas Co., WV (son of Harper Greathouse and Hazel Bennett), d. Feb 5 1997 in Washington, D.C.
Children:
    1323 i.   Richard⁹ Greathouse, II.

974. **David F.⁸ Varner** (656.Jessie⁷ Lambert, 344.Sallie Denie⁶ Mullenax, 157.James B.⁵, 50.William Isaac⁴, 7.James W.³, 2.Abraham², 1.Mary Elizabeth¹ Arbogast), b. Mar 22 1930.
He Married **Marilyn (Unknown)**.
Children:
    1324 i.   Catherine Elizabeth⁹ Varner.
    1325 ii. James Brafrord Varner.

976. **Ernest McKinley⁸ Arbogast** (657.Rhoda Martha⁷ Lambert, 344.Sallie Denie⁶ Mullenax, 157.James B.⁵, 50.William Isaac⁴, 7.James W.³, 2.Abraham², 1.Mary Elizabeth¹ Arbogast), b. Oct 18 1939 in Cass, Pocahontas Co., WV, d. May 6 1994 in Brooklyn Heights, Cleveland Co., OH.
Married Feb 14 1960 in Cleveland, Cuyahoga Co., OH, **Norma Jean Bohannon**, b. Mar 20 1940 in Marshall Co., KY (daughter of James Bohannon and Novalee Rose).

Children:
+ 1326 i.   Steven Allen⁹ Arbogast b. Jan 27 1961.
+ 1327 ii. James McKinley Arbogast b. Apr 28 1963.
+ 1328 iii. Richard Wayne Arbogast b. Jun 25 1966.

977. **Betty⁸ Lambert** (658.Dewey Judy⁷, 344.Sallie Denie⁶ Mullenax, 157.James B.⁵, 50.William Isaac⁴, 7.James W.³, 2.Abraham², 1.Mary Elizabeth¹ Arbogast), b. Jan 20 1945.
(1) She Married **Lawrence Wilber Starr**, b. Nov 10 1942.

(2) Married Nov 23 1962 in Arbovale Cem., Arbovale, Pocahontas Co., WV, **Orville Swecker**, b. Aug 24 1938 in Randolph Co., WV.
Children:
    1329 i.   Gary Allen⁹ Swecker b. Jun 23 1964.
+ 1330 ii. Melissa Ann Swecker b. Aug 26 1966.
+ 1331 iii. Dennis James Swecker b. Mar 17 1968.

(3) Married Apr 19 1990, **Richard Wallace Allen**, b. Jul 10 1935.

978. **Edward Judy⁸ Lambert** (658.Dewey Judy⁷, 344.Sallie Denie⁶ Mullenax, 157.James B.⁵, 50.William Isaac⁴, 7.James W.³, 2.Abraham², 1.Mary Elizabeth¹ Arbogast), b. Nov 16 1947.
He Married **Jacqueline Matis**, b. Dec 24 1948.
Children:
    1332 i.   Edward Judy⁹ Lambert, II b. Aug 6 1968, d. Feb 22 1969.
    1333 ii. Dawn Marie Lambert b. Nov 1 1970.
              She Married **Robert Carline**.

979. **Roger Lee⁸ Lambert** (658.Dewey Judy⁷, 344.Sallie Denie⁶ Mullenax, 157.James B.⁵, 50.William Isaac⁴, 7.James W.³, 2.Abraham², 1.Mary Elizabeth¹ Arbogast), b. Jul 28 1948.
He Married **Catherine Ethel Timblin**, b. Aug 13 1950.
Children:
    1334 i.   Roger Lee⁹ Lambert, II b. Jul 28 1971.
    1335 ii. Richard David Russell Lambert b. Feb 5 1978.
    1336 iii. Carol Marie Lambert b. Feb 15 1980.

980. **James Eugene⁸ Lambert** (658.Dewey Judy⁷, 344.Sallie Denie⁶ Mullenax, 157.James B.⁵, 50.William Isaac⁴, 7.James W.³, 2.Abraham², 1.Mary Elizabeth¹ Arbogast), b. Jul 3 1951.
(1) He Married **Deborah Kay Praisiner**.
Children:
- 1337 i. Heidi Lynn⁹ Lambert b. Oct 23 1975.
- 1338 ii. Renae Hope Lambert b. Aug 24 1977.

(2) He Married **Carol Lynda Marinba**, b. Oct 30 1951.
Children:
- 1339 iii. Timothy Michael Lambert b. Oct 30 1970.

982. **Larry Dale⁸ Lambert** (658.Dewey Judy⁷, 344.Sallie Denie⁶ Mullenax, 157.James B.⁵, 50.William Isaac⁴, 7.James W.³, 2.Abraham², 1.Mary Elizabeth¹ Arbogast), b. May 19 1955.
(1) He Married **Beverly Sue Bleasdale**.

(2) He Married **Jody Elaine Inserra**, b. Aug 16 1962.
Children:
- 1340 i. Larry Dale⁹ Lambert, II b. May 25 1991.
- 1341 ii. Dewey Judy Lambert b. `.

(3) He Married **(unknown) Labarr**.
Children:
- 1342 iii. Heather Nicole Labarr b. Oct 16 1983.
- 1343 iv. Brandon James Labarr b. May 12 1987.
- 1344 v. Brittney Marie Labarr b. May 2 1988.
- 1345 vi. Brandy Amber Labarr b. Apr 9 1995.

983. **Debra Kay⁸ Lambert** (658.Dewey Judy⁷, 344.Sallie Denie⁶ Mullenax, 157.James B.⁵, 50.William Isaac⁴, 7.James W.³, 2.Abraham², 1.Mary Elizabeth¹ Arbogast), b. Jun 1 1957.
(1) She Married **Kenneth Earl Heister**, b. Aug 31 1948.
Children:
- 1346 i. Kami Leann⁹ Heister b. Mar 12 1981.
- 1347 ii. Lisa Kay Heister b. Jan 29 1987.

(2) She Married **Joseph Arthur Kounovsky**, b. Feb 13 1948.
Children:
- 1348 iii. Jonathon David Kounovsky b. Oct 23 1980.
- 1349 iv. Mary Elizabeth Kounovsky b. Nov 1 1982.
- 1350 v. Katherine Christinne Kounovsky b. Sep 24 1984.

984. **Patty Jean⁸ Lambert** (658.Dewey Judy⁷, 344.Sallie Denie⁶ Mullenax, 157.James B.⁵, 50.William Isaac⁴, 7.James W.³, 2.Abraham², 1.Mary Elizabeth¹ Arbogast), b. Aug 31 1958.
She Married **Thomas Eugene Burns**, b. Apr 5 1958.
Children:
- 1351 i. Christopher Lee⁹ Burns b. Jan 2 1986.
- 1352 ii. Justin Arthur Burns b. Jan 2 1986.

985. **Brenda Lee⁸ Lambert** (658.Dewey Judy⁷, 344.Sallie Denie⁶ Mullenax, 157.James B.⁵, 50.William Isaac⁴, 7.James W.³, 2.Abraham², 1.Mary Elizabeth¹ Arbogast), b. Sep 26 1962.
She Married **Dan Patrick McDonough**, b. Jan 19 1952.
Children:
- 1353 i. Dan Patrick⁹ McDonough, II b. Oct 6 1978.
- 1354 ii. Matthew Dereck McDonough b. Jan 21 1986.
- 1355 iii. Nathan Paul McDonough b. Dec 19 1987.

1356 iv. Joshua Todd McDonough b. Oct 12 1989.

986. **Ralph David**[8] **Waybright** (660.Sherron Virginia[7] Calhoun, 347.Nellie Mae[6] Mullenax, 162.Solomon Key[5], 50.William Isaac[4], 7.James W.[3], 2.Abraham[2], 1.Mary Elizabeth[1] Arbogast), b. Apr 19 1949 in Pocahontas Co., WV.
Married Aug 24 1970 in Bath Co., VA, **Marie Alice Bond**, b. Feb 05 1953 in Mineral Co., NV.
Children:
1357 i. Jeremiah David[9] Waybright b. Jan 20 1977 in Randolph Co., WV.
1358 ii. Andrew Zephaniah Waybright b. Mar 12 1990 in Randolph Co., WV.

987. **Charles Edward**[8] **Bryant** (660.Sherron Virginia[7] Calhoun, 347.Nellie Mae[6] Mullenax, 162.Solomon Key[5], 50.William Isaac[4], 7.James W.[3], 2.Abraham[2], 1.Mary Elizabeth[1] Arbogast), b. Mar 17 1938.
Married c1963 in Pocahontas Co., WV, **Patricia Augusta Browne**, b. Oct 27 1937 in San Diego, San Diego Co., CA.
Children:
+ 1359 i. Collen Marie[9] Bryant b. Aug 24 1960.
1360 ii. Karen Elizabeth Bryant b. Aug 24 1962.
1361 iii. Thomas Edward Bryant b. Dec 19 1965.
+ 1362 iv. Margaret Sharron Bryant b. Nov 19 1967.

988. **Harold McQuain**[8] **Bryant** (660.Sherron Virginia[7] Calhoun, 347.Nellie Mae[6] Mullenax, 162.Solomon Key[5], 50.William Isaac[4], 7.James W.[3], 2.Abraham[2], 1.Mary Elizabeth[1] Arbogast), b. Mar 17 1938.

He Married **Hope Bolton**.
Children:
1363 i. Charles Michael[9] Bryant b. Feb 06 1956.
+ 1364 ii. Dana Lynn Bryant b. Jun 10 1958.

989. **Richard Gale**[8] **Bryant** (660.Sherron Virginia[7] Calhoun, 347.Nellie Mae[6] Mullenax, 162.Solomon Key[5], 50.William Isaac[4], 7.James W.[3], 2.Abraham[2], 1.Mary Elizabeth[1] Arbogast), b. Aug 16 1941.
He Married **Irene Sweeney**.
Children:
1365 i. Richard[9] Bryant b. Feb 19 1962.
1366 ii. Steven Bryant b. Aug 08 1967.

1004. **Helen Grethel**[8] **Kyer** (690.Grethel Mae[7] Buckbee, 405.Lena Ester[6] Mullenax, 169.Martin[5], 51.John Wesley[4], 7.James W.[3], 2.Abraham[2], 1.Mary Elizabeth[1] Arbogast), b. Aug 29 1925.
Married May 06 1950 in Weston, Lewis Co., WV, **Fred William Fest, Jr.**, b. Nov 20 1924 in Martins Ferry, Belmont Co., OH.
Children:
+ 1367 i. Fred William[9] Fest, III b. Aug 21 1950.
1368 ii. Barbara Ann Fest b. Jul 06 1953 in Waynesburg, Greene Co., PA.
1369 iii. David Phillip Fest b. May 02 1958 in Waynesburg, Greene Co., PA.
1370 iv. Charles Edward Fest b. Apr 20 1962 in Washington, PA.

1006. **Lucille Zenna**[8] **Kyer** (690.Grethel Mae[7] Buckbee, 405.Lena Ester[6] Mullenax, 169.Martin[5], 51.John Wesley[4], 7.James W.[3], 2.Abraham[2], 1.Mary Elizabeth[1] Arbogast).
Married Aug 02 1951, **John Weber**, b. May 08 1927 in Weston, Lewis Co., WV.
Children:
+ 1371 i. Glenna Sue[9] Weber b. Jun 11 1952.

1007. **John Herbert**[8] **Kyer, Jr.** (690.Grethel Mae[7] Buckbee, 405.Lena Ester[6] Mullenax, 169.Martin[5], 51.John Wesley[4], 7.James W.[3], 2.Abraham[2], 1.Mary Elizabeth[1] Arbogast), b. Jun 03 1940 in Weston, Lewis Co., WV.

He Married **Beverly Ann Engle**, b. Nov 16 1939 in Peru, Miami Co., IN.
Children:
+ 1372   i.   Denise Ann⁹ Kyer b. May 14 1964.
  1373   ii. Melissa Ann Kyer b. May 28 1968 in Aurora, Arapahoe Co., CO.
  1374   iii. Deborah Ann Kyer b. Sep 17 1971 in Sumter Co., SC.

1013. **Linda Carol⁸ Wilfong** (704.Mabel Caroline⁷ Collins, 424.Lillie⁶ Raines, 189.Elizabeth A.⁵ Lambert, 65.Susan⁴ Calhoun, 12.Elizabeth Ann³ Mullenax, 2.Abraham², 1.Mary Elizabeth¹ Arbogast), b. Apr 28 1938 in Bartow, Pocahontas Co., WV.
She Married **Wayne Bonifant**.
Children:
1375   i.   (infant)⁹ Wilfong b. Feb 1 1956 in Bartow, Pocahontas Co., WV, d. Feb 1 1956 in Bartow, Pocahontas Co., WV.

1020. **Phyllis Jean⁸ Wilfong** (704.Mabel Caroline⁷ Collins, 424.Lillie⁶ Raines, 189.Elizabeth A.⁵ Lambert, 65.Susan⁴ Calhoun, 12.Elizabeth Ann³ Mullenax, 2.Abraham², 1.Mary Elizabeth¹ Arbogast), b. Nov 20 1946 in Bartow, Pocahontas Co., WV.
She Married **Stephen Plyler**, b. Dec 1 1945 in Pocahontas Co., WV, d. Sep 24 1985 in Quakertown, Bucks Co., PA, buried in Arbovale Cem., Arbovale, Pocahontas Co., WV. **Stephen**: Ref: Pocahontas 1981: 398 Dates and name of son from obituary S/o Luther Oren and Bertha (Hoover) Plyler.
Children:
1376   i.   Stephen Todd⁹ Plyler.

1022. **Ralph Scott⁸ Simmons** (709.Fannie May⁷ Hinkle, 432.Elbridge L.⁶, 198.William⁵, 68.Phoebe (Susan)⁴ Calhoun, 12.Elizabeth Ann³ Mullenax, 2.Abraham², 1.Mary Elizabeth¹ Arbogast), b. Jan 18 1903 in Blue Grass Cem., Highland Co., VA, d. Feb 27 1970.
He Married **Erma Lillian Waybright**, b. Jan 10 1912 in Cherry Grove, Pendleton Co., WV (daughter of Jesse Waybright and Attie Bessie Rexrode), d. Nov 9 1986 in Waynesboro, Augusta Co., VA, buried in Blue Grass Cem., Highland Co., VA.
Children:
1377   i.   Joy Lou⁹ Simmons b. Nov 5 1933 in Virginia, d. Aug 13 1963.
            She Married Thomas L. Mitchell.

1028. **Virgil⁸ Rymer** (711.Clyde⁷, 433.Susan⁶ Hinkle, 198.William⁵, 68.Phoebe (Susan)⁴ Calhoun, 12.Elizabeth Ann³ Mullenax, 2.Abraham², 1.Mary Elizabeth¹ Arbogast), b. Nov 03 1908, d. Oct 18 1978.
Married Jun 04 1927, **Hazel Ferrebee**.
Children:
1378   i.   Marie⁹ Ferrebee.
1379   ii. Donna Ferrebee.
1380   iii. Debbie Ferrebee.

1031. **Elmer P.⁸ Phares** (713.Cleat⁷, 435.Eliza Ann⁶ Hinkle, 198.William⁵, 68.Phoebe (Susan)⁴ Calhoun, 12.Elizabeth Ann³ Mullenax, 2.Abraham², 1.Mary Elizabeth¹ Arbogast), b. 1908, d. Jan-02-1972.
He Married **Myrtle M Sponaugle**, b. Dec-13-1908 (daughter of Herman Henry Sponaugle and Etta Beulah Warner), d. Nov-27-1970 in Cherry Grove, Pendleton Co., WV.
Children:
+ 1381   i.   Richard Cleat⁹ Phares b. May-16-1928.
+ 1382   ii. Ina Lee Phares b. Aug-07-1930.
+ 1383   iii. James H. Phares b. Oct-19-1932.
+ 1384   iv. Raymond Phares b. Sep-20-1934.
+ 1385   v.   Mary June Phares b. Dec-15-1936.
+ 1386   vi. Dottie Lou Phares b. Aug-02-1944.

1042. **Lowell Jene**[8] **Collins** (752.Harold Cecil[7], 453.Cecil Morgan[6], 206.Louella Maer[5] Grogg, 72.Emily Jane[4] Mullenax, 16.John H.[3], 3.Jacob[2], 1.Mary Elizabeth[1] Arbogast), b. Aug 09 1939.
(1) He Married **Susan Alkire**.
Children:
1387   i.   Kelly Sue[9] Collins.

(2) He Married **Sharon Johnson**.
Children:
1388   ii.   Christine Collins.
1389   iii.   Andrew Jon Collins.

1043. **Atlos Martin**[8] **Collins** (752.Harold Cecil[7], 453.Cecil Morgan[6], 206.Louella Maer[5] Grogg, 72.Emily Jane[4] Mullenax, 16.John H.[3], 3.Jacob[2], 1.Mary Elizabeth[1] Arbogast), b. Oct 25 1942 in Pocahontas Co., WV.
(1) He Married **Judith Elaine Gill**.
Children:
1390   i.   Dawnne Renee[9] Collins b. Oct 01 1964.
1391   ii.   Ribin Leigh Collins b. Aug 01 1965.
1392   iii.   Virginia Lynn Collins b. Aug 19 1967.

(2) He Married **Tammy Jo Farnham**.
Children:
1393   iv.   Sonja Michelle Collins b. Feb 02 1979.

1044. **Carol Lee**[8] **Collins** (754.Bernard Morris[7], 453.Cecil Morgan[6], 206.Louella Maer[5] Grogg, 72.Emily Jane[4] Mullenax, 16.John H.[3], 3.Jacob[2], 1.Mary Elizabeth[1] Arbogast).
She Married **Bill Waco Lambert**.
Children:
1394   i.   Janie Marie[9] Lambert.
1395   ii.   Billy W Lambert.
1396   iii.   Jody Lynn Lambert.
1397   iv.   Pamela Carol Lambert.
1398   v.   Julie Ann Lambert.

1045. **Rebecca Jeanne**[8] **Collins** (754.Bernard Morris[7], 453.Cecil Morgan[6], 206.Louella Maer[5] Grogg, 72.Emily Jane[4] Mullenax, 16.John H.[3], 3.Jacob[2], 1.Mary Elizabeth[1] Arbogast).
(1) She Married **Bob Shepherd**.
Children:
1399   i.   Kelly Ann[9] Shepherd.
1400   ii.   Gred Rob Shepherd.

(2) She Married **Tom Nohe**.
Children:
1401   iii.   Thomas Nohe.

1060. **Quinten**[8] **Arbogast** (774.David Lee[7], 512.Samual Henry[6], 238.Wilbur[5], 88.Cordelia[4] Waybright, 24.Christina[3] Mullenax, 5.William[2], 1.Mary Elizabeth[1] Arbogast), b. Aug 21 1970.
Children:
1402   i.   Ashley Marie[9] Arbogast b. Jan 21 1993.

1088. **Louis Scott**[8] **Townsend** (806.Lester Lou[7], 560.Hazel Marie[6] Mulnanx, 289.James Lewis[5] Mulanax, 124.William Dallas[4], 33.Miles Elliott[3], 6.Joseph[2], 1.Mary Elizabeth[1] Arbogast), b. Sep 07 1953 in Manhattan, Riley Co., KS.
He Married **Debra Hoke**.

Children:
1403   i.   Luke E^9 Townsend b. Aug 06 1988 in Manhattan, Riley Co., KS.

1089. **Harry Steve^8 Townsend** (806.Lester Lou^7, 560.Hazel Marie^6 Mulnanx, 289.James Lewis^5 Mulanax, 124.William Dallas^4, 33.Miles Elliott^3, 6.Joseph^2, 1.Mary Elizabeth^1 Arbogast), b. Nov 11 1958.
<u>Married</u> Feb 16 1980, **Tina Haid**.
    Children:
1404   i.   Michael Steven^9 Gaid b. May 13 1990 in Topeka, Shawnee Co., KS.
1405   ii.   Samantha Louise Townsend b. Jun 23 1983 in Topeka, Shawnee Co., KS.
1406   iii.   Kristi Townsend b. May 19 1986 in Topeka, Shawnee Co., KS.

1090. **Kevin Lee^8 Townsend** (806.Lester Lou^7, 560.Hazel Marie^6 Mulnanx, 289.James Lewis^5 Mulanax, 124.William Dallas^4, 33.Miles Elliott^3, 6.Joseph^2, 1.Mary Elizabeth^1 Arbogast), b. Nov 03 1959 in Manhattan, Riley Co., KS.
(1) <u>Married</u> Feb 25 1978 in Dover, Shawnee Co., KS, **Dana Springer**, b. Jul 09 1959.
    Children:
1407   i.   Sean Michael^9 Townsend b. Oct 11 1979 in Topeka, Shawnee Co., KS.
1408   ii.   Matteau Steven Townsend b. Aug 04 1980 in Topeka, Shawnee Co., KS.
1409   iii.   Ryan Scott Townsend b. Sep 27 1982 in Topeka, Shawnee Co., KS.

(2) He <u>Married</u> **Gloria K. Giegert**.
    Children:
1410   iv.   Chelsea Kathleen Townsend b. Mar 07 1990 in Topeka, Shawnee Co., KS.

1092. **Beverly Sue^8 Barnes** (810.Jane Earline^7 Nelson, 568.Maggie May^6 Blaikie, 293.Flora Adeline^5 Mulanax, 125.John Greenbury^4, 33.Miles Elliott^3, 6.Joseph^2, 1.Mary Elizabeth^1 Arbogast), b. Jun 30 1948 in Mena, Polk Co., AR.
<u>Married</u> Jun 11 1966, **Dwight Powell**.
    Children:
+ 1411   i.   Deanna Sue^9 Powell b. Aug 13 1968.
+ 1412   ii.   Duane Lloyd Powell b. Jun 05 1970.
   1413   iii.   Dennis Loran Powell b. Mar 23 1971.

1093. **Joane Sue^8 Barnes** (810.Jane Earline^7 Nelson, 568.Maggie May^6 Blaikie, 293.Flora Adeline^5 Mulanax, 125.John Greenbury^4, 33.Miles Elliott^3, 6.Joseph^2, 1.Mary Elizabeth^1 Arbogast), b. Dec 15 1950 in Mena, Polk Co., AR.
<u>Married</u> Aug 16 1967 in Mena, Polk Co., AR, **Dale Powell**.
    Children:
+ 1414   i.   Donita Laneel^9 Powell b. Mar 05 1969.
   1415   ii.   Darrell Powell b. Feb 10 1974 in Russellville, Pope Co., AR.

1094. **Betty Lovella^8 Barnes** (810.Jane Earline^7 Nelson, 568.Maggie May^6 Blaikie, 293.Flora Adeline^5 Mulanax, 125.John Greenbury^4, 33.Miles Elliott^3, 6.Joseph^2, 1.Mary Elizabeth^1 Arbogast), b. Oct 05 1952 in Cleburne, Johnson Co., TX.
<u>Married</u> Jul 04 1968 in Fayetteville, Washington Co., AR, **Ivan Kiersey**.
    Children:
+ 1416   i.   Lannie Gene^9 Kiersey b. Dec 08 1969.
   1417   ii.   Russell Scott Kiersey b. Mar 10 1971 in Mena, Polk Co., AR.
                <u>Married</u> Aug 20 1993 in Kunache, HI, April Wilson, b. Jun 13 1972.

1096. **Randy Gale^8 Franklin** (812.Francis Billey^7, 574.Bessie Lee^6 Osburn, 301.Mary Aceneth^5 Mulanax, 127.Matthew Elliott^4, 35.William R.^{3}, 6.Joseph^2, 1.Mary Elizabeth^1 Arbogast), b. Jun 26 1951 in Eugene, Lane Co., OR.
(1) <u>Married</u> Mar 08 1970 in Arkansas City, KS, **Micki Michelle Woolsey**.

Children:
1418 i.   Stephanie Gail⁹ Franklin b. Oct 04 1970 in Arkansas City, KS.

(2) <u>Married</u> Apr 17 1976 in Enid, Garfield Co., OK, **Cindy Ruth Chrisman**.
Children:
1419 ii.   Amiee Ruth Franklin b. Jan 08 1977 in Enid, Garfield Co., OK.

(3) He <u>Married</u> **Ronni Carter**.
Children:
1420 iii. Leslie Gale Franklin b. Apr 24 1978 in Enid, Garfield Co., OK.
1421 iv.   Geoffery Wayne Franklin b. Jun 07 1979 in Enid, Garfield Co., OK.
1422 v.   Christi Jo Franklin b. Jul 13 1980 in Enid, Garfield Co., OK.

1098. **Cheryl Lynn⁸ Franklin** (812.Francis Billey⁷, 574.Bessie Lee⁶ Osburn, 301.Mary Aceneth⁵ Mulanax, 127.Matthew Elliott⁴, 35.William R.³, 6.Joseph², 1.Mary Elizabeth¹ Arbogast), b. Aug 07 1954 in Springfield, Greene Co., MO.
<u>Married</u> Mar 08 1976, **Richard Shrope**.
Children:
1423 i.   Tera Lea Danelle⁹ Franklin b. Mar 23 1981 in Arkansas City, KS.

1099. **Ricky Michael⁸ Franklin** (813.Vernon Newton⁷, 574.Bessie Lee⁶ Osburn, 301.Mary Aceneth⁵ Mulanax, 127.Matthew Elliott⁴, 35.William R.³, 6.Joseph², 1.Mary Elizabeth¹ Arbogast), b. Aug 16 1950 in Pekin, Tazewell Co., IL, d. Feb 20 1981 in Mexico.
<u>Married</u> Sep 27 1970, **Debbie Ann Limbach**, b. Jul 26 1952 in Illinois.
Children:
1424 i.   Heather Michelle⁹ Franklin b. Apr 09 1971.
1425 ii.   Heidi Nicole Franklin b. Jun 01 1975.

1100. **Brent Mitchell⁸ Franklin** (813.Vernon Newton⁷, 574.Bessie Lee⁶ Osburn, 301.Mary Aceneth⁵ Mulanax, 127.Matthew Elliott⁴, 35.William R.³, 6.Joseph², 1.Mary Elizabeth¹ Arbogast), b. Dec 31 1952 in Pekin, Tazewell Co., IL.
<u>Married</u> Dec 22 1972, **Julie Ann Root**, b. Feb 22 1954 in Pekin, Tazewell Co., IL.
Children:
1426 i.   Thadus Jacob⁹ Franklin b. m10271975 in Peoria, Peoria Co., IL.

1101. **Kevin Kyle⁸ Franklin** (813.Vernon Newton⁷, 574.Bessie Lee⁶ Osburn, 301.Mary Aceneth⁵ Mulanax, 127.Matthew Elliott⁴, 35.William R.³, 6.Joseph², 1.Mary Elizabeth¹ Arbogast), b. Mar 19 1958 in Pekin, Tazewell Co., IL.
<u>Married</u> Nov 04 1976, **Dennie June Dobbs**, b. Jan 19 1958 in Pekin, Tazewell Co., IL.
Children:
1427 i.   Delta Lee⁹ Franklin b. Sep 30 1977 in Pekin, Tazewell Co., IL, d. Oct 05 1977 in Pekin, Tazewell Co., IL.
1428 ii.   Dawn Lynn Franklin b. Sep 30 1977 in Pekin, Tazewell Co., IL.
1429 iii. Cody Lyle Franklin b. Oct 17 1979 in Pekin, Tazewell Co., IL.

1103. **Galen Wayne⁸ Franklin** (814.Wayne Russell⁷, 574.Bessie Lee⁶ Osburn, 301.Mary Aceneth⁵ Mulanax, 127.Matthew Elliott⁴, 35.William R.³, 6.Joseph², 1.Mary Elizabeth¹ Arbogast), b. May 01 1952 in Eugene, Lane Co., OR.
<u>Married</u> May 08 1982 in Eugene, Lane Co., OR, **Candice Lynn Hobart**, b. Apr 20 1852 in Eugene, Lane Co., OR.
Children:
1430 i.   Garrett Eayne⁹ Franklin b. Jun 21 1983 in Eugene, Lane Co., OR.

1105. **Terry Lynn⁸ Franklin** (814.Wayne Russell⁷, 574.Bessie Lee⁶ Osburn, 301.Mary Aceneth⁵ Mulanax, 127.Matthew Elliott⁴, 35.William R.³, 6.Joseph², 1.Mary Elizabeth¹ Arbogast), b. Oct 12 1955 in Eugene, Lane Co., OR.
Married Jun 10 1978 in Springfield, Lane Co., OR, **Ronda Lou Smith**, b. Jul 05 1958 in Eugene, Lane Co., OR.

Children:
- 1431 i. Kristina Lou⁹ Franklin b. f08261980.

1106. **Shirley Ann⁸ Bruce** (815.Maty Ann⁷ Franklin, 574.Bessie Lee⁶ Osburn, 301.Mary Aceneth⁵ Mulanax, 127.Matthew Elliott⁴, 35.William R.³, 6.Joseph², 1.Mary Elizabeth¹ Arbogast), b. Mar 04 1941 in Eugene, Lane Co., OR.
Married Feb 12 1972 in Elmira. Lane Co., OR, **Michael Allen Whitney**, b. Aug 13 1949.

Children:
- 1432 i. Joshua Earl⁹ Whitney b. Oct 19 1973 in Eugene, Lane Co., OR.
- 1433 ii. Amanda Marie Whitney b. Sep 30 1976 in Eugene, Lane Co., OR.
- 1434 iii. Hannah Kristeen Whitney b. Aug 07 1979 in Eugene, Lane Co., OR.
- 1435 iv. Rebecca Suzanne Whitney b. Apr 29 1981 in Eugene, Lane Co., OR.

1107. **Janell Kay⁸ Bruce** (815.Maty Ann⁷ Franklin, 574.Bessie Lee⁶ Osburn, 301.Mary Aceneth⁵ Mulanax, 127.Matthew Elliott⁴, 35.William R.³, 6.Joseph², 1.Mary Elizabeth¹ Arbogast), b. Nov 20 1953.
She Married **Kenneth Lee Howland, Jr.**, b. Jul 16 1952 in Hastings, Adams Co., NE.

Children:
- 1436 i. Rachelle Lea⁹ Howland b. Feb 16 1978 in Eugene, Lane Co., OR.

1108. **Liessa Gay⁸ Bruce** (815.Maty Ann⁷ Franklin, 574.Bessie Lee⁶ Osburn, 301.Mary Aceneth⁵ Mulanax, 127.Matthew Elliott⁴, 35.William R.³, 6.Joseph², 1.Mary Elizabeth¹ Arbogast), b. Aug 15 1961 in Eugene, Lane Co., OR.
Married Apr 05 1985, **James Patrick Boytz**, b. Oct 17 1960.

Children:
- 1437 i. Mathew James⁹ Boytz b. Jul 02 1990 in Eugene, Lane Co., OR.

1109. **Harry James⁸ Crabtree** (816.Gladys Faye⁷ Franklin, 574.Bessie Lee⁶ Osburn, 301.Mary Aceneth⁵ Mulanax, 127.Matthew Elliott⁴, 35.William R.³, 6.Joseph², 1.Mary Elizabeth¹ Arbogast), b. Mar 23 1951 in Eugene, Lane Co., OR.
(1) Married Sep 14 1971 in Reno, Washoe Co., NV, **Carolyn Kay Bunsh**, b. Dec 06 1964.

Children:
- 1438 i. Hillaire Ray⁹ Crabtree b. Jul 14 1973 in Eugene, Lane Co., OR.
- 1439 ii. Lindsay Kay Crabtree b. Apr 04 1978 in Eugene, Lane Co., OR.
- 1440 iii. Erin Michale Crabtree b. Nov 08 1979 in Eugene, Lane Co., OR.
- 1441 iv. Harry James Crabtree, Jr. b. Mar 20 1986 in Eugene, Lane Co., OR.

(2) He Married **Collean Shey**, b. Aug 25 1957.

1113. **Charmaine Marie⁸ Fennimore** (817.Lois Ruth⁷ Franklin, 574.Bessie Lee⁶ Osburn, 301.Mary Aceneth⁵ Mulanax, 127.Matthew Elliott⁴, 35.William R.³, 6.Joseph², 1.Mary Elizabeth¹ Arbogast), b. Jul 15 1957 in Silverton, Marion Co., OR.
Married Mar 15 1979, **Joel Dean Adams**, b. Apr 02 1955.

Children:
- 1442 i. Elizabeth Marie⁹ Adams b. Jul 06 1980 in Corvallis, Benton Co., OR.
- 1443 ii. Daniel J. Adams b. May 26 1982 in Corvallis, Benton Co., OR.
- 1444 iii. David Paul Adams b. Jan 06 1985 in Corvallis, Benton Co., OR.
- 1445 iv. Kevin James Adams b. Oct 06 1986 in Corvallis, Benton Co., OR.
- 1446 v. Keith Joel Adams b. Apr 14 1989 in Corvallis, Benton Co., OR.

1114. **Gilman Joseph⁸ Fennimore, Jr.** (817.Lois Ruth⁷ Franklin, 574.Bessie Lee⁶ Osburn, 301.Mary Aceneth⁵ Mulanax, 127.Matthew Elliott⁴, 35.William R.³, 6.Joseph², 1.Mary Elizabeth¹ Arbogast), b. Jul 23 1958 in Dallas, Polk Co., OR.
He Married **Mary Larraine**, b. Sep 01 1959.
Children:
- 1447 i. Benjamin Joseph⁹ Fennimore b. Sep 07 1985.
- 1448 ii. Stephanie Ann Fennimore b. Jun 07 1989.

1115. **Cassandra Lou⁸ Fennimore** (817.Lois Ruth⁷ Franklin, 574.Bessie Lee⁶ Osburn, 301.Mary Aceneth⁵ Mulanax, 127.Matthew Elliott⁴, 35.William R.³, 6.Joseph², 1.Mary Elizabeth¹ Arbogast), b. Aug 21 1960.
Married Nov 20 1982, **Rand William Cooper**, b. Apr 29 1958.
Children:
- 1449 i. Kelly Rand⁹ Cooper b. Jul 28 1986.

1116. **Teresa Jean⁸ Hoag** (818.Betty Jean⁷ Franklin, 574.Bessie Lee⁶ Osburn, 301.Mary Aceneth⁵ Mulanax, 127.Matthew Elliott⁴, 35.William R.³, 6.Joseph², 1.Mary Elizabeth¹ Arbogast), b. Jun 08 1957 in Springfield, Lane Co., OR.
Married May 07 1957 in Springfield, Lane Co., OR, **Ramond Paul Nickoli**, b. Jan 07 1950 in Huron, Erie Co., OH.
Children:
- 1450 i. Darci LeAnn⁹ Nickoli b. May 06 1979 in Eugene, Lane Co., OR.
- 1451 ii. Tanna June Nickoli b. Jan 19 1981 in Eugene, Lane Co., OR.

1119. **Gregory Allen⁸ Larson** (819.Bonnie Jean⁷ Franklin, 574.Bessie Lee⁶ Osburn, 301.Mary Aceneth⁵ Mulanax, 127.Matthew Elliott⁴, 35.William R.³, 6.Joseph², 1.Mary Elizabeth¹ Arbogast), b. Jul 08 1956 in Coburg, Lane Co., OR.
Married Oct 16 1976 in Coburg, Lane Co., OR, **Roberta June Savage**, b. Apr 18 1958.
Children:
- 1452 i. Jeremy Allen⁹ Larson b. Feb 16 1978 in Eugene, Lane Co., OR.
- 1453 ii. Mindy Sue Larson b. Sep 27 1979.
- 1454 iii. Nathan Lars Larson b. Jan 18 1981.

1120. **Michael Ray⁸ Larson** (819.Bonnie Jean⁷ Franklin, 574.Bessie Lee⁶ Osburn, 301.Mary Aceneth⁵ Mulanax, 127.Matthew Elliott⁴, 35.William R.³, 6.Joseph², 1.Mary Elizabeth¹ Arbogast), b. Feb 02 1958.
He Married **Belinda Jo De Hart**, b. Jul 21 1962.
Children:
- 1455 i. Christopher MIchael⁹ Larson b. Apr 18 1983.
- 1456 ii. Callie Jean Larson b. Apr 13 1987.

1124. **William Douglas⁸ Franklin** (820.James Lee⁷, 574.Bessie Lee⁶ Osburn, 301.Mary Aceneth⁵ Mulanax, 127.Matthew Elliott⁴, 35.William R.³, 6.Joseph², 1.Mary Elizabeth¹ Arbogast), b. Feb 17 1963 in Eugene, Lane Co., OR.
Married Nov 12 1983, **Jeanette Michael**, b. Oct 17 1965.
Children:
- 1457 i. Stephanie Elizabeth⁹ Franklin b. Nov 27 1984.
- 1458 ii. Samantha Kay Franklin b. Oct 20 1986.
- 1459 iii. William Henry Franklin b. Apr 09 1989.

1126. **Brandel Allen⁸ Franklin** (821.John Allen⁷, 574.Bessie Lee⁶ Osburn, 301.Mary Aceneth⁵ Mulanax, 127.Matthew Elliott⁴, 35.William R.³, 6.Joseph², 1.Mary Elizabeth¹ Arbogast), b. Aug 16 1960 in Eugene, Lane Co., OR.
He Married **Joy McKafka**.

Children:

1460   i.   Bryan James[9] Franklin b. Jun 02 1978 in Springfield, Lane Co., OR.

1131. **Tony Ray[8] Franklin** (822.Alman Ray[7], 574.Bessie Lee[6] Osburn, 301.Mary Aceneth[5] Mulanax, 127.Matthew Elliott[4], 35.William R.[3], 6.Joseph[2], 1.Mary Elizabeth[1] Arbogast), b. Sep 14 1963 in Springfield, Lane Co., OR.
Married Jun 19 1983, **Shelli Lyn Sneed**, b. Oct 13 1963.

Children:

1461   i.   Ashley Dawn[9] Franklin b. Sep 20 1984.
1462   ii.   Karin Noel Franklin b. Apr 29 1988.

1133. **Donald Gene[8] Arnold** (823.Ethel Fern[7] Osburn, 575.Charley Calvin[6], 301.Mary Aceneth[5] Mulanax, 127.Matthew Elliott[4], 35.William R.[3], 6.Joseph[2], 1.Mary Elizabeth[1] Arbogast), b. Jan 14 1951 in Baker Co., OR.
Married Jun 04 1969 in Payette, Payette Co., WA, **Kathy Jean Griffin**, b. Jan 26 1952 (daughter of Ray Griffin).

Children:

+ 1463   i.   Candice Dawn[9] Arnold b. Mar 26 1972.
1464   ii.   Damion Blue Arnold b. Apr 16 1974.

1134. **Shelly Lynn[8] Arnold** (823.Ethel Fern[7] Osburn, 575.Charley Calvin[6], 301.Mary Aceneth[5] Mulanax, 127.Matthew Elliott[4], 35.William R.[3], 6.Joseph[2], 1.Mary Elizabeth[1] Arbogast), b. Jun 23 1956 in Ontario, Malheur Co., OR.
She Married **Andrew Fredrick Knipe, Jr.**, b. Oct 27 1955 in Scotia, Humboldt Co., CA (son of Andrew Fredrick Knipe and Marie Stratton).

Children:

1465   i.   Autumn Lynn[9] Knipe b. Apr 06 1979 in Portland, Multnomah Co., OR.
1466   ii.   Ashley Amber Knipe b. Jan 20 1981 in Portland, Multnomah Co., OR.
1467   iii.   Allison Nicole Knipe b. Jan 02 1983 in Weiser, Washington Co., ID.
1468   iv.   Anthony Andrew Knipe b. Mar 17 1984 in Weiser, Washington Co., ID.

1135. **Juanita Raquelle[8] Fagerburg** (825.Billie Lorreen[7] Osburn, 575.Charley Calvin[6], 301.Mary Aceneth[5] Mulanax, 127.Matthew Elliott[4], 35.William R.[3], 6.Joseph[2], 1.Mary Elizabeth[1] Arbogast), b. Jan 10 1960 in Mt. Vernon, Skagit Co., WA.
(1) Married Jun 04 1982, **Frank Lewis Nicklin, Jr.**.

Children:

1469   i.   Tiffany Skye[9] Fagerburg b. Oct 13 1978.

(2) She Married **Victor Manuel Lerma**, b. Dec 23 1919 in Mexico City, Mexico.

1136. **Martin Kerry[8] Fagerburg** (825.Billie Lorreen[7] Osburn, 575.Charley Calvin[6], 301.Mary Aceneth[5] Mulanax, 127.Matthew Elliott[4], 35.William R.[3], 6.Joseph[2], 1.Mary Elizabeth[1] Arbogast), b. Jan 06 1961 in Mt. Vernon, Skagit Co., WA.
He Married **Kate Louise Du Chow**, b. Jul 22 1961 in St. Peter, Nicolette Co., MN (daughter of Wayne Lincoln De Chow and Charlotte Ann Schultz).

Children:

1470   i.   Claire Luisa[9] Fagerburg b. May 07 1982 in Munich, Germany.
1471   ii.   Meghan Elizabeth Fagerburg b. May 06 1985 in Portland, Multnomah Co., OR.
1472   iii.   Olivia Kerry Fagerburg b. Jan 02 1987 in Portland, Multnomah Co., OR.

1138. **Kimberly Cherise[8] Vail** (826.Kathryn Machiel[7] Osburn, 575.Charley Calvin[6], 301.Mary Aceneth[5] Mulanax, 127.Matthew Elliott[4], 35.William R.[3], 6.Joseph[2], 1.Mary Elizabeth[1] Arbogast), b. Oct 02 1960 in Bellingham, Whatcom Co., WA.
She Married **Kevin Pflugar**, b. Aug 01 1960 in Bellingham, Whatcom Co., WA.

Children:
- 1473 i. Nichole Alexandria⁹ Pflugar b. Mar 25 1986 in Bellingham, Whatcom Co., WA.
- 1474 ii. Mathew Thomas Pflugar b. Oct 08 1987 in Bellingham, Whatcom Co., WA.

1164. **Leland Gary⁸ Schnell** (839.Betty Jane⁷ Osburn, 577.Samual Stephen⁶, 301.Mary Aceneth⁵ Mulanax, 127.Matthew Elliott⁴, 35.William R.³, 6.Joseph², 1.Mary Elizabeth¹ Arbogast), b. 7 Apr 1858 in Walla Walla, Walla Walla Co., WA.
Married 28 Nov 1982 in Glendale, Los Angeles Co., CA, **Sandra Slyvania Swantes**, b. 17 Jun 1960 in Rio De Janeiro, Brazil.
Children:
- 1475 i. Andrew James⁹ Schnell b. 13 Sep 1990 in Redlands, San Bernardino Co., CA.

1166. **Heather Susan⁸ Schnell** (839.Betty Jane⁷ Osburn, 577.Samual Stephen⁶, 301.Mary Aceneth⁵ Mulanax, 127.Matthew Elliott⁴, 35.William R.³, 6.Joseph², 1.Mary Elizabeth¹ Arbogast), b. 1 Dec 1966 in Tempe, Maricopa Co., AZ.
Married 26 Mar 1988, **Tona Campa**.
Children:
- 1476 i. Skylar Spartakus⁹ Campa b. 14 Dec 1988 in Boise, Ada Co., ID.
- 1477 ii. Gabriella Jordan Campa b. 20 Jan 1990 in Nampa, AZ.

1171. **Rebecca Rae⁸ Sisco** (846.Doris Acentha⁷ Allen, 579.Mable Marie⁶ Osburn, 301.Mary Aceneth⁵ Mulanax, 127.Matthew Elliott⁴, 35.William R.³, 6.Joseph², 1.Mary Elizabeth¹ Arbogast), b. 17 Oct 1953 in Roseburg, Douglas Co., OR.
Married 25 Nov 1974 in Springfield, Lane Co., OR, **Rocky Lee Brown**.
Children:
- 1478 i. Rocky Charles⁹ Brown b. 31 Jul 1976 in Eugene, Lane Co., OR.
- 1479 ii. Tiffany Ann Brown b. 17 Apr 1981 in Eugene, Lane Co., OR.
- 1480 iii. LeAnn Marie Brown b. 2 Nov 1986 in Portland, Multnomah Co., OR.

1172. **Tanya Mae⁸ Sisco** (846.Doris Acentha⁷ Allen, 579.Mable Marie⁶ Osburn, 301.Mary Aceneth⁵ Mulanax, 127.Matthew Elliott⁴, 35.William R.³, 6.Joseph², 1.Mary Elizabeth¹ Arbogast), b. 17 Oct 1955.
Married 19 Feb 1976 in Idaho Falls, Bonneville Co., ID, **David Lawrence Wach**, b. 28 Dec 1953 in Eugene, Lane Co., OR.
Children:
- 1481 i. Mariah Acentha⁹ Wach b. 28 Apr 1978 in Eugene, Lane Co., OR.
- 1482 ii. Selima Davina Wach b. 21 May 1979 in Eugene, Lane Co., OR.
- 1483 iii. Lavina Marie Wach b. 22 May 1981 in Eugene, Lane Co., OR.
- 1484 iv. Wesley LaGranda Wach b. 11 Jan 1984 in Eugene, Lane Co., OR, d. 11 Mar 1984 in Eugene, Lane Co., OR.
- 1485 v. Alexis Wach b. 22 Oct 1984 in Eugene, Lane Co., OR, d. 22 Oct 1984.
- 1486 vi. Apollo Wach b. 11 Apr 1986 in Eugene, Lane Co., OR, d. 11 Apr 1986 in Eugene, Lane Co., OR.
- 1487 vii. Lolita Elizabeth Wach b. 25 Apr 1987 in Eugene, Lane Co., OR.

1173. **Wesley Ray⁸ Sisco, Jr.** (846.Doris Acentha⁷ Allen, 579.Mable Marie⁶ Osburn, 301.Mary Aceneth⁵ Mulanax, 127.Matthew Elliott⁴, 35.William R.³, 6.Joseph², 1.Mary Elizabeth¹ Arbogast), b. 25 Mar 1959 in San Diego, San Diego Co., CA.
He Married **Dorothy Ann Leonardi**.
Children:
- 1488 i. Wesley Ray⁹ Sisco, III b. 22 Oct 1986 in Phoenix, Jackson Co., AZ.
- 1489 ii. Franco Philip Sisco b. 1989 in Lebanon, Linn Co., OR.
- 1490 iii. Sara Lavern Sisco b. 30 Nov 1992.

Generation Nine

1209. **Sue Ellen**[9] **Arbogast** (886.Rev. James Bert[8], 613.Rella K[7] Waybright, 334.Amby Stanton[6], 153.Mary Permelia Catherine[5] Mullenax, 50.William Isaac[4], 7.James W.[3], 2.Abraham[2], 1.Mary Elizabeth[1] Arbogast).
Ref: Stalnaker 259.
She Married **Lynn Doddrill**.
Children:
    1491 i. Matthew[10] Doddrill.

1210. **Sherry**[9] **Lynnarbogast** (886.Rev. James Bert[8] Arbogast, 613.Rella K[7] Waybright, 334.Amby Stanton[6], 153.Mary Permelia Catherine[5] Mullenax, 50.William Isaac[4], 7.James W.[3], 2.Abraham[2], 1.Mary Elizabeth[1] Arbogast).
She Married **Dana Lemasters**.
Children:
    1492 i. Lisa Marie[10] Lemasters.

1219. **Steven Guy**[9] **Hartman** (905.Mildred Mary[8] Warner, 631.Verlie[7], 338.Lura[6] Mullenax, 155.Elijah[5], 50.William Isaac[4], 7.James W.[3], 2.Abraham[2], 1.Mary Elizabeth[1] Arbogast).
He Married **Robin Shull**.
Children:
    1493 i. April[10] Hartman.
    1494 ii. Adriana Hartman.

1237. **Mary Ann**[9] **Carter** (941.Janice Lee[8] Mullenax, 649.Paul[7], 343.Emory R[6], 157.James B.[5], 50.William Isaac[4], 7.James W.[3], 2.Abraham[2], 1.Mary Elizabeth[1] Arbogast), b. Nov 21 1976.
Married Sep 18 1999, **Scott Wachter**.
Children:
    1495 i. Hunter[10] Wachter b. Nov. 2000.

1238. **Ronald**[9] **Gordon** (943.Louise Grey[8] Mullenax, 649.Paul[7], 343.Emory R[6], 157.James B.[5], 50.William Isaac[4], 7.James W.[3], 2.Abraham[2], 1.Mary Elizabeth[1] Arbogast), b. Aug 23 1975.
Married 27 Aug 2005, **Lakisha Renee Johnson**, b. Dec 31 1982 in Marlinton, Pocahontas Co., WV (daughter of Ricky Lee Johnston and Brenda Jane Sharp).
Children:
    1496 i. Blanton Davis[10] Loudermilk b. 8 Apr 2003 in Pocahontas Co., WV.
    1497 ii. Branson Lee Gordon b. 20 Jul 2006 in Pocahontas Co., WV.
    1498 iii. Remmington Cain Gordon b. 9 Sep 2008 in Pocahontas Co., WV.

1242. **James Richard**[9] **Cassell** (944.Connie Jean[8] Mullenax, 650.Richard Emory[7], 343.Emory R[6], 157.James B.[5], 50.William Isaac[4], 7.James W.[3], 2.Abraham[2], 1.Mary Elizabeth[1] Arbogast), b. Aug 19 1967.
Shelia lived wit, but not Married to, James.
(1) He Married **Shelia Ann Ray**, b. Nov 11 1968 in Marlinton, Pocahontas Co., WV (daughter of Harold Douglas Moore and Sally Kay Ray).
Children:
    1499 i. James Michael[10] Cassell b. Nov 4 1987 in Davis Memorial Hospital, Elkins, Randolph Co., WV, d. Nov 4 1987 in Davis Memorial Hospital, Elkins, Randolph Co., WV.
    1500 ii. Christopher Bradley Cassell b. Dec 30 1988.

(2) He Married **Stephanie Arbogast** (daughter of Glenn William Arbogast and Debra Jean Nottingham).
Children:

1501 iii. Madison Faith Cassell b. Sep 8 2004 in Davis Memorial Hospital, Elkins, Randolph Co., WV.

(3) Married Aug 31 1991, **Jacqueline Hubbert**, b. Mar 18 1968 (daughter of Walter Hubbert and Barbara Friel).

Children:
1502 iv. Joshua Devore Kincaid b. Nov 18 1985.
Stepchild. Delmar Devore Kincaid II b 2/5/1964 is father.
1503 v. Chelsie Renee Kincaid b. Dec 14 1988.
Stepchild. Delmar Devore Kincaid II b 2/5/1964 is father.
1504 vi. Shena Marie Cassell b. Jul 13 1990.

1243. **Crissy Jo^9 Cassell** (944.Connie Jean^8 Mullenax, 650.Richard Emory^7, 343.Emory R^6, 157.James B.^{5}, 50.William Isaac^4, 7.James W.^{3}, 2.Abraham^2, 1.Mary Elizabeth^1 Arbogast), b. Nov 14 1969 in Davis Memorial Hospital, Elkins, Randolph Co., WV.
Married Jul 2 1991 in Monterey, Highland Co., VA, **Ronnie Terry Lambert**, b. Oct 10 1965 in Elkins, Randolph Co., WV (son of Oakland Lambert and Virginia Vandevender).

Children:
1505 i. Alecia Janine^{10} Lambert b. Oct 5 1990 in Elkins, Randolph Co., WV.

1244. **Lauri Ann^9 Hess** (945.Sonya^8 Mullenax, 650.Richard Emory^7, 343.Emory R^6, 157.James B.^{5}, 50.William Isaac^4, 7.James W.^{3}, 2.Abraham^2, 1.Mary Elizabeth^1 Arbogast).
(1) Married Jun 25 1993 in Harrisonburg, Rockingham Co., VA, **Michael Lynn Taylor**, b. Jun 25 1973 in Harrisonburg, Rockingham Co., VA (son of Roy Hiner Taylor and Myra Jean Shinaberry).

Children:
1506 i. Kaitlynn Rae^{10} Taylor b. Jul 21 1994 in Davis Memorial Hospital, Elkins, Randolph Co., WV.

(2) Married Mar 27 1999, **David Andrew Greene**, b. Nov 21 (son of David Greene and Barbara Burner).

Children:
1507 ii. Alexis Marie Greene b. Nov 21 1999 in Winchester, Frederick Co., VA.

1248. **John E.^{9} Crabtree** (948.Shirley Ann^8 Warner, 651.Gus^7, 344.Sallie Denie^6 Mullenax, 157.James B.^{5}, 50.William Isaac^4, 7.James W.^{3}, 2.Abraham^2, 1.Mary Elizabeth^1 Arbogast), b. 9 Jan 1951.
He Married **Lou Ann (unknown)**.

Children:
1508 i. Christian^{10} Crabtree b. 3 Nov 1980.
1509 ii. Brendon Crabtree b. 12 Feb 1983.
1510 iii. Courtney Crabtree b. 9 Nov 1984.
1511 iv. Travis Crabtree b. 12 Mar 1991.

1252. **Lertie^9 Simmons** (951.Dewey Hunter^8, 652.Georgia^7 Lambert, 344.Sallie Denie^6 Mullenax, 157.James B.^{5}, 50.William Isaac^4, 7.James W.^{3}, 2.Abraham^2, 1.Mary Elizabeth^1 Arbogast), b. Oct 16 1948.
He Married **Patty Ellen Westfall**, b. Jun 17 1961.

Children:
1512 i. Letrie Allen^{10} Simmons, II b. Jun 16 1982.

1253. **Shirley Marie^9 Simmons** (951.Dewey Hunter^8, 652.Georgia^7 Lambert, 344.Sallie Denie^6 Mullenax, 157.James B.^{5}, 50.William Isaac^4, 7.James W.^{3}, 2.Abraham^2, 1.Mary Elizabeth^1 Arbogast), b. Apr 3 1950.
She Married **Willard Arbogast**, b. Sep 6 1949.

Children:

+ 1513 i. James[10] Arbogast b. Oct 5 1970.
  1514 ii. Valerie Arbogast b. Feb 3 1972.
  1515 iii. Glorie Arbogast.
  1516 iv. Michael Arbogast b. Jan 1 1972.

1254. **Rose Mary**[9] **Simmons** (951.Dewey Hunter[8], 652.Georgia[7] Lambert, 344.Sallie Denie[6] Mullenax, 157.James B.[5], 50.William Isaac[4], 7.James W.[3], 2.Abraham[2], 1.Mary Elizabeth[1] Arbogast), b. Feb 1 1953.
She Married **Delmar Lambert, II**, b. Jan 3 1950.
     Children:
+ 1517 i. Pamela Sue[10] Lambert b. May 5 1970.
+ 1518 ii. Dale Lambert b. Jan 20 1973.
  1519 iii. James Stewart Lambert.
  1520 iv. Stacy Lambert b. Dec 12 1974.

1259. **Barbara Joan**[9] **Simmons** (952.Edward Lee[8], 652.Georgia[7] Lambert, 344.Sallie Denie[6] Mullenax, 157.James B.[5], 50.William Isaac[4], 7.James W.[3], 2.Abraham[2], 1.Mary Elizabeth[1] Arbogast), b. Aug 18 1953.
(1) She Married **Donald Wiles**.

(2) She Married **Steve Davis**.
     Children:
  1521 i. Lawrence Edward[10] Davis.
  1522 ii. Ronald Davis.
  1523 iii. Mary Davis.

1260. **Sondra**[9] **Simmons** (952.Edward Lee[8], 652.Georgia[7] Lambert, 344.Sallie Denie[6] Mullenax, 157.James B.[5], 50.William Isaac[4], 7.James W.[3], 2.Abraham[2], 1.Mary Elizabeth[1] Arbogast), b. Dec 6 1955.
(1) She Married **Denver Arbogast**.
     Children:
  1524 i. Robert[10] Arbogast b. Oct. 1976.

(2) She Married **Edward Moore**.
     Children:
  1525 ii. Nick Moore.

1261. **Kathleen Marie**[9] **Simmons** (952.Edward Lee[8], 652.Georgia[7] Lambert, 344.Sallie Denie[6] Mullenax, 157.James B.[5], 50.William Isaac[4], 7.James W.[3], 2.Abraham[2], 1.Mary Elizabeth[1] Arbogast), b. Dec 24 1958.
She Married **Bobby Allen Chenoweth**, b. Nov 16 1955.
     Children:
  1526 i. Daniel Taylor[10] Chenoweth, II b. Apr 15 1972.
  1527 ii. Waleene Chenoweth b. Mar 18 1974.
  1528 iii. Laramie Angel Chenoweth b. Apr 3 1974.
  1529 iv. Linda May Chenoweth b. May 8 1976.
  1530 v. Heidi Francis Chenoweth b. Aug 30 1982.

1262. **Judy**[9] **Simmons** (952.Edward Lee[8], 652.Georgia[7] Lambert, 344.Sallie Denie[6] Mullenax, 157.James B.[5], 50.William Isaac[4], 7.James W.[3], 2.Abraham[2], 1.Mary Elizabeth[1] Arbogast), b. Oct 26 1960.
(1) She Married **Hubert Reed**.
     Children:
  1531 i. Floyd Hubert[10] Reed, II b. June 1979.
  1532 ii. Cynthia Elaine Reed b. Dec 18 1981.

(2) She Married **Glen Koon**.

1263. **Georgie Elizabeth⁹ Simmons** (952.Edward Lee⁸, 652.Georgia⁷ Lambert, 344.Sallie Denie⁶ Mullenax, 157.James B.⁵, 50.William Isaac⁴, 7.James W.³, 2.Abraham², 1.Mary Elizabeth¹ Arbogast), b. Sep 24 1962.
She Married **John Weese**.
Children:
- 1533 i. Billy Lee¹⁰ Weese b. 1978.
- 1534 ii. Chrystie Lunn Weese b. Sep 3 1981.

1264. **Kevin Lee⁹ Simmons** (952.Edward Lee⁸, 652.Georgia⁷ Lambert, 344.Sallie Denie⁶ Mullenax, 157.James B.⁵, 50.William Isaac⁴, 7.James W.³, 2.Abraham², 1.Mary Elizabeth¹ Arbogast), b. May 3 1964.
He Married **Ginger (Unknown)**.
Children:
- 1535 i. Erin Elizabeth¹⁰ Simmons b. May 18 1991.

1266. **Charles Blaine⁹ Simmons** (952.Edward Lee⁸, 652.Georgia⁷ Lambert, 344.Sallie Denie⁶ Mullenax, 157.James B.⁵, 50.William Isaac⁴, 7.James W.³, 2.Abraham², 1.Mary Elizabeth¹ Arbogast), b. Nov 4 1971.
He Married **Traci (Unknown)**.
Children:
- 1536 i. Edward Blaine¹⁰ Simmons b. Oct 26 1996.

1267. **Bruce Allen⁹ Simmons** (953.Roy Lester⁸, 652.Georgia⁷ Lambert, 344.Sallie Denie⁶ Mullenax, 157.James B.⁵, 50.William Isaac⁴, 7.James W.³, 2.Abraham², 1.Mary Elizabeth¹ Arbogast), b. Feb 28 1957.
(1) He Married **Robin Henske**.
Children:
- 1537 i. Yvonne Renee¹⁰ Simmons.

(2) He Married **Carolyn Cole**.
Children:
- 1538 ii. Lorene Elizabeth Simmons b. Sep 25 1987.
- 1539 iii. Geri Nicole Simmons b. Jun 17 1991.

1268. **Roy Lester⁹ Simmons** (953.Roy Lester⁸, 652.Georgia⁷ Lambert, 344.Sallie Denie⁶ Mullenax, 157.James B.⁵, 50.William Isaac⁴, 7.James W.³, 2.Abraham², 1.Mary Elizabeth¹ Arbogast), b. Jun 23 1958.
He Married **Mary Callen Sullivan**.
Children:
- 1540 i. Roy James¹⁰ Simmons b. Nov 12 1982.
- 1541 ii. Kaityln Elizabeth Simmons b. Apr 5 1985.
- 1542 iii. Jared Michael Simmons b. Aug 29 1990.

1269. **Roxanna Yuvonne⁹ Simmons** (953.Roy Lester⁸, 652.Georgia⁷ Lambert, 344.Sallie Denie⁶ Mullenax, 157.James B.⁵, 50.William Isaac⁴, 7.James W.³, 2.Abraham², 1.Mary Elizabeth¹ Arbogast), b. May 4 1963.
She Married **Richard Lynn Baughman**.
Children:
- 1543 i. Michayla Lynn¹⁰ Baughman b. Jun 23 1999.

1280. **Cheryl Annetta**^{9} **Hayse** (957.Clara^8 Simmons, 652.Georgia^7 Lambert, 344.Sallie Denie^6 Mullenax, 157.James B.^{5}, 50.William Isaac^4, 7.James W.^{3}, 2.Abraham^2, 1.Mary Elizabeth^1 Arbogast), b. Jan 2 1959.
She Married **Einar Finvik**.
Children:
 1544 i. Jennifer Erin^{10} Finvik b. Nov 4 1982.
 1545 ii. Atephanie Kay Finvik b. Nov 25 1989.

1281. **Darlene Francis**^{9} **Hayse** (957.Clara^8 Simmons, 652.Georgia^7 Lambert, 344.Sallie Denie^6 Mullenax, 157.James B.^{5}, 50.William Isaac^4, 7.James W.^{3}, 2.Abraham^2, 1.Mary Elizabeth^1 Arbogast), b. May 25 1960.
(1) She Married **Chris Peterson**.

(2) She Married **Tom Christenson**, b. Jan 30 1959.
Children:
 1546 i. Adam Gabriel^{10} Christenson b. Mar 8 1984.
 1547 ii. Ryan Zachary Christenson b. Jan 29 1987.

1283. **Theresa**^{9} **Lambert** (958.Sadie^8 Simmons, 652.Georgia^7 Lambert, 344.Sallie Denie^6 Mullenax, 157.James B.^{5}, 50.William Isaac^4, 7.James W.^{3}, 2.Abraham^2, 1.Mary Elizabeth^1 Arbogast), b. Nov 14 1966.
Married Sep 24 1988, **Harry Cooper**, b. Feb 3 1963.
Children:
 1548 i. Misty^{10} Cooper b. Feb 16 1989.
 1549 ii. Lee Cooper b. Jan 27 1991.

1284. **Diana F.**^{9} **Lambert** (958.Sadie^8 Simmons, 652.Georgia^7 Lambert, 344.Sallie Denie^6 Mullenax, 157.James B.^{5}, 50.William Isaac^4, 7.James W.^{3}, 2.Abraham^2, 1.Mary Elizabeth^1 Arbogast), b. Oct 17 1967.
Married Dec 14 1990, **Robert A. Jackson**, b. Nov 11 1964.
Children:
 1550 i. Chrifstal D.^{10} Jackson b. May 19 1993.
 1551 ii. Ryan A. Jackson b. Apr 11 1997.

1285. **Richard W.**^{9} **Lambert** (958.Sadie^8 Simmons, 652.Georgia^7 Lambert, 344.Sallie Denie^6 Mullenax, 157.James B.^{5}, 50.William Isaac^4, 7.James W.^{3}, 2.Abraham^2, 1.Mary Elizabeth^1 Arbogast), b. May 19 1971.
Married Jul 22 1993, **Norma Butcher**, b. Jul 7 1972.
Children:
 1552 i. Tasaha M.^{10} Lambert b. Oct 25 1993.

1287. **Carolyn Sue**^{9} **Brown** (959.Janet Lee^8 Lambert, 653.Roy D.^{7}, 344.Sallie Denie^6 Mullenax, 157.James B.^{5}, 50.William Isaac^4, 7.James W.^{3}, 2.Abraham^2, 1.Mary Elizabeth^1 Arbogast), b. Feb 16 1957.
Children:
 1553 i. Jerry Lee Morris^{10} Brown b. Mar 26 1981.

1288. **Phyllis Ann**^{9} **Brown** (959.Janet Lee^8 Lambert, 653.Roy D.^{7}, 344.Sallie Denie^6 Mullenax, 157.James B.^{5}, 50.William Isaac^4, 7.James W.^{3}, 2.Abraham^2, 1.Mary Elizabeth^1 Arbogast), b. Jun 4 1958.
Married Mar 11 1978, **Don Morris**.
Children:
 1554 i. Melanie Ann^{10} Morris b. Sep 9 1978.
 1555 ii. Melinda Sue Morris b. Apr 4 1982.
 1556 iii. Marie Elizabeth Morris b. Nov 3 1984.

1289. **Barbara Sue**[9] **Brown** (959.Janet Lee[8] Lambert, 653.Roy D.[7], 344.Sallie Denie[6] Mullenax, 157.James B.[5], 50.William Isaac[4], 7.James W.[3], 2.Abraham[2], 1.Mary Elizabeth[1] Arbogast), b. May 30 1960.
   Children:
   1557 i. Chad Michael[10] Brown b. Nov 30 1987.

1290. **Roberta Jane**[9] **Brown** (959.Janet Lee[8] Lambert, 653.Roy D.[7], 344.Sallie Denie[6] Mullenax, 157.James B.[5], 50.William Isaac[4], 7.James W.[3], 2.Abraham[2], 1.Mary Elizabeth[1] Arbogast), b. Apr 9 1961.
   She Married **Ernest Ware**, b. Mar 21 1959.
   Children:
   1558 i. Virginia Lynn[10] Ware b. Jun 29 1979.
   1559 ii. Ernest Lee Ware b. Apr 11 1984.

1293. **Brenda Kay**[9] **Howeyshell** (960.Francis[8] Lambert, 653.Roy D.[7], 344.Sallie Denie[6] Mullenax, 157.James B.[5], 50.William Isaac[4], 7.James W.[3], 2.Abraham[2], 1.Mary Elizabeth[1] Arbogast), b. May 21 1961.
   She Married **Levi Shelter**.
   Children:
   1560 i. Brenda Marie[10] Shelter b. Oct 5 1981.
   1561 ii. Tekisha Lynn Shelter b. Mar 10 1983.
   1562 iii. Latasha Shelter b. Feb 3 1996.

1294. **Lewis Earl**[9] **Turner** (960.Francis[8] Lambert, 653.Roy D.[7], 344.Sallie Denie[6] Mullenax, 157.James B.[5], 50.William Isaac[4], 7.James W.[3], 2.Abraham[2], 1.Mary Elizabeth[1] Arbogast), b. Mar 9 1965.
   He Married **Mary Jane Bullick**, b. Jul 14 1966.
   Children:
   1563 i. Heather Marie[10] Turner b. Oct 28 1992.
   1564 ii. Ellen May Turner.
   1565 iii. Brent Allen Turner.
   1566 iv. Drenna Nicole Turner b. Aug 12 1995.

1295. **Jeffery Allen**[9] **Lambert** (961.Keith Fallen[8], 653.Roy D.[7], 344.Sallie Denie[6] Mullenax, 157.James B.[5], 50.William Isaac[4], 7.James W.[3], 2.Abraham[2], 1.Mary Elizabeth[1] Arbogast), b. Apr 18 1971.
   He Married **Kara Lynn Francis**.
   Children:
   1567 i. Emily Grace[10] Lambert b. Aug 19 2000.

1297. **Robert Allen**[9] **Woods, II** (962.Joan Dare[8] Lambert, 653.Roy D.[7], 344.Sallie Denie[6] Mullenax, 157.James B.[5], 50.William Isaac[4], 7.James W.[3], 2.Abraham[2], 1.Mary Elizabeth[1] Arbogast), b. May 14 1961.
   He Married **Donna Sharp**, b. Feb 16 1961.
   Children:
   1568 i. Jeremy Allen[10] Woods b. Jun 21 1981.
   1569 ii. Melinda Jane Woods b. May 24 1984.
   1570 iii. Robert Scott Woods b. Jan 18 1988.

1298. **Robert Lynn**[9] **Woods** (962.Joan Dare[8] Lambert, 653.Roy D.[7], 344.Sallie Denie[6] Mullenax, 157.James B.[5], 50.William Isaac[4], 7.James W.[3], 2.Abraham[2], 1.Mary Elizabeth[1] Arbogast), b. Aug 21 1963.
   He Married **Angela Marie**.
   Children:
   1571 i. Jessica Ann[10] Woods b. Jul 11 1983.

1572 ii. Nathaniel Robert Woods b. Jul 9 1988.

1300. **Sherrie Marie**[9] **Deeter** (964.Charlotte[8] Lambert, 653.Roy D.[7], 344.Sallie Denie[6] Mullenax, 157.James B.[5], 50.William Isaac[4], 7.James W.[3], 2.Abraham[2], 1.Mary Elizabeth[1] Arbogast), b. Aug 2 1970.
She Married **Michael Bennett**, b. Jul 11 1972.
Children:
1573 i. Angela Marie[10] Bennett b. Mar 28 1987.
1574 ii. Tiffany Dawn Bennett b. Apr 9 1997.

1307. **Carolyn Sue**[9] **Lambert** (968.Kenneth[8], 654.Russell[7], 344.Sallie Denie[6] Mullenax, 157.James B.[5], 50.William Isaac[4], 7.James W.[3], 2.Abraham[2], 1.Mary Elizabeth[1] Arbogast) (See marriage to number 936.)

1309. **Sandra Jean**[9] **Sheets** (969.Hilda Josephine[8] Lambert, 655.Orie Basil[7], 344.Sallie Denie[6] Mullenax, 157.James B.[5], 50.William Isaac[4], 7.James W.[3], 2.Abraham[2], 1.Mary Elizabeth[1] Arbogast), b. Mar 29 1950 in Marlinton, Pocahontas Co., WV.
Married Feb 14 1970 in Durbin, Pocahontas Co., WV, **Bobby Merl Craig**, b. Dec 19 1947 in Milan, Sullivan Co., MO.
Children:
1575 i. Tamera Leah[10] Craig b. Oct 20 1976.
Married Jun 2 2002 in St. Leo's Church, Fairfax Co., VA, **Jamie Andres Rodrigues**, b. Jun 11 1975.

1310. **Donna Faye**[9] **Sheets** (969.Hilda Josephine[8] Lambert, 655.Orie Basil[7], 344.Sallie Denie[6] Mullenax, 157.James B.[5], 50.William Isaac[4], 7.James W.[3], 2.Abraham[2], 1.Mary Elizabeth[1] Arbogast), b. Aug 12 1951 in Marlinton, Pocahontas Co., WV.
Married Feb 6 1972, **James Allen Gragg**, b. Dec 28 1950 in Frank, Pocahontas Co., WV (son of Hallie Arbogast and Paul Craig).
Children:
1576 i. James Allen[10] Gragg, II b. Mar 10 1972 in Elkins, Randolph Co., WV.
1577 ii. Patrick Allen Gragg b. Dec 27 1978 in Elkins, Randolph Co., WV, d. Jun 2 1982 in Marlinton, Pocahontas Co., WV.

1311. **Larry Allen**[9] **Sheets** (969.Hilda Josephine[8] Lambert, 655.Orie Basil[7], 344.Sallie Denie[6] Mullenax, 157.James B.[5], 50.William Isaac[4], 7.James W.[3], 2.Abraham[2], 1.Mary Elizabeth[1] Arbogast), b. Dec 6 1952 in Bartow, Pocahontas Co., WV.
Married May 25 1974 in Brethren Church, Durbin, Pocahontas Co., WV, **Donna Jean Risley**, b. Nov 14 1953 in Winston, Jo Daviess Co., IL.
Children:
1578 i. Michelle Denise[10] Sheets b. Apr 1 1976 in Manassas, Prince Co., VA.
1579 ii. Melissa Dawn Sheets b. Dec 7 1979 in Manassas, Prince Co., VA.

1312. **Diana Kay**[9] **Sheets** (969.Hilda Josephine[8] Lambert, 655.Orie Basil[7], 344.Sallie Denie[6] Mullenax, 157.James B.[5], 50.William Isaac[4], 7.James W.[3], 2.Abraham[2], 1.Mary Elizabeth[1] Arbogast), b. Jun 3 1954 in Marlinton, Pocahontas Co., WV.
Married Jul 6 1973 in Boyer, Pocahontas Co., WV, **Lewis Ray Arbogast**, b. Mar 26 1952 in Durbin, Pocahontas Co., WV (son of Green Arbogast and Dorothy Ryder).
Children:
1580 i. Lewis Ray[10] Arbogast, II b. Mar 13 1974 in Elkins, Randolph Co., WV.
(1) He Married **Melissa Kay Cosner**, b. Oct 8 1974 in Virginia.
(2) Married Apr 1 2000 in Frank, Pocahontas Co., WV, **Jessie L. Walton**.
1581 ii. Michael Lee Arbogast b. Mar 4 1978.
He Married **Lelly Noel Day**.

1313. **Teresa Allen⁹ Sheets** (969.Hilda Josephine⁸ Lambert, 655.Orie Basil⁷, 344.Sallie Denie⁶ Mullenax, 157.James B.⁵, 50.William Isaac⁴, 7.James W.³, 2.Abraham², 1.Mary Elizabeth¹ Arbogast), b. Dec 16 1959 in Bartow, Pocahontas Co., WV.
Married Jun 6 1981 in United Methodist Church, Marlinton, Pocahontas Co., WV, **David Dewayne Rhea**, b. May 11 1954 in Marlinton, Pocahontas Co., WV.

    Children:
- 1582 i. Mathew Eric¹⁰ Rhea b. May 5 1982.
Married Jul 3 2004, **Kristie Kane**.
- 1583 ii. Jessica Lynn Reah b. Jul 29 1984.

1314. **Thomas Wayne⁹ Sheets** (969.Hilda Josephine⁸ Lambert, 655.Orie Basil⁷, 344.Sallie Denie⁶ Mullenax, 157.James B.⁵, 50.William Isaac⁴, 7.James W.³, 2.Abraham², 1.Mary Elizabeth¹ Arbogast), b. Dec 22 1964 in Marlinton, Pocahontas Co., WV.
Married Sep 3 1983 in Bartow, Pocahontas Co., WV, **Diana Denise Nelson**, b. Sep 3 1966 in Marlinton, Pocahontas Co., WV.

    Children:
- 1584 i. Thomas Wayne¹⁰ Sheets, II b. Mar 13 1984.
- 1585 ii. Alannah Brook Sheets b. Jan 10 1992 in Davis Memorial Hospital, Elkins, Randolph Co., WV.

1315. **Vickie Lynn⁹ Funkhouser** (971.Gladys Marie⁸ Lambert, 655.Orie Basil⁷, 344.Sallie Denie⁶ Mullenax, 157.James B.⁵, 50.William Isaac⁴, 7.James W.³, 2.Abraham², 1.Mary Elizabeth¹ Arbogast), b. May 10 1960.
She Married **Douglas McLean**.

    Children:
- 1586 i. Stephen¹⁰ McLean b. Oct 11 1991.
- 1587 ii. Kathryn Marie McLean b. Sep 21 1995.
- 1588 iii. Johathon Lambert McLean b. Sep 21 1995.

1318. **Travis Lee⁹ Roach** (972.Shirley Mae⁸ Lambert, 655.Orie Basil⁷, 344.Sallie Denie⁶ Mullenax, 157.James B.⁵, 50.William Isaac⁴, 7.James W.³, 2.Abraham², 1.Mary Elizabeth¹ Arbogast), b. Jun 20 1962.
(1) Married Aug 4 1984 in Durbin, Pocahontas Co., WV, **Phyllis Marie Grogg**, b. Aug 6 1963 (daughter of Donald Grogg and Mary McDonald).

    Children:
- 1589 i. Carrie Louise¹⁰ Roach b. Jul 13 1987 in Davis Memorial Hospital, Elkins, Randolph Co., WV.
- 1590 ii. Jessica Renee Roach b. Oct 3 1995 in Woodbridge, Prince William Co., VA.

(2) He Married **Michelle Leigh Marshall**, b. Aug 2 1969.

    Children:
- 1591 iii. Travis Lee Roach, II b. Mar 24 1989.
- 1592 iv. Daniel Matthew Roach b. Dec 6 1991.

1320. **Tina Marie⁹ Roach** (972.Shirley Mae⁸ Lambert, 655.Orie Basil⁷, 344.Sallie Denie⁶ Mullenax, 157.James B.⁵, 50.William Isaac⁴, 7.James W.³, 2.Abraham², 1.Mary Elizabeth¹ Arbogast), b. Mar 25 1968.
She Married **John Aaron Nicely**, b. Oct 30 1965.

    Children:
- 1593 i. John Partick¹⁰ Nicely b. Sep 26 1989.
- 1594 ii. Kevin Aaron Nicely b. Jun 27 1996.

1321. **Kathy Lunn⁹ Roach** (972.Shirley Mae⁸ Lambert, 655.Orie Basil⁷, 344.Sallie Denie⁶ Mullenax, 157.James B.⁵, 50.William Isaac⁴, 7.James W.³, 2.Abraham², 1.Mary Elizabeth¹ Arbogast), b. Feb 7 1970.
She Married **Richie Mason**.
Children:
    1595 i. Samatha Nichole¹⁰ Mason b. Jul 26 1993 in Potomac Hospital, Woodbridge, Prince William Co., VA.

1322. **Beth Ann⁹ Roach** (972.Shirley Mae⁸ Lambert, 655.Orie Basil⁷, 344.Sallie Denie⁶ Mullenax, 157.James B.⁵, 50.William Isaac⁴, 7.James W.³, 2.Abraham², 1.Mary Elizabeth¹ Arbogast), b. Oct 2 1971.
Married Oct 13 2003 in Picture Rocks, Lycoming Co., PA, **Robert H. Baylor, II**.
Children:
    1596 i. Zachary Robert¹⁰ Baylor b. Feb 19 2003 in Williamsport, Lycoming Co., PA.

1326. **Steven Allen⁹ Arbogast** (976.Ernest McKinley⁸, 657.Rhoda Martha⁷ Lambert, 344.Sallie Denie⁶ Mullenax, 157.James B.⁵, 50.William Isaac⁴, 7.James W.³, 2.Abraham², 1.Mary Elizabeth¹ Arbogast), b. Jan 27 1961 in Cleveland, Cuyahoga Co., OH.
(1) He Married **Dana Gosnay**, b. Aug 29 1963 in Texas City, Galveston Co., TX (daughter of Frank Gosnay).

(2) Married May 3 1986 in Virginia Beach, Princess Anne Co., VA, **Dawn Denise Barrack**, b. Sep 9 1961 in Charleston, Charleston Co., SC (daughter of Francis Barrack and Eleanor Powell).

Children:
    1597 i. Jason Douglas¹⁰ Arbogast b. Nov 30 1986.

1327. **James McKinley⁹ Arbogast** (976.Ernest McKinley⁸, 657.Rhoda Martha⁷ Lambert, 344.Sallie Denie⁶ Mullenax, 157.James B.⁵, 50.William Isaac⁴, 7.James W.³, 2.Abraham², 1.Mary Elizabeth¹ Arbogast), b. Apr 28 1963 in Cleveland, Cuyahoga Co., OH.
Married Oct 19 1991 in Faith UMC, Cleveland, OH, **Kimberly Louise Emert**, b. Aug 28 1969 in Cleveland, Cuyahoga Co., OH (daughter of John Emert and Beverly Thwatt).

Children:
    1598 i. Anne Katherine¹⁰ Arbogast b. Nov 20 1995 in Cleveland, Cuyahoga Co., OH.
    1599 ii. Adam James Arbogast b. Apr 16 1998 in Cleveland, Cuyahoga Co., OH.
    1600 iii. Aaron Richard Arbogast b. Apr 16 1998 in Cleveland, Cuyahoga Co., OH.

1328. **Richard Wayne⁹ Arbogast** (976.Ernest McKinley⁸, 657.Rhoda Martha⁷ Lambert, 344.Sallie Denie⁶ Mullenax, 157.James B.⁵, 50.William Isaac⁴, 7.James W.³, 2.Abraham², 1.Mary Elizabeth¹ Arbogast), b. Jun 25 1966 in Cleveland, Cuyahoga Co., OH.
Married May 8 1999 in Middleburg Heights, OH, **Christine Jessica Pearson**, b. Dec 13 1978 in Summers Heights, Ocean Co., NJ.
Children:
    1601 i. Eligah Christian¹⁰ Arbogast b. Aug 10 2000 in Fairview General Hosp., Cleveland, OH.
    1602 ii. Julieanna Dawn Arbogast b. Sep 18 2001.

1330. **Melissa Ann⁹ Swecker** (977.Betty⁸ Lambert, 658.Dewey Judy⁷, 344.Sallie Denie⁶ Mullenax, 157.James B.⁵, 50.William Isaac⁴, 7.James W.³, 2.Abraham², 1.Mary Elizabeth¹ Arbogast), b. Aug 26 1966 in Pocahontas Co., WV.
(1) She Married **Michael Reed**.
Children:
    1603 i. Katie Ann¹⁰ Reed b. Jan 7 1996.

(2) Married Aug 20 1997, **Doug Sanner**.

1331. **Dennis James**[9] **Swecker** (977.Betty[8] Lambert, 658.Dewey Judy[7], 344.Sallie Denie[6] Mullenax, 157.James B.[5], 50.William Isaac[4], 7.James W.[3], 2.Abraham[2], 1.Mary Elizabeth[1] Arbogast), b. Mar 17 1968.
(1) He Married **Angela Kessler**.
Children:
- 1604 i. Aliesha Marie[10] Swecker b. Sep 16 1994.
- 1605 ii. Nicole Kathryn Swecker b. Jan 11 2000.

(2) He Married **Shannon Lee Brumbugh**.
Children:
- 1606 iii. Anthony James Swecker b. Jun 5 1991.

1359. **Collen Marie**[9] **Bryant** (987.Charles Edward[8], 660.Sherron Virginia[7] Calhoun, 347.Nellie Mae[6] Mullenax, 162.Solomon Key[5], 50.William Isaac[4], 7.James W.[3], 2.Abraham[2], 1.Mary Elizabeth[1] Arbogast), b. Aug 24 1960.
Married April 1980, **Robert Cade**.
Children:
- 1607 i. Danielle Rene[10] Cade.
- 1608 ii. Jason Bryant Cade.
- 1609 iii. Aaron Robert Cade.

1362. **Margaret Sharron**[9] **Bryant** (987.Charles Edward[8], 660.Sherron Virginia[7] Calhoun, 347.Nellie Mae[6] Mullenax, 162.Solomon Key[5], 50.William Isaac[4], 7.James W.[3], 2.Abraham[2], 1.Mary Elizabeth[1] Arbogast), b. Nov 19 1967.
She Married **Daniel Alexander Gainer**.
Children:
- 1610 i. Gabrielle Augusta[10] Gainer b. Jan 13 1989.

1364. **Dana Lynn**[9] **Bryant** (988.Harold McQuain[8], 660.Sherron Virginia[7] Calhoun, 347.Nellie Mae[6] Mullenax, 162.Solomon Key[5], 50.William Isaac[4], 7.James W.[3], 2.Abraham[2], 1.Mary Elizabeth[1] Arbogast), b. Jun 10 1958.
Married Oct 1978, **Bryon Foster**.
Children:
- 1611 i. Kristi Rose[10] Foster b. Nov 14 1979.

1367. **Fred William**[9] **Fest, III** (1004.Helen Grethel[8] Kyer, 690.Grethel Mae[7] Buckbee, 405.Lena Ester[6] Mullenax, 169.Martin[5], 51.John Wesley[4], 7.James W.[3], 2.Abraham[2], 1.Mary Elizabeth[1] Arbogast), b. Aug 21 1950.
(1) Married Jul 20 1974 in Later Divorced, **Kathryn Harriett Nelson**, b. Feb 21 1951.
Children:
- 1612 i. Lindsay Kira[10] Fest b. Aug 21 1981 in Flagstaff, Coconino Co., AZ.

(2) He Married **Helen Patricia Hessinger**, b. Oct 29 1951 in Binghamton, Broome Co., NY.
Children:
- 1613 ii. Morgan Helen Fest b. Dec 19 1985 in Flagstaff, Coconino Co., AZ.
- 1614 iii. Michelle Kimberley Fest b. Apr 28 1990 in Flagstaff, Coconino Co., AZ.

1371. **Glenna Sue**[9] **Weber** (1006.Lucille Zenna[8] Kyer, 690.Grethel Mae[7] Buckbee, 405.Lena Ester[6] Mullenax, 169.Martin[5], 51.John Wesley[4], 7.James W.[3], 2.Abraham[2], 1.Mary Elizabeth[1] Arbogast), b. Jun 11 1952 in Weston, Lewis Co., WV.
She Married **Richard K. Kleinkauf**, b. Nov 10 1948 in Trenton, Mercer Co., NJ.
Children:
- 1615 i. Paul Larwence[10] Kleinkauf b. Sep 28 1976 in Fort Riley, Geary Co., KS.

1616 ii. Valerie Lynn Kleinkauf b. Sep 21 1978 in Fort Riley, Geary Co., KS.

1372. **Denise Ann^9 Kyer** (1007.John Herbert^8, 690.Grethel Mae^7 Buckbee, 405.Lena Ester^6 Mullenax, 169.Martin^5, 51.John Wesley^4, 7.James W.^{3}, 2.Abraham^2, 1.Mary Elizabeth^1 Arbogast), b. May 14 1964 in Kokomo, Howard Co., IN.
Married Jan 12 1985 in Parker, Douglas Co., CO, **Ronald Edwin Stelly**.
Children:
1617 i. Jessica Ann^{10} Kyer b. Jun 23 1989.

1381. **Richard Cleat^9 Phares** (1031.Elmer P.^{8}, 713.Cleat^7, 435.Eliza Ann^6 Hinkle, 198.William^5, 68.Phoebe (Susan)^4 Calhoun, 12.Elizabeth Ann^3 Mullenax, 2.Abraham^2, 1.Mary Elizabeth^1 Arbogast), b. May-16-1928.
He Married **Ruth M. Stites**, b. Oct-01-1933 (daughter of L.B. Sites and Gertrude Hoffman).

Children:
1618 i. Pamala Karla^{10} Phares b. Jul-15-1932.
  She Married **Steven J. Kulback**, b. Jul-21-1953.
+ 1619 ii. Richard Clete Phares, Jr. b. Dec-25-1953.
+ 1620 iii. Kimberly Lynn Phares b. Dec-20-1957.
 1621 iv. Sonnee Dee Phares b. Feb-14-1965.
  She Married **Kevin Barkley**, b. Dec-31-1958.

1382. **Ina Lee^9 Phares** (1031.Elmer P.^{8}, 713.Cleat^7, 435.Eliza Ann^6 Hinkle, 198.William^5, 68.Phoebe (Susan)^4 Calhoun, 12.Elizabeth Ann^3 Mullenax, 2.Abraham^2, 1.Mary Elizabeth^1 Arbogast), b. Aug-07-1930.
She Married **Blake R. Hedrick**, b. 102119255 (son of Glenn Hedrick and Myrtle Raines).
Children:
1622 i. Cathy Dianna^{10} Hedrick b. Feb-04-1953.
  She Married **Harry McMorrow**, b. Jul-07-1951.
1623 ii. Patsy L. Hedrick b. Mar-16-1955.
  She Married **Douglas H. Wimer**.

1383. **James H.^{9} Phares** (1031.Elmer P.^{8}, 713.Cleat^7, 435.Eliza Ann^6 Hinkle, 198.William^5, 68.Phoebe (Susan)^4 Calhoun, 12.Elizabeth Ann^3 Mullenax, 2.Abraham^2, 1.Mary Elizabeth^1 Arbogast), b. Oct-19-1932.
He Married **Beverly June Huffman**, b. Jun-12-1939 (daughter of Hensel Huffman and Wilma Raines).
Children:
1624 i. James Allen^{10} Phares b. Oct-08-1956.
  He Married **Lenita Jill Calliton**.
1625 ii. Thomas Lee Phares b. May-29-1958.
  He Married **Cheryl Lynn Cooper**.
1626 iii. Benjamin Loren Phares b. Nov-23-1964.
1627 iv. Matthew H Phares b. Mar-11-1971.
1628 v. Marianne M. Phares b. Mar-11-1971.

1384. **Raymond^9 Phares** (1031.Elmer P.^{8}, 713.Cleat^7, 435.Eliza Ann^6 Hinkle, 198.William^5, 68.Phoebe (Susan)^4 Calhoun, 12.Elizabeth Ann^3 Mullenax, 2.Abraham^2, 1.Mary Elizabeth^1 Arbogast), b. Sep-20-1934.
He Married **Alta Rose Elkins**, b. May-07-1942 (daughter of Walter G Elkins and Ida Mae Miller).
Children:
+ 1629 i. Michael Elmer^{10} Phares b. Dec-03-1963.
+ 1630 ii. Raymond Edward Phares b. Aug-04-1965.
 1631 iii. Georgia Lynn Phares b. Mar-17-1969.

1385. **Mary June**[9] **Phares** (1031.Elmer P.[8], 713.Cleat[7], 435.Eliza Ann[6] Hinkle, 198.William[5], 68.Phoebe (Susan)[4] Calhoun, 12.Elizabeth Ann[3] Mullenax, 2.Abraham[2], 1.Mary Elizabeth[1] Arbogast), b. Dec-15-1936.
Married Jan-10-1958, **Henry E. Bennett**, b. Dec-17-1932 (son of Henry Bennett and Virginia C. Vest).
Children:
 1632 i. Scott Allen[10] Bennett b. Jan-15-1971.

1386. **Dottie Lou**[9] **Phares** (1031.Elmer P.[8], 713.Cleat[7], 435.Eliza Ann[6] Hinkle, 198.William[5], 68.Phoebe (Susan)[4] Calhoun, 12.Elizabeth Ann[3] Mullenax, 2.Abraham[2], 1.Mary Elizabeth[1] Arbogast), b. Aug-02-1944.
She Married **Jerry M. Warner**.
Children:
+ 1633 i. Jeffery[10] Warner b. Jan-14-1966.
 1634 ii. Melissa Daun Warner b. Jun-25-1965.
    She Married **Larry Allen Hoover**, b. Apr-01-1965 (son of Wilson Hoover and Betty Jean Warner).

1411. **Deanna Sue**[9] **Powell** (1092.Beverly Sue[8] Barnes, 810.Jane Earline[7] Nelson, 568.Maggie May[6] Blaikie, 293.Flora Adeline[5] Mulanax, 125.John Greenbury[4], 33.Miles Elliott[3], 6.Joseph[2], 1.Mary Elizabeth[1] Arbogast), b. Aug 13 1968 in Texarkana, Bowie Co., TX.
Married Nov 11 1987, **John Skipper, II**.
Children:
 1635 i. John[10] Skipper III b. Jul 24 1988 at De Queen, Sevier Co., AR.
 1636 ii. Sara Ann Skipper b. Mar 31 1990 in De Queen, Sevier Co., AR.
 1637 iii. Steffania Skipper b. Mar 31 1990 in De Queen, Sevier Co., AR.
 1638 iv. Ashlae Nicole Skipper b. Apr 02 1993 in De Queen, Sevier Co., AR.

1412. **Duane Lloyd**[9] **Powell** (1092.Beverly Sue[8] Barnes, 810.Jane Earline[7] Nelson, 568.Maggie May[6] Blaikie, 293.Flora Adeline[5] Mulanax, 125.John Greenbury[4], 33.Miles Elliott[3], 6.Joseph[2], 1.Mary Elizabeth[1] Arbogast), b. Jun 05 1970.
She Married **Catherine Reed**.
Children:
 1639 i. Jessica Lee[10] Powell b. Nov 10 1989 in Mena, Polk Co., AR.
 1640 ii. Cassie Powell b. Jun 11 1993 in Mena, Polk Co., AR.

1414. **Donita Laneel**[9] **Powell** (1093.Joane Sue[8] Barnes, 810.Jane Earline[7] Nelson, 568.Maggie May[6] Blaikie, 293.Flora Adeline[5] Mulanax, 125.John Greenbury[4], 33.Miles Elliott[3], 6.Joseph[2], 1.Mary Elizabeth[1] Arbogast), b. Mar 05 1969 in Mena, Polk Co., AR.
Married Mar 12 1958 in Mena, Polk Co., AR, **James Christopher Gann**.
Children:
 1641 i. Nathen Christopher[10] Gann b. Jun 01 1989 in Russellville, Pope Co., AR.
 1642 ii. Whitney Brooke Gann b. Aug 11 1990 in Russellville, Pope Co., AR.

1416. **Lannie Gene**[9] **Kiersey** (1094.Betty Lovella[8] Barnes, 810.Jane Earline[7] Nelson, 568.Maggie May[6] Blaikie, 293.Flora Adeline[5] Mulanax, 125.John Greenbury[4], 33.Miles Elliott[3], 6.Joseph[2], 1.Mary Elizabeth[1] Arbogast), b. Dec 08 1969 in Fayetteville, Washington Co., AR.
He Married **Shannon Leigh Barr**, b. in Mena, Polk Co., AR.
Children:
 1643 i. Aaron Ray[10] Kiersey b. Oct 22 1988 in Mena, Polk Co., AR.

1463. **Candice Dawn**[9] **Arnold** (1133.Donald Gene[8], 823.Ethel Fern[7] Osburn, 575.Charley Calvin[6], 301.Mary Aceneth[5] Mulanax, 127.Matthew Elliott[4], 35.William R.[3], 6.Joseph[2], 1.Mary Elizabeth[1] Arbogast), b. Mar 26 1972 in Weiser, Washington Co., ID.

Married May 17 1991 in Weiser, Washington Co., ID, **Kenneth John Kelley**, b. Jul 25 1970 in Boise, Ada Co., ID (son of Kenneth Crow and Joan Lorraine Bee).

> ***Children:***
> 1644   i.   Stephanie Jean^{10} Kelly b. Dec 03 1991.

Generation Ten

1513. **James^{10} Arbogast** (1253.Shirley Marie^9 Simmons, 951.Dewey Hunter^8, 652.Georgia^7 Lambert, 344.Sallie Denie^6 Mullenax, 157.James B.^{5}, 50.William Isaac^4, 7.James W.^{3}, 2.Abraham^2, 1.Mary Elizabeth^1 Arbogast), b. Oct 5 1970.
He Married **Gloria (Unknown)**.
> ***Children:***
> 1645   i.   Shasta^{11} Arbogast b. Oct 22 1992.
> 1646   ii.   James Richard Arbogast.

1517. **Pamela Sue^{10} Lambert** (1254.Rose Mary^9 Simmons, 951.Dewey Hunter^8, 652.Georgia^7 Lambert, 344.Sallie Denie^6 Mullenax, 157.James B.^{5}, 50.William Isaac^4, 7.James W.^{3}, 2.Abraham^2, 1.Mary Elizabeth^1 Arbogast), b. May 5 1970.
She Married **James Stewart**.
> ***Children:***
> 1647   i.   Asley Cerria^{11} Stewart b. Jan 13 1996.

1518. **Dale^{10} Lambert** (1254.Rose Mary^9 Simmons, 951.Dewey Hunter^8, 652.Georgia^7 Lambert, 344.Sallie Denie^6 Mullenax, 157.James B.^{5}, 50.William Isaac^4, 7.James W.^{3}, 2.Abraham^2, 1.Mary Elizabeth^1 Arbogast), b. Jan 20 1973.
He Married **Stacy**.
> ***Children:***
> 1648   i.   Tistvan^{11} Lambert b. Nov 21 1995.

1619. **Richard Clete^{10} Phares, Jr.** (1381.Richard Cleat^9, 1031.Elmer P.^{8}, 713.Cleat^7, 435.Eliza Ann^6 Hinkle, 198.William^5, 68.Phoebe (Susan)^4 Calhoun, 12.Elizabeth Ann^3 Mullenax, 2.Abraham^2, 1.Mary Elizabeth^1 Arbogast), b. Dec-25-1953.
He Married **Lisa Yvonne Launder**, b. May-01-1961 (daughter of Ruben Phares and Beverly Noel).
> ***Children:***
> 1649   i.   Richard Clete^{11} Phares, III b. Jun-08-1990.

1620. **Kimberly Lynn^{10} Phares** (1381.Richard Cleat^9, 1031.Elmer P.^{8}, 713.Cleat^7, 435.Eliza Ann^6 Hinkle, 198.William^5, 68.Phoebe (Susan)^4 Calhoun, 12.Elizabeth Ann^3 Mullenax, 2.Abraham^2, 1.Mary Elizabeth^1 Arbogast), b. Dec-20-1957.
She Married **John Edsel Gowdin**, b. Jun 1953 (son of Charles Gowdin and Wilda Moore).
> ***Children:***
> 1650   i.   John Richard^{11} Gowdin b. Aug-29-1988.

1629. **Michael Elmer^{10} Phares** (1384.Raymond^9, 1031.Elmer P.^{8}, 713.Cleat^7, 435.Eliza Ann^6 Hinkle, 198.William^5, 68.Phoebe (Susan)^4 Calhoun, 12.Elizabeth Ann^3 Mullenax, 2.Abraham^2, 1.Mary Elizabeth^1 Arbogast), b. Dec-03-1963.
He Married **Jill F. Phares**.
> ***Children:***
> 1651   i.   Joshua Michael^{11} Phares b. Nov-12-1990.

1630. **Raymond Edward**[10] **Phares** (1384.Raymond[9], 1031.Elmer P.[8], 713.Cleat[7], 435.Eliza Ann[6] Hinkle, 198.William[5], 68.Phoebe (Susan)[4] Calhoun, 12.Elizabeth Ann[3] Mullenax, 2.Abraham[2], 1.Mary Elizabeth[1] Arbogast), b. Aug-04-1965.
He Married **Susanna Thompson**.
   Children:
   1652   i.   Stephen Edward[11] Phares b. Nov-25-1990.

1633. **Jeffery**[10] **Warner** (1386.Dottie Lou[9] Phares, 1031.Elmer P.[8], 713.Cleat[7], 435.Eliza Ann[6] Hinkle, 198.William[5], 68.Phoebe (Susan)[4] Calhoun, 12.Elizabeth Ann[3] Mullenax, 2.Abraham[2], 1.Mary Elizabeth[1] Arbogast), b. Jan-14-1966.
He Married **Pamala J. Craig**, b. Jun-18-1975.
   Children:
   1653   i.   Clara Dawn[11] Craig b. Dec-01-1989.

Descendants of Michael Arbogast Forth Child of Michael and Mary Elizabeth Samuels

Generation One

1. **Michael¹ Arbogast**, b. About 1768 in Augusta Co., VA (son of Michael Arbogast and Mary Elizabeth Samuels Amanapas), d. About 1813 in Springfield, Clark Co., OH.
Migrated to Champaign Co., now Clark Co., OH, about 1811, killed there in 1813. Land Bounty for war service? Relocated with brothers, David and Peter. Father of several children. See *Biographical Album of Clark and Greene Cos.,* by Chapman Bros., 1890, page 295. Also Court Records of Clark Co. This information from AAF..

More About Michael Arbogast, Jr.:
Emigration: 1811, Moorefield Township, Clark Co. Ohio
Residence: 1811, Moorefield Township, Clark Co., Ohio
    Rosemary Pickett a descendant has done extensive research in and around Clark Co., OH and from her home over several years has provided well documented family group records for Michael, Jr. and each of his children. On the son, George, Rosemary's data was augmented by research of Theodore B. James who is descended from George's daughter Annie Eliza and research of Margaret Sievers, National DAR # 527614 who is descended from George's son, James Henry Arbogast. On the son, Eli McKinley, all of the research is by Rosemary since this is her line and includes this line of her ancestors as well as her own descendants. Children listed may not be in order of birth. Rosemary cites, Portraits and   Biographies Album of Greene and Clark Counties, Ohio, Vols. I & II, Chapman Bros., Chicago, 1890, as a source and extracted the text pointing out the error that all of Michael's children were not born in Ohio and he came to Ohio prior to 1816. Rosemary's work may be referred to hereafter as THE PICKETT PAPERS.
    Other sources cited by Rosemary Pickett are: Clark Co., OH Marriage Records (researched 4 Apr 1991).Also see, Ohio Wills & Estates to 1850: An Index, by Carol W. Bell, 1981, Michael's estate filed 1814.
Early Clark Co., OH Families, Vol. I & II, by Friends of the Library General
Research Group. History of Clark Co., OH, by W.H. Beers & Co. as well as, A
Standard History of Springfield & Clark Co., OH, 1922, by Dr. Benjamin F. Price.

Michael, Jr. was a farmer. His year of death is from his Estate papers, Champaign Co., OH, Common Pleas Court minute book, 5, p. 24, 1814.
Married About 1792 in Pendleton Co., WV, **Barbara Buzzard**, b. About 1772 in Virginia (daughter of Heinrich 'henry' Buzzard and Elizabeth Ault), d. About 1824 in Springfield, Clark Co., OH. **Barbara**: Name from Amanda Arbogast Forbes research confirmed by Rosemary Pickett including approx. year and state of birth as well as approx. year and place of death, and names of parents. Ardath L. Brown of Covington, GA. cites "Buzzard - Alt" book, p. 110 as documentation of virtually identical information. She indicates the Buzzards.

                      Children:
- + 2   i.   George² Arbogast b. Aug 10 1793.
- + 3   ii.   Silas Arbogast b. About 1796.
- + 4   iii.   Eli McKinley Arbogast b. Nov 01 1799.
- + 5   iv.   Solomon Arbogast b. Aug 10 1804.
-     6   v.   Enoch Arbogast. Clark Co., OH Marriage Book 2, p. 5. He Married Mary Anzel.
- + 7   vi.   Elizabeth (Betsy) Arbogast b. About 1812.
- + 8   vii.   Catherine Kate Arbogast b. 1805.

Generation Two

2. **George² Arbogast** (1.Michael¹), b. Aug 10 1793 in Pendleton Co., WV, d. Apr 02 1868 in Springfield, Clark Co., OH, buried in Newcomers Cem., Springfield, Clark Co., OH.
Rosemary Pickett research papers cites, Portraits and Biographies Album of Greene and Clark Counties, Ohio, Chapman Bros., 1890, Vol. I, p. 295 for George and his son Eli McKinley Arbogast. George was a farmer in Moorefield Twp. and later lived in Springfield Twp., Clark Co., OH. Children are probably not in correct order of birth. Ancestral File (AFN:13LS-9C7) Spouse: Elizabeth HOLLINGER (AFN:GP96-17) Married 25 Dec 1817 Place: Champaign Co., Oh
Married Dec 25 1817 in Champaign Co., OH, **Elizabeth Hullinger**, b. About 1797 in Virginia.

   Children:
   + 9   i.   Catherine³ Arbogast b. About 1812.
     10   ii.   (unknown) Arbogast b. About 1818 in Champaign Co., OH.
   + 11   iii. Nancy Arbogast b. About 1822.
   + 12   iv.   Enoch G. Arbogast b. Dec 23 1825.
   + 13   v.   Melinda Arbogast b. May 14 1828.
   + 14   vi.   Matilda Arbogast b. May 14 1828.
   + 15   vii. Eli McKinley Arbogast b. Mar 04 1830.
   + 16   viii. Charles Ward Arbogast b. About 1830.
   + 17   ix.   James Harvey Arbogast b. Apr 03 1832.
   + 18   x.   Seth Arbogast b. About 1834.
   + 19   xi.   Elizabeth Ann Arbogast b. Mar 11 1837.
   + 20   xii. William Henry Arbogast b. Jun 12 1841.
   + 21   xiii. John A. Arbogast b. About 1842.

3. **Silas² Arbogast** (1.Michael¹), b. About 1796 in Pendleton Co., WV, d. Nov 05 1865 in Bloomfield Twp., Logan Co., OH, buried in Hodge Cem., Bloom Center, Logan Co., OH.
From Rosemary Pickett research. Date of birth and death estimated from 1850 and 1860 census of Bloomfield Twp., Logan Co., OH. Children from 1830 Clark Co., OH census and 1840, 50 and 60 Logan Co., OH census. There may be more children. Additional and more definitive information from records of Barbara (Coleman) Dove of San Antonio, TX. Complete names of 6 children and some spouse.
Barbara's notes indicate Silas' original will is in the Logan County Genealogical Society files. Silas lived in Clark Co., OH, (Cincinnati, OH, land officerecords28 Jan 1835, Range 8, Twp. 12, Sect. 32) before he moved to Logan County. Logan Co. formed 1818 from Champaign County. Silas tombstone standing and inscription legible. The cemetery is on a hill overlooking the Miami River Valley a few miles from the farm where he lived most of his life. Birth records were not required in the early 1800's in Ohio.
Married Apr 10 1816 in Champaign Co., OH, **Hannah Coulter** (daughter of William Coulter).

   Children:
   + 22   i.   Barbara Jane³ Arbogast b. About 1817.
   + 23   ii.   David Arbogast b. Mar 24 1822.

4. **Eli McKinley² Arbogast** (1.Michael¹), b. Nov 01 1799 in Pendleton Co., WV, d. Jul 01 1876 in Clark Co., OH, buried in Pleasant Hill Cem., Clark Co., OH.
From THE ROSEMARY PICKETT PAPERS in file. Sources include Eli's will, Clark Co., OH marriage records, cemetery records, census of 1830-1880, various histories of Clark Co., "Henckel Genealogy" by Junkin and correspondents with some descendants. Rosemary is also a descendant of this line through the son, Reuben. Eli was a farmer. There were nine children but only eight are listed, one has never been identified as to sex or date of birth.
Married Apr 01 1824 in Clark Co., OH, **Nancy Henkle** (daughter of Jacob Henkle and Elizabeth Forsee).

***Children*:**

+ 24	i.	Louisa³ Arbogast b. Aug 12 1825.
+ 25	ii.	Helena Jane Arbogast b. Jun 10 1827.
26	iii.	John F. Arbogast b. 1832 in Clark Co., OH.
27	iv.	Mahalia Arbogast b. Feb 20 1833 in Clark Co., OH.
+ 28	v.	Reuben H. Arbogast b. Apr 20 1835.
29	vi.	Flara Arbogast b. Jun 07 1838 in Clark Co., OH.
30	vii.	Nancy Arbogast b. Sep 22 1841 in Clark Co., OH.

5. **Solomon² Arbogast** (1.Michael¹), b. Aug 10 1804 in Augusta Co., VA, d. Apr 24 1870 in Roundhead Village, Hardin Co., OH, buried in Pleasant Hill Cem., Hardin Co., OH.
From ROSEMARY PICKETT PAPERS. Pleasant Hill Cemetery is between Alger and Houndhead Village in Hardin Co., OH. According to Rosemary's extract from "The History of Hardin Co., OH" by Warner & Beers, Chicago, Solomon was as early settler of Roundhead Twp. settling on Scioto Marsh where he farmed and then in the Bowdle settlement. They then lived in Roundhead Village where he was involved in teamin until his death. Member of the Society of the Bowdle Church which was affiliated with the Methodist Episcopal Church. He and Mary had four sons and five daughters, seven living in 1883, four in Roundhead Village.
Married Oct 20 1834 in Champaign Co., OH, **Mary Barrington**.

***Children*:**

31	i.	Elizabeth³ Arbogast b. 1836.
+ 32	ii.	George Washington Arbogast b. Oct 05 1837.
+ 33	iii.	Harrison Arbogast b. Nov 15 1840.
34	iv.	Dianna Arbogast b. About 1845 in Clark Co., OH.
35	v.	Eli Arbogast b. About 1846 in Clark Co., OH.
36	vi.	Mary M. Arbogast b. About 1850 in Clark Co., OH.
37	vii.	Margaret Elizabeth Arbogast b. Sep 19 1851 in Hardin Co., OH, d. Dec 21 1921 in Roundhead Village, Hardin Co., OH.
38	viii.	Bishop Arbogast b. About 1856 in Ohio, d. Feb 5 1917 in Old Fellows Home, Walla Walla Co., WA.

7. **Elizabeth (Betsy)² Arbogast** (1.Michael¹), b. About 1812 in Ohio, d. After1883.
From ROSEMARY PICKETT PAPERS. From "History of Hardin Co., OH" by Warner, Beers & Co., Chicago, 1883, Betsy living at Somerford, Madison Co., OH. Married Recorded in Clark Co., OH, Vol I-B, p. 295. 1850 Census, Jefferson Twp., Logan Co., OH.
Married Mar 29 1831 in Clark Co., OH, **Thomas McKinnon**.

***Children*:**

39	i.	Margaret³ McKinnon b. About 1833 in Clark Co., OH.
40	ii.	Amanda A. McKinnon b. About 1835, d. in Clark Co., OH.
41	iii.	Matilda A. McKinnon b. About 1838 in Clark Co., OH.
+ 42	iv.	Louisa A. McKinnon b. About 1841.
43	v.	Kitty Jane McKinnon b. About 1845 in Logan Co., OH.

8. **Catherine Kate² Arbogast** (1.Michael¹), b. 1805 in Pendleton Co., VA, d. 1935 in Madison Co., IN.
Title: Public Member Trees
Author: Ancestry.com
Publication: Online publication - Provo, UT, USA: The Generations Network, Inc., 2006.Original data - Family trees submitted by Ancestry members. Original data: Family trees submitted by Ancestry members.
This information comes from 1 or more individual Ancestry Family Tree files. This source citation points you to a current version of those files. Note: The owners of these tree files may have remove d or changed information since this source citation was created.
Page: 1 or more individual Ancestry Family Tree files were combined to create this source citation. Information extracted from various family tree data submitted to Ancestry.com and The Generations Network Text: http://trees.ancestry.com/pt/AMTCitationRedir.aspx?tid=3521207&pid=-1433950130

Married 1818 in Clark Co., OH, **Joseph Mulanax**, b. a 1795 (son of James Mullenax and Mary Elizabeth Arbogast), d. Apr 12 1864 in Green City, Hickory Co., MO. **Joseph**: Title: Roots, Ancestors & Wings Family Records & Stories
Author: Kathy Taylor Spivey
Note:
These are records and stories handed down from family members and published records.
Page: Joseph Mullenax and his family were part of the great migration Westward
Date: 1816
Note: Joseph Mulanax and his family were part of the great migration Westward to settle and make homes in the wilderness. From Virginia he pioneered in Clark County, Ohio in about 1816; then in Madison County, Indiana, and finally in Green County, Missouri, in about 1848, where he lived until he died in 1864 at the age of 69.
Text: Joseph Mulanax and his family were part of the great migration Westward to settle and make homes in the wilderness. From Virginia he pioneered in Clark County, Ohio in about 1816; then in Madison County , Indiana, and finally in Green County, Missouri, in about 1848, where he lived until he died in1864 at the age of 69.Joseph Mullenax was born about 1795 in Virginia and died on April 12, 1864 in Gree ne County, Missouri. His first wife was Catherine "Kate" Arbogast, daughter of Michael Arbogast, Jr., and Barbara Buzzard. He Married Kate in about 1818. Kate died in Madison County, Indiana. Joseph married Mary Ann Davis in the same county in 1836. Mary Ann died on June 12, 1907. She was living with her daughter, Martha (Mrs. Cires Cowan) at the time of her death in Sparks, Oklahoma. Joseph Mulana x served as a private in the 5th Regiment, Virginia Militia during the war of 1812. He was a farmer, a carpenter, and a miller .Joseph Mullenax first appeared as head of a family in the 1820 Federal Census of Clark County, Ohio. They lived in Pleasant Township. Kate and Joseph were between the ages of 16-25 and they had one son under ten. Miles Elliot Mulanax, was born on September 20, 1820, so perhaps she was the son indicated in this census. Kate's mother Barbara Arbogast, lived on a farm in the same township and was listed in the same 1820 census as a widow between the ages of 26-44 with six boy s and two girls, all under the ages of 25.Joseph was a farmer most of his life. The 1830 Federal Census listed him and his family in Clark County, Ohio. He and Kate had 2 sons and 4 daughters at that time. Sometime after 1830, Joseph Mullenax and his family along with other friends and relatives, migrated to Madison County, Indiana. The land records of Madison County, Indiana show that Joseph Mulanax b ought 57.5 acres of land on June 13, 1833 and paid $71.88 for his land. This record was found in Book 4, Page 332 in the County Court House in Anderson, Indiana. This land was in Anderson Township, clos e to the town of Anderson, Indiana. The exact location was: Township 19 North, Range 7 East, the East half of the northwest quarter in Section 10. The land was close to the Moss Islands in the White River just west of the city of Anderson, Indiana. Joseph's land is a beautiful flat farming land. He built the Moss Island Mills on this tract of land. In the "History of Madison County" by Samuel Harden (1874), there is a picture of the Moss Island Mills with this notation: "Moss Island Mills, these mills were built about the year 1836 by Joseph Mullenax. This mill was consumed by fire in 1873. This mil l is located 2 miles west of Anderson and is supplied with water from White River. The mill derived its name from a small island in the river. Frank Damis owned the mills after Joseph Mullenax. the 56. 5 acres were later owned by I. Moss in 1880."Joseph and Kate Mullenax had seven children who grew to adulthood. They were: Miles, Sarah, William, Catharine, Greenberry, Elizabeth, and Mary. Kate died ab out 1835 in Madison County, Indiana. She had a daughter, Catharine, who was born in1835, so she may have died following childbirth. On June 7, 1836, Joseph Married Mary Ann Davis in Anderson, Indiana . She was also called "Polly." Mary Ann and Joseph had two children while they lived in Madison County, Indiana. They were Clotillaand Josephine. They had ten other children who were born in Missouri . They were: Joseph, Mahalia, Eliza, Alfred, Martha, Francis, Jacob, James, George, and John. Joseph and his second wife, Mary Ann, may have lived in the northwest corner of Missouri in Andrew, Buchanan o r Platte Counties for a short time in the 1840's and later moved down south to Green County, Missouri Federal Census of Missouri, in green County in Boone Township. In this census Joseph was 56, Mary An n, his wife, was 30 years of age and they had eleven children still at home. Joseph bought land from Joseph Moss on May 6, 1848. It was 80 Acres plus. Its' location was in the east half of the south west one quarter of Section 23, Township 31 (Boone Township), Range 24. He also bought part of the northwest and part of the southwest quarters of the same section transaction was found in Book F, Page 176 in the Greene County, Missouri Court Records. On April 1, 1852, Joseph bought 320 acres of land

from Samuel Julian. It was the southwest quarter of the northwest quarter in Section 34. This transaction was found in Book D, Page 131. Joseph received 80 acres of bounty land fro having served during the War of 1812. This was on May 29, 1856, Land Warrant No. 31078. It was located in Township 27, Section 11, Range 33 and was the West half of the Northeast quarter of Section 11.

Children:

+	44	i.	Miles Elliott³ Mullenax b. Sep 06 1820.
+	45	ii.	Elizabeth J. Mullenax b. 1827.
+	46	iii.	William R. Mullenax b. Oct 10 1832.
	47	iv.	Greenberry Mullenax b. 1821 in Madison Co., IN.
	48	v.	Mary Mullenax b. 1929 in Ohio. Married Feb 04 1849 in Andrew Co., MO, **William Cass**.
	49	vi.	Sarah Mullenax b. 1830 in Clark Co., OH. Married Mar 13 1852 in Andrew Co., MO, **Joseph Dandrivan**, b. 1826 in Ohio.
	50	vii.	Catherine Mullenax b. 1935 in Madison Co., IN.

Generation Three

9. **Catherine³ Arbogast** (2.George², 1.Michael¹), b. About 1812, d. 1835 in Madison Co., IN. She Married **John Wierack**.

Children:

+ 51   i.   Martin⁴ Wierack.
   52   ii.   Wilson Wierack.
              He Married **Eva Kibling**.
   53   iii.   Elizabeth Wierack.
              She Married **Mort Shupp**.

11. **Nancy³ Arbogast** (2.George², 1.Michael¹), b. About 1822 in Ohio.
Married Mar 18 1847 in Ohio, **William Maggart**, b. About 1818 in Onoto, Pocahontas Co., WV.

Children:

54   i.   George⁴ Maggart b. About 1848 in Ohio.
        Married **Miss Burns**
55   ii.   David W. Maggart b. March 1850 in Ohio, d. Feb 02 1851 in Ohio.
56   iii.   Charles Maggart b. About 1852 in Ohio.
57   iv.   James McKee Maggart b. About 1854 in Onoto, Pocahontas Co., WV.
58   v.   Albert (Alonzo) Maggart b. About 1859 in Ohio.

12. **Enoch G.³ Arbogast** (2.George², 1.Michael¹), b. Dec 23 1825, d. Jun 24 1903.
He Married **Lavinia Harmon**.

Children:

59   i.   Schuyler C⁴ Arbogast.
        Married **Charlotte Stauffer**
60   ii.   James Oscar Arbogast b. About 1852.
        Married **Mary Ellen Boward**, b. Abt 1851, MD
        Married **Bessie Haney Harvey**
61   iii.   Emma J. Arbogast b. About 1858.
        She Married **John N. Davis** 31 May 1888 Clark Co., OH.
62   iv.   Anna R. Arbogast b. About 1860, d. 1882.
63   v.   Nettie C. Arbogast b. About 1866, d. Jun 24 1947.
64   vi.   William Edward Arbogast b. Nov 21 1867, d. Jan 13 1939.
        Married **Glenna B. Mc Mahan**, b. 31 May 1870, Springfield, , Oh, d. 31 May 1898, Springfield, , Oh

		Married Harriet Lyons
		Married Claire Louise Welch, b. 29 Aug 1880, Springfield, Clark Co., Oh, d. 26 Feb 1942
65	vii.	Charles H. Arbogast b. About 1869.
		He Married **Carrie Rush**.
66	viii.	Walter H. Arbogast b. About 1871. They had four children; Pauline, Dorothy, George, and Robert.
		Married Jennie Hallan
67	ix.	Mary E. Arbogast b. About 1872. Springfield, Clark, Oh
		Married Robert Morley
		Married Harry E. Wadsworth
68	x.	Nancy Elizabeth Arbogast b. Oct 26 1873 Springfield, Clark, Oh

13. **Melinda³ Arbogast** (2.George², 1.Michael¹), b. May 14 1828 in Ohio, d. Jul 25 1892.
Married c 1842 in Clark Co., OH, **James Driscoll**, b. Jan 09 1817 in Greene Co., OH (son of John Driscoll and Mary Jones).

   Children:

69	i.	Rebecca J.⁴ Driscoll b. About 1843 in Ohio.
		She Married **Alfred Miller**.
+ 70	ii.	George W. Driscoll b. Jan 09 1844.
+ 71	iii.	John H. Driscoll b. About 1845.
72	iv.	Charles E. Driscoll b. About 1856 in Ohio.
		He Married **Anna Smiley**.

14. **Matilda³ Arbogast** (2.George², 1.Michael¹), b. May 14 1828, d. Jan 17 1901.
She Married **Jacob Carpender McBride**.

   Children:

73	i.	Annie Eliza⁴ McBride b. Jun 20 1854, d. Apr 23 1877.
74	ii.	Mary Elizabeth McBride b. Mar 17 1856, d. Jun 04 1890.
75	iii.	Lillian Viola McBride b. Nov 17 1857, d. Nov 02 1917.
76	iv.	James Henry McBride b. Sep 16 1859, d. Nov. 1912.
		He Married **Estelle Dox**.
77	v.	Rebecca Jane McBride b. Sep 15 1861 in Logan Co., OH, d. Mar 12 1887. She Married **Willis Routzahn**, b. Aug 28 1883 in Springfield, Clark Co., OH.
78	vi.	Nancy Ellen McBride b. Sep 15 1861, d. May 06 1862.

15. **Eli McKinley³ Arbogast** (2.George², 1.Michael¹), b. Mar 04 1830 in Ohio.
ELI MCKINDEY Arbogast can number among his ancestors two of the early settlers of this part of Ohio, and he himself was born in this county, and has ever since made his home here, with the exception of a year elsewhere. In his business as a contractor and builder he has done a great deal to promote the growth of Springfield, his place of residence, and the surrounding country. When he came here in early manhood the city was but a village of three or four thousand people, and he has seen it grow from a mere commercial town, the metropolis of an agricultural community, to be one of the most flourishing manufacturing cities in the State, with a population of nearly forty thousand inhabitants.
(1) Married Nov 06 1851 in Ohio, **Catherine M. Coffield**, b. About 1825 in Butler, Richland County. OH.

   Children by Catherine M. Coffield:

79	i.	John Hamilton⁴ Arbogast b. Dec 24 1855 in Ohio, d. Jul 24 1926.
80	ii.	George W. Arbogast b. Oct 29 1856 in Ohio, d. Oct 04 1891.
81	iii.	William Arbogast b. About 1860.

(2) He Married **Anne Elliott**.

16. **Charles Ward³ Arbogast** (2.George², 1.Michael¹), b. About 1830, d. About 1863.

He Married **Rebecca W. Sellers**, b. About 1833 in Ohio.

> ### *Children*:
> 82   i.   Whitcomb^4 Arbogast.
> 83   ii.   Clara B. Arbogast b. Jul 16 1854.
> 84   iii.   Lizzie Arbogast b. About 1857.
> 85   iv.   John Forrest Arbogast b. About 1859.
> 86   v.   Charles Elmer Arbogast b. Sep 22 1862.

17. **James Harvey^3 Arbogast** (2.George^2, 1.Michael^1), b. Apr 03 1832, d. Nov 16 1911.
    He Married **Augustine Dabe**, b. Nov 01 1833 in Paris, France.

    > ### *Children*:
    > 87   i.   James Rodney^4 Arbogast b. Aug 05 1856, d. Oct 20 1918.
    >   He Married **Nettie Bauer**.
    > 88   ii.   Frank M. Arbogast b. About 1859.
    > 89   iii.   Cora M. Arbogast b. About 1862.
    > 90   iv.   Alice D. Arbogast b. About 1864.
    > 91   v.   Ida Rose Arbogast b. Nov 15 1870.
    > 92   vi.   Nelle Arbogast b. Mar 03 1873, d. Sep 03 1957.
    >   She Married **Alfred Long Kay**.

18. **Seth^3 Arbogast** (2.George^2, 1.Michael^1), b. About 1834, d. Before 1913.
    He Married **Anne R. Trimmer**, b. About 1836.

    > ### *Children*:
    > 93   i.   Sheridan^4 Arbogast b. Before 1864, d. Oct 14 1914.

19. **Elizabeth Ann^3 Arbogast** (2.George^2, 1.Michael^1), b. Mar 11 1837 in Clark Co., OH, d. Feb 26 1911.
    She Married **Ambrose Petticrew**.

    > ### *Children*:
    > 94   i.   Alice^4 Petticrew.
    > 95   ii.   Lulu Petticrew.

20. **William Henry^3 Arbogast** (2.George^2, 1.Michael^1), b. Jun 12 1841, d. Apr 12 1903.
    He Married **Elizabeth Ann Willard**.

    > ### *Children*:
    > 96   i.   Albert Willard^4 Arbogast b. Jan 06 1869, d. Mar 06 1873.
    > 97   ii.   Victor R. Arbogast b. Feb 20 1872, d. May 07 1936.
    > 98   iii.   Clarence W. Arbogast b. Apr 30 1873, d. Oct 13 1914.
    > 99   iv.   Genevieve M Arbogast b. Mar 06 1876.
    >   She Married **Forrest M. Trimmins**.
    > 100   v.   Mary Gertrude Arbogast b. 1877, d. Mar 13 1933.

21. **John A.^{3} Arbogast** (2.George^2, 1.Michael^1), b. About 1842, d. Jan 03 1924.
    He Married **Mary Ann Walker**, b. About 1841 in Ohio.

    > ### *Children*:
    > 101   i.   Clinton D.^{4} Arbogast b. Nov 22 1868.
    > 102   ii.   Elizabeth Lydia Arbogast b. Jul 01 1870.
    > 103   iii.   Harry G. Arbogast b. Oct 12 1876, d. Feb 76 1879.
    > 104   iv.   James Harvey Arbogast b. Sep 06 1878.

22. **Barbara Jane^3 Arbogast** (3.Silas^2, 1.Michael^1), b. About 1817 in Champaign Co., OH.
    Married Dec 30 1836 in Bloomfield Twp., Logan Co., OH, **Isaac Dove**.

    > ### *Children*:
    > 105   i.   Michael Ely^4 Dove.
    > 106   ii.   Isaac Dove b. About 1837 in Bloomfield Twp., Logan Co., OH.

- 107 iii. George W. Dove b. Feb 12 1842 in Bloomfield Twp., Logan Co., OH.
- 108 iv. John M. Dove b. Dec 30 1845 in Bloomfield Twp., Logan Co., OH.
- 109 v. Silis P. Dove b. About 1846 in Bloomfield Twp., Logan Co., OH.
- 110 vi. Hannah Dove b. About 1847 in Bloomfield Twp., Logan Co., OH.
- 111 vii. Jennie Miriah Dove b. 1852 in Bloomfield Twp., Logan Co., OH.

23. **David^3 Arbogast** (3.Silas^2, 1.Michael^1), b. Mar 24 1822 in Bloomfield Twp., Logan Co., OH, d. Jan 17 1873 in Shelby, Richland Co., OH.
    Married Apr 14 1851 in Shelby, Richland Co., OH, **Melinda Catherine Mitchell**.
    ### *Children*:
    - 112 i. Charlotte^4 Arbogast b. March 1852.
    - 113 ii. William Arbogast b. Feb 1854.
    - 114 iii. Luella A. Arbogast b. About 1863.
    - 115 iv. John Arbogast b. Dec 1863.
    - 116 v. Ulysses S, Arbogast b. May 1865.
    - 117 vi. Rene M. Arbogast b. About 1867 in Ohio.
    - 118 vii. Etta Arbogast b. Mar 15 1870 in Shelby Co., OH.
    - 119 viii. Emma C. Arbogast b. About 1873 in Ohio.

24. **Louisa^3 Arbogast** (4.Eli McKinley^2, 1.Michael^1), b. Aug 12 1825 in Clark Co., OH, d. Jun 11 1891 in Clark Co., OH.
    Married Sep 17 1843 in Clark Co., OH, **Adam M. Brandle**.
    ### *Children*:
    - 120 i. Elizs A.^{4} Brandle b. About 1844 in Clark Co., OH.
    - 121 ii. Eli Brandle b. May 1847 in Clark Co., OH.
    - 122 iii. Reuben Brandle b. Sept 1849 in Clark Co., OH.
    - 123 iv. Harry S, Brandle b. About 1851 in Clark Co., OH.

25. **Helena Jane^3 Arbogast** (4.Eli McKinley^2, 1.Michael^1), b. Jun 10 1827 in Clark Co., OH, d. Aug 29 1851 in Clark Co., OH.
    Died giving birth to twin daughters, one daughter lived a little more than a week, and the other almost 2 weeks before death.
    Married May 18 1847 in Clark Co., OH, **Christian Brandle**.
    ### *Children*:
    - 124 i. Lemuel H.^{4} Brandle b. About 1848 in Moorefield TWP., Clark Co., OH.
      Married Feb-09-1875 in Clark Co., OH, Rilla C. Payne.
    - 125 ii. Ann E. Brandle b. Aug 29 1851 in Moorefield TWP., Clark Co., OH, d. Sept. 1851 in Moorefield TWP., Clark Co., OH.
    - 126 iii. Helena J. Brandle b. Aug 29 1851 in Moorefield TWP., Clark Co., OH, d. Sept 1851 in Moorefield TWP., Clark Co., OH.

28. **Reuben H.^{3} Arbogast** (4.Eli McKinley^2, 1.Michael^1), b. Apr 20 1835 in Clark Co., OH, d. Mar 28 1873 in Moorefield TWP., Clark Co., OH.
    He Married **Caroline Sheeder**, b. Oct 30 1839 in Moorefield TWP., Clark Co., OH.
    ### *Children*:
    - 127 i. Nancy Maud^4 Arbogast b. Jul 14 1870 in Moorefield TWP., Clark Co., OH.
    - 128 ii. Louisa May Arbogast b. Jul 14 1870 in Moorefield TWP., Clark Co., OH.
    - 129 iii. Reubin Sheeder Arbogast b. Sep 12 1873 in Moorefield TWP., Clark Co., OH.

32. **George Washington^3 Arbogast** (5.Solomon^2, 1.Michael^1), b. Oct 05 1837 in Clark Co., OH, d. Feb 04 1904 in Hardin Co., OH.
    Married May 08 1873 in Hardin Co., OH, **Sarah A. Warren**.
    ### *Children*:
    - 130 i. Charles^4 Arbogast b. Apr 29 1874 in Hardin Co., OH.
    - 131 ii. Gurnie Arbogast b. Feb 22 1877 in Hardin Co., OH.

      132   iii.   Leander Arbogast b. 2-20-1882 in Hardin Co., OH, d. Feb 7- 1959.

33. **Harrison^3 Arbogast** (5.Solomon^2, 1.Michael^1), b. Nov 15 1840 in Clark Co., OH, d. Jun 30 1927. Married May 04 1880, **Ellen Griffin**.

              Children:
- 133 i. Jennie^4 Arbogast b. Feb 20 1882.
- 134 ii. Cleta Arbogast b. Aug 19 1882.
- 135 iii. Roy Arbogast b. Aug 22 1883.
- 136 iv. Alta Arbogast b. Mar 12 1886.
- 137 v. Earnest Arbogast b. Mar 16 1888.
- 138 vi. Beatrice Arbogast b. Sep 30 1890.
- 139 vii. Guy Arbogast b. Jan 21 1895 in Hardin Co., OH.
- 140 viii. Scott Arbogast b. Mar 20 1898 in Hardin Co., OH.

42. **Louisa A.^{3} McKinnon** (7.Elizabeth (Betsy)^2 Arbogast, 1.Michael^1), b. About 1841 in Clark Co., OH. She Married **Hamilton P. Franks, MD**, b. Mar 8 1849 in Hardin Co., OH (son of Peter Franks and Mary Brown).

              Children:
- 141 i. Jessie M.^{4} Franks b. 8 Nov 1972.
- 142 ii. Mary O. Franks b. 18 Nov 1981.

44. **Miles Elliott^3 Mullenax** (8.Catherine Kate^2 Arbogast, 1.Michael^1), b. Sep 06 1820 in Clark Co., OH, d. Mar 22 1896 in Jackson Co., KS.
Married Dec 10 1848 in Missouri, **Rachel Ellen Miller**, b. Oct 27 1833 in Ohio, d. 0616102 in Jackson Co., KS.

              Children:
- \+ 143 i. Clotilda Adeline^4 Mullenax b. May 05 1853.
- \+ 144 ii. William Dallas Mullenax b. Dec 02 1854.
- \+ 145 iii. John Greenbury Mullenax b. Aug 27 1856.

45. **Elizabeth J.^{3} Mullenax** (8.Catherine Kate^2 Arbogast, 1.Michael^1), b. 1827 in Ohio, d. 1886. She Married **Jacob Matheny**.

              Children:
- 146 i. Martha Jane^4 Matheny.

46. **William R.^{3} Mullenax** (8.Catherine Kate^2 Arbogast, 1.Michael^1), b. Oct 10 1832 in Madison Co., IN, d. May 10 1901 in Holton, Jackson Co., KS.
Title: Family Data Collection - Individual Records Author: Edmund West, comp.
Publication: Online publication - Provo, UT, USA: The Generations Network, Inc., 2000.
Married Dec 13 1855 in Andrew Co., MO, **Mary Ann Kincade**, b. Jan 07 1833 in Illinois, d. Dec 23 1906 in Holton, Jackson Co., KS.

              Children:
- \+ 147 i. Matthew Elliott^4 Mullenax b. Jun 07 1858.
- 148 ii. Elizabeth Jane Mullenax b. Jan 02 1860 in Holton, Jackson Co., KS.
  Married 28 Nov 1880 in Jackson Co., KS, **William Coleman**.
- 149 iii. Rachel Elizabeth Mullenax b. Apr 15 1862 in Kansas.
  (1) She Married **Jake Helm**.
  (2) She Married **Floyd Beauchamp**.
- \+ 150 iv. Jacob Allen Mullenax b. Oct 10 1864.
- 151 v. Katherine Mullenax b. Jan 19 1866 in Kansas.
  Married 20 May 1983, **Milton Curtis**.
- 152 vi. Mary L. Mullenax b. May 30 1868 in Kansas. (
  1) She Married **Joe Lightbody**.
  (2) Married 17 Feb 1886, **Jake Helm**.
- \+ 153 vii. John William Mullenax b. Jan 07 1871.

154 viii. Nellie Mullenax b. About 1876 in Jackson Co., KS, d. Sept. 1907.
  Married 6 Jun 1893 in Jackson Co., KS, **Bruce Fouch**.
155 ix. Sarah E. Mullenax b. 2-11-1876.
+ 156 x. Lucy Adeline Mullenax b. Aug 27 1878.
157 xi. Jesse E. Mullenax b. Apr 28 1882, d. 9 Jan 1900.
  He Married **(unknown) Perry**.

Generation Four

51. **Martin^4 Wierack** (9.Catherine^3 Arbogast, 2.George^2, 1.Michael^1).
He Married **Elizabeth Reed**.
  Children:
  158 i. Myrtle^5 Wierack.

70. **George W.^{4} Driscoll** (13.Melinda^3 Arbogast, 2.George^2, 1.Michael^1), b. Jan 09 1844 on Ohio.
Married Sep 27 1866 in Clark Co., OH, **Rosa Gwyn**, b. Nov 13 1843 in Barcelona, Spain (daughter of John Edward Gwyn and Isabella Turnbull).
  Children:
  159 i. Minnie^5 Driscoll b. About 1874 in Ohio.
  + 160 ii. James Gwyn Driscoll b. Mar 02 1883.
  161 iii. Edward Driscoll b. Feb 25 1886 in Ohio.

71. **John H.^{4} Driscoll** (13.Melinda^3 Arbogast, 2.George^2, 1.Michael^1), b. About 1845 in Springfield, Clark Co., OH.
Married About 1873 in Ohio, **Emme Kennedy**, b. About 1854 in Ohio.
  Children:
  162 i. Albert^5 Driscoll b. About 1874 in Ohio.
  163 ii. Robert Driscoll b. About 1876 in Ohio.
  164 iii. John H. Driscoll, Jr. b. About 1879 in Ohio.

143. **Clotilda Adeline^4 Mullenax** (44.Miles Elliott^3, 8.Catherine Kate^2 Arbogast, 1.Michael^1), b. May 05 1853 in Montana, d. Jun 01 1920 in Jackson Co., KS.
Married Jan 02 1873 in Kansas, **John H. Renfro**, b. About 1849 in Missouri.
USA Notes of Dorothy Mullenax. Dorothy is the wife of Lewis Mullenax, Anita's cousin.
  Children:
  165 i. Mary Agnus.^{5} Renfro b. 1873.
    She Married **Henry Ray**.
  166 ii. Rachel Ann Renfro b. 1875.
    Married 1898, **Lewis England**.
  167 iii. Jesse Renfro b. 1879.
  168 iv. Lucy Renfro b. 1882.
  169 v. Flora Renfro b. 1883.
    Married 1911, **John Krumrey**.

144. **William Dallas^4 Mullenax** (44.Miles Elliott^3, 8.Catherine Kate^2 Arbogast, 1.Michael^1), b. Dec 02 1854 in Missouri, d. Jun 01 1920 in Jackson Co., MO.
Married Sep 17 1876, **Mary Renfro**, b. in Missouri (daughter of James Renfro and Ann Overly), buried in South Cedar Cem., Denison, Jackson Co., KS, d. May 04 1884 in Denison, Jackson Co., KS.
  Children:
  + 170 i. James Lewis^5 Mullenax b. Jul 27 1877.

    171   ii.   Arthur Dallas Mullenax b. Oct 17 1880 in Kansas, d. Sep 28 1945 in Topeka, Shawnee Co., KS.
He Married **Mary E. Campbell**.

    172   iii.   Harry Edgar Mullenax b. Dec 13 1881 in Kansas, buried in Holton, Jackson Co., KS, d. Aug 06 1955 in Holton, Jackson Co., KS.
Married Dec 25 1901 in Holton, Jackson Co., KS, **Cora Spiker**.

    173   iv.   George Ellet Mullenax b. Apr 29 1884, buried in Cassoday, Butler Co., KS, d. Oct 31 1951 in Cassoday, Butler Co., KS.
Married Mar 22 1905 in Topeka, Shawnee Co., KS, **Myrtle Martin**.

145.   **John Greenbury⁴ Mullenax** (44.Miles Elliott³, 8.Catherine Kate² Arbogast, 1.Michael¹), b. Aug 27 1856 in Missouri, d. Aug 20 1930 in Denison, Jackson Co., KS, buried in South Cedar Cem., Denison, Jackson Co., KS.
Title: 1880 United States Federal Census
   (1) Married Sep 05 1977 in Denison, Jackson Co., KS, **Flora Ellen Kirkpatrick**, b. Dec 27 1858 in Muskingum Co., OH (daughter of James W. Kirkpatrick and Eleanor Ann Lyons), buried in South Cedar Cem., Denison, Jackson Co., KS, d. Jun 20 1889 in Denison, Jackson Co., KS.

           Children *by Flora Ellen Kirkpatrick:*
+ 174   i.   Flora Adeline⁵ Mullenax b. 0828879.
   175   ii.   Rachel Ellen Mullenax b. Aug 28 1878 in Donison, Jackson Co., KS, d. Apr 04 1957.
   176   iii.   Ida May Mullenax b. Apr 27 1883 in Kansas, d. Aug 05 1919 in Kansas.
   177   iv.   (infant) Mullenax b. May 17 1884 in Jackson Co., KS, d. May 17 1884 in Jackson Co., KS.
   178   v.   John W. Mullenax b. Aug 26 1886 in Kansas, d. Mar 29 1905 in Kansas.
   179   vi.   Anna M. Mullenax b. Jun 01 1889 in Kansas, d. Aug 16 1889 in Kansas.

   (2) He Married **Rachel McRaynolds**, d. 1930 in Kansas.

147.   **Matthew Elliott⁴ Mullenax** (46.William R.³, 8.Catherine Kate² Arbogast, 1.Michael¹), b. Jun 07 1858 in Grant Twp., Jackson Co., KS, d. Aug 11 1928 in Mayetta, Jackson Co., KS, buried Aug 13 1928 in Mayetta, Jackson Co., KS. Married Feb 13 1881 in Doniphan Co., KS, **Olive Lavina Payne**.

           Children:
   180   i.   Joseph M.⁵ Mullenax b. Jun 26 1886 in Jackson Co., KS, buried in Olive Hill Cem., Horton, Brown Co., KS, d. Jun 08 1894 in Jackson Co., KS.
   181   ii.   Walter Mullenax b. Nov 09 1888 in Jackson Co., KS, d. Oct 08 1964.
He Married **Bessie Sharrai**.
+ 182   iii.   Mary Aceneth Mullenax b. Oct 10 1890.
   183   iv.   Kate Mullenax b. Sep 17 1892 in Jackson Co., KS, d. Sep 1962 in Topeka, Shawnee Co., KS.
She Married **Jess Martin**.
   184   v.   Grace Mullenax b. Aug 23 1895, buried in Olive Hill Cem., Horton, Brown Co., KS, d. Dec 05 1895 in Jackson Co., KS.
   185   vi.   Leroy Mullenax b. May 10 1896 in Jackson Co., KS, d. Aug 15 1961 in Jackson Co., KS.
He Married **Elizabeth Lavier**.
+ 186   vii.   Louis Mullenax b. Oct 19 1898.
+ 187   viii.   Alfred Mullenax b. Feb 11 1901.

150.   **Jacob Allen⁴ Mullenax** (46.William R.³, 8.Catherine Kate² Arbogast, 1.Michael¹), b. Oct 10 1864 in Jackson Co., KS, d. 19 Apr 1944 in Torrington, Goshen Co., WY.
Married 15 Feb 1992 in Pottawattamie Co., KS, **Maymie Alice Brooks Bennett**, b. 1854, d. 1929 in Laramie, Laramie Co., WY.

           Children:
   188   i.   Violet⁵ Mullenax b. 27 Jan 1896, d. 26 Apr 1930.
She Married **William Alvin Shaw**.

189   ii.   Bessie Mullenax.
190   iii.   Hazel Mullenax d. 1964.
              She Married **Fred Cooley**.
191   iv.   Raymond Mullenax.
192   v.   Ed Barnett Mullenax.

153. **John William**[4] **Mullenax** (46.William R.[3], 8.Catherine Kate[2] Arbogast, 1.Michael[1]), b. Jan 07 1871 in Kansas, d. 28 Dec 1938 in Lafayette, Yamhill Co., OR, buried in Evergreen Cem., McMinnville, Yamhill Co., OR.
Married 23 Dec 1896 in Jackson Co., KS, **Sarah Ellen Osburn**, b. 25 Aug 1876 in Havensville, Pottawatomie Co., KS, d. 18 Sep 1940 in Lafayette, Yamhill Co., OR, buried in Evergreen Cem., McMinnville, Yamhill Co., OR.

             Children:
      193   i.   Gertrude May[5] Mullenax b. 10 Mar 1898 in Havensville, Pottawatomie Co., KS, d. 5 Oct 1961.
+   194   ii.   Calvin Silas Mullenax b. 16 Aug 1903.
      195   iii.   Alice Ruby Mullenax b. 21 May 1907.
+   196   iv.   Edith Pearl Mullenax b. 25 May 1909.
+   197   v.   Ruby Ann Mullenax b. 25 Aug 1916.

156. **Lucy Adeline**[4] **Mullenax** (46.William R.[3], 8.Catherine Kate[2] Arbogast, 1.Michael[1]), b. Aug 27 1878 in Denison, Jackson Co., KS, d. 24 Nov 1945 in Douglas, Converse Co., WY, buried in Holton, Jackson Co., KS.
Married 10 Mar 1897 in Jackson Co., KS, **James William Hager**, b. 17 Apr 1872 at Avoca, Jackson Co., KS (son of David Hammond Hagar and Laura Gish), d. 17 Nov 1937 in Topeka, Shawnee Co., KS, buried in Holton, Jackson Co., KS.

             Children:
      198   i.   Estella May[5] Hager b. 1 Oct 1898 in Avoca, Jackson Co., KS, d. 17 Feb 1952 in Kansas, buried in Holton, Jackson Co., KS.
             Married About 1922, **Frank Zibell**.
      199   ii.   Edith Asele Hager b. 18 Dec 1900 in Avoca, Jackson Co., KS, buried in Holton, Jackson Co., KS, d. 17 Jan 1978 in Arkansas.
             Married 27 Mar 1920, **Ray A. McKinsey**.
+   200   iii.   William Roy Hager b. 7 Jan 1903.
      201   iv.   Laura Maude Hagar b. 28 Dec 1904 in Avoca, Jackson Co., KS, d. About 1987 in Douglas, Converse Co., WY.
             Married 3 Mar 1923, **John S. Townend**.

Generation Five

160. **James Gwyn**[5] **Driscoll** (70.George W.[4], 13.Melinda[3] Arbogast, 2.George[2], 1.Michael[1]), b. Mar 02 1883 in Ohio.
He Married **Vera Ross**.

             Children:
      202   i.   Jack[6] Driscoll.

170. **James Lewis**[5] **Mullenax** (144.William Dallas[4], 44.Miles Elliott[3], 8.Catherine Kate[2] Arbogast, 1.Michael[1]), b. Jul 27 1877 in Kansas, buried in Denison, Jackson Co., KS, d. Nov 24 1952 in Abilene, Dickinson Co., KS.
Married Nov 04 1896 in Meriden, Jefferson Co., KS, **Mary Willella Bales**, b. Feb 14 1878 in Hancock Co., IN (daughter of John Bales and Sarah Jane Smith), d. Oct 01 1960 in Abilene, Dickinson Co., KS.

Children:

203   i.   Claude Arthur[6] Mulnanx b. Nov 27 1900 in Kansas, d. Nov 09 1986 in Riverside, Riverside Co., CA.
(1) Married Aug 07 1921, **Grace Moore**.
(2) He Married **Dolly Millikan**.

204   ii.   Curtis Mulnanx b. Mar 16 1901 in Jackson Co., KS, d. Mar 16 1901 in Jackson Co., KS.

+ 205   iii.   Hazel Marie **Mulnanx** b. Jun 01 1904.

206   iv.   Louise Ernest Mulnanx b. Sep 09 1907 in Denison, Jackson Co., KS, d. Sep 15 1972 in Enterprise, Dickinson Co., KS.
He Married **Velma A. Cline**.

207   v.   (infancy) Mulnanx b. Mar 29 1910 in Denison, Jackson Co., KS, d. Mar 29 1910 in Denison, Jackson Co., KS.

+ 208   vi.   Alvin Edgar Mulnanx b. Apr 01 1912.

209   vii.   Lyle Verne Mullenax b. May 22 1914 in Denison, Jackson Co., KS, d. Nov 19 1973 in Abilene, Dickinson Co., KS.
Married Nov 12 1935 in Enterprise, Dickinson Co., KS, **Marian A. Knox**.

210   viii.   Faye Ammelia Mullenax b. Nov 26 1916 in Denison, Jackson Co., KS.
Married Jun 21 1936 in Enterprise, Dickinson Co., KS, **Harold Laughlin**.

174. **Flora Adeline**[5] **Mullenax** (145.John Greenbury[4], 44.Miles Elliott[3], 8.Catherine Kate[2] Arbogast, 1.Michael[1]), b. 0828879 in Jackson Co., KS, d. Jan 12 1953 in Springtown, Benton Co., AR.
Married Oct 02 1895 in Holden, Jackson Co., KS, **Frank Francis Blaikie**, b. Oct 05 1862 in Coldingham, Scotland, buried in Gentry Cem., Gentry, Benton Co., AR, d. Nov 15 1941 in Springtown, Benton Co., AR.

Children:

211   i.   Maude[6] Blaikie b. Jul 26 1896 in Kansas, d. Sep 08 1976 in Oklahoma.

212   ii.   Flora Jane Blaikie b. Sep 23 1897 in Kansas, d. Jan 19 1985 in Oklahoma.

+ 213   iii.   Maggie May Blaikie b. Jun 19 1899.

214   iv.   Ellen E. Blaikie b. Oct 22 1900 in Jackson Co., KS, d. Oct 20 1987 in Oklahoma.

215   v.   John W. Blaikie b. Jul 20 1902 in Jackson Co., KS, d. May 21 1966 in Oklahoma.

216   vi.   Jessie A. Blaikie b. Dec 22 1905 in Jackson Co., KS.

217   vii.   Nora Bell Blaikie b. Jun 03 1911.

218   viii.   Robert F. Blaikie b. Jul 22 1912, d. in Gentry, Benton Co., AR.

182. **Mary Aceneth**[5] **Mullenax** (147.Matthew Elliott[4], 46.William R.[3], 8.Catherine Kate[2] Arbogast, 1.Michael[1]), b. Oct 10 1890 in Denison, Jackson Co., KS, d. Sep 03 1955.
Married May 03 1905 in Jackson Co., KS, **Riley Newton Osburn**, b. Apr 27 1881 in Havensville, Pottawatomie Co., KS (son of Stephen Osburn and Perthena Ann Smalley), d. Mar 22 1942 in McMinnville, Yamhill Co., OR.

Children:

+ 219   i.   Bessie Lee[6] Osburn b. Feb 24 1906.
+ 220   ii.   Charley Calvin Osburn b. Jul 24 1907.
+ 221   iii.   Cleo Faye Osburn b. Feb 03 1909.
+ 222   iv.   Samuel Stephen Osburn b. Oct 23 1910.
+ 223   v.   Parthena Ann Osburn b. Oct 25 1912.
+ 224   vi.   Mable Marie Osburn b. Apr 23 1915.
+ 225   vii.   Myrtle May Osburn b. Apr 23 1915.
+ 226   viii.   Minnie Belle Osburn b. Oct 30 1916.
+ 227   ix.   Francis Paul Osburn b. Oct 14 1928.
+ 228   x.   Theodore Harvey Osburn b. Oct 13 1920.
+ 229   xi.   Mary Helen Rose Osburn b. Feb 26 1922.

230   xii.   Jim Conrad Burton Osburn b. Jun 17 1924, buried in Marcola Cem., Lane Co., OR, d. Apr 16 1989 in Marcola, Lane Co., OR. He

Married **Clarabelle Jones**, b. 13 Aug 1930 in Ontario, Vernon Co., WI (daughter of William Samuel Jones and Claudia Bell Todd).
231   xiii.   Riley Matthew Osburn b. Jul 05 1926 in Ontario, Malheur Co., OR.
He Married **Beatrice Faye Guther**, b. 20 Jan 1923 in Lakeview, Lake Co., OR.
+ 232   xiv.   Zella Jane Osburn b. Oct 04 1928.
233   xv.   Vance Vernon Osburn b. Jan 18 1931 in Payette, Payette Co., ID.

186. **Louis^5 Mullenax** (147.Matthew Elliott^4, 46.William R.^{3}, 8.Catherine Kate^2 Arbogast, 1.Michael^1), b. Oct 19 1898 in Jackson Co., KS, d. Mar 1963 in Mayetta, Jackson Co., KS.
Married 27 Jan 1921 in Jackson Co., KS, **Eunice Lavier** (daughter of Joe Lavier and Martha Battesse).

    Children:
234   i.   James Matthew^6 Mullenax b. in Jackson Co., KS.
Married 18 Jul 1953 in Jackson Co., KS, **Dorothy Nozhachum**.
235   ii.   Kenneth Mullenax.
Married 29 Jul 1967 in Jackson Co., KS, **Elizabeth Stueve**.
236   iii.   Irvan Mulanax.
(1) He Married **Jeanie Hannerhan**.
(2) He Married **Janice Thompson**.
237   iv.   William Mulanax b. in Jackson Co., KS.
He Married **Mary Fitzgerald**.
238   v.   Elta Vera Mulanax b. in Jackson Co., KS.
She Married **Clayton H. Ray**.
239   vi.   Cora Vivena Mulanax b. in Jackson Co., KS.
She Married **Abe Walkenstick**.

187. **Alfred^5 Mulanax** (147.Matthew Elliott^4, 46.William R.^{3}, 8.Catherine Kate^2 Arbogast, 1.Michael^1), b. Feb 11 1901 in Jackson Co., KS, buried in Evergreen Cem., McMinnville, Yamhill Co., OR, d. Aug 1956.
He Married **Ruby Ann Mulanax**, b. 25 Aug 1916 (daughter of John William Mulanax and Sarah Ellen Osburn), d. 21 Dec 1966 in Evergreen Cem., McMinnville, Yamhill Co., OR.

    Children:
240   i.   Matthew William^6 Mulanax b. 1940.

194. **Calvin Silas^5 Mulanax** (153.John William^4, 46.William R.^{3}, 8.Catherine Kate^2 Arbogast, 1.Michael^1), b. 16 Aug 1903 in Havensville, Pottawatomie Co., KS, buried in Evergreen Cem., McMinnville, Yamhill Co., OR, d. 24 Apr 1966 in Portland, Multnomah Co., OR.
Married 20 Mar 1927 in Portland, Multnomah Co., OR, **Marguerite Barbara Deets**, b. 11 Sep 1906 in Kearny Co., KS, buried in Evergreen Cem., McMinnville, Yamhill Co., OR, d. 2 Apr 1994.

    Children:
+ 241   i.   Dorothy Ellen^6 Mulanax b. 3 Apr 1929.

196. **Edith Pearl^5 Mulanax** (153.John William^4, 46.William R.^{3}, 8.Catherine Kate^2 Arbogast, 1.Michael^1), b. 25 May 1909.
She Married **Ernest Alexander**.

    Children:
242   i.   Bidwell William^6 Alexander.

197. **Ruby Ann^5 Mulanax** (153.John William^4, 46.William R.^{3}, 8.Catherine Kate^2 Arbogast, 1.Michael^1)
(See marriage to number 187.)

200. **William Roy^5 Hager** (156.Lucy Adeline^4 Mulanax, 46.William R.^{3}, 8.Catherine Kate^2 Arbogast, 1.Michael^1), b. 7 Jan 1903 in Avoca, Jackson Co., KS, buried in Casper City Cem., Casper, WY, d. 26 Feb 1971 in Casper, Natrona Co., KY.
(1) Married 14 Apr 1923, **Pearl McQueen**.

(2) Married 21 Dec 1925 in Douglas, Converse Co., WY, **Martha Markytan**, b. 14 Jun 1908 in Clarkston, Colfax Co., NE (daughter of John Markyston and Julie Koukal), buried in Casper City Cem., Casper, WY, d. 22 Dec 1977 in Casper, Natrona Co., KY.

Children by Martha Markytan:
+ 243   i.   Ardath Lenore^6 Hagar b. 23 Feb 1937.

Generation Six

205. **Hazel Marie^6 Mulnanx** (170.James Lewis^5 Mulanax, 144.William Dallas^4, 44.Miles Elliott^3, 8.Catherine Kate^2 Arbogast, 1.Michael^1), b. Jun 01 1904 in Denison, Jackson Co., KS.
Married May 15 1922, **Lester Earl Townsend**, b. Jun 26 1900 in Jackson Co., KS, buried in Denison, Jackson Co., KS, d. Sep 23 1969 in Topeka, Shawnee Co., KS.

Children:
    244   i.   (infant)^7 Townsend b. 1922, d. 1923.
    245   ii.   Virginia Louise Townsend b. Jul 13 1924 in Denison, Jackson Co., KS, buried in Denison, Jackson Co., KS, d. May 02 1971 in Topeka, Shawnee Co., KS.
+ 246   iii.   Lester Lou Townsend b. Sep 09 1927.

208. **Alvin Edgar^6 Mulnanx** (170.James Lewis^5 Mulanax, 144.William Dallas^4, 44.Miles Elliott^3, 8.Catherine Kate^2 Arbogast, 1.Michael^1), b. Apr 01 1912 in Denison, Jackson Co., KS, buried in Denison Cem., Jackson Co., KS, d. Apr 24 1987 in Manhattan, Riley Co., KS. He
Married **Alma Katherine Schiller, R.n.**, b. Sep 04 1914 in Kirwin, Phillips Co., KS (daughter of Frank William Schiller and Edith May Thomas).

Children:
+ 247   i.   Roger Lewis^7 Mulanax b. Jul 15 1945.

213. **Maggie May^6 Blaikie** (174.Flora Adeline^5 Mulanax, 145.John Greenbury^4, 44.Miles Elliott^3, 8.Catherine Kate^2 Arbogast, 1.Michael^1), b. Jun 19 1899 in Jackson Co., KS, d. Oct 13 1929 in Grant Co., OK.
Married May 15 1925 in Bentonville, Benton Co., OK, **Leslie Howard Nelson**, b. Oct 16 1900 in Columbia, Kingfish Co., OK (son of George Monroe Nelson and Nellie Beatty Moore), buried in Cherry Hill, Polk Co., AR, d. Feb 02 1990 in Mena, Polk Co., AR.

Children:
    248   i.   Vera Dean^7 Nelson b. Apr 02 1926 in Pond Creek, Grant Co., OK, d. Apr 13 1926 in Pond Creek, Grant Co., OK.
    249   ii.   Jean Earl Nelson b. Dec 20 1927 in Pond Creek, Grant Co., OK, d. Dec 26 1927 in Pond Creek, Grant Co., OK.
+ 250   iii.   Jane Earline Nelson b. Dec 20 1927.
    251   iv.   Cleo May Nelson b. Oct 13 1929 in Perry, Noble Co., OK, d. Oct 13 1929 in Perry, Noble Co., OK.

219. **Bessie Lee^6 Osburn** (182.Mary Aceneth^5 Mulanax, 147.Matthew Elliott^4, 46.William R.^{3}, 8.Catherine Kate^2 Arbogast, 1.Michael^1), b. Feb 24 1906, buried in Springfield, Lane Co., OR, d. Jul 16 1976 in Springfield, Lane Co., OR.
Married Sep 08 1924 in Idaho, **James William Newton Franklin**, b. Apr 06 1883 in Buffalo, Dallas Co., MO (son of James Benton Franklin and Liza Slack), d. May 29 1954 in Silverton, Marion Co., OR.

Children:
+ 252   i.   Francis Billey^7 Franklin b. Jun 23 1925.
+ 253   ii.   Vernon Newton Franklin b. Feb 27 1927.
+ 254   iii.   Wayne Russell Franklin b. Oct 12 1928.
+ 255   iv.   Maty Ann Franklin b. Jul 10 1930.

+ 256   v.   Gladys Faye Franklin b. Mar 28 1932.
+ 257   vi.   Lois Ruth Franklin b. Mar 06 1934.
+ 258   vii.   Betty Jean Franklin b. Nov 10 1935.
+ 259   viii.   Bonnie Jean Franklin b. Sep 10 1937.
+ 260   ix.   James Lee Franklin b. Sep 10 1937.
+ 261   x.   John Allen Franklin b. Apr 09 1939.
+ 262   xi.   Alman Ray Franklin b. Sep 05 1941.

220. **Charley Calvin**[6] **Osburn** (182.Mary Aceneth[5] Mulanax, 147.Matthew Elliott[4], 46.William R.[3], 8.Catherine Kate[2] Arbogast, 1.Michael[1]), b. Jul 24 1907 in Paxton, Harvey Co., KS, buried in Riverside Cem., Payette Co., ID, d. Nov 02 1973 in Bellingham, Whatcom Co., WA.
Married Oct 06 1931 in Payette, Payette Co., WA, **Agnus Virenda Corbit**, b. Feb 02 1924 in Idaho Falls, Bonneville Co., ID (daughter of Ira Alfred Corbit and Susie A. Meeds), buried in Riverside Cem., Payette Co., ID, d. Feb 27 1974 near Bellingham, Whatcom Co., WA.

       Children:
+ 263   i.   Ethel Fern[7] Osburn b. Aug 24 1932.
   264   ii.   Charleyn Joy Osburn b. Apr 19 1934 in Wendell, Gooding Co., ID.
             Married Nov 26 1965 in Oregon Falls, OR, **Clarie Gerald Harris**.
+ 265   iii.   Billie Lorreen Osburn b. May -2 1936.
+ 266   iv.   Kathryn Michael Osburn b. Mar 22 1939.

221. **Cleo Faye**[6] **Osburn** (182.Mary Aceneth[5] Mulanax, 147.Matthew Elliott[4], 46.William R.[3], 8.Catherine Kate[2] Arbogast, 1.Michael[1]), b. Feb 03 1909, d. May 29 1968.
She Married **Christopher Thomas Soron**, b. Jul 26 1898 in Denver, Arapaho Co., CO (son of Thomas Soran and Anne Meade).

       Children:
+ 267   i.   Mary Virginia[7] Soron b. Aug 10 1929.
   268   ii.   Annastasia Soran b. Jan 17 1913, d. Jun 1931.
+ 269   iii.   Thomas Christopher Soran b. Jan 31 1933.
   270   iv.   Rita (Louise) Soran b. Jun 02 1934.
             Married Sep 11 1954, **Leo Echel**.
   271   v.   Patricia Soran b. Jul 08 1935.
             She Married **Lenard McMahan**.
   272   vi.   Christopher Soran b. Apr 17 1937 in Boise, Ada Co., ID, d. Jan 02 1939.
   273   vii.   Michael Thomas Soran b. Jan 26 1941.
             Married 1958, **Donna McHugh**.
+ 274   viii.   Cordelia Soran b. Jan 20 1941.
+ 275   ix.   Stephen Michael Soran b. Dec 10 1943.
   276   x.   Phillip Stephen Soran b. May 21 1945 in Denver, Denver Co., CO.
             Married Nov 11 1967, **Mary Theresa Thurston**.
   277   xi.   Matthew Richard Soran b. Jul 29 1947 in Twin Falls Co., ID, d. 1967.
             He Married Barbara **Ann Friskie**.

222. **Samuel Stephen**[6] **Osburn** (182.Mary Aceneth[5] Mulanax, 147.Matthew Elliott[4], 46.William R.[3], 8.Catherine Kate[2] Arbogast, 1.Michael[1]), b. Oct 23 1910 in Avoca, Jackson Co., KS, buried in Midvale, Washington Co., ID, d. Dec 1984 in Midvale, Washington Co., ID.
Married Apr 04 1934 in Payette, Payette Co., ID, **Thelma Head**, b. Jun 24 1914 (daughter of Marion Head and Alzona Head).

       Children:
+ 278   i.   Patricia Lee[7] Osburn b. Jun 29 1935.
+ 279   ii.   Betty Jane Osburn b. Jun 19 1937.
+ 280   iii.   Linda Gail Osburn b. Jun 15 1940.
+ 281   iv.   John Franklin Osburn b. Aug 31 1943.
+ 282   v.   Connie Jean Osburn b. Mar 02 1950.

223. **Parthena Ann**[6] **Osburn** (182.Mary Aceneth[5] Mulanax, 147.Matthew Elliott[4], 46.William R.[3], 8.Catherine Kate[2] Arbogast, 1.Michael[1]), b. Oct 25 1912 in Emmett, Pottawatomie Co., KS.
Married 20 Jun 1934 in Boise, Ada Co., ID, **Floyd Edward Van Horn**, b. 3 Mar 1908 in Solomon, Dixon Co., KS.

    Children:
- 283   i.   Billie Floyd[7] Van Horn b. 2 Nov 1936 in Boise, Ada Co., ID.
  Married 5 May 1956, **Marilyn Jean King**.
- 284   ii.   Jackie Dean Van Horn b. 2 Dec 1939 in Boise, Ada Co., ID.
  Married 25 May 1961, **Dorris Lea De Mott**.
- 285   iii.   Judith Ann Van Horn b. 21 Sep 1941 in Boise, Ada Co., ID.
  Married 5 Jun 1959, **Delloyd Bowen**.

224. **Mable Marie**[6] **Osburn** (182.Mary Aceneth[5] Mulanax, 147.Matthew Elliott[4], 46.William R.[3], 8.Catherine Kate[2] Arbogast, 1.Michael[1]), b. Apr 23 1915 in Elkton, Mower Co., MN, buried in Marcola, Lane Co., OR, d. May 17 1981 in Springfield, Lane Co., OR.
Married 16 Apr 1933 in Payette, Payette Co., ID, **Archaball Allen**, b. 7 Dec 1909 in Deerhead, Barber Co., KS, d. in Marcola, Lane Co., OR.

    Children:
- + 286   i.   Doris Acentha[7] Allen b. 22 Feb 1934.
- + 287   ii.   Opal Jane Allen b. 30 May 1935.

225. **Myrtle May**[6] **Osburn** (182.Mary Aceneth[5] Mulanax, 147.Matthew Elliott[4], 46.William R.[3], 8.Catherine Kate[2] Arbogast, 1.Michael[1]), b. Apr 23 1915 in Elkton, Mower Co., MN.
Married 20 Oct 1931 in Vale, Malheur Co., OR, **Carol Thomas Fulton**, b. 9 Jun 1910 in Iowa.

    Children:
- + 288   i.   Eunice Marie[7] Fulton b. 12 May 1932.
- 289   ii.   Lamont Fulton b. 29 Dec 1942 in Payette, Payette Co., ID.
  Married 1951, **Carol Thornton**.

226. **Minnie Belle**[6] **Osburn** (182.Mary Aceneth[5] Mulanax, 147.Matthew Elliott[4], 46.William R.[3], 8.Catherine Kate[2] Arbogast, 1.Michael[1]), b. Oct 30 1916 in Payette, Payette Co., ID, buried in Jupiter Haven Cem., Prineville, Crook Co., OR, d. Jun 03 1994 in Prineville, Crook Co., OR.
She Married **Lester Thomas Garside**, b. 19 Jul 1914 in Ontario, Malheur Co., OR.

    Children:
- 290   i.   Lawrence Addison[7] Garside b. 25 Jul 1934 in Payette, Payette Co., ID.
  He Married **Ruby Smith**.
- 291   ii.   Mearl Lester Garside b. 25 Nov 1935 in Payette, Payette Co., ID.
- 292   iii.   Cinthea Loreda Garside b. 15 Jul 1945 in Lakeview, Lake Co., OR.
  She Married **Duane Morgan**.

227. **Francis Paul**[6] **Osburn** (182.Mary Aceneth[5] Mulanax, 147.Matthew Elliott[4], 46.William R.[3], 8.Catherine Kate[2] Arbogast, 1.Michael[1]), b. Oct 14 1928 in Poapie, Mower Co., MN, d. Jul 29 1989 in Vancouver, Clark Co., WA.
(1) Married 17 Apr 1941 in Weiser, Washington Co., ID, **Dorothy Grace Windle**, b. 24 May 1925 in Payette, Payette Co., ID.

    Children by Dorothy Grace Windle:
- 293   i.   Ronald[7] Osburn b. 22 Oct 1942 in La Grange, Cook Co., OR.
  (1) Married 1966, Lillian Hardy. (
  2) Married Mar 1971, Diane Slone.
- 294   ii.   Mary Osburn b. 1 Apr 1944 in Payette, Payette Co., ID. (
  1) Married 2 May 1964, Wilber Skinner.
  (2) Married 23 Nov 1971, Norman Johnson.
  (3) She Married (unknown) Fraizer.
- 295   iii.   Joyce Osburn b. 13 Oct 1945 in Ontario, Malheur Co., OR.
  She Married (unknown) Gilbertson.

(2) He Married **Dessa Evelon Wilson**, b. 29 Jun 1950 in Plymouth, Payette Co., ID.
> ***Children*** *by Dessa Evelon Wilson:*

296   iv.   Andrea Osburn b. 14 Dec 1950.
           Married Aug 1973, **Richard Guthery**.
297   v.   Daniel Osburn b. 16 Feb 1952.
298   vi.   Julie Osburn b. 27 Apr 1953.
           She Married **Ivan Lamarr**.
299   vii.   Lynn Osburn b. 3 Jan 1955.
300   viii.   Stanley Osburn.
301   ix.   Jerry Osburn b. 6 Apr 1958.

228. **Theodore Harvey⁶ Osburn** (182.Mary Aceneth⁵ Mulanax, 147.Matthew Elliott⁴, 46.William R.³, 8.Catherine Kate² Arbogast, 1.Michael¹), b. Oct 13 1920 in Plainview, Wabasha Co., MN, buried in Riverside Cem., Payette Co., ID, d. Aug 03 1985 in Payette, Payette Co., ID.
(1) He Married **Ellen Lila Windle**, b. 11 Jun 1921 in Payette, Payette Co., ID (daughter of Burrel Windle and Elizabeth Mickelson).
> ***Children*** *by Ellen Lila Windle:*

+ 302   i.   Sandra⁷ Osburn b. 1 Oct 1941.
+ 303   ii.   Laurie Joan Osburn b. 22 May 1943.
  304   iii.   (infant) Osburn b. 1945, d. 1945.

(2) He Married **Edith Hoyle Tomasson**.
> ***Children*** *by Edith Hoyle Tomasson:*

305   iv.   Stephen Wayne Osburn b. 27 Jun 1956 in Ontario, Malheur Co., OR. He Married **Connie Haines**.
306   v.   Rita Faye Osburn b. 1957, d. 1970.
307   vi.   Teddy Lea Osburn b. 13 Sep 1958.

229. **Mary Helen Rose⁶ Osburn** (182.Mary Aceneth⁵ Mulanax, 147.Matthew Elliott⁴, 46.William R.³, 8.Catherine Kate² Arbogast, 1.Michael¹), b. Feb 26 1922 in Plainview, Wabasha Co., MN.
Married 20 Sep 1942 in Payette, Payette Co., ID, **Jesse William Compton**, d. 1969.
> ***Children***:

+ 308   i.   Carlotta Aceneth⁷ Compton b. 13 Sep 1942.
+ 309   ii.   Jesse William Compton, Jr. b. 1 Oct 1946.
  310   iii.   Timothy Jay Compton b. 16 Jun 1949, d. 18 Mar 1973.

232. **Zella Jane⁶ Osburn** (182.Mary Aceneth⁵ Mulanax, 147.Matthew Elliott⁴, 46.William R.³, 8.Catherine Kate² Arbogast, 1.Michael¹), b. Oct 04 1928 near Wenatchee, Chelan Co., WA.
She Married **Lyle Ames Wheeler**, b. 19 Oct 1922 in Kennewick, Benton Co., WA.
> ***Children***:

+ 311   i.   Lyle Anthony⁷ Wheeler b. 5 Aug 1957.
  312   ii.   Scott Matthew Wheeler. He
           Married **Connie Hayes**, b. 29 Dec 1958 in Springfield, Lane Co., OR.

241. **Dorothy Ellen⁶ Mulanax** (194.Calvin Silas⁵, 153.John William⁴, 46.William R.³, 8.Catherine Kate² Arbogast, 1.Michael¹), b. 3 Apr 1929 in Portland, Multnomah Co., OR.
She Married **Curtis Fay Myrick**, b. 31 Jan 1927 in Pendleton, Umatilla Co., OR.
> ***Children***:

+ 313   i.   Clinton Jay⁷ Myrick b. 1 Jun 1953.
+ 314   ii.   Calvin Curtis Myrick b. 4 Feb 1957.
+ 315   iii.   Cynthia Marguerite Myrick b. 9 Apr 1963.

243. **Ardath Lenore⁶ Hagar** (200.William Roy⁵ Hager, 156.Lucy Adeline⁴ Mulanax, 46.William R.³, 8.Catherine Kate² Arbogast, 1.Michael¹), b. 23 Feb 1937 in Douglas, Converse Co., WY.

Married 10 Dec 1954 in Lincoln, Lancaster Co., NE, **Paul Elton Brown**, b. 7 Oct 1932 in Cochran, Bleckley Co., GA.

    Children:
- 316 i. Martha Laree[7] Brown b. 4 Jan 1958 in Atlanta, Fulton Co., GA.
- 317 ii. Lenore Ann Brown b. 18 Jul 1959 in De Kalb Co., GA.
  Married 8 Nov 1991 in Knoxville, Knox Co., TN, **Gary Eugene Poteat**.

Generation Seven

246. **Lester Lou[7] Townsend** (205.Hazel Marie[6] Mulnanx, 170.James Lewis[5] Mulanax, 144.William Dallas[4], 44.Miles Elliott[3], 8.Catherine Kate[2] Arbogast, 1.Michael[1]), b. Sep 09 1927.
Married Aug 07 1948, **Peggy Redro**, b. Sep 04 1928 in Junction City, Geary Co., KS.

    Children:
- 318 i. Lester John[8] Townsend b. Nov 24 1949 in Manhattan, Riley Co., KS.
- + 319 ii. Louis Scott Townsend b. Sep 07 1953.
- + 320 iii. Harry Steve Townsend b. Nov 11 1958.
- + 321 iv. Kevin Lee Townsend b. Nov 03 1959.

247. **Roger Lewis[7] Mulanax** (208.Alvin Edgar[6] Mulnanx, 170.James Lewis[5] Mulanax, 144.William Dallas[4], 44.Miles Elliott[3], 8.Catherine Kate[2] Arbogast, 1.Michael[1]), b. Jul 15 1945 in Hot Springs, Garland Co., AR.
Married Jun 01 1970 in Manhattan, Riley Co., KS, **Joann Lefeber**, b. Nov 02 1947 in Chicago, Cook Co., IL (daughter of John Lefeber and Hazel Ann Sterrett).

    Children:
- 322 i. Douglas Lefeber[8] Mulanax b. Jun 03 1972 in Youngstown, Mahoning Co., OH.

250. **Jane Earline[7] Nelson** (213.Maggie May[6] Blaikie, 174.Flora Adeline[5] Mulanax, 145.John Greenbury[4], 44.Miles Elliott[3], 8.Catherine Kate[2] Arbogast, 1.Michael[1]), b. Dec 20 1927 in Pond Creek, Grant Co., OK.
Married Jun 14 1947 in Mena, Polk Co., AR, **William Jackson Barnes**, b. Sep 02 1927 in Mena, Polk Co., AR (son of Harvey L. Barnes and Gertrude Kellar).

    Children:
- + 323 i. Beverly Sue[8] Barnes b. Jun 30 1948.
- + 324 ii. Joane Sue Barnes b. Dec 15 1950.
- + 325 iii. Betty Lovella Barnes b. Oct 05 1952.
- 326 iv. William Jack Barnes b. Sep 05 1954.
  (1) Married Jun 01 1974 in Mena, Polk Co., AR, **Barbara Bell**.
  (2) He Married **Scheryl Campbell**`.

252. **Francis Billey[7] Franklin** (219.Bessie Lee[6] Osburn, 182.Mary Aceneth[5] Mulanax, 147.Matthew Elliott[4], 46.William R.[3], 8.Catherine Kate[2] Arbogast, 1.Michael[1]), b. Jun 23 1925 in Twin Falls Co., ID.
Married Apr 23 1950 in Springfield, Greene Co., MO, **Eunice Marie Loony**, b. Apr 23 1932 in Halfway, Polk Co., MO.

    Children:

- + 327 i. Randy Gale[8] Franklin b. Jun 26 1951.
- 328 ii. Ronald Dale Franklin b. Dec 18 1952 in Springfield, Greene Co., MO.
  He Married Mary Jane Edwards, b. Aug 12 1960.
- + 329 iii. Cheryl Lynn Franklin b. Aug 07 1954.

253. **Vernon Newton**[7] **Franklin** (219.Bessie Lee[6] Osburn, 182.Mary Aceneth[5] Mulanax, 147.Matthew Elliott[4], 46.William R.[3], 8.Catherine Kate[2] Arbogast, 1.Michael[1]), b. Feb 27 1927 in Denver, Denver Co., CO.
Married Apr 10 1948 in Buffalo, Dallas Co., MO, **Ailene Oleta Cansler**, b. Sep 09 1931 in Halfway, Polk Co., MO.

    Children:
- \+ 330   i.   Ricky Michael[8] Franklin b. Aug 16 1950.
- \+ 331   ii.   Brent Mitchell Franklin b. Dec 31 1952.
- \+ 332   iii.   Kevin Kyle Franklin b. Mar 19 1958.
-    333   iv.   Darren Vern Franklin b. Mar 08 1965 in Pekin, Tazewell Co., IL.

254. **Wayne Russell**[7] **Franklin** (219.Bessie Lee[6] Osburn, 182.Mary Aceneth[5] Mulanax, 147.Matthew Elliott[4], 46.William R.[3], 8.Catherine Kate[2] Arbogast, 1.Michael[1]), b. Oct 12 1928.
He Married **Lois Ann Jones**, b. Jan 01 1935 in Ontario, Vernon Co., WI.

    Children:
- \+ 334   i.   Galen Wayne[8] Franklin b. May 01 1952.
-    335   ii.   Gary Lee Franklin b. Jul 28 1954 in Eugene, Lane Co., OR.
Married Sep 21 1985 in Eugene, Lane Co., OR, **Debbie Faye Keefe**, b. May 05 1955 in Eugene, Lane Co., OR.
- \+ 336   iii.   Terry Lynn Franklin b. Oct 12 1955.

255. **Maty Ann**[7] **Franklin** (219.Bessie Lee[6] Osburn, 182.Mary Aceneth[5] Mulanax, 147.Matthew Elliott[4], 46.William R.[3], 8.Catherine Kate[2] Arbogast, 1.Michael[1]), b. Jul 10 1930 in Buffalo, Dallas Co., MO.
Married Aug 24 1950 in Reno, Washoe Co., NV, **Earl Claude Bruce**, b. Aug 06 1928.

    Children:
- \+ 337   i.   Shirley Ann[8] Bruce b. Mar 04 1941.
- \+ 338   ii.   Janell Kay Bruce b. Nov 20 1953.
- \+ 339   iii.   Liessa Gay Bruce b. Aug 15 1961.

256. **Gladys Faye**[7] **Franklin** (219.Bessie Lee[6] Osburn, 182.Mary Aceneth[5] Mulanax, 147.Matthew Elliott[4], 46.William R.[3], 8.Catherine Kate[2] Arbogast, 1.Michael[1]), b. Mar 28 1932 in Long Lane, Dallas Co., MO.
Married May 23 1950 in Reno, Washoe Co., NV, **Harry Wayne Crabtree**, b. Dec 16 1926 in Missouri.

    Children:
- \+ 340   i.   Harry James[8] Crabtree b. Mar 23 1951.
-    341   ii.   Sheldon DeWayne Crabtree b. May 18 1952 in Eugene, Lane Co., OR, d. Mar 23 1952 in Eugene, Lane Co., OR.
-    342   iii.   Sonya Faye Crabtree b. Aug 28 1953 in Silverton, Marion Co., OR, d. Apr 01 1956 in Eugene, Lane Co., OR.
-    343   iv.   Larry Dean Crabtree b. Mar 12 1955 near Silverton, Marion Co., OR.
Married Sep 14 1971 in Reno, Washoe Co., NV, **Carolyn Kay Bunch**, b. Dec 06 1958.

257. **Lois Ruth**[7] **Franklin** (219.Bessie Lee[6] Osburn, 182.Mary Aceneth[5] Mulanax, 147.Matthew Elliott[4], 46.William R.[3], 8.Catherine Kate[2] Arbogast, 1.Michael[1]), b. Mar 06 1934 in Long Lane, Dallas Co., MO.
Married Jun 06 1934 in Springfield, Lane Co., OR, **Gilman Joseph Fennimore**, b. Mar 24 1932 in Silverton, Marion Co., OR.

Children:
- \+ 344 i. Charmaine Marie[8] Fennimore b. Jul 15 1957.
- \+ 345 ii. Gilman Joseph Fennimore, Jr. b. Jul 23 1958.
- \+ 346 iii. Cassandra Lou Fennimore b. Aug 21 1960.

258. **Betty Jean[7] Franklin** (219.Bessie Lee[6] Osburn, 182.Mary Aceneth[5] Mulanax, 147.Matthew Elliott[4], 46.William R.[3], 8.Catherine Kate[2] Arbogast, 1.Michael[1]), b. Nov 10 1935.
Married Nov 11 1961 in Reno, Washoe Co., NV, **Vernon George Hoag**, b. Sep 25 1935 in Dixon, Logan Co., ND.
Children:
- \+ 347 i. Teresa Jean[8] Hoag b. Jun 08 1957.
- 348 ii. Valerie Lea Hoag b. Jun 23 1962 in Eugene, Lane Co., OR.
- 349 iii. Todd Vernon Hoag b. Jul 19 1963 in Eugene, Lane Co., OR.

259. **Bonnie Jean[7] Franklin** (219.Bessie Lee[6] Osburn, 182.Mary Aceneth[5] Mulanax, 147.Matthew Elliott[4], 46.William R.[3], 8.Catherine Kate[2] Arbogast, 1.Michael[1]), b. Sep 10 1937, d. Jul 06 1989 in Eugene, Lane Co., OR.
Married Jan 30 1955 in Woodburn, Marion Co., OR, **Oscar Larson, Jr.**, b. May 01 1955 in Oshkosh, Winnebago Co., WI.
Children:
- \+ 350 i. Gregory Allen[8] Larson b. Jul 08 1956.
- \+ 351 ii. Michael Ray Larson b. Feb 02 1958.
- 352 iii. Kimberly Lee Larson b. Oct 01 1960 in Springfield, Lane Co., OR.

260. **James Lee[7] Franklin** (219.Bessie Lee[6] Osburn, 182.Mary Aceneth[5] Mulanax, 147.Matthew Elliott[4], 46.William R.[3], 8.Catherine Kate[2] Arbogast, 1.Michael[1]), b. Sep 10 1937.
He Married **Tomi Jean Hatfield**, b. Jul 10 1939 in Buckholts, Milam Co., TX.
Children:
- 353 i. Colleen Ann[8] Franklin b. Jan 04 1958 in Eugene, Lane Co., OR.
  Married Jul 02 1981 in Eugene, Lane Co., OR, **Bryan Clough**, b. May 19 1959 in Fresno, Fresno Co., CA.
- 354 ii. John James Franklin b. May 09 1959.
- \+ 355 iii. William Douglas Franklin b. Feb 17 1963.
- 356 iv. James Paul Franklin b. Oct 26 1968 in Eugene, Lane Co., OR.

261. **John Allen[7] Franklin** (219.Bessie Lee[6] Osburn, 182.Mary Aceneth[5] Mulanax, 147.Matthew Elliott[4], 46.William R.[3], 8.Catherine Kate[2] Arbogast, 1.Michael[1]), b. Apr 09 1939.
Married Jan 16 1960 in Springfield, Lane Co., OR, **Malba May Sizemore**, b. Dec 31 1942.
Children:
- \+ 357 i. Brandel Allen[8] Franklin b. Aug 16 1960.
- 358 ii. Mark Lee Franklin b. Sep 26 1962 in Springfield, Lane Co., OR.
- 359 iii. Angelia Joy Franklin b. May 19 1964 in Springfield, Lane Co., OR.
- 360 iv. Melissa Robyn Franklin b. Apr 04 1966 in Springfield, Lane Co., OR.
- 361 v. Robyn Melinda Franklin b. Aug 29 1968 in Springfield, Lane Co., OR.

262. **Alman Ray[7] Franklin** (219.Bessie Lee[6] Osburn, 182.Mary Aceneth[5] Mulanax, 147.Matthew Elliott[4], 46.William R.[3], 8.Catherine Kate[2] Arbogast, 1.Michael[1]), b. Sep 05 1941.
Married Jul 03 1962 in Springfield, Lane Co., OR, **Shirley Dawn Nelson**, b. Nov 21 1942 in Chicago, Cook Co., IL.
Children:
- \+ 362 i. Tony Ray[8] Franklin b. Sep 14 1963.
- 363 ii. Wendy Lee Franklin b. May 05 1968.

263. **Ethel Fern[7] Osburn** (220.Charley Calvin[6], 182.Mary Aceneth[5] Mulanax, 147.Matthew Elliott[4], 46.William R.[3], 8.Catherine Kate[2] Arbogast, 1.Michael[1]), b. Aug 24 1932 in Boise, Ada Co., ID.

Married Jun 19 1950 in Winnemucca, Humboldt Co., NV, **Charles Isadore Arnold, Jr.**, b. Jul 03 1928 in Azalea, Green Co., IA (son of Charles Isadore Arnold and Pearl Mable Berry).

Children:

+ 364 i. Donald Gene[8] Arnold b. Jan 14 1951.
+ 365 ii. Shelly Lynn Arnold b. Jun 23 1956.

265. **Billie Lorreen**[7] **Osburn** (220.Charley Calvin[6], 182.Mary Aceneth[5] Mulanax, 147.Matthew Elliott[4], 46.William R.[3], 8.Catherine Kate[2] Arbogast, 1.Michael[1]), b. May -2 1936 in Payette, Payette Co., ID. Married Apr 04 1959 in Bellingham, Whatcom Co., WA, **Keith Duane Fagerburg**, b. May 05 1934 in Kirtland, King Co., WA (son of Theodore Fagerburd and Edna Lura Bluch).

Children:

+ 366 i. Juanita Raquelle[8] Fagerburg b. Jan 10 1960.
+ 367 ii. Martin Kerry Fagerburg b. Jan 06 1961.

266. **Kathryn Machiel**[7] **Osburn** (220.Charley Calvin[6], 182.Mary Aceneth[5] Mulanax, 147.Matthew Elliott[4], 46.William R.[3], 8.Catherine Kate[2] Arbogast, 1.Michael[1]), b. Mar 22 1939 in Payette, Payette Co., ID. She Married **Harold Glen Vail**, b. Oct 12 1933 in Sumas, Whatcom Co., WA (son of Glen Burton Vail and Sadie L. House).

Children:

 368 i. Charles Anthony[8] Vail b. Apr 24 1959 in Bellingham, Whatcom Co., WA. He Married Paula Huffine, b. May 12 1960 in Wichita, Sedgwick Co., KS.
+ 369 ii. Kimberly Cherise Vail b. Oct 02 1960.

267. **Mary Virginia**[7] **Soron** (221.Cleo Faye[6] Osburn, 182.Mary Aceneth[5] Mulanax, 147.Matthew Elliott[4], 46.William R.[3], 8.Catherine Kate[2] Arbogast, 1.Michael[1]), b. Aug 10 1929 in Emmett, Gem Co., ID, d. Nov 23 1990 in Spokane, Spokane Co., WA.
She Married **Robert Sullivan**, b. in Butte, Silver Bow Co., MT, buried in Holy Cross Cem., Spokane, WA.

Children:

 370 i. Delores Ann[8] Sullivan.
    Married in Spokane, Spokane Co., WA, **Gene Bonderman**.
 371 ii. Faye Elizabeth Sullivan.
    She Married **Scott Ellern**.
 372 iii. Dayle Marie Sullivan b. in Spokane, Spokane Co., WA.
    She Married **Randy L. Lewis**.
 373 iv. Timothy Albert Sullivan b. in Spokane, Spokane Co., WA.
    Married in Spokane, Spokane Co., WA, **Laurie Bonderman**.
 374 v. John Albert Sullivan.
 375 vi. Patricia J. Sullivan.
 376 vii. Michelle T. Sullivan.
 377 viii. Rita J. Sullivan.
 378 ix. Robert Patrick Sullivan.
 379 x. Todd Tyse Sullivan.

269. **Thomas Christopher**[7] **Soran** (221.Cleo Faye[6] Osburn, 182.Mary Aceneth[5] Mulanax, 147.Matthew Elliott[4], 46.William R.[3], 8.Catherine Kate[2] Arbogast, 1.Michael[1]), b. Jan 31 1933.
Married Aug 25 1956, **Cscelia Schweiger**.

Children:

 380 i. Thomas Christophor[8] Soran b. in Hoquiam, Grays Harbor Co., WA.
 381 ii. Joseph Soran b. in Hoquiam, Grays Harbor Co., WA.
 382 iii. Mary Soran.
 383 iv. Louise Soran.
 384 v. Steve Soran.
 385 vi. Tony Soran. Married in Tacoma, Pierce Co., WA, **Mary Fitzpatrick**.

386   vii.   Christopher Soran.
387   viii. Tim Soran.
388   ix.   Joan Soran b. 1968 in Everett, Snohomish Co., WA.

274. **Cordelia**[7] **Soran** (221.Cleo Faye[6] Osburn, 182.Mary Aceneth[5] Mulanax, 147.Matthew Elliott[4], 46.William R.[3], 8.Catherine Kate[2] Arbogast, 1.Michael[1]), b. Jan 20 1941 in Boise, Ada Co., ID.
(1) Married 1958, **Byron James Hobbs**.
(2) Married Jun 09 1973 in Coeur d'Alene, Kootenai Co., ID, **Paul Charles Kemble**, b. May 30 1937 in Martinez, Contra Costa, CA.
   Children by Paul Charles Kemble:
389   i.   Samuel Crispin[8] Kemble b. Jan 30 1976 in Spokane, Spokane Co., WA, d. Jan 31 1976.
390   ii. Kyle Crispin Kemble b. Sep 15 1978 in Spokane, Spokane Co., WA.

275. **Stephen Michael**[7] **Soran** (221.Cleo Faye[6] Osburn, 182.Mary Aceneth[5] Mulanax, 147.Matthew Elliott[4], 46.William R.[3], 8.Catherine Kate[2] Arbogast, 1.Michael[1]), b. Dec 10 1943 in Denver, Denver Co., CO.
Married Jul 05 1969 in Spokane, Spokane Co., WA, **Roberta Ann Schell**, b. Sep 09 1946 in Spokane, Spokane Co., WA (daughter of Robert Schell and Elsie Baldasty).
   Children:
391   i.   Eric[8] Soran b. Oct 01 1980 in Tacoma, Pierce Co., WA.
392   ii. Elizabeth Jo Beth Soran b. May 06 1985 in Tacoma, Pierce Co., WA.

278. **Patricia Lee**[7] **Osburn** (222.Samual Stephen[6], 182.Mary Aceneth[5] Mulanax, 147.Matthew Elliott[4], 46.William R.[3], 8.Catherine Kate[2] Arbogast, 1.Michael[1]), b. Jun 29 1935 in Payette, Payette Co., ID.
She Married **Lawrence Wade Kitchek**, b. 1 Apr 1956 in Eugene, Lane Co., OR.
   Children:
393   i.   Vance Wade[8] Kitchek b. 12 Oct 1956 in Eugene, Lane Co., OR.
394   ii. Kim Bryan Kitchek b. 10 Jan 1958 in Eugene, Lane Co., OR.

279. **Betty Jane**[7] **Osburn** (222.Samual Stephen[6], 182.Mary Aceneth[5] Mulanax, 147.Matthew Elliott[4], 46.William R.[3], 8.Catherine Kate[2] Arbogast, 1.Michael[1]), b. Jun 19 1937 in Payette, Payette Co., ID.
Married 2 Jun 1957 in Eugene, Lane Co., OR, **Alvin Delano Schnell**, b. 20 Apr 1937 in Council, Adams Co., ID (son of Walter Schnell and Louise Heinrick).
   Children:
+ 395   i.   Leland Gary[8] Schnell b. 7 Apr 1858.
  396   ii. Danise Dawn Schnell b. 1 Jul 1990 in Midvale, Washington Co., ID.
             Married 1 Jul 1990 in Midvale, Washington Co., ID, **Ivan Ray Wolfe**, b. 10 Aug 1970 in Ontario, Malheur Co., OR (son of Janes Wolfe and Carol Matthews).
+ 397   iii. Heather Susan Schnell b. 1 Dec 1966.

280. **Linda Gail**[7] **Osburn** (222.Samual Stephen[6], 182.Mary Aceneth[5] Mulanax, 147.Matthew Elliott[4], 46.William R.[3], 8.Catherine Kate[2] Arbogast, 1.Michael[1]), b. Jun 15 1940.
Married 5 May 1962 in Las Vegas, Clark Co., NV, **Robert Pyanowski**.
   Children:
398   i.   Douglas Kent[8] Pyanowski b. 26 Nov 1962 in Loma Linda, San Bernardino Co., CA.

281. **John Franklin**[7] **Osburn** (222.Samual Stephen[6], 182.Mary Aceneth[5] Mulanax, 147.Matthew Elliott[4], 46.William R.[3], 8.Catherine Kate[2] Arbogast, 1.Michael[1]), b. Aug 31 1943.
Married 23 Nov 1963 in Newport, Washington Co., OH, **Marjorie Bailor**.
   Children:
399   i.   Jeffery Todd[8] Osburn b. 21 Nov 1966 in Eugene, Lane Co., OR.

282. **Connie Jean**[7] **Osburn** (222.Samual Stephen[6], 182.Mary Aceneth[5] Mulanax, 147.Matthew Elliott[4], 46.William R.[3], 8.Catherine Kate[2] Arbogast, 1.Michael[1]), b. Mar 02 1950.

Married April 1970, **Runen Plates**.
Children:
- 400   i.   Angeline Alicia^8 Plates b. 26 Oct 1970 in Eugene, Lane Co., OR.
- 401   ii.   Enoc Ruben Plates b. 5 Jun 1973 in Maryland.

286. **Doris Acentha^7 Allen** (224.Mable Marie^6 Osburn, 182.Mary Aceneth^5 Mulanax, 147.Matthew Elliott^4, 46.William R.^{3}, 8.Catherine Kate^2 Arbogast, 1.Michael^1), b. 22 Feb 1934 at Payette, Payette Co., ID.
Married 28 Sep 1952 in Springfield, Lane Co., OR, **Wesley Ray Sisco**, b. 13 Apr 1933 in Soper, Choctaw Co., OK.
Children:
- + 402   i.   Rebecca Rae^8 Sisco b. 17 Oct 1953.
- + 403   ii.   Tanya Mae Sisco b. 17 Oct 1955.
- + 404   iii.   Wesley Ray Sisco, Jr. b. 25 Mar 1959.

287. **Opal Jane^7 Allen** (224.Mable Marie^6 Osburn, 182.Mary Aceneth^5 Mulanax, 147.Matthew Elliott^4, 46.William R.^{3}, 8.Catherine Kate^2 Arbogast, 1.Michael^1), b. 30 May 1935 in Payette, Payette Co., ID, d. 17 Nov 1992 in Eugene, Lane Co., OR.
(1) Married 25 Nov 1954, **Donald Lewis O'Brien**.
Children by Donald Lewis O'Brien:
- 405   i.   Clayton Lewis^8 O'Brien b. Nov 1955 in Roseburg, Douglas Co., OR.
  Married 30 Aug 1974, Nancy Jean Hill, b. 31 Mar 1956 in Eugene, Lane Co., OR.

(2) She Married **Francis Merle Wallace**
Children by Francis Merle Wallace:
- 406   ii.   Allen Merle Wallace b. 20 Apr 1965.
- 407   iii.   Christopher Loy Wallace.

288. **Eunice Marie^7 Fulton** (225.Myrtle May^6 Osburn, 182.Mary Aceneth^5 Mulanax, 147.Matthew Elliott^4, 46.William R.^{3}, 8.Catherine Kate^2 Arbogast, 1.Michael^1), b. 12 May 1932 in Payette, Payette Co., ID.
Married 30 Mar 1951, **David Norman Swafford**, b. 24 Nov 1931 in Wendling, Lane Co., OR.
Children:
- 408   i.   Debra L.^{8} Swafford b. 21 Jul 1951 in Roseburg, Douglas Co., OR.
- 409   ii.   Michelle M. Swafford b. 20 Jan 1955.
- 410   iii.   Jeff N. Swafford b. 4 Feb 1959.
- 411   iv.   Steve J. Swafford b. 1 Jan 1961.

302. **Sandra^7 Osburn** (228.Theodore Harvey^6, 182.Mary Aceneth^5 Mulanax, 147.Matthew Elliott^4, 46.William R.^{3}, 8.Catherine Kate^2 Arbogast, 1.Michael^1), b. 1 Oct 1941 in Coos Bay, Coos Co., OR.
(1) She Married **Wallace Zielienski**.
(2) She Married **Lawrence Martin**.

Children by Lawrence Martin:
- 412   i.   John Lawrence^8 Martin b. 1 Aug 1962.
- 413   ii.   Terry Lila Martin b. 1 Jul 1963.
- 414   iii.   David Vernon Martin.

(3) She Married **Steve Black**
Children by Steve Black:
- 415   iv.   Nathan Milo Black b. 26 Apr 1975.
- 416   v.   Amy Rachel Black b. 5 Jul 1976.

303. **Laurie Joan⁷ Osburn** (228.Theodore Harvey⁶, 182.Mary Aceneth⁵ Mulanax, 147.Matthew Elliott⁴, 46.William R.³, 8.Catherine Kate² Arbogast, 1.Michael¹), b. 22 May 1943 in Payette, Payette Co., ID.
She Married **Jerry Loomis**, b. 1 Jul 1966 in Mountain Grove, Ozarks Co., MO.
        Children:
    417   i.   Brenden Phillips⁸ Loomis b. 8 May 1968.
    418   ii.   Deborah Kate Lommis b. 1 Mar 1970.

308. **Carlotta Aceneth⁷ Compton** (229.Mary Helen Rose⁶ Osburn, 182.Mary Aceneth⁵ Mulanax, 147.Matthew Elliott⁴, 46.William R.³, 8.Catherine Kate² Arbogast, 1.Michael¹), b. 13 Sep 1942 in Boise, Ada Co., ID.
(1) She Married **Smith B. Prowell**.
(2) She Married **Robert Bunnell**.
        Children by Smith B. Prowell:
    419   i.   Randy Ray⁸ Prowell b. 5 May 1959 in Roseburg, Douglas Co., OR.
    420   ii.   Ronnie Jay Prowell b. 23 Jun 1960 in Roseburg, Douglas Co., OR.
    421   iii.   Diane Kay Prowell b. 60 Apr 1966 in Springfield, Lane Co., OR.
        He Married **Linda Lydie**.

309. **Jesse William⁷ Compton, Jr.** (229.Mary Helen Rose⁶ Osburn, 182.Mary Aceneth⁵ Mulanax, 147.Matthew Elliott⁴, 46.William R.³, 8.Catherine Kate² Arbogast, 1.Michael¹), b. 1 Oct 1946.
(1) Married 23 Sep 1970, **Myrna Ricken**.
(2) He Married **Carol McCarty**. , b. 5 Sep 1952 in San Angelo, Tom Green Co., TX.
        Children by Carol McCarty:
    422   i.   Jesse Caleb⁸ Compton b. 31 Dec 1976 in Eugene, Lane Co., OR.
    423   ii.   Lacey Celine Compton b. 5 Mar 1979 in Eugene, Lane Co., OR.

    (3) He Married **Terry Lynn Langnes**
        Children by Terry Lynn Langnes:
    424   iii.   Kelley Corrine Compton b. 6 Mar 1984 in Eugene, Lane Co., OR.

311. **Lyle Anthony⁷ Wheeler** (232.Zella Jane⁶ Osburn, 182.Mary Aceneth⁵ Mulanax, 147.Matthew Elliott⁴, 46.William R.³, 8.Catherine Kate² Arbogast, 1.Michael¹), b. 5 Aug 1957 in Springfield, Lane Co., OR.
He Married **Patricia Conner**, b. 17 Apr 1958.
        Children:
    425   i.   Shannon Diane⁸ Wheeler b. 15 Feb 1988 in Portland, Multnomah Co., OR.

313. **Clinton Jay⁷ Myrick** (241.Dorothy Ellen⁶ Mulanax, 194.Calvin Silas⁵, 153.John William⁴, 46.William R.³, 8.Catherine Kate² Arbogast, 1.Michael¹), b. 1 Jun 1953.
He Married **Kathleen Marie Forsman**, b. 13 Oct 1954 in Fort Ord, Monterey Co., CA.
        Children:
    426   i.   Daniel Jay⁸ Myrick b. 26 Feb 1980 in Dover, Kent Co., DE.
    427   ii.   David Curtis Myrick b. 9 Jul 1982 in Dover, Kent Co., DE.

314. **Calvin Curtis⁷ Myrick** (241.Dorothy Ellen⁶ Mulanax, 194.Calvin Silas⁵, 153.John William⁴, 46.William R.³, 8.Catherine Kate² Arbogast, 1.Michael¹), b. 4 Feb 1957 in Portland, Multnomah Co., OR.
(1) Married 9 Apr 1977, **Donna A. Hamilton**. , b. 9 Sep 1959 in Boulder, Boulder Co., CO.

    (2) He Married **Vicki Kay Eckert**
        Children by Vicki Kay Eckert:
    428   i.   Marissa Mary⁸ Myrick b. 29 May 1988 in Honolulu, Honolulu Co., HI.

315. **Cynthia Marguerite**[7] **Myrick** (241.Dorothy Ellen[6] Mulanax, 194.Calvin Silas[5], 153.John William[4], 46.William R.[3], 8.Catherine Kate[2] Arbogast, 1.Michael[1]), b. 9 Apr 1963 in Portland, Multnomah Co., OR.
She Married **Dunan Arthur Howell**, b. 4 Apr 1963 in Hawaii.

Children:

429	i.	Anna Elizabeth[8] Howell b. 23 May 1985 in Upper Haayford, Oxfordshire, England.
430	ii.	Jamin Arthur Howell b. 10 May 1988 in Milwaukie, Clackamas Co., OR.
431	iii.	Rebecca Estella Howell b. in Milwaukie, Clackamas Co., OR.

Generation Eight

319. **Louis Scott**[8] **Townsend** (246.Lester Lou[7], 205.Hazel Marie[6] Mulnanx, 170.James Lewis[5] Mulanax, 144.William Dallas[4], 44.Miles Elliott[3], 8.Catherine Kate[2] Arbogast, 1.Michael[1]), b. Sep 07 1953 in Manhattan, Riley Co., KS.
He Married **Debra Hoke**.

Children:

432 i. Luke E[9] Townsend b. Aug 06 1988 in Manhattan, Riley Co., KS.

320. **Harry Steve**[8] **Townsend** (246.Lester Lou[7], 205.Hazel Marie[6] Mulnanx, 170.James Lewis[5] Mulanax, 144.William Dallas[4], 44.Miles Elliott[3], 8.Catherine Kate[2] Arbogast, 1.Michael[1]), b. Nov 11 1958.
Married Feb 16 1980, **Tina Haid**.

Children:

433	i.	Michael Steven[9] Gaid b. May 13 1990 in Topeka, Shawnee Co., KS.
434	ii.	Samantha Louise Townsend b. Jun 23 1983 in Topeka, Shawnee Co., KS.
435	iii.	Kristi Townsend b. May 19 1986 in Topeka, Shawnee Co., KS.

321. **Kevin Lee**[8] **Townsend** (246.Lester Lou[7], 205.Hazel Marie[6] Mulnanx, 170.James Lewis[5] Mulanax, 144.William Dallas[4], 44.Miles Elliott[3], 8.Catherine Kate[2] Arbogast, 1.Michael[1]), b. Nov 03 1959 in Manhattan, Riley Co., KS.
(1) Married Feb 25 1978 in Dover, Shawnee Co., KS, **Dana Springer**, b. Jul 09 1959.

Children by Dana Springer:

436	i.	Sean Michael[9] Townsend b. Oct 11 1979 in Topeka, Shawnee Co., KS.
437	ii.	Matteau Steven Townsend b. Aug 04 1980 in Topeka, Shawnee Co., KS.
438	iii.	Ryan Scott Townsend b. Sep 27 1982 in Topeka, Shawnee Co., KS.

(2) He Married **Gloria K. Giegert**.

Children by Gloria K. Giegert:

439 iv. Chelsea Kathleen Townsend b. Mar 07 1990 in Topeka, Shawnee Co., KS.

323. **Beverly Sue**[8] **Barnes** (250.Jane Earline[7] Nelson, 213.Maggie May[6] Blaikie, 174.Flora Adeline[5] Mulanax, 145.John Greenbury[4], 44.Miles Elliott[3], 8.Catherine Kate[2] Arbogast, 1.Michael[1]), b. Jun 30 1948 in Mena, Polk Co., AR.
Married Jun 11 1966, **Dwight Powell**.

Children:

+	440	i.	Deanna Sue[9] Powell b. Aug 13 1968.
+	441	ii.	Duane Lloyd Powell b. Jun 05 1970.
	442	iii.	Dennis Loran Powell b. Mar 23 1971.

324. **Joane Sue**[8] **Barnes** (250.Jane Earline[7] Nelson, 213.Maggie May[6] Blaikie, 174.Flora Adeline[5] Mulanax, 145.John Greenbury[4], 44.Miles Elliott[3], 8.Catherine Kate[2] Arbogast, 1.Michael[1]), b. Dec 15 1950 in Mena, Polk Co., AR.
Married Aug 16 1967 in Mena, Polk Co., AR, **Dale Powell**.

Children:
- \+ 443   i.   Donita Laneel[9] Powell b. Mar 05 1969.
- 444   ii.   Darrell Powell b. Feb 10 1974 in Russellville, Pope Co., AR.

325. **Betty Lovella[8] Barnes** (250.Jane Earline[7] Nelson, 213.Maggie May[6] Blaikie, 174.Flora Adeline[5] Mulanax, 145.John Greenbury[4], 44.Miles Elliott[3], 8.Catherine Kate[2] Arbogast, 1.Michael[1]), b. Oct 05 1952 in Cleburne, Johnson Co., TX.
Married Jul 04 1968 in Fayetteville, Washington Co., AR, **Ivan Kiersey**.
Children:
- \+ 445   i.   Lannie Gene[9] Kiersey b. Dec 08 1969.
- 446   ii.   Russell Scott Kiersey b. Mar 10 1971 in Mena, Polk Co., AR.
Married Aug 20 1993 in Kunache, HI, **April Wilsom**, b. Jun 13 1972.

327. **Randy Gale[8] Franklin** (252.Francis Billey[7], 219.Bessie Lee[6] Osburn, 182.Mary Aceneth[5] Mulanax, 147.Matthew Elliott[4], 46.William R.[3], 8.Catherine Kate[2] Arbogast, 1.Michael[1]), b. Jun 26 1951 in Eugene, Lane Co., OR.
(1) Married Mar 08 1970 in Arkansas City, KS, **Micki Michelle Woolsey**.
Children by Micki Michelle Woolsey:
- 447   i.   Stephanie Gail[9] Franklin b. Oct 04 1970 in Arkansas City, KS.

(2) Married Apr 17 1976 in Enid, Garfield Co., OK, **Cindy Ruth Chrisman**.
Children by Cindy Ruth Chrisman:
- 448   ii.   Amiee Ruth Franklin b. Jan 08 1977 in Enid, Garfield Co., OK.

(3) He Married **Ronni Carter**.
Children by Ronni Carter:
- 449   iii.   Leslie Gale Franklin b. Apr 24 1978 in Enid, Garfield Co., OK.
- 450   iv.   Geoffery Wayne Franklin b. Jun 07 1979 in Enid, Garfield Co., OK.
- 451   v.   Christi Jo Franklin b. Jul 13 1980 in Enid, Garfield Co., OK.

329. **Cheryl Lynn[8] Franklin** (252.Francis Billey[7], 219.Bessie Lee[6] Osburn, 182.Mary Aceneth[5] Mulanax, 147.Matthew Elliott[4], 46.William R.[3], 8.Catherine Kate[2] Arbogast, 1.Michael[1]), b. Aug 07 1954 in Springfield, Greene Co., MO.
Married Mar 08 1976, **Richard Shrope**.
Children:
- 452   i.   Tera Lea Danelle[9] Franklin b. Mar 23 1981 in Arkansas City, KS.

330. **Ricky Michael[8] Franklin** (253.Vernon Newton[7], 219.Bessie Lee[6] Osburn, 182.Mary Aceneth[5] Mulanax, 147.Matthew Elliott[4], 46.William R.[3], 8.Catherine Kate[2] Arbogast, 1.Michael[1]), b. Aug 16 1950 in Pekin, Tazewell Co., IL, d. Feb 20 1981 in Mexico.
Married Sep 27 1970, **Debbie Ann Limbach**, b. Jul 26 1952 in Illinois.
Children:
- 453   i.   Heather Michelle[9] Franklin b. Apr 09 1971.
- 454   ii.   Heidi Nicole Franklin b. Jun 01 1975.

331. **Brent Mitchell[8] Franklin** (253.Vernon Newton[7], 219.Bessie Lee[6] Osburn, 182.Mary Aceneth[5] Mulanax, 147.Matthew Elliott[4], 46.William R.[3], 8.Catherine Kate[2] Arbogast, 1.Michael[1]), b. Dec 31 1952 in Pekin, Tazewell Co., IL.
Married Dec 22 1972, **Julie Ann Root**, b. Feb 22 1954 in Pekin, Tazewell Co., IL.
Children:
- 455   i.   Thadus Jacob[9] Franklin b. m10271975 in Peoria, Peoria Co., IL.

332. **Kevin Kyle**[8] **Franklin** (253.Vernon Newton[7], 219.Bessie Lee[6] Osburn, 182.Mary Aceneth[5] Mulanax, 147.Matthew Elliott[4], 46.William R.[3], 8.Catherine Kate[2] Arbogast, 1.Michael[1]), b. Mar 19 1958 in Pekin, Tazewell Co., IL.
Married Nov 04 1976, **Dennie June Dobbs**, b. Jan 19 1958 in Pekin, Tazewell Co., IL.
Children:
- 456 i. Delta Lee[9] Franklin b. Sep 30 1977 in Pekin, Tazewell Co., IL, d. Oct 05 1977 in Pekin, Tazewell Co., IL.
- 457 ii. Dawn Lynn Franklin b. Sep 30 1977 in Pekin, Tazewell Co., IL.
- 458 iii. Cody Lyle Franklin b. Oct 17 1979 in Pekin, Tazewell Co., IL.

334. **Galen Wayne**[8] **Franklin** (254.Wayne Russell[7], 219.Bessie Lee[6] Osburn, 182.Mary Aceneth[5] Mulanax, 147.Matthew Elliott[4], 46.William R.[3], 8.Catherine Kate[2] Arbogast, 1.Michael[1]), b. May 01 1952 in Eugene, Lane Co., OR.
Married May 08 1982 in Eugene, Lane Co., OR, **Candice Lynn Hobart**, b. Apr 20 1852 in Eugene, Lane Co., OR.
Children:
- 459 i. Garrett Eayne[9] Franklin b. Jun 21 1983 in Eugene, Lane Co., OR.

336. **Terry Lynn**[8] **Franklin** (254.Wayne Russell[7], 219.Bessie Lee[6] Osburn, 182.Mary Aceneth[5] Mulanax, 147.Matthew Elliott[4], 46.William R.[3], 8.Catherine Kate[2] Arbogast, 1.Michael[1]), b. Oct 12 1955 in Eugene, Lane Co., OR.
Married Jun 10 1978 in Springfield, Lane Co., OR, **Ronda Lou Smith**, b. Jul 05 1958 in Eugene, Lane Co., OR.
Children:
- 460 i. Kristina Lou[9] Franklin b. f08261980.

337. **Shirley Ann**[8] **Bruce** (255.Maty Ann[7] Franklin, 219.Bessie Lee[6] Osburn, 182.Mary Aceneth[5] Mulanax, 147.Matthew Elliott[4], 46.William R.[3], 8.Catherine Kate[2] Arbogast, 1.Michael[1]), b. Mar 04 1941 in Eugene, Lane Co., OR.
Married Feb 12 1972 in Elmira. Lane Co., OR, **Michael Allen Whitney**, b. Aug 13 1949.
Children:
- 461 i. Joshua Earl[9] Whitney b. Oct 19 1973 in Eugene, Lane Co., OR.
- 462 ii. Amanda Marie Whitney b. Sep 30 1976 in Eugene, Lane Co., OR.
- 463 iii. Hannah Kristeen Whitney b. Aug 07 1979 in Eugene, Lane Co., OR.
- 464 iv. Rebecca Suzanne Whitney b. Apr 29 1981 in Eugene, Lane Co., OR.

338. **Janell Kay**[8] **Bruce** (255.Maty Ann[7] Franklin, 219.Bessie Lee[6] Osburn, 182.Mary Aceneth[5] Mulanax, 147.Matthew Elliott[4], 46.William R.[3], 8.Catherine Kate[2] Arbogast, 1.Michael[1]), b. Nov 20 1953. She Married **Kenneth Lee Howland, Jr.**, b. Jul 16 1952 in Hastings, Adams Co., NE.
Children:
- 465 i. Rachelle Lea[9] Howland b. Feb 16 1978 in Eugene, Lane Co., OR.

339. **Liessa Gay**[8] **Bruce** (255.Maty Ann[7] Franklin, 219.Bessie Lee[6] Osburn, 182.Mary Aceneth[5] Mulanax, 147.Matthew Elliott[4], 46.William R.[3], 8.Catherine Kate[2] Arbogast, 1.Michael[1]), b. Aug 15 1961 in Eugene, Lane Co., OR.
Married Apr 05 1985, **James Patrick Boytz**, b. Oct 17 1960.
Children:
- 466 i. Mathew James[9] Boytz b. Jul 02 1990 in Eugene, Lane Co., OR.

340. **Harry James**[8] **Crabtree** (256.Gladys Faye[7] Franklin, 219.Bessie Lee[6] Osburn, 182.Mary Aceneth[5] Mulanax, 147.Matthew Elliott[4], 46.William R.[3], 8.Catherine Kate[2] Arbogast, 1.Michael[1]), b. Mar 23 1951 in Eugene, Lane Co., OR.
(1) Married Sep 14 1971 in Reno, Washoe Co., NV, **Carolyn Kay Bunsh**, b. Dec 06 1964
Children by Carolyn Kay Bunsh:

467	i.	Hillaire Ray^9 Crabtree b. Jul 14 1973 in Eugene, Lane Co., OR.
468	ii.	Lindsay Kay Crabtree b. Apr 04 1978 in Eugene, Lane Co., OR.
469	iii.	Erin Michale Crabtree b. Nov 08 1979 in Eugene, Lane Co., OR.
470	iv.	Harry James Crabtree, Jr. b. Mar 20 1986 in Eugene, Lane Co., OR.

(2) He <u>Married</u> **Collean Shey**, b. Aug 25 1957.

344. **Charmaine Marie^8 Fennimore** (257.Lois Ruth^7 Franklin, 219.Bessie Lee^6 Osburn, 182.Mary Aceneth^5 Mulanax, 147.Matthew Elliott^4, 46.William R.^{3}, 8.Catherine Kate^2 Arbogast, 1.Michael^1), b. Jul 15 1957 in Silverton, Marion Co., OR.
<u>Married</u> Mar 15 1979, **Joel Dean Adams**, b. Apr 02 1955.

Children:

471	i.	Elizabeth Marie^9 Adams b. Jul 06 1980 in Corvallis, Benton Co., OR.
472	ii.	Daniel J. Adams b. May 26 1982 in Corvallis, Benton Co., OR.
473	iii.	David Paul Adams b. Jan 06 1985 in Corvallis, Benton Co., OR.
474	iv.	Kevin James Adams b. Oct 06 1986 in Corvallis, Benton Co., OR.
475	v.	Keith Joel Adams b. Apr 14 1989 in Corvallis, Benton Co., OR.

345. **Gilman Joseph^8 Fennimore, Jr.** (257.Lois Ruth^7 Franklin, 219.Bessie Lee^6 Osburn, 182.Mary Aceneth^5 Mulanax, 147.Matthew Elliott^4, 46.William R.^{3}, 8.Catherine Kate^2 Arbogast, 1.Michael^1), b. Jul 23 1958 in Dallas, Polk Co., OR.
He <u>Married</u> **Mary Larraine**, b. Sep 01 1959.

Children:

476	i.	Benjamin Joseph^9 Fennimore b. Sep 07 1985.
477	ii.	Stephanie Ann Fennimore b. Jun 07 1989.

346. **Cassandra Lou^8 Fennimore** (257.Lois Ruth^7 Franklin, 219.Bessie Lee^6 Osburn, 182.Mary Aceneth^5 Mulanax, 147.Matthew Elliott^4, 46.William R.^{3}, 8.Catherine Kate^2 Arbogast, 1.Michael^1), b. Aug 21 1960.
<u>Married</u> Nov 20 1982, **Rand William Cooper**, b. Apr 29 1958.

Children:

478	i.	Kelly Rand^9 Cooper b. Jul 28 1986.

347. **Teresa Jean^8 Hoag** (258.Betty Jean^7 Franklin, 219.Bessie Lee^6 Osburn, 182.Mary Aceneth^5 Mulanax, 147.Matthew Elliott^4, 46.William R.^{3}, 8.Catherine Kate^2 Arbogast, 1.Michael^1), b. Jun 08 1957 in Springfield, Lane Co., OR.
<u>Married</u> May 07 1957 in Springfield, Lane Co., OR, **Ramond Paul Nickoli**, b. Jan 07 1950 in Huron, Erie Co., OH.

Children:

479	i.	Darci LeAnn^9 Nickloi b. May 06 1979 in Eugene, Lane Co., OR.
480	ii.	Tanna June Nickoli b. Jan 19 1981 in Eugene, Lane Co., OR.

350. **Gregory Allen^8 Larson** (259.Bonnie Jean^7 Franklin, 219.Bessie Lee^6 Osburn, 182.Mary Aceneth^5 Mulanax, 147.Matthew Elliott^4, 46.William R.^{3}, 8.Catherine Kate^2 Arbogast, 1.Michael^1), b. Jul 08 1956 in Coburg, Lane Co., OR.
<u>Married</u> Oct 16 1976 in Coburg, Lane Co., OR, **Roberta June Savage**, b. Apr 18 1958.

Children:

481	i.	Jeremy Allen^9 Larson b. Feb 16 1978 in Eugene, Lane Co., OR.
482	ii.	Mindy Sue Larson b. Sep 27 1979.
483	iii.	Nathan Lars Larson b. Jan 18 1981.

351. **Michael Ray^8 Larson** (259.Bonnie Jean^7 Franklin, 219.Bessie Lee^6 Osburn, 182.Mary Aceneth^5 Mulanax, 147.Matthew Elliott^4, 46.William R.^{3}, 8.Catherine Kate^2 Arbogast, 1.Michael^1), b. Feb 02 1958.
He <u>Married</u> **Belinda Jo De Hart**, b. Jul 21 1962.

Children:
- 484 i. Christopher MIchael[9] Larson b. Apr 18 1983.
- 485 ii. Callie Jean Larson b. Apr 13 1987.

355. **William Douglas[8] Franklin** (260.James Lee[7], 219.Bessie Lee[6] Osburn, 182.Mary Aceneth[5] Mulanax, 147.Matthew Elliott[4], 46.William R.[3], 8.Catherine Kate[2] Arbogast, 1.Michael[1]), b. Feb 17 1963 in Eugene, Lane Co., OR.
Married Nov 12 1983, **Jeanette Michael**, b. Oct 17 1965.
   Children:
   - 486 i. Stephanie Elizabeth[9] Franklin b. Nov 27 1984.
   - 487 ii. Samantha Kay Franklin b. Oct 20 1986.
   - 488 iii. William Henry Franklin b. Apr 09 1989.

357. **Brandel Allen[8] Franklin** (261.John Allen[7], 219.Bessie Lee[6] Osburn, 182.Mary Aceneth[5] Mulanax, 147.Matthew Elliott[4], 46.William R.[3], 8.Catherine Kate[2] Arbogast, 1.Michael[1]), b. Aug 16 1960 in Eugene, Lane Co., OR.
He Married **Joy McKafka**.
   Children:
   - 489 i. Bryan James[9] Franklin b. Jun 02 1978 in Springfield, Lane Co., OR.

362. **Tony Ray[8] Franklin** (262.Alman Ray[7], 219.Bessie Lee[6] Osburn, 182.Mary Aceneth[5] Mulanax, 147.Matthew Elliott[4], 46.William R.[3], 8.Catherine Kate[2] Arbogast, 1.Michael[1]), b. Sep 14 1963 in Springfield, Lane Co., OR.
Married Jun 19 1983, **Shelli Lyn Sneed**, b. Oct 13 1963.
   Children:
   - 490 i. Ashley Dawn[9] Franklin b. Sep 20 1984.
   - 491 ii. Karin Noel Franklin b. Apr 29 1988.

364. **Donald Gene[8] Arnold** (263.Ethel Fern[7] Osburn, 220.Charley Calvin[6], 182.Mary Aceneth[5] Mulanax, 147.Matthew Elliott[4], 46.William R.[3], 8.Catherine Kate[2] Arbogast, 1.Michael[1]), b. Jan 14 1951 in Baker Co., OR.
Married Jun 04 1969 in Payette, Payette Co., WA, **Kathy Jean Griffin**, b. Jan 26 1952 (daughter of Ray Griffin).
   Children:
   - + 492 i. Candice Dawn[9] Arnold b. Mar 26 1972.
   - 493 ii. Damion Blue Arnold b. Apr 16 1974.

365. **Shelly Lynn[8] Arnold** (263.Ethel Fern[7] Osburn, 220.Charley Calvin[6], 182.Mary Aceneth[5] Mulanax, 147.Matthew Elliott[4], 46.William R.[3], 8.Catherine Kate[2] Arbogast, 1.Michael[1]), b. Jun 23 1956 in Ontario, Malheur Co., OR.
She Married **Andrew Fredrick Knipe, Jr.**, b. Oct 27 1955 in Scotia, Humboldt Co., CA (son of Andrew Fredrick Knipe and Marie Stratton).
   Children:
   - 494 i. Autuma Lynn[9] Knipe b. Apr 06 1979 in Portland, Multnomah Co., OR.
   - 495 ii. Ashley Amber Knipe b. Jan 20 1981 in Portland, Multnomah Co., OR.
   - 496 iii. Allison Nicole Knipe b. Jan 02 1983 in Weiser, Washington Co., ID.
   - 497 iv. Anthony Andrew Knipe b. Mar 17 1984 in Weiser, Washington Co., ID.

366. **Juanita Raquelle[8] Fagerburg** (265.Billie Lorreen[7] Osburn, 220.Charley Calvin[6], 182.Mary Aceneth[5] Mulanax, 147.Matthew Elliott[4], 46.William R.[3], 8.Catherine Kate[2] Arbogast, 1.Michael[1]), b. Jan 10 1960 in Mt. Vernon, Skagit Co., WA.
(1) Married Jun 04 1982, **Frank Lewis Nicklin, Jr.**.
   Children by Frank Lewis Nicklin, Jr.:
   - 498 i. Tiffany Skye[9] Fagerburg b. Oct 13 1978.

(2) She Married **Victor Manuel Lerma**, b. Dec 23 1919 in Mexico City, Mexico.

367. **Martin Kerry⁸ Fagerburg** (265.Billie Lorreen⁷ Osburn, 220.Charley Calvin⁶, 182.Mary Aceneth⁵ Mulanax, 147.Matthew Elliott⁴, 46.William R.³, 8.Catherine Kate² Arbogast, 1.Michael¹), b. Jan 06 1961 in Mt. Vernon, Skagit Co., WA.
He Married **Kate Louise Du Chow**, b. Jul 22 1961 in St. Peter, Nicolette Co., MN (daughter of Wayne Lincoln De Chow and Charlotte Ann Schultz).
  Children:
  - 499 i.   Claire Luisa⁹ Fagerburg b. May 07 1982 in Munich, Germany.
  - 500 ii. Meghan Elizabeth Fagerburg b. May 06 1985 in Portland, Multnomah Co., OR.
  - 501 iii. Olivia Kerry Fagerburg b. Jan 02 1987 in Portland, Multnomah Co., OR.

369. **Kimberly Cherise⁸ Vail** (266.Kathryn Machiel⁷ Osburn, 220.Charley Calvin⁶, 182.Mary Aceneth⁵ Mulanax, 147.Matthew Elliott⁴, 46.William R.³, 8.Catherine Kate² Arbogast, 1.Michael¹), b. Oct 02 1960 in Bellingham, Whatcom Co., WA.
She Married **Kevin Pflugar**, b. Aug 01 1960 in Bellingham, Whatcom Co., WA.
  Children:
  - 502 i.   Nichole Alexandria⁹ Pfluger b. Mar 25 1986 in Bellingham, Whatcom Co., WA.
  - 503 ii. Mathew Thomas Pfluger b. Oct 08 1987 in Bellingham, Whatcom Co., WA.

395. **Leland Gary⁸ Schnell** (279.Betty Jane⁷ Osburn, 222.Samual Stephen⁶, 182.Mary Aceneth⁵ Mulanax, 147.Matthew Elliott⁴, 46.William R.³, 8.Catherine Kate² Arbogast, 1.Michael¹), b. 7 Apr 1858 in Walla Walla, Walla Walla Co., WA.
Married 28 Nov 1982 in Glendale, Los Angeles Co., CA, **Sandra Slyvania Swantes**, b. 17 Jun 1960 in Rio De Janeiro, Brazil.
  Children:
  - 504 i.   Andrew James⁹ Schnell b. 13 Sep 1990 in Redlands, San Bernardino Co., CA.

397. **Heather Susan⁸ Schnell** (279.Betty Jane⁷ Osburn, 222.Samual Stephen⁶, 182.Mary Aceneth⁵ Mulanax, 147.Matthew Elliott⁴, 46.William R.³, 8.Catherine Kate² Arbogast, 1.Michael¹), b. 1 Dec 1966 in Tempe, Maricopa Co., AZ.
Married 26 Mar 1988, **Tona Campa**.
  Children:
  - 505 i.   Skylar Spartakus⁹ Campa b. 14 Dec 1988 in Boise, Ada Co., ID.
  - 506 ii. Gabriella Jordan Campa b. 20 Jan 1990 in Nampa, AZ.

402. **Rebecca Rae⁸ Sisco** (286.Doris Acentha⁷ Allen, 224.Mable Marie⁶ Osburn, 182.Mary Aceneth⁵ Mulanax, 147.Matthew Elliott⁴, 46.William R.³, 8.Catherine Kate² Arbogast, 1.Michael¹), b. 17 Oct 1953 in Roseburg, Douglas Co., OR.
Married 25 Nov 1974 in Springfield, Lane Co., OR, **Rocky Lee Brown**.
  Children:
  - 507 i.   Rocky Charles⁹ Brown b. 31 Jul 1976 in Eugene, Lane Co., OR.
  - 508 ii. Tiffany Ann Brown b. 17 Apr 1981 in Eugene, Lane Co., OR.
  - 509 iii. LeAnn Marie Brown b. 2 Nov 1986 in Portland, Multnomah Co., OR.

403. **Tanya Mae⁸ Sisco** (286.Doris Acentha⁷ Allen, 224.Mable Marie⁶ Osburn, 182.Mary Aceneth⁵ Mulanax, 147.Matthew Elliott⁴, 46.William R.³, 8.Catherine Kate² Arbogast, 1.Michael¹), b. 17 Oct 1955.
Married 19 Feb 1976 in Idaho Falls, Bonneville Co., ID, **David Lawrence Wach**, b. 28 Dec 1953 in Eugene, Lane Co., OR.
  Children:
  - 510 i.   Mariah Acentha⁹ Wach b. 28 Apr 1978 in Eugene, Lane Co., OR.
  - 511 ii. Selima Davina Wach b. 21 May 1979 in Eugene, Lane Co., OR.
  - 512 iii. Lavina Marie Wach b. 22 May 1981 in Eugene, Lane Co., OR.

513 iv. Wesley LaGranda Wach b. 11 Jan 1984 in Eugene, Lane Co., OR, d. 11 Mar 1984 in Eugene, Lane Co., OR.
514 v. Alexis Wach b. 22 Oct 1984 in Eugene, Lane Co., OR, d. 22 Oct 1984.
515 vi. Apollo Wach b. 11 Apr 1986 in Eugene, Lane Co., OR, d. 11 Apr 1986 in Eugene, Lane Co., OR.
516 vii. Lolita Elizabeth Wach b. 25 Apr 1987 in Eugene, Lane Co., OR.

404. **Wesley Ray^8 Sisco, Jr.** (286.Doris Acentha^7 Allen, 224.Mable Marie^6 Osburn, 182.Mary Aceneth^5 Mulanax, 147.Matthew Elliott^4, 46.William R.^{3}, 8.Catherine Kate^2 Arbogast, 1.Michael^1), b. 25 Mar 1959 in San Diego, San Diego Co., CA.
He Married **Dorothy Ann Leonardi**.
Children:
517 i. Wesley Ray^9 Sisco, III b. 22 Oct 1986 in Phoenix, Jackson Co., AZ.
518 ii. Franco Philip Sisco b. 1989 in Lebanon, Linn Co., OR.
519 iii. Sara Lavern Sisco b. 30 Nov 1992.

Generation Nine

440. **Deanna Sue^9 Powell** (323.Beverly Sue^8 Barnes, 250.Jane Earline^7 Nelson, 213.Maggie May^6 Blaikie, 174.Flora Adeline^5 Mullenax, 145.John Greenbury^4, 44.Miles Elliott^3, 8.Catherine Kate^2 Arbogast, 1.Michael^1), b. Aug 13 1968 in Texarkana, Bowie Co., TX.
Married Nov 11 1987, **John Skipper, II**.
Children:
520 i. John^{10} Skipper III b. Jul 24 1988 at De Queen, Sevier Co., AR.
521 ii. Sara Ann Skipper b. Mar 31 1990 in De Queen, Sevier Co., AR.
522 iii. Steffania Skipper b. Mar 31 1990 in De Queen, Sevier Co., AR.
523 iv. Ashlae Nicole Skipper b. Apr 02 1993 in De Queen, Sevier Co., AR.

441. **Duane Lloyd^9 Powell** (323.Beverly Sue^8 Barnes, 250.Jane Earline^7 Nelson, 213.Maggie May^6 Blaikie, 174.Flora Adeline^5 Mullenax, 145.John Greenbury^4, 44.Miles Elliott^3, 8.Catherine Kate^2 Arbogast, 1.Michael^1), b. Jun 05 1970.
She Married **Catherine Reed**.
Children:
524 i. Jessica Lee^{10} Powell b. Nov 10 1989 in Mena, Polk Co., AR.
525 ii. Cassie Powell b. Jun 11 1993 in Mena, Polk Co., AR.

443. **Donita Laneel^9 Powell** (324.Joane Sue^8 Barnes, 250.Jane Earline^7 Nelson, 213.Maggie May^6 Blaikie, 174.Flora Adeline^5 Mullenax, 145.John Greenbury^4, 44.Miles Elliott^3, 8.Catherine Kate^2 Arbogast, 1.Michael^1), b. Mar 05 1969 in Mena, Polk Co., AR.
Married Mar 12 1958 in Mena, Polk Co., AR, **James Christopher Gann**.
Children:
526 i. Nathen Christopher^{10} Gann b. Jun 01 1989 in Russellville, Pope Co., AR.
527 ii. Whitney Brooke Gann b. Aug 11 1990 in Russellville, Pope Co., AR.

445. **Lannie Gene^9 Kiersey** (325.Betty Lovella^8 Barnes, 250.Jane Earline^7 Nelson, 213.Maggie May^6 Blaikie, 174.Flora Adeline^5 Mullenax, 145.John Greenbury^4, 44.Miles Elliott^3, 8.Catherine Kate^2 Arbogast, 1.Michael^1), b. Dec 08 1969 in Fayetteville, Washington Co., AR.
He Married **Shannon Leigh Barr**, b. in Mena, Polk Co., AR.
Children:
528 i. Aaron Ray^{10} Kiersey b. Oct 22 1988 in Mena, Polk Co., AR.

492. **Candice Dawn^9 Arnold** (364.Donald Gene^8, 263.Ethel Fern^7 Osburn, 220.Charley Calvin^6, 182.Mary Aceneth^5 Mullenax, 147.Matthew Elliott^4, 46.William R.^{3}, 8.Catherine Kate^2 Arbogast, 1.Michael^1), b. Mar 26 1972 in Weiser, Washington Co., ID.
Married May 17 1991 in Weiser, Washington Co., ID, **Kenneth John Kelley**, b. Jul 25 1970 in Boise, Ada Co., ID (son of Kenneth Crow and Joan Lorraine Bee).

    Children:
 529 i. Stephanie Jean^{10} Kelly b. Dec 03 1991.

Descendants of Dorothy Arbogast Fifth Child of Michael and Mary Elizabeth Samuels

Generation One

1. **Dorothy "Dolly"¹ Arbogast**, b. 1765/1769 in Crabbottom, Highland Co., VA (daughter of Michael Arbogast and Mary Elizabeth Samuels Amanapas), d. 1839 in Pendleton Co., WV. She Married c 1785 in Augusta Co., VA, **Jacob Gum**, b. 1755/1765 in Highland Co., VA (son of John Gum and Alice Fisher), d. 1820 in Pendleton Co., WV.

    Children:

    2   i.   Sarah² Gum, b. About 1788 in Augusta Co., VA, d. in Bond Co., IL.
             From family record by Amanda Arbogast Forbes. Named in Madison Co., OH deed in 1839. From, Leaves *From The Gum Tree*, by Muriel Martens Hoffman, 1984, family was in Champaign Co., OH, in 1820, then to Madison Co., IN, for land purchases 1823-1836; in Bond Co., IL, in 1850. In 1860, Sarah and Henry in household of Morgan, probably a son, his wife, Ellen 24, and a 3 month old child, Bond Co., IL. There were many Syberts and Gums wherever Sarah and Henry located, so it is impossible to construct a family group sheet. We do have the following information from Madison Co., IN, in 1830. In addition to Sarah and Henry, there was 1 male 20-30; 1 male 10-15; 1 male 5-10; 2 males under 5; 1 female 15-20; 1 female 10-15; 1 female under 5. In 1840 Madison Co., IN, Three additional females were added and an older male was gone.
             She Married **Harry Seybert**.
    + 3 ii. Isaac Gum b. Mar 07 1790.
    + 4 iii. Mary M. Gum b. Jul 24 1792.
    + 5 iv. Adam Gum b. About 1794.
    + 6 v.   Jacob Jr. Gum b. About 1798.
       7 vi. Edith "Eddy" Gum, b. 1794 - 1800 in Augusta Co., VA, d. in Madison Co., IN.
             In Highland Co., VA History by Morton. Also named in Madison Co., IN, deed in 1839 with husband. From, Leaves From The Gum Tree, 1984, by Muriel Martens Hoffman, on the 1830 Madison Co., IN, census are the following children; 1 male under 5; 2 females 5-10; 1 female under 5. In 1840, same place, three more males and one female added to family. We do not know if this family went with others to Bond Co., IL.
             Married Feb 17 1820 in Pendleton Co., WV, **Henry Seybert, Jr.**.
    + 8 vii. Elleder Gum b. Oct 30 1804.
    + 9 viii.Jesse Gum b. Jun 01 1804.

Generation Two

3. **Isaac² Gum** (1.Dorothy "Dolly"¹ Arbogast), b. Mar 07 1790 in Virginia, d. Mar 7 1847 in Bond Co., IL.
    (1) Married BEF 1807, **(unknown) Gum**, b. in Scotland, UK, d. 1825 in Madison Co., IN.

    Children by (unknown) Gum:
    + 10 i.   Henry³ Gum b. ABT 1807.
    + 11 ii. Jacob Gum b. 1810.
    + 12 iii. Sarah Gum b. 1812.

+ 13	iv.	Jesse S. Gum b. ABT 1815.
+ 14	v.	Isaac C. Gum b. May 9 1818.
+ 15	vi.	Catherine Gum b. OCT 1820.
+ 16	vii.	John Finley Gum b. 1821.
+ 17	viii.	James Riley Gum b. Jul 10 1822.
+ 18	ix.	Elizabeth Gum b. Jan 11 1825.

(2) He Married **Roenna Fletcher**.

Children by Roenna Fletcher:

19	x.	William Gum b. 1827 in Madison Co., IN, d. Jun 25 1892.
		(1) Married Oct 24 1851 in Bond Co., IL, **Catherine Miles**.
		(2) Married Oct 24 1851, **Nancy E. Jennings**.
+ 20	xi.	Jeremiah C. Gum b. 1828.
+ 21	xii.	Olive Gum b. Feb 6 1832.
22	xiii.	Matilda Caroline Gum b. ABT 1835 in Madison Co., IN, d. Mar 22 1880 in Bond Co., IL.
		Married Jun 24 1854 in Bond Co., IL, Augustus Shelton.
+ 23	xiv.	Perry O. Gum b. Jan 13 1836.
24	xv.	Moses Gum b. ABT 1840 in Bond Co., IL, d. Nov 11 1871.
25	xvi.	Milberry Gum b. ABT 1845 in Bond Co., IL, d. ABT 26 JUL 1883 in Missouri.
		Married Nov 1 1873 in Bond Co., IL, George M. Daggett.

4. **Mary M.[2] Gum** (1.Dorothy "Dolly"[1] Arbogast), b. Jul 24 1792 in Augusta Co., VA, d. 1859 in Rochester, Andrews Co., MO.
Mary named in Fayette Co., OH deed in 1839. From, Leaves From The Gum Tree, 1984, by Muriel Martens Hoffman, the 1830 Fayette Co., OH, census of Hi Point Twp., lists #13, William Fisher (Flescher?), #14 Jacob Dundle, and #9 Jesse Flesher. In Jefferson Twp. of same county, at the same time were Jacob Gum, Peter Fisher, Jacob Jenkins, John
Flesher and Peter Flesher.
Married Dec 28 1866 in Pendleton Co., WV, **William Flesher, Sr.**, b. 1792 in Highland Co., VA (son of Henry Flesher and Susan Catherine Peninger), d. Dec 28 1866 in Rochester, Andrews Co., MO.

Children:

26	i.	Katharine[3] Flesher b. in Ohio, d. in Dallas Co., MO.
		She Married James K. Eson., d. in Dallas Co., MO.
27	ii.	Mary Flesher b. in Virginia, d. in Oklahoma.
28	iii.	Ruth Flesher.
+ 29	iv.	Adam Flesher b. Oct 12 1813.
30	v.	Mahalia Flesher b. 1815 in Highland Co., VA.
		(1) She Married **Allen Gum**, b. About 1815.
		(2) She Married **Jacob Jr. Gum**, b. About 1798 in Augusta Co., VA (son of Jacob Gum and Dorothy "Dolly" Arbogast), d. About 1871 in Andrews Co., MO. Jacob:. Jacob, his brother, Jesse, sisters, Mary and Elinor and all their spouse of Fayette Co., OH, and sisters, Sarah and Eddy, and their spouse of Madison Co., IN, transfer by deed to Henry Gum, their interest in land owned by their mother following her death, dated 5 Sep 1839; Pendleton Co. Deed Book 14, p. 531. Jacob apparently migrated to Andrew Co., MO, in about 1840 probably by way of Bond Co., IL.
		From, Leaves from the Gum Tree, 1984, by Muriel Martens Hoffman, Samuel B. Gum, son and heir, appointed Administrator of Jacob Gum estate on 22 Dec 1871. Other heirs were the widow, Rachel, and Rachel Couch, Andrew Co., MO, and the heirs of Miles Gum in Bond Co., IL. Rochester Twp., Andrew Co., MO.
+ 31	vi.	Henry Flesher b. About 1817.
+ 32	vii.	Sarah Jane Flesher b. Oct 20 1819.
+ 33	viii.	Absalom Flesher b. 1821.
+ 34	ix.	William Seybert Flesher b. Jul 19 1824.

35	x.	Caroline Flesher b. 1829 in Ohio, d. in Rochester, Andrews Co., MO. <u>Married</u> in Andrews Co., MO, **John Devault**, b. 1833.
36	xi.	Ellen Flesher b. 1830 in Fayette Co., OH, d. 1909 in Rochester, Andrews Co., MO. She <u>Married</u> **Thomas Janes**, b. 1828 in Indiana.
37	xii.	Dorothy Flesher b. 1833 in Ohio, d. 1909.
+ 38	xiii.	Louesa K Flesher b. Aug 17 1839.

5. **Adam² Gum** (1.Dorothy "Dolly"¹ Arbogast), b. About 1794 in Augusta Co., VA, d. March 1847. From family group record of Amanda Arbogast Forbes. Adam in History of Highland Co., VA by Morton, died 1846, Eleven children and their descendants from, Leaves From The Gum Tree, by Muriel Martens Hoffman, 1984, Fairbury, IL, Cornbelt Press. Adam was the only child of Jacob's eight children who remained in Virginia. All of the others migrated to new land in Ohio, Indiana and Missouri.
<u>Married</u> Nov 15 1810 in Highland Co., VA, **Susanna Lantz**.

   ### *Children*:

+ 39	i.	Matilda³ Gum b. 1812.
+ 40	ii.	Henry Gum b. 1813.
+ 41	iii.	Sabina Gum b. Aug 1814.
42	iv.	Peter Gum b. 1819.
+ 43	v.	Amos Gum b. 1820.
44	vi.	Christine Gum.
45	vii.	Adam Gum. b. 1822, d Mar 1857 <u>Married</u> **Lucinda Mullenax** b 1832 – d. 26 Dec 1886 married 30 Apr 1855
46	viii.	Ellender (Nelly) Gum b. 1826.
47	ix.	Elizabeth Gum.
48	x.	Susanna Gum b. 1828. <u>Married</u> **Mathew Gum** (b. abt 1819 – d. abt 1880) married on 15 Jun 1855
49	xi.	Eliza Gum b. 1829.
	xii.	Matilda Gum b 1843, <u>Married</u> **Adam F Nicholas** b. 06 Jan 1831 – d. 12 Apr 1914)

6. **Jacob Jr.² Gum** (1.Dorothy "Dolly"¹ Arbogast), b. About 1798 in Augusta Co., VA, d. About 1871 in Andrews Co., MO.
. Jacob, his brother, Jesse, sisters, Mary and Elinor and all their spouse of Fayette Co., OH, and sisters, Sarah and Eddy, and their spouse of Madison Co., IN, transfer by deed to Henry Gum, their interest in land owned by their mother following her death, dated 5 Sep 1839; Pendleton Co. Deed Book 14, p. 531. Jacob apparently migrated to Andrew Co., MO, in about 1840 probably by way of Bond Co., IL.
   From, Leaves From The Gum Tree, 1984, by Muriel Martens Hoffman, Samuel B.
Gum, son and heir, appointed Administrator of Jacob Gum estate on 22 Dec 1871.
Other heirs were the widow, Rachel, and Rachel Couch, Andrew Co., MO, and the
heirs of Miles Gum in Bond Co., IL. Rochester Twp., Andrew Co., MO.
(1) <u>Married</u> Jan 13 1818 in Pendleton Co., WV, **Isabella Cunningham**.

   ### *Children* by Isabella Cunningham:

50	i.	Miles³ Gum b. 1820 in Virginia.

(2) He <u>Married</u> **Mahalia Flesher**, b. 1815 in Highland Co., VA (daughter of William Flesher, Sr. and Mary M. Gum).

8. **Ellender² Gum** (1.Dorothy "Dolly"¹ Arbogast), b. Oct 30 1804 in Pendleton Co., WV, d. Oct 5 1975 in Fayette Co., OH.,
(1) <u>Married</u> Jan 27 1825 in Pendleton Co., WV, **Andrew Jenkins**, b. in Pendleton Co., WV.

   ### *Children* by Andrew Jenkins:

+ 51	i.	Sarah³ Jenkins.
52	ii.	Polly Jenkins .

	53	iii.	Edith Emaline Jenkins b. Feb 16 1830 in Pendleton Co., WV.
	54	iv.	Andrew Jackson Jenkins b. Sep 9 1833.
	55	v.	Martha J. Jenkins b. 1836.
	56	vi.	Henry A Jenkins b. 1838.
	57	vii.	Peter H Jenkins b. 1844.
	58	viii.	Peter H Jenkins b. 1845.
	59	ix.	Rachel Jenkins b. 1851.
	60	x.	(infant) Jenkins b. 1852.
	61	xi.	Aletha Jenkins b. Dec 5 1934.

9. **Jesse² Gum** (1.Dorothy "Dolly"¹ Arbogast), b. Jun 01 1804 in Pendleton Co., WV, d. Aug 26 1854 in Lawrence Co., MO.

    Jesse went to Fayette Co., OH after death of mother and later went to Lawrence Co., MO where he was killed in 1854. Named in Fayette Co., OH deed in 1839. From, Leaves From The Gum Tree, 1984, by Muriel Martens Hoffman, records land sales in Virginia during the mid 1820's. Jesse followed his brother, Jacob and sister Nelly (Gum) Jenkins to Fayette Co., OH. They were there for the 1830 census. A number of other Virginia families are also recorded there in 1830,ie, Dunkles, Claypools, Fisher (Flesher), Jenkins, etc. Jesse married in 1832. Shortly after signing the deed to dispose of his mother's land, he migrated to Barry Co., MO, along with John Dunkle, his brother-in-law, and possibly others. Jesse filed for patent lands in Barry Co. in Nov. and Dec. 1839. Barry Co. became part of Dade Co. in 1842, which merger into Lawrenc.Co.in 1845. According to family stories, Jesse was killed by guerilla raiders in the border fights before Kansas became a state. Children, their spouse and Descendants from this book. Credits in the book are to Edrie M. Graham of St. Louis, MO, Mrs. Irene Whittenberg, Carthage, MO and Nolan Gunter, Miller, MO. Fred Mieswinkel, Mt. Vernon, MO, supplied records from Lawrence County Cemeteries and Court Records, 1975.

    Married Nov 26 1832 in Fayette Co., OH, **Aletha Dunkle**, b. Aug 14 1812 in Pendleton Co., WV, d. Mar 10 1902 in Lawrence Co., MO.

    ### *Children*:

+	62	i.	Lewis W.³ Gum b. Jan 17 1833.
	63	ii.	James H Gum b. Jul 06 1835, d. Sep 17 1862 in Old Ripley, Bond Co., IL.
+	64	iii.	William Madison Gum b. Jun 26 1839.
+	65	iv.	George Washington Gum b. Jun 26 1839.
+	66	v.	Jesse M Gum b. Mar 18 1842.
+	67	vi.	Mary Ellen Gum b. Jul 31 1844.
+	68	vii.	Martha Jane Gum b. Sep 10 1846.
+	69	viii.	Sarah Elizabeth Gum b. Mar 14 1849.
+	70	ix.	Talitha Gum b. May 29 1851.

Generation Three

10. **Henry³ Gum** (3.Isaac², 1.Dorothy "Dolly"¹ Arbogast), b. ABT 1807 in Pendleton Co., WV, d. AFT 1850.

    Married ABT 1830 in Madison Co., IN, **Jane (Unknown)**.

    ### *Children*:

	71	i.	Enoch⁴ Gum b. About 1831.
	72	ii.	Sarah Gum b. About 1832.
	73	iii.	Isaac Gum b. About 1833. Possibly the Isaac who married Catherine McDonald, 22 Apr 1869, Bond Co., IL
	74	iv.	Isabel Gum b. About 1840.
	75	v.	Elijah Gum b. About 1841. Possibly the Elijah Gum who enlisted 5 Sep 1862, carpenter from Bond Co., IL, died 23 Feb 1863, Memphis, TN. (War Records, IL Archives
	76	vi.	William Gum b. About 1845.

This couple lived in Madison, IL and their kids were most likely all born there.

11. **Jacob³ Gum** (3.Isaac², 1.Dorothy "Dolly"¹ Arbogast), b. 1810 in Pendleton Co., WV, d. JUN 1847 in Bond Co., IL.
    Married Jul 18 1844 in Bond Co., IN, **Susan Seybert**.
    ### *Children*:
    + 77   i.   James V.⁴ Gum b. Feb 14 1847.

12. **Sarah³ Gum** (3.Isaac², 1.Dorothy "Dolly"¹ Arbogast), b. 1812 in Ohio, d. 1898 in Bond Co., IL.
    Married Oct 19 1848 in Bond Co., IL, **Charles Wall**.
    ### *Children*:
    78   i.   Thomas⁴ Wall b. About 1842.
    79   ii.   Danial Wall b. About 1851.

13. **Jesse S.³ Gum** (3.Isaac², 1.Dorothy "Dolly"¹ Arbogast), b. ABT 1815 in Columbus, Franklin Co., OH, d. BEF 1847 in Bond Co., IL.
    Married BEF 1834 in Indiana, **Sarah (Unknown)**, b. in Scotland, UK.
    ### *Children*:
    + 80   i.   Louisa Janetta⁴ Gum b. Jan 29 1835.
    81   ii.   Elizabeth Ellen Gum b. ABT 1838.
             Married Jun 21 1855, **John M. Goodson**.
    82   iii.   James Gum b. ABT 1840.
    83   iv.   Mahalia Gum b. ABT 1842.
    84   v.   Mary Gum.

14. **Isaac C.³ Gum** (3.Isaac², 1.Dorothy "Dolly"¹ Arbogast), b. May 9 1818 in Ohio, d. Dec 4 1869 in Bond Co., IL.
    (1) Married 1842 in Madison Co., IN, **Clarissa Davenport**.

    ### *Children* by Clarissa Davenport:
    + 85   i.   William Jefferson⁴ Gum b. Jun 02 1843 Bond co., I d. Feb 13 1865IL Harriett
             Married **Elizabeth Hegler** Jul 24 1863
             Married Margaret Shields
    86   ii.   Eliza Jane Gum b. About 1845, d. before 1863.
             Married Apr 17 1861 in Bond Co., IL, **John William Dugan**, d. after1883. John: Son of Christopher SCHMOLLINGER and Dora LAWRENCE.
    + 87   iii.   Lemuel B. Gum b. About 1846. 1870 census Farmer, Pleasant Mound, IL 1870, age 22; Frances, 18; Augustus, 2 mos; Mary Gum, 9 years old.
    88   iv.   Matilda E. Gum b. after 1846.
    + 89   v.   John Royal Gum b. Nov 22 1851d. Jan 10 1916
             Married Matilda E. Barth, **b.** 14 Feb 1856, **d.** 4 Sep 1907 Several children
    + 90   vi.   James Johnson Gum b. April 1854 d. Jul 17 1931
             Married Theresa Elizabeth Barth, b. 1854, d. 1941
    + 91   vii.   Martha E. Gum b. About 1858.
             Married **Henry Schmollenge**
    r   + 92   viii.   Mary C. Caroline Gum b. About 1861.

    (2) He Married **Sarah Elizabeth Merritt**, b. Mar 1 1831 in Tennessee, d. Feb 12 1880.
    ### *Children* by Sarah Elizabeth Merritt:
    93   ix.   David Gum b. About 1866.

15. **Catherine³ Gum** (3.Isaac², 1.Dorothy "Dolly"¹ Arbogast), b. OCT 1820 in Ohio, d. AFT 1900 in Andrews Co., MO.
    She Married **Lemuel B. Gum**, b. About 1819 in Ohio.
    ### *Children*:

	94	i.	Marian⁴ Gum b. 1851.
			She Married **John Misner**.
	95	ii.	Rachel Gum b. 1853.
	96	iii.	John R Gum b. 1855.
	97	iv.	Sarah C Gum.

16. **John Finley³ Gum** (3.Isaac², 1.Dorothy "Dolly"¹ Arbogast), b. 1821 in Columbus, Franklin Co., OH, d. BEF 1870 in Bond Co., IL.
Married Apr 15 1850 in Bond Co., IL, **Elizabeth Hill**.
   Children:
   + 98   i.   Samuel A⁴ Gum b. 1855.
     99   ii. Louisa Gum b. 1857.
    100   iii. John D Gum b. 1857.

17. **James Riley³ Gum** (3.Isaac², 1.Dorothy "Dolly"¹ Arbogast), b. Jul 10 1822 in Columbus, Franklin Co., OH, d. Jan 31 1895 in Bond Co., IL.
Married Mar 13 1845 in Bond Co., IL, **Almira J. File**, d. Aug 14 1876 in Bond Co., IL, buried in Gum Cem., Bond Co., IL. Almira: Daughter of Daniel File and Martha H. James.
   Children:
    101   i.   Martha E.⁴ Gum b. Jun 15 1846, d. 1850-1860.
   + 102 ii. Sarah Jane Gum b. Feb 20 1850.
    103   iii. Henry Gum b. Dec 02 1854, d. Dec 03 1858.
   + 104 iv. Isaac Daniel Gum b. Apr 14 1858.
   + 105 v.   Enoch Riley Gum b. Feb 24 1863.

18. **Elizabeth³ Gum** (3.Isaac², 1.Dorothy "Dolly"¹ Arbogast), b. Jan 11 1825 in Madison Co., IN, d. 1903 in Bond Co., IL.
   (1) Married May 5 1849 in Bond Co., IL, **Daniel File**.
      Children by Daniel File:
   + 106 i.   Sarah M.⁴ File.

   (2) She Married **James Jones**.

20. **Jeremiah C.³ Gum** (3.Isaac², 1.Dorothy "Dolly"¹ Arbogast), b. 1828 in Madison Co., IN, d. Apr 27 1867 in Bond Co., IL.
Married Feb 8 1853 in Bond Co., IL, **Elwina Ray**, d. 1860.
   Children:
    107   i.   Rosetta Elvina⁴ Gum b. About 1854.
              (1) Married Nov 26 1872 in Bond Co., IL, **Peter Hay**.
              (2) Married Jul 3 1887, **Robert Bruff**.
    108   ii. Jannetta Gum b. About 1854.
              (1) Married Jan 11 1873 in Bond Co., IL, **Elias Munson**.
              (2) Married Dec 25 1876, **Charles Morris Harnett**.

21. **Olive³ Gum** (3.Isaac², 1.Dorothy "Dolly"¹ Arbogast), b. Feb 6 1832 in Madison Co., IN, d. Apr 22 1891 in Madison Co., IN. Married May 22 1851 in Bond Co., IL, **Addison Ray**.
   Children:
    109   i.   Mere⁴ Ray b. About 1852.
    110   ii. William R Ray b. Mar 20 1854, d. Mar 22 1932.
              Married Dec 27 1877, **Susan Emely Owens**.
    111   iii. George F. Ray.
    112   iv. Sara A. Ray.

23. **Perry O.³ Gum** (3.Isaac², 1.Dorothy "Dolly"¹ Arbogast), b. Jan 13 1836 in Madison Co., IN, d. Dec 25 1911 in Alton, Madison Co., IL.

Married Oct 4 1856 in Bond Co., IL, **Camilla Ann File**, b. Nov 10 1840, d. Dec 16 1911 in Alton, Madison Co., IL.

> ### *Children*:
>
> + 113   i.   Olive[4] Gum b. 1856.
>   114   ii.   Emma Gum b. 1859.
>   She Married **Preston Hubbard**.
>   115   iii.   Lydia Gum b. 1861, d. 1931.
>   She Married **Charles Lemon**.
>   116   iv.   Mary Gum b. 1865, d. 1930.
>   She Married **Luther Hester**.
>   117   v.   Hamtom Gum b. 1865.
>   118   vi.   Daniel Lee Gum b. 1868, d. 1894 in Omaha, Douglas Co., NE.
>   119   vii.   Ida Gum b. 1871.
>   120   viii.   Nellie Etta Gum b. Jun 21 1874.
>   Married Jun 21 1892 in Alton, Madison Co., IL, **John Elbert Russell**.
>   121   ix.   Guy Gum b. 1878, d. 1908.

29. **Adam**[3] **Flesher** (4.Mary M.[2] Gum, 1.Dorothy "Dolly"[1] Arbogast), b. Oct 12 1813 in Highland Co., VA, d. May 05 1893 in Andrews Co., MO.
(1) Married Aug 01 1831 in Fayette Co., OH, **Elizabeth Simmons**, b. 1815 in Virginia, d. 1850 in Missouri.

> ### *Children* by Elizabeth Simmons:
>
>   122   i.   Lucinda[4] Flesher b. 1832 in Fayette Co., OH, d. c 1832.
>   123   ii.   Sarah Jane Flesher b. 1834 in Fayette Co., OH.
>   Married Jan 1859 in Andrews Co., MO, **Marion King**, b. About 1834 in Union Star, Dekalb Co., MO.
> + 124   iii.   Amanda Ellen Flesher b. 1836.
>   125   iv.   Marion Flesher b. 1838 in Fayette Co., OH.
>   126   v.   William Flesher b. 1839.
>   127   vi.   Emaline Flesher b. 1840 in Andrews Co., MO, d. After 1896.
>   She Married **George Patton**.
> + 128   vii.   Angeline Flesher b. Dec 24 1843.
> + 129   viii.   Greenberry Flesher b. 1846.
> + 130   ix.   Henry Flesher b. 1849.

(2) Married Jul 04 1852 in Buchanan Co., MO, **Pheobe Janes**, b. 1808 in Virginia.
(3) Married c 1875, **Cassandra Turnipseed**, b. 1818.

31. **Henry**[3] **Flesher** (4.Mary M.[2] Gum, 1.Dorothy "Dolly"[1] Arbogast), b. About 1817 in Highland Co., VA, d. in Mill Grove, Poweshiek Co., IA.
(1) He Married **Rachel Farm**, b. About 1817.
(2) He Married **Sophia Low**, b. About 1817.
 (3) Married Jan 01 1846 in Andrews Co., MO, **Sophia Cruse**, b. c 1826 in Tennessee, d. Jun 09 1912 in Sonoma Co., CA.

> ### *Children* by Sophia Cruse:
>
>   131   i.   Mary Jane[4] Flesher b. Apr 19 1841 in Missouri, d. Mar 17 1923 in Canby, Clackamas Co., OR.
>   She Married **Joseph Layton**, b. Oct 04 1832 in Montgomery Co., IN, d. Feb 02 1910 in Pottawattamie Co., IA.
>   132   ii.   Sarah E Flesher b. 1847 in Missouri.
>   Married Oct 19 1868 in Pottawattamie Co., IA, **Rueben E Raynolds**.
>   133   iii.   William Flesher b. 1849 in Missouri, d. Dec 15 1919 in Placer Co., CA.
>   Married Jul 03 1872, **Susan F Wright**, b. May 1851 in Kentucky, d. Feb 11 1914.
>   134   iv.   Henrietta E Flesher b. 1850.
>   135   v.   Benjamin F Flesher b. 1851 in Missouri, d. Aug 15 1935.

		Married c 1881, **Eda Morris**, b. About 1851.
136	vi.	Harriet E Flesher b. 1853 in Missouri.
		Married Jul 01 1870 in Pottawattamie Co., IA, **H D Johnson**.
137	vii.	James Alvin Flesher b. 1855 in Missouri.
138	viii.	Joseph J Flesher b. 1857-58 in Missouri, d. Jan 25 1926.
139	ix.	Margaret Louisa Flesher b. 1859 in Iowa.
+ 140	x.	Emerson B Flesher b. Feb 05 1862.
+ 141	xi.	Harry Seldom Flesher b. Apr 12 1864.

32. **Sarah Jane³ Flesher** (4.Mary M.² Gum, 1.Dorothy "Dolly"¹ Arbogast), b. Oct 20 1819 in Highland Co., VA, d. May 19 1875 in Girard, Crawford Co., KS.
Married Apr 21 1839 in Fayette Co., OH, **John Cibert Dunkle**, b. Jun 26 1816 in Crawford Co., KS (son of Jacob Dunkle and Ellender Nellie), d. c 1900 in Girard, Crawford Co., KS, buried in Meyers Cem., Girard, Crawford County KA.

   Children:

142	i.	Mary E⁴ Dunkle b. 1840 in Missouri.
		Married Rev. **Phillip Thompsom Foust** b. Sep 15 1836. Knox Co., TN, d Nov 17 1924 Greene Co., MO
143	ii.	Malinda Dunkle b. 1842 in Missouri.
144	iii.	Sarah Jane Dunkle b. 1843 in Missouri
		Married. **Hewey Ellis Morrison Born 1843, d. Feb 20.1915**
145	iv.	Melvina Dunkle b. 1845 in Missouri.
146	v.	William Dunkle b. 1848 in Missouri.
147	vi.	Martha Dunkle b. 1850 in Missouri.
+ 148	vii.	Aletha Adaline Dunkle b. Jun 07 1852.

33. **Absolum³ Flesher** (4.Mary M.² Gum, 1.Dorothy "Dolly"¹ Arbogast), b. 1821 in Highland Co., VA. He Married **Melinda Taylor**.

   Children:

149	i.	Ellen⁴ Flesher.
150	ii.	Franklin Flesher.
151	iii.	Jane Flesher.
152	iv.	Katie Flesher.
153	v.	Mary Flesher.
154	vi.	Robert Flesher.
155	vii.	George Flesher.
156	viii.	Marion Flesher.

34. **William Seybert³ Flesher** (4.Mary M.² Gum, 1.Dorothy "Dolly"¹ Arbogast), b. Jul 19 1824 in Fayette Co., OH, d. Apr 13 1894 in Hoyt, Jackson Co., KS.
William Seybert Flesher was born in Fayette County, Ohio on July 19, 1828,
died April 13, 1894 in Jackson County, Kansas, buried in South Cedar
Cemetery, also known as Coleman Cemetery, four miles South of Denison,
Kansas, Northeast of Hoyt. He moved with his parents to Lexington,
Illinois, then to Dade County, Missouri where he
Married in 1849 Emeline Smith, born in Kentucky 1833, died in November 1857 in Andrews County, Missouri. They moved to Andrews County, Missouri in 1851 with their first 2 children. Their 4 children: John Henry, Mary E., Benjamin W., and Louisa J.
After Emeline's death William Married in Andrews County, Missouri on January 22, 1860 to **Sarah Annas (Smith) Hunt**. She had been Married briefly to Henry Hunt. He left for Ohio on horseback to collect his inheritance and was never seen again. The incoherent deathbed confession of a neighbor led Sarah to believe Henry had been murdered and thrown in a river. Sarah was a daughter of William Smith. She was born in Jackson County, Indiana on September 30, 1842. In February, 1960 William and Sarah moved to Jackson County, Kansas (Douglas Township) where they remained until William's death in 1894. Sarah then moved to Guthrie, Oklahoma where

two of her Married daughters were living. She died on February 28, 1922. She's buried in Tuttle, Oklahoma, Fairview Cemetery.

(1) Married April 1848 in Dade Co., MO, **Emeline E Smith**, b. 1833 in Kentucky, d. Nov 1857 in Andrews Co., MO.

    Children by Emeline E Smith:

+ 157   i.   John Henry[4] Flesher b. Aug 25 1849.
+ 158   ii.   Mary Elizabeth Flesher b. Mar 04 1851.
+ 159   iii.   Benjamin W Flesher b. Nov 16 1854.
+ 160   iv.   Louisa J Flesher b. 1857.

(2) Married Jan 22 1860 in Howard Co., MO, **Sarah Smith**, b. Sep 30 1842 in Tuttle, Grady Co., OK, d. Feb 22 1922 in Jackson Co., IN.

    Children by Sarah Smith:

 161   v.   Tabitha S Flesher b. Oct 17 1860 in Kansas, d. Oct 14 1935.
    (1) She Married **(unknown) Smith**.
    (2) Married Apr 08 1879 in Jackson Co., KS, **John William Boyce**, b. Nov 20 1843, d. May 28 1919.
 162   vi.   Marion L Flesher b. Sep 15 1862 in Kansas, d. Nov 09 1956.
+ 163   vii.   Sarah Ellen Flesher b. Jul 18 1865.
+ 164   viii.   Thomas Edward Flesher b. Aug 30 1867.
 165   ix.   Matilda Frances Flesher b. Nov 12 1869 in Kansas.
    Married Dec 31 1887 in Holden, Jackson Co., KS, **William Jess Hubberd**, b. 1865 in Kansas.
 166   x.   Lucinda Adaline Flesher b. Jan 18 1871 in Kansas. She Married **Eli Shelton**.
 167   xi.   Jasesus Flesher b. Mar 17 1873.
 168   xii.   Josiah H. Flesher b. Feb 12 1874, d. Nov 16 1874.
 169   xiii.   Mary Ida Flesher b. Aug 12 1875 in Kansas. She Married **William L. Morris**.
 170   xiv.   Netta B. Flesher b. Nov 23 1878, d. Jun 24 1914.
 171   xv.   Emma Rita Flesher b. Jul 25 1882, d. Dec 19 1955 in Carthage, Jasper Co., MO. She Married **Samuel Moore**, b. Sep 25 1860 in Carthage, Jasper Co., MO, d. Oct 30 1930 in Carthage, Jasper Co., MO.

38. **Louisa K**[3] **Flesher** (4.Mary M.[2] Gum, 1.Dorothy "Dolly"[1] Arbogast), b. Aug 17 1839 in OH or MO, d. Nov 20 1900 in Andrews Co., MO.
Married Jun 28 1860 in Lon Branch Church Cem., Andrew Co., MO., **William Kizamore Miller**, b. Jul 11 1840 in Ohio, d. Nov 07 1899.

    Children:

 172   i.   William D[4] Miller.
 173   ii.   James Henry Miller b. 1863.
    He Married Lucy Belle Elgin, b. 1863.
 174   iii.   John Adam Miller.
 175   iv.   Albert E Miller.
 176   v.   Mary Catherine Miller.
+ 177   vi.   George Riley Miller b. Apr 27 1872.
 178   vii.   Charles Kizamore Miller b. Mar 6 1876.
 179   viii.   Thomas R Miller.
 180   ix.   Laura Ellen Miller.
 181   x.   Joseph Miller.
 182   xi.   Alice Miller.
 183   xii.   Jacob Oscar Miller b. Nov 6 1878.

39. **Matilda**[3] **Gum** (5.Adam[2], 1.Dorothy "Dolly"[1] Arbogast), b. 1812.
Married Jan 31 1830 in Pendleton Co., WV, **George Nicholas**.

Children:

184	i.	Adam F^4 Nicholas b. About 1831.
185	ii.	Cynthia Nicholas b. About 1834.
186	iii.	James W Nicholas b. About 1837.
187	iv.	Frensceenor Nicholas b. 1839.
188	v.	Mary A Nicholas b. About 1841.
189	vi.	Renick L Nicholas b. About 1843.
190	vii.	Jones Nicholas b. About 1850.
191	viii.	George Nicholas b. About 1850.

40. **Henry^3 Gum** (5.Adam^2, 1.Dorothy "Dolly"^{1} Arbogast), b. 1813.
    <u>Married</u> Apr 02 1831 in Pendleton Co., WV, **Margaret Chew**. Margaret: Lived in Lewis County, Freemans Dist., VA.

    ### Children:

192	i.	Alcy^4 Gum b. About 1833.
193	ii.	William J Gum b. About 1833.
+ 194	iii.	Joseph Gum b. June 1836.
+ 195	iv.	Peter Gum b. Dec 1839.
+ 196	v.	Boyd Gum b. Oct 1842.
197	vi.	Sayer Gum b. About 1845.
198	vii.	Adam Gum b. About 1849.

41. **Sabina^3 Gum** (5.Adam^2, 1.Dorothy "Dolly"^{1} Arbogast), b. Aug 1814 in Pendleton Co., WV, d. Jan 30 1859 in McLean Co., IL, buried in Hopewell Cem., Downs, IL.
    <u>Married</u> Mar 20 1834 in Pendleton Co., WV, **William Benjamin Colaw**, b. Jun 30 1813 in Virginia, d. Sep 03 1896 in Downs, Mclean Co., IL. Son of George Colaw and Elizabeth Wimer.

    ### Children:

+ 199	i.	William^4 Colaw, Jr b. Jul 19 1829.
200	ii.	Laban Colaw b. Nov 27 1834, d. Dec 17 1858.
201	iii.	Harmon Colaw b. Oct 14 1836, d. Oct 22 1858.
+ 202	iv.	Benjamin Watters Colaw b. About 1840.
203	v.	Sarah Ellen Colaw b. Mar 1843, d. Sep 05 1871. <u>Married</u> Aug 11 1867, **William H. Staten.**
+ 204	vi.	Dyer W Colaw b. Feb 20 1846.
205	vii.	Martha Jane Colaw b. Sep 03 1850, d. Feb 08 1897.
206	viii.	Amos Kendall Colaw b. About 1856.

43. **Amos^3 Gum** (5.Adam^2, 1.Dorothy "Dolly"^{1} Arbogast), b. 1820, d. c 1900.
    He <u>Married</u> **Frances Terry**.

    ### Children:

+ 207	i.	Thomas Marion^4 Gum b. Jul 31 1861.
+ 208	ii.	James Otho Gum b. Jul 14 1867.

51. **Sarah^3 Genkins** (8.Elleder^2 Gum, 1.Dorothy "Dolly"^{1} Arbogast). Born in **Ohio,** USA on 26 Sep 1841 died 3 Apr 1916 in Oklahoma City, OK
    She <u>Married</u> **John Easter Shockey**. Born in Highland, Ohio, **USA** on **15 Apr 1837** to Isaac Shockey and Airy Barker. John Easter married Sarah Ellen Jenkins and had 14 children. He passed away on **26 Nov 1908** in Redd Starr, OK

    ### Children:

209	i.	Grover Charles^4 Shockey b. 1833 in Hardin Co., OH.
210	ii.	Rebecca Shockey b. 1860 in Fayette Co., OH. She passed away on **1898** <u>Married</u> **Gillingham Garwood** and had 9 children.
211	iii.	John Henry Shockey b. 1862 in Fayette Co., OH. Born in **Fayette, Ohio, USA** on **1862**. He passed away on 1877 in Hale, Hardin, Ohio
212	iv.	Almeda May Shockey Born in **Fayette, Ohio, USA** on **1866** to

		Married **Leroy Swampton Ramsey** and had 8 children. She passed away on **1922** in **CO.**
213	v.	Jacob Andrew Shockey b. 1867 in Fayette Co., OH.
		Married **Hester Jane Roberts** and had 7 children. He passed away on **1955** in Adair, MO
214	vi.	Isaac Shockey b. 1869 in Pike Co., OH.
		Married Fanny Adkins and had 3 children. Isaac married Laura Ward. He passed away on **27 Apr 1903** in MO
215	vii.	William Shockey b. 1870 in Pike Co., OH.D. 1882 in Hale, Hardin, Ohio
216	viii.	Orvil A Shockey b. 1872 in Hardin Co., OH.
		Married **Fanny Adkins**
		Married **Wardie Hunsacker**. He passed away on 1923 in Dayton, Montgomery Co. OH,
217	ix.	Jasper Shockey b. 1877 in Hardin Co., OH.
		Married **Minnie Holt** and had 8 children. He passed away on **1920**.
+ 218	x.	Gertrude Ethel Shockey b. 1878.
+ 219	xi.	Rosa Vera Shockey b. 1882.

62. **Lewis W.³ Gum** (9.Jesse², 1.Dorothy "Dolly"¹ Arbogast), b. Jan 17 1833 in Fayette Co., OH, d. Mar 14 1916 in Lawrence Co., MO.
Married 1860, **Cordelia Elizabeth Yancey**, b. Jan 03 1839, d. Nov 19 1892.

   Children:
220	i.	Mary Elizabeth⁴ Gum b. 1865.
221	ii.	Francis E. Gum b. May 02 1867, d. Oct 10 1920.
222	iii.	Tecumsia Sherman Gum b. May 1869. D 10 Oct 1920 in Lawrence, Missouri
223	iv.	Josephine Gum b. Dec 1870, buried in Gum Cem., near Old Ripley, Bond Co., IL.
224	v.	Grant Gum b. Dec 1870.
225	vi.	Thomas Gum b. About 1874.
226	vii.	Will S. Gum b. Nov 02 1875, d. Jul 05 1907 in Old Ripley, Bond Co., IL.
227	viii.	Robert Gum b. Nov 1876.
228	ix.	Gussie Gum b. Sept 1881.

64. **William Madison³ Gum** (9.Jesse², 1.Dorothy "Dolly"¹ Arbogast), b. Jun 26 1839, d. Dec 30 1926, buried in Hood Cem., Lawrence Co., MO.
Married Nov 18 1869 in Lawrence Co., MO, **Nancy J Lewis**, b. About 1840.

   Children:
229	i.	Elmer E.⁴ Gum b. About 1871.
		lived in Kingsville, TX and worked on King Ranch. Had child Kay Rand Gum.
+ 230	ii.	Gerthe Gum b. 1874.
231	iii.	William W Gum b. 1878.
		He Married **Byrt West**.
+ 232	iv.	Thomas Otto Gum b. Mar 1883.
233	v.	Wilber Gum.

65. **George Wasgington³ Gum** (9.Jesse², 1.Dorothy "Dolly"¹ Arbogast), b. Jun 26 1839 in Highland Co., VA, d. Aug 01 1899, buried in Sycamore Cem., Lewis Co., WV.
Married Oct 18 1868 in Lawrence Co., MO, **Margaret Ruark**, b. Mar 06 1845, d. Jun 22 1926, buried in Sycamore Cem., Lewis Co., WV.

   Children:
+ 234	i.	Nathaniel Meade⁴ Gum b. Oct 20 1869.
+ 235	ii.	William Oliver Gum b. Jul 30 1871.
+ 236	iii.	Andrew Newton Gum b. Dec 22 1872.
+ 237	iv.	Effie Gum b. Jul 06 1875.
+ 238	v.	Edgar Haddon Gum b. Sep 15 1877.

+ 239   vi.   Albert Gum b. May 12 1880.
+ 240   vii.   Ida May Gum b. Oct 06 1883.

66. **Jesse M³ Gum** (9.Jesse², 1.Dorothy "Dolly"¹ Arbogast), b. Mar 18 1842, d. Aug 01 1899, buried in Hood Cem., Lawrence Co., MO. Jesse was a private in the Union Army, enlisted Mar 31 1863 at Springfield, MO, transferred to 4th Reg. Calv.
Married Mar 06 1870 in Springfield, Greene Co., MO, **Nancy Skean**.
   Children:
   241   i.   Jesse W⁴ Gum b. Jan 08 1877, d. Feb 14 1877.
   242   ii.   Earnest Gum b. Apr 28 1891, d. May 10 1891.

67. **Mary Ellen³ Gum** (9.Jesse², 1.Dorothy "Dolly"¹ Arbogast), b. Jul 31 1844, d. Sep 06 1887, buried in Hood Cem., Lawrence Co., MO.
She Married **Robert L Yancy**, b. Feb 02 1847, d. Sep 13 1906, buried in Gum Cem., Bond Co., IL.
   Children:
   243   i.   Thomas Sherman⁴ Yancy b. About 1869.
   244   ii.   James E Yancy b. About 1871.
   245   iii.   Mary Elizabeth Yancy b. About 1874.
   246   iv.   Effie C Yancy b. About 1875.
   247   v.   Ella C Yancy b. About 1880.
   248   vi.   John Yancy b. About 1880.

68. **Martha Jane³ Gum** (9.Jesse², 1.Dorothy "Dolly"¹ Arbogast), b. Sep 10 1846, d. Dec 05 1891, buried in Hood Cem., Lawrence Co., MO.
She Married **Benjamin W Stinson**, b. Mar 20 1841, d. Jan 22 1889, buried in Hood Cem., Lawrence Co., MO.
   Children:
   249   i.   William W⁴ Stinson b. About 1871.
   250   ii.   Jesse M Stinson b. About 1873.
   251   iii.   Loren L Stinson b. About 1878.
   252   iv.   John Stinson.
   253   v.   George Stinson.
   254   vi.   Ben Stinson b. Aug 1885.
   255   vii.   Mary Stinson.

69. **Sarah Elizabeth³ Gum** (9.Jesse², 1.Dorothy "Dolly"¹ Arbogast), b. Mar 14 1849, d. Feb 26 1935, buried in Dunkle Cem., Lawrence Co., MO.
She Married **Thomas Westley McNeal**, b. Jun 08 1856, d. Oct 18 1936, buried in Dunkle Cem., Lawrence Co., MO.
   Children:
+ 256   i.   Pearl⁴ McNeal b. Dec 06 1885.
+ 257   ii.   William Wesley McNeal b. May 21 1890.
   258   iii.   Earl Moss McNeal b. Sep 13 1891, d. Sep 22 1910.

70. **Talitha³ Gum** (9.Jesse², 1.Dorothy "Dolly"¹ Arbogast), b. May 29 1851, d. Jul 24 1921, buried in Sycamore Cem., Lewis Co., WV.
Married Aug 03 1871 in Lawrence Co., MO, **James L Stinson**, b. 1851.
   Children:
   259   i.   William Sherman⁴ Stinson b. Sep 21 1872, d. Feb 23 1963.
+ 260   ii.   Sarah Jane Stinson b. Jul 05 1874.
   261   iii.   James Madison Stinson b. Jan 04 1877, d. Feb 08 1896.
   262   iv.   Thomas Andrew Stinson b. Nov 26 1878, d. Dec 06 1878.
+ 263   v.   Pearl Stinson b. Jul 12 1880.
+ 264   vi.   Fred Stinson b. Jan 26 1884.
+ 265   vii.   Lula Stinson b. Jun 26 1886.

+ 266   viii.   Grace Stinson b. Feb 26 1889.
+ 267   ix.   Dallas Stinson b. Jan 12 1892.

Generation Four

77. **James V.^{4} Gum** (11.Jacob^3, 3.Isaac^2, 1.Dorothy "Dolly"^{1} Arbogast), b. Feb 14 1847, d. May 5 1927. Married c 1873, **Eliza Parton**.
    ### Children:
    268   i.   Lucinda^5 Gum b. About 1873.
    269   ii.   John Henry Gum b. 1875.

80. **Louisa Janetta^4 Gum** (13.Jesse S.^{3}, 3.Isaac^2, 1.Dorothy "Dolly"^{1} Arbogast), b. Jan 29 1835 in Illinois, d. Sep 24 1901, buried in Miami Cem.; Miami, Ottawa Co., OK.
    Married Dec 12 1850, **Green Berry Huffstedtler**, b. Dec 10 1831 in Illinois, d. Jun 20 1873, buried in Old Mt. Nebo Cem.; Sorento, Bond Co., IL. **Green**: 1850 Federal Census lists Greenbury as a member of the John Huffstudler household. This would lead me to believe that this is is father and his mother is Rachel. Brothers & sisters listed are David -23, Adaline-14, Maranda-10, Harriet-9, Emily-6, Caroline-3, Elizabeth-17?, Clementine-4 mos. Green's age is listed as 17, putting his date of birth as 1833, different from F. Englands records as 1831.
    ### Children:
    270   i.   Maurice M.^{5} Huffstedtler b. Feb 9 1852, d. Dec 19 1854.
    + 271   ii.   Sarah Elizabeth Huffstedtler b. Dec 4 1853.
    272   iii.   Louis Fred Huffstedtler b. Oct 26 1855, d. Jan 20 1879, buried in Old Mt. Nebo Cem.; Sorento, Bond Co., IL.
    273   iv.   James W. Huffstedtler b. Jan 30 1857, d. Dec 14 1899, buried in Old Mt. Nebo Cem.; Sorento, Bond Co., IL.
    274   v.   Mary Frances Huffstedtler b. Mar 21 1859, buried in Fly Creek Cem., Faulkner, Cherokee Co., KS.
    275   vi.   Narcissa Ellen Huffstedtler b. Dec 1 1862, d. 1878.
    276   vii.   Mahalia C. Huffstedtler b. Nov 5 1864, d. Jan 4 1931, buried in Fairmount Cem., Follett, Lipscomb Co., TX.
    277   viii.   Margaret L. Huffstedtler b. Apr 28 1867, d. Dec 6 1868, buried in Old Mt. Nebo Cem.; Sorento, Bond Co., IL.

85. **William Jefferson^4 Gum** (14.Isaac C.^{3}, 3.Isaac^2, 1.Dorothy "Dolly"^{1} Arbogast), b. Jun 02 1843, d. Jun 10 1925.
    (1) Married Jul 30 1883 in Bond Co., IL, **Harriette Elizabeth Hagler**, b. Oct 23 1843, d. Nov 15 1864, buried in Payne Cem., Bond Co., IL.
    ### Children by Harriette Elizabeth Hagler:
    278   i.   Roberts M.^{5} Gum b. Jun 11 1864, d. May 09 1865.

    (2) Married Aug 24 1865,.**Martha Margaret Shields**, b. About 1849, d. Dec 28 1911
    ### Children by Martha Margaret Shields:
    279   ii.   Sarah Gum b. Sep 14 1868.
    280   iii.   Icy D. Gum b. About 1869 in Illinois.
    281   iv.   F. A. Gum b. About 1871.
    282   v.   C. V. Gum b. About 1874.
    283   vi.   Louiza Gum b. About 1876.
    284   vii.   Lewy A. Gum b. About 1878.
    285   viii.   (infant) Gum b. About 1880.

87. **Lemuel B.**^{4} **Gum** (14.Isaac C.^{3}, 3.Isaac^2, 1.Dorothy "Dolly"^{1} Arbogast), b. About 1846 in Illinois.
Married Dec 12 1867 in Fayette Co., IL, **Francis Davis**, b. About 1852.
   ### *Children*:
   - 286   i.   William F.^{5} Gum b. About 1870.
   - 287   ii.   Arnold O. Gum b. About 1877 in Fayette Co., IL.
     Married Sep 29 1911 in Fayette Co., IL, **Clara L. White**, b. 1877 in Christian Co., IL. Clara: Daughter of Stephen WHITE and Mary TRAVIS.

89. **John Royal**^{4} **Gum** (14.Isaac C.^{3}, 3.Isaac^2, 1.Dorothy "Dolly"^{1} Arbogast), b. Nov 22 1851 in Pleasant Mound Twp., Bond Co., IL, d. Oct 01 1916.
Married Aug 22 1875 in Bond Co., IL, **Matilda E. Barth**, d. Sep 04 1907 in Paine Cem., Bond Co., IL. **Matilda**: Daughter of Jacob BARTH and Elisabeth GETNER Gunther.
   ### *Children*:
   - + 288   i.   Edward Gustavus^5 Gum b. About 1876.
   - + 289   ii.   Clara (Elizabeth?) Gum b. About 1879.
   - 290   iii.   George Washington Gum b. About 1882.
   - 291   iv.   Millard A. Gum b. Aug 14 1884, d. Sep 16 1884 in St. Louis, St. Louis Co., MO.
   - 292   v.   Annie B. Gum b. Oct 1889.
   - + 293   vi.   Bert E. Gum b. Jan 15 1892.

90. **James Johnson**^{4} **Gum** (14.Isaac C.^{3}, 3.Isaac^2, 1.Dorothy "Dolly"^{1} Arbogast), b. April 1854 in Illinois, d. Jul 17 1931 in Illinois.
Married Nov 22 1874 in Bond Co., IL, **Theresa E. Barth**, d. Aug 31 1941, buried in Payne Cem., Bond Co., IL. **Theresa**: Daughter of Jacob BARTH and Elisabeth GETNER Gunther.
   ### *Children*:
   - + 294   i.   Jacob I.^{5} Gum b. 1876.
   - 295   ii.   Isaac Gum b. 1876.
   - + 296   iii.   John Leonard Gum b. Oct 1877.
   - + 297   iv.   James Edward Gum b. Apr 1884.
   - + 298   v.   Luther Randolph Gum b. Mar 28 1888.

91. **Martha E.**^{4} **Gum** (14.Isaac C.^{3}, 3.Isaac^2, 1.Dorothy "Dolly"^{1} Arbogast), b. About 1858 in Bond Co., IL.
Married Mar 23 1879, **Henry L Schmollinger**, b. About 1856 in Philadelphia, Philadelphia Co., PA. **Henry**: Son of Christopher Schmollinger and Dora Lawrence.
   ### *Children*:
   - 299   i.   Samual^5 Schmollinger.
   - 300   ii.   Millard Schmollinger.
   - 301   iii.   Tracy Schmollinger.

92. **Mary C. Caroline**^{4} **Gum** (14.Isaac C.^{3}, 3.Isaac^2, 1.Dorothy "Dolly"^{1} Arbogast), b. About 1861 in Bond Co., IL, d. Mar 31 1890, buried in Payne Cem., Bond Co., IL.
Son of Jacob BARTH and Elisabeth GETNER Gunther
Married Mar 04 1883 in Bond Co., IL, **Jacob Barth**, b. Jun 02 1858 in Bond Co., IL, d. Apr 17 1929 in Payne Cem., Bond Co., IL.
   ### *Children*:
   - 302   i.   Lizzie C^5 Barth b. Nov 29 1883, d. Sep 26 1898.

98. **Samuel A**^{4} **Gum** (16.John Finley^3, 3.Isaac^2, 1.Dorothy "Dolly"^{1} Arbogast), b. 1855.
Married Oct 10 1878, **Louise Davenport**.
   ### *Children*:
   - 303   i.   John L^5 Gum b. 1880.

102. **Sarah Jane**^{4} **Gum** (17.James Riley^3, 3.Isaac^2, 1.Dorothy "Dolly"^{1} Arbogast), b. Feb 20 1850, d. Jun 28 1932, buried in Montrose Cem., Greenville, Bond Co., IL.

(1) Married Jul 15 1866 in Bond Co., IL, **David Causey**, b. Oct 20 1842, d. May 06 1875.
   Children *by David Causey:*
   304 i.   Mary Elizabeth^5 Causey b. Jul 07 1867, d. Jun 20 1932.
             Married c 1882, William Lindley (son of Eligah Lindley and Clarissa Gum).
   305 ii. Harriett Ellen Causey b. Feb 20 1869, d. Jul 15 1954.
             Married Feb 21 1888, William A. Michael.
   306 iii. Lucy Jane Causey b. Aug 07 1871, d. 1951.
             She Married Emil Duchenne.
   307 iv. William Riley Causey b. Dec 13 1873 in Hutchinson, Reno Co., KS, d. Feb 19 1946.
             He Married **Bertha Gottgetreu**.

(2) Married Mar 05 1882, **Elisha Ray**, b. Oct 27 1852 in Bond Co., IL. **Elisha**: Son of William Ra and Matilda T Paine.
   Children *by Elisha Ray:*
   308 v.   Mitlida Almira Ray b. May 23 1883, d. Apr 15 1951.
              Married Mar 05 1903, **Benjamin File**.
   309 vi.   Enoch Albert Ray b. Jul 03 1885, d. Mar 28 1942.
              He Married **Blanche Faulk**.
   310 vii. Laura Edith Ray b. Aug 08 1889, d. Mar 22 1964.
              Married Apr 10 1916, **Landolin Houseman.**
 + 311 viii. Blanche Mahalia Ray b. Apr 07 1894.

104. **Isaac Daniel^4 Gum** (17.James Riley^3, 3.Isaac^2, 1.Dorothy "Dolly"^{1} Arbogast), b. Apr 14 1858, d. Sep 25 1927.
Married Oct 30 1879 in Bond Co., IL, **Elizabeth A. Ray**, b. Jan 04 1858, d. Mar 15 1934 in Greenville, Bond Co., IL.
   Children*:*
   312 i.   Alice Ethel^5 Gum b. Nov 08 1888. She
             Married **Henry Garfield Gates**.
 + 313 ii. William Riley Gum, M.d. b. Jan 01 1894.

105. **Enoch Riley^4 Gum** (17.James Riley^3, 3.Isaac^2, 1.Dorothy "Dolly"^{1} Arbogast), b. Feb 24 1863, d. Jun 30 1953.
Married Jul 03 1887 in Bond Co., IL, **Rosella Paterson**, b. Jan 11 1872, d. Jan 12 1964.
   Children*:*
   314 i.   Mabel^5 Gum b. Sep 21 1888. She
             Married **Charles E. Lewis**.
   315 ii. Clarence Enoch Gum b. Jun 17 1890 in Bond Co., IL, d. Mar 1898.
   316 iii. Sarah Florence Gum b. Sep 1891, d. 1992.
   317 iv. Elva Gum b. Jan 31 1894 in Bond Co., MO.
   318 v.   Eva Gum b. Jan 31 1894 in Bond Co., MO.
   319 vi. Clara Elizabeth Gum b. Jul 31 1899 in Pocahontas Co., WV.

106. **Sarah M.^{4} File** (18.Elizabeth^3 Gum, 3.Isaac^2, 1.Dorothy "Dolly"^{1} Arbogast).
Married Feb 27 1868 in Bethalto, Madison Co., IL, **Jasper Starkey**, d. 1906/1907.
   Children*:*
   320 i.   Eva Arlene^5 Starkey.
   321 ii.   Fay Starkey. Died as an infant
   322 iii. Rupert Starkey. Died as an infant
   323 iv.   Emmet Starkey. Died as an infant
 + 324 v.   Lee Starkey b. 1874.
   325 vi.   Edward Starkey b. 1882.
 + 326 vii. David Daniel Starkey.
 + 327 viii. Hillery Herbert Starkey.
 + 328 ix.   Louella Starkey.

113. **Olive**[4] **Gum** (23.Perry O.[3], 3.Isaac[2], 1.Dorothy "Dolly"[1] Arbogast), b. 1856, d. 1911.
   Married 1876 in Madison Co., IL, **Richard Linder**.

   Children:
   - 329   i.   Jessica[5] Linder.
   - 330   ii.   Mehitabel Linder.
   - 331   iii. Perry Linder.
   - 332   iv.   Richard Linder, Jr..
   - 333   v.   Anna Linder.
   - 334   vi.   Katherine Linder.
   - 335   vii. Ruth Linder.
   - 336   viii. James Linder.
   - 337   ix.   Hope Linder.
   - 338   x.   Daniel Linder.
   - 339   xi.   Nellie Linder.
   - 340   xii. Leona Linder.

124. **Amanda Ellen**[4] **Flesher** (29.Adam[3], 4.Mary M.[2] Gum, 1.Dorothy "Dolly"[1] Arbogast), b. 1836 in Fayette Co., OH, d. 1868.
   Married Dec 1855 in Buchanan Co., MO, **Henry C Janes**, b. 1831, d. 1875.

   Children:
   - 341   i.   Adam[5] Janes.
   - 342   ii.   Elizabeth Jane Janes b. 1860 in Missouri, d. 1891.
   - 343   iii. Ida F Janes b. 1863 in Missouri, d. 1884.
   - 344   iv.   Thomas Newton Janes b. Apr 10 1865.

128. **Angeline**[4] **Flasher** (29.Adam[3] Flesher, 4.Mary M.[2] Gum, 1.Dorothy "Dolly"[1] Arbogast), b. Dec 24 1843 in Berry Co., MO, d. Sep 13 1903 in Pittsburg, Crawford Co., KS.
   Married 1864 in St. Joseph, Buchanan Co., MO, **John Danial Patton**, b. Apr 03 1842 in Virginia, d. Oct 18 1910 in Denver, Arapaho Co., CO, buried in Pittsburg, Crawford Co., KS.

   Children:
   - + 345 i.   Mattie[5] Patton b. 1865.
   -   346 ii.   Janette Alice Patton b. Dec 23 1869.
   -   347 iii. Liz Patton b. Mar 17 1870.
   - + 348 iv.   Lillie May Patton b. Oct 01 1874.
   -   349 v.   Thomas Patton b. Aug 15 1878, d. Jul 28 1921 in Pittsburg, Crawford Co., KS.
   -   350 vi.   John Henry Patton b. Dec 1881 in Andrews Co., MO, d. Jan 11 1883 in Andrews Co., MO.
   - + 351 vii. Minnie Belle Patton b. Nov 21 1884.

129. **Greenberry**[4] **Flesher** (29.Adam[3], 4.Mary M.[2] Gum, 1.Dorothy "Dolly"[1] Arbogast), b. 1846 in Andrews Co., MO.
   (1) He Married **Margaret Jane Patton**, b. in Kidder, Caldwell Co., MO. .

   Children by *Margaret Jane Patton*:
   -   352 i.   Angeline[5] Flesher.
   -   353 ii.   Dora Flesher.
   -   354 iii. Richard Flesher.
   - + 355 iv.   Edward Henry Flesher b. Feb 25 1877.
   -   356 v.   William A Flesher b. 1879 in Missouri.
   -   357 vi.   Ida Flesher b. July 1882 in Missouri.
   -   358 vii. Maude Flesher b. Sep 6 1883 in Missouri.
   -   359 viii. Lulu Flesher b. Mar 1883.
   -   360 ix.   Earlic Flesher b. Oct 1889.

   (2) He Married **Cynthia King**, b. c 1845

Children by Cynthia King:
- 361   x.   Cora Flesher.
- 362   xi.   Anna Flesher.
- 363   xii.   Alice Flesher b. 1870 in Missouri.

130. **Henry⁴ Flesher** (29.Adam³, 4.Mary M.² Gum, 1.Dorothy "Dolly"¹ Arbogast), b. 1849 in Andrews Co., MO.
Married Sep 20 1883 in Barnard, Nodaway Co., MO, **Emma Sweet**, b. 1866 in Union Star, Dekalb Co., MO.

Children:
- 364   i.   Mary Jane⁵ Flesher.
- 365   ii.   Benjamin Flesher.
- 366   iii.   (unknown) Flesher.

140. **Emerson B⁴ Flesher** (31.Henry³, 4.Mary M.² Gum, 1.Dorothy "Dolly"¹ Arbogast), b. Feb 05 1862, d. Feb 26 1929 in Pottawattamie Co., IA.
Married Dec 12 1888, **Belle Walker**, b. Apr 08 1867, d. Feb 01 1953.

Children:
- 367   i.   Claire⁵ Flesher b. c 1889.

141. **Harry Seldom⁴ Flesher** (31.Henry³, 4.Mary M.² Gum, 1.Dorothy "Dolly"¹ Arbogast), b. Apr 12 1864 in Pottawattamie Co., IA, d. 1939 in California.
Married c1895, **Ora Almeda Thomas**, b. 1876 in Iowa, d. 1956 in California.

Children:
- + 368   i.   Elsie Vera⁵ Flesher b. Dec 24 1895.
- + 369   ii.   Seldon Elmo Flesher b. May 05 1901.
- 370   iii.   Milton Henry Flesher b. Apr 14 1906 in Graton, Sonoma Co., CA, d. Sep 10 2000 in Santa Rosa, Sonoma Co., CA.
- 371   iv.   Lola Flesher b. Aft 1906, d. Bef 1974.

148. **Aletha Adaline⁴ Dunkle** (32.Sarah Jane³ Flesher, 4.Mary M.² Gum, 1.Dorothy "Dolly"¹ Arbogast), b. Jun 07 1852 in Lawrenceburg, Lawrence Co., MO, d. May 13 1880.
Married in Missouri, **Robert Allen Smalling**, b. May 19 1841 in Meigs or McMinn Co., TN, d. in Missouri, buried in Rock Creek Cem., Halltown, Lawrence Co., MO.

Children:
- + 372   i.   Ida Josephine⁵ Smalling b. Apr 17 1872.

157. **John Henry⁴ Flesher** (34.William Seybert³, 4.Mary M.² Gum, 1.Dorothy "Dolly"¹ Arbogast), b. Aug 25 1849 in Howard Co., MO, d. Oct 20 1917 in Jackson Co., KS.
John Henry Flesher died on a train en route to visit his daughter in
Clayton, New Mexico. John Henry and Lucinda are buried in the Hoyt
Cemetery, two miles west of Hoyt, Kansas.
Married Mar 06 1870, **Lucinda Elizabeth Liggett**, b. Apr 29 1849 in Howard Co., MO, d. Jan 13 1917 in Hoyt, Jackson Co., KS, buried in Hoyt, Jackson Co., KS.

Children:
- 373   i.   Amanda⁵ Flesher b. Nov 27 1870, d. Dec 04 1871.
- 374   ii.   Hiram Flesher b. Nov 06 1872, d. Oct 29 1874.
- + 375   iii.   Paul Flesher b. Jul 12 1875.
- 376   iv.   Mary Jane Flesher b. Dec 29 1877 in Kansas, d. Aug 07 1947.
  Married 1898 in Kansas, **William Baker**, b. About 1877.
- 377   v.   Laure E Flesher b. Oct 01 1881, d. Mar 31 1885.
- + 378   vi.   John William Flesher b. Oct 01 1885.
- 379   vii.   Bertha M Flesher b. Jul 24 1888 in Kansas, d. Nov 07 1953.
  Married 1907, **Bruce Kennedy**.
- 380   viii.   John Henry Flesher b. Oct 1895 in Kansas.

158. **Mary Elizabeth**[4] **Flesher** (34.William Seybert[3], 4.Mary M.[2] Gum, 1.Dorothy "Dolly"[1] Arbogast), b. Mar 04 1851 in Dade Co., MO, d. May 18 1910, buried in Little Cross Creek Cem., Hoyt, Jackson Co., KA.
Married Mar 06 1870, **John Colombus Liggett**, b. Dec 19 1844 (son of William Liggett and Lucinda Elgin), d. Mar 12 1914 in Denver, Arapaho Co., CO.
- *Children*:
  - 381   i.   Laura Belle[5] Liggett.

159. **Benjamin W**[4] **Flesher** (34.William Seybert[3], 4.Mary M.[2] Gum, 1.Dorothy "Dolly"[1] Arbogast), b. Nov 16 1854 in Andrews Co., MO, d. May 05 1916 in Jackson Co., KS.
He Married **Clarissa B. Smith**, b. Nov 14 1858 in Missouri, d. Nov 25 1922 in Douglas Twp., Jackson Co., KS.
- *Children*:
  - 382   i.   Anna R[5] Flesher b. 1876 in Kansas.
  - 383   ii. Luisa F Flesher b. 1879 in Kansas.
  - 384   iii. Emma A Flesher b. July 1881 in Kansas.
  - 385   iv. Minnie A Flesher b. July 1888 in Kansas.

160. **Louisa J**[4] **Flesher** (34.William Seybert[3], 4.Mary M.[2] Gum, 1.Dorothy "Dolly"[1] Arbogast), b. 1857 in Andrews Co., MO.
(1) Married in Jackson Co., KS, **Albert Richard**, b. 1857. .
- *Children* by Albert Richard:
  - + 386   i.   Charles Francis[5] Richard b. Jun 2 1878.
  -   387   ii. Henry William Richard.
  -   388   iii. Nellie May Richard.
  -   389   iv. Frank Floyd Richard.

(2) She Married **Jasper Brownfield**

163. **Sarah Ellen**[4] **Flesher** (34.William Seybert[3], 4.Mary M.[2] Gum, 1.Dorothy "Dolly"[1] Arbogast), b. Jul 18 1865 in Kansas.
She Married **Stephen J. Hubbard**, b. 1862 in Missouri.
- *Children*:
  - 390   i.   Willie A.[5] Hubbard b. Dec 31 1882, d. Jan 03 1883.

164. **Thomas Edward**[4] **Flesher** (34.William Seybert[3], 4.Mary M.[2] Gum, 1.Dorothy "Dolly"[1] Arbogast), b. Aug 30 1867 in Holton, Jackson Co., KS, d. Feb 18 1938 in Klamath Co., OR.
Married Sept 1894 in St. Joseph, Buchanan Co., MO, **Ella Alice Foster**, b. Mar 28 1873, d. Feb 04 1939 in Klamath Co., OR.
- *Children*:
  - 391   i.   Sarah Ellen[5] Flesher b. Feb 27 1894, d. May 27 1962 in Tidewater, Lincoln Co., OR.
  - 392   ii.   Mary Elizabeth Flesher b. Nov 07 1896, d. Sep 26 1958 in Klamath Co., OR.
  - 393   iii. William Edward Flesher b. Feb 10 1899, d. Aug 11 1962.
  - 394   iv.   Laura Frances Flesher b. Jan 27 1901, d. Apr 28 1973.
  - 395   v.   Roy Marion Flesher b. Jan 01 1903, d. 1963.
  - 396   vi.   Benjamin Silas Flesher b. Aug 10 1905, d. Aug 08 1959.
  - 397   vii. Iva Edna Flesher b. 1908 in Tidewater, Lincoln Co., OR.
  - 398   viii. Bertie L. Flesher b. 1908 in Tidewater, Lincoln Co., OR.
  - 399   ix.   Martha Anna Flesher b. Aug 12 1915 in Tidewater, Lincoln Co., OR, d. Nov 12 1981 in Milwaukie, Clackamas Co., OR. She
    Married **Henry Morris Minnick**, b. About 1915.

177. **George Riley**[4] **Miller** (38.Louesa K[3] Flesher, 4.Mary M.[2] Gum, 1.Dorothy "Dolly"[1] Arbogast), b. Apr 27 1872, d. Nov 14 1939.

He Married **Flora Elvira Dickson**, b. Jun 29 1876, d. Sep 11 1957.

Children:
- \+ 400   i.   Audra S.^{5} Miller b. Jun 8 1897.
- 401   ii.   Sarah Louisa Miller b. Nov 4 1899. She Married **Lewis Zimmerman**.
- \+ 402   iii.   Blanche Pearl Miller b. Jul 24 1901.
- \+ 403   iv.   Goldia Bell Miller b. Jan 1 1903.
- \+ 404   v.   Claudine Miller b. Jan 31 1905.
- \+ 405   vi.   Lily Virginia Miller b. Nov 22 1907.
- \+ 406   vii.   Glen Washington Miller b. Jul 18 1909.
- 407   viii.   William Forest Miller b. Feb 27 1912. He Married **Iris Stubbs**.

194. **Joseph^4 Gum** (40.Henry^3, 5.Adam^2, 1.Dorothy "Dolly"^{1} Arbogast), b. June 1836. Lived in Lewis County, VA
He Married **Margaret (Unknown)**, b. Dec 1843.

Children:
- 408   i.   Perry^5 Gum b. Nov 1864.
- \+ 409   ii.   Charles M Gum b. Nov 1870.

195. **Peter^4 Gum** (40.Henry^3, 5.Adam^2, 1.Dorothy "Dolly"^{1} Arbogast), b. Dec 1839. Lived in Lewis County, Freemans Dist., VA
Married About 1872, **Almeda (Unknown)**.

Children:
- 410   i.   Edie R^5 Gum b. Aug 1872. Lived in Lewis County, Freemans Dist., VA
- 411   ii.   Henry D Gum b. Dec 1875. Lived in Lewis County, Freemans Dist., VA
- 412   iii.   Emory B Gum b. Feb 1878. Lived in Lewis County, Freemans Dist., VA
- 413   iv.   Daisy Gum b. Oct 1882. Lived in Lewis County, Freemans Dist., VA

196. **Boyd^4 Gum** (40.Henry^3, 5.Adam^2, 1.Dorothy "Dolly"^{1} Arbogast), b. Oct 1842. Lived in Lewis County, Freemans Dist., VA
He Married **Mary M (Unknown)**.

Children:
- 414   i.   Alda J^5 Gum b. Jun 1882. Lived in Lewis County, Freemans Dist., VA
- 415   ii.   Wesley Gum b. May 1883. Lived in Lewis County, Freemans Dist., VA
- 416   iii.   Thomas Gum b. July 1887. Lived in Lewis County, Freemans Dist., VA

199. **William^4 Colaw, Jr** (41.Sabina^3 Gum, 5.Adam^2, 1.Dorothy "Dolly"^{1} Arbogast), b. Jul 19 1829, d. Aug 04 1928. Cpl. F Co., 96th IL Vol.. Fought at Vicksburg.
Married Aug 19 1866, **Mary Elizabeth Jones**, b. Jul 03 1845, d. Apr 10 1918.

Children:
- \+ 417   i.   Della I^5 Colaw b. Feb 18 1871.

202. **Benjamin Watters^4 Colaw** (41.Sabina^3 Gum, 5.Adam^2, 1.Dorothy "Dolly"^{1} Arbogast), b. About 1840, d. 1898 in Kansas.
(1) He Married **Martha Matilda Savage**, b. About 1840 in Downs, Mclean Co., IL, d. 1884 in Kansas. .

Children by Martha Matilda Savage:
- \+ 418   i.   George William^5 Colaw b. 1866.
- \+ 419   ii.   Mary Rosetta Colaw b. 1868.
- \+ 420   iii.   John Harmon Colaw b. 1871.
- \+ 421   iv.   Franklin Robert Colaw b. May 30 1873.
- \+ 422   v.   Harry Albert Colaw b. 1876.
- 423   vi.   Orry Omar Colaw b. Jan 7 1878, d. Nov 1966. He Married **Doris Richmond**.

+ 424 vii. Ella May Colaw b. 1881.
425 viii. Clida Colaw b. 1884, d. 1884.

(2) He Married **Amanda Blackwood**
Children by Amanda Blackwood:
+ 426 ix. Bernard Colaw b. 1893.
427 x. Burris Colaw.

204. **Dyer W^4 Colaw** (41.Sabina^3 Gum, 5.Adam^2, 1.Dorothy "Dolly"^{1} Arbogast), b. Feb 20 1846, d. Jan 20 1923.
Married Sep 15 1867, **Mary Jane Garr**, b. Dec 30 1843 (daughter of Joseph Garr and Margaret Galloway), d. Jan 20 1923.
Children:
+ 428 i. Alphorus^5 Colaw b. Sep 19 1868.
429 ii. Lillian Colaw b. May 21 1872, d. Apr 13 1947.

207. **Thomas Marion^4 Gum** (43.Amos^3, 5.Adam^2, 1.Dorothy "Dolly"^{1} Arbogast), b. Jul 31 1861 in Highland Co., VA, d. Jun 9 1952 in Pocahontas Co., WV, buried in Dunmore Cem., Dunmore, Pocahontas Co., WV. S/o Amos and Frances (Terry) Gum
Married Jul 9 1891 in Pocahontas Co., WV, **Margaret Louella Elsie Dilley**, b. Feb 25 1872 in Pocahontas Co., WV (daughter of Martin Clark Dilley and Margaret Jane Arbogast), d. Mar 4 1956 in Pocahontas Co., WV, buried in Dunmore Cem., Dunmore, Pocahontas Co., WV. **Margaret**: Ref: Jim and Rita Wooddell records, January 1994 Gave details of dates, burial, name of husband and his parents.
Children:
+ 430 i. Otie Viola^5 Gum b. May 30 1892.
+ 431 ii. Roy McKinley Gum b. Dec 9 1894.
432 iii. Russell O. Gum b. Apr 11 1896.
+ 433 iv. Wardell Clark Gum b. Sep 13 1898.
434 v. Paul Gum.
435 vi. Thomas Mack Gum b. July 1901.

208. **James Otho^4 Gum** (43.Amos^3, 5.Adam^2, 1.Dorothy "Dolly"^{1} Arbogast), b. Jul 14 1867 in Highland Co., VA, d. Dec 12 1952 in Pocahontas County Memorial Hospital, Marlinton, WV, buried Dec 15 1952 in Dunmore Cem., Dunmore, Pocahontas Co., WV.
Information from family records of Sylvia (Taylor) Gum of Green Bank, WV, in file. Son of Amos and Frances Terry Gum.
Married Jul 9 1891 in Pocahontas Co., WV, **Naomi Elizabeth Dilley**, b. Jan 29 1874 in Pocahontas Co., WV (daughter of Martin Clark Dilley and Margaret Jane Arbogast), d. May 27 1967 in Crawford Co., PA, buried in Dunmore Cem., Dunmore, Pocahontas Co., WV.
Children:
436 i. Harry W.^{5} Gum b. Apr 14 1892 in Dunmore, Pocahontas Co., WV, d. Jul 29 1974 in Townville, Crawford Co., PA.
Married in Crabbottom, Highland Co., VA, **Louella E. Fisher**, b. May 31 1891 in Crabbottom, Highland Co., VA.
+ 437 ii. Ida Omega Gum b. Jan 23 1902.
+ 438 iii. Merritt Moore Gum b. Apr 4 1904.
+ 439 iv. Robert Sterling Gum b. May 3 1909.

218. **Gertrude Ethel^4 Shockey** (51.Sarah^3 Genkins, 8.Elleder^2 Gum, 1.Dorothy "Dolly"^{1} Arbogast), b. 1878 in Hardin Co., OH.
She Married **Levi Willman**.
Children:
+ 440 i. Homer Burrell^5 Willman b. Oct 23 1908.

219. **Rosa Vera**[4] **Shockey** (51.Sarah[3] Genkins, 8.Elleder[2] Gum, 1.Dorothy "Dolly"[1] Arbogast), b. 1882 in Ridgeway Twp., Harden Co., OH, d. 1924 in Glencoe, Payne Co., OK, buried in Bethel Cem., Payne Co., OK.
Married 1898 in Kirksville, Adair Co., MO, **Oscar O. Stewart**, b. 1875 in Kirksville, Adair Co., MO.

   Children:
   - 441   i.   Bertha[5] Stewart b. 1899 in Western OK.
   - 442   ii. John L. Stewart b. 1901 in Western OK.
   - 443   iii. Glen Ernest Stewart b. 1903 in Bethany, Oklahoma Co., OK. He Married **Lena Mae Hodgett**, b. 1908 in Whitley Twp., Crawford Co., AR.
   - 444   iv. Lona Agnes Stewart b. 1905 in Western OK.
   - 445   v.   Goldie Stewart b. 1907 in Western OK.
   - 446   vi. Eugene Stewart b. 1908 in Oklahoma City, Oklahoma Co., OK.
   - 447   vii. Frank O. Stewart b. 1910 in Oklahoma City, Oklahoma Co., OK.
   - 448   viii. Catherine Stewart b. 1912 in Oklahoma City, Oklahoma Co., OK.
   - 449   ix. Ruben Raymond Stewart b. 1914 in Oklahoma City, Oklahoma Co., OK.
   - 450   x.   Lloyd Edward Stewart b. 1917 in Oklahoma City, Oklahoma Co., OK.
   - 451   xi. Dorothy Marie Stewart b. 1921 in Oklahoma.

230. **Gerthe**[4] **Gum** (64.William Madison[3], 9.Jesse[2], 1.Dorothy "Dolly"[1] Arbogast), b. 1874.
She Married **Charles Henry**.

   Children:
   - 452   i.   Dean[5] Henry b. in Miller Co., MO.
   - 453   ii. Wannalou Henry. Lived in Miller, MO
             She Married **Willard Strine**, b. in Versailles, Morgan Co., MO.

232. **Thomas Otto**[4] **Gum** (64.William Madison[3], 9.Jesse[2], 1.Dorothy "Dolly"[1] Arbogast), b. Mar 1883, d. Mar 25 1963.
Married May 10 1908, **Cora Boyd**, b. Oct 28 1887, d. Sep 26 1973.

   Children:
   - 454   i.   Vaughn[5] Gum b. About 1913.
             Vaughn Married a **Maxine ?** and had children: Neil, Bruce and Glenda Gum Barber.
   - 455   ii. Betty Gum b. About 1915.

234. **Nathaniel Meade**[4] **Gum** (65.George Wasgington[3], 9.Jesse[2], 1.Dorothy "Dolly"[1] Arbogast), b. Oct 20 1869, d. Dec 15 1955.
He Married **Leatha Viola Ramsey**, b. Oct 22 1873, d. Sep 19 1957.

   Children:
   - + 456   i.   Oscar Clarence[5] Gum b. Dec 16 1893.
   -   457   ii. Homer Ethmer Gum b. Jun 08 1897, d. Feb 15 1968.
                Lived in CA
                He Married **Pearl Workman**.
   -   458   iii. Zelma Edyth Gum b. Oct 14 1902, d. Feb 02 1974.
                She Married **Henry Gaben**.
   - + 459   iv. Freda May Gum b. Sep 20 1906.
   - + 460   v.   George William Gum b. Dec 29 1908.
   -   461   vi. Ida Irene Gum b. Jun 19 1912.
                Lived in Carthage, MO
                She Married **Gerald Whittenburg**.

235. **William Oliver**[4] **Gum** (65.George Wasgington[3], 9.Jesse[2], 1.Dorothy "Dolly"[1] Arbogast), b. Jul 30 1871 in Missouri, d. Mar 03 1960.
Married Jul 03 1895, **Carrie Marsh**, d. 1945.

   Children:
   - + 462   i.   Roy Calvin[5] Gum b. May 02 1895.

236. **Andrew Newton**[4] **Gum** (65.George Wasgington[3], 9.Jesse[2], 1.Dorothy "Dolly"[1] Arbogast), b. Dec 22 1872, d. Dec 15 1955.
Married Nov 06 1898, **Fannie Lieuallen**, d. 1956.
Children:
+ 463   i.   Willis Herbert[5] Gum b. Nov 09 1899.
+ 464   ii.   Melvin Gum b. Dec 11 1914.

237. **Effie**[4] **Gum** (65.George Wasgington[3], 9.Jesse[2], 1.Dorothy "Dolly"[1] Arbogast), b. Jul 06 1875, d. Mar 01 1920.
Married 1903, **Will Vance**, d. Aug 01 1922.
Children:
+ 465   i.   Willard C[5] Vance b. Dec 25 1904.
  466   ii.   Berenice Vance b. Jan 15 1907, d. Apr 11 1910.

238. **Edgar Haddon**[4] **Gum** (65.George Wasgington[3], 9.Jesse[2], 1.Dorothy "Dolly"[1] Arbogast), b. Sep 15 1877, d. May 08 1950.
Married Feb 05 1899, **Bertha Hughes**, d. Jun 28 1962.
Children:
  467   i.   Connie Gretchen[5] Gum b. Jun 23 1901 in Modesto, Stanislaus Co., CA. (1) Married in Divorced, **Walter Andrews**. (2) She Married **William Westmoreland**, d. 1971.
+ 468   ii.   Lois T Gum b. Apr 26 1903.
  469   iii.   Maud Eldridge Gum b. April 1905, d. Mar 1908.
  470   iv.   Edgar Herschel Gum b. Oct 1917, d. Oct 1917.
+ 471   v.   Rowland Hughes Gum b. May 29 1920.

239. **Albert**[4] **Gum** (65.George Wasgington[3], 9.Jesse[2], 1.Dorothy "Dolly"[1] Arbogast), b. May 12 1880, d. Nov 15 1968.
Married Dec 24 1907, **Anna Schmickle**, d. Jun 11 1962.
Children:
  472   i.   Godfrey H[5] Gum b. Apr 14 1909.
        Married in Lived in Springfield, Greene Co., MO, **Isabel McLaughlin**.
  473   ii.   Francis Henry Gum b. Mar 12 1911. Married in Lived in Springfield, Greene Co., MO, **Thelma Williams**.
  474   iii.   Meadfred Gum b. Oct 01 1913, d. Mar 26 1971. He Married Mildred Hailey.
  475   iv.   Leonard Gum b. Oct 26 1917.
        Married in Lived in Ash Grove, Greene Co., MO, **Virginia Taylor**.

240. **Ida May**[4] **Gum** (65.George Wasgington[3], 9.Jesse[2], 1.Dorothy "Dolly"[1] Arbogast), b. Oct 06 1883, d. Nov 26 1969.
She Married **Frederick H Miller**, b. Aug 05 1884, d. Dec 04 1963.
Children:
+ 476   i.   Edrie Maurine[5] Miller b. Jan 10 1909.
+ 477   ii.   Eva Marie Miller b. Aug 22 1910.

256. **Pearl**[4] **McNeal** (69.Sarah Elizabeth[3] Gum, 9.Jesse[2], 1.Dorothy "Dolly"[1] Arbogast), b. Dec 06 1885, d. Oct 11 1941.
She Married **Earnest McHenry**.
Children:
  478   i.   Lucille[5] McHenry.
  479   ii.   Lavern McHenry.
  480   iii.   Nelson McHenry.

257. **William Wesley**[4] **McNeal** (69.Sarah Elizabeth[3] Gum, 9.Jesse[2], 1.Dorothy "Dolly"[1] Arbogast), b. May 21 1890.

He Married **Montie Mae Adcock**.

Children:
- 481   i.   Donald[5] McNeal b. Aug 01 1915, d. Aug 01 1915.
- + 482   ii.   William Wayne McNeal b. Sep 01 1919.
- + 483   iii.   Carl Thomas McNeal b. May 05 1923.

260. **Sarah Jane[4] Stinson** (70.Talitha[3] Gum, 9.Jesse[2], 1.Dorothy "Dolly"[1] Arbogast), b. Jul 05 1874, d. 1937. She
Married **Marion Cantrell**, b. Apr 01 1860, d. Aug 08 1937.

Children:
- + 484   i.   James Virgil[5] Cantrell b. Dec 09 1892.
- 485   ii.   Francis Leonord Cantrell b. May 10 1894, d. Oct 23 1910.
- 486   iii.   Ethmer Pearl Cantrell b. Jul 11 1900, d. Nov 10 1949.
  He Married **Hazel Helen Hearrell**, b. Oct 26 1901, d. Mar 05 1973.
- + 487   iv.   Reggie Bernard Cantrell b. Feb 06 1904.
- 488   v.   Herbert Hadley Cantrell b. Jul 04 1911.

263. **Pearl[4] Stinson** (70.Talitha[3] Gum, 9.Jesse[2], 1.Dorothy "Dolly"[1] Arbogast), b. Jul 12 1880, d. Apr 16 1911.
She Married **Donald B. Hinkle**, b. Jan 24 1874, d. Mar 03 1925.

Children:
- 489   i.   Audrea Lela[5] Hinkle b. Jan 05 1897, d. Jan 21 1920.
- 490   ii.   Clyde Cleo Hinkle b. Apr 09 1901, d. Nov 25 1974.
  He Married **Eva Lucille Palmer**, b. Jul 07 1913, d. Aug 30 1966.
- 491   iii.   Opal Lizzia Hinkle b. Mar 25 1903.
  She Married **Ott Armstrong**, b. Oct 04 1888, d. Nov 24 1966.
- + 492   iv.   Emil Fred Hinkle b. Jan 08 1907.

264. **Fred[4] Stinson** (70.Talitha[3] Gum, 9.Jesse[2], 1.Dorothy "Dolly"[1] Arbogast), b. Jan 26 1884, d. Aug 08 1972.
Married in Divorced, **Delia Glidewell**.

Children:
- + 493   i.   Joel[5] Stinson b. Jul 05 1909.

265. **Lula[4] Stinson** (70.Talitha[3] Gum, 9.Jesse[2], 1.Dorothy "Dolly"[1] Arbogast), b. Jun 26 1886, d. Jan 30 1912.
She Married **William Earnest Ruark**, b. Apr 20 1884.

Children:
- + 494   i.   Juanita Mildred[5] Ruark b. Apr 19 1908.
- + 495   ii.   William Lloyd Ruark b. Jul 03 1909.

266. **Grace[4] Stinson** (70.Talitha[3] Gum, 9.Jesse[2], 1.Dorothy "Dolly"[1] Arbogast), b. Feb 26 1889, d. Oct 18 1914.
She Married **Oran Glascock**, b. May 05 1887, d. Jan 11 1914.

Children:
- 496   i.   Rayme[5] Glascock b. Jun 29 1907, d. Dec 26 1922.

267. **Dallas[4] Stinson** (70.Talitha[3] Gum, 9.Jesse[2], 1.Dorothy "Dolly"[1] Arbogast), b. Jan 12 1892, d. Sep 15 1973 in Jackson, Amador Co., CA.
(1) She Married **Roy Jones**, b. Dec 07 1889.

Children by Roy Jones:
- 497   i.   Vandolyn[5] Jones b. May 27 1911, d. Jan 22 1912.

(2) She Married **Teva Stinson**, b. Dec 20 1896.

Generation Five

271. **Sarah Elizabeth^5 Huffstedtler** (80.Louisa Janetta^4 Gum, 13.Jesse S.^{3}, 3.Isaac^2, 1.Dorothy "Dolly"^{1} Arbogast), b. Dec 4 1853 in Pocahontas, Bond Co., IL, d. Mar 4 1938 in Picher, Ottawa Co., OK, buried in Swars Prairie Cem.; Seneca, Newton Co., MO.
Married Feb 2 1871 in Old Ripley, Bond Co., IL, **John Williamson Page**, b. Mar 27 1848 in New Douglas, Madison Co., IL, d. Nov 14 1906 in Seneca, Newton Co., MO, buried in Swars Prairie Cem.; Seneca, Newton Co., MO.
   Children:
   - 498   i.   Nancy Ellen^6 Page b. Nov 4 1871 in Old Ripley, Bond Co., IL, d. Oct 13 1936 in Lacygne, Linn Co., KS, buried in Lacygne Cem., Linn Co., KS.
   - + 499 ii. Louisa Jeanetta Page b. Mar 24 1873.
   - 500   iii. Albert Allen Page b. Jun 28 1875 in Old Ripley, Bond Co., IL, d. Aug 7 1876, buried in Cox Cem., Mt. Vernon City, IL.
   - 501   iv. William Silas Page b. Sep 18 1878.
   - 502   v.   Charles F. Page b. Feb 7 1881 in Old Ripley, Bond Co., IL, d. Sep 1 1912.
   - 503   vi. Henry Leslie Page.
   - 504   vii. Louis Alvin Page b. Mar 17 1885.
   - 505   viii. Mary Jane Page b. Dec 6 1887 in Fontana, Miami Co., KS.
   - 506   ix. Clarence Miami Page b. Dec 1 1891.
   - 507   x.   Jesse Edward Page b. Jan 21 1894.

288. **Edward Gustavus^5 Gum** (89.John Royal^4, 14.Isaac C.^{3}, 3.Isaac^2, 1.Dorothy "Dolly"^{1} Arbogast), b. About 1876 in Bond Co., IL, d. 1938.
Married Jun 28 1904 in Bond Co., IL, **Anna Marie Carroll**, b. Apr 13 1881 in Tamalco, Bond Co., IL, d. Dec 13 1941 in St. Louis, St. Louis Co., MO. **Anna**: Daughter of Thomas P. CARROLL and Mary Ellen BRUNER.
   Children:
   - + 508 i.   Melvin C.^{6} Gum b. Jun 19 1907.
   - + 509 ii. Elvin George Gum b. Oct 20 1911.

289. **Clara (Elizabeth?)^5 Gum** (89.John Royal^4, 14.Isaac C.^{3}, 3.Isaac^2, 1.Dorothy "Dolly"^{1} Arbogast), b. About 1879.
Married May 09 1898 in Bond Co., IL, **Elias Barcroft**, b. About 1879. **Elias**: Son of John BARCROFT and Margaret Jane NELSON.
   Children:
   - 510   i.   Victor^6 Barcroft b. c 1899.
   - 511   ii. Berle Barcroft b. Apr 10 1902, d. Dec 6 1912.

293. **Bert E.^{5} Gum** (89.John Royal^4, 14.Isaac C.^{3}, 3.Isaac^2, 1.Dorothy "Dolly"^{1} Arbogast), b. Jan 15 1892 in Illinois, d. Mar 28 1973.
He Married **Lena Hord**, b. Aug 07 1891, d. Feb 20 1972, buried in McKendree Church Cem., Bond Co., IL.
   Children:
   - 512   i.   Bert E.^{6} Gum b. Aug 4 1930, d. Aug 5 1930.

294. **Jacob I.⁵ Gum** (90.James Johnson⁴, 14.Isaac C.³, 3.Isaac², 1.Dorothy "Dolly"¹ Arbogast), b. 1876 in Bond Co., IL, d. after 1926.
Married Feb 27 1898 in Bond Co., IL, **Sarah Gertrude Duckworth**, b. Jan 20 1881 in Bond Co., IL, d. Mar 05 1926 in Granit City, IL, buried in Paine Cem., Bond Co., IL. **Sarah**: Daughter of Thomas DUCKWORTH and Sarah ETHRIDGE.

Children:
- 513   i.   Opal⁶ Gum.
- 514   ii.   Erma Violet Gum b. Jan 16 1902, d. Jan 23 1902 in Paine Cem., Bond Co., IL.
- 515   iii.   Maggie Gum b. Before 1926.
- 516   iv.   Harold Fern Gum b. Before 1926.
- 517   v.   Gilbert Gum.

296. **John Leonard⁵ Gum** (90.James Johnson⁴, 14.Isaac C.³, 3.Isaac², 1.Dorothy "Dolly"¹ Arbogast), b. Oct 1877 in Bond Co., IL.
Married Nov 10 1897 in Bond Co., IL, **Elizabeth Jane (Minnie) McCuskey**, b. in Floyd Co., IL, d. 1949 in Payne Cem., Bond Co., IL, buried in Payne, Paulding Co., OH. **Elizabeth**: Daughter of William MCCUSKEY and Elizabeth J. WINTERS.

Children:
- 518   i.   Vivian E.⁶ Gum b. Oct 1899.
  - (1) She Married **Clarence Summers**, b. About 1897.
  - (2) She Married **Lloud Kennett**.
- 519   ii.   Dena Daisy Gum b. Nov 23 1900.
- 520   iii.   Willis Luther Gum b. Jul 07 1903, d. Feb 05 1904.
- + 521   iv.   Marie M. Gum.
- 522   v.   Ruby Gum.
  - She Married **Verne Hartline**.
- + 523   vi.   Hurlius Gum.
- 524   vii.   Faye Gum.
  - She Married **Lee Summers**.
- + 525   viii.   Vera Gum.
- 526   ix.   Cecil Gum b. May 21 1907, buried in Payne Cem., Bond Co., IL.

297. **James Edward⁵ Gum** (90.James Johnson⁴, 14.Isaac C.³, 3.Isaac², 1.Dorothy "Dolly"¹ Arbogast), b. Apr 1884 in Bond Co., IL, d. Jul 01 1957 in Nashville, Washington Co., IL.
(1) Married Apr 10 1915 in Bond Co., IL, **Blanche Matthews**. **Blanche**: Daughter of John Jefferson MATTHEWS and Fredonia Alice RENCH.

Children by Blanche Matthews:
- + 527   i.   Clyde Everett⁶ Gum b. Jul 18 1915.
- + 528   ii.   Erma Charlotte Gum b. Oct 09 1917.
- + 529   iii.   Ardelene Mardell Gum b. Oct 27 1919.
- 530   iv.   Leland Relmot Gum b. Aug 1922, d. Oct 04 1922.
- + 531   v.   Luthur Aaron Gum b. Sep 12 1923.
- + 532   vi.   Mary Edyth Gum b. Nov 07 1924.
- + 533   vii.   Gorden Isaac Gum b. Apr 28 1926.
- + 534   viii.   Marvin Udell Gum b. Jul 24 1928.
- 535   ix.   Paul Henry Gum b. Jul 23 1932, d. Jul 23 1932 in Portage, Potter Co., IN.
- + 536   x.   Zepha Edan Gum b. Sep 30 1933.

(2) Married Nov 26 1902 in Bond Co., IL, **Mary Belle Coin**, b. Nov 11 1883, d. Oct 26 1911. **Mary**: Daughter of Tom Coin and Arilla Ogle.

Children by Mary Belle Coin:
- + 537   xi.   Maggie Alberta Gum b. Apr 12 1903.
- + 538   xii.   Dallas Edward Gum b. Feb 27 1905.
- + 539   xiii.   Howard Schubert Gum b. May 14 1907.

298. **Luther Randolph⁵ Gum** (90.James Johnson⁴, 14.Isaac C.³, 3.Isaac², 1.Dorothy "Dolly"¹ Arbogast), b. Mar 28 1888, d. Jul 25 1963.
Married Sep 09 1903 in Bond Co., IL, **Mamie Hohl**, b. Dec 13 1885 in Bond Co., IL, d. Jun 13 1958, buried in McKendree Church Cem., Bond Co., IL. **Mamie**: Daughter of Andrew HOHL and Margaret L. (Maggie) CURRAN.
        Children:
- \+ 540   i.   Homer Benjamin⁶ Gum b. Jul 10 1904.
- \+ 541   ii.   Clara Alberta Gum b. May 03 1907.
- 542   iii.   Elmer Lloyd Curren Gum b. Jul 14 1909, d. May 01 1972.

311. **Blanche Mahalia⁵ Ray** (102.Sarah Jane⁴ Gum, 17.James Riley³, 3.Isaac², 1.Dorothy "Dolly"¹ Arbogast), b. Apr 07 1894, d. Oct 06 1964.
Married Oct 04 1911 in Greenville, Bond Co., IL, **Samuel Weber Kell**, d. Nov 20 1956 in Mt. Auburn Cem., Greenville, Christian Co., IL. **Samuel**: Son of Noah Kell and Ella Norman.
        Children:
- 543   i.   Laurel Samual⁶ Kell b. Apr 16 1913, d. Apr 17 1913.
- \+ 544   ii.   Ellen Jane Kell b. Jul 26 1917.

313. **William Riley⁵ Gum, M.d.** (104.Isaac Daniel⁴, 17.James Riley³, 3.Isaac², 1.Dorothy "Dolly"¹ Arbogast), b. Jan 01 1894, d. Mar 25 1968.
Married May 24 1916, **Hazel Irene Starkey**, b. May 24 1896, d. Mar 03 1965 in St. Louis, St. Louis Co., MO.
        Children:
- 545   i.   Elizabeth Joan⁶ Gum b. Jun 06 1919 in St. Louis, St. Louis Co., MO, d. Mar 09 1920 in St. Louis, St. Louis Co., MO.
- 546   ii.   Audrey Irene Gum b. Jan 09 1921.
  She Married **Robert Sherrard**.
- \+ 547   iii.   William Riley Gum b. Jan 29 1924.

324. **Lee⁵ Starkey** (106.Sarah M.⁴ File, 18.Elizabeth³ Gum, 3.Isaac², 1.Dorothy "Dolly"¹ Arbogast), b. 1874.
He Married **Lillian Warnick**.
        Children:
- 548   i.   Louise⁶ Starkey.
  Louise Married and has one daughter and one son.

326. **David Daniel⁵ Starkey** (106.Sarah M.⁴ File, 18.Elizabeth³ Gum, 3.Isaac², 1.Dorothy "Dolly"¹ Arbogast).
He Married **Maude Smith**.
        Children:
- 549   i.   Elizabeth⁶ Starkey.
- 550   ii.   Derrell Starkey.
- 551   iii.   Jayne Starkey.

327. **Hillery Herbert⁵ Starkey** (106.Sarah M.⁴ File, 18.Elizabeth³ Gum, 3.Isaac², 1.Dorothy "Dolly"¹ Arbogast).
She Married **Ester Mae Thrailkill**.
        Children:
- 552   i.   Evelyn Mae⁶ Starkey b. 1916.
  She Married **Edwin Haskell**.
- \+ 553   ii.   Herbert Standeford Starkey b. 1918.
- 554   iii.   Victoria Margaretta Starkey b. 1921.
  She Married **John A. McKenzie**.
- 555   iv.   Willys Lee Starkey b. 1928.
- 556   v.   Joseph Ralph Starkey b. 1931.

328. **Louella**[5] **Starkey** (106.Sarah M.[4] File, 18.Elizabeth[3] Gum, 3.Isaac[2], 1.Dorothy "Dolly"[1] Arbogast). She Married **Oliver Sanders**.
Children:
- 557　i.　Jasper Lee[6] Sanders.
- 558　ii.　Perry Orin Sanders.
  He Married **Mary Elizabeth Hinton**.
- 559　iii.　Kenneth Sanders.
  Died As an infant.

345. **Mattie**[5] **Patton** (128.Angeline[4] Flasher, 29.Adam[3] Flesher, 4.Mary M.[2] Gum, 1.Dorothy "Dolly"[1] Arbogast), b. 1865. She Married **William Moreland**.
Children:
- 560　i.　Fred[6] Moreland.
- 561　ii.　Frank Moreland.

348. **Lillie May**[5] **Patton** (128.Angeline[4] Flasher, 29.Adam[3] Flesher, 4.Mary M.[2] Gum, 1.Dorothy "Dolly"[1] Arbogast), b. Oct 01 1874.
She Married **Henry Farris**, b. 1869.
Children:
- 562　i.　Katie[6] Farris b. 1894.

351. **Minnie Belle**[5] **Patton** (128.Angeline[4] Flasher, 29.Adam[3] Flesher, 4.Mary M.[2] Gum, 1.Dorothy "Dolly"[1] Arbogast), b. Nov 21 1884 in Marysville, Union Co., OH, d. Feb 05 1938 in Denver, Arapaho Co., CO.
Married May 26 1908 in Denver, Arapaho Co., CO, **John Daniel Kennedy**, b. July 1886 in Denver, Arapaho Co., CO (son of Thomas Kennedy and Katherine McCue), d. Dec. 1918 in Denver, Arapaho Co., CO.
Children:
- 563　i.　John Daniel[6] Kennedy b. Jul 27 1909, d. April 1955.
- 564　ii.　Robert Logan Kennedy b. May 14 1911 on Denver, Arapaho Co., CO, d. Jul 22 1976.
- 565　iii.　James Daniel Kennedy b. Nov 22 1913 in Denver, Arapaho Co., CO, d. May 19 1958 in Lakewood, Jefferson Co., CO.
- 566　iv.　John Patton Kennedy b. May 14 1915 in Denver, Arapaho Co., CO, d. Oct 08 1981 in Denver, Arapaho Co., CO.
  He Married **Charlotte Gertrude Hoelsken**.
- 567　v.　Mildred Pearl Kennedy b. Jun 04 1917 in Denver, Arapaho Co., CO, d. Dec 07 1990.

355. **Edward Henry**[5] **Flesher** (129.Greenberry[4], 29.Adam[3], 4.Mary M.[2] Gum, 1.Dorothy "Dolly"[1] Arbogast), b. Feb 25 1877 in Missouri.
Married Dec 28 1905, **Flora Mae Brown**, b. Apr 13 1889, d. Sep 26 1969.
Children:
- 568　i.　Cecil[6] Flesher b. Oct 13 1906, d. 1966.
  He Married in 1906.
- 569　ii.　Virgil G Flesher b. Apr 07 1908 in Osborn, Clinton Co., MO, d. Sep 26 1989 in Cameron, Clinton County MO.
  Married Oct 1931 in Marysville, Union Co., OH, **Oleva Mae Browmley**, b. Nov 06 1909 in Marysville, Union Co., OH, d. Jul 03 1993 in Cameron, Clinton County MO.
- 570　iii.　Gladys Ethal Flesher b. Jan 13 1910 in Osborn, Clinton Co., MO, d. Nov 02 1993 in Marysville, Union Co., OH.
  Gladys also Married an **unknown Bromley**.
  She Married **Roy E Hatch**, b. 1930.
- 571　iv.　William Quintin Flesher b. Dec 09 1912, d. May 14 1977.
- 572　v.　Phyllis Vernil Flesher b. Nov 30 1914, d. Dec 18 1989.
  She Married **Dale Lovitt**, b. Sep 26 1907, d. Nov 09 1996.

573 vi. Earl Flesher b. 1915, d. 1915.
574 vii. James Flesher b. Jan 09 1917, d. Jan 06 1979.
James Married a women born in 1920 and another women after 1979.
575 viii. Mary Larranine Flesher b. Apr 08 1919, d. Feb 13 1986.
Mary Married but not sure who.
576 ix. Donald Francis Flesher b. Nov 27 1921.

368. **Elsie Vera⁵ Flesher** (141.Harry Seldom⁴, 31.Henry³, 4.Mary M.² Gum, 1.Dorothy "Dolly"¹ Arbogast), b. Dec 24 1895, d. Sep 29 1974.
Married Mar 7 1915 in Sebastopol, Sonoma Co., CA, **John Martin Davis**, b. Feb 21 1890 in Sonoma Co., CA.
Children:
577 i. Vera⁶ Davis.
578 ii. Lora Davis.
579 iii. Norma Davis.
580 iv. Raymond Davis.

369. **Seldon Elmo⁵ Flesher** (141.Harry Seldom⁴, 31.Henry³, 4.Mary M.² Gum, 1.Dorothy "Dolly"¹ Arbogast), b. May 05 1901 in Sebastopol, Sonoma Co., CA, d. Nov 27 1980 in Santa Rosa, Sonoma Co., CA.
Married Jun 21 1921, **Eunice Mae Baughman**, b. Jan 2 1899 in Cottage Grove. Lane Co., OR.
Children:
+ 581 i. Wayne Elmo⁶ Flesher b. May 16 1923.
+ 582 ii. Nona Mae Flesher b. Jan 29 1929.

372. **Ida Josephine⁵ Smalling** (148.Aletha Adaline⁴ Dunkle, 32.Sarah Jane³ Flesher, 4.Mary M.² Gum, 1.Dorothy "Dolly"¹ Arbogast), b. Apr 17 1872 in Lawrence Co., MO, d. Jan 13 1937 in Billings, Yellowstone Co., MT.
She Married **Marcus Right Hendricks**, b. Feb 23 1860 in Billings, Greene Co., MO, d. Jun 4 1960 in Billings, Greene Co., MO.
Children:
+ 583 i. Ada Angeline⁶ Hendricks b. Sep 1 1891.

375. **Paul⁵ Flesher** (157.John Henry⁴, 34.William Seybert³, 4.Mary M.² Gum, 1.Dorothy "Dolly"¹ Arbogast), b. Jul 12 1875 in Kansas, d. Oct 1959.
Married Mar 22 1899 in Holton, Jackson Co., KS, **Sarah Stella Holt**, b. Feb 23 1875 in Indiana (daughter of Sebastian Holt and Phoebe King), d. Jun 9 1959.
Children:
+ 584 i. Claude B.⁶ Flesher b. Aug 12 1900.
585 ii. Marguerite Flesher b. Nov 21 1901 in Kansas.
(1) She Married **Raymond Fletcher**, b. Oct 13 1903, d. Mar 25 1945.
(2) Married 1211941, **Harry Burke**.
+ 586 iii. Gorman B. Flesher b. Jun 23 1905.
587 iv. John Reginald Flesher b. Jan 21 1907 in Kansas.
Married 1928, **Pauline P. Driver**, b. Oct 5 1907 in Indiana.
588 v. Pauline Mercedes Flesher b. 1910 in Kansas.
She Married **Victor F. Spathelf** (son of Eugene H. Spathelf).
589 vi. (unknown) Flesher.

378. **John William⁵ Flesher** (157.John Henry⁴, 34.William Seybert³, 4.Mary M.² Gum, 1.Dorothy "Dolly"¹ Arbogast), b. Oct 01 1885 near Holden, Jackson Co., KS, d. Jul 15 1915 in Arlington, Reno Co., KS.
He Married **Lora Jane Wilderson**, b. Sep 28 1889 in Pratte Co., MO.
Children:

590 i. Murray Orville[6] Flesher b. Jul 3 1910 in Hoyt, Jackson Co., KS, d. Nov 23 1972 in La Mirada, Los Angeles Co., CA.
(1) Married Jun 3 1991 in Topeka, Shawnee Co., KS, **Bernadette Richie Levett**, b. Oct 4 1911 in Topeka, Shawnee Co., KS.
(2) Married Jun 17 1937 in Marysville, Union Co., OH, **Irene Mae King**, b. Sep 1 1921 in Grantville, Calhoun Co., KS.

591 ii. Opal Flesher b. Oct 15 1912 in Hoyt, Jackson Co., KS, d. Oct 11 1994 in Topeka, Shawnee Co., KS.
(1) She Married **Lawrence Kent**.
(2) She Married **Floyd Barnes**.

386. **Charles Francis[5] Richard** (160.Louisa J[4] Flesher, 34.William Seybert[3], 4.Mary M.[2] Gum, 1.Dorothy "Dolly"[1] Arbogast), b. Jun 2 1878.
He Married **Grace Adeline Schaffer**, b. 1879.
Children:
592 i. George Harold[6] Richard.
He Married **Dorothy Maye Bennaka**.

400. **Audra S.[5] Miller** (177.George Riley[4], 38.Louesa K[3] Flesher, 4.Mary M.[2] Gum, 1.Dorothy "Dolly"[1] Arbogast), b. Jun 8 1897, d. Apr 3 1966.
(1) He Married **Elsie Wise**. .
Children by Elsie Wise:
593 i. Victor Earl[6] Miller.
594 ii. Vernon Lloyd Miller.

(2) He Married **Neva Steidley**

402. **Blanche Pearl[5] Miller** (177.George Riley[4], 38.Louesa K[3] Flesher, 4.Mary M.[2] Gum, 1.Dorothy "Dolly"[1] Arbogast), b. Jul 24 1901.
She Married **Charles Kapp Moutray**.
Children:
595 i. Marjorie Ellen[6] Moutray.
596 ii. Margaret Juanita Moutray.
597 iii. Charles Kapp Moutray , Jr..
598 iv. Evelyn Berenice Moutray.

403. **Goldia Bell[5] Miller** (177.George Riley[4], 38.Louesa K[3] Flesher, 4.Mary M.[2] Gum, 1.Dorothy "Dolly"[1] Arbogast), b. Jan 1 1903.
She Married **Jess Moutray**.
Children:
599 i. George Franklin[6] Moutray.
600 ii. Harold Eugene Moutray.
601 iii. Gary Keith Moutray.

404. **Claudine[5] Miller** (177.George Riley[4], 38.Louesa K[3] Flesher, 4.Mary M.[2] Gum, 1.Dorothy "Dolly"[1] Arbogast), b. Jan 31 1905, d. Mar 15 1978.
She Married **Henry Eli Fletchall**.
Children:
602 i. R.g.[6] Fletchall.

405. **Lily Virginia[5] Miller** (177.George Riley[4], 38.Louesa K[3] Flesher, 4.Mary M.[2] Gum, 1.Dorothy "Dolly"[1] Arbogast), b. Nov 22 1907.
She Married **Frank A. Gunselman**.
Children:
603 i. Wavalea[6] Gunselman.

406. **Glen Washington[5] Miller** (177.George Riley[4], 38.Louesa K[3] Flesher, 4.Mary M.[2] Gum, 1.Dorothy "Dolly"[1] Arbogast), b. Jul 18 1909.
He Married **Wilma Marie Roesti**.
  Children:
  604 i. Glenna Marie[6] Miller.

409. **Charles M[5] Gum** (194.Joseph[4], 40.Henry[3], 5.Adam[2], 1.Dorothy "Dolly"[1] Arbogast), b. Nov 1870.
Married About 1895, **Nancy C (Unknown)**.
  Children:
  605 i. Georgia[6] Gum b. About 1899.

417. **Della I[5] Colaw** (199.William[4], 41.Sabina[3] Gum, 5.Adam[2], 1.Dorothy "Dolly"[1] Arbogast), b. Feb 18 1871, d. Jun 27 1966.
She Married **Owen Lester Scott**, b. Oct 19 1868, d. Jul 31 1948.
  Children:
  606 i. Edna[6] Scott.
           She Married **Downey Phillips**.
  607 ii. Alta Scott b. Apr 02 1895, d. Dec 21 1969.
           She Married **Forrest Watson**.
  608 iii. Imo Scott b. Apr 02 1895, d. Dec 21 1969.
           She Married **Floyd Cole**.
  609 iv. Hazel Scott.
           She Married **Lynn Lanier**.
  610 v. Inez Scott.

418. **George William[5] Colaw** (202.Benjamin Watters[4], 41.Sabina[3] Gum, 5.Adam[2], 1.Dorothy "Dolly"[1] Arbogast), b. 1866.
He Married **Winnie Green**.
  Children:
  611 i. Martha Ellen[6] Colaw.
  612 ii. Naomi Colaw.
           She Married **George Davis** (son of George Russell Davis and Eleanor Elizabeth Nottingham). George: Information from Mary E. (Nottingham) Skelton of Jamestown, PA.

419. **Mary Rosetta[5] Colaw** (202.Benjamin Watters[4], 41.Sabina[3] Gum, 5.Adam[2], 1.Dorothy "Dolly"[1] Arbogast), b. 1868.
She Married **Webster Stevens**.
  Children:
  613 i. Viola May[6] Colaw b. 1891.
  614 ii. Ethel May Colaw b. Feb 11 1895, d. Jan 9 1975.
  615 iii. Ida Gertrude Colaw b. 1896, d. Feb 20 1980.

420. **John Harmon[5] Colaw** (202.Benjamin Watters[4], 41.Sabina[3] Gum, 5.Adam[2], 1.Dorothy "Dolly"[1] Arbogast), b. 1871.
He Married **Ella Cusey**.
  Children:
  + 616 i. Charles Benjamin[6] Colaw b. Apr 30 1895.
  + 617 ii. Donald Colaw.
  + 618 iii. John Orval Colaw b. 1902.
  + 619 iv. Ray Kenneth Colaw b. 1906.
  + 620 v. Ben Wilson Colaw.

421. **Franklin Robert⁵ Colaw** (202.Benjamin Watters⁴, 41.Sabina³ Gum, 5.Adam², 1.Dorothy "Dolly"¹ Arbogast), b. May 30 1873, d. Jan 21 1944.
Married Feb 12 1896, **Lillie Belle Kirk**, b. Jul 28 1876, d. 1960.
Children:
+ 621   i.   Robert Ray⁶ Colaw b. Sep 8 1897.

422. **Harry Albert⁵ Colaw** (202.Benjamin Watters⁴, 41.Sabina³ Gum, 5.Adam², 1.Dorothy "Dolly"¹ Arbogast), b. 1876.
He Married **Sarah Olive Davis**.

Children:

+ 622   i.   Mamie Bell⁶ Colaw b. 1901.
    623   ii.   Imogene Matilda Colaw b. 1906.

424. **Ella May⁵ Colaw** (202.Benjamin Watters⁴, 41.Sabina³ Gum, 5.Adam², 1.Dorothy "Dolly"¹ Arbogast), b. 1881.
She Married **Charles Wolfe**.
Children:
+ 624   i.   Doris⁶ Wolfe b. 1904.
+ 625   ii.   Herbert William Wolfe b. 1909.

426. **Bernard⁵ Colaw** (202.Benjamin Watters⁴, 41.Sabina³ Gum, 5.Adam², 1.Dorothy "Dolly"¹ Arbogast), b. 1893.
He Married **Nellie Woods**.
Children:
    626   i.   Adele⁶ Colaw.
    627   ii.   Albert Eugene Colaw.
    628   iii.   Janice Colaw.

428. **Alphorus⁵ Colaw** (204.Dyer W⁴, 41.Sabina³ Gum, 5.Adam², 1.Dorothy "Dolly"¹ Arbogast), b. Sep 19 1868 in Illinois, d. 1939.
He Married **Bertha Viola Ketterman**, b. Dec 30 1874 (daughter of Nicholas Harper Ketterman and Elizabeth Teter), d. Apr 4 1942.
Children:
+ 629   i.   Wayne⁶ Colaw b. Jan 28 1897.
+ 630   ii.   Grace Colaw.
+ 631   iii.   Glen Dyer Colaw b. Apr 20 1907.
+ 632   iv.   Merle C. Colaw b. Apr 20 1907.
    633   v.   Dorothy Colaw b. Jan 19 1909, d. Jul 30 1984.
           Married Nov 1947 in Las Vegas, Clark Co., NV, **Don Jeneves**.
+ 634   vi.   Thornton Colaw b. May 19 1914.

430. **Otie Viola⁵ Gum** (207.Thomas Marion⁴, 43.Amos³, 5.Adam², 1.Dorothy "Dolly"¹ Arbogast), b. May 30 1892 in Naples, Collier Co., VA, d. Feb 5 1962 in Durbin, Pocahontas Co., WV.
Married Feb 21 1912 in Marlinton, Pocahontas Co., WV, **Cecil Clay Houchin**, b. Apr 26 1882 (son of Thomas Houchin and Mary McNeil), d. Nov 18 1977 in Elkins, Randolph Co., WV.
Children:
    635   i.   Helen Lee⁶ Houchin b. May 31 1824.
           She Married **Lanty Dale Ryder**, b. May 5 1825, d. Jul 30 1883.
+ 636   ii.   Clay T. Houchin b. 1915.
    637   iii.   Wardell Houchin b. 1920 in Durbin, Pocahontas Co., WV, d. Feb 18 1986 in Lancaster General Hospital, Lancaster, PA.
           He Married **Ella Mae Brenner**.

+ 638 iv. Virginia Houchin.
+ 639 v. Margaret Houchin.
+ 640 vi. Paul Russell Houchin b. 1922.
641 vii. Ray Houchin.
He Married **Phyllis Greathouse**.
+ 642 viii. Audrey Houchin.

431. **Roy McKinley**[5] **Gum** (207.Thomas Marion[4], 43.Amos[3], 5.Adam[2], 1.Dorothy "Dolly"[1] Arbogast), b. Dec 9 1894 in Naples, Collier Co., VA, d. Dec 2 1955 in South Charleston, Kanawha Co., WV.
Married Jan 23 1921, **Helen Moffett Moore**, b. Dec 7 1898 (daughter of Harry Moffett Moore and Cora Elvira Jones).

Children:
643 i. Roy McKinley[6] Gum II b. Jun 16 1924, d. Jun 19 1924.
644 ii. Helen Alaine Gum b. Aug 13 1925, d. Jul 10 1977 in Virginia Beach, Princess Anne Co., VA. S
She Married **Pierre Arthur Verdin III**, b. Dec 8 1922.
+ 645 iii. Corrinne Ann Gum b. Nov 2 1930.
646 iv. Donna Moore Gum b. Feb 25 1935.
She Married **Frederick Neale**.

433. **Wardell Clark**[5] **Gum** (207.Thomas Marion[4], 43.Amos[3], 5.Adam[2], 1.Dorothy "Dolly"[1] Arbogast), b. Sep 13 1898 in Frost, Pocahontas Co., WV, d. Sep 3 1982 in Elkins, Randolph Co., WV.
Married Mar 7 1925 in Green Bank, Pocahontas Co., WV, **Anna Mary Sharp**, b. Sep 9 1907 in Dunmore, Pocahontas Co., WV (daughter of Samuel Sharp and Vivian Buterbaugh), d. Jan 16 1977 in Ruby Memorial Hospital, Morgantown, Monongalia Co., WV.

Children:
+ 647 i. Paul Roy[6] Gum b. Jun 10 1927.
+ 648 ii. Mary Agatha Gum b. Oct 9 1928.
649 iii. Wardell Chad Gum.

437. **Ida Omega**[5] **Gum** (208.James Otho[4], 43.Amos[3], 5.Adam[2], 1.Dorothy "Dolly"[1] Arbogast), b. Jan 23 1902, d. Apr 15 1988 in Conneautville, Crawford Co., PA.
Information from Mrs. Sylvia (Taylor) Gum of Green Bank, WV by letter 9 Jan 1993 in file.
She Married **Frank Wardell Galford**, b. Aug 4 1894 (son of John Allan Galford and Mary Catherine McLaughlin), d. Jan 16 1977 in Meadville, Crawford Co., PA.

Children:
650 i. Hazel[6] Galford b. 1922. She
Married **Forrest W. Goodwill**.
651 ii. E. Kathryn Galford.
Married Nov 20 1945, **Amon L. McQuiston**.
652 iii. Eula G. Galford.
Married Aug 7 1949, **Meredith K. Orr**.
653 iv. Virginia Dare Galford b. Jul 27 1923 in Dunmore, Pocahontas Co., WV.
Married Aug 26 1943, **Roscoe Bertram Roat**.
654 v. James Allen Galford.
655 vi. (infant) Galford b. Sep 18 1929, d. Oct 16 1929.
656 vii. Harold Wayne Galford b. Aug 5 1935.
Married May 21 1955, **Mary Elizabeth Spaid**.
657 viii. Frances Pauline Galford b. Jul 10 1941. She Married **Roy Weed**.

438. **Merritt Moore**[5] **Gum** (208.James Otho[4], 43.Amos[3], 5.Adam[2], 1.Dorothy "Dolly"[1] Arbogast), b. Apr 4 1904 in Green Bank, Pocahontas Co., WV, d. Sep 28 1978 in Memorial General Hospital, Elkins, Randolph Co., WV, buried in Dunmore Cem., Dunmore, Pocahontas Co., WV.
Married Aug 4 1925 in Marlinton, Pocahontas Co., WV, **Sylvia Leone Taylor**, b. May 23 1905 in Dunmore, Pocahontas Co., WV (daughter of William Harrison Taylor and Victoria Jane

Nottingham), d. Apr 6 1994 in Mercy Hospital. Pittsburgh, Allegheny Co., PA. **Sylvia** : Information from Mrs. Sylvia (Taylor) Gum of Green Bank, WV by = 1993 in file. Sylvia writes that she is 88 years old and is able = and care for herself in her own home.

    Children:

- 658 i. Daniel Lorain^6 Gum b. Jul 17 1926 in Dunmore, Pocahontas Co., WV, d. Aug 4 1950 in Hinton, Summers Co., WV, buried in Dunmore Cem., Dunmore, Pocahontas Co., WV.
  Information from Mrs. Sylvia (Taylor) Gum of Green Bank, WV by = 1993 in file. Daniel never Married.
- 659 ii. Kerth Elmo Gum b. Apr 4 1935 in Dunmore, Pocahontas Co., WV.
  Kerth is Sylvia's only living child according to = lives in New Cumberland, WV.
  Married Mar 11 1957 in Cumberland, Allegheny Co., MD, **Barbara Ann Strope**, b. Jan 1 1938 in Weirton, Weirton, WV.

439. **Robert Sterling**^{5} **Gum** (208.James Otho^4, 43.Amos^3, 5.Adam^2, 1.Dorothy "Dolly"^{1} Arbogast), b. May 3 1909 in Dunmore, Pocahontas Co., WV, d. Nov 9 1981.
Married **Ruby Seelee** of Kentucky.
He Married **Ruby Alice Salee**, b. Jul 4 1911 in Kentucky, d. Sep 21 1993 in Weirton, Weirton, WV.

    Children:
- 660 i. Robert^6 Gum.
- 661 ii. Trudy Gum. She Married **(unknown) McClelland**.
- 662 iii. Joyce Gum. She Married **(unknown) Swartzonill**.

440. **Homer Burrell**^{5} **Willman** (218.Gertrude Ethel^4 Shockey, 51.Sarah^3 Genkins, 8.Elleder^2 Gum, 1.Dorothy "Dolly"^{1} Arbogast), b. Oct 23 1908, d. May 23 1977 in Crescent City, Del Norte Co., CA.
Married Aug 15 1930 in Oklahoma, **Viola May Wagoner**, b. Sep 29 1912.

    Children:
- 663 i. John Burrell^6 Willman b. Aug 16 1934 in Stillwater, Payne Co., OK.
- 664 ii. Barbara Ellen Willman b. Feb 12 1943.

456. **Oscar Clarence**^{5} **Gum** (234.Nathaniel Meade^4, 65.George Wasgington^3, 9.Jesse^2, 1.Dorothy "Dolly"^{1} Arbogast), b. Dec 16 1893, d. Feb 15 1968. Lived in CA
He Married **Helen Mae Baker** born Apr 12 1906, died Jan 2, 1983 in ,d. Jul 13 1995, Jasper Co., MN.

    Children:
- 665 i. Gary^6 Gum.

459. **Freda May**^{5} **Gum** (234.Nathaniel Meade^4, 65.George Wasgington^3, 9.Jesse^2, 1.Dorothy "Dolly"^{1} Arbogast), b. Sep 20 1906 Kansas City. MO. D Jul 13 1995, Reeds, MO. Lived in Albuquerque, NM in 1975
She Married **Willis Earl Hitchcock**. B Jul 2, 1916 Jasper Co., MO, d Feb 12

    Children:
- 666 i. Max Hitchcock. 1996 alameda, CA.

460. **George William**^{5} **Gum** (234.Nathaniel Meade^4, 65.George Wasgington^3, 9.Jesse^2, 1.Dorothy "Dolly"^{1} Arbogast), b. Dec 29 1908, d. Oct 26 1970. Lived in Joplin, MO
He Married **Hazel Long**.

    Children:
- + 667 i. Freda Jeanne^6 Gum.

462. **Roy Calvin**^{5} **Gum** (235.William Oliver^4, 65.George Wasgington^3, 9.Jesse^2, 1.Dorothy "Dolly"^{1} Arbogast), b. May 02 1895, d. Jul 30 1968.
He Married **Edith Winifred**.

    Children:

        668   i.   Edgar Allen⁶ Gum b. Sep 03 1919.
Lived in Lakeland Village, WA
He <u>Married</u> **Hazel Radford**.
+ 669   ii.   Nell Katherine Gum b. Jul 22 1921.
  670   iii.   Georgiua Geraldine Gum b. Aug 16 1923, d. Aug 21 1923.
  671   iv.   Helen Erline Gum b. Aug 18 1926, d. Aug 18 1968.
She <u>Married</u> **Harvey D Oder**.
+ 672   v.   George Richard Gum b. Apr 03 1933.
  673   vi.   Earl Gum b. Jan 27 1935.

463. **Willis Herbert⁵ Gum** (236.Andrew Newton⁴, 65.George Wasgington³, 9.Jesse², 1.Dorothy "Dolly"¹ Arbogast), b. Nov 09 1899.
Lived in Springfield, MO
He <u>Married</u> **Edith Yant**.
         Children:
  674   i.   Arele⁶ Gum.
She <u>Married</u> **William Rule**. William: Lived in Dallas, TX.

464. **Melvin⁵ Gum** (236.Andrew Newton⁴, 65.George Wasgington³, 9.Jesse², 1.Dorothy "Dolly"¹ Arbogast), b. Dec 11 1914.
He <u>Married</u> **Maxine Gerry**.
         Children:
  675   i.   Lemoine⁶ Gum.

465. **Willard C⁵ Vance** (237.Effie⁴ Gum, 65.George Wasgington³, 9.Jesse², 1.Dorothy "Dolly"¹ Arbogast), b. Dec 25 1904.
He <u>Married</u> **Faye Macy**.
         Children:
  676   i.   Macy William⁶ Vance. <u>Married</u> May 01 1971 in Lived in Monroeville, Allegheny Co., PA, **Sharon Maline**.

468. **Lois T⁵ Gum** (238.Edgar Haddon⁴, 65.George Wasgington³, 9.Jesse², 1.Dorothy "Dolly"¹ Arbogast), b. Apr 26 1903, d. Sep 12 1973.
She <u>Married</u> **Willis Amerine**, d. 1975.
         Children:
+ 677   i.   Merwin Wells⁶ Amerine b. Apr 21 1923.
+ 678   ii.   Reagan Haddon Amerine b. Apr 10 1924.
+ 679   iii.   Richard Dean Amerine.

471. **Rowland Hughes⁵ Gum** (238.Edgar Haddon⁴, 65.George Wasgington³, 9.Jesse², 1.Dorothy "Dolly"¹ Arbogast), b. May 29 1920.
<u>Married</u> in Modesto, Stanislaus Co., CA, **Lavivian Melgren**.
         Children:
+ 680   i.   Russell Lynn⁶ Gum b. Feb 11 1943.
+ 681   ii.   Martin Louis Gum b. Jan 17 1950.
  682   iii.   Stephen Hughes Gum b. Apr 15 1956.

476. **Edrie Maurine⁵ Miller** (240.Ida May⁴ Gum, 65.George Wasgington³, 9.Jesse², 1.Dorothy "Dolly"¹ Arbogast), b. Jan 10 1909. Was living in St. Louise, MO in 1984
She <u>Married</u> **A Rudd Graham**. A Rudd: From Paducah, KY.
         Children:
+ 683   i.   Byron Rudd⁶ Graham b. Jul 02 1940.
  684   ii.   James Miller Graham b. Oct 16 1945.
He <u>Married</u> **Linda Kay Edwards**, b. in Springfield, Greene Co., MO.

477. **Eva Marie⁵ Miller** (240.Ida May⁴ Gum, 65.George Wasgington³, 9.Jesse², 1.Dorothy "Dolly"¹ Arbogast), b. Aug 22 1910 in Carthage, Jasper Co., MO.
She Married **Edgar C Ruppert**.
                    Children:
+ 685   i.   Richard E⁶ Ruppert b. Apr 08 1948.
   686   ii. Sara Ann Ruppert b. Nov 13 1949.
              She Married **Steven J Stone**.

482. **William Wayne⁵ McNeal** (257.William Wesley⁴, 69.Sarah Elizabeth³ Gum, 9.Jesse², 1.Dorothy "Dolly"¹ Arbogast), b. Sep 01 1919, d. Jan 03 1954.
He Married **Lela May Whorton**.
                    Children:
   687   i.   Norman Wayne⁶ McNeal.
   688   ii. James Wesley McNeal.

483. **Carl Thomas⁵ McNeal** (257.William Wesley⁴, 69.Sarah Elizabeth³ Gum, 9.Jesse², 1.Dorothy "Dolly"¹ Arbogast), b. May 05 1923.
He Married **Phyllis Nicholson**. Phyllis: Lived in Houston, TX.
                    Children:
   689   i.   Carla Sue⁶ McNeal.
   690   ii.   Phillip Wayne McNeal.
   691   iii. Mary Elizabeth McNeal.
   692   iv. Thomas Allen McNeal.

484. **James Virgil⁵ Cantrell** (260.Sarah Jane⁴ Stinson, 70.Talitha³ Gum, 9.Jesse², 1.Dorothy "Dolly"¹ Arbogast), b. Dec 09 1892, d. Mar 07 1970.
Married Feb 13 1913, **May Pendergrass**, b. Feb 26 1895.
                    Children:
   693   i.   Nina Marie⁶ Cantrell b. Aug 06 1914.
              She Married **Robert Sperry**.
+ 694   ii. Winfield Winson Cantrell b. Feb 25 1918.
+ 695   iii. Vergie Francis Cantrell.
+ 696   iv. James Paul Cantrell b. Aug 20 1932.

487. **Reggie Bernard⁵ Cantrell** (260.Sarah Jane⁴ Stinson, 70.Talitha³ Gum, 9.Jesse², 1.Dorothy "Dolly"¹ Arbogast), b. Feb 06 1904.
He Married **Gladys (Unknown)**.
                    Children:
   697   i.   Dixie⁶ Crantell.

492. **Emil Fred⁵ Hinkle** (263.Pearl⁴ Stinson, 70.Talitha³ Gum, 9.Jesse², 1.Dorothy "Dolly"¹ Arbogast), b. Jan 08 1907.
He Married **Juanita E Pauge**, b. Apr 13 1920.
                    Children:
   698   i.   Richard Wayne⁶ Hinkle b. Nov 13 1938.
+ 699   ii. Randell Glenn Hinkle b. Feb 25 1942.

493. **Joel⁵ Stinson** (264.Fred⁴, 70.Talitha³ Gum, 9.Jesse², 1.Dorothy "Dolly"¹ Arbogast), b. Jul 05 1909.
He Married **Beulah Wetencamp**, b. Dec 08 1913.
                    Children:
   700   i.   Juanita Louise⁶ Stinson b. Apr 14 1942.
              She Married **John S Scoma Ruano**.

494. **Juanita Mildred**^{5} **Ruark** (265.Lula^4 Stinson, 70.Talitha^3 Gum, 9.Jesse^2, 1.Dorothy "Dolly"^{1} Arbogast), b. Apr 19 1908.
She Married **John Smith Dunn**, b. Jul 30 1899, d. Jan 06 1969.
  Children:
  701 i. Dennis Eugene^6 Dunn b. Feb 05 1948, d. Apr 05 1964.

495. **William Lloyd**^{5} **Ruark** (265.Lula^4 Stinson, 70.Talitha^3 Gum, 9.Jesse^2, 1.Dorothy "Dolly"^{1} Arbogast), b. Jul 03 1909.
He Married **Mary Spielman**, b. Dec 08 1915.
  Children:
  + 702 i. William Larry^6 Ruark b. Jan 06 1938.
  + 703 ii. Linda Suzanna Ruark b. May 15 1945.

Generation Six

499. **Louisa Jeanetta**^{6} **Page** (271.Sarah Elizabeth^5 Huffstedtler, 80.Louisa Janetta^4 Gum, 13.Jesse S.^{3}, 3.Isaac^2, 1.Dorothy "Dolly"^{1} Arbogast), b. Mar 24 1873 in Old Ripley, Bond Co., IL, d. Mar 17 1956, buried in Fontana, Miami Co., KS.
Married Oct 29 1893 in Fontana, Miami Co., KS, **Joseph William Graham**, b. Jul 16 1870 in Fort Scott, Bourbon Co., KS (Found family on 1870 Federal census which was taken on August 24, 1870, but asked for those living at residence on June 1, 1870. Thus he is not listed as a child of the family at that time.), d. Jun 22 1956, buried in Fontana, Miami Co., KS. Joseph: Newspaper article dated 4/29/1938? about Joseph, from the Western Spirit. Describes his occupation/avocation of hunting and trapping; particularly wolves. Also traps skunks and mink. Mentions his "grandfather" Andy McCoy. This is news to me and don't think this is accurate. Will research McCoy and see if there is a link. Nickname is "Bush". Paper says he came to Miami County in 1861, an obvious error as he was only born in 1870.

Found an original copy of above article from Mom & Dad that shows that the copy I used at the Miami Co Gen. Soc. had omitted the final 4 or 5 lines of the first column which states he is talking about his Grandpa Hart and McCoy is only a friend.
  Children:
  + 704 i. Florence Wauneta^7 Graham b. Dec 17 1904.
    705 ii. George Lester Graham b. in Fontana, Miami Co., KS, d. Aug 20 1894 in Paola, Miami Co., KS, buried Aug 24 1984 in Osawatomie, Miami Co., KS.

508. **Melvin C.**^{6} **Gum** (288.Edward Gustavus^5, 89.John Royal^4, 14.Isaac C.^{3}, 3.Isaac^2, 1.Dorothy "Dolly"^{1} Arbogast), b. Jun 19 1907.
Married Aug 23 1927, **Grace Mills**, b. Dec 08 1910.
  Children:
  + 706 i.   Royal Edward^7 Gum.
    707 ii. Stanley Carrol Gum b. Mar 01 1936.
    708 iii. Raymond Alvin Gum b. Dec 30 1938.

509. **Elvin George**^{6} **Gum** (288.Edward Gustavus^5, 89.John Royal^4, 14.Isaac C.^{3}, 3.Isaac^2, 1.Dorothy "Dolly"^{1} Arbogast), b. Oct 20 1911.
He Married **Bernice (Unknown)**.
  Children:
  709 i.   Earl^7 Gum.
  710 ii. Roger Gum.
  711 iii. John Gum.
  712 iv. Mary Gum.

521. **Marie M.**[6] **Gum** (296.John Leonard[5], 90.James Johnson[4], 14.Isaac C.[3], 3.Isaac[2], 1.Dorothy "Dolly"[1] Arbogast).
She Married **Lowell Hampton**.
Children:
+ 713 i. Lowell[7] Hampton, Jr..

523. **Hurlius**[6] **Gum** (296.John Leonard[5], 90.James Johnson[4], 14.Isaac C.[3], 3.Isaac[2], 1.Dorothy "Dolly"[1] Arbogast).
He Married **Lucille (Unknown)**.
Children:
714 i. Wayne[7] Gum.

525. **Vera**[6] **Gum** (296.John Leonard[5], 90.James Johnson[4], 14.Isaac C.[3], 3.Isaac[2], 1.Dorothy "Dolly"[1] Arbogast).
She Married **Lee Wood**.
Children:
715 i. Joyce[7] Wood.

527. **Clyde Everett**[6] **Gum** (297.James Edward[5], 90.James Johnson[4], 14.Isaac C.[3], 3.Isaac[2], 1.Dorothy "Dolly"[1] Arbogast), b. Jul 18 1915, d. Dec 21 1973.
He Married **Vera Sussen**.
Children:
716 i. Clyde Roger[7] Gum.
717 ii. Ronald Gum.
718 iii. Linda C. Gum.
719 iv. Veralyn Gene Gum.
720 v. Monty Gum.

528. **Erma Charlotte**[6] **Gum** (297.James Edward[5], 90.James Johnson[4], 14.Isaac C.[3], 3.Isaac[2], 1.Dorothy "Dolly"[1] Arbogast), b. Oct 09 1917, d. Apr 04 1974.
She Married **Raymond Vonburg**.
Children:
+ 721 i. Raymond Edward[7] Vonburg b. Nov 27 1936.
+ 722 ii. Erma Jean Vonburg b. Jul 14 1938.
+ 723 iii. Paul Laverne Vonburg b. May 18 1940.

529. **Ardelene Mardell**[6] **Gum** (297.James Edward[5], 90.James Johnson[4], 14.Isaac C.[3], 3.Isaac[2], 1.Dorothy "Dolly"[1] Arbogast), b. Oct 27 1919, d. Apr 14 1978.
She Married **Benjamin Marshall Vonburg**.
Children:
+ 724 i. Benjamin J.[7] Vonburg, Jr..
+ 725 ii. Steven Blair Vonburg b. Mar 27 1951.
+ 726 iii. Susan Mardell Vonburg b. Oct 13 1952.

531. **Luthur Aaron**[6] **Gum** (297.James Edward[5], 90.James Johnson[4], 14.Isaac C.[3], 3.Isaac[2], 1.Dorothy "Dolly"[1] Arbogast), b. Sep 12 1923.
Married Jan 07 1945, **Elizabeth Nanni**.
Children:
+ 727 i. Judith Rosemary[7] Gum b. 1946.

532. **Mary Edyth**[6] **Gum** (297.James Edward[5], 90.James Johnson[4], 14.Isaac C.[3], 3.Isaac[2], 1.Dorothy "Dolly"[1] Arbogast), b. Nov 07 1924.
She Married **Alfonso Buvarskis**.

Children:
+ 728   i.   Gordon Alan⁷ Buvarskis b. Oct 31 1948.

533. **Gorden Isaac⁶ Gum** (297.James Edward⁵, 90.James Johnson⁴, 14.Isaac C.³, 3.Isaac², 1.Dorothy "Dolly"¹ Arbogast), b. Apr 28 1926.
He Married **Faye Lucille Koontz**.
    Children:
+ 729   i.   Brenda Lucille⁷ Gum b. 1950.
   730   ii.   Lonnie Gordon Gum b. 1954.
+ 731   iii.   Diana Faye Gum b. 1954.

534. **Marvin Udell⁶ Gum** (297.James Edward⁵, 90.James Johnson⁴, 14.Isaac C.³, 3.Isaac², 1.Dorothy "Dolly"¹ Arbogast), b. Jul 24 1928.
Married c 1947, **Harriett Ilene Brown**.
    Children:
+ 732   i.   Marvin Blaine⁷ Gum b. 1948.
+ 733   ii.   Janis Ilene Gum.
+ 734   iii.   Dennis Lynn Gum b. 1951.
   735   iv.   Kevin Gum b. Feb 21 1961, d. Feb 21 1961.
   736   v.   Karen June Gum b. Sep 23 1963.
   737   vi.   Kieth James Gum b. Mar 26 1969.

536. **Zepha Edan⁶ Gum** (297.James Edward⁵, 90.James Johnson⁴, 14.Isaac C.³, 3.Isaac², 1.Dorothy "Dolly"¹ Arbogast), b. Sep 30 1933. \
She Married **Robert Ivan Painter**.
    Children:
+ 738   i.   Sharlyn Lavon⁷ Painter b. 1953.
   739   ii.   Robin Lynn Painter b. 1955.
               Married 1976, **Russell Clifton Bradford**.
   740   iii.   Christopher Robert Painter b. 1969.

537. **Maggie Alberta⁶ Gum** (297.James Edward⁵, 90.James Johnson⁴, 14.Isaac C.³, 3.Isaac², 1.Dorothy "Dolly"¹ Arbogast), b. Apr 12 1903.
Married Dec 15 1924, **Virgil Norwood Williams**.
    Children:
   741   i.   Melvin Norris⁷ Williams b. Jan 01 1931.
               Married Nov 24 1954, **Ethlyn Hunsacker**.
+ 742   ii.   Reba Arlene Williams b. Feb 20 1933.

538. **Dallas Edward⁶ Gum** (297.James Edward⁵, 90.James Johnson⁴, 14.Isaac C.³, 3.Isaac², 1.Dorothy "Dolly"¹ Arbogast), b. Feb 27 1905, d. May 1970.
He Married **Ethel Goodin**, d. Sep 06 1981.
    Children:
+ 743   i.   Thomas Edward⁷ Gum b. Mar 01 1931.

539. **Howard Schubert⁶ Gum** (297.James Edward⁵, 90.James Johnson⁴, 14.Isaac C.³, 3.Isaac², 1.Dorothy "Dolly"¹ Arbogast), b. May 14 1907.
(1) He Married **Naome Edna Lewey**, b. Nov 11 1909, d. Jan 19 1974.
    Children by Naome Edna Lewey:
+ 744   i.   Robert Edward⁷ Gum b. 1928.
+ 745   ii.   William Kenneth Gum b. Apr 22 1929.
+ 746   iii.   Mary Alice Gum.
+ 747   iv.   Clara Lou Gum b. Sep 21 1934.
   748   v.   Gary Lee Gum b. Oct 19 1935.

*(2) He Married **Delores Seaman**.*

Children *by Delores Seaman:*
- 749 vi. Paul Howard Gum
- 750 vii. James Russell Gum.
- 751 viii. Delores Ilene Gum.
- 752 ix. Theresa Ruth Gum.
- 753 x. Joan Gum.
- 754 xi. Ellen Gum.
- 755 xii. Mary Lou Gum b. 1951, d. 1951.
- 756 xiii. Julie Kay Gum b. 1962.

540. **Homer Benjamin^6 Gum** (298.Luther Randolph^5, 90.James Johnson^4, 14.Isaac C.^{3}, 3.Isaac^2, 1.Dorothy "Dolly"^{1} Arbogast), b. Jul 10 1904.
Married Aug 02 1924, **Clarissa Ann Carver**.
Children:
- 757 i. William^7 Gum.
- 758 ii. Monty Gum.
- 759 iii. Nadine Gum.

541. **Clara Alberta^6 Gum** (298.Luther Randolph^5, 90.James Johnson^4, 14.Isaac C.^{3}, 3.Isaac^2, 1.Dorothy "Dolly"^{1} Arbogast), b. May 03 1907.
Married Feb 20 1949, **Byron C. Taylor**, b. Jul 13 1907, d. Nov 26 1964.
Children:
- 760 i. Sharon^7 Taylor b. Dec 12 1949.
  Married Apr 10 1982, **Delbert Ladell Kirt**.

544. **Ellen Jane^6 Kell** (311.Blanche Mahalia^5 Ray, 102.Sarah Jane^4 Gum, 17.James Riley^3, 3.Isaac^2, 1.Dorothy "Dolly"^{1} Arbogast), b. Jul 26 1917.
Married Aug 15 1937 in St. Charles Co., MO, **Oral Mauricelce Tevis**, b. Apr 20 1916 in Fayette Co., IL. **Oral**: Son of Morgan Tevis and Eva Edyth Eakle.
Children:
- 761 i. Cecelia Kay^7 Tevis b. Feb 13 1938, d. Mar 24 1938.
- + 762 ii. Lana Janice Tevis b. Dec 17 1940.

547. **William Riley^6 Gum** (313.William Riley^5, 104.Isaac Daniel^4, 17.James Riley^3, 3.Isaac^2, 1.Dorothy "Dolly"^{1} Arbogast), b. Jan 29 1924.
Married Apr 21 1946, **Eleanor Wilcox Wilson**.
Children:
- 763 i. William Riley^7 Gum, Jr. b. Dec 30 1951.
- 764 ii. Steven Boyce Gum b. May 27 1954.
  Married 1978, **Dorothy Routt**.
- 765 iii. Michael Gum b. Jun 14 1958.

553. **Herbert Standeford^6 Starkey** (327.Hillery Herbert^5, 106.Sarah M.^{4} File, 18.Elizabeth^3 Gum, 3.Isaac^2, 1.Dorothy "Dolly"^{1} Arbogast), b. 1918.
He Married **Ann Williams**.
Children:
- 766 i. Judy Ann^7 Starkey.

581. **Wayne Elmo^6 Flesher** (369.Seldon Elmo^5, 141.Harry Seldom^4, 31.Henry^3, 4.Mary M.^{2} Gum, 1.Dorothy "Dolly"^{1} Arbogast), b. May 16 1923 in Santa Rosa, Sonoma Co., CA.
He Married **Germaine Ida Becker**, b. Jul 27 1927 in St. Joseph, Kossuth Co., IA.

Children:
- 767 i. Shawn Paul[7] Flesher b. Dec 9 1962 in Craig, Moffat Co., CO, d. Apr 7 1991 in Leadville, Lake Co., CO.

582. **Nona Mae**[6] **Flesher** (369.Seldon Elmo[5], 141.Harry Seldom[4], 31.Henry[3], 4.Mary M.[2] Gum, 1.Dorothy "Dolly"[1] Arbogast), b. Jan 29 1929 in Sebastopol, Sonoma Co., CA, d. Dec 4 1990 in Lakeport, Lake Co., CA.
(1) She Married **Darrell Jake Goss**, b. Jul 17 1926 in Loma, Mesa Co., CO.
(2) She Married **Carl Milton Brown**, b. Aug 25 1927 in Meeker, Rio Blanco Co., CO.
   Children by Carl Milton Brown:
   - 768 i. Andy Joe[7] Brown b. Jan 1962.

583. **Ada Angeline**[6] **Hendricks** (372.Ida Josephine[5] Smalling, 148.Aletha Adaline[4] Dunkle, 32.Sarah Jane[3] Flesher, 4.Mary M.[2] Gum, 1.Dorothy "Dolly"[1] Arbogast), b. Sep 1 1891 in Billings, Greene Co., IA.
She Married **Merrick Thayer**, b. Oct 7 1883.
   Children:
   - 769 i. Julia Blanch[7] Thayer b. Nov 24 1926 in Lawrence Co., MO.
     She Married Ivan Leroy Rose.

584. **Claude B.**[6] **Flesher** (375.Paul[5], 157.John Henry[4], 34.William Seybert[3], 4.Mary M.[2] Gum, 1.Dorothy "Dolly"[1] Arbogast), b. Aug 12 1900 in Kansas or Colorado.
Married 1923, **Freda Ruby**, b. 1904 in Michigan (daughter of John E. Ruby).
   Children:
   - 770 i. John Stanford[7] Flesher b. 1925 in Michigan.
     He Married Joanne Melke.

586. **Gorman B.**[6] **Flesher** (375.Paul[5], 157.John Henry[4], 34.William Seybert[3], 4.Mary M.[2] Gum, 1.Dorothy "Dolly"[1] Arbogast), b. Jun 23 1905 in Oklahoma.
He Married **Kathleen Prier**, b. 1907 in Michigan (daughter of William M. Prier).
   Children:
   - 771 i. Donald[7] Flesher b. 1928 in Michigan.
   - 772 ii. Ann Flesher b. 1929 in Michigan.

616. **Charles Benjamin**[6] **Colaw** (420.John Harmon[5], 202.Benjamin Watters[4], 41.Sabina[3] Gum, 5.Adam[2], 1.Dorothy "Dolly"[1] Arbogast), b. Apr 30 1895.
Charlie farmed Kansas land around High Prairie, Fredonia, Rest, Bufand Chanute until the early 1940's. He worked for the Sheriff's office and Police Force from 1944-1964 in Independence, Kansas and Emma would bake goodies and take to the prisoners. Charlie worked for Shiel Plumbing Shop in Fredonia, Kansas from 1968 until he died. They were active in the Nazarene church.
Married in High Prairie, Leavenworth Co., KS, **Emma Sarilda Powell**, b. Sep 25 1897 in Kansas, d. April 1980 in Oklahoma.
   Children:
   - + 773 i. Charles Benjamin[7] Colaw, Jr. b. 1919.
   - + 774 ii. Emerson J. Colaw b. Nov 13 1921.
   - + 775 iii. Marjorie Neil Colaw.

617. **Donald**[6] **Colaw** (420.John Harmon[5], 202.Benjamin Watters[4], 41.Sabina[3] Gum, 5.Adam[2], 1.Dorothy "Dolly"[1] Arbogast), d. Jul 18 1962.
He Married **Nora Sullivan**.
   Children:
   - 776 i. Victor[7] Colaw d. 1971.
   - 777 ii. Orrie Colaw.
   - 778 iii. Max Colaw.

618. **John Orval⁶ Colaw** (420.John Harmon⁵, 202.Benjamin Watters⁴, 41.Sabina³ Gum, 5.Adam², 1.Dorothy "Dolly"¹ Arbogast), b. 1902.
He Married **Francis Kennison**, b. 1912.
Children:
+ 779   i.   John Orval⁷ Colaw, Jr. b. 1930.

619. **Ray Kenneth⁶ Colaw** (420.John Harmon⁵, 202.Benjamin Watters⁴, 41.Sabina³ Gum, 5.Adam², 1.Dorothy "Dolly"¹ Arbogast), b. 1906.
He Married **Clara Muninger**, b. Feb 10 1910, d. 1986.
Children:
+ 780   i.   Frank Edwin⁷ Colaw.
   781   ii.   Ray Kenneth Colaw, Jr..
He Married **Billie Brown**. Billie: Ray was Married again, but do not know who. He has at least one child, Carolyn Rae Colaw who Married **Christopher Joseph**, as well as 2 adopted children Timothy and Carrie.

620. **Ben Wilson⁶ Colaw** (420.John Harmon⁵, 202.Benjamin Watters⁴, 41.Sabina³ Gum, 5.Adam², 1.Dorothy "Dolly"¹ Arbogast).
He Married **Cleora M. Follmer**, b. 1914.
Children:
+ 782   i.   Richard William⁷ Colaw b. 1940.
+ 783   ii.   Jackson Ben Colaw b. 1945.

621. **Robert Ray⁶ Colaw** (421.Franklin Robert⁵, 202.Benjamin Watters⁴, 41.Sabina³ Gum, 5.Adam², 1.Dorothy "Dolly"¹ Arbogast), b. Sep 8 1897, d. Jul 8 1947.
Married Feb 12 1921, **Dorothy Lapham**, b. Sep 19 1896, d. Dec 10 1982.
Children:
+ 784   i.   David Lapham⁷ Colaw b. Oct 3 1923.
+ 785   ii.   Roberta Rea Colaw b. Aug 21 1925.

622. **Mamie Bell⁶ Colaw** (422.Harry Albert⁵, 202.Benjamin Watters⁴, 41.Sabina³ Gum, 5.Adam², 1.Dorothy "Dolly"¹ Arbogast), b. 1901.
She Married **Walter Noltensmeyer**.
Children:
+ 786   i.   Charles Null⁷ Noltensmeyer.

624. **Doris⁶ Wolfe** (424.Ella May⁵ Colaw, 202.Benjamin Watters⁴, 41.Sabina³ Gum, 5.Adam², 1.Dorothy "Dolly"¹ Arbogast), b. 1904.
She Married **George Hess**.
Children:
+ 787   i.   Charles⁷ Hess b. 1925.
+ 788   ii.   George Robert Hess b. 1926.
   789   iii.   Joan Hess.
+ 790   iv.   Gary Lee Hess b. 1933.
+ 791   v.   Delores Jean Hess b. 1935.
   792   vi.   Lavon Irean Hess b. 1941.
   793   vii.   Donald Richard Hess b. 1946.
   794   viii.   James Erwin Hess b. 1949.

625. **Herbert William⁶ Wolfe** (424.Ella May⁵ Colaw, 202.Benjamin Watters⁴, 41.Sabina³ Gum, 5.Adam², 1.Dorothy "Dolly"¹ Arbogast), b. 1909.
He Married **Helen Lavine Cain**.
Children:

+ 795 i. Harve Wesley[7] Wolfe b. 1931.
+ 796 ii. Carolyn Darl Wolfe b. 1934.

629. **Wayne[6] Colaw** (428.Alphorus[5], 204.Dyer W[4], 41.Sabina[3] Gum, 5.Adam[2], 1.Dorothy "Dolly"[1] Arbogast), b. Jan 28 1897, d. July 1971.
He Married **Bertha Wilson**.
Children:
797 i. Betty[7] Colaw.
798 ii. Donald Colaw.

630. **Grace[6] Colaw** (428.Alphorus[5], 204.Dyer W[4], 41.Sabina[3] Gum, 5.Adam[2], 1.Dorothy "Dolly"[1] Arbogast).
She Married **(unknown) Weaver**.
Children:
799 i. Darrell[7] Weaver.

631. **Glen Dyer[6] Colaw** (428.Alphorus[5], 204.Dyer W[4], 41.Sabina[3] Gum, 5.Adam[2], 1.Dorothy "Dolly"[1] Arbogast), b. Apr 20 1907, d. May 1980.
He Married **Leal Manahan**.
Children:
+ 800 i. Russell G.[7] Colaw b. Mar 28 1941.

632. **Merle C.[6] Colaw** (428.Alphorus[5], 204.Dyer W[4], 41.Sabina[3] Gum, 5.Adam[2], 1.Dorothy "Dolly"[1] Arbogast), b. Apr 20 1907, d. May, 1980.
He Married **Lois Lee**.
Children:
801 i. Lee[7] Colaw.

634. **Thornton[6] Colaw** (428.Alphorus[5], 204.Dyer W[4], 41.Sabina[3] Gum, 5.Adam[2], 1.Dorothy "Dolly"[1] Arbogast), b. May 19 1914, d. Jan 1984.
He Married **Bessie Compton**.
Children:
802 i. Sandra[7] Colaw.
803 ii. Suzanne Colaw.

636. **Clay T.[6] Houchin** (430.Otie Viola[5] Gum, 207.Thomas Marion[4], 43.Amos[3], 5.Adam[2], 1.Dorothy "Dolly"[1] Arbogast), b. 1915, d. Aug 4 1997 in St. Albans, Kanawha Co., WV.
He Married **Hester E. (Unknown)**.
Children:
804 i. Cecil C.[7] Houchin.

638. **Virginia[6] Houchin** (430.Otie Viola[5] Gum, 207.Thomas Marion[4], 43.Amos[3], 5.Adam[2], 1.Dorothy "Dolly"[1] Arbogast).
She Married **Bert Theodore Hevener** (son of Robert Hevener and Lucy Gragg).
Children:
805 i. Nancy J.[7] Hevener b. 1944 in Lancaster, Lancaster Co., PA, d. Feb 8 1998 in Manheim, Lancaster Co., PA.
Married Sep 20 1961, **Gerald L. Weachter**.

639. **Margaret[6] Houchin** (430.Otie Viola[5] Gum, 207.Thomas Marion[4], 43.Amos[3], 5.Adam[2], 1.Dorothy "Dolly"[1] Arbogast).
She Married **Guy Stone** (son of Scott Winfield Stone and Lela Mae Keller).
Children:
806 i. Daniel Richard[7] Stone.

Daniel and Debra had these children; Amanda Stone and Stacy Stone
Married Nov. 1979 in Gatewood Brethren Church, Fayetteville, Fayette Co., WV, **Debra Ruth Fox**.

640. **Paul Russell[6] Houchin** (430.Otie Viola[5] Gum, 207.Thomas Marion[4], 43.Amos[3], 5.Adam[2], 1.Dorothy "Dolly"[1] Arbogast), b. 1922, d. Feb 16 1993 in Lancaster General Hospital, Lancaster, PA. Paul was a step child.
He Married **Martha Marie Hevener**, b. Nov 20 1925 (daughter of John Hevener and Elva Calhoun), d. Oct 10 1991.

Children:
- 807 i. Charlotte M.[7] Houchin.
- 808 ii. Shirley F. Houchin.

642. **Audrey[6] Houchin** (430.Otie Viola[5] Gum, 207.Thomas Marion[4], 43.Amos[3], 5.Adam[2], 1.Dorothy "Dolly"[1] Arbogast).
She Married **Loman Bryant Pugh**, b. Nov 21 1923 in Arbovale Cem., Arbovale, Pocahontas Co., WV (son of Bryan Pugh and Elva Wilfong), d. Dec 1 1978 in King Daughter Hospital, Staunton, VA.

Children:
- + 809 i. Ronnie[7] Pugh.
- + 810 ii. Roger L. Pugh.
- 811 iii. Judy Pugh. Stepchild.
  She Married **Ronnie White**.
- 812 iv. Karen Pugh.
  Stepchild.
  She Married **Alan Warner**.
- 813 v. Wanda Pugh.
  Stepchild.
  She Married **Denny Gene Wimer**.

645. **Corrinne Ann[6] Gum** (431.Roy McKinley[5], 207.Thomas Marion[4], 43.Amos[3], 5.Adam[2], 1.Dorothy "Dolly"[1] Arbogast), b. Nov 2 1930.
(1) Married May 28 1948 in Charleston, Kanawha Co., WV, **William Richardson**. .

Children by William Richardson:
- 814 i. Ann Leslie[7] Richardson b. Jan 15 1950.

(2) She Married **Eugene Lee Slack**

Children by Eugene Lee Slack:
- 815 ii. Kimberly Gene Slack b. Jul 22 1960.

647. **Paul Roy[6] Gum** (433.Wardell Clark[5], 207.Thomas Marion[4], 43.Amos[3], 5.Adam[2], 1.Dorothy "Dolly"[1] Arbogast), b. Jun 10 1927.
Married Jul 28 1961 in Hagerstown, Washington Co., MD, **Bertha Lee Galford**, b. Jan 28 1940 (daughter of Paul Ardell Galford and Ora Gray Buzzard).

Children:
- 816 i. Kevin Timothy[7] Gum b. Nov 18 1964.
  Married 2001, **Regina Zelda Cassell**, b. Aug 18 1955.

648. **Mary Agatha[6] Gum** (433.Wardell Clark[5], 207.Thomas Marion[4], 43.Amos[3], 5.Adam[2], 1.Dorothy "Dolly"[1] Arbogast), b. Oct 9 1928.
She Married **Eldon Gray Galford**, b. Feb 17 1925 (son of Bernard Galford and Elvettie Friel).

Children:
- 817 i. Patrice Sue[7] Galford b. Sep 4 1950 in Marlinton, Pocahontas Co., WV.
- 818 ii. Sharon Ann Galford b. Feb 16 1951 in Marlinton, Pocahontas Co., WV.
- 819 iii. Eldon Gray Galford II b. Nov 7 1957 in Marlinton, Pocahontas Co., WV.

    820   iv.   Steven Galford.

667. **Freda Jeanne**[6] **Gum** (460.George William[5], 234.Nathaniel Meade[4], 65.George Wasgington[3], 9.Jesse[2], 1.Dorothy "Dolly"[1] Arbogast). Lived in Texas, 1975
She Married **A J Christman**.
    Children:
    821   i.   Keri[7] Christman.
    822   ii.   David Christman.

669. **Nell Katherine**[6] **Gum** (462.Roy Calvin[5], 235.William Oliver[4], 65.George Wasgington[3], 9.Jesse[2], 1.Dorothy "Dolly"[1] Arbogast), b. Jul 22 1921. Lived in Twist, WA
She Married **Kenneth R Duncan**.
    Children:
    823   i.   Kenneth Roy[7] Duncan b. Jun 14 1943.

672. **George Richard**[6] **Gum** (462.Roy Calvin[5], 235.William Oliver[4], 65.George Wasgington[3], 9.Jesse[2], 1.Dorothy "Dolly"[1] Arbogast), b. Apr 03 1933. Lived in Hutchison, KS
He Married **Dorothy Anna Nevius**.
    Children:
    824   i.   Dorothea Louise[7] Gum b. Aug 23 1958.
    825   ii.   Patricia Ann Gum b. Aug 09 1959.
    826   iii.   Barbara Lynn Gum b. Oct 09 1960.
    827   iv.   Penny Laurene Gum b. May 22 1966.

677. **Merwin Wells**[6] **Amerine** (468.Lois T[5] Gum, 238.Edgar Haddon[4], 65.George Wasgington[3], 9.Jesse[2], 1.Dorothy "Dolly"[1] Arbogast), b. Apr 21 1923.
He Married **Nancy Cavan**, b. in Detroit, Wayne Co., MI.
    Children:
    828   i.   Cavan Wells[7] Amerine b. Mar 01 1944.
    829   ii.   Barbara Joyce Amerine b. Oct 06 1948.

678. **Reagan Haddon**[6] **Amerine** (468.Lois T[5] Gum, 238.Edgar Haddon[4], 65.George Wasgington[3], 9.Jesse[2], 1.Dorothy "Dolly"[1] Arbogast), b. Apr 10 1924 in Oakdale, Stanislaus Co., CA.
He Married **Jean Pilcher**, b. in Denver, Arapaho Co., CO.
    Children:
    830   i.   Ronald Reagan[7] Amerine b. Feb 11 1947.
    831   ii.   Gary Dean Amerine b. Jun 24 1950.

679. **Richard Dean**[6] **Amerine** (468.Lois T[5] Gum, 238.Edgar Haddon[4], 65.George Wasgington[3], 9.Jesse[2], 1.Dorothy "Dolly"[1] Arbogast).
Married in Modesto, Stanislaus Co., CA, **Carolyn Schoenfield**.
    Children:
    832   i.   Richard Dana[7] Amerine b. Oct 21 1951.
    833   ii.   David Mitchell Amerine b. Aug 31 1952.
    834   iii.   Corinne Dee Amerine b. Oct 19 1954.

680. **Russell Lynn**[6] **Gum** (471.Rowland Hughes[5], 238.Edgar Haddon[4], 65.George Wasgington[3], 9.Jesse[2], 1.Dorothy "Dolly"[1] Arbogast), b. Feb 11 1943. Lives in Tucson, AZ
He Married **Nancy Raper**, b. in Modesto, Stanislaus Co., CA.
    Children:
    835   i.   Richard Bryan[7] Gum b. Jun 28 1962.

681. **Martin Louis**[6] **Gum** (471.Rowland Hughes[5], 238.Edgar Haddon[4], 65.George Wasgington[3], 9.Jesse[2], 1.Dorothy "Dolly"[1] Arbogast), b. Jan 17 1950.

Children:
836   i.   Aaron[7] Gum b. 1973.

683. **Byron Rudd[6] Graham** (476.Edrie Maurine[5] Miller, 240.Ida May[4] Gum, 65.George Wasgington[3], 9.Jesse[2], 1.Dorothy "Dolly"[1] Arbogast), b. Jul 02 1940 in St. Louis, St. Louis Co., MO.
He Married **Janice Elaine Beacom**, b. in Arlington National Cem., Arlington, VA.
Children:
837   i.   Jennifer Dawn[7] Graham b. Aug 02 1974.

685. **Richard E[6] Ruppert** (477.Eva Marie[5] Miller, 240.Ida May[4] Gum, 65.George Wasgington[3], 9.Jesse[2], 1.Dorothy "Dolly"[1] Arbogast), b. Apr 08 1948.
He Married **Donna Stanley**.
Children:
838   i.   Angela Kay[7] Ruppert b. Dec 27 1970.
839   ii.   Cynthia Ruppert b. Nov 1973.

694. **Winfield Winson[6] Cantrell** (484.James Virgil[5], 260.Sarah Jane[4] Stinson, 70.Talitha[3] Gum, 9.Jesse[2], 1.Dorothy "Dolly"[1] Arbogast), b. Feb 25 1918.
He Married **Ruth Lamb**.
Children:
+ 840   i.   Wilma Jean[7] Cantrell b. May 26 1939.
+ 841   ii.   Barbara Dean Cantrell b. May 05 1941.
+ 842   iii.   Patricia Ann Cantrell.

695. **Vergie Francis[6] Cantrell** (484.James Virgil[5], 260.Sarah Jane[4] Stinson, 70.Talitha[3] Gum, 9.Jesse[2], 1.Dorothy "Dolly"[1] Arbogast).
Married c 1941, **James Herbert Hicks**, b. Sep 23 1920.
Children:
843   i.   James William[7] Hicks b. Jun 12 1942.
844   ii.   Dixie Francis Hicks b. Sep 23 1943.
845   iii.   Walter Herbert Hicks b. Feb 17 1949.
846   iv.   Melodie Lee Hicks b. Oct 02 1952.
847   v.   Nina Jo Hicks b. Mar 29 1957.

696. **James Paul[6] Cantrell** (484.James Virgil[5], 260.Sarah Jane[4] Stinson, 70.Talitha[3] Gum, 9.Jesse[2], 1.Dorothy "Dolly"[1] Arbogast), b. Aug 20 1932.
He Married **Margiele Pearl Sharon**, b. May 08 1930.
Children:
848   i.   Randell Lee[7] Cantrell b. Oct 07 1955.
849   ii.   Wendell Kent Cantrell b. Jan 09 1959.
850   iii.   Lyndell Brent Cantrell b. May 13 1962.
851   iv.   Kelly Marie Cantrell b. Jul 30 1964.
852   v.   Kathi Sue Cantrell b. Nov 06 1968.

699. **Randell Glenn[6] Hinkle** (492.Emil Fred[5], 263.Pearl[4] Stinson, 70.Talitha[3] Gum, 9.Jesse[2], 1.Dorothy "Dolly"[1] Arbogast), b. Feb 25 1942.
He Married **Edna Jo Osborn**.
Children:
853   i.   Wesley Kevin[7] Hinkle.
854   ii.   Michael Glenn Hinkle.
855   iii.   Shawn Christopher Hinkle.
856   iv.   Dustin Timothy Hinkle.

702. **William Larry⁶ Ruark** (495.William Lloyd⁵, 265.Lula⁴ Stinson, 70.Talitha³ Gum, 9.Jesse², 1.Dorothy "Dolly"¹ Arbogast), b. Jan 06 1938.
He Married **Linda Lou Beaty**, b. Aug 26 1940.
Children:
- 857 i. Kristie Kay⁷ Ruark.
- 858 ii. William Shea Ruark.
- 859 iii. Sherri Ann Ruark.

703. **Linda Suzanna⁶ Ruark** (495.William Lloyd⁵, 265.Lula⁴ Stinson, 70.Talitha³ Gum, 9.Jesse², 1.Dorothy "Dolly"¹ Arbogast), b. May 15 1945.
She Married **Michael Richardson**, b. Jan 06 1944.
Children:
- 860 i. Michael David⁷ Richardson.
- 861 ii. Angela Suzanne Richardson.

Generation Seven

704. **Florence Wauneta⁷ Graham** (499.Louisa Jeanetta⁶ Page, 271.Sarah Elizabeth⁵ Huffstedtler, 80.Louisa Janetta⁴ Gum, 13.Jesse S.³, 3.Isaac², 1.Dorothy "Dolly"¹ Arbogast), b. Dec 17 1904 in Fontana, Miami Co., KS, d. Dec 15 1984, buried in Elm Grove; Cadmus Co., KS.
Married Jan 10 1923 in Paola, Miami Co., KS, **Virgil Osborn England**, b. Feb 24 1905 in Lincoln, Logan Co., IL, d. Jun 25 1988, buried in Elm Grove; Cadmus Co., KS.
Children:
- 862 i. Wanda Madge⁸ England b. Oct 21 1923 in Fontana, Miami Co., KS.
  Married May 17 1942 in Fontana, Miami Co., KS, **Herman Eldon Keitel**, b. Oct 11 1922.
- 863 ii. Virgil Lavern England b. Dec 6 1925 in Fontana, Miami Co., KS.

706. **Royal Edward⁷ Gum** (508.Melvin C.⁶, 288.Edward Gustavus⁵, 89.John Royal⁴, 14.Isaac C.³, 3.Isaac², 1.Dorothy "Dolly"¹ Arbogast).
Married Jun 09 1950, **Beverly Ann Neumann**.
Children:
- 864 i. Janet Sue⁸ Gum b. Feb 09 1952.
- 865 ii. Shirley Diane Gum b. Jul 07 1953.
- 866 iii. Nancy Kay Gum b. Jan 10 1959.

713. **Lowell⁷ Hampton, Jr.** (521.Marie M.⁶ Gum, 296.John Leonard⁵, 90.James Johnson⁴, 14.Isaac C.³, 3.Isaac², 1.Dorothy "Dolly"¹ Arbogast).
Children:
- 867 i. Dennis⁸ Hampton.
- 868 ii. John Hampton.
- 869 iii. Donald Hampton.

721. **Raymond Edward⁷ Vonburg** (528.Erma Charlotte⁶ Gum, 297.James Edward⁵, 90.James Johnson⁴, 14.Isaac C.³, 3.Isaac², 1.Dorothy "Dolly"¹ Arbogast), b. Nov 27 1936.
Married 1958, **Barbara Wilson**.
Children:
- 870 i. Brenda Jo⁸ Vonburg.
- 871 ii. Pamela Vonburg.
- 872 iii. Patricia Vonburg.
- 873 iv. Karen Vonburg.

874	v.	John Vonburg.
875	vi.	Brian Vonburg.
876	vii.	Jeff Vonburg.
877	viii.	Michael Vonburg.

722. **Erma Jean**[7] **Vonburg** (528.Erma Charlotte[6] Gum, 297.James Edward[5], 90.James Johnson[4], 14.Isaac C.[3], 3.Isaac[2], 1.Dorothy "Dolly"[1] Arbogast), b. Jul 14 1938.
She Married **Jack Wall**.
> *Children:*
> 878   i.   Jack[8] Wall, Jr..
> 879   ii.   Sherrill Wall.
> 880   iii.   James Wall.

723. **Paul Laverne**[7] **Vonburg** (528.Erma Charlotte[6] Gum, 297.James Edward[5], 90.James Johnson[4], 14.Isaac C.[3], 3.Isaac[2], 1.Dorothy "Dolly"[1] Arbogast), b. May 18 1940.
He Married **Shirley (Unknown)**.
> *Children:*
> 881   i.   Vernon Ray[8] Vonburg.
> 882   ii.   David Vonburg.
> 883   iii.   Mary Vonburg.
> 884   iv.   Paula Vonburg.
> 885   v.   Tammy Vonburg.
> 886   vi.   Scott Vonburg.
> 887   vii.   Chad Everett.

724. **Benjamin J.**[7] **Vonburg, Jr.** (529.Ardelene Mardell[6] Gum, 297.James Edward[5], 90.James Johnson[4], 14.Isaac C.[3], 3.Isaac[2], 1.Dorothy "Dolly"[1] Arbogast), d. 1946.
He Married **Susan Hasselblock**.
> *Children:*
> 888   i.   Craig Allen[8] Vonburg.
> 889   ii.   Christina Ann Vonburg.

725. **Steven Blair**[7] **Vonburg** (529.Ardelene Mardell[6] Gum, 297.James Edward[5], 90.James Johnson[4], 14.Isaac C.[3], 3.Isaac[2], 1.Dorothy "Dolly"[1] Arbogast), b. Mar 27 1951.
He Married **Peggy Salatino**.
> *Children:*
> 890   i.   Matthew[8] Vonburg.
> 891   ii.   Anthony Vonburg.

726. **Susan Mardell**[7] **Vonburg** (529.Ardelene Mardell[6] Gum, 297.James Edward[5], 90.James Johnson[4], 14.Isaac C.[3], 3.Isaac[2], 1.Dorothy "Dolly"[1] Arbogast), b. Oct 13 1952.
She Married **George Dudley**.
> *Children:*
> 892   i.   Krissa Suzanna[8] Vonburg.

727. **Judith Rosemary**[7] **Gum** (531.Luthur Aaron[6], 297.James Edward[5], 90.James Johnson[4], 14.Isaac C.[3], 3.Isaac[2], 1.Dorothy "Dolly"[1] Arbogast), b. 1946.
She Married **Eric Bridge**.
> *Children:*
> 893   i.   Rachel[8] Bridge.
> 894   ii.   Morgan Bridge.

728. **Gordon Alan**[7] **Buvarskis** (532.Mary Edyth[6] Gum, 297.James Edward[5], 90.James Johnson[4], 14.Isaac C.[3], 3.Isaac[2], 1.Dorothy "Dolly"[1] Arbogast), b. Oct 31 1948.
(1) He Married **Barbara June Snyder**. .

Children by *Barbara June Snyder:*
- 895 i. Gordon Richard[8] Buvarskis b. 1967.

(2) Married Jul 30 1983, **Loretta Rose Nevarro**

729. **Brenda Lucille**[7] **Gum** (533.Gorden Isaac[6], 297.James Edward[5], 90.James Johnson[4], 14.Isaac C.[3], 3.Isaac[2], 1.Dorothy "Dolly"[1] Arbogast), b. 1950.
She Married **Larry Wayne Eyman**.
Children:
- 896 i. Kevin[8] Eyman.
- 897 ii. Janara Eyman.

731. **Diana Faye**[7] **Gum** (533.Gorden Isaac[6], 297.James Edward[5], 90.James Johnson[4], 14.Isaac C.[3], 3.Isaac[2], 1.Dorothy "Dolly"[1] Arbogast), b. 1954.
She Married **David Ritter**.
Children:
- 898 i. Nicole[8] Ritter.

732. **Marvin Blaine**[7] **Gum** (534.Marvin Udell[6], 297.James Edward[5], 90.James Johnson[4], 14.Isaac C.[3], 3.Isaac[2], 1.Dorothy "Dolly"[1] Arbogast), b. 1948.
Married 1979, **Mary Elizabeth Tokum**.
Children:
- 899 i. Aaron Nicholas[8] Gum.
- 900 ii. Andrew Christopher Gum.
- 901 iii. Melvin Alexander Gum.

733. **Janis Ilene**[7] **Gum** (534.Marvin Udell[6], 297.James Edward[5], 90.James Johnson[4], 14.Isaac C.[3], 3.Isaac[2], 1.Dorothy "Dolly"[1] Arbogast).
She Married **Andrew Boren**.
Children:
- 902 i. Sheila Ilene[8] Boren.
- 903 ii. Shawn Alfred Owen.

734. **Dennis Lynn**[7] **Gum** (534.Marvin Udell[6], 297.James Edward[5], 90.James Johnson[4], 14.Isaac C.[3], 3.Isaac[2], 1.Dorothy "Dolly"[1] Arbogast), b. 1951.
Married 1974, **Karen Ann Chambers**.
Children:
- 904 i. Julie Ann[8] Gum.
- 905 ii. Dennis Lynn Gum III.
- 906 iii. Melissa Elizabeth Gum.
- 907 iv. Donald Eric Gum.
- 908 v. Karol Ryne Gum.

738. **Sharlyn Lavon**[7] **Painter** (536.Zepha Edan[6] Gum, 297.James Edward[5], 90.James Johnson[4], 14.Isaac C.[3], 3.Isaac[2], 1.Dorothy "Dolly"[1] Arbogast), b. 1953.
She Married **Curtis Robert Woodall**.
Children:
- 909 i. Melissa Lavon[8] Woodall.

742. **Reba Arlene**[7] **Williams** (537.Maggie Alberta[6] Gum, 297.James Edward[5], 90.James Johnson[4], 14.Isaac C.[3], 3.Isaac[2], 1.Dorothy "Dolly"[1] Arbogast), b. Feb 20 1933.
Married Oct 24 1954, **Robert Hunsacker**.
Children:
- 910 i. Ursula Fay[8] Hunsacker b. 1955.

911   ii.   Laura Mae Hunsacker b. 1955.
912   iii.   Renita Jane Hunsacker b. 1957.

743. **Thomas Edward**[7] **Gum** (538.Dallas Edward[6], 297.James Edward[5], 90.James Johnson[4], 14.Isaac C.[3], 3.Isaac[2], 1.Dorothy "Dolly"[1] Arbogast), b. Mar 01 1931.
He Married **Norma Jean Dirks**, b. Aug 02 1927.
                 Children:
913   i.   Thomas Edward[8] Gum b. 1955.
914   ii.   Robert Daniel Gum b. 1956.
915   iii.   David Wyett Gum b. 1957.
916   iv.   Richard Gum b. 1960.
917   v.   Mary Katherine Gum b. 1963.

744. **Robert Edward**[7] **Gum** (539.Howard Schubert[6], 297.James Edward[5], 90.James Johnson[4], 14.Isaac C.[3], 3.Isaac[2], 1.Dorothy "Dolly"[1] Arbogast), b. 1928, d. 1965.
He Married **Eudora Nadine Watkins**.
                 Children:
918   i.   Cathy Rae[8] Gum b. 1956.

745. **William Kenneth**[7] **Gum** (539.Howard Schubert[6], 297.James Edward[5], 90.James Johnson[4], 14.Isaac C.[3], 3.Isaac[2], 1.Dorothy "Dolly"[1] Arbogast), b. Apr 22 1929.
He Married **Margaret Greeley**.
                 Children:
919   i.   Sara Jane[8] Gum.

746. **Mary Alice**[7] **Gum** (539.Howard Schubert[6], 297.James Edward[5], 90.James Johnson[4], 14.Isaac C.[3], 3.Isaac[2], 1.Dorothy "Dolly"[1] Arbogast).
She Married **Robert Grant**.
                 Children:
920   i.   Joe Lynn[8] Grant b. 1950.
921   ii.   Gayla Jean Grant b. 1952.
922   iii.   Trudy Layne Grant b. 1954.
923   iv.   Bobbi Kay Grant b. 1957.
924   v.   Kevin Lee Grant.
925   vi.   Shelley Rene Grant b. 1960.

747. **Clara Lou**[7] **Gum** (539.Howard Schubert[6], 297.James Edward[5], 90.James Johnson[4], 14.Isaac C.[3], 3.Isaac[2], 1.Dorothy "Dolly"[1] Arbogast), b. Sep 21 1934.
She Married **Harold Lorraine Osborne**.
                 Children:
926   i.   Terry Lorraine[8] Osborne b. 1953.
927   ii.   Gary Gene Osborne b. 1956.

762. **Lana Janice**[7] **Tevis** (544.Ellen Jane[6] Kell, 311.Blanche Mahalia[5] Ray, 102.Sarah Jane[4] Gum, 17.James Riley[3], 3.Isaac[2], 1.Dorothy "Dolly"[1] Arbogast), b. Dec 17 1940.
Married Jul 04 1965 in Homer, Cortland Co., NY, **Gerald Gorden Griffin**, b. Jul 12 1940 in Cortland Co., NY. **Gerald**: Son or Gorden Herbert Griffin and Gertrude Anne Nuttall.
                 Children:
+ 928   i.   David Gerald[8] Griffin b. Dec 14 1969.
929   ii.   Janice Kathleen Griffin b. Nov 04 1971 in Falls Church, Fairfax Co., VA.

773. **Charles Benjamin**[7] **Colaw, Jr.** (616.Charles Benjamin[6], 420.John Harmon[5], 202.Benjamin Watters[4], 41.Sabina[3] Gum, 5.Adam[2], 1.Dorothy "Dolly"[1] Arbogast), b. 1919 in Log cabin, High Prairie Church, Leavenworth Co., KS.
Chuck farmed all his life until 1946. He also worked for Standard Oil

and in a weapons shell loading plant at Parsons, Kansas during WWII. He began his first pastorate November, 1946 in rural Sabetha, Kansas then Sharon Springs Kansas for three years and then Oakley Kansas for 3 years. In 1956, he became District Superintendent and pastored a church in Blackwell, Oklahoma. He started the Wesleyan Church in Bartlesville Oklahoma in September 1959 and served for 4 years. He returned to Bartlesville and retired July, 1990 as District Superintendent with 34years of service. After retirement, he served as interim Pastor/Administrator of Bartlesville First Wesleyan for 10 months. He was instrumental in locating Bartlesville Wesleyan College and arranging for the purchase of the present property. They bestowed a honorary Doctor's Degree on him in May, 1986. He continues to serve as Chairman of the Board of Trustees for the college and travels some for them as a "Good Will Ambassador." Recently, he was awarded a high honor in Rotary, "Paul Harris Fellow" award. They have traveled extensively, including a John Wesley Study Tour in England and two mission tours to Africa.

Married Aug 22 1937, **Mabel Estella Kauth**, b. Sep 27 1917 in Rural Wilson County.
Children:
+ 930   i.   Charles Dwayne^8 Colaw b. 1938.
+ 931   ii.   Nathan Rena Colaw b. 1941.
+ 932   iii.   Max Arthur Colaw b. 1945.
+ 933   iv.   Stephen Olin Colaw b. 1947.
   934   v.   Judith Charlene Colaw b. 1954.
   935   vi.   Joseph Wayne Colaw b. 1955.

774. **Emerson J.^{7} Colaw** (616.Charles Benjamin^6, 420.John Harmon^5, 202.Benjamin Watters^4, 41.Sabina^3 Gum, 5.Adam^2, 1.Dorothy "Dolly"^{1} Arbogast), b. Nov 13 1921 in Wilson Co., KS.
He Married **Jane (Unknown)**.
Children:
+ 936   i.   Prudence Elaine^8 Colaw.
   937   ii.   Deborah Jane Colaw.
   938   iii.   Marcella Louise Colaw.
   939   iv.   David Emerson Colaw.

775. **Marjorie Neil^7 Colaw** (616.Charles Benjamin^6, 420.John Harmon^5, 202.Benjamin Watters^4, 41.Sabina^3 Gum, 5.Adam^2, 1.Dorothy "Dolly"^{1} Arbogast).
She Married **Calvin Jantz**.
Children:
   940   i.   Carolyn M. Joel^8 Colaw.

779. **John Orval^7 Colaw, Jr.** (618.John Orval^6, 420.John Harmon^5, 202.Benjamin Watters^4, 41.Sabina^3 Gum, 5.Adam^2, 1.Dorothy "Dolly"^{1} Arbogast), b. 1930.
He Married **Verda Mahanay**, b. 1932.
Children:
   941   i.   John Orval^8 Colaw, III b. 1956.
   942   ii.   Debra Ann Colaw b. 1958.
   943   iii.   Sandra Kay Colaw b. 1966.

780. **Frank Edwin^7 Colaw** (619.Ray Kenneth^6, 420.John Harmon^5, 202.Benjamin Watters^4, 41.Sabina^3 Gum, 5.Adam^2, 1.Dorothy "Dolly"^{1} Arbogast).
He Married **Ellen Ginzelman**.
Children:
   944   i.   Frank Dean^8 Colaw.
   945   ii.   John Michael Colaw.

782. **Richard William^7 Colaw** (620.Ben Wilson^6, 420.John Harmon^5, 202.Benjamin Watters^4, 41.Sabina^3 Gum, 5.Adam^2, 1.Dorothy "Dolly"^{1} Arbogast), b. 1940.

He Married **Bettie Kincade**, b. 1941.
Children:
- 946   i.   Deborah Renae[8] Colaw b. 1961.
- 947   ii. Tracy Lynn Colaw b. 1965.

783. **Jackson Ben[7] Colaw** (620.Ben Wilson[6], 420.John Harmon[5], 202.Benjamin Watters[4], 41.Sabina[3] Gum, 5.Adam[2], 1.Dorothy "Dolly"[1] Arbogast), b. 1945.
He Married **Judith Mary Martin**, b. 1946.
Children:
- 948   i.   Lisa Christina[8] Colaw b. 1968.
- 949   ii. Julie Marie Colaw b. 1971.

784. **David Lapham[7] Colaw** (621.Robert Ray[6], 421.Franklin Robert[5], 202.Benjamin Watters[4], 41.Sabina[3] Gum, 5.Adam[2], 1.Dorothy "Dolly"[1] Arbogast), b. Oct 3 1923.
Married Jul 19 1946, **Helen Louise Lehr**, b. Mar 26 1925.
Children:
- + 950   i.   Barbara Sue[8] Colaw b. Jun 27 1947.
-   951   ii. Sandra Louise Colaw b. Nov 5 1949.
- + 952   iii. Virginia Marie Colaw b. Sep 12 1956.

785. **Roberta Rea[7] Colaw** (621.Robert Ray[6], 421.Franklin Robert[5], 202.Benjamin Watters[4], 41.Sabina[3] Gum, 5.Adam[2], 1.Dorothy "Dolly"[1] Arbogast), b. Aug 21 1925.
Married May 31 1953, **John Francis Moran**.
Children:
- 953   i.   Bruce[8] Moran b. Oct 30 1954.
- 954   ii. Mark Moran b. Sep 13 1956.
- 955   iii. Jeralyn Moran b. 1959.
  Married Oct 26 1985, **Patrick J. Cady**.
- 956   iv. Steven Moran.

786. **Charles Null[7] Noltensmeyer** (622.Mamie Bell[6] Colaw, 422.Harry Albert[5], 202.Benjamin Watters[4], 41.Sabina[3] Gum, 5.Adam[2], 1.Dorothy "Dolly"[1] Arbogast).
He Married **Doris Manley**.
Children:
- 957   i.   Thomas[8] Noltensmeyer.
- 958   ii. Ronda Noltensmeyer. She
  Married **Gary Wilson**.
- 959   iii. Karen Noltensmeyer.

787. **Charles[7] Hess** (624.Doris[6] Wolfe, 424.Ella May[5] Colaw, 202.Benjamin Watters[4], 41.Sabina[3] Gum, 5.Adam[2], 1.Dorothy "Dolly"[1] Arbogast), b. 1925.
He Married **Shirley Johnson**.
Children:
- 960   i.   John[8] Hess b. 1958.
  John was an adopted child.
- 961   ii. Bradley Hess b. 1960.
  Bradley was an adopted child.
- 962   iii. Lisa Ann.

788. **George Robert[7] Hess** (624.Doris[6] Wolfe, 424.Ella May[5] Colaw, 202.Benjamin Watters[4], 41.Sabina[3] Gum, 5.Adam[2], 1.Dorothy "Dolly"[1] Arbogast), b. 1926.
He Married **Thelma Hartzell**.
Children:
- 963   i.   Deborah[8] Hess b. 1953.

964 ii. Cynthia Joan Hess b. 1959.

790. **Gary Lee⁷ Hess** (624.Doris⁶ Wolfe, 424.Ella May⁵ Colaw, 202.Benjamin Watters⁴, 41.Sabina³ Gum, 5.Adam², 1.Dorothy "Dolly"¹ Arbogast), b. 1933.
He Married **Joan Copenhafer**.
    Children:
965 i. Kevin⁸ Hess b. 1967.

791. **Delores Jean⁷ Hess** (624.Doris⁶ Wolfe, 424.Ella May⁵ Colaw, 202.Benjamin Watters⁴, 41.Sabina³ Gum, 5.Adam², 1.Dorothy "Dolly"¹ Arbogast), b. 1935.
She Married **Henry Kirk**.
    Children:
966 i. Richard Douglass⁸ Kirk b. 1967.
967 ii. Tracey Kirk b. 1968.
968 iii. Angela Kirk b. 1968.

795. **Harve Wesley⁷ Wolfe** (625.Herbert William⁶, 424.Ella May⁵ Colaw, 202.Benjamin Watters⁴, 41.Sabina³ Gum, 5.Adam², 1.Dorothy "Dolly"¹ Arbogast), b. 1931.
He Married **Lora S. McPherren**, b. 1931.
    Children:
969 i. Steven Wesley⁸ Wolfe b. 1954.
970 ii. Kimberly Darl Wolfe b. 1956.
971 iii. Richard McPherren Wolfe b. 1958.
972 iv. Kathleen Darl Wolfe b. 1959.
973 v. Charles William Wolfe b. 1961.

796. **Carolyn Darl⁷ Wolfe** (625.Herbert William⁶, 424.Ella May⁵ Colaw, 202.Benjamin Watters⁴, 41.Sabina³ Gum, 5.Adam², 1.Dorothy "Dolly"¹ Arbogast), b. 1934.
She Married **Peter Allen Nei**, b. 1932.
    Children:
974 i. Mark Allen⁸ Nei b. 1955.
975 ii. Scott William Nei b. 1957.
976 iii. Bric Lee Nei b. 1962.

800. **Russell G.⁷ Colaw** (631.Glen Dyer⁶, 428.Alphorus⁵, 204.Dyer W⁴, 41.Sabina³ Gum, 5.Adam², 1.Dorothy "Dolly"¹ Arbogast), b. Mar 28 1941, d. May 4 1984. (
1) He Married **Denny Holub**, b. in Wyoming.
    Children by *Denny Holub*:
977 i. Glenn⁸ Colaw.
    Lived in Normal, IL
978 ii. Gail Colaw b. in card.
    Lives in Farmington, IL
979 iii. Gary Colaw b. in Perkin, Tazewell Co., IL.

(2) Married in Bloomington, McLean Co., IL, **Dixie Harmon**.

809. **Ronnie⁷ Pugh** (642.Audrey⁶ Houchin, 430.Otie Viola⁵ Gum, 207.Thomas Marion⁴, 43.Amos³, 5.Adam², 1.Dorothy "Dolly"¹ Arbogast).
Married Jun 14 1885 in Oakland, Garrett Co., MD, **Barbara Kisner** (daughter of William Kisner).
    Children:
980 i. Aaron⁸ Pugh.
981 ii. Calep Pugh.
982 iii. Noah Pugh.
983 iv. Ethan Pugh.

810. **Roger L.**[7] **Pugh** (642.Audrey[6] Houchin, 430.Otie Viola[5] Gum, 207.Thomas Marion[4], 43.Amos[3], 5.Adam[2], 1.Dorothy "Dolly"[1] Arbogast). Stepchild.
He Married **Jeannie Kerr**.
   Children:
   + 984 i. Bryan[8] Pugh.

840. **Wilma Jean**[7] **Cantrell** (694.Winfield Winson[6], 484.James Virgil[5], 260.Sarah Jane[4] Stinson, 70.Talitha[3] Gum, 9.Jesse[2], 1.Dorothy "Dolly"[1] Arbogast), b. May 26 1939.
She Married **Leonard Avon Snyder**, b. Aug 21 1938.
   Children:
   985 i. David Scott[8] Snyder.
   986 ii. Mary Ann Snyder.

841. **Barbara Dean**[7] **Cantrell** (694.Winfield Winson[6], 484.James Virgil[5], 260.Sarah Jane[4] Stinson, 70.Talitha[3] Gum, 9.Jesse[2], 1.Dorothy "Dolly"[1] Arbogast), b. May 05 1941.
She Married **Gary Lynn Graton**, b. Jun 21 1940.
   Children:
   987 i. Gary[8] Graton.
   988 ii. Jeffery Dan Graton.
   989 iii. Roger Dale Graton.
   990 iv. Susan Lynn Graton.

842. **Particia Ann**[7] **Cantrell** (694.Winfield Winson[6], 484.James Virgil[5], 260.Sarah Jane[4] Stinson, 70.Talitha[3] Gum, 9.Jesse[2], 1.Dorothy "Dolly"[1] Arbogast).
She Married **Jerry Lynn Hood**, b. Jun 1936.
   Children:
   991 i. Melissa Kay[8] Hood.
   992 ii. Pamela Hood.

Generation Eight

928. **David Gerald**[8] **Griffin** (762.Lana Janice[7] Tevis, 544.Ellen Jane[6] Kell, 311.Blanche Mahalia[5] Ray, 102.Sarah Jane[4] Gum, 17.James Riley[3], 3.Isaac[2], 1.Dorothy "Dolly"[1] Arbogast), b. Dec 14 1969 in Falls Church, Fairfax Co., VA. Married Before 1980 in Henry Co., VA, **Julie Lauraine Ryder**, b. 27 Dec 1965 (daughter of James Ishmal Ryder and Dorothy Kay Smallwood).
   Children:
   993 i. Jennifer Lauraine[9] Grifffin b. 31 May 1980.
   + 994 ii. Joanne Dawn Griffin b. 28 Jul 1981.

930. **Charles Dwayne**[8] **Colaw** (773.Charles Benjamin[7], 616.Charles Benjamin[6], 420.John Harmon[5], 202.Benjamin Watters[4], 41.Sabina[3] Gum, 5.Adam[2], 1.Dorothy "Dolly"[1] Arbogast), b. 1938. He Married **June R. Burton**, b. 1938.
   Children:
   995 i. David Dwayne[9] Colaw b. 1959.
   996 ii. Kathy Leutta Colaw b. 1961.
   997 iii. Lucinda Ann Colaw b. 1964.

931. **Nathan Rena**[8] **Colaw** (773.Charles Benjamin[7], 616.Charles Benjamin[6], 420.John Harmon[5], 202.Benjamin Watters[4], 41.Sabina[3] Gum, 5.Adam[2], 1.Dorothy "Dolly"[1] Arbogast), b. 1941. He Married **Betty Ann Friend**.
   Children:
   998 i. Shari Renee[9] Colaw b. 1965.

999 ii. Derrel Emerson Colaw b. 1967.
1000 iii. Sheila Suzanne Colaw b. 1969.

932. **Max Arthur⁸ Colaw** (773.Charles Benjamin⁷, 616.Charles Benjamin⁶, 420.John Harmon⁵, 202.Benjamin Watters⁴, 41.Sabina³ Gum, 5.Adam², 1.Dorothy "Dolly"¹ Arbogast), b. 1945. He Married **Ruth Ann Maness**.
    Children:
    1001 i. Stephen Lloyd⁹ Colaw b. 1970.

933. **Stephen Olin⁸ Colaw** (773.Charles Benjamin⁷, 616.Charles Benjamin⁶, 420.John Harmon⁵, 202.Benjamin Watters⁴, 41.Sabina³ Gum, 5.Adam², 1.Dorothy "Dolly"¹ Arbogast), b. 1947. He Married **Vanita Kay Barrows**.
    Children:
    1002 i. Julie Michelle⁹ Colaw b. 1970.

936. **Prudence Elaine⁸ Colaw** (774.Emerson J.⁷, 616.Charles Benjamin⁶, 420.John Harmon⁵, 202.Benjamin Watters⁴, 41.Sabina³ Gum, 5.Adam², 1.Dorothy "Dolly"¹ Arbogast). She Married **Larry Klinger**.
    Children:
    1003 i. Jeff⁹ Klinger b. 1967.
    1004 ii. Robbie Klinger b. 1970.
    1005 iii. Kristin Klinger b. 1975.

950. **Barbara Sue⁸ Colaw** (784.David Lapham⁷, 621.Robert Ray⁶, 421.Franklin Robert⁵, 202.Benjamin Watters⁴, 41.Sabina³ Gum, 5.Adam², 1.Dorothy "Dolly"¹ Arbogast), b. Jun 27 1947. Married Jun 14 1969, **Alan Yurkshat**, b. Jul 24 1947.
    Children:
    1006 i. Tara Laigh⁹ Yurkshat b. Jul 14 1971.
    1007 ii. Jason Alan Yurkshat b. Mar 12 1974.

952. **Virginia Marie⁸ Colaw** (784.David Lapham⁷, 621.Robert Ray⁶, 421.Franklin Robert⁵, 202.Benjamin Watters⁴, 41.Sabina³ Gum, 5.Adam², 1.Dorothy "Dolly"¹ Arbogast), b. Sep 12 1956. Married Aug 26 1978, **Leroy Schmidt**, b. Nov 10 1954.
    Children:
    1008 i. Joshua David⁹ Schmidt b. Jul 8 1981.
    1009 ii. Corrie Rene Schmidt b. Aug 28 1983.

984. **Bryan⁸ Pugh** (810.Roger L.⁷, 642.Audrey⁶ Houchin, 430.Otie Viola⁵ Gum, 207.Thomas Marion⁴, 43.Amos³, 5.Adam², 1.Dorothy "Dolly"¹ Arbogast).
    He Married **Amanda Marie Wright**, b. Nov 19 1881 (daughter of Alan Wright and Tammy Gragg).
    Children:
    1010 i. Hailey Marie⁹ Pugh b. Jan 31 1904 in Davis Memorial Hospital, Elkins, Randolph Co., WV.

Generation Nine

994. **Joanne Dawn⁹ Griffin** (928.David Gerald⁸, 762.Lana Janice⁷ Tevis, 544.Ellen Jane⁶ Kell, 311.Blanche Mahalia⁵ Ray, 102.Sarah Jane⁴ Gum, 17.James Riley³, 3.Isaac², 1.Dorothy "Dolly"¹ Arbogast), b. 28 Jul 1981.
    She Married **(unknown) Hall**.
    Children:

1011 i. Holly Johna[10] Hall.

About The Author

Nancy Elizabeth Arbogast, a fourth generation off spring rom German born Michael Arbogast ,produced a sixth generation male child who gave a dam about his relatives . This chap is the product of four pioneering families who settled in the heart of the Alleghany Mountains, and with the help of other pioneers turned the wilderness into a most hospitable place to live.

Edyth Laura Morrison had gone to Pocahontas County in 1916 to teach school in Frost. On September 3, 1923 she and Mitchell Sharp were married. Curtis was their third child, born October 31 1929 in his parent's home on Knapps Creek, two days after the October 29, 1929 bank crash. The land on which the house stood was a part of the holdings acquired by pioneer John Sharp (born c1757). It had passed from Pioneer John through multiple Sharp generations to Mitchell. Two years later Mitchell and Edyth lost the land and house for debts owed to a brother, cousin, neighbor and sister-in-law. The goodness and greatness of the Morrison family burst forward, and Mitchell, Edyth and the three boys had a place to land.

From 1931 through his retirement in 1994, Curtis rarely returned to Pocahontas County. After retirement, he began accumulating genealogical data and history on the ancestors of his four grandparents. *John Sharp and Margaret Blain Sharp Family History* was published in 2014., and *A Morrison Family, History and Descendants of Nathaniel Morrison* in 2016. This volume is a third result of that 20 plus year effort.

Curtis has been married to Peggy Bell Sharp for 60 years, has 4 children, 11 grandchildren and one great grandchild. This, a three volume effort, will be his sixth book since retirement. The first, *Blessings and Burdens, Growing up Poor and Rich,* is about his parent's upbringing, their downfall and recovery, and his early life. Being born poor and being the child of Mitchell and Edyth are among his greatest blessings.

His 40-year professional career with the U. S. Department of Agriculture focused on using vegetation for solving soil and water conservation problems. His forth post retirement book, *Conservation Plants, A USDA Success Story*, discussed the people and products resulting from the first 75 years history of this Program.

Index

(Unknown), Almeda, 184
(Unknown), Bernice, 201
(Unknown), Carolyn, 103, 107
(Unknown), Fransina, 42
(Unknown), Ginger, 122
(Unknown), Gladys, 200
(Unknown), Gloria, 131
(Unknown), Hester E., 207
(Unknown), Jane, 169, 215
(Unknown), Lorena, 75
(unknown), Lou Ann, 120
(Unknown), Lucille, 202
(Unknown), Margaret, 184
(Unknown), Marilyn, 108
(Unknown), Marla, 91
(Unknown), Martha, 16
(Unknown), Mary M, 184
(Unknown), Minnie V., 74
(Unknown), Nancy, 34
(Unknown), Nancy C, 195
(Unknown), Sarah, 170
(Unknown), Sheryl, 106
(Unknown), Shirley, 212
(Unknown), Traci, 122
(Unknown), Zelda, 73
, Charles Kapp Moutray, Jr., 194
A.Grogg, 66
Adams, Daniel J., 115, 161
Adams, David Paul, 115, 161
Adams, Elizabeth Marie, 115, 161
Adams, Joel Dean, 115, 161
Adams, Keith Joel, 115, 161
Adams, Kevin James, 115, 161
Adamson, Albert C, 55
Adamson, Fred A., 54
Adamson, Glenn, 55
Adamson, John Robert, 54
Adamson, Nellie C., 54
Adamson, Rosa N., 54
Adamson, Rula K., 55
Adamson, Verner C., 55
Adamson. Grace, 51
Adcock, Montie Mae, 188
Adkin , Fanny, 176
Afflack, Fred, 21
Alaexander, Bidwell William, 62, 146
Alaexander, Ernest, 62, 146
Alkire, Susan, 112

Allen, Archaball, 79, 149
Allen, Doris Acentha, 79, 98, 149, 156
Allen, John R., 48
Allen, Opal Jane, 79, 99, 149, 156
Allen, Richard Wallace, 108
Alt, (unknown), 83
Alton, Samantha Azlee, 21
Amanapas, Mary Elizabeth Samuals, 12, 29, 133, 166
Amerine, Barbara Joyce, 209
Amerine, Cavan Wells, 209
Amerine, Corinne Dee, 209
Amerine, David Mitchell, 209
Amerine, Gary Dean, 209
Amerine, Merwin Wells, 199, 209
Amerine, Reagan Haddon, 199, 209
Amerine, Richard Dana, 209
Amerine, Richard Dean, 199, 209
Amerine, Ronald Reagan, 209
Amerine, Willis, 199
Amstrong, Mary Ruth, 82
Andrews, Walter, 187
Ann, Lisa, 216
Anzel, Mary, 133
Arbogast, (unknown), 134
Arbogast, Aaron Richard, 127
Arbogast, Ada Leah, 23, 27
Arbogast, Adam Crawford, 82
Arbogast, Adam James, 127
Arbogast, Albert Adair, 15, 19
Arbogast, Albert Willard, 139
Arbogast, Alfred, 19
Arbogast, Alice D., 139
Arbogast, Alta, 141
Arbogast, Ann, 28
Arbogast, Anna Abigail, 12, 13
Arbogast, Anna Belle, 20
Arbogast, Anna R., 137
Arbogast, Anne, 28
Arbogast, Anne Katherine, 127

Arbogast, Ashley Marie, 112
Arbogast, Barbara Jane, 134, 139
Arbogast, Barbary, 12, 14
Arbogast, Beatrice, 141
Arbogast, Benjamin, 15
Arbogast, Benjamin Hays, 18
Arbogast, Betty Virginia, 57
Arbogast, Birdie, 20
Arbogast, Bishop, 135
Arbogast, Bruce, 17
Arbogast, Carl Lee, 57
Arbogast, Catherine, 134, 137
Arbogast, Catherine Kate, 32, 133, 135
Arbogast, Charles, 140
Arbogast, Charles Elmer, 139
Arbogast, Charles H., 138
Arbogast, Charles Preston, 17
Arbogast, Charles Ward, 134, 138
Arbogast, Charlotte, 140
Arbogast, Chloe, 43
Arbogast, Claire, 28
Arbogast, Clara B., 139
Arbogast, Clarence W., 139
Arbogast, Clarissa C, 17
Arbogast, Claude, 23
Arbogast, Cleta, 141
Arbogast, Clifford Rudolph, 23
Arbogast, Clinton D., 139
Arbogast, Connie Sue, 75, 92
Arbogast, Cora M., 139
Arbogast, Daniel Huffman, 13
Arbogast, David, 10, 12, 134, 140
Arbogast, David Daniel, 15, 18
Arbogast, David Lee, 75, 92
Arbogast, Denver, 121
Arbogast, Dianna, 135
Arbogast, Donald, 75, 92
Arbogast, Donna Darlene, 75
Arbogast, Dora L, 17
Arbogast, Dorothy "Dolly", 10, 166, 167
Arbogast, Doyle Edward, 75
Arbogast, Duane, 92
Arbogast, Earnest, 141
Arbogast, Eli, 135

Arbogast, Eli McKinley, 133, 134, 138
Arbogast, Eligah Christian, 127
Arbogast, Elizabeth, 12, 135
Arbogast, Elizabeth (Betsy), 133, 135
Arbogast, Elizabeth Ann, 134, 139
Arbogast, Elizabeth Lyda, 139
Arbogast, Elliott, 28
Arbogast, Elmore James, 27, 28
Arbogast, Emma C., 140
Arbogast, Emma J., 137
Arbogast, Enoch, 133
Arbogast, Enoch G., 134, 137
Arbogast, Enos, 12, 13, 14, 19
Arbogast, Enos James, 18, 23
Arbogast, Enos Miles, 15
Arbogast, Ernest McKinley, 87, 108
Arbogast, Essie Opal, 23
Arbogast, Ethan Allan, 18
Arbogast, Ethan Allen, 18
Arbogast, Etta, 19, 140
Arbogast, Flara, 135
Arbogast, Framk M., 139
Arbogast, Frances Isabella, 18, 22
Arbogast, Genevieve M, 139
Arbogast, George, 10, 17, 30, 133, 134
Arbogast, George L, 14, 17
Arbogast, George W., 138
Arbogast, George Washington, 135, 140
Arbogast, Glenn William, 119
Arbogast, Glorie, 121
Arbogast, Grace, 22
Arbogast, Green, 125
Arbogast, Grover C., 22, 26
Arbogast, Gurnie, 140
Arbogast, Guy, 141
Arbogast, Hallie, 125
Arbogast, Hannah, 30
Arbogast, Harrison, 135, 141
Arbogast, Harry G., 139
Arbogast, Hazel Mae, 43
Arbogast, Helena Jane, 135, 140
Arbogast, Henry, 10
Arbogast, Henry Clay, 43
Arbogast, Henry J, 13
Arbogast, Henry J., 15, 19
Arbogast, Henry Lawrence, 23
Arbogast, Henry Miles, 12, 13, 18
Arbogast, Henry Parker, 82
Arbogast, Hugh, 14, 17
Arbogast, Ida Alice, 19, 23
Arbogast, Ida E, 17
Arbogast, Ida Rose, 139
Arbogast, Irene May, 103
Arbogast, Isaac, 12
Arbogast, Isaac Newton, 19
Arbogast, Jacob, 12, 15
Arbogast, Jacob C., 40
Arbogast, James, 121, 131
Arbogast, James Edward, 76
Arbogast, James Harvey, 134, 139
Arbogast, James Lawrence, 87
Arbogast, James McKinley, 108, 127
Arbogast, James Oscar, 137
Arbogast, James Richard, 131
Arbogast, James Rodney, 139
Arbogast, Jane, 14
Arbogast, Jason Douglas, 127
Arbogast, Jasper, 43
Arbogast, Jennie, 141
Arbogast, John, 140
Arbogast, John A., 134, 139
Arbogast, John B. (Jack), 43
Arbogast, John C., 10
Arbogast, John F., 135
Arbogast, John Forrest, 139
Arbogast, John Hamilton, 138
Arbogast, John Lewis, 16, 20
Arbogast, John Lynn, 25, 28
Arbogast, John Wesley, 17
Arbogast, Julieanna Dawn, 127
Arbogast, Laura Louisa, 15
Arbogast, Leander, 141
Arbogast, Lester James, 23
Arbogast, Lewis Ray, 125
Arbogast, Lewis Ray, II, 125
Arbogast, Linda, 75, 92
Arbogast, Lizzie, 139
Arbogast, Lona, 22
Arbogast, Lora Alice, 23
Arbogast, Louisa, 135, 140
Arbogast, Louisa Acenith, 18
Arbogast, Louisa Catherine, 19
Arbogast, Louisa May, 140
Arbogast, Lovie May, 57, 75
Arbogast, Luella A., 140
Arbogast, Lydia Ann, 14
Arbogast, M.D., 17
Arbogast, Mahala, 135
Arbogast, Margaret, 57
Arbogast, Margaret Elizabeth, 135
Arbogast, Margaret Jane, 185
Arbogast, Mary, 10, 13, 16
Arbogast, Mary E., 138
Arbogast, Mary Elizabeth, 10, 20, 25, 29, 136
Arbogast, Mary Gertude, 139
Arbogast, Mary M., 135
Arbogast, Mary Susan, 43
Arbogast, Matilda, 134, 138
Arbogast, Maude Isabella, 23
Arbogast, May Lavonne, 23
Arbogast, Meade Estella, 23, 27
Arbogast, Melinda, 134, 138
Arbogast, Michael, 10, 12, 29, 32, 121, 133, 166
Arbogast, Michael Lee, 125
Arbogast, Mildred, 27
Arbogast, Millie Jane, 16
Arbogast, Misty Lea, 93
Arbogast, Moses, 12
Arbogast, Myrtle M., 36
Arbogast, Nancy, 134, 135, 137
Arbogast, Nancy Elizabeth, 138
Arbogast, Nancy Jane, 15
Arbogast, Nancy Luverta, 68
Arbogast, Nancy Maud, 140
Arbogast, Nelle, 139
Arbogast, Nettie C., 137
Arbogast, Nichol, 92
Arbogast, Odessus Adam, 10
Arbogast, Ollie A., 44
Arbogast, Paul B., 25
Arbogast, Pauline Faye, 57
Arbogast, Perlie, 43, 56
Arbogast, Peter, 10, 14
Arbogast, Quinten, 92, 112
Arbogast, Rachel, 35, 41, 52
Arbogast, Rene M., 140
Arbogast, Reuben H., 135, 140
Arbogast, Reubin Sheeder, 140

Arbogast, Rev. James Bert, 82, 101
Arbogast, Rhoda, 17
Arbogast, Richard Wayne, 108, 127
Arbogast, Robert, 121
Arbogast, Robert Allen, 75
Arbogast, Robert Guy, 27
Arbogast, Robert Sprole, 18, 22
Arbogast, Roger Lee, 76, 93
Arbogast, Ronald Jones, 44
Arbogast, Rose Joy, 57
Arbogast, Roselee, 57
Arbogast, Roy, 141
Arbogast, Ruby Jane, 57
Arbogast, Rudolphus George, 19, 23
Arbogast, Samual Henry, 57, 75
Arbogast, Samuel Henry, 43
Arbogast, Sanford Albert, 15, 18
Arbogast, Sanford Barton, 19
Arbogast, Sarah (Sally), 12, 15
Arbogast, Sarah Catherine, 18, 22
Arbogast, Sarah E., 20
Arbogast, Schuyler C, 137
Arbogast, Scott, 141
Arbogast, Sellah Ray, 23
Arbogast, Seth, 134, 139
Arbogast, Shasta, 131
Arbogast, Sheridan, 139
Arbogast, Silas, 133, 134
Arbogast, Solomon, 133, 135
Arbogast, Stella Amanda, 17, 21
Arbogast, Stephanie, 119
Arbogast, Stephen Faust, 18
Arbogast, Steven Allen, 108, 127
Arbogast, Straud Deluca, 23, 27
Arbogast, Sue Ellen, 101, 119
Arbogast, Sylva May, 26
Arbogast, Thomas Jonathan, 19
Arbogast, Travis, 92
Arbogast, Ulysses S,, 140
Arbogast, Valerie, 121
Arbogast, Vera Kathryn, 25, 28
Arbogast, Victor R., 139
Arbogast, Walter H., 138
Arbogast, Whitcomb, 139
Arbogast, Wilbur, 43, 57
Arbogast, Wilbur Junior, 57, 76
Arbogast, Willard, 120
Arbogast, William, 12, 13, 16, 28, 138, 140
Arbogast, William David, 23
Arbogast, William Edward, 137
Arbogast, William Goodin, 17
Arbogast, William Henderson, 20, 25
Arbogast, William Henry, 44, 134, 139
Arbogast, Zebulon Brevard (Zeb),, 19
Arbogast, Zeria W., 17
Armentrout, Carney L., 51
Armentrout, Christiphor, 51
Armentrout, Elva T., 51
Armentrout, Letha, 66
Armentrout, Ola E., 51
Armentrout, Vergie F., 51
Armentrout, Vista G., 51
Armstrong, Eli, 82
Armstrong, Ott, 188
Arnold, Candice Dawn, 117, 130, 162, 165
Arnold, Charles Isadore, 96, 154
Arnold, Charles Isadore, Jr., 96, 154
Arnold, Damion Blue, 117, 162
Arnold, Donald Gene, 96, 117, 154, 162
Arnold, Shelly Lynn, 96, 117, 154, 162
Arthur, Addie, 17
Arthur, Athelinda, 17, 21
Arthur, Daniel, 17, 22
Arthur, Henry H., 17
Arthur, John, 17
Arthur, John D., 17
Arthur, Joseph Glasgow, 14
Arthur, Mary J., 17
Arthur, Oliver Wendell, 22
Ash, Carl Thomas, 57
Ault, Elizabeth, 133
Auvil, Nobel Edward, 58
Back, Stanley Miller, 59
Bailor, Marjorie, 98, 155
Baker, E, 26
Baker, Helen, 198
Baker, William, 182
Baldasty, Elsie, 98, 155
Bales, John, 60, 144
Bales, Mary Willella, 60, 144
Banton, Barbara Jean, 89
Barb, Mildred, 56
Barcroft, Berle, 189
Barcroft, Elias, 189
Barcroft, Victor, 189
Barkley, Kevin, 129
Barnes, Betty Lovella, 94, 113, 151, 159
Barnes, Beverly Sue, 94, 113, 151, 158
Barnes, Emma L, 17
Barnes, Floyd, 194
Barnes, Harvey L., 94, 151
Barnes, Joane Sue, 94, 113, 151, 158
Barnes, William Jack, 94, 151
Barnes, William Jackson, 94, 151
Barr, Shannon Leigh, 130, 164
Barrack, Dawn Denise, 127
Barrack, Francis, 127
Barrington, Mary, 135
Barrows, Vanita Kay, 219
Barth, Jacob, 179
Barth, Lizzie C, 179
Barth, Matilda E., 179
Barth, Theresa E., 179
Battesse, Martha, 61, 146
Bauer, Nettie, 139
Baughman, Eunice Mae, 193
Baughman, Michayla Lynn, 122
Baughman, Richard Lynn, 122
Baylor, Robert H., II, 127
Baylor, Zacharp Robert, 127
Beachler, Jerome, 15
Beacom, Janice Elaine, 210
Beard, Nell Lorraine, 84
Beard, Samuel Bryant Monroe, 84
Beaty, Linda Lou, 211
Beauchamp, Floyd, 37, 141
Beck, Elnora Elizabeth, 15
Becker, Germaine Ida, 204
Beckwith, Beth Ann, 91
Beckwith, Robert Nicholas, 91
Beckwith, Tracy Lynn, 91

Beckwith, Walton, 91
Bee, Joan Lorraine, 131, 165
Bell, Barbara, 94, 151
Bell, Mary, 75
Benbow, Cordelia Grace, 23
Bennaka, Dorothy Maye, 194
Bennett, Ada, 90
Bennett, Amanda M., 48
Bennett, America, 34
Bennett, Angela Marie, 125
Bennett, Azora M., 49
Bennett, Charlie N, 90
Bennett, Charlotte Ellen, 48
Bennett, Cora Ellen, 49
Bennett, Edward J., 49
Bennett, Elemuel Jefferson, 49
Bennett, Florrie Dean, 49, 67
Bennett, Grace Marie, 67, 88
Bennett, Hazel, 108
Bennett, Henry, 130
Bennett, Henry E., 130
Bennett, Ida Florence, 49
Bennett, John, 90
Bennett, John Adam, 49
Bennett, Katie, 49
Bennett, Martha (Mattie), 49
Bennett, Mary Elizabeth, 57
bennett, Maymie Alice Brooks, 46, 143
Bennett, Merle, 67
Bennett, Michael, 125
Bennett, Nimrod, 39
Bennett, Oscela Martin, 49, 67
Bennett, Paul, 67
Bennett, Paul Lowell, 64
Bennett, Ray, 51
Bennett, Robert C., 63
Bennett, Ruth, 84
Bennett, Sallie Dean, 48
Bennett, Scott Allen, 130
Bennett, Thomas J., 49
Bennett, Tiffany Dawn, 125
Bennett, Toy Helen, 58
Bennett, Tressie, 82
Bennett, Willie, 49
Bennett, Zenia, 49
Berry, Ava, 21
Berry, Pearl Mable, 96, 154
Beverage, Loleta Ann, 86
Biehl, Alta Menry, 25
Biehl, Henry,, 25
Birdette, Vern Niles, 55
Black, Amy Rachel, 99, 156
Black, Nathan Milo, 99, 156

Black, Steve, 99, 156
Blackwood, Amanda, 184
Blaikie, Ellen E., 60, 145
Blaikie, Flora Jane, 60, 145
Blaikie, Frank Francis, 45, 60, 145
Blaikie, Jessie A., 60, 145
Blaikie, John W., 60, 145
Blaikie, Maggie May, 60, 77, 145, 147
Blaikie, Maude, 60, 145
Blaikie, Nora Bell, 60, 145
Blaikie, Robert F., 60, 145
Blazer, Betty, 66
Bleasdale, Beverly Sue, 109
Blessings and Burdens, 221
Bluch, Edna Lura, 96, 154
Bogard, Hannah, 29
Bohannon, James, 108
Bohannon, Norma Jean, 108
Bohlin, Anna Thelita, 81
Bohlin, Stanley Carl, 81
Bohlin, Timothy Carl, 81
Bolton, Hope, 110
Bond, Marie Alice, 110
Bonderman, Gene, 97, 154
Bonderman, Laurie, 97, 154
Bonifant, Wayne, 111
Boren, Andrew, 213
Boren, Sheila Ilene, 213
Borrow, Marquerite Rowe, 87
Botkin, Jack, 58
Botkin, James, 58
Botkin, John, 58
Botkin, Margaret, 58
Botkin, Odes, 58
Botkin, Susan, 58
Botkin, Thomas, 58
Botkin, Wanda, 58
Bowen, Delloyd, 79, 149
Bower, Henery Theodore, 24
Bower, Rena Ann, 24
Bowers, Mary, 21, 25
Bowling, Lacy, 64
Boyce, John William, 174
Boyd, Cora, 186
Boytz, James Patrick, 115, 160
Boytz, Mathew James, 115, 160
Bradford, Russell Clifton, 203
Bragg, Joseph, 42
Bramdle, Eli, 140
Bramdle, Harry S,, 140

Bramdle, Reuben, 140
Brandle, Adam M., 140
Brandle, Ann E., 140
Brandle, Christian, 140
Brandle, Elizs A., 140
Brandle, Lemuel H., 140
Brasher, Amrynth, 21
Bratton, Cornelia, 107
Brenner, Ella Mae, 196
Brevard, Mercy, 18
Brewer, Edna Lois, 74
Brewster, Andrew, 56
Bridat, Nina, 49
Bridge, Eric, 212
Bridge, Morgan, 212
Bridge, Rachel, 212
Bright, Phoebe Rebecca, 73
Brock, Jo Ann Hull, 88
Brock, William, 107
Brock, William Wilson, 107
Brooks, Daniel, 22
Brooks, Emery W., 22
Brooks, Enos, 22
Brooks, Ethel, 22
Brooks, Ira S., 22
Brooks, James W., 22
Brooks, Laura Dell, 22
Brooks, Marietta Acenith, 22
Browmley, Oleva Mae, 192
Brown, Ada Viola, 21, 26
Brown, Andy Joe, 205
Brown, Barbara Sue, 106, 124
Brown, Betty, 67
Brown, Billie, 206
Brown, Carl Milton, 205
Brown, Carolyn Sue, 105, 123
Brown, Chad Michael, 124
Brown, Charles Robert,, 22
Brown, Flora Mae, 192
Brown, George Washington, 21
Brown, George Washington Jr., 22
Brown, Gertrude Harriet, 21
Brown, Harriett Ilene, 203
Brown, Harry Franklin, 22
Brown, Ida Mae, 21
Brown, James Cooper, 22
Brown, James Madison, 20
Brown, Jerry Lee Morris, 123
Brown, John Arthur, 21
Brown, Joseph Edgar, 21
Brown, Joseph Lynn, 106
Brown, Lawrence, 89

Brown, LeAnn Marie, 118, 163
Brown, Lenore Ann, 80, 151
Brown, Martha Laree, 80, 151
Brown, Mary, 141
Brown, Mary Inez, 84
Brown, Ola Elizabeth, 21
Brown, Paul Elton, 80, 151
Brown, Phyllis Ann, 105, 123
Brown, Robert Lee, 105, 106
Brown, Roberta Jane, 106, 124
Brown, Rocky Charles, 118, 163
Brown, Rocky Lee, 118, 163
Brown, Tiffany Ann, 118, 163
Brown, Warren, 105
Brown, Zorado Jane, 20
Browne, Patricia Augusta, 110
Brownfield, Jasper, 183
Bruce, Earl Claude, 95, 152
Bruce, Janell Kay, 95, 115, 152, 160
Bruce, Liessa Gay, 95, 115, 152, 160
Bruce, Shirley Ann, 95, 115, 152, 160
Bruff, Robert, 171
Brumbugh, Shannon Lee, 128
Bryan, Doris, 73
Bryan, Gertude, 73
Bryan, Gilbert Jennings, 73
Bryan, Henry Lee, 73
Bryan, Lorraine, 73
Bryant, Charles Edward, 87, 110
Bryant, Charles Michael, 110
Bryant, Collen Marie, 110, 128
Bryant, Dana Lynn, 110, 128
Bryant, Harold McQuain, 87, 110
Bryant, Karen Elizabeth, 110
Bryant, Margaret Sharron, 110, 128
Bryant, Richard, 110
Bryant, Richard Gale, 87, 110
Bryant, Steven, 110
Bryant, Thomas Edward, 110
Buckbee, Grethel Mae, 68, 88
Buckbee, Guy Carleston, 68
Buckbee, Johna Elmer, 68
Buckbee, Jonah Elmer, 51
Buckbee, Maudie Irene, 68
Bullick, Mary Jane, 124
Bunch, Carolyn Kay, 95, 152
Bunnell, Robert, 100, 157
Bunsh, Carolyn Kay, 115, 160
Burke, Harry, 193
Burner, Barbara, 120
Burns, Christopher Lee, 109
Burns, Justin Arthur, 109
Burns, Maude, 103
Burns, Thomas Eugene, 109
Burton, June R., 218
Butcher, Alva, 105
Butcher, Buck, 105
Butcher, Charlene, 105
Butcher, Debra, 105
Butcher, Delores, 105
Butcher, Geraldene, 105
Butcher, Norma, 123
Butcher, Randall, 105
Butcher, Shelda, 105
Buterbaugh, Vivian, 197
Butts, (unknown), 101
Buvarskis, Alfonso, 202
Buvarskis, Gordon Alan, 203, 212
Buvarskis, Gordon Richard, 213
Buzzard, Barbara, 32, 133
Buzzard, Heinrich 'henry', 133
Buzzard, Ora Gray, 208
Cade, Aaron Robert, 128
Cade, Danielle Rene, 128
Cade, Jason Bryant, 128
Cade, Robert, 128
Cady, Patrick J., 216
Cain, Helen Lavine, 206
Calhoun, Allen, 34
Calhoun, Annie Catherine, 34, 40
Calhoun, Carry Evans, 87
Calhoun, Eli, 34
Calhoun, Elizabeth Susan, 36
Calhoun, Elva, 208
Calhoun, Ephraim, 34
Calhoun, Harold Kay, 66, 87
Calhoun, Harrison, 36
Calhoun, Jackson, 34
Calhoun, James, 34
Calhoun, Martha, 34
Calhoun, Phoebe (Susan), 34
Calhoun, Phoebe Susan, 40
Calhoun, Ronald Victor, 66
Calhoun, Sarah, 35
Calhoun, Schallace Tiffin, 87
Calhoun, Shellace Tiffin, 66, 87
Calhoun, Sherron Virginia, 66, 87
Calhoun, Susan, 34, 40
Calhoun, Virgil McQuain, 66
Calhoun, Virgil Mullenax, 66
Calhoun, Winifred, 36
Call, Hosea, 21
Calliton, Lenita Jill, 129
Campa, Gabriella Jordan, 118, 163
Campa, Skylar Spartakus, 118, 163
Campa, Tona, 118, 163
Campbell, Mary E., 45, 143
Campbell`, Scheryl, 94, 151
Cansler, Ailene Oleta, 94, 152
Cantrell, Barbara Dean, 210, 218
Cantrell, Ethmer Pearl, 188
Cantrell, Francis Leonord, 188
Cantrell, Herbert Hadley, 188
Cantrell, James Paul, 200, 210
Cantrell, James Virgil, 188, 200
Cantrell, Kathi Sue, 210
Cantrell, Kelly Marie, 210
Cantrell, Lyndell Brent, 210
Cantrell, Marion, 188
Cantrell, Nina Marie, 200
Cantrell, Particia Ann, 210, 218
Cantrell, Randell Lee, 210
Cantrell, Reggie Bernard, 188, 200
Cantrell, Vergie Francis, 200, 210
Cantrell, Wendell Kent, 210
Cantrell, Wilma Jean, 210, 218
Cantrell, Winfield Winson, 200, 210
Carline, Robert, 108
Carpenter, Thelma Gertrude, 72
Carr, Florna Jane, 55
Carr, Vincent, 43
Carroll, Anna Marie, 189

Carter, Mary Ann, 103, 119
Carter, Richard Stanley, 103
Carter, Ronni, 114, 159
Carver, Clarissa Ann, 204
Cass, William, 32, 137
Cassell, Christopher Bradley, 119
Cassell, Crissy Jo, 103, 120
Cassell, Edward Clarence, 103
Cassell, Gayle Marie, 85
Cassell, James Edward, 103
Cassell, James Michael, 119
Cassell, James Richard, 103, 119
Cassell, Madison Faith, 120
Cassell, Regina, 93
Cassell, Regina Zelda, 208
Cassell, Shena Marie, 120
Cassell, Willis, 85
Causey, David, 180
Causey, Harriett Ellen, 180
Causey, Lucy Jane, 180
Causey, Mary Elizabeth, 180
Causey, William Riley, 180
Cavan, Nancy, 209
Chambers, Karen Ann, 213
Chenoweth, Bobby Allen, 121
Chenoweth, Daniel Taylor, II, 121
Chenoweth, Heidi Francis, 121
Chenoweth, Laramie Angel, 121
Chenoweth, Linda May, 121
Chenoweth, Waleene, 121
Chew, Margaret, 175
Chow, Kate Louise Du, 117, 163
Chrisman, Cindy Ruth, 114, 159
Christebson, Leonard, 44
Christenson, Adam Gabriel, 123
Christenson, Ryan Zachary, 123
Christenson, Tom, 123
Christman, A J, 209
Christman, David, 209
Christman, Keri, 209
Cinders, Ann, 49
Clark, Dorothy Elvira, 72
Clark, Edra Mae, 72
Clark, Ethel, 72, 90
Clark, Florence Ruth, 72
Clark, Leman Dwight, 72
Clark, Luther Curtis, 71
Clark, Marie, 47
Clark, Mary, 47
Clark, Olive Arlene, 72
Clark, Robert William, 72
Clark, Walter, 71
Clark, Walter Dale, 72
Clayton, Henery Harrison, 42
Clayton, Sophia Catherine, 43
Cline, Velma A., 60, 145
Clingerman, William Russell, 58
Close, Vernon E., 72
Clough, Bryan, 96, 153
Cobb, Ida, 32
Cody, Christine, 104
Coffield, Catherine M., 138
Coin, Mary Belle, 190
Colaw, Adele, 196
Colaw, Albert Eugene, 196
Colaw, Alphorus, 185, 196
Colaw, Amos Kendall, 175
Colaw, Barbara Sue, 216, 219
Colaw, Ben Wilson, 195, 206
Colaw, Benjamin Watters, 175, 184
Colaw, Bernard, 185, 196
Colaw, Betty, 207
Colaw, Burris, 185
Colaw, Carolyn M. Joel, 215
Colaw, Catherine, 13
Colaw, Charles Benjamin, 195, 205
Colaw, Charles Benjamin, Jr., 205, 214
Colaw, Charles Dwayne, 215, 218
Colaw, Clida, 185
Colaw, David Dwayne, 218
Colaw, David Emerson, 215
Colaw, David Lapham, 206, 216
Colaw, Deborah Jane, 215
Colaw, Deborah Renae, 216
Colaw, Debra Ann, 215
Colaw, Della I, 184, 195
Colaw, Derrel Emerson, 219
Colaw, Donald, 195, 205, 207
Colaw, Dorothy, 196
Colaw, Dyer W, 175, 185
Colaw, Ella May, 185, 196
Colaw, Emerson J., 205, 215
Colaw, Ethel May, 195
Colaw, Frank Dean, 215
Colaw, Frank Edwin, 206, 215
Colaw, Franklin Robert, 184, 196
Colaw, Gail, 217
Colaw, Gary, 217
Colaw, George William, 184, 195
Colaw, Glen Dyer, 196, 207
Colaw, Glenn, 217
Colaw, Grace, 196, 207
Colaw, Harmon, 175
Colaw, Harry Albert, 184, 196
Colaw, Ida Gertrude, 195
Colaw, Imogene Matilda, 196
Colaw, Jackson Ben, 206, 216
Colaw, Janice, 196
Colaw, John Harmon, 184, 195
Colaw, John Michael, 215
Colaw, John Orval, 195, 206
Colaw, John Orval, III, 215
Colaw, John Orval, Jr., 206, 215
Colaw, Joseph Wayne, 215
Colaw, Judith Charlene, 215
Colaw, Julie Marie, 216
Colaw, Julie Michelle, 219
Colaw, Kathy Leutta, 218
Colaw, Laban, 175
Colaw, Lee, 207
Colaw, Lillian, 185
Colaw, Lisa Christina, 216
Colaw, Lucinda Ann, 218
Colaw, Mamie Bell, 196, 206
Colaw, Marcella Louise, 215
Colaw, Marjorie Neil, 205, 215
Colaw, Martha Ellen, 195
Colaw, Martha Jane, 175
Colaw, Mary Rosetta, 184, 195
Colaw, Max, 205
Colaw, Max Arthur, 215, 219
Colaw, Merle C., 196, 207
Colaw, Naomi, 195
Colaw, Nathan Rena, 215, 218
Colaw, Orrie, 205
Colaw, Orry Omar, 184
Colaw, Prudence Elaine, 215, 219

Colaw, Ray Kenneth, 195, 206
Colaw, Ray Kenneth, Jr., 206
Colaw, Richard William, 206, 215
Colaw, Robert Ray, 196, 206
Colaw, Roberta Rea, 206, 216
Colaw, Russell G., 207, 217
Colaw, Sandra, 207
Colaw, Sandra Kay, 215
Colaw, Sandra Louise, 216
Colaw, Sarah Ellen, 175
Colaw, Shari Renee, 218
Colaw, Sheila Suzanne, 219
Colaw, Stephen Lloyd, 219
Colaw, Stephen Olin, 215, 219
Colaw, Suzanne, 207
Colaw, Thornton, 196, 207
Colaw, Tracy Lynn, 216
Colaw, Victor, 205
Colaw, Viola May, 195
Colaw, Virginia Marie, 216, 219
Colaw, Wayne, 196, 207
Colaw, William Benjamin, 175
Colaw, William, Jr, 175, 184
Cole, Carolyn, 122
Cole, Floyd, 195
Cole, Roberta Ruth, 24
Coleman, William, 37, 141
Collins, Adam, 52, 68
Collins, Andrew Jon, 112
Collins, Andrew Morgan, 53
Collins, Atlos Martin, 91, 112
Collins, Bernard Morris, 74, 91
Collins, Carol Lee, 91, 112
Collins, Cecil Morgan, 54, 73
Collins, Christine, 112
Collins, Dale, 68
Collins, Dawnne Renee, 112
Collins, Delbert, 68
Collins, Donald Eugene, 73
Collins, Floyd William, 54, 73
Collins, Franklin D., 68
Collins, Goldie, 68
Collins, Harold Cecil, 73, 91
Collins, Karyl Lynn, 90
Collins, Kaye Adair, 90
Collins, Kelly Sue, 112
Collins, Lowell Jene, 91, 112
Collins, Mabel Caroline, 69, 89
Collins, Mamie Katherine, 44
Collins, Nors, 68
Collins, Paul Hunter, 73, 90
Collins, Rebecca Jeanne, 91, 112
Collins, Ribin Leigh, 112
Collins, Ruby Mae, 74
Collins, Sonja Michelle, 112
Collins, Virginia Lynn, 112
Collins, Wilma Dell, 74
Compton, Bessie, 207
Compton, Carlotta Aceneth, 80, 99, 150, 157
Compton, Jesse Caleb, 100, 157
Compton, Jesse William, 80, 150
Compton, Jesse William, Jr., 80, 100, 150, 157
Compton, Kelley Corrine, 100, 157
Compton, Lacey Celine, 100, 157
Compton, Timothy Jay, 80, 150
Conner, Patricia, 100, 157
Conrad, Angela Mae, 93
Conrad, Christie Lynn, 93
Conrad, Darla Renna, 93
Conrad, Debra, 75, 93
Conrad, Heidi, 92
Conrad, Jerry, 75, 93
Conrad, Jerry Lee, 93
Conrad, Jonathan, 93
Conrad, Justin Lloyd, 93
Conrad, Larry Francis, 75, 92
Conrad, Lloyd Francis, 75
Conrad, Michael, 75
Conrad, Nichole, 92
Conrad, Patricia Ann, 75, 93
Conrad, Randy, 75, 92
Conrad, Ricky Gene, 75
Conrad, Robert Lee, 93
Conrad, Vivien, 28
Conservation Plants, 221
Cook, Sallie, 90
Cooley, Fred, 46, 144
Cooper, Cheryl Lynn, 129
Cooper, Harry, 123
Cooper, Kelly Rand, 116, 161
Cooper, Lee, 123
Cooper, Misty, 123
Cooper, Rand William, 116, 161
Copenhafer, Joan, 217
Corbit, Agnus Virenda, 78, 148
Corbit, Ira Alfred, 78, 148
Corysager, 104
Cosner, Melissa Kay, 125
Cotherman, Donna, 59
Coulter, Hannah, 134
Coulter, William, 134
Cowan, Cires, 32
Cox, Rebecca M., 44
Crabtree, Brendon, 120
Crabtree, Christian, 120
Crabtree, Courtney, 120
Crabtree, Edward J., 104
Crabtree, Edward Louis, 104
Crabtree, Erin Michale, 115, 161
Crabtree, Etta, 24
Crabtree, Harry James, 95, 115, 152, 160
Crabtree, Harry James, Jr., 115, 161
Crabtree, Harry Wayne, 95, 152
Crabtree, Hillaire Ray, 115, 161
Crabtree, John E., 104, 120
Crabtree, Larry Dean, 95, 152
Crabtree, Lindsay Kay, 115, 161
Crabtree, Sheldon DeWayne, 95, 152
Crabtree, Sonya Faye, 95, 152
Crabtree, Ted L., 104
Crabtree, Travis, 120
Craig, Bobby Merl, 125
Craig, Clara Dawn, 132
Craig, Pamala J., 132
Craig, Paul, 125
Craig, Tamera Leah, 125
Crantell, Dixie, 200
Crantz, Helen, 22
Cree, Iva Marie, 75
Creed, Richard, 101
Crow, Kenneth, 131, 165
Cruse, Sophia, 172
Cummingham, Anna B., 64
Cummings, Linda, 92
Cunningham, Abraham Lantz, 69
Cunningham, Arthena, 42
Cunningham, Chloe, 70

Cunningham, Ellen Jane, 52
Cunningham, Elva Bebecca, 51
Cunningham, Henry, 42
Cunningham, Hinkle, 70
Cunningham, Isabella, 168
Cunningham, Lu Cinda, 70
Cunningham, Vella J, 70
Cunningham, Willie, 69
Cunningham, Zena, 69
Curl, Nancy, 17
Curt, Jeremiah, 17
Curtis, Milton, 37, 141
Cusey, Ella, 195
Dabe, Agustine, 139
Daggett, George M., 167
Dahmer, Ella Vaiden, 44
Dandrivan, Joseph, 32, 137
Danison, Myrtle, 26
Darr, Kramer, 57
DarthulaTarter, Emily, 23
Davenport, Clarissa, 170
Davenport, Louise, 179
Davenport, Roger, 66
Davis, Francis, 179
Davis, George, 195
Davis, George Russell, 195
Davis, James P., 35
Davis, John Martin, 193
Davis, John N., 137
Davis, Larwence Edward, 121
Davis, Lora, 193
Davis, Mary, 121
Davis, Mary Ann, 32
Davis, Maxine, 28
Davis, Norma, 193
Davis, Raymond, 193
Davis, Ronald, 121
Davis, Sarah Olive, 196
Davis, Steve, 121
Davis, Sue, 75
Davis, Vera, 193
Davis, William, 89
Day, Lelly Noel, 125
De Chow, Wayne Lincoln, 117, 163
De Hart, Belinda Jo, 116, 161
De Mott, Dorris Lea, 79, 149
Dean, Kathy, 92
Deeter, Albert, 65
Deeter, Sherrie Marie, 106, 125
Deeter, William Edward, 106
Deeter, William Edward, II, 106
Deets, Marguerite Barbara, 62, 146
Dell, Janer, 66
Denison, Edward H, 21
Denison, Lindsey H, 26
Devault, John, 168
Dickson, Flora Elvira, 184
Dilley, Margaret Louella Elsie, 185
Dilley, Martin Clark, 185
Dilley, Naomi Elizabeth, 185
Dillon, George William, 103
Dillon, Kristi Dare, 103
Dirks, Norma Jean, 214
Dobbs, Dennie June, 114, 160
Doddrill, Lynn, 119
Doddrill, Matthew, 119
Dolin, Maudie, 59
Dolly, Dorothy, 54
Dove, George W., 140
Dove, Hannah, 140
Dove, Isaac, 139
Dove, Jennie Miriah, 140
Dove, John M., 140
Dove, Mary, 29
Dove, Michael Ely, 139
Dove, Silis P., 140
Dove, Virginia, 50
Dox, Estelle, 138
Driscoll, John, 138
Driscoll, Albert, 142
Driscoll, Charles E., 138
Driscoll, Edward, 142
Driscoll, George W., 138, 142
Driscoll, Jack, 144
Driscoll, James, 138
Driscoll, James Gwyn, 142, 144
Driscoll, John H., 138, 142
Driscoll, John H., Jr., 142
Driscoll, Minnie, 142
Driscoll, Rebecca J., 138
Driscoll, Robert, 142
Driver, Pauline P., 193
Drumheller, Eva Pearl, 85
Duchenne, Emil, 180
Duckworth, Bessie, 22
Duckworth, Sarah Gertrude, 190
Dudley, George, 212
Dugan, John William, 170
Duncan, Kenneth R, 209
Duncan, Kenneth Roy, 209
Dunkle, Aletha, 169
Dunkle, Aletha Adaline, 173, 182
Dunkle, Jacob, 173
Dunkle, John Cibert, 173
Dunkle, Malinda, 173
Dunkle, Martha, 173
Dunkle, Mary E, 173
Dunkle, Melvina, 173
Dunkle, Sarah Jane, 173
Dunkle, William, 173
Dunn, Dennis Eugene, 201
Dunn, John Smith, 201
Easter, Karl, 26
Easter, William, 26
Easter, William K., 26
Echel, Leo, 78, 148
Eckert, Vicki Kay, 100, 157
Edwards, Linda Kay, 199
Edwards, Mary Jane, 94, 151
Elgin, Lucinda, 183
Elgin, Lucy Belle, 174
Elizabeth, Rachel, 68
Elkins, Alta Rose, 129
Elkins, Walter G, 129
Ellern, Scott, 97, 154
Elliott, Anne, 138
Elliott, Miles, 12
Elmore, Pearl, 27
Elza, Alpha Hollie, 55
Elza, Carl, 81
Elza, Clinton Charles, 81
Emert, John, 127
Emert, Kimberly Louise, 127
England, Lewis, 45, 142
England, Virgil Lavern, 211
England, Virgil Osborn, 211
England, Wanda Madge, 211
Engle, Beverly Ann, 111
Ervine, Bertie Ruth, 73
Ervine, Chessa Lee, 89
Ervine, Dewey Hunter, 88
Ervine, Donald Robert, 88
Ervine, Edward Newton, 73
Ervine, Effie Bly, 89
Ervine, Jason Edward, 88
Ervine, Robert Francis, 88
Everett, Chad, 212
Eye, Harry Srtife, 83
Eye, James Lee, 83
Eye, Myrtle Nellie, 66
Eye, Pauline Elza, 82
Eye, Richard Hull, 83
Eye, Terry Sue, 83
Eyman, Janara, 213
Eyman, Kevin, 213

Eyman, Larry Wayne, 213
Fagerburd, Theodore, 96, 154
Fagerburg, Claire Luisa, 117, 163
Fagerburg, Jaunita Raquelle, 96, 117, 154, 162
Fagerburg, Keith Duane, 96, 154
Fagerburg, Martin Kerry, 96, 117, 154, 163
Fagerburg, Meghan Elizabeth, 117, 163
Fagerburg, Olivia Kerry, 117, 163
Fagerburg, Tiffany Skye, 117, 162
Fansler, Dollie Vorden, 91
Farabough, George Marvin, 21
Farence, Patsey Ethel, 55
Farm, Rachel, 172
Farmer, Henry Ardillon, 21
Farnham, Tammy Jo, 112
Farris, Henry, 192
Farris, Katie, 192
Faulk, Blanche, 180
Fencemaker, George, 65
Fennimore, Benjamin Joseph, 116, 161
Fennimore, Cassandra Lou, 95, 116, 153, 161
Fennimore, Charmaine Marie, 95, 115, 153, 161
Fennimore, Gilman Joseph, 95, 152
Fennimore, Gilman Joseph, Jr., 95, 116, 153, 161
Fennimore, Stephanie Ann, 116, 161
Ferrebee, Debbie, 111
Ferrebee, Donna, 111
Ferrebee, Hazel, 111
Ferrebee, Marie, 111
Fest, Barbara Ann, 110
Fest, Charles Edward, 110
Fest, David Phillip, 110
Fest, Fred William, III, 110, 128
Fest, Fred William, Jr., 110
Fest, Lindsay Kira, 128
Fest, Michelle Kimberley, 128
Fest, Morgan Helen, 128
File, Almira J., 171
File, Benjamin, 180
File, Camilla Ann, 172
File, Daniel, 171
File, Sarah M., 171, 180
Finvik, Atephanie Kay, 123
Finvik, Einar, 123
Finvik, Jennifer Erin, 123
Fisher, Alice, 166
Fisher, Louella E., 185
Fitzgerald, Mary, 61, 146
Fitzpatrick, Mary, 97, 154
Flasher, Angeline, 172, 181
Fleiisher, Barbarea Ellen, 44
Fleisher, Elizabeth, 12
Fleisher, Peter, 12
Fleming, Catherine, 14
Flemming, Edward Earl, 57
Flesher, (unknown), 182, 193
Flesher, Absolum, 167, 173
Flesher, Adam, 167, 172
Flesher, Alice, 182
Flesher, Amanda, 182
Flesher, Amanda Ellen, 172, 181
Flesher, Angeline, 181
Flesher, Ann, 205
Flesher, Anna, 182
Flesher, Anna R, 183
Flesher, Benjamin, 182
Flesher, Benjamin F, 172
Flesher, Benjamin Silas, 183
Flesher, Benjamin W, 174, 183
Flesher, Bertha M, 182
Flesher, Bertie L., 183
Flesher, Caroline, 168
Flesher, Cecil, 192
Flesher, Claire, 182
Flesher, Claude B., 193, 205
Flesher, Cora, 182
Flesher, Donald, 205
Flesher, Donald Francis, 193
Flesher, Dora, 181
Flesher, Dorothy, 168
Flesher, Earl, 193
Flesher, Earlic, 181
Flesher, Edward Henry, 181, 192
Flesher, Ellen, 168, 173
Flesher, Elsie Vera, 182, 193
Flesher, Emaline, 172
Flesher, Emerson B, 173, 182
Flesher, Emma A, 183
Flesher, Emma Rita, 174
Flesher, Franklin, 173
Flesher, George, 173
Flesher, Gladys Ethal, 192
Flesher, Gorman B., 193, 205
Flesher, Greenberry, 172, 181
Flesher, Harriet E, 173
Flesher, Harry Seldom, 173, 182
Flesher, Henretta E, 172
Flesher, Henry, 167, 172, 182
Flesher, Hiram, 182
Flesher, Ida, 181
Flesher, Iva Edna, 183
Flesher, James, 193
Flesher, James Alvin, 173
Flesher, Jane, 173
Flesher, Jasesus, 174
Flesher, John Henry, 174, 182
Flesher, John Reginald, 193
Flesher, John Stanford, 205
Flesher, John William, 182, 193
Flesher, Joseph J, 173
Flesher, Josiah H., 174
Flesher, Katharine, 167
Flesher, Katie, 173
Flesher, Laura Frances, 183
Flesher, Laure E, 182
Flesher, Lola, 182
Flesher, Louesa K, 168, 174
Flesher, Louisa, 173
Flesher, Louisa J, 174, 183
Flesher, Lucinda, 172
Flesher, Lucinda Adaline, 174
Flesher, Luisa F, 183
Flesher, Lulu, 181
Flesher, Mahalia, 167, 168
Flesher, Marguerite, 193
Flesher, Marion, 172, 173
Flesher, Marion L, 174
Flesher, Martha Anna, 183
Flesher, Mary, 167, 173
Flesher, Mary Elizabeth, 174, 183
Flesher, Mary Ida, 174
Flesher, Mary Jane, 172, 182
Flesher, Mary Larranine, 193
Flesher, Matilda Frances, 174
Flesher, Maude, 181
Flesher, Milton Henry, 182
Flesher, Minnie A, 183
Flesher, Murray Orville, 194
Flesher, Netta B., 174
Flesher, Nona Mae, 193, 205
Flesher, Opal, 194
Flesher, Paul, 182, 193
Flesher, Pauline Mercedes, 193

Flesher, Phyllis Vernil, 192
Flesher, Richard, 181
Flesher, Robert, 173
Flesher, Roy Marion, 183
Flesher, Ruth, 167
Flesher, Sarah E, 172
Flesher, Sarah Ellen, 174, 183
Flesher, Sarah Jane, 167, 172, 173
Flesher, Seldon Elmo, 182, 193
Flesher, Shawn Paul, 205
Flesher, Tabitha S, 174
Flesher, Thomas Edward, 174, 183
Flesher, Virgil G, 192
Flesher, Wayne Elmo, 193, 204
Flesher, William, 172
Flesher, William A, 181
Flesher, William Edward, 183
Flesher, William Quintin, 192
Flesher, William Seybert, 167, 173
Flesher, William, Sr., 167, 168
Fletchall, Henry Eli, 194
Fletchall, R.g., 194
Fletcher, Raymond, 193
Fletcher, Roenna, 167
Fogus, Bessie, 107
Follmer, Cleora M., 206
Fordyce, Mary Jane, 76
Forsee, Elizabeth, 134
Forsman, Kathleen Marie, 100, 157
Forthun, Mabel, 82
Foster, Bryon, 128
Foster, Ella Alice, 183
Foster, Kristi Rose, 128
Fouch, Bruce, 37, 142
Fox, Debra Ruth, 208
Fox, Roscoe W., 44
Fraizer, (unknown), 79, 149
Francis, Kara Lynn, 124
Franklin, Alman Ray, 78, 96, 148, 153
Franklin, Amiee Ruth, 114, 159
Franklin, Angelia Joy, 96, 153
Franklin, Ashley Dawn, 117, 162
Franklin, Betty Jean, 77, 95, 148, 153
Franklin, Bonnie Jean, 77, 96, 148, 153
Franklin, Brandel Allen, 96, 116, 153, 162
Franklin, Brent Mitchell, 94, 114, 152, 159
Franklin, Bryan James, 117, 162
Franklin, Cheryl Lynn, 94, 114, 151, 159
Franklin, Christi Jo, 114, 159
Franklin, Cody Lyle, 114, 160
Franklin, Colleen Ann, 96, 153
Franklin, Darren Vern, 95, 152
Franklin, Dawn Lynn, 114, 160
Franklin, Delta Lee, 114, 160
Franklin, Francis Billey, 77, 94, 147, 151
Franklin, Galen Wayne, 95, 114, 152, 160
Franklin, Garrett Eayne, 114, 160
Franklin, Gary Lee, 95, 152
Franklin, Geoffery Wayne, 114, 159
Franklin, Gladys Faye, 77, 95, 148, 152
Franklin, Heather Michelle, 114, 159
Franklin, Heidi Micole, 114, 159
Franklin, James Benton, 77, 147
Franklin, James Lee, 77, 96, 148, 153
Franklin, James Paul, 96, 153
Franklin, James William Newton, 77, 147
Franklin, John Allen, 77, 96, 148, 153
Franklin, John James, 96, 153
Franklin, Karin Noel, 117, 162
Franklin, Kevin Kyle, 95, 114, 152, 160
Franklin, Kristina Lou, 115, 160
Franklin, Leslie Gale, 114, 159
Franklin, Lois Ruth, 77, 95, 148, 152
Franklin, Mark Lee, 96, 153
Franklin, Maty Ann, 77, 95, 147, 152
Franklin, Melissa Robyn, 96, 153
Franklin, Randy Gale, 94, 113, 151, 159
Franklin, Ricky Michael, 94, 114, 152, 159
Franklin, Robyn Melinda, 96, 153
Franklin, Ronald Dale, 94, 151
Franklin, Samantha Kay, 116, 162
Franklin, Stephanie Elizabeth, 116, 162
Franklin, Stephanie Gail, 114, 159
Franklin, Tera Lea Danelle, 114, 159
Franklin, Terry Lynn, 95, 115, 152, 160
Franklin, Thadus Jacob, 114, 159
Franklin, Tony Ray, 96, 117, 153, 162
Franklin, Vernon Newton, 77, 94, 147, 152
Franklin, Wayne Russell, 77, 95, 147, 152
Franklin, Wendy Lee, 96, 153
Franklin, William Douglas, 96, 116, 153, 162
Franklin, William Henry, 116, 162
Franks, Jessie M., 141
Franks, Mary O., 141
Franks, Peter, 141
Frazier, Georgia Goodsell, 90
Freeland, John Russell II, 90
Friel, Barbara, 120
Friel, Elvettie, 208
Friend, Betty Ann, 218
Friskie, Barbara Ann, 78, 148
Frost, Jeff, 92
Frost, Jonathan, 92
Frost, Joshua, 92
Frost, Kenneth, 92
Fuller, Carl Lindsey, 21
Fuller, David Smith, 21, 25
Fuller, Fred Elmer, 21
Fuller, George H, 21
Fuller, Grace, 21

Fuller, Hazel, 25
Fuller, Iris Icelona, 21, 26
Fuller, Josephus, 21
Fuller, Walter W, 25
Fuller, Wayne McKinley, 25
Fuller, Willard Smith, 25
Fuller, William, 25
Fulton, Carol Thomas, 79, 149
Fulton, Eunice Marie, 79, 99, 149, 156
Fulton, Lamont, 79, 149
Funkhouser, Daniel, 107
Funkhouser, Daniel Curtis, 107
Funkhouser, Douglas, 107
Funkhouser, Vickie Lynn, 107, 126
Gaben, Henry, 186
Gaid, Michael Steven, 113, 158
Gainer, Daniel Alexander, 128
Gainer, Gabrielle Augusta, 128
Galford, (infant), 197
Galford, Bernard, 208
Galford, Bertha Lee, 208
Galford, E. Kathryn, 197
Galford, Eldon Gray, 208
Galford, Eldon Gray II, 208
Galford, Eula G., 197
Galford, Frances Pauline, 197
Galford, Frank Wardell, 197
Galford, Harold Wayne, 197
Galford, Hazel, 197
Galford, James Allen, 197
Galford, John Allan, 197
Galford, Patrica Sue, 208
Galford, Paul Ardell, 208
Galford, Rachel Nettie, 82
Galford, Sharon Ann, 208
Galford, Steven, 209
Galford, Virginia Dare, 197
Galloway, Margaret, 185
Gann, James Christopher, 130, 164
Gann, Nathen Christopher, 130, 164
Gann, Whitney Brooke, 130, 164
Gardner, Mary Hester, 25
Garr, Joseph, 185
Garr, Mary Jane, 185
Garris, Noah Vernon, 72
Garside, Cinthea Loreda, 79, 149
Garside, Lawerence Addison, 79, 149
Garside, Lester Thomas, 79, 149
Garside, Mearl Lester, 79, 149
Garwood, Gillingham, 175
Gasch, David Noel, 88
Gasch, Richard Donald, 88
Gates, Henry Garfield, 180
Gatewood, Willie Nathen, 58
Gatewood, Wilma, 58
Gatto, George Clarence, 74
Gatto, Kathryn Mae, 74, 91
Genkins, (infant), 169
Genkins, Aletha, 169
Genkins, Andrew Jackson, 169
Genkins, Henry A, 169
Genkins, Martha J., 169
Genkins, Peter H, 169
Genkins, Polly, 168
Genkins, Rachel, 169
Genkins, Sarah, 168, 175
Gennette, Erma Blanche, 56
George Duncan, 18
Gerry, Maxine, 199
Gibson, Alonzo John, 50
Gibson, Eddie Oliver, 50
Gibson, Effie Viola, 50
Gibson, Ethel Victoria, 50
Gibson, Flossie Margaret, 50
Gibson, John, 50
Gibson, Mary Catherine, 50
Gibson, William, 50
Giegert, Gloria K., 113, 158
Gilbertson, (unknown), 79, 149
Gill, Judith Elaine, 112
Gillespie, Harry Clifford, 67
Gillespie, Lula Mae, 67
Gillespy, Rachel, 22
Gim, Sarah, 178
Ginkins, Andrew, 168
Ginzelman, Ellen, 215
Gish, Laura, 47, 144
Gladwell, Meno C., 68
Gladwell, William Alexander, 68
Glascock, Oran, 188
Glascock, Rayme, 188
Glenn, Margaret, 24
Glidewell, Delia, 188
Goodin, Ethel, 203
Goodson, John M., 170
Goodwill, Forrest W., 197
Gordan, Branson Lee, 119
Gordilla, Josea, 106
Gordon, Elizabeth, 15
Gordon, Philip, 15
Gordon, Remmington Cain, 119
Gordon, Ronald, 103, 119
Gosnay, Dana, 127
Gosnay, Frank, 127
Goss, Darrell Jake, 205
Goss, Nancy Emiline, 47
Gottgetreu, Bertha, 180
Gowdin, Charles, 131
Gowdin, John Edsel, 131
Gowdin, John Richard, 131
Gragg, James Allen, 125
Gragg, James Allen, II, 125
Gragg, Lucy, 207
Gragg, Patrick Allen, 125
Gragg, Tammy, 219
Graham, A Rudd, 199
Graham, Byron Rudd, 199, 210
Graham, Florence Wauneta, 201, 211
Graham, George Lester, 201
Graham, James Miller, 199
Graham, Jennifer Dawn, 210
Graham, Joseph William, 201
Grant, Bobbi Kay, 214
Grant, Gayla Jean, 214
Grant, Joe Lynn, 214
Grant, Kevin Lee, 214
Grant, Robert, 214
Grant, Shelley Rene, 214
Grant, Trudy Layne, 214
Graton, Gary, 218
Graton, Gary Lynn, 218
Graton, Jeffery Dan, 218
Graton, Roger Dale, 218
Graton, Susan Lynn, 218
Greathouse, Harper, 108
Greathouse, Phyllis, 197
Greathouse, Richard D., 108
Greathouse, Richard, II, 108
Greeley, Margaret, 214
Green, Winnie, 195
Greene, Alexis Marie, 120
Greene, David, 120
Greene, David Andrew, 120
Gregory, Helen, 59
Griddin, Janice Kathlene, 214
Grifffin, Jennifer Lauraine, 218
Griffin, David Gerald, 214,

218
Griffin, Ellen, 141
Griffin, Gerald Gorden, 214
Griffin, Joanne Dawn, 218, 219
Griffin, Kathy Jean, 117, 162
Griffin, Ray, 117, 162
Griffin, Ruby, 86
Grimes, Catherine, 33
Groce, Anita Lorraine, 62, 81
Groce, Cecil Leroy, 62
Groce, Don Romaine, 62
Groce, Glen Ramon, 62
Groce, Terrance Renaldo, 62
Grogg, Donald, 126
Grogg, James J., 41
Grogg, Louella Maer, 41, 53
Grogg, Phyllis Marie, 126
Grossman, Thomas, 65
Gum, (infant), 178
Gum, (unknown), 166
Gum, Aaron, 210
Gum, Aaron Nicholas, 213
Gum, Adam, 30, 166, 168, 175
Gum, Albert, 177, 187
Gum, Alcy, 175
Gum, Alda J, 184
Gum, Alice Ethel, 180
Gum, Allen, 167
Gum, Amos, 168, 175
Gum, Andrew Christopher, 213
Gum, Andrew Newton, 176, 187
Gum, Annie B., 179
Gum, Ardelene Mardell, 190, 202
Gum, Arele, 199
Gum, Arnold O., 179
Gum, Audrey Irene, 191
Gum, Barbara Lynn, 209
Gum, Bert E., 179, 189
Gum, Betty, 186
Gum, Beverly Ann, 101
Gum, Boyd, 175, 184
Gum, Brenda Lucille, 203, 213
Gum, C. V., 178
Gum, Catherine, 167, 170
Gum, Cathy Rae, 214
Gum, Cecil, 190
Gum, Charles M, 184, 195
Gum, Christine, 168
Gum, Clara (Elizabeth?), 179, 189

Gum, Clara Alberta, 191, 204
Gum, Clara Elizabeth, 180
Gum, Clara Lou, 203, 214
Gum, Clarence Enoch, 180
Gum, Clarissa, 180
Gum, Clyde Everett, 190, 202
Gum, Clyde Roger, 202
Gum, Connie Gretchen, 187
Gum, Corrinne Ann, 197, 208
Gum, Daisy, 184
Gum, Dallas Edward, 190, 203
Gum, Daniel Lee, 172
Gum, Daniel Lorain, 198
Gum, David, 170
Gum, David Sterling, 101
Gum, David Wyett, 214
Gum, Delores Ilene, 204
Gum, Dena Daisy, 190
Gum, Dennis Lynn, 203, 213
Gum, Dennis Lynn III, 213
Gum, Diana Faye, 203, 213
Gum, Donald Eric, 213
Gum, Donna Lee, 101
Gum, Donna Moore, 197
Gum, Dorothea Louise, 209
Gum, Earl, 199, 201
Gum, Earnest, 177
Gum, Edgar Allen, 199
Gum, Edgar Haddon, 176, 187
Gum, Edgar Herschel, 187
Gum, Edie R, 184
Gum, Edith "Eddy", 166
Gum, Edward Gustavus, 179, 189
Gum, Effie, 176, 187
Gum, Elijah, 169
Gum, Eliza, 168
Gum, Eliza Jane, 170
Gum, Elizabeth, 167, 168, 171
Gum, Elizabeth Ellen, 170
Gum, Elizabeth Joan, 191
Gum, Elleder, 166, 168
Gum, Ellen, 204
Gum, Ellender (Nelly), 168
Gum, Elmer E., 176
Gum, Elmer Lloyd Curren, 191
Gum, Elva, 180
Gum, Elvin George, 189, 201
Gum, Emma, 172
Gum, Emory B, 184

Gum, Enoch, 169
Gum, Enoch Riley, 171, 180
Gum, Erma Charlotte, 190, 202
Gum, Erma Violet, 190
Gum, Eva, 180
Gum, F. A., 178
Gum, Faye, 190
Gum, Francis E., 176
Gum, Francis Henry, 187
Gum, Freda Jeanne, 198, 209
Gum, Freda May, 186, 198
Gum, Gary, 198
Gum, Gary Lee, 203
Gum, George Richard, 199, 209
Gum, George Wasgington, 169, 176
Gum, George Washington, 179
Gum, George William, 186, 198
Gum, Georgia, 195
Gum, Georgiua Geraldine, 199
Gum, Gerthe, 176, 186
Gum, Gilbert, 190
Gum, Godfrey H, 187
Gum, Gorden Isaac, 190, 203
Gum, Grant, 176
Gum, Gussie, 176
Gum, Guy, 172
Gum, Hamtom, 172
Gum, Harold Fern, 190
Gum, Harry W., 185
Gum, Helen Alaine, 197
Gum, Helen Erline, 199
Gum, Henry, 166, 168, 169, 171, 175
Gum, Henry D, 184
Gum, Homer Benjamin, 191, 204
Gum, Homer Ethmer, 186
Gum, Howard Schubert, 190, 203
Gum, Hurlius, 190, 202
Gum, Icy D., 178
Gum, Ida, 172
Gum, Ida Irene, 186
Gum, Ida May, 177, 187
Gum, Ida Omega, 185, 197
Gum, Isaac, 166, 169, 179
Gum, Isaac C., 167, 170
Gum, Isaac Daniel, 171, 180
Gum, Isabel, 169
Gum, Jacob, 166, 167, 170

Gum, Jacob I., 179, 190
Gum, Jacob Jr., 166, 167, 168
Gum, Jacqueline Jean, 101
Gum, James, 170
Gum, James Edward, 179, 190
Gum, James H, 169
Gum, James Johnson, 170, 179
Gum, James Otho, 175, 185
Gum, James Riley, 167, 171
Gum, James Russell, 204
Gum, James V., 170, 178
Gum, Janet Sue, 211
Gum, Janis Ilene, 203, 213
Gum, Jennetta, 171
Gum, Jeremiah C., 167, 171
Gum, Jesse, 166, 169
Gum, Jesse M, 169, 177
Gum, Jesse S., 167, 170
Gum, Jesse W, 177
Gum, Joan, 204
Gum, John, 166, 201
Gum, John D, 171
Gum, John Finley, 167, 171
Gum, John Henry, 178
Gum, John L, 179
Gum, John Leonard, 179, 190
Gum, John R, 171
Gum, John Royal, 170, 179
Gum, Joseph, 175, 184
Gum, Josephine, 176
Gum, Joyce, 198
Gum, Judith Rosemary, 202, 212
Gum, Julie Ann, 213
Gum, Julie Kay, 204
Gum, Karen June, 203
Gum, Karol Ryne, 213
Gum, Kerth Elmo, 198
Gum, Kevin, 203
Gum, Kevin Timothy, 208
Gum, Kieth James, 203
Gum, Leland Relmot, 190
Gum, Lemoine, 199
Gum, Lemuel B., 170
Gum, Lemuel B., 170, 179
Gum, Leonard, 187
Gum, Lewis W., 169, 176
Gum, Lewy A., 178
Gum, Linda C., 202
Gum, Lois T, 187, 199
Gum, Lonnie Gordon, 203
Gum, Louisa, 171
Gum, Louisa Janetta, 170, 178

Gum, Louiza, 178
Gum, Lucinda, 178
Gum, Luther Randolph, 179, 191
Gum, Luthur Aaron, 190, 202
Gum, Lydia, 172
Gum, Mabel, 180
Gum, Maggie, 190
Gum, Maggie Alberta, 190, 203
Gum, Mahala, 170
Gum, Marian, 171
Gum, Marie M., 190, 202
Gum, Marilyn Lee, 89
Gum, Martha E., 170, 171, 179
Gum, Martha Jane, 169, 177
Gum, Martin Louis, 199, 209
Gum, Marvin Blaine, 203, 213
Gum, Marvin Udell, 190, 203
Gum, Mary, 170, 172, 201
Gum, Mary Agatha, 197, 208
Gum, Mary Alice, 203, 214
Gum, Mary C. Caroline, 170, 179
Gum, Mary Edyth, 190, 202
Gum, Mary Elizabeth, 176
Gum, Mary Ellen, 169, 177
Gum, Mary Katherine, 214
Gum, Mary Lou, 204
Gum, Mary M., 166, 167, 168
Gum, Matilda, 168, 174
Gum, Matilda Caroline, 167
Gum, Matilda E., 170
Gum, Maud Eldridge, 187
Gum, Meadfred, 187
Gum, Melissa Elizabeth, 213
Gum, Melvin, 187, 199
Gum, Melvin Alexander, 213
Gum, Melvin C., 189, 201
Gum, Merritt Moore, 185, 197
Gum, Michael, 204
Gum, Milberry, 167
Gum, Miles, 168
Gum, Millard A., 179
Gum, Monty, 202, 204
Gum, Moses, 167
Gum, Nadine, 204
Gum, Nancy Kay, 211
Gum, Nathaniel Meade, 176, 186
Gum, Nell Katherine, 199, 209

Gum, Nellie Etta, 172
Gum, Olive, 167, 171, 172, 181
Gum, Opal, 190
Gum, Oscar Clarence, 186, 198
Gum, Otie Viola, 185, 196
Gum, Pamela Marie, 101
Gum, Patricia Ann, 209
Gum, Patricia Jo, 101
Gum, Paul, 185
Gum, Paul Henry, 190
Gum, Paul Howard, 204
Gum, Paul Roy, 197, 208
Gum, Penny Laurene, 209
Gum, Perry, 184
Gum, Perry O., 167, 171
Gum, Peter, 168, 175, 184
Gum, Rachel, 171
Gum, Raymond Alvin, 201
Gum, Richard, 214
Gum, Richard Bryan, 209
Gum, Robert, 176, 198
Gum, Robert Dale, 89
Gum, Robert Daniel, 214
Gum, Robert Edward, 203, 214
Gum, Robert Sterling, 185, 198
Gum, Roberts M., 178
Gum, Roger, 201
Gum, Ronald, 202
Gum, Rosetta Elvina, 171
Gum, Rowland Hughes, 187, 199
Gum, Roy Calvin, 186, 198
Gum, Roy McKinley, 185, 197
Gum, Roy McKinley II, 197
Gum, Royal Edward, 201, 211
Gum, Ruby, 190
Gum, Russell Lynn, 199, 209
Gum, Russell O., 185
Gum, Sabina, 168, 175
Gum, Samual A, 171, 179
Gum, Sandra, 101
Gum, Sara Jane, 214
Gum, Sarah, 166, 169, 170
Gum, Sarah C, 171
Gum, Sarah Elizabeth, 169, 177
Gum, Sarah Florence, 180
Gum, Sarah Jane, 171, 179
Gum, Sayer, 175
Gum, Shirley Diane, 211

Gum, Stanley Carrol, 201
Gum, Stephen Hughes, 199
Gum, Sterling Bruce, 81
Gum, Sterling Lee, 81, 101
Gum, Steven Boyce, 204
Gum, Susan, 168
Gum, Talitha, 169, 177
Gum, Tamara, 101
Gum, Tecumsia Sherman, 176
Gum, Theresa Ruth, 204
Gum, Thomas, 176, 184
Gum, Thomas Edward, 203, 214
Gum, Thomas Mack, 185
Gum, Thomas Marion, 175, 185
Gum, Thomas Otto, 176, 186
Gum, Trudy, 198
Gum, Vaughn, 186
Gum, Vera, 190, 202
Gum, Veralyn Gene, 202
Gum, Vivian E., 190
Gum, Wardell Chad, 197
Gum, Wardell Clark, 185, 197
Gum, Wayne, 202
Gum, Wesley, 184
Gum, Wilber, 176
Gum, Will S., 176
Gum, William, 167, 169, 204
Gum, William Crawford, 81
Gum, William F., 179
Gum, William J, 175
Gum, William Jefferson, 170, 178
Gum, William Kenneth, 203, 214
Gum, William Madison, 169, 176
Gum, William Oliver, 176, 186
Gum, William Riley, 191, 204
Gum, William Riley, Jr., 204
Gum, William Riley, M.d., 180, 191
Gum, William W, 176
Gum, Willis Herbert, 187, 199
Gum, Willis Luther, 190
Gum, Zelma Edyth, 186
Gum, Zepha Edan, 190, 203
Gunselman, Frank A., 194
Gunselman, Wavalea, 194
Guther, Beatrice Faye, 61, 146
Guthery, Richard, 79, 150
Guy, Freda Fay, 72
Gwyn, John Edward, 142
Gwyn, Rosa, 142
Hadrick, Will, 86
Hagar, Ardath Lenore, 62, 80, 147, 150
Hagar, David Hammond, 47, 144
Hagar, Laura Maude, 47, 144
Hager, Edith Asele, 47, 144
Hager, Estella May, 47, 144
Hager, James William, 47, 144
Hager, William Roy, 47, 62, 144, 146
Hagler, Harriette Elizabeth, 178
Haid, Tina, 113, 158
Hailey, Mildred, 187
Haines, Connie, 80, 150
Hair, A. Forbes, 102
Hair, John II, 102
Hal, Joseph Wesley, 23
Hall, (unknown), 219
Hall, Chester Roy,, 23
Hall, Christopher Luther, 23
Hall, Ethel Mercy,, 23
Hall, Florence Gertrude, 23
Hall, Glen Wood, 23
Hall, Herbert Hillary, 23
Hall, Herschel Emit, 23
Hall, Holly Johna, 220
Hallan, Jennie, 138
Hallon, Wilma J., 52
Halterman, (unknown), 83
Halterman, Charlsie, 65, 84
Halterman, Fairy Dare, 65, 84
Halterman, Jesse, 65
Halterman, Joseph Clark, 48, 65
Halterman, Joseph R., 65
Halterman, Lena Virginia, 65, 84
Halterman, Mary Jane, 65
Halterman, Silas Clark, 48
Halterman, Violet, 65
Hamel, Eve, 89
Hamilton, Betty Jean, 28
Hamilton, Charles Merrill, 27
Hamilton, Donna A., 100, 157
Hamilton, Esther Cordelia, 27
Hamilton, James Andrew, 27, 28
Hamilton, Lois Roberta, 27
Hamilton, Mary Isabella, 27
Hamilton, Paul Harrick, 27
Hamilton, Pearl May, 21
Hamilton, Ruby Rea, 27, 28
Hamilton, William Everett, 27
Hammacker, Unknown, 66
Hammer, C. E., 59
Hammer, Edith C, 90
Hammer, Glen, 59
Hammer, John William, 26
Hammer, Luther, 59
Hammer, Lyle Frederick, 26
Hammer, Robert G., 59
Hammer, Sarah Catherine, 53
Hammer, Vera, 26
Hampton, Dennis, 211
Hampton, Donald, 211
Hampton, John, 211
Hampton, Lowell, 202
Hampton, Lowell, Jr., 202, 211
Hamrick, Sarah M, 91
Hannerhan, Jeanie, 61, 146
Hardy, Effie May, 57
Hardy, Lillian, 79, 149
Harmon, Dixie, 217
Harmon, Lavinia, 137
Harnett, Charles Morris, 171
Harper, Amby, 36
Harper, Donald, 8
Harper, Howard Dice, 38
Harper, Mary, 101
Harper, Pheobe, 33
Harper, Simeon, 42
Harris, Clarie Gerald, 78, 148
Harris, Joseph Jerome, 88
Harris, Mary, 22
Harrold, Frances, 13
Hart, Wila Jenieva, 57
Hartley, Mary Matilda, 20
Hartline, Verne, 190
Hartman, Adriana, 119
Hartman, April, 119
Hartman, Charles Okey, 82
Hartman, Dorothy Louise, 102
Hartman, Elemuel Ake, 102
Hartman, Maxine Carrie, 82
Hartman, Steven Guy, 102, 119
Hartman, Warden Guy, 102

Hartzell, Thelma, 216
Haskell, Edwin, 191
Hasselblock, Susan, 212
Hatch, Roy E, 192
Hatfield, Tomi Jean, 96, 153
Hay, Peter, 171
Hayes, Connie, 80, 150
Hays, Isabella, 18
Hays, James, 18
Hayse, Cheryl Annetta, 105, 123
Hayse, Darlene Francis, 105, 123
Hayse, Gragery Allen, 105
Hayse, Harold, 105
Hazelton, Sarah A., 18
Head, Alzona, 78, 148
Head, Marion, 78, 148
Head, Thelma, 78, 148
Hearrell, Hazel Helen, 188
Heath, Harold V, 55
Heath, William, 55
Hebb, Richard theodore, 76
Hebb, Sherry Lynn, 76
Hebert, Peter, 102
Hedrick, Artie Dolly, 74
Hedrick, Blake R., 129
Hedrick, Cathy Dianna, 129
Hedrick, Glenn, 129
Hedrick, Maggie, 82
Hedrick, Martha, 86
Hedrick, Ona T., 51
Hedrick, Patsy L., 129
Hedrick, Sylvia, 86
Hedrick, Walter, 43
Heinrick, Louise, 98, 155
Heister, Kami Leann, 109
Heister, Kenneth Earl, 109
Heister, Lisa Kay, 109
Helm, Jake, 37, 141
Helmick, Abraham, 39
Helmick, Abraham, Jr., 39
Helmick, Catherine, 38
Helmick, Lillie, 40
Henderson, Catherine Okey, 20
Hendricks, Ada Angeline, 193, 205
Hendricks, John, 85
Hendricks, Marcus Right, 193
Henkle, Jacob, 134
Henkle, Nancy, 134
Henry, Anna, 22
Henry, Charles, 186
Henry, Dean, 186
Henry, Wannalou, 186
Henske, Robin, 122
Hess, Bradley, 216
Hess, Charles, 206, 216
Hess, Cynthia Joan, 217
Hess, Deborah, 216
Hess, Delores Jean, 206, 217
Hess, Donald Richard, 206
Hess, Gary Lee, 206, 217
Hess, George, 206
Hess, George Robert, 206, 216
Hess, James Erwin, 206
Hess, Joan, 206
Hess, John, 216
Hess, Kevin, 217
Hess, Lauri Ann, 104, 120
Hess, Lavon Irean, 206
Hess, Raymond, 104
Hessinger, Helen Patricia, 128
Hester, Luther, 172
Hevener, Bert Theodore, 207
Hevener, Edward, 35
Hevener, Emily Gertrude, 35
Hevener, Jacob Pinkley, 35
Hevener, John, 208
Hevener, John H., 58
Hevener, Kathleen Hope, 58
Hevener, Madelyn Gayle, 58, 76
Hevener, Martha Marie, 208
Hevener, Nancy J., 207
Hevener, Robert, 207
Hevener, William, 35
Hickman, Evalene S, 91
Hicks, Dixie Francis, 210
Hicks, James Herbert, 210
Hicks, James William, 210
Hicks, Melodie Lee, 210
Hicks, Nina Jo, 210
Hicks, Walter Herbert, 210
Higgins, Donnie Ray, 92
Higgins, Heather, 92
Higgins, Samual Raymond, 92
High, Norval, 36
Hill, Elizabeth, 171
Hill, Nancy Jean, 99, 156
Hinkle, (unknown), 53
Hinkle, Audrea Lela, 188
Hinkle, Catherine Beam, 52, 69
Hinkle, Clara, 69
Hinkle, Clyde Cleo, 188
Hinkle, Donald B., 188
Hinkle, Dustin Timothy, 210
Hinkle, Edward, 87
Hinkle, Elbridge L., 52, 69
Hinkle, Eliza Ann, 52, 69
Hinkle, Elizabeth C, 48, 52, 69
Hinkle, Emil Fred, 188, 200
Hinkle, Fannie May, 69, 89
Hinkle, Isaac Harness, 53, 70
Hinkle, Isaac Harness, Jr., 70
Hinkle, Jasper Triplett, 53
Hinkle, Leonard Harper, 53
Hinkle, Martha Ann, 70, 90
Hinkle, Mary Harper, 39
Hinkle, Michael Glenn, 210
Hinkle, Mildred, 87
Hinkle, Opal Lizzia, 188
Hinkle, Pauline, 53
Hinkle, Philip M., 53
Hinkle, Randell Glenn, 200, 210
Hinkle, Richard Wayne, 200
Hinkle, Salma, 70
Hinkle, Shawn Christopher, 210
Hinkle, Solomon, 40
Hinkle, Susan, 52, 69
Hinkle, Wesley Kevin, 210
Hinkle, William, 40, 48, 52
Hinton, Mary Elizabeth, 192
Hise, Benjamin Jeremiah, 102
Hise, Clarence Wilmer II, 84
Hise, Clarence Wimer, 84
Hise, Laure, 102
Hise, Lee, 102
Hise, Luke, 102
Hise, Nancy Louise, 84
Hise, Ralph Gerald II, 84, 102
Hise, Shirley Marie, 84
Hitchcock, Earl, 198
Hitchcock, Max, 198
Hite, (unknown), 52
Hix, Belinda, 76
Hoag, Teresa Jean, 95, 116, 153, 161
Hoag, Todd Vernon, 95, 153
Hoag, Valerie Lea, 95, 153
Hoag, Vernon George, 95, 153
Hobart, Candice Lynn, 114, 160
Hobbs, Byron James, 97, 155
Hodgett, Lena Mae, 186
Hoelsken, Charlotte

Gertrude, 192
Hoffa, Kathryn, 85
Hoffman, Brown, 101
Hoffman, Gertrude, 129
Hoffman, Rheba, 101
Hohl, Mamie, 191
Hoke, Debra, 112, 158
Holcomb, Fredwin, 55
Hollenback, Lottie, 17
Hol<u>t, Minnie,</u> 176
Holt, Sarah Stella, 193
Holt, Sebastian, 193
Holtz, Arthur, 82
Holtz, Lois Ann, 82
Holub, Denny, 217
Hood, Jerry Lynn, 218
Hood, Melissa Kay, 218
Hood, Pamela, 218
Hoover, Larry Allen, 130
Hoover, Mamie, 65
Hoover, William Ashley, 44
Hoover, Wilson, 130
Hoppes, Dwayne Allen, 91
Hoppes, Dwight Gorden, 91
Hord, Lena, 189
Hottle, Roy, 43
Houchin, Audrey, 197, 208
Houchin, Cecil C., 207
Houchin, Cecil Clay, 196
Houchin, Charlotte M., 208
Houchin, Clay T., 196, 207
Houchin, Helen Lee, 196
Houchin, Margaret, 197, 207
Houchin, Paul Russell, 197, 208
Houchin, Ray, 197
Houchin, Shirley F., 208
Houchin, Virginia, 197, 207
Houchin, Wardell, 196
Houghin, Thomas, 196
Hourhood, Elizabeth, 33
House, Sadie L., 97, 154
Houseman, Landolin, 180
Hover, William, 45
Howell, Anna Elizabeth, 100, 158
Howell, Dunan Arthur, 100, 158
Howell, Jamin Arthur, 100, 158
Howell, Mae, 106
Howell, Rebecca Estella, 100, 158
Howeyshell, (unknown), 106
Howeyshell, Brenda Kay, 106, 124

Howland, Kenneth Lee, Jr., 115, 160
Howland, Rachelle Lea, 115, 160
Hubbard, Preston, 172
Hubbard, Stephen J., 183
Hubbard, Willie A., 183
Hubberd, William Jess, 174
Hubbert, Jacqueline, 120
Hubbert, Walter, 120
Huffine, Paula, 97, 154
Huffman, Beverly June, 129
Huffman, Christian, 13
Huffman, David, 42
Huffman, Frank, 54
Huffman, Hensel, 129
Huffman, Marian A., 42
Huffman, Mary, 13
Huffman, Mary Marcella, 42, 55
Huffman, Phoebe Jane, 54
Huffstedtler, Green Berry, 178
Huffstedtler, James W., 178
Huffstedtler, Louis Fred, 178
Huffstedtler, Mahala C., 178
Huffstedtler, Marget L., 178
Huffstedtler, Mary Frances, 178
Huffstedtler, Maurice M., 178
Huffstedtler, Narcissa Ellen, 178
Huffstedtler, Sarah Elizabeth, 178, 189
Huggins, Brandy, 92
Hughes, Bertha, 187
Hull, Brown, 68
Hull, William, 35
Hullinger, Elizabeth, 134
Hulver, David Frederick, 65
Hulver, Hinkle, 65
Hulver, Irene, 65
Hulver, Mildred, 65
Humphrey, Philope, 43
Hunsacker, Ethlyn, 203
Hunsacker, Laura Mae, 214
Hunsacker, Renita Jane, 214
Hunsacker, Robert, 213
Hunsacker, Ursula Fay, 213
Hunsacker., Wardie, 176
Hunter, Autumn Grace, 94
Hursey, John R., 72
I, John Russell Freeland, 90
Inserra, Jody Elaine, 109
Isner, Allen, 43

J.Brandle, Helena, 140
Jackson, Agnes, 23
Jackson, Chrifstal D., 123
Jackson, Douglas Lee, 28
Jackson, Gilbert Lee, 28
Jackson, R, 26
Jackson, Robert A., 123
Jackson, Ryan A., 123
James K. Eson., 167
Janes, Adam, 181
Janes, Elizabeth Jane, 181
Janes, Henry C, 181
Janes, Ida F, 181
Janes, Pheobe, 172
Janes, Thomas, 168
Janes, Thomas Newton, 181
Jantz, Calvin, 215
Jaynes, Anna, 12
Jeans, (unknown), 89
Jeneves, Don, 196
Jennings, Nancy E., 167
Jerman, James Arthur, 59
Jerman, James Arthur, Jr., 59
John Sharp and Margaret Blain Sharp, 221
Johnson, Anna Ethel, 22
Johnson, Grace, 105
Johnson, H D, 173
Johnson, Lakisha Renee, 119
Johnson, Mary Leta, 82, 101
Johnson, Norman, 79, 149
Johnson, Richard Allen, 85
Johnson, Ruby M., 84
Johnson, Sharon, 112
Johnson, Shirley, 216
Johnson, Solomon, 64
Johnston, Ann Lynn, 82
Johnston, Buford C, 82, 101
Johnston, Cletis, 64, 82
Johnston, CLETUS, 64
Johnston, Dotty, 102
Johnston, Emma, 16
Johnston, Francis, 16
Johnston, Georgia Ellen, 64, 83
Johnston, James, 16
Johnston, Janet L, 102
Johnston, Jesse, 64, 82
Johnston, John, 16
Johnston, Judith, 64
Johnston, Mary Ann, 101
Johnston, Merle, 64
Johnston, Mildred, 64
Johnston, Mona, 64
Johnston, Nancy, 16
Johnston, Odell Raines, 83

Johnston, Otis, 64
Johnston, Ricky, 102
Johnston, Ricky Lee, 119
Johnston, Solomon Harvey, 64
Johnston, Virginia, 64
Johnston, William, 64
Jones, Clarabelle, 61, 146
Jones, Cora Elvira, 197
Jones, James, 171
Jones, Leslie, 27
Jones, Leslie, Jr., 27
Jones, Lois Ann, 95, 152
Jones, Mary, 138
Jones, Mary Elizabeth, 184
Jones, Robert Neal, 27
Jones, Roy, 188
Jones, Vandolyn, 188
Jones, William Samuel, 61, 146
Jordan, Clorinda, 39
Jordan, Fleet, 55
Jordan, Glen Weed, 55
Jordan, Hetzel (John), 42
Judy, Adam, 39
Judy, Early Thomas, 102
Judy, Mary Catherine, 39
Judy, Norma, 102
Judy, Olie, 63
Judy, Patricia Louvon, 102
Judy, Tina, 63
Kane, Kristie, 126
Kauth, Mabel Estella, 215
Kay, Alfred Long, 139
Keefe, Debbie Faye, 95, 152
Keitel, Herman Eldon, 211
Kell, Ellen Jane, 191, 204
Kell, Laurel Samual, 191
Kell, Samuel Weber, 191
Kellar, Gertrude, 94, 151
Keller, Lela Mae, 207
Kelley, Anna Jane, 47, 62
Kelley, G. Vernon, 47
Kelley, Hobart William, 47
Kelley, Irene Marie, 47
Kelley, James Fay, 47
Kelley, Joseph Henry, 47
Kelley, Kenneth John, 131, 165
Kelley, Luther Elliot, 47
Kelley, Mary Evelyn, 47, 62
Kelley, Milton Ephram, 47
Kelley, Robert Harold, 47
Kelley, Thelma Louise, 47, 62
Kelley, Thomas Benton, 47

Kelly, Stephanie Jean, 131, 165
Kemble, Kyle Crispin, 98, 155
Kemble, Paul Charles, 97, 155
Kemble, Samual Crispin, 97, 155
Kendall, Jane, 21
Kennedy, Arthur, 27
Kennedy, Bruce, 182
Kennedy, Emme, 142
Kennedy, James Daniel, 192
Kennedy, John Daniel, 192
Kennedy, John Patton, 192
Kennedy, Mildred Pearl, 192
Kennedy, Rev. Harold, 27
Kennedy, Robert Logan, 192
Kennedy, Thomas, 192
Kennett, Lloud, 190
Kennison, Francis, 206
Kent, Lawrence, 194
Kenton, Richard, 76
Kerr, Earl Frederick, 55, 74
Kerr, Jeannie, 218
Kerr, Margaret Ann, 74, 91
Kerr, Orville Erry, 74
Kessler, Angela, 128
Ketterman, Bertha Viola, 196
Ketterman, Nicholas Harper, 196
Kibling, Eva, 137
Kidwell, Jesse, 24
Kiersey, Aaron Ray, 130, 164
Kiersey, Ivan, 113, 159
Kiersey, Lannie Gene, 113, 130, 159, 164
Kiersey, Russell Scott, 113, 159
Kile, George, 29
Kile, Mary Hannah, 29
Kincade, Bettie, 216
Kincade, Mary Ann, 37, 141
Kincaid, Chelsie Renee, 120
Kincaid, David, 30
Kincaid, George, 35
Kincaid, Joshua Devore, 120
King, Billy, 93
King, Cynthia, 181
King, Irene Mae, 194
King, Marion, 172
King, Marlyn Jean, 79, 149
King, Phoebe, 193
King, William Authur, 93
Kirk, Angela, 217
Kirk, Henry, 217

Kirk, Lillie Belle, 196
Kirk, Richard Douglass, 217
Kirk, Tracey, 217
Kirkpatrick, Flora Ellen, 45, 143
Kirkpatrick, James W., 45, 143
Kirkpatrick, Maria Bertha, 75
Kirt, Delbert Ladell, 204
Kisamore, Bernetti Ann, 75
Kisamore, Byron Stanley, 55
Kisamore, Diana Marie, 75, 91
Kisamore, Elaine, 55
Kisamore, Ethel May, 55
Kisamore, Gary, 56
Kisamore, Gary Williams, 75
Kisamore, Glen, 57, 75
Kisamore, Glen, Jr., 75
Kisamore, Gloria Dale, 75
Kisamore, Gola, 55
Kisamore, Goldie, 57
Kisamore, Grace, 56
Kisamore, Guy, 57, 75
Kisamore, Harry, 56
Kisamore, Hayes Wheeler, 55
Kisamore, Margie, 56, 74
Kisamore, Marjorie Ettie, 55
Kisamore, Mary Frances, 55
Kisamore, Nina Elizabeth, 55
Kisamore, Olive Pearl, 75, 92
Kisamore, Oliver Wayne, 55
Kisamore, Ralph Hugh, 57
Kisamore, Ruth Virginia, 55
Kisamore, Troy, 57, 74
Kisamore, Troy Eugene, 75
Kisamore, Troy, Jr., 75
Kisamore, Valley, 57
Kisamore, Zernie, 55
Kisner, Barbara, 217
Kisner, William, 217
Kitchek, Kim Bryan, 98, 155
Kitchek, Lawrence Wade, 98, 155
Kitchek, Vance Wade, 98, 155
Kittle, Okey, 57
Kizer, Rhoda, 20
Kleinkauf, Paul Larwence, 128
Kleinkauf, Richard K., 128
Kleinkauf, Valerie Lynn, 129
Kline, Belva, 104
Klinger, Jeff, 219
Klinger, Kristin, 219

Klinger, Larry, 219
Klinger, Robbie, 219
Knapps Creek, 221
Knipe, Allison Nicole, 117, 162
Knipe, Andrew Fredfick, 117, 162
Knipe, Andrew Fredrick, Jr., 117, 162
Knipe, Anthony Andrew, 117, 162
Knipe, Ashley Amber, 117, 162
Knipe, Autuma Lynn, 117, 162
Knotts, Ethel Cora, 40
Knox, Marian A., 60, 145
Koon, Glen, 122
Koontz, Faye Lucille, 203
Koukal, Julie, 62, 147
Kounovsky, Jonathon David, 109
Kounovsky, Joseph Arthur, 109
Kounovsky, Katherine Christinne, 109
Kounovsky, Mary Elizabeth, 109
Krumrey, John, 45, 142
Kulback, Steven J., 129
Kyer, Deborah Ann, 111
Kyer, Denise Ann, 111, 129
Kyer, Gearldene Marie, 89
Kyer, Helen Grethel, 89, 110
Kyer, Jessica Ann, 129
Kyer, John Herbert, 88
Kyer, John Herbert, Jr., 89, 110
Kyer, Lucille Zenna, 89, 110
Kyer, Melissa Ann, 111
Labarr, (unknown), 109
Labarr, Brandon James, 109
Labarr, Brandy Amber, 109
Labarr, Brittney Marie, 109
Labarr, Heather Nicole, 109
Lamarr, Ivan, 80, 150
Lamb, Nettie, 39
Lamb, Ruth, 210
Lambert, Albinus, 40
Lambert, Albinus, Jr., 40
Lambert, Alecia Janine, 120
Lambert, Arnetta C., 51
Lambert, Bessie Ann, 52
Lambert, Beth, 89
Lambert, Betty, 87, 108
Lambert, Bill Waco, 112

Lambert, Billy W, 112
Lambert, Brenda Lee, 87, 109
Lambert, Cadden, 40
Lambert, Callie Coetta, 40
lambert, Cam, 82
Lambert, Carol Marie, 108
Lambert, Carolyn Sue, 103, 107, 125
Lambert, Charlotte, 86, 106
Lambert, Cluetta, 40
Lambert, Crystal, 106
Lambert, Curtis C., 51, 68
Lambert, Dale, 121, 131
Lambert, David Russell, 107
Lambert, Dawn Marie, 108
Lambert, Debra Kay, 87, 109
Lambert, Delmar, II, 121
Lambert, Dewey Judy, 65, 87, 109
Lambert, Diana F., 105, 123
Lambert, Donald Curtis, 86, 106
Lambert, Donald Woodrow, 68, 89
Lambert, Doris Ann, 86, 108
Lambert, Earl Russell, 86, 106
Lambert, Edward Judy, 87, 108
Lambert, Edward Judy, II, 108
Lambert, Eli H., 40
Lambert, Elizabeth, 34, 106
Lambert, Elizabeth A., 40, 52
Lambert, Elsie Bird, 52
Lambert, Emily Grace, 124
Lambert, Ethel Marie, 86
Lambert, Fallen, 65
Lambert, Flotie V., 52, 68
Lambert, Francis, 68, 86, 106
Lambert, Francis Arnold, 40
Lambert, Gary Allen, 87
Lambert, George Edward, 52
Lambert, George Washington, 40
Lambert, Georgia, 65, 85
Lambert, Gladys Marie, 86, 107
Lambert, Heidi Lynn, 109
Lambert, Hester Jane, 40
Lambert, Hilda Josephine, 86, 107
Lambert, Hugh, 51
Lambert, Ida, 52
Lambert, Ira, 40

Lambert, J. Elmer, 82
Lambert, James Eugene, 87, 109
Lambert, James Stewart, 121
Lambert, Janet Lee, 86, 105
Lambert, Janie Marie, 112
Lambert, Jay, 40, 51, 52
Lambert, Jeffery Allen, 106, 124
Lambert, Jessie, 65, 86
Lambert, Joan Dare, 86, 106
Lambert, Job, 39
Lambert, Jody Lynn, 112
Lambert, John, 34
Lambert, Julie Ann, 112
Lambert, Keith, 107
Lambert, Keith Fallen, 86, 106
Lambert, Kenneth, 86, 103, 107
Lambert, Kimberly, 107
Lambert, Lannas, 89
Lambert, Larry Dale, 87, 109
Lambert, Larry Dale, II, 109
Lambert, Levi, 39
Lambert, Lillie, 52, 68
Lambert, Lucretia, 40
Lambert, Lynn, 82
Lambert, Mahala P., 40
Lambert, Margaret Ann, 40
Lambert, Margaret Deanie, 86
Lambert, Mary H., 40
Lambert, Michael David, 106
Lambert, Mildred, 83
Lambert, Misty, 107
Lambert, Moody, 52
Lambert, Oakland, 120
Lambert, Orie Basil, 65, 86
Lambert, Otha, 64
Lambert, Pamela Carol, 112
Lambert, Pamela Sue, 121, 131
Lambert, Patty Jean, 87, 109
Lambert, Peggy L., 105
Lambert, Philbert, 40
Lambert, Renae Hope, 109
Lambert, Rhoda Martha, 65, 87
Lambert, Richard David Russell, 108
Lambert, Richard W., 105, 123
Lambert, Robert, 52
Lambert, Roger Lee, 87, 108
Lambert, Roger Lee, II, 108

Lambert, Ronnie Terry, 120
Lambert, Roy Allen, 86
Lambert, Roy D., 65, 86
Lambert, Russell, 65, 86
Lambert, Shirley Mae, 86, 107
Lambert, Soloman K., 40, 52
Lambert, Stacy, 121
Lambert, Statten, 40
Lambert, Tasaha M., 123
Lambert, Theresa, 105, 123
Lambert, Timothy Michael, 109
Lambert, Tistvan, 131
Lambert, Tony, 107
Lambert, Turlie, 52
Lambert, Uxter, 52, 68
Lambert, Viva Georgia, 82
Lambert, Walter W., 42
Lambert, William L., 68
Lambert, Wilmouth, 105
Lambert, Winefred, 33
Langenbacker, Jessie, 47
Langnes, Terry Lynn, 100, 157
Lanier, Lynn, 195
Lantz, Susanna, 168
Lapham, Dorothy, 206
Larraine, Mary, 116, 161
Larson, Callie Jean, 116, 162
Larson, Christopher MIchael, 116, 162
Larson, Gregory Allen, 96, 116, 153, 161
Larson, Jeremy Allen, 116, 161
Larson, Kimberly Lee, 96, 153
Larson, Michael Ray, 96, 116, 153, 161
Larson, Mindy Sue, 116, 161
Larson, Nathan Lars, 116, 161
Larson, Oscar, Jr., 96, 153
Laughlin, Harold, 60, 145
Launder, Lisa Yvonne, 131
Lavier, Elizabeth, 46, 143
Lavier, Eunice, 61, 146
Lavier, Joe, 61, 146
Lawrence, Susan, 36
Layfield, George, 41
Layfield, William, 41
Layton, Joseph, 172
Lee, Lois, 207
Lefeber, Joann, 94, 151
Lefeber, John, 94, 151

Lehr, Helen Louise, 216
Lemasters, Dana, 119
Lemasters, Lisa Marie, 119
Lemon, Charles, 172
Lemon, Mary Jane (Chambers), 53
Leonardi, Dorothy Ann, 118, 164
Lerma, Victor Manuel, 117, 163
Levett, Bernadette Richie, 194
Lewey, Naome Edna, 203
Lewis, Charles E., 180
Lewis, Mary A., 42
Lewis, Nancy J, 176
Lewis, Randy L., 97, 154
Lieuallen, Fannie, 187
Liggett, John Colombus, 183
Liggett, Laura Belle, 183
Liggett, Lucinda Elizabeth, 182
Liggett, William, 183
Lightbody, Joe, 37, 141
Limbach, Debbie Ann, 114, 159
Linder, Anna, 181
Linder, Daniel, 181
Linder, Hope, 181
Linder, James, 181
Linder, Jessica, 181
Linder, Katherine, 181
Linder, Leona, 181
Linder, Mehitabel, 181
Linder, Nellie, 181
Linder, Perry, 181
Linder, Richard, 181
Linder, Richard, Jr., 181
Linder, Ruth, 181
Lindley, Eligah, 180
Lindley, William, 180
Livingston, Itonia May, 23
Livingston, James W., 23
Loftice, (unknown), 87
Loftice, Brenda, 88
Loftice, Brent, 88
Loftice, Kimberly, 88
Lommis, Deborah Kate, 99, 157
Long, Abel, 30
Long, George A., 30
Long, Hazel, 198
Loomis, Brenden Phillips, 99, 157
Loomis, Jerry, 99, 157
Loony, Eunice Marie, 94, 151

Loudenslager, Nona, 26
Loudermilk, Blanton Davis, 119
Loughrey, Georgia Virginia, 56
Loughrey, James Patrick, 56
Loughrey, Nathan Andrew Warren, 56
Loughrey, Rosa Lee, 56
Loughrey, Rosalie, 56
Loughrey, Viola, 56
Loughry, Wilbur Gay, 43
Louk, Jessie Lucy, 74
Lovitt, Dale, 192
Low, Sophia, 172
Lunsford, Phoebe J., 35
Lydie, Linda, 100, 157
Lynnarbogast, Sherry, 101, 119
Lyons, Eleanor Ann, 45, 143
Lyons, Harriet, 138
Macy, Faye, 199
Maequess, Gertrude, 59
Maggart, Albert (Alonzo), 137
Maggart, Charles, 137
Maggart, David W., 137
Maggart, George, 137
Maggart, James, 137
Maggart, William, 137
Mahanay, Verda, 215
Mahler, Barbara Joy, 62
Mahler, Charles, 62
Mahler, Charles Hobart, 62
Mahler, Mary, 62
Malberg, (unknown), 54
Maline, Sharon, 199
Mallow, Annie Pressie, 83
Mallow, Carl, 64
Mallow, Gladys, 51
Mallow, Juanita, 102
Mallow, Opal Amy, 51
Manahan, Leal, 207
Maness, Ruth Ann, 219
Manley, Doris, 216
Marie, Angela, 124
Marinba, Carol Lynda, 109
Markom, Olga, 91
Markyston, John, 62, 147
Markytan, Martha, 62, 147
Marsh, Carrie, 186
Marshall, Michelle Leigh, 126
Martin, David Vernon, 99, 156

Martin, Jess, 46, 143
Martin, John Lawrence, 99, 156
Martin, Judith Mary, 216
Martin, Lawrence, 99, 156
Martin, Myrtle, 45, 143
Martin, Terry Lila, 99, 156
Mason, Richie, 127
Mason, Samatha Nichole, 127
Matheney, Elizabeth, 64
Matheny, Jacob, 37, 141
Matheny, Martha Jane, 37, 141
Matis, Jacqueline, 108
Matthews, Blanche, 190
Matthews, Carol, 98, 155
Matts, Martha Ann, 32
Mc Bride, Varenda, 19
McBride, Annie Eliza, 138
McBride, Gladys Mae, 86
McBride, Jacob Carpender, 138
McBride, James Henry, 138
McBride, Lillian Viola, 138
McBride, Mary Elizabeth, 138
McBride, Nancy Ellen, 138
McBride, Rebecca Jane, 138
McCarty, Carol, 100, 157
McCarty, Vickie Lynn, 93
McClelland, (unknown), 198
McClintic, Mary Belle, 43
McConkey, J Wes, 17
McCue, Katherine, 192
McCuskey, Elizabeth Jane (Minnie), 190
McDermott, Lyda, 87
McDonald, Mary, 126
McDonald, William Shirley, 56
McDonough, Dan Patrick, 109
McDonough, Dan Patrick, II, 109
McDonough, Joshua Todd, 110
McDonough, Matthew Dereck, 109
McDonough, Nathan Paul, 109
McGraff, Madeline V., 47
McHenry, Earnest, 187
McHenry, Lavern, 187
McHenry, Lucille, 187
McHenry, Nelson, 187

McHugh, Donna, 78, 148
McKafka, Joy, 116, 162
McKee, Lauretta Sternes, 67
McKenzie, John A., 191
McKinley, Anna B, 20, 26
McKinley, Charles Lewis, 16, 20
McKinley, Cornelia, 25
McKinley, Earl, 25
McKinley, George Haines, 17
McKinley, George Patrick, 26
McKinley, Harriet Esther, 20, 25
McKinley, James F, 25
McKinley, Jessie Alice, 21
McKinley, Joan, 26
McKinley, John Schuyler, 20
McKinley, John Warner, 16, 20
McKinley, Joseph, 25
McKinley, Joseph Franklin, 20, 25
McKinley, Laura Susan, 17
McKinley, Mattie Susan, 20, 25
McKinley, Maxie Edith, 21
McKinley, Robert, 16
McKinley, Robert A, 20
McKinley, Robert Frederick, 21
McKinley, Samuel A, 20, 26
McKinley, William, 16, 25
McKinnon, Amanda A., 135
McKinnon, Kitty Jane, 135
McKinnon, Louisa A., 135, 141
McKinnon, Margaret, 135
McKinnon, Matilda A., 135
McKinnon, Thomas, 135
McKinsey, Ray A., 47, 144
McLamb, Cager, 82
Mclamb, Oddie, 82
McLaughlin, Isabel, 187
McLaughlin, Mary Catherine, 197
McLean, Douglas, 126
McLean, Johathon Lambert, 126
McLean, Kathryn Marie, 126
McLean, Stephen, 126
McMahan, Lenard, 78, 148
McMorrow, Harry, 129
McNeal, Carl Thomas, 188, 200

McNeal, Carla Sue, 200
McNeal, Donald, 188
McNeal, Earl Moss, 177
McNeal, James Wesley, 200
McNeal, Mary Elizabeth, 200
McNeal, Norman Wayne, 200
McNeal, Pearl, 177, 187
McNeal, Phillip Wayne, 200
McNeal, Thomas Allen, 200
McNeal, Thomas Westley, 177
McNeal, William Wayne, 188, 200
McNeal, William Wesley, 177, 187
McNeil, Mary, 196
McPherren, Lora S., 217
McQuain, Rosa Bell, 67
McQueen, Pearl, 62, 146
McQuiston, Amon L., 197
McRaynolds, Rachel, 46, 143
MD, Hamilton P. Franks,, 141
Meade, Anne, 78, 148
Means, (unknown), 101
Mechem, Walter, 63
Meeds, Susie A., 78, 148
Melgren, Lavivian, 199
Melke, Joanne, 205
Merritt, Sarah Elizabeth, 170
Metts, Elizabeth, 32
Michael, Jeanette, 116, 162
Michael, William A., 180
Mick, Daisy Margaret, 49
Mickelson, Elizabeth, 80, 150
Miles, Catherine, 167
Miller, Albert E, 174
Miller, Alfred, 138
Miller, Alice, 174
Miller, Audra S., 184, 194
Miller, Blanche Pearl, 184, 194
Miller, Charles Kizamore, 174
Miller, Claudine, 184, 194
Miller, Edrie Maurine, 187, 199
Miller, Eva Marie, 187, 200
Miller, Frederick H, 187
Miller, George Riley, 174, 183
Miller, Glen Washington, 184, 195
Miller, Glenna Marie, 195
Miller, Goldia Bell, 184, 194

Miller, Ida Mae, 129
Miller, Jacob Oscar, 174
Miller, James Henry, 174
Miller, John Adam, 174
Miller, Joseph, 174
Miller, Laura Ellen, 174
Miller, Lily Virginia, 184, 194
Miller, Louisa A, 26
Miller, Mary Catherine, 174
Miller, Rachel Ellen, 37, 141
Miller, Sarah Louisa, 184
Miller, Thomas R, 174
Miller, Vernon Lloyd, 194
Miller, Victor Earl, 194
Miller, Violet Elizabeth, 58
Miller, William D, 174
Miller, William Forest, 184
Miller, William Kizamore, 174
Millikan, Dolly, 60, 145
Mills, Grace, 201
Minnick, Henry Morris, 183
Misner, John, 171
Mitchell, Melinda Catherine, 140
Mitchell, Thomas L., 111
Moines, Mary Des, 18
Moore, Edward, 121
Moore, Grace, 60, 145
Moore, Harold Douglas, 119
Moore, Harry Moffett, 197
Moore, Helen Moffett, 197
Moore, Margaret A., 53
Moore, Nellie Beatty, 77, 147
Moore, Nick, 121
Moore, Samuel, 174
Moore, Wilda, 131
Moran, Bruce, 216
Moran, Jeralyn, 216
Moran, John Francis, 216
Moran, Mark, 216
Moran, Steven, 216
Moreland, Frank, 192
Moreland, Fred, 192
Moreland, William, 192
Morgan, Duane, 79, 149
Morgan, Mary, 13
Morley, Robert, 138
Morris, Alma, 72
Morris, Charity, 22
Morris, Dana, 72
Morris, Don, 123
Morris, Eda, 173
Morris, Farnsworth, 72
Morris, Irvine James, 72

Morris, Marie Elizabeth, 123
Morris, Melanie Ann, 123
Morris, Melinda Sue, 123
Morris, William Harvey, 21
Morris, William L., 174
Morrison, Arthur C, 5
Morrison, Leonard, 5
Moss, Alexandria, 14, 18
Moss, Alfred Rulon, 19, 24
Moss, Amanda, 14
Moss, Anna (Angelia), 16
Moss, Belimira, 14
Moss, C. E., 15
Moss, Catherine, 13, 16
Moss, Chester A., 18
Moss, E. M., 15
Moss, Eliza, 13, 14, 16, 17
Moss, Frank H., 18
Moss, G. W., 15
Moss, Harriet, 14
Moss, Harrison, 14
Moss, Henry, 14, 15
Moss, Henry S., 14
Moss, Isaac, 13, 16
Moss, Isabel Nora, 15, 20
Moss, J. Thomas, 16
Moss, Jacob, 15
Moss, James, 13, 16
Moss, John Crabtree, 24
Moss, John L., 15
Moss, John M., 13
Moss, Josephine M., 18
Moss, Josephine Winifred, 20
Moss, Lavinia Mary, 24
Moss, Lee Eugene, 24
Moss, Leroy Franklin, 15
Moss, Leroy Hartley, 20
Moss, Lucinda, 15
Moss, Mabelle K., 20
Moss, Mable A., 18
Moss, Margaret, 16
Moss, Margaret Ann, 15
Moss, Matilda, 15
Moss, Maud Betsy, 13
Moss, Maude A., 18
Moss, Melvin Henery, 24
Moss, Mike, 16
Moss, Minnie Bell, 19
Moss, Montezuma, 13, 15
Moss, N. A., 15
Moss, Nancy Jane, 15
Moss, Naomi Mary, 24
Moss, Paul Simeon, 24
Moss, Polly Ann Lewarky, 13
Moss, Rachel Aradene, 24

Moss, Roma, 16
Moss, Ruth Crabtree, 24
Moss, Ruth Margaret, 24
Moss, S. A., 15
Moss, Samuel Robeson, 15, 19
Moss, Sanford Ross, 15, 19
Moss, Simeon Martindale, 19, 24
Moss, Vernon Laurence, 19, 24
Moss, William B., 16
Moss, William Jefferson, 13, 15, 19, 24
Motes, Flora Eva, 30
Moutray, Charles Kapp, 194
Moutray, Evelyn Berniece, 194
Moutray, Gary Keith, 194
Moutray, George Franklin, 194
Moutray, Harold Eugene, 194
Moutray, Jess, 194
Moutray, Margaret Juanita, 194
Moutray, Marjorie Ellen, 194
Mowery, Mary, 36
Moyers, Sarah, 36
Mulanax, (infant), 46, 143
Mulanax, Alfred, 46, 61, 143, 146
Mulanax, Alice Ruby, 46, 144
Mulanax, Anna Louisa, 38, 47
Mulanax, Anna M., 46, 143
Mulanax, Arthur Dallas, 45, 143
Mulanax, Bertie, 38
Mulanax, Bessie, 46, 144
Mulanax, Calvin Silas, 46, 61, 144, 146
Mulanax, Catherine, 32, 137
Mulanax, Clotilda Adeline, 37, 45, 141, 142
Mulanax, Cora Vivena, 61, 146
Mulanax, Dorothy Ellen, 62, 80, 146, 150
Mulanax, Douglas Lefeber, 94, 151
Mulanax, Ed Barnett, 46, 144
Mulanax, Edith Pearl, 46, 62, 144, 146
Mulanax, Elizabeth J., 32, 37, 137, 141

Mulanax, Elizabeth Jane, 37, 141
Mulanax, Ella, 38
Mulanax, Elta Vera, 61, 146
Mulanax, Faye Ammelia, 60, 145
Mulanax, Flora Adeline, 45, 60, 143, 145
Mulanax, George Cazwell, 37
Mulanax, George Ellet, 45, 143
Mulanax, Gertrude May, 46, 144
Mulanax, Grace, 46, 143
Mulanax, Greenberry, 32, 137
Mulanax, Harry Edgar, 45, 143
Mulanax, Hazel, 46, 144
Mulanax, Ida May, 46, 143
Mulanax, Irvan, 61, 146
Mulanax, Jacob Allen, 37, 46, 141, 143
Mulanax, James Harvey, 38
Mulanax, James Lewis, 45, 60, 142, 144
Mulanax, James Matthew, 61, 146
Mulanax, Jessee E., 37, 142
Mulanax, John Greenbury, 37, 45, 141, 143
Mulanax, John W., 46, 143
Mulanax, John William, 37, 46, 61, 141, 144, 146
Mulanax, Joseph, 29, 31, 136
Mulanax, Joseph M., 46, 143
Mulanax, Kate, 46, 143
Mulanax, Katherine, 37, 141
Mulanax, Kenneth, 61, 146
Mulanax, Leroy, 46, 143
Mulanax, Lillian, 38
Mulanax, Louis, 46, 61, 143, 146
Mulanax, Lucy Adeline, 37, 47, 142, 144
Mulanax, Lyle Verne, 60, 145
Mulanax, Mary, 32, 137
Mulanax, Mary Aceneth, 46, 60, 143, 145
Mulanax, Mary L., 37, 141
Mulanax, Mary S., 37
Mulanax, Matthew Elliott, 37, 46, 141, 143
Mulanax, Matthew William, 61, 146
Mulanax, Miles Elliott, 32, 36, 137, 141
Mulanax, Nellie, 37, 142
Mulanax, Oliver Elliott, 38
Mulanax, Rachal Elizabeth, 37, 141
Mulanax, Rachel Ellen, 46, 143
Mulanax, Raymond, 46, 144
Mulanax, Roger Lewis, 77, 94, 147, 151
Mulanax, Ruby Ann, 47, 61, 62, 144, 146
Mulanax, Sarah, 32, 137
Mulanax, Sarah E., 37, 142
Mulanax, Steven N., 37
Mulanax, Thomas Luther, 38
Mulanax, Violet, 46, 143
Mulanax, Walter, 46, 143
Mulanax, William, 61, 146
Mulanax, William Dallas, 37, 45, 141, 142
Mulanax, William R., 32, 37, 137, 141
Mulenax, Crystabelle, 49
Mullenax, (infant) Daughter, 36
Mullenax, (infant) Son, 35
Mullenax, Aaron C., 36, 44
Mullenax, Abraham, 29, 30, 33
Mullenax, Abraham, Jr., 30
Mullenax, Adam D., 36
Mullenax, Alfred C., 32
Mullenax, Almira J., 34
Mullenax, Alphra, 39
Mullenax, Ann R., 41
Mullenax, Anna C., 36
Mullenax, Annie Jane, 38, 48
Mullenax, Arthur, 38
Mullenax, Basil Kay, 49
Mullenax, Benjamin A., 33
Mullenax, Benjamin W., 44
Mullenax, Betty Alice, 48, 65
Mullenax, Bishop Marvin, 50
Mullenax, Bonnie, 66, 88
Mullenax, Brenda Lyn, 102
Mullenax, Brooks Burdette, 64, 84
Mullenax, Calhoun, 44
Mullenax, Carolyn Jean, 84, 102
Mullenax, Cassie E., 36
Mullenax, Catharine, 30, 34
Mullenax, Catherine, 33, 39
Mullenax, Charity Margaret, 33, 39
Mullenax, Charles B., 51
Mullenax, Charles Edward Vivan, 50, 67
Mullenax, Charlie, 36
Mullenax, Christina, 30, 35, 36
Mullenax, Claris Ella, 44, 59
Mullenax, Claude, 36
Mullenax, Connie, 88
Mullenax, Connie Jean, 85, 103
Mullenax, Conrad, 29, 35
Mullenax, David Lee, 84, 102
Mullenax, David Pillow, 41, 54
Mullenax, Debra Elizabeth, 67, 88
Mullenax, Dolly, 48, 64
Mullenax, Donald C., 66, 88
Mullenax, Dora, 38
Mullenax, Doris Lee, 84
Mullenax, Douglas, 67
Mullenax, Edith Virginia, 44
Mullenax, Edward, 30, 36
Mullenax, Edward J., 39
Mullenax, Edward Lee, 49, 67
Mullenax, Elijah, 38, 48
Mullenax, Eliza C., 32
Mullenax, Elizabeth, 30, 40
Mullenax, Elizabeth Ann, 30, 33
Mullenax, Elizabeth P., 39
Mullenax, Elizabeth S, 36, 44
Mullenax, Ellen, 48
Mullenax, Elva, 44, 49
Mullenax, Elva Lenor, 50
Mullenax, Emily, 36
Mullenax, Emily Jane, 34, 41
Mullenax, Emma, 36
Mullenax, Emory R, 48, 65
Mullenax, Ephriam A., 41
Mullenax, Ernest, 36
Mullenax, Esta Belle, 44
Mullenax, Etta, 50
Mullenax, Fannie Margaret, 66
Mullenax, Francis Benjamin, 32
Mullenax, Fred, 44
Mullenax, Galen, 66
Mullenax, Garnett, 35
Mullenax, Geneva Katherine,

Mullenax, George, 30, 34, 35, 41
Mullenax, George Fry, 66
Mullenax, George W., 32
Mullenax, Gerald Allen, 49
Mullenax, Geraldine M., 74
Mullenax, Gladys Mae, 44
Mullenax, Halcie, 65, 84
Mullenax, Harlan, 64, 84
Mullenax, Harnass, 50
Mullenax, Haxel, 44
Mullenax, Hazel Gray, 44
Mullenax, Helen, 66, 87
Mullenax, Helen J., 67, 88
Mullenax, Henry A., 41
Mullenax, Henry Clay, 30, 35
Mullenax, Henry Walter, 36, 44
Mullenax, Ida, 36
Mullenax, Ida Florance, 34
Mullenax, Ida Jane, 50
Mullenax, Inez Catherine, 49, 67
Mullenax, Isaac J., 39, 49
Mullenax, Isaac S., 33, 39
Mullenax, Jacob, 29, 30, 33
Mullenax, Jacob C., 30
Mullenax, Jacob E., 34
Mullenax, Jacob L., 32
Mullenax, James, 29, 36, 136
Mullenax, James B., 38, 48
Mullenax, James K., 30, 36
Mullenax, James P., 33
Mullenax, James W., 29, 32
Mullenax, James Wilson, 32
Mullenax, Janice Lee, 85, 103
Mullenax, Jeddy D., 50
Mullenax, Jesse, 38
Mullenax, John, 29, 36
Mullenax, John A., 39
Mullenax, John B., 32, 41
Mullenax, John H., 30, 34
Mullenax, John W., 50
Mullenax, John Wesley, 33, 39
Mullenax, John William, 44, 50
Mullenax, Joseph, 30, 35, 44
Mullenax, Joseph Riley, 32, 37
Mullenax, Karen Sue, 85, 103
Mullenax, Katie E., 50
Mullenax, Kelley M., 83
Mullenax, Kelly Blaine, 85, 104
Mullenax, Kenneth Oscar, 51
Mullenax, Kenton Dexter, 44, 59
Mullenax, Kenton Dexter, Jr., 59
Mullenax, Kenton L., 35, 44
Mullenax, Lena Ester, 51, 68
Mullenax, Lester, 44
Mullenax, Letha Carol, 66
Mullenax, Levie, 50
Mullenax, Lillie, 51
Mullenax, Lonnie Lee, 102
Mullenax, Louisa, 38
Mullenax, Louisa K., 41
Mullenax, Louise Grey, 85, 103
Mullenax, Lucinda, 30
Mullenax, Lucy Bell, 36
Mullenax, Luetta, 40
Mullenax, Lura, 48, 64
Mullenax, Mahala J, 32
Mullenax, Margaret, 30, 33, 34
Mullenax, Margaret A, 40
Mullenax, Margaret Ann, 38
Mullenax, Martha, 31, 34, 35, 36, 41
Mullenax, Martha (Mattie), 36
Mullenax, Martha A., 32
Mullenax, Martha Ann, 49
Mullenax, Martha E., 41
Mullenax, Martha Ellen, 48, 64
Mullenax, Martin, 39, 51
Mullenax, Martin, Jr., 51
Mullenax, Mary, 30, 33
Mullenax, Mary J., 36
Mullenax, Mary Jane, 39, 49
Mullenax, Mary Permelia Catherine, 38, 47
Mullenax, Mary Virginia, 38
Mullenax, Mattie, 50
Mullenax, Maude, 35
Mullenax, Mavis A., 35, 44, 58
Mullenax, May, 35
Mullenax, Mcclelland, 48, 64
Mullenax, Merle, 44
Mullenax, Michael, 85
Mullenax, Minor, 36, 48
Mullenax, Monna Lee, 44, 59
Mullenax, Nellie Mae, 49, 65
Mullenax, Nellie Susan, 44, 59
Mullenax, Noah, 40
Mullenax, Ollie Elizabeth, 44, 59
Mullenax, Paul, 65, 85
Mullenax, Paula Marie, 85
Mullenax, Pheobe, 40
Mullenax, Pheobe Ann, 50
Mullenax, Phoebe, 35, 39, 51
Mullenax, Phoebe Ellen, 39
Mullenax, Rachel, 29, 51
Mullenax, Randall, 67
Mullenax, Ray, 44
Mullenax, Raymond, 67
Mullenax, Raymond Rafe, 49, 66
Mullenax, Regania, 40
Mullenax, Richard Dickson, 51
Mullenax, Richard Emory, 65, 85
Mullenax, Ruby mae, 44
Mullenax, Ruhana, 30, 35
Mullenax, Salathial, 30, 33
Mullenax, Salathiel, 40
Mullenax, Salisbury, 36
Mullenax, Sallie Denie, 48, 65
Mullenax, Samual B., 30
Mullenax, Sandra Jean, 85
Mullenax, Sarah A., 33
Mullenax, Sarah C., 35
Mullenax, Sarah F., 41
Mullenax, Sedgwick L., 50
Mullenax, Sidney E., 40
Mullenax, Silvie P., 50
Mullenax, Solomon, 30
Mullenax, Solomon Key, 39, 48
Mullenax, Sonya, 85, 103
Mullenax, Stanley Domaine, 49
Mullenax, Stella, 51
Mullenax, Stephen Grover, 41
Mullenax, Steven Grove, 54, 74
Mullenax, Strickler J., 50
Mullenax, Susan, 30
Mullenax, Thelma Gertrude, 44
Mullenax, Thomas Jefferson, 39, 50
Mullenax, Thorald Tiffin, 66
Mullenax, Tiffin Rienhart, 49, 66

Mullenax, Tiffin Rinehart, 66
Mullenax, Tilden, 35
Mullenax, Valley, 51
Mullenax, Viola, 50
Mullenax, Virgie, 48
Mullenax, Virgil Craig, 49, 66
Mullenax, Virginia, 36
Mullenax, Virginia Susan, 39, 50
Mullenax, Vivian Lucille, 49
Mullenax, Wanda Dran, 59, 76
Mullenax, Wandy F., 50
Mullenax, William, 29, 30, 35
Mullenax, William Alexander, 38, 48
Mullenax, William Benny, 38
Mullenax, William Carter, 40
Mullenax, William Isaac, 32, 38
Mullenax, William Kay, 66
Mullenax, William Vivin, 49
Mullenax, Willie, 38
Mullenax, Wilma Grethel, 49, 66
Mullin, (unknown), 101
Mulnanx, (infany), 60, 145
Mulnanx, Alvin Edgar, 60, 77, 145, 147
Mulnanx, Claude Arthur, 60, 145
Mulnanx, Curtis, 60, 145
Mulnanx, Hazel Marie, 60, 77, 145, 147
Mulnanx, Louise Ernest, 60, 145
Muninger, Clara, 206
Munson, Elias, 171
Murphy, Louise, 48
Murphy, Nancy Ann, 30
Murphy, Permelia, 32
Murphy, Walter, 32
Murray, Lisa, 93
Murray, Narhon Scott, 93
Murray, Sherry, 93
Musetta, Helen, 67
Musser, Mary, 64
Mxkenley, Cornelius, 16
Myers, John William, 49
Myers, Rosetta, 49
Myrick, Calvin Curtis, 80, 100, 150, 157
Myrick, Clinton Jay, 80, 100, 150, 157

Myrick, Curtis Fay, 80, 150
Myrick, Cynthia Marguerite, 80, 100, 150, 158
Myrick, Daniel Jay, 100, 157
Myrick, David Curtis, 100, 157
Myrick, Marissa Mary, 100, 157
Nanni, Elizabeth, 202
Nash, Charles Lewis, 23
Neace, Filmore, 56
Neal, Leah Philena, 22
Neale, Frederick, 197
Neel, Della Mae, 22
Neel, Goldie Demoine,, 22, 27
Neel, John A, 22
Neel, Ruth Ellen, 22, 27
Nei, Bric Lee, 217
Nei, Mark Allen, 217
Nei, Peter Allen, 217
Nei, Scott William, 217
Nellie, Ellender, 173
Nelson, Anderson, 38
Nelson, Charlotte, 63
Nelson, Cleo May, 77, 147
Nelson, David, 66
Nelson, Diana Denise, 126
Nelson, Donna, 66
Nelson, Elizabeth, 38
Nelson, George Monroe, 77, 147
Nelson, Helen, 66
Nelson, Jane Earline, 77, 94, 147, 151
Nelson, Jean Earl, 77, 147
Nelson, Jerry, 66
Nelson, John, 66
Nelson, Kathryn Harriett, 128
Nelson, Leslie Howard, 77, 147
Nelson, Lester, 66
Nelson, Margaret, 30
Nelson, Robert J., 34
Nelson, Sarah S, 69
Nelson, Shirley Dawn, 96, 153
Nelson, Sylvestor, 36
Nelson, Vera Dean, 77, 147
Nestor, John, 57
Neumann, Beverly Ann, 211
Nevarro, Loretta Rose, 212
Nevius, Dorothy Anna, 209
Newcomb, Elizabeth, 16
Newman, Linnie M, 60
Newman, Margaret, 36

Newman, Vernon Harold, 84
Nicely, John Aaron, 126
Nicely, John Partick, 126
Nicely, Kevin Aaron, 126
Nicholas, Adam F, 175
Nicholas, Cynthia, 175
Nicholas, Frensceenor, 175
Nicholas, George, 174, 175
Nicholas, James W, 175
Nicholas, Jones, 175
Nicholas, Mary A, 175
Nicholas, Phoebe J Stone, 70
Nicholas, Renick L, 175
Nicholson, Phyllis, 200
Nicklin, Frank Lewis, Jr., 117, 162
Nickloi, Darci LeAnn, 116, 161
Nickoli, Ramond Paul, 116, 161
Nickoli, Tanna June, 116, 161
Nims, Edith, 26
Noel, Beverly, 131
Nohe, Thomas, 112
Nohe, Tom, 112
Noltensmeyer, Charles Null, 206, 216
Noltensmeyer, Karen, 216
Noltensmeyer, Ronda, 216
Noltensmeyer, Thomas, 216
Noltensmeyer, Walter, 206
Norman, Mary Ann, 24
North, Zachery T., 21
Nottingham, Adam, 10
Nottingham, Addison, 10
Nottingham, Debra Jean, 119
Nottingham, Eleanor Elizabeth, 195
Nottingham, Grace Marie, 24
Nottingham, Henry, 10, 11
Nottingham, Mahala Patsy, 10
Nottingham, Margaret, 10
Nottingham, Mary, 10
Nottingham, Nancy Jane, 10
Nottingham, Victoria Jane, 198
Nottingham, William III, 10
Nottingham, William, Jr., 10
Nottinghan, William, Sr., 10
Nozhachum, Dorothy, 61, 146
O'Brien, Clayton Lewis, 99, 156
O'Brien, Donald Lewis, 99,

156
O'brien, Susannah, 10
Oder, Harvey D, 199
Offutt, (unknown), 101
O'neal, Peggy Marie, 106
Orr, Flora Mabel, 26
Orr, James Henry, 26
Orr, Meredith K., 197
Orrahood, Elizabeth Ann, 41
Oryall, Alice, 66
Osborn, Edna Jo, 210
Osborne, Gary Gene, 214
Osborne, Harold Lorraine, 214
Osborne, Terry Lorraine, 214
Osburn, (infant), 80, 150
Osburn, Andrea, 79, 150
Osburn, Bessie Lee, 61, 77, 145, 147
Osburn, Betty Jane, 78, 98, 148, 155
Osburn, Billie Lorreen, 78, 96, 148, 154
Osburn, Charley Calvin, 61, 78, 145, 148
Osburn, Charleyn Joy, 78, 148
Osburn, Cleo Faye, 61, 78, 145, 148
Osburn, Connie Jean, 78, 98, 148, 155
Osburn, Daniel, 80, 150
Osburn, Ethel Fern, 78, 96, 148, 153
Osburn, Francis Paul, 61, 79, 145, 149
Osburn, Jeffery Todd, 98, 155
Osburn, Jerry, 80, 150
Osburn, Jim Conrad Burton, 61, 145
Osburn, John Franklin, 78, 98, 148, 155
Osburn, Joyce, 79, 149
Osburn, Julie, 80, 150
Osburn, Kathryn Machiel, 78, 97, 148, 154
Osburn, Laurie Joan, 80, 99, 150, 157
Osburn, Linda Gail, 78, 98, 148, 155
Osburn, Lynn, 80, 150
Osburn, Mable Marie, 61, 79, 145, 149
Osburn, Mary, 79, 149
Osburn, Mary Helen Rose, 61, 80, 145, 150
Osburn, Minnie Belle, 61, 79, 145, 149
Osburn, Myrtle May, 61, 79, 145, 149
Osburn, Parthena Ann, 61, 78, 145, 149
Osburn, Patricia Lee, 78, 98, 148, 155
Osburn, Riley Matthew, 61, 146
Osburn, Riley Newton, 61, 145
Osburn, Rita Faye, 80, 150
Osburn, Ronald, 79, 149
Osburn, Samual Stephen, 61, 78, 145, 148
Osburn, Sandra, 80, 99, 150, 156
Osburn, Sarah Ellen, 46, 61, 144, 146
Osburn, Stanley, 80, 150
Osburn, Stephen, 61, 145
Osburn, Stephen Wayne, 80, 150
Osburn, Teddy Lea, 80, 150
Osburn, Theodore Harvey, 61, 80, 145, 150
Osburn, Vance Vernon, 61, 146
Osburn, Zella Jane, 61, 80, 146, 150
Overly, Ann, 45, 142
Owen, Shawn Alfred, 213
Owens, Susan Emely, 171
Page, Albert Allen, 189
Page, Charles F., 189
Page, Clarence Miami, 189
Page, Henry Leslie, 189
Page, Jesse Edward, 189
Page, John Williamson, 189
Page, Louis Alvin, 189
Page, Louisa Jeanetta, 189, 201
Page, Mary Jane, 189
Page, Nancy Ellen, 189
Page, William Silas, 189
Painter, Christopher Robert, 203
Painter, Robert Ivan, 203
Painter, Robin Lynn, 203
Painter, Sharlyn Lavon, 203, 213
Painter, Zella, 40
Palmer, Eva Lucille, 188
Parsons, Arthur B, 43
Parsons, Edith, 44
Parton, Eliza, 178
Paterson, Rosella, 180
Patton, George, 172
Patton, Janette Alice, 181
Patton, John Danial, 181
Patton, John Henry, 181
Patton, Julia, 22
Patton, Lillie May, 181, 192
Patton, Liz, 181
Patton, Margaret Jane, 181
Patton, Mattie, 181, 192
Patton, Michael R., 63
Patton, Minnie Belle, 181, 192
Patton, Patrick H., 63
Patton, Raymond, 62
Patton, Thomas, 181
Pauge, Juanita E, 200
Payne, Minerva, 14
Payne, Olive Lavina, 46, 143
Payne, Rilla C., 140
Pearson, Christine Jessica, 127
Pendergrass, May, 200
Peninger, Susan Catherine, 167
Pennington, Josephine, 58
Perry, (unknown), 37, 142
Perryman, Mary Louise, 37
Perryman, Thomas, 37
Perryman, William A., 32
Personeus, David, 91
Personeus, Mary Alicia, 92
Personeus, Melissa, 92
Peterson, Chris, 123
Petra, Mary, 89
Petros, Louise, 23
Petticrew, Alice, 139
Petticrew, Ambrose, 139
Petticrew, Lulu, 139
Pflugar, Kevin, 117, 163
Pfluger, Mathew Thomas, 118, 163
Pfluger, Nichole Alexandria, 118, 163
Phares, Abigail, 35
Phares, Adam Harness, 33
Phares, Benjamin B., 69
Phares, Benjamin Loren, 129
Phares, Bulah, 69
Phares, Cleat, 69, 90
Phares, Dottie Lou, 111, 130
Phares, Elizabeth, 33
Phares, Elmer P., 90, 111
Phares, Georgia Lynn, 129

Phares, Ina Lee, 111, 129
Phares, James Allen, 129
Phares, James H., 111, 129
Phares, Jill F., 131
Phares, Joshua Michael, 131
Phares, Kimberly Lynn, 129, 131
Phares, Marianne M., 129
Phares, Martha, 69
Phares, Mary, 87
Phares, Mary June, 111, 130
Phares, Matthew H, 129
Phares, Michael Elmer, 129, 131
Phares, Myrtle K, 90
Phares, Pamala Karla, 129
Phares, Raymond, 111, 129
Phares, Raymond Edward, 129, 132
Phares, Richard, 64
Phares, Richard Cleat, 111, 129
Phares, Richard Clete, Jr., 129, 131
Phares, Ruben, 131
Phares, Sonnee Dee, 129
Phares, Stephen Edward, 132
Phares, Thomas Lee, 129
Phares,III, Richard Clete, 131
Phillips, Downey, 195
Phillips, Ronald John, 65
Pilcher, Jean, 209
Pinnock, Gladys Evelyn, 24
Plates, Angeline Alicia, 98, 156
Plates, Enoc Ruben, 98, 156
Plates, Runen, 98, 156
Plyler, Anna Pauline, 88
Plyler, Calvin Kieth, 67
Plyler, Stephen, 111
Plyler, Stephen Todd, 111
Polize, Nadine, 92
Posten, Susannah, 32
Poteat, Gary Eugene, 81, 151
Potter, Matthew, 36
Powell, Arthur Thomas, 25
Powell, Cassie, 130, 164
Powell, Dale, 113, 158
Powell, Darrell, 113, 159
Powell, Deanna Sue, 113, 130, 158, 164
Powell, Delma Esther, 26
Powell, Dennis Loran, 113, 158
Powell, Dewett McKinley, 26
Powell, Donita Laneel, 113, 130, 159, 164
Powell, Duane Lloyd, 113, 130, 158, 164
Powell, Dwight, 113, 158
Powell, Eleanor, 127
Powell, Emma Sarilda, 205
Powell, Jessica Lee, 130, 164
Powell, Rachel Jane, 29
Powell, Rosella Zorada, 26
Praisiner, Deborah Kay, 109
Price, Dr. William T., 5, 6
Prier, Kathleen, 205
Prier, William M., 205
Prowell, Diane Kay, 100, 157
Prowell, Randy Ray, 100, 157
Prowell, Ronnie Jay, 100, 157
Prowell, Smith B., 99, 157
Puffenbarger, Herman, 84
Puffenbarger, Rheda Catherine, 86
Puffenbarger, Thorton George, 52
Pugh, Aaron, 217
Pugh, Bryan, 208, 218, 219
Pugh, Calep, 217
Pugh, Ethan, 217
Pugh, Hailey Marie, 219
Pugh, Judy, 208
Pugh, Karen, 208
Pugh, Loman Bryant, 208
Pugh, Noah, 217
Pugh, Roger L., 208, 218
Pugh, Ronnie, 208, 217
Pugh, Wanda, 208
Pyanowski, Douglas Kent, 98, 155
Pyanowski, Robert, 98, 155
Radford, Hazel, 199
Raines, Delbert, 69
Raines, Fred, 52
Raines, Kate, 52
Raines, Kenney, 52
Raines, Lillie, 52, 68
Raines, Marshall, 52, 69
Raines, Martha, 52
Raines, Monna, 82
Raines, Myrtle, 129
Raines, Russell, 69
Raines, Stewart, 52
Raines, Sylvia, 52
Raines, Una, 69
Raines, Walter, 52
Raines, Wilma, 129
Ralston, Margaret, 16
Ralston, Samuel, 36
Ramsey, Leatha Viola, 186
Ramsey, Leroy Swampton, 176
Ramsey, Othelia Ann, 43
Raper, Nancy, 209
Ray, Addison, 171
Ray, Blanche Mahalia, 180, 191
Ray, Clayton H., 61, 146
Ray, Elisha, 180
Ray, Elizabeth A., 180
Ray, Elwina, 171
Ray, Enoch Albert, 180
Ray, George F., 171
Ray, Henry, 45, 142
Ray, Laura Edith, 180
Ray, Mere, 171
Ray, Mitlida Almira, 180
Ray, Sally Kay, 119
Ray, Sara A., 171
Ray, Shelia Ann, 119
Ray, William R, 171
Raynolds, Rueben E, 172
Reagan, Elizabeth, 22
Reah, Jessica Lynn, 126
Redro, Peggy, 94, 151
Reed, Catherine, 130, 164
Reed, Cynthia Elaine, 121
Reed, Elizabeth, 142
Reed, Floyd Hubert, II, 121
Reed, Hubert, 121
Reed, Katie Ann, 127
Reed, Michael, 127
Reeser, Harriet, 26
Reeser, Margaret, 26
Reeser, Ora H, 26
Reeser, William Henry, 26
Reiber, Catherine, 25
Reid, Dr. John H., 25
Reid, Harlan E., 25
Reid, L. Wayne, 25
Renfro, Flora, 45, 142
Renfro, James, 45, 142
Renfro, Jesse, 45, 142
Renfro, John H., 45, 142
Renfro, Lucy, 45, 142
Renfro, Mary, 45, 142
Renfro, Mary Agnus., 45, 142
Renfro, Rachel Ann, 45, 142
Rexroad, Arthur, 44
Rexroad, Benjamin, 45
Rexroad, Clinton D, 44
Rexroad, Edwin C, 60
Rexroad, Forrest, 45

Rexroad, Grace, 45
Rexroad, Ira H, 45
Rexroad, Jefferson D, 44
Rexroad, Kemper D, 44, 60
Rexroad, Lena, 45
Rexroad, Mary E, 45
Rexroad, Nicholas, 44
Rexroad, Robert, 45
Rexrode, Attie Bessie, 59, 69, 111
Rexrode, Cecil Clark, 101
Rexrode, Christian, 34
Rexrode, Ellen Catherine, 44
Rexrode, James Morgan, 101
Rexrode, Kim, 101
Rexrode, Lewis, 30
Rexrode, Mary Ettie, 59
Rexrode, Nora, 36
Rexrode, Rachel, 34
Rexrode, Theresa Iola, 101
Rhea, David Dewayne, 126
Rhea, Mathew Eric, 126
Rhodes, Kitty Lou, 58
Richard, Albert, 183
Richard, Charles Francis, 183, 194
Richard, Frank Floyd, 183
Richard, George Harold, 194
Richard, Henry William, 183
Richard, Nellie May, 183
Richards, Rev. Donald E., 74
Richardson, Angela Suzanne, 211
Richardson, Ann Leslie, 208
Richardson, Michael, 211
Richardson, Michael David, 211
Richardson, William, 208
Richmond, Doris, 184
Ricken, Myrna, 100, 157
Risley, Donna Jean, 125
Ritchie, Donald, 106
Ritter, David, 213
Ritter, Nicole, 213
Roach, Beth Ann, 107, 127
Roach, Carrie Louise, 126
Roach, Daniel Matthew, 126
Roach, Darrell Dwayne, 107
Roach, Dorral Dainwood, 107
Roach, James, 107
Roach, Jessica Renee, 126
Roach, Kathy Lunn, 107, 127
Roach, Thomas, 55
Roach, Tina Marie, 107, 126
Roach, Travis Lee, 107, 126
Roach, Travis Lee, II, 126
Roat, Roscoe Bertram, 197
Roberts, Hester Jane, 176
Robertson, J. Stanley, 49
Rodrigues, Jamie Andres, 125
Roesti, Wilma Marie, 195
Root, Julie Ann, 114, 159
Rose, Ivan Leroy, 205
Rose, Novalee, 108
Ross, Christopher Guy, 92
Ross, Hattie Luvernia, 21
Ross, Henry, 92
Ross, Henry, Jr., 92
Ross, Selena, 92
Ross, Vera, 144
Roth, Mary Ann, 19
Routt, Dorothy, 204
Routzahn, Willis, 138
Roy, Estaline, 20
Roy, Gladys, 43
Roy, Lester Lee, 67
Roy, Seymore, 67
Roy, Stilman, 67
Ruano, John S Scoma, 200
Ruark, Juanita Mildred, 188, 201
Ruark, Kristie Kay, 211
Ruark, Linda Suzanna, 201, 211
Ruark, Margaret, 176
Ruark, Sherri Ann, 211
Ruark, William Earnest, 188
Ruark, William Larry, 201, 211
Ruark, William Lloyd, 188, 201
Ruark, William Shea, 211
Ruby, Freda, 205
Ruby, John E., 205
Ruggles, Kathlene, 104
Rule, William, 199
Rulon, Mary Ruth, 19
Ruppert, Angela Kay, 210
Ruppert, Cynthia, 210
Ruppert, Edgar C, 200
Ruppert, Richard E, 200, 210
Ruppert, Sara Ann, 200
Rush, Carrie, 138
Russell, John Elbert, 172
Ryder, Dorothy, 125
Ryder, James Ishmal, 218
Ryder, Julie Lauraine, 218
Ryder, Lanty Dale, 196
Ryder, Millie, 76
Rymer, Clyde, 69, 90
Rymer, Jacob Harper, 69
Rymer, Mary, 90
Rymer, Mattie, 69
Rymer, Sudie R, 69, 90
Rymer, Virgil, 90, 111
Sager, Jordan, 104
Sager, Michael Allen, 104
Salatino, Peggy, 212
Salee, Ruby Alice, 198
Sanders, Jasper Lee, 192
Sanders, Kenneth, 192
Sanders, Oliver, 192
Sanders, Perry Orin, 192
Sanner, Doug, 127
Sappington, Gary, 93
Sappington, Martha Elizabeth, 17
Saum, Jr., George Daniel, 88
Saum, Sr., George Daniel, 88
Sausaman, Golda Wreathel, 23
Savage, Martha Matilda, 184
Savage, Roberta June, 116, 161
Saybert, Henry, Jr., 166
Sayre, Anna Mae, 76
Schaffer, Grace Adeline, 194
Schaumann, Holger Heinrich, 24
Scheitlin, Williard James, 56
Schell, Robert, 98, 155
Schell, Roberta Ann, 98, 155
Schiller, Alma Katherine, R.n., 77, 147
Schiller, Frank Wiliam, 77, 147
Schmickle, Anna, 187
Schmidt, Corrie Rene, 219
Schmidt, Joshua David, 219
Schmidt, Leroy, 219
Schmollinger, Henry L, 179
Schmollinger, Millard, 179
Schmollinger, Samual, 179
Schmollinger, Tracy, 179
Schnell, Alvin Delano, 98, 155
Schnell, Andrew James, 118, 163
Schnell, Danise Dawn, 98, 155
Schnell, Heather Susan, 98, 118, 155, 163
Schnell, Leland Gary, 98, 118, 155, 163
Schnell, Walter, 98, 155
Schoenfield, Carolyn, 209

Schriener, Mildred, 72
Schultz, Charlotte Ann, 117, 163
Schweiger, Cscelia, 97, 154
Scott, Alta, 195
Scott, Edna, 195
Scott, Hazel, 195
Scott, Imo, 195
Scott, Inez, 195
Scott, Owen Lester, 195
Seaman, Delores, 204
Seeley, Ann Marie, 85
Seeley, Carmen Cora, 85
Seeley, Clarence Walter, 85
Seiler, Alice, 101
Sellers, Rebecca W., 139
Senger, Gerald Wayne II, 103
Senger, Gerald Wayne III, 103
Senger, Jonathan Paul, 103
Senger, Kara Anna- Marie, 103
Seybert, Harry, 166
Seybert, Leah, 34
Seybert, Susan, 170
Sharon, Margiele Pearl, 210
Sharp, Anna Mary, 197
Sharp, Brenda Jane, 119
Sharp, Donna, 124
Sharp, Eliza Jane, 41
Sharp, Samuel, 197
Sharrai, Bessie, 46, 143
Shaw, William Alvin, 46, 143
Sheeder, Caroline, 140
Sheets, Alannah Brook, 126
Sheets, Bryan Robert, 103
Sheets, Clawson, 107
Sheets, Clawson Emerson, II, 107
Sheets, Diana Kay, 107, 125
Sheets, Donna Faye, 107, 125
Sheets, Grover Cleveland, 84
Sheets, Larry Allen, 107, 125
Sheets, Mary Frances, 84, 102
Sheets, Melissa Dawn, 125
Sheets, Melvina, 103
Sheets, Michelle Denise, 125
Sheets, Robert Clark, 84, 103
Sheets, Roy Wetzel, 84, 103
Sheets, Sandra Jean, 107, 125
Sheets, Stephen Mark, 103
Sheets, Teresa Allen, 107, 126
Sheets, Thomas Wayne, 107, 126
Sheets, Thomas Wayne, II, 126
Sheets, Todd Loran, 103
Sheets, William Wetzel, 103
Sheets, William Winfred, 84
Shelter, Brenda Marie, 124
Shelter, Latasha, 124
Shelter, Levi, 124
Shelter, Tekisha Lynn, 124
Shelton, Augustus, 167
Shelton, Eli, 174
Shepherd, Bob, 112
Shepherd, Gred Rob, 112
Shepherd, Kelly Ann, 112
Shepler, Janet, 91
Sherrard, Robert, 191
Shey, Collean, 115, 161
Shields, Martha Margaret, 178
Shinaberry, Brandon Christin, 103
Shinaberry, Henry, 103
Shinaberry, Howard Ellet, 103
Shinaberry, Joshua Daryl, 103
Shinaberry, Myra Jean, 120
Shinaberry, Seth Adam, 103
Shockey, Almeda May, 175
Shockey, Gertrude Ethel, 176, 185
Shockey, Grover Charles, 175
Shockey, Isaac, 176
Shockey, Jacob Andrew, 176
Shockey, Jasper, 176
Shockey, John Easter, 175
Shockey, John Henry, 175
Shockey, Orvil A, 176
Shockey, Rebecca, 175
Shockey, Rosa Vera, 176, 186
Shockey, Wiliam, 176
Shrope, Richard, 114, 159
Shull, Robin, 119
Shupp, Mort, 137
Simions, Irma, 85
Simmions, Roy James, 122
Simmons, Aaron Sharon, 41, 53
Simmons, Abraham, 33, 34
Simmons, Albert, 89
Simmons, Amos, 68
Simmons, Ann R., 34
Simmons, Barbara Joan, 104, 121
Simmons, Bessie Catherine, 87
Simmons, Bruce Allen, 105, 122
Simmons, Charles Blaine, 104, 122
Simmons, Clara, 85, 105
Simmons, Dewey Hunter, 85, 104
Simmons, Dewey Hunter, II, 104
Simmons, Edward Blaine, 122
Simmons, Edward Lee, 85, 104
Simmons, Elbridge H, 89
Simmons, Elizabeth, 172
Simmons, Emery, 41
Simmons, Emma, 85
Simmons, Emmett, 53
Simmons, Erin Elizabeth, 122
Simmons, Ethel S, 89
Simmons, Everret, 53
Simmons, Georgie Elizabeth, 104, 122
Simmons, Geri Nicole, 122
Simmons, Gladys, 104, 107
Simmons, Huldah C. Or Ulda, 41
Simmons, James Alfred, 34
Simmons, James Lester, 85
Simmons, James Orie, 104
Simmons, Jared Michael, 122
Simmons, John, 33
Simmons, John Wesley, 34, 41
Simmons, Joy Lou, 111
Simmons, Judy, 104, 121
Simmons, Kaitlyn Elizabeth, 122
Simmons, Kathleen Marie, 104, 121
Simmons, Keith, 85
Simmons, Kevin Lee, 104, 122
Simmons, Larry, 104
Simmons, Lertie, 104, 120
Simmons, Letrie Allen, II, 120
Simmons, Lorene Elizabeth, 122
Simmons, Lucinda, 35
Simmons, Mahulda, 33
Simmons, Martha M., 85,

Simmons, Mary, 41
Simmons, Minor K., 36
Simmons, Nettie, 36
Simmons, Norah A., 41
Simmons, Paul, 104
Simmons, Ralph Scott, 89, 111
Simmons, Rose Mary, 104, 121
Simmons, Roxanna Yuvonne, 105, 122
Simmons, Roxie, 89
Simmons, Roy, 89
Simmons, Roy Lester, 85, 105, 122
Simmons, Sadie, 85, 105
Simmons, Sarah, 41
Simmons, Sarah Lavina, 41, 53
Simmons, Shirley Marie, 104, 120
Simmons, Sondra, 104, 121
Simmons, Sylvia H, 89
Simmons, Vesta, 53
Simmons, Will, 69
Simmons, William, 41
Simmons, Winnie B, 53
Simmons, Yuvonne Renee, 122
Sinnett, Mary, 34
Sisco, Franco Philip, 118, 164
Sisco, Rebecca Rae, 99, 118, 156, 163
Sisco, Sara Lavern, 118, 164
Sisco, Tanya Mae, 99, 118, 156, 163
Sisco, Wesley Ray, 98, 156
Sisco, Wesley Ray, III, 118, 164
Sisco, Wesley Ray, Jr., 99, 118, 156, 164
Sites, John, 42
Sites, L.B., 129
Sizemore, Malba May, 96, 153
Skean, Nancy, 177
Skinner, Wilber, 79, 149
Skipper, Ashlae Nicole, 130, 164
Skipper, John III, 130, 164
Skipper, John, II, 130, 164
Skipper, Sara Ann, 130, 164
Skipper, Steffania, 130, 164
Slack, Eugene Lee, 208

Slack, Kimberly Gene, 208
Slack, Liza, 77, 147
Slaven, Dallas, 101
Slaven, Thelma Delores, 101
Slayton, Floyd Jr., 68
Slayton, Floyd Sr., 68
Slone, Diane, 79, 149
Smalley, Perthena Ann, 61, 145
Smalling, Ida Josephine, 182, 193
Smalling, Robert Allen, 182
Smallwood, Dorothy Kay, 218
Smiley, Anna, 138
Smiley, Nancy, 15
Smith, (unknown), 174
Smith, Alice, 73
Smith, Andrew, 102
Smith, Blanche Alma, 53, 70
Smith, Boinnie, 105
Smith, Charles W., 53, 73
Smith, Clarissa B., 183
Smith, Clifford Clem, 73
Smith, Dale, 73
Smith, Dane Avery, 73
Smith, Emeline E, 174
Smith, Evajene Faynell, 73
Smith, Ezra J., 53, 70
Smith, Frank K., 105
Smith, George, 102
Smith, Herman Ray, 73
Smith, Jacob, 53
Smith, Leland D., 70
Smith, Leslie R., 24
Smith, Mary Elizabeth, 53, 72
Smith, Mary Frances, 102
Smith, Mary Francis, 102
Smith, Maude, 191
Smith, Mirta B. Or Myrtle, 53, 72
Smith, Myrtle Marie, 73
Smith, Neal, 91
Smith, Richard, 73
Smith, Richard Ralph, 53, 73
Smith, Robert, 40
Smith, Robert Louis, 53
Smith, Ronda Lou, 115, 160
Smith, Ruby, 79, 149
Smith, Sarah, 174
Smith, Sarah Jane, 60, 144
Smith, Texanna, 67
Smith, Virgina, 70
Sneed, Shelli Lyn, 117, 162
Snider, Elizabeth, 41, 54

Snyder, Barbara June, 212
Snyder, David Scott, 218
Snyder, Leonard Avon, 218
Snyder, Mary Ann, 218
Soran, Annastasia, 78, 148
Soran, Christophor, 78, 97, 148, 155
Soran, Cordelia, 78, 97, 148, 155
Soran, Elizabeth Jo Beth, 98, 155
Soran, Eric, 98, 155
Soran, Joan, 97, 155
Soran, Joseph, 97, 154
Soran, Louise, 97, 154
Soran, Mary, 97, 154
Soran, Matthew Richard, 78, 148
Soran, Michael Thomas, 78, 148
Soran, Patricia, 78, 148
Soran, Phillip Stephen, 78, 148
Soran, Rita (Louise), 78, 148
Soran, Stephen Michael, 78, 98, 148, 155
Soran, Steve, 97, 154
Soran, Thomas, 78, 148
Soran, Thomas Christopher, 78, 97, 148, 154
Soran, Thomas Christophor, 97, 154
Soran, Tim, 97, 155
Soran, Tony, 97, 154
Soron, Christopher Thomas, 78, 148
Soron, Mary Virginia, 78, 97, 148, 154
Spaid, Mary Elizabeth, 197
Spathelf, Eugene H., 193
Spathelf, Victor F., 193
Spencer, Virginia Lee, 65
Sperry, Robert, 200
Spielman, Mary, 201
Spiker, Cora, 45, 143
Sponaughe, Ona Lucy, 83
Sponaugle, Bead, 63
Sponaugle, Billy Roy, 83
Sponaugle, Brenda, 83
Sponaugle, Brison Jay, 83
Sponaugle, Conda Roy, 83
Sponaugle, Genevieve, 83
Sponaugle, Gilbert Kenton, 83
Sponaugle, Harold Michael, 83, 102

Sponaugle, Herbert Charles, 101
Sponaugle, Herman Henry, 63, 111
Sponaugle, Jenny K., 83
Sponaugle, John Alonzo, 83
Sponaugle, Kitty Belle, 63
Sponaugle, M. Elaine, 83
Sponaugle, Monna Roxie, 102
Sponaugle, Myrtle M, 111
Sponaugle, Norms Jean, 83
Sponaugle, Patrica, 101
Sponaugle, Sally Nola "Sallie", 101
Sponaugle, Tamara Jo, 102
Springer, Dana, 113, 158
Stacy, 131
Stalnaker, Forrest, 50
Stalnaker, Mary Ann, 101
Stanley, Donna, 210
Starkey, David Daniel, 180, 191
Starkey, Derrell, 191
Starkey, Edward, 180
Starkey, Elizabeth, 191
Starkey, Emmet, 180
Starkey, Eva Arlene, 180
Starkey, Evelyn Mae, 191
Starkey, Fay, 180
Starkey, Hazel Irene, 191
Starkey, Herbert Standeford, 191, 204
Starkey, Hillery Herbert, 180, 191
Starkey, Jasper, 180
Starkey, Jayne, 191
Starkey, Joseph Ralph, 191
Starkey, Judy Ann, 204
Starkey, Lee, 180, 191
Starkey, Louella, 180, 192
Starkey, Louise, 191
Starkey, Victoria Margaretta, 191
Starkey, Willys Lee, 191
Starks, George, 81
Starr, Larwence Wilber, 108
Staten, William H., 175
Staton, Larry Addison, 102
Staton, Max Addison, 102
Steidley, Neva, 194
Stelly, Ronald Edwin, 129
Stephens, Howard E.,, 27
Stephens, Roger, 27
Stephens, Simon Harness,, 27
Sterrett, Hazel Ann, 94, 151
Stevens, Webster, 195
Stewart, Asley Cerria, 131
Stewart, Bertha, 186
Stewart, Catherine, 186
Stewart, Debbie, 93
Stewart, Dorothy Marie, 186
Stewart, Eugene, 186
Stewart, Frank O., 186
Stewart, Glen Ernest, 186
Stewart, Goldie, 186
Stewart, James, 131
Stewart, Jimmy, 102
Stewart, John L., 186
Stewart, Lloyd Edward, 186
Stewart, Lona Agnes, 186
Stewart, Oscar O., 186
Stewart, Ruben Raymond, 186
Stiner, August Edward Van Der Wastein Or, 81
Stinson, Ben, 177
Stinson, Benjamin W, 177
Stinson, Dallas, 178, 188
Stinson, Fred, 177, 188
Stinson, George, 177
Stinson, Grace, 178, 188
Stinson, James L, 177
Stinson, James Madison, 177
Stinson, Jesse M, 177
Stinson, Joel, 188, 200
Stinson, John, 177
Stinson, Juanita Louise, 200
Stinson, Loren L, 177
Stinson, Lula, 177, 188
Stinson, Mary, 177
Stinson, Pearl, 177, 188
Stinson, Sarah Jane, 177, 188
Stinson, Teva, 188
Stinson, Thomas Andrew, 177
Stinson, William Sherman, 177
Stinson, William W, 177
Stites, Ruth M., 129
Stone, Daniel Richard, 207
Stone, Guy, 207
Stone, Scott Winfield, 207
Stone, Steven J, 200
Stratton, Marie, 117, 162
Strine, Willard, 186
Strope, Barbara Ann, 198
Stubbs, Iris, 184
Stueve, Elizabeth, 61, 146
Sullivan, Dayle Marie, 97, 154
Sullivan, Delores Ann, 97, 154
Sullivan, Faye Elizabeth, 97, 154
Sullivan, John Albert, 97, 154
Sullivan, Mary Callen, 122
Sullivan, Michelle T., 97, 154
Sullivan, Nora, 205
Sullivan, Patricia J., 97, 154
Sullivan, Rita J., 97, 154
Sullivan, Robert, 97, 154
Sullivan, Robert Partick, 97, 154
Sullivan, Timothy Albert, 97, 154
Sullivan, Todd Tyse, 97, 154
Summers, Clarence, 190
Summers, Lee, 190
Sussen, Vera, 202
Sutton, Rubina Ruth, 81
Swadley, Cameron, 41
Swadley, Nicholas, 41
Swafford, David Norman, 99, 156
Swafford, Debra L., 99, 156
Swafford, Jeff N., 99, 156
Swafford, Michelle M., 99, 156
Swafford, Steve J., 99, 156
Swanson, Fred Garfield, 23
Swantes, Sandra Slyvania, 118, 163
Swartzonill, (unknown), 198
Swecker, Aliesha Marie, 128
Swecker, Anthony James, 128
Swecker, Dennis James, 108, 128
Swecker, Gery Allen, 108
Swecker, John, 44
Swecker, Melissa Ann, 108, 127
Swecker, Nicole Kathryn, 128
Swecker, Orville, 108
Sweeney, Irene, 110
Sweet, Emma, 182
Swisher, Margaret, 17
Tallman, Bonnie, 67
Tallman, Harlan, 67
Taylor, Byron C., 204
Taylor, George, 22
Taylor, Helen Jean, 72
Taylor, Kaitlynn Rae, 120
Taylor, Lucille, 75
Taylor, Mamie Tennessee, 74

Taylor, Melinda, 173
Taylor, Michael Lynn, 120
Taylor, Nina Elizabeth, 84
Taylor, Robert Daniel, 72
Taylor, Roy Hiner, 120
Taylor, Sharon, 204
Taylor, Sylvia Leone, 197
Taylor, Virginia, 187
Taylor, William Harrison, 197
Teeple, Bonita, 88
Teeple, Craig, 88
Teeple, Harry, 88
Teeple, Jennifer, 88
Teeple, John, 88
Teeter, Frances Ina, 39
Terer, James Albert, 39
Terner, Sondra Jat, 76
Terry, Frances, 175
Teter, Elizabeth, 196
Teter, Frances Ina, 51
Teter, Gertrude Ellen, 43
Teter, Jada, 68
Teter, Lucinda, 40
Teter, Noah, 39
Teter, Rachel Elizabeth, 51
Teter, Ramsey, 90
Tevis, Cecelia Kay, 204
Tevis, Lana Janice, 204, 214
Tevis, Oral Mauricelce, 204
Thayer, Julia Blanch, 205
Thayer, Merrick, 205
Thomas, Bernard, 57
Thomas, Edith May, 77, 147
Thomas, Ora Almeda, 182
Thompson, Ernest A., 58
Thompson, George, Sr, 29
Thompson, Janice, 61, 146
Thompson, Joseph, 29
Thompson, Susanna, 132
Thompson, Zoe Etta, 83
Thornburg, Martha, 20
Thornton, Carol, 79, 149
Thrailkill, Ester Mae, 191
Thurston, Mary Theresa, 78, 148
Thwatt, Beverly, 127
Timblin, Catherine Ethel, 108
Tingler, Lena, 84
Todd, Claudia Bell, 61, 146
Tokum, Mary Elizabeth, 213
Tolliver, Betty Loraine, 56
Tomasson, Edith Hoyle, 80, 150
Toothman, Cora Eleanor, 58
Townend, John S., 47, 144

Townsend, (infant), 77, 147
Townsend, Chelsea Kathleen, 113, 158
Townsend, Harry Steve, 94, 113, 151, 158
Townsend, Kevin Lee, 94, 113, 151, 158
Townsend, Kristi, 113, 158
Townsend, Lester Earl, 77, 147
Townsend, Lester John, 94, 151
Townsend, Lester Lou, 77, 94, 147, 151
Townsend, Louis Scott, 94, 112, 151, 158
Townsend, Luke E, 113, 158
Townsend, Matteau Steven, 113, 158
Townsend, Ryan Scott, 113, 158
Townsend, Samantha Louise, 113, 158
Townsend, Sean Michael, 113, 158
Townsend, Virginia Louise, 77, 147
Trimmer, Anne R., 139
Trimmins, Forrest M., 139
Tuck, (unknown), 89
Turnbull, Isabella, 142
Turner, Brent Allen, 124
Turner, Bruce Ian, 28
Turner, Darlene, 84
Turner, Drenna Nicole, 124
Turner, Earl, 106
Turner, Ellen May, 124
Turner, Heather Marie, 124
Turner, Lewis Earl, 106, 124
Turner, Lynn, 28
Turner, Rachel, 54
Turner, Russell C, Jr., 76
Turner, Sherren Lee, 76
Turner, Sylvia Warren, 28
Turner, Vera Lynn, 28
Turnipseed, Cassandra, 172
Vail, Charles Anthony, 97, 154
Vail, Glen Burton, 97, 154
Vail, Harold Glen, 97, 154
Vail, Kimberly Cherise, 97, 117, 154, 163
Van Horn, Billie Floyd, 78, 149
Van Horn, Floyd Edward, 78, 149

Van Horn, Jackie Dean, 79, 149
Van Horn, Judith Ann, 79, 149
Vance, Bereneice, 187
Vance, Christina, 30
Vance, Macy William, 199
Vance, Martha E, 54
Vance, Mary J, 54
Vance, Perry, 54
Vance, Phoebe C., 54
Vance, Sarah, 54
Vance, Solomon, 30
Vance, Will, 187
Vance, Willard C, 187, 199
Vandervender, Danny, 102
Vandervender, Ruby, 49
Vandervender, William, 101
Vandevander, Arlie, 101
Vandevander, Billy D., 84
Vandevander, Charles, 81
Vandevander, Dollie Irene, 81
Vandevander, Eliza, 36
Vandevander, Eugene Charles, 82
Vandevander, Francis Marie, 82
Vandevander, Grant, 82
Vandevander, Helen Kathleen, 82
Vandevander, Lottie Mae, 81
Vandevander, Mary Dessie, 83
Vandevander, Merle, 81
Vandevander, Patricia, 101
Vandevander, Randall, 84
Vandevander, Robert, 84
Vandevander, Vervie, 81
Vandevander, Virgil, 84
Vandevander, Wayne, 84
Vandevaner, (unknown), 105
Vandevender, George, 34
Vandevender, Margie Marie, 85
Vandevender, Virginia, 120
Vandevender, Wayne Sylvester, 84
Varner, Catherine Elizabeth, 108
Varner, Clinton Lee, 86
Varner, David F., 86, 108
Varner, David Mauzy, 86
Varner, Eva Jean, 66
Varner, James Brafrord, 108
Varner, Jenifer Lynn, 77

Varner, Margie K, 63
Varner, Mildred Lee, 91
Varner, Miller David, 86
Varner, Penelope Kaye, 77, 94
Varner, William Dale, 76
Varner, William Oaklyn, 76
Verdin, Pierre Arthur III, 197
Vest, Virginia C., 130
Vinson, Sally, 15
Vivav, 51
Vonburg, Anthony, 212
Vonburg, Benjamin J., Jr., 202, 212
Vonburg, Benjamin Marshall, 202
Vonburg, Brenda Jo, 211
Vonburg, Brian, 212
Vonburg, Christina Ann, 212
Vonburg, Craig Allen, 212
Vonburg, David, 212
Vonburg, Erma Jean, 202, 212
Vonburg, Jeff, 212
Vonburg, John, 212
Vonburg, Karen, 211
Vonburg, Krissa Suzanna, 212
Vonburg, Mary, 212
Vonburg, Matthew, 212
Vonburg, Michael, 212
Vonburg, Pamela, 211
Vonburg, Patricia, 211
Vonburg, Paul Laverne, 202, 212
Vonburg, Paula, 212
Vonburg, Raymond, 202
Vonburg, Raymond Edward, 202, 211
Vonburg, Scott, 212
Vonburg, Steven Blair, 202, 212
Vonburg, Susan Mardell, 202, 212
Vonburg, Tammy, 212
Vonburg, Vernon Ray, 212
Voyles, Thelma, 27
Wach, Alexis, 118, 164
Wach, Apollo, 118, 164
Wach, David Lawrence, 118, 163
Wach, Lavina Marie, 118, 163
Wach, Lolita Elizabeth, 118, 164
Wach, Mariah Acentha, 118, 163
Wach, Selima Davina, 118, 163
Wach, Wesley LaGranda, 118, 164
Wachter, Hunter, 119
Wachter, Scott, 119
Wadsworth, Harry E., 138
Wagoner, Viola May, 198
Walkenstick, Abe, 61, 146
Walker, Belle, 182
Walker, Mary Ann, 139
Wall, Charles, 170
Wall, Danial, 170
Wall, Jack, 212
Wall, Jack, Jr., 212
Wall, James, 212
Wall, Sherrill, 212
Wall, Thomas, 170
Wallace, Allen Merle, 99, 156
Wallace, Christopher Loy, 99, 156
Wallace, Francis Merle, 99
Wallace, Louise, 37
Wallace, Sarah, 18
Walton, Jessie L., 125
Ware, Ernest, 124
Ware, Ernest Lee, 124
Ware, Jacob G., 91
Ware, Roy, 91
Ware, Virginia Lynn, 124
Warner, Alan, 208
Warner, Ann, 90
Warner, Argle, 64
Warner, Bertie Catherine, 63, 82
Warner, Betty, 64, 83
Warner, Betty Jean, 130
Warner, Caroline Ruth, 83
Warner, Charles, 64
Warner, Charles A, 90
Warner, Charles J, 90
Warner, Dennis, 83
Warner, Elizabeth J., 48
Warner, Emory J., 63
Warner, Etta Beulah, 63, 111
Warner, Evelyn, 64
Warner, Florence, 53
Warner, Francis, 83
Warner, Gail, 83
Warner, Geneva, 83
Warner, Genevieve, 90
Warner, Gus, 65, 85
Warner, Harold, 90
Warner, Hilda, 83
Warner, Isaac Grant, 40
Warner, Jack T, 90
Warner, Jeffery, 130, 132
Warner, Jenna, 64
Warner, Jerrol, 83
Warner, Jerry M., 130
Warner, Jimmy, 83
Warner, John Edward, 90
Warner, John W., 63
Warner, Johnnie, 83
Warner, Judith, 64, 83
Warner, Kate, 82
Warner, Kermit, 83
Warner, Melissa Daun, 130
Warner, Mildred Mary, 83, 102
Warner, Myrtle R., 63
Warner, Ollice C, 64
Warner, Ollie K., 82
Warner, Pet, 64
Warner, Robert G., 85
Warner, Roscoe, 49
Warner, Shirley Ann, 85, 104
Warner, Tina, 63
Warner, Verlie, 64, 83
Warnick, Lillian, 191
Warren, Sarah A., 140
Warwick, Lee Ann, 107
Warwick, Pat Ann, 106
Washburn, Ollie, 73
Watkins, Eudora Nadine, 214
Watson, Forrest, 195
Watts, Hattie, 82
Waybright, (infant), 54
Waybright, (unknown), 74, 76
Waybright, Abraham, 35, 41, 42
Waybright, Albert, 41, 54
Waybright, Alice, 48
Waybright, Amby Stanton, 48, 63
Waybright, Andrew Zephaniah, 110
Waybright, Annie, 35
Waybright, Anthony Burl, 76
Waybright, Arthur, 54
Waybright, Bert, 54, 74
Waybright, Betty Jean, 57
Waybright, Billy Keith, 91
Waybright, Bricel, 74, 91
Waybright, Bricel Roy, 91
Waybright, Burley McCoy, 43, 58
Waybright, Cecil, 42
Waybright, Charla, 36

Waybright, Churchill, 48
Waybright, Clara Ann, 48
Waybright, Clarence, 87
Waybright, Clarice June, 57
Waybright, Clifton Mason, 43, 57
Waybright, Columbus P., 41, 54
Waybright, Cordelia, 35, 43
Waybright, Daniel, 35, 41, 52
Waybright, Daniel, Jr., 35, 41
Waybright, Darl Blaine, 56, 74
Waybright, Delbert, 87
Waybright, Diana Kay, 76
Waybright, Dollie Elizabeth, 59, 76
Waybright, Donald Henry, 56
Waybright, Dove, 56
Waybright, Edger Roy, 43
Waybright, Edna Alice, 63, 82
Waybright, Edna Margaret, 43, 58
Waybright, Edsel, 74
Waybright, Elijah, 38
Waybright, Elizabeth, 44
Waybright, Ella Catherine, 58
Waybright, Ellis Paul, 58, 76
Waybright, Elmer Lewis, 57
Waybright, Emery Henry, 63
Waybright, Erma Lillian, 111
Waybright, Esther, 59
Waybright, Ethel Virginia, 43
Waybright, Eve Frances, 42, 55
Waybright, Fransina Lee, 48, 63
Waybright, George Samual, 59
Waybright, George Samual, Sr., 59, 76
Waybright, George Samuel, Jr., 76, 93
Waybright, Gerald, 74
Waybright, Gerald Mason, 57
Waybright, Gertrude Lee, 63, 81
Waybright, Glenn McCoy, 58
Waybright, Grace Elizabeth, 63, 81
Waybright, Grace Marie, 58
Waybright, Guy Daniel, 43, 58
Waybright, Harold Burton, 57
Waybright, Henry Clay, 35
Waybright, Henry V., 54
Waybright, Ica Chloe, 42
Waybright, Iona Patrica, 63, 73, 81
Waybright, Ira, 59
Waybright, Isaac Perry, 35, 42
Waybright, James Albert, 43
Waybright, James Buckhannan, 48
Waybright, James Herman, 56
Waybright, Jasper, 54
Waybright, Javan Seth, 93
Waybright, Jeffrey Lynn, 76
Waybright, Jeremiah David, 110
Waybright, Jesse, 59, 66, 69, 111
Waybright, Jessie Susan, 43
Waybright, John Edward, 35, 43
Waybright, June Elizabeth, 58
Waybright, Kagun Eugene, 93
Waybright, Katheryn Mary, 57
Waybright, Kenneth Gene, 91
Waybright, Kenny, 59
Waybright, Lemuel, 36
Waybright, Leonard Thaddeus, 56
Waybright, Lettie S., 35
Waybright, Lloyd, 54
Waybright, Lucille Mae, 59
Waybright, Luther, 42
Waybright, Margaret Ann, 38
Waybright, Martha Ann, 48, 52
Waybright, Martha Elizabeth, 43
Waybright, Martha J., 54
Waybright, Martha Jane, 54, 69
Waybright, Mary, 55, 74
Waybright, Mary Bella, 54
Waybright, Mary Christina, 42, 54
Waybright, Mary J, 42
Waybright, Mary Jane, 41, 42, 54
Waybright, Mary Margaret, 35, 42, 55
Waybright, Mona, 54
Waybright, Morris, 63
Waybright, Myrtle, 54
Waybright, Nevette Lagina, 93
Waybright, Ocie Aaron, 60
Waybright, Oliver, 42
Waybright, Ollie Katherine, 63, 81
Waybright, Oscar Blaine, 42, 56
Waybright, Paul, 55
Waybright, Ralph David, 87, 110
Waybright, Randolph Ray, 59
Waybright, Ray, 59
Waybright, Rella K, 63, 81
Waybright, Retha, 91
Waybright, Rettia C., 42, 56
Waybright, Richard L., 91
Waybright, Robert Lewis, 58
Waybright, Rosetta, 42
Waybright, Rosie, 54
Waybright, Ruth V., 74
Waybright, Sarah P, 48
Waybright, Silva Gladys, 42
Waybright, Solomon Robert, 42, 56
Waybright, Stanley Guy, 58
Waybright, Thaddeus, 42, 55
Waybright, Thomas L., 91
Waybright, Timothy Scott, 76
Waybright, Vavil Virginia, 58
Waybright, Verlin, 56
Waybright, Verna, 42
Waybright, Virgil Lee, 43
Waybright, Walter C., 42
Waybright, Wilber Allen, 48, 63, 73
Waybright, William Nevin, 59, 76, 93
Waybright, William Washington, 35, 42
Weachter, Gerald L., 207
Weaver, (unknown), 207
Weaver, Darrell, 207
Webb, Lemuell R., 15
Weber, Glenna Sue, 110, 128
Weber, John, 110
Weed, Roy, 197
Weese, Billy Lee, 122
Weese, Chrystie Lunn, 122

Weese, Delia, 45
Weese, John, 122
Welch, Claire Louise, 138
Welch, Lucille Faye, 72
Wenger, Leonard C., 59
Wenger, Naomi Gay, 59
Wertz, Chester, 20
Wertz, Florence Marie, 20
Wertz, Francis Marion, 20
Wertz, Jesse, 20
Wertz, Leroy Franklin, 20
West, Byrt, 176
Westfall, Patty Ellen, 120
Westmoreland, William, 187
Wetencamp, Beulah, 200
Wheeler, Lyle Ames, 80, 150
Wheeler, Lyle Anthony, 80, 100, 150, 157
Wheeler, Scott Matthew, 80, 150
Wheeler, Shannon Diane, 100, 157
White, Clara L., 179
White, Debra, 93
White, Edward, 40
White, Mary Elizabeth, 68
White, Otis, 66
White, Ronnie, 208
White, Sena, 63, 73
White, Zadie, 52
Whitney, Amanda Marie, 115, 160
Whitney, Hannah Kristeen, 115, 160
Whitney, Joshua Earl, 115, 160
Whitney, Michael Allen, 115, 160
Whitney, Rebecca Suzanne, 115, 160
Whittenburg, Gerald, 186
Whorton, Lela May, 200
Wiant, Henry, 31
Wierack, Elizabeth, 137
Wierack, John, 137
Wierack, Martin, 137, 142
Wierack, Myrtle, 142
Wierack, Wilson, 137
Wilderson, Lora Jane, 193
Wiles, Donald, 121
Wilfong, (infant), 111
Wilfong, Anna B., 76
Wilfong, Archie, 89
Wilfong, Daniel James, 89
Wilfong, Deloris Kay, 89
Wilfong, Dharl Lane, 89

Wilfong, Earl Cranson, 89
Wilfong, Elva, 208
Wilfong, Erlene, 89
Wilfong, Gerald Gray, 89
Wilfong, Greta Jewell, 89
Wilfong, Jessie, 101
Wilfong, Linda Carol, 89, 111
Wilfong, Norman J., 89
Wilfong, Patricia Lou, 89
Wilfong, Phyllis Jean, 89, 111
Wilfong, Robert Cranston, 89
Wilfong, Winnifred, 30
Willard, Elizabeth Ann, 139
Willey, W.l., 64
Williams, Ann, 204
Williams, Elizabeth, 105
Williams, Kenneth, 105
Williams, Kenneth J., 105
Williams, Melvin Norris, 203
Williams, Patricia Russell, 105
Williams, Reba Arlene, 203, 213
Williams, Thelma, 187
Williams, Trenia, 105
Williams, Virgil Norwood, 203
Willman, Barbara Ellen, 198
Willman, Homer Burrell, 185, 198
Willman, John Burrell, 198
Willman, Levi, 185
Wilsom, April, 113, 159
Wilson, Barbara, 211
Wilson, Bertha, 207
Wilson, Dessa Evelon, 79, 150
Wilson, Elenor Wilcox, 204
Wilson, Gary, 216
Wilson, L. Merton, 72
Wimer, Arbelia, 44
Wimer, Berlie Brooks, 82
Wimer, Bobby MCarthur, 82, 101
Wimer, Charles Amos, 83
Wimer, Denny Gene, 208
Wimer, Dessie Ina, 82
Wimer, Douglas H., 129
Wimer, Eldon J, 83
Wimer, Eston Jennings, 82
Wimer, Floyd Herman, 82
Wimer, Fred Marshall, 82
Wimer, Gennie Belle, 35
Wimer, George, Jr., 35

Wimer, Hassie Blanche, 58
Wimer, Homer Sylvarius, 82
Wimer, Housten, 35
Wimer, James, 35
Wimer, Jeremiah Emanuel, 44
Wimer, Leila Modelia, 52
Wimer, Mary, 29
Wimer, Mary Ellen, 87
Wimer, MaryEllen, 64
Wimer, Mona, 102
Wimer, Nathan, 35
Wimer, Omer John, 82
Wimer, Timothy Allen, 101
Winch, Allie, 55
Windle, Burrel, 80, 150
Windle, Dorothy Grace, 79, 149
Windle, Ellen Lila, 80, 150
Windsor, Ruby, 20
Winifred, Edith, 198
Wise, Elsie, 194
Wolfe, Camon, 69
Wolfe, Carolyn Darl, 207, 217
Wolfe, Charles, 196
Wolfe, Charles William, 217
Wolfe, Doris, 196, 206
Wolfe, Harve Wesley, 207, 217
Wolfe, Herbert William, 196, 206
Wolfe, Ivan Ray, 98, 155
Wolfe, Janes, 98, 155
Wolfe, Kathleen Darl, 217
Wolfe, Kimberly Darl, 217
Wolfe, Richard McPherren, 217
Wolfe, Steven Wesley, 217
Wood, Joyce, 202
Wood, Lee, 202
Woodall, Curtis Robert, 213
Woodall, Melissa Lavon, 213
Wooddell, Baine Wesley, 85
Wooddell, Charles Stewart Warwick, 65
Wooddell, Cora Belle, 65
Wooddell, Crystal Belle, 85
Woods, James, 106
Woods, Jeremy Allen, 124
Woods, Jessica Ann, 124
Woods, Melinda Jane, 124
Woods, Nathaniel Robert, 125
Woods, Nellie, 196
Woods, Robert Allen, 106

Woods, Robert Allen, II, 106, 124
Woods, Robert Lynn, 106, 124
Woods, Robert Scott, 124
Woolsey, Micki Michelle, 113, 159
Workman, Pearl, 186
Wratchford, Sarah Christina, 41
Wright, Alan, 219
Wright, Amanda Marie, 219
Wright, Collin David, 104
Wright, Grover, 103
Wright, John, 104
Wright, John Allen, 104
Wright, Karen Kay, 103
Wright, Susan F, 172
Wyson, Robert, 15
Yancey, Cordelia Elizabeth, 176
Yancy, Effie C, 177
Yancy, Ella C, 177
Yancy, James E, 177
Yancy, John, 177
Yancy, Mary Elizabeth, 177
Yancy, Robert L, 177
Yancy, Thomas Sherman, 177
Yant, Edith, 199
Yeager, Catherine, 30
Young, Dorothea Marie, 28
Yurkshat, Alan, 219
Yurkshat, Jason Alan, 219
Yurkshat, Tara Laigh, 219
Zibell, Frank, 47, 144
Zickafoose, Mary Wade, 53
Zickefoose, Susannah, 35
Zielienski, Wallace, 99, 156
Zimmerman, Lewis, 184

---

[i] Price

Made in the USA
Middletown, DE
23 September 2022